OPENING THE GATES OF HELL

OSPREY
PUBLISHING

RICHARD HARGREAVES

OPENING THE GATES OF HELL

OPERATION BARBAROSSA, JUNE–JULY 1941

OSPREY PUBLISHING
Bloomsbury Publishing Plc
Kemp House, Chawley Park, Cumnor Hill, Oxford OX2 9PH, UK
Bloomsbury Publishing Ireland Limited,
29 Earlsfort Terrace, Dublin 2, D02 AY28, Ireland
1385 Broadway, 5th Floor, New York, NY 10018, USA
E-mail: info@ospreypublishing.com
www.ospreypublishing.com

OSPREY is a trademark of Osprey Publishing Ltd

First published in Great Britain in 2025

A catalogue record for this book is available from the British Library

ISBN: HB 9781472869463; eBook 9781472869449; ePDF 9781472869425; XML 9781472869432

25 26 27 28 29   10 9 8 7 6 5 4 3 2 1

Image credits are given in full in the List of Illustrations (pp.6–7)

Maps by www.bounford.com
Index by Angela Hall

Typeset by Deanta Global Publishing Services, Chennai, India
Printed and bound in Great Britain by Clays Ltd, Elcograf S.p.A.

Osprey Publishing supports the Woodland Trust, the UK's leading woodland conservation charity.

To find out more about our authors and books visit www.ospreypublishing.com. Here you will find extracts, author interviews, details of forthcoming events and the option to sign up for our newsletter.

For product safety related questions contact productsafety@bloomsbury.com

CONTENTS

LIST OF ILLUSTRATIONS AND MAPS

ILLUSTRATIONS

A 5cm Pak 38 fires at a Soviet bunker on the far bank of the Bug at first light on 22 June. (Author's collection)

A horse-drawn 7.5cm infantry gun crosses the border near Sokal, north of Lvov. (Author's collection)

Troops of 101st Light Division cross the railway bridge over the San at Przemyśl. (Author's collection)

German troops comb through the ruins of the citadel in Brest fortress. (Author's collection)

A motorised German column pauses on the outskirts of Grodno. (Author's collection)

Elements of Otto Lasch's advanced detachment moves through the burning suburbs of Riga. (Author's collection)

Armour of 4th Panzer Division moves through the outskirts of Minsk at the end of June. (Author's collection)

Ukrainians give the Hitler salute to passing motorcycle troops of 12th Panzer Division. (Author's collection)

Rigans salute the arrival of German assault guns on the edge of the old town. (Author's collection)

A Red Army truck burns next to a knocked-out OT-130 flamethrower tank and T-34 at Jeziornica, near Slonim. (NARA)

A German 3.7cm anti-tank gun takes up position at Dubno. (Author's collection)

A German soldier inspects a disabled T-34 as a column of trucks files past on the embankment. (Author's collection)

German troops stare at the corpses of murdered Soviet prisoners at Varėna in Lithuania, 24 June. (Author's collection)

Russians captured in the Białystok–Minsk pockets await their fate on the edge of the Byelorussian capital. (Author's collection)

A crowd of Lithuanians and German soldiers watch Jews bludgeoned to death at Kaunas' Lietūkis garage. (Vilna Gaon State Jewish Museum)

Lvov citizens file past corpses in the grounds of Zamarstynów prison. (Author's collection)

German infantrymen await another Soviet breakout attempt on the edge of the Volkovysk–Minsk pocket. (Author's collection)

5th Infantry Division's ranks move through the steppe. (Author's collection)

Endless lines of German infantry move down a dusty Byelorussian road. (Author's collection)

MAPS

INTRODUCTION

It is well that war is so terrible, otherwise we should grow too fond of it.

General Robert E. Lee

On a cool mid-summer day in Lithuania's second city of Kaunas, a taxi pulls up outside my hotel. I clamber into the back and, having settled down, tell the driver: 'Septintas Fortas.' *Seventh Fort.*

He nods.

'Devintasis Fortas.' *Ninth Fort.*

I shake my head. 'Septintas, Septintas Fortas…'

The driver is confused. His surprise is understandable. Fort IX is a national monument, a large memorial complex and museum to victims of the Nazi occupation on the northwestern outskirts of the city, a site of pilgrimage for thousands of fellow countrymen – and the occasional foreign visitor – every year.

The much smaller Fort VII, three miles away, is largely forgotten, at the end of a nondescript road lined by blocks of flats and fine post-Communist-era villas. Until recently, it's been derelict.

I pull out a map and point out the fort to him.

He sees the road name and nods. 'Ah, Archyvo. Septintas Fortas…'

No taxi driver in Brest needs directions. There is only one *krepost* – fortress – in the gateway to Belarus. It is the city's principal tourist attraction – it has been for more than half a century. It too became a place of pilgrimage, one of a small number of sites and cities granted the honorific 'Hero' by Soviet leaders. Long after they – and their regime – have faded into history, the fortress remains a draw for visitors: Germans, Russians, Belarusians and a trickle of military historians and enthusiasts from across the globe.

In June and July 1941 fire and fury swept through these two 19th-century forts. They embody the essence of the opening few days of Operation *Barbarossa,* the fire of the greatest invasion in history which ran – unexpectedly – into a bulwark of fanatical defenders in places such as Brest, the fury of unchecked historic, racial and ideological prejudices unleashed across the Baltic states, Belarus and western Ukraine.

This combination of unprecedented, rapid military victories coupled with state-sponsored and spontaneous atrocities makes the opening fortnight of the German invasion of the Soviet Union unique in the annals of modern warfare, a bloodletting unparalleled. It is impossible to separate the two. Ideological and racial murders were built into the *Barbarossa* plan from the outset. Killing at the front occurred simultaneously with killing *behind* the front – on both sides. As German arms swept forward, political instructors in the Red Army – commissars – as well as Jews, the intelligentsia and anyone the Nazis deemed a threat, were systematically executed, individual or en masse. And as the Soviet authorities fell back, there was no time to empty the overflowing prisons. Stalin's security services butchered the inmates, the methods used at times medieval. In many cases, their discovery sparked a wave of pogroms – some stoked by the German 'liberators', others purely nationalist affairs – unsurpassed in scale and brutality in the 20th century.

The account which follows is therefore a contrast of heroism and horror, of brave, dedicated, determined soldiers on both sides, fighting for what they believed were just causes, of unchecked primeval, bestial impulses and actions, of the joy of apparent liberation and the barbarity of hatred unrestrained. As a result, at times it is a difficult, almost impossible read. Even nearly a century later the horrors are beyond the imagination of many a bloodthirsty Hollywood director. And while some accounts and testimonies may have been embellished to suit new masters, the atrocities of June–July 1941 are thoroughly documented in contemporary official documents, personal diaries, letters and court papers, even captured on film. Alongside newsreels and newspapers, later memoirs and testimonies, monographs and studies, and military histories in half a dozen languages scattered across the archives, libraries and museums of Europe, visited during more than a decade's research, they serve as the bedrock of this work.

Our story ends in early July 1941 – five months before *Barbarossa* stuttered to a halt in the snow outside Moscow, none of its goals fulfilled – for two reasons. One is the sheer challenge of continuing in the same vein until the year's end. But secondly, and more importantly, because the rest of the *Barbarossa* campaign never matched the opening days. Never again was the German advance as rapid as it was in the first ten days of the campaign in the East – and certainly not on every front simultaneously. There were stunning victories for German arms: with more than 1,200,000 prisoners taken, the encirclements at Kiev in September and around

Bryansk and Vyazma the following month eclipsed the triumph of the Białystok–Minsk pockets. There were breakthroughs and breakneck panzer dashes, notably again at Bryansk and Vyazma. In June and early July 1941, these were the rule. Thereafter they were the exception. There was still the widespread murder of Jews in the Baltic and Ukraine in the wake of the panzers – most infamously at Babi Yar in Kiev in September. But the popular uprisings, the spontaneous pogroms, were beginning to give way to more organised, 'orderly' mass executions at the hands of German security services joined, in time, by collaborators from the lands the Third Reich had 'liberated' from Soviet rule.

By the time Joseph Stalin addressed his people on the morning of 3 July 1941 for the first time since the invasion began, the first phase of the German onslaught was largely over. The war in the East was not. For the ordinary soldier – the German *Landser*, the Soviet *frontovik* – the fighting would continue until the Hammer and Sickle was raised over the Reichstag in Berlin in May 1945. For ordinary citizens there were three or more years to endure under the Nazi yoke: repression, arbitrary acts, starvation, deportation as slave labourers. And for the Jews of the occupied territories, there was death: death in the ghettos their new masters quickly established, then death on an industrial scale in the killing factories of Majdanek, Treblinka and Auschwitz.

For anyone swept up by Operation *Barbarossa* in June and July 1941, this was just the beginning. The Germans had merely opened the gates to Hell.

A NOTE ON PLACE NAMES

The map of Central and Eastern Europe was re-drawn repeatedly in the 20th century, with borders moved, towns, villages and regions frequently swapping nations and changing their names. For the most part, I have used the names of towns as they were in June 1941 in the countries they were then located, unless there is a well-known English-language title. So it is Lvov, not the German Lemberg, Polish Lwów or present-day Ukrainian Lviv; and Kiev, the common spelling in 1941, not Kyiv; Kaunas rather than Kauen or Kovno; and Liepāja, not Libau or Libava.

ACKNOWLEDGEMENTS

The staff of the Bundesarchiv in Freiburg proved as helpful as ever, as did the staff of the Department of Documents at the Imperial War Museum, London; NIOD in Amsterdam; the National Archives in Kew; the British Library; Hampshire Library Service; I would also like to thank Craig Luther, who has produced three recent monumental works on *Barbarossa*, kindly shared much of his source material with me; Jan-Hendrik Wendler, for help with rare unit histories; Jason Mark and his colleagues at the Eastern Front Research Forum pointed me in the direction of sources and frequently helped with translation; Regent Holidays for providing guides/translators in Brest and at the Stalin Line Museum; Michael Miller for his help with SS, SD and police authorities; Prit Buttar, Tom Houlihan, Bill Russ, Yan Mann and Iain Ballantyne for general advice, support and proofreading. And Kate Moore and her team at Osprey have been wonderfully encouraging and done a superb job editing the manuscript. The book which follows is all the richer for their input.

1

ONE MORE BLITZKRIEG

This is a war on the grandest scale, the likes of which history has never seen.

Non-commissioned officer, German 121st Infantry Division

'IT'S QUIET, BUT ONLY FOR THE TIME BEING...'
BREST, SATURDAY 21 JUNE 1941

Spring, the people of Brest say with a certain degree of pride, arrives two weeks earlier than in Minsk. This year it was late. It was mid-June, and though the River Bug dropped a few more centimetres each day, it was still higher than usual. Throughout the morning motorboats had been running up and down the river, hugging the right bank, their crews clearly soldiers, but dressed in civilian clothes. Ostensibly they were recording the water level. In reality they were scanning the Bug's left bank not 250ft away. Through the dense foliage of alder, poplars and willows, they could see nothing. The boats disappeared up an arm of the Mukhavets, whose peaty brown waters muddy the Bug as the two rivers merge. Here Slavic tribes of the Kievan Rus had settled 'Berestye' at the beginning of the second millennium. And here, eight centuries later, the land's now-Russian rulers sought to safeguard the Moscow–Warsaw road – and later railway – which ran through Brest by building a great fortress with the island formed by the two arms of the languid Mukhavets at its heart. Despite being strengthened and improved to keep pace with the changing face of war, it had been unable to withstand the fall of empires or the march of armies. In the past 25 years, it had traded rulers more than half a dozen times – rarely peacefully – most recently the Third Reich for the Soviet Union in September 1939. Pregnable though the fortress of Brest had proven to be – repeatedly – it was not yet redundant.

This Saturday the sprawling complex was mostly at peace. After a morning of drill to the music of military bands on the fortress's central island, many of the 9,000 soldiers, plus 300 of their family members living within its grounds, were looking forward to an afternoon and evening off. Homesick company commander Akaki 'Kako' Shevardnadze yearned to escape and return to his village, a few miles from the eastern shore of the Black Sea. 'To my parents, to my brother Laie,' the 21-year-old senior sergeant wrote. 'Dear Laie, send me your photograph. I live here just like anywhere else. I long for you. And I long for my Georgia. Everything is peaceful here. My duties will soon be over. I hug you. Kako.'

Many of Shevardnadze's comrades headed the mile or so into the city, transplanted eastwards when the fortress was built and now a thriving community of 70,000 souls. Given Brest's varied recent history, its inhabitants – they preferred to call themselves 'locals' rather than Soviets or Russians – fraternised easily with these 'foreigners': Ukrainians, White Russians, Georgians, Armenians, Jews, Christians, even one German Communist. But in recent weeks, the foreigners had noticed the mood and attitude of the people of Brest change. Government communiqués denying any worsening of relations with Berlin did nothing to ease the tension. In shops there was a run on salt, bread, flour, sugar, soap, shoes. Tailors, shoemakers and watchmakers willingly took orders from garrison troops, but were in no hurry to give customers their suits, boots or watches; they were stockpiling them, ready to sell to the Germans when they invaded. The disquiet among the populace rubbed off on the men of the garrison. 'A storm is brewing and when it comes it'll probably be worse than the Finnish one,' one junior officer wrote home. Junior commissar Vladimir Abyzov also felt compelled to warn his family. 'Our neighbour is unreliable – despite the fact that we have treaties with him,' the 20-year-old wrote. 'We need to be at combat readiness to protect our borders at any moment and, if we have to, to smash the enemy on his own soil.' The wife of a commissar admitted to friends that she'd been 'thinking about war a great deal. *Da*, in all likelihood, we'll have to fight. But God forbid that we're sucked into this inferno.' For more than a year, Gregory Davidovich Derevyanko had been convinced Hitler's Germany and Stalin's Russia would clash. The only question was when – and in June 1941 the 24-year-old committed Communist dismissed the imminence of war with Germany. 'Certainly not this year, but in, two, three, five years' time – and it will be decisive,' he wrote. 'I believe we're waiting for the right moment, when all the other countries have been weakened. For the time being it's quiet, but only for the time being…'[1]

Save a few recently erected observation towers rising above the trees, the left bank of the Bug betrayed no signs of warlike intentions. But beneath the canopy were men, panzers, mortars, howitzers, motorcycles, horse-drawn and self-propelled guns, flak, armoured cars, horses, trucks – four divisions massed on the short stretch of the Bug opposite Brest alone. While the garrison of the fortress was converging on the May 1st Park or strolling into the city, German radio operator Walter Stoll fell in alongside his comrades in front of their company commander. With a serious expression, Lieutenant Helmstedt stepped forward and began to read a leaflet, '*Soldaten der Ostfront!*' – Soldiers of the Eastern Front! – and the words of Adolf Hitler. 'Having been weighed down by grave burdens and forced to remain silent for many months, the moment has finally come to speak openly…' For the next half hour Helmstedt struggled through the four-page document as the Führer surveyed a quarter century of European history: England's long-standing envy and hatred of Germany and her industrial strength, Germany's defeat in World War I at the hands of 'internal strife', the 'Jews, Bolsheviks and reactionaries' who had opposed the German resurgence under the National Socialists, the pact with Moscow in August 1939 and how, ever since, the Soviet Union had undermined the alliance, attacked, carved up or simply swallowed the peaceful nations of Eastern Europe – Finland, the Baltic states, Bessarabia – and tried to stir up unrest in the Balkans. And now, armies were massing along the German–Soviet frontier – 150 divisions – waiting for the right moment 'to crush the German Reich and Italy'. The time had come, the Reich's leader declared, 'when continuing to simply watch would not merely be a sin of omission, but a crime against the German people, indeed against all of Europe'. And so, the Führer had acted. 'Soldiers of the Eastern Front! Right now, the largest, most extensive military build-up the world has ever seen has taken place.' From the Arctic to the Black Sea, it was time 'to save all of Europe's culture and civilisation'. After nearly 30 minutes, Helmstedt reached the appeal's concluding paragraphs: 'German soldiers! You are embarking on a difficult struggle, burdened with responsibility, for the fate of Europe, the future of the German Reich, the existence of our people are now in your hands. May the Lord help us all in this struggle!'

The officer now turned to the company's mission: cross the Bug south of Brest, eliminate a series of bunkers four miles from the fortress, and forge a bridgehead – all under the umbrella of a tremendous artillery barrage. 'Now everyone had to hurry,' Walter Stoll remembered. 'Dismantle tents, load vehicles, reel in the telephone wires, collect iron rations and ammunition – it all took place in a blur.' For good measure, the men also grabbed chocolate, cognac and beer. The regimental band played its final march before the musicians sent their instruments to the rear and joined the ranks as stretcher bearers. 'There was evidently hard fighting ahead,' the young radio operator observed.

A few miles away, 40-year-old chaplain Rudolf Gschöpf led the staff of 45th Infantry Division in a final act of worship at their tented headquarters, located in a forest off the main road to Warsaw. 'Everything passed in a very serious, collected mood,' the Austrian wrote 15 years later. And well it might, for on the coming day Gschöpf's division had to storm the fortress of Brest. The men of the 45th had been practising for their mission for six weeks: the men, by 'attacking' Fort Okęcie, a late-19th-century fortification on the southwestern edge of Warsaw; their senior officers, by studying every detail of Brest – old plans, aerial photographs, panoramas and accounts of previous assaults on the citadel.

As darkness fell, the staff struck their tents and moved to the border town of Terespol, where their command post had been established in a World War I bunker built next to the municipal cemetery. The troops too abandoned their bivouacs and silently made for the marshes by the Bug. Pioneers hauled inflatable boats towards the river's edge. Artillery pieces – 15, 21, 28cm mortars and new multiple rocket launchers – were pushed and pulled along specially laid corduroy roads. Walter Stoll and his comrades passed through a village near the Bug which was crammed with *Sturmgeschütze*, self-propelled artillery, ready to cross the river when the bridgehead was secure. The watchword throughout was silence. For the 45th Infantry's commander Fritz Schlieper, these were the most uncertain hours of the operation. If the Russians across the river noticed or heard his men moving into position, would they order a pre-emptive barrage, catching his men in the open, smashing some of the assault boats, perhaps even detonating the stockpiles of ammunition? Schlieper need not have worried. 'Everything is calm on the Russian side,' he recorded in his diary. The only noise crossing the peacefully babbling waters of the Bug: locomotives shunting in the sidings at Brest's station and the usual sounds coming from the fortress.[2]

Perhaps not the only noise. In the May 1st Park, barely half a mile from the fortress, lectures by the political officers of the Red Army proclaiming there was no need to fear war with Germany, that relations between the two countries had never been better, had given way to music – orchestras and brass bands. Single soldiers invariably ended up in Brest's bars and dance halls, but officers and their families had congregated in the park, where they were joined by the city's inhabitants, enjoying free entertainment on a fine mid-summer's evening. 'Back then it was the only place where you could enjoy yourself,' Brest resident Georgii Karbuk remembered. 'There was dancing, people were happy. It was pleasant and beautiful.' Soldiers who'd chosen to remain in the fortress were treated to an evening of political instruction from their commissars followed by films – all good Soviet fare, naturally: a documentary about the 'liberation' of Bessarabia the previous summer, the fictionalised account of a peasant leader from the Russian Civil War, or *Ruslan and Ludmila*, Pushkin's fairy tale given the cinematic treatment. Other members of their garrison drew their entertainment from alcohol. As the bottles grew emptier, the noise grew louder, Erich Bunke remembered, 'occasionally turning into a chorus at whose end we could just make out: *Vivat Stalin, vivat Stalin.*' Eventually, the din faded and the singing stopped. It was now past midnight. Saturday had turned to Sunday, 22 June 1941, the day when the world would hold its breath.[3]

Nearly three months had now passed since Adolf Hitler had underlined his irrevocable decision to attack the Soviet Union. He had chosen Sunday 30 March to treat his senior military commanders and staff officers to a two-and-a-half-hour *tour d'horizon* at his imposing New Reich Chancellery in Berlin, outlining the strategic situation since the fall of France, focusing, above all, on why Britain had failed to make peace. The reason was simple: Russia. It had been the constant theme of his strategic thinking ever since he had first asked his armed forces to consider an invasion of the Soviet Union the previous July. The tentative plans of the summer and autumn of 1940 took on more definite form shortly before the year's end, when efforts to divert Moscow's gaze from Europe and carve up the British Empire jointly with Germany had been rejected. Seven days before Christmas 1940, the Führer ordered his military 'to smash Soviet Russia in a rapid campaign', an operation he codenamed *Barbarossa*.

Nothing in the intervening three months had persuaded Adolf Hitler to change his mind. 'We are now presented with the opportunity of laying Russia low while our rear is free – and we will not be presented with such an opportunity again for some time,' he told his generals this Sunday morning. 'It would be a crime against the German people's future if I did not seize this opportunity.' And seize it he would, brushing aside the threat posed by the Soviet military. The ordinary Russian soldier was tough and determined, but poorly led, while the Red Army may have possessed the largest tank force in the world, but most vehicles were obsolete. The Red Air Force was similarly large but mostly outdated. The Führer was not entirely oblivious to the scale of the task facing his armed forces, however. The Soviet Union was vast, and despite the size and strength of the Wehrmacht and its allies, the panzers and Luftwaffe would have to concentrate their efforts at specific points. Where they did, Hitler predicted, 'the Russians will crumple under their massive impact'. The industrial centres of Leningrad, Moscow and southern Russia would be smashed, Ukraine occupied and exploited.

So far this was the usual fare. But now the German leader began to liken the forthcoming campaign to a 20th-century crusade – 'very different from that in the West'. War with Russia would be like none which had gone before it in the modern age. It was not merely a clash of arms but a clash between two 'faiths': National Socialism and Bolshevism. 'Peace in Europe is unimaginable without a clash between Germany and Russia,' he explained. If Germany wanted peace for the coming generations, European Russia had to be smashed once and for all.[4]

'WAR AGAINST GERMANY IS INEVITABLE…' THE SOVIET UNION, SPRING 1941

The first day of May was a leaden Thursday in Kiev. All morning clouds had filled the sky. The darkened heavens did not deter inhabitants from lining both sides of the kilometre-long Kreshchatik, the city's principal boulevard. The first day of May meant a public holiday and the annual May Day parade. Children held small red Soviet flags in eager anticipation of proceedings beginning at 10am. First to appear was the class of 1941, the graduates of the schools of the Kiev Military District, all junior lieutenants. They were followed by paratroopers, then sailors of the Red Fleet in their white caps. Mighty horses pulled cannons across Dumska Square, towards the northern end of Kreshchatik. And then the future: motorised infantry in trucks, anti-aircraft guns, quadruple-mounted machine-guns, tractors with caterpillar tracks hauling howitzers. The crowd cheered – this was what they had come to see. On the platform erected for Ukraine's political and military leaders, the district's artillery commander leaned over to a comrade. 'It's a pity that we do not have more of this technology!' he whispered. 'But just you wait – in two years' time things will look better!' The noise of the tractors was quickly drowned out by the rattle of tanks on Kreshchatik's cobbles – cleared of the usual trolleybuses for this festive occasion. Light tanks, three abreast, then the heavy armour – the street was only wide enough to accommodate two side-by-side. Again Kievans were delighted. They did not know that the multi-turreted T-35 tanks on display were already obsolete and about to be withdrawn. Nor that the newest models on display – the T-34 with its turret perched forward over sloped armour, or the monstrous 45-tonne KV tanks – were pretty much all the district had; troops were still mastering the few others which had reached front-line units. Barely had the last tanks rolled across the square than the air shook with the roar of low-flying fighters, I-16s. Small, stubby, manoeuvrable, it had been a revelation when introduced in the mid-1930s. Now it was becoming increasingly outdated, but it remained the Red Air Force's principal interceptor. Only a small formation of modern fast fighters, MiG-3s, appeared over Kiev. As with the new heavy tanks, crews had not yet mastered them.

The fly-past of the MiGs brought the military element of the parade to an end. Now came the workers, carrying huge portraits of Stalin or banners, some proclaiming the latest increase in production figures, others depicting factory workers and collective farm employees standing shoulder-to-shoulder, weapons in their hands. Echoing off the three-, four- and five-storey buildings towering over the crowds in Kreshchatik, the most popular song of the day, sung by one group of workers after another, '*Esli zavtra voina*' – If War Comes Tomorrow – from the film of the same name:

> If there is war tomorrow,
> If the enemy attacks,
> If the forces of darkness descend,
> Like one man the entire Soviet people
> Will rise up to defend their beloved Motherland.

In all, more than half a million Soviet citizens paraded down Kiev's main street that Thursday. No-one who watched the three-hour spectacle could have failed to be impressed.

As the brass bands disappeared down Kreshchatik, a small man with a round face, rather shabbily dressed in an old raincoat and peaked cap, a *stalinka*, stepped down from the tribune and began meeting the crowds. Nikita Khrushchev, head of the Communist Party in Ukraine, knew both the strengths – and weaknesses – on show. Parades like this bolstered public morale. But the former metal worker also knew such displays 'covered up the faults of our army and deluded us into thinking we were safe'.[5]

May Day parades such as those in Kiev, Minsk, Leningrad, Smolensk, Kharkov and, of course, the Red Square showed the public face of the Soviet armed forces. Four days later, Joseph Stalin revealed the true state of affairs in a reception for 1,500 graduates of the Soviet Union's military academies. Before dining, Stalin treated his guests to a 40-minute assessment of the state of his nation's armed forces in the spring of 1941 as well as the wider international situation. The graduates had been away from the front-line Red Army for between three and four years completing their studies. 'When you return to its ranks, you will not recognise it,' Stalin assured his listeners. The rifle division of 1941 – the designation 'rifle' was preferred to 'infantry' – was smaller than those which had gone before, but much more mobile. There were more motorised divisions and armoured divisions equipped with the latest tanks – heavily armed *and* armoured. The Red Air Force too was being transformed. New aircraft with top speeds of more than 400mph were entering service in large numbers – a good thing, the Soviet leader conceded, for if the Red Air Force's existing fleet was thrown into action today, 'they would be shot down immediately'. Yet for all the new equipment, for all the armed forces had learned from their experiences in Finland and by observing the German campaign in France from afar, their training and tactics lagged behind this technology. Teaching in the academies – the very institutions his audience had just passed out of – was outdated, their instructors too lazy to study the latest developments. The head of the academies visibly blanched as the *vozhd* – leader – listed their shortcomings. But Stalin did not stop there. The entire nation had to change its attitude from defence to attack. Training. Propaganda. Newspapers. Radio. All had to adjust. 'The Red Army is a modern army – and a modern army is an offensive army.'

As for the lessons of the current war, Joseph Stalin told the gathering of officers that there was 'nothing special' about Germany's panzers or her Luftwaffe. 'The Germans think their army is ideal, outstanding, invincible. On these points they are mistaken,' he declared. 'There are no invincible armies and there never have been in this world.' Complacency and arrogance were taking hold in the ranks of the German Army. But these were not its greatest shortcoming, Stalin told his audience. 'When Napoleon waged war under the banner of liberation from bondage, he found sympathy and support – and succeeded. When he switched to wars of conquest, he made many enemies and was bound to fail ultimately.' Germany had fought to make good what it had lost at Versailles – and succeeded. Now Berlin was waging a war of conquest. It would fail. 'No victory will be granted to a German Army which wages war under the banner of subjugating other nations and peoples.'

After dining, various officers arose to propose a succession of toasts which, despite loudspeakers peppered around the Kremlin, were often barely audible. Drunk on vodka, wine and champagne, the men's mood was boisterous as Stalin saluted the artillery – 'the god of war' – the cavalry, the infantry, the tank crews and airmen. Finally, a tank general stood up and began to toast his leader's foreign policy. The *vozhd* interrupted him. Yes, he had pursued a policy which had guaranteed peace for the Soviet Union. But friendly relations with Berlin had failed to materialise. 'War against Germany is inevitable,' Stalin told his audience before turning to his foreign minister. 'If Comrade Molotov and the apparatus of the People's Commissariat of Foreign Affairs are able to delay the outbreak of war then we're lucky.'[6]

Throughout the spring, evidence of this inevitable war with Germany accumulated by the day. By the time of Stalin's speech in the Kremlin, his intelligence services estimated there were more than 100 German divisions in Poland – three dozen of them arriving in the past couple of months. The Luftwaffe violated Soviet air space daily. Moscow protested, but went no further. It did nothing for fear of provoking precisely the attack the Germans were planning. When Japanese foreign minister Yōsuke Matsuoka left the Soviet capital for Berlin after signing a non-aggression pact with the USSR, Stalin and Molotov unexpectedly appeared at the railway station. Leaving his Far Eastern guests, the *vozhd* sought out German ambassador Friedrich-Werner Graf von der Schulenburg and, uncharacteristically, put his arm around the reserved diplomat's shoulders. 'We must remain friends and you must now do everything to that end!' The Soviet leader was similarly convivial with deputy military attaché Hans Krebs: 'We will remain friends with you – whatever happens!' The monocled Krebs, a die-hard Nazi, concluded that Stalin would 'do anything to avoid war and would give way on every issue short of making territorial concessions'.

The German Embassy in Moscow fed such snippets and other reports – Muscovites were predicting war would begin on 20 May, the British Embassy on 22 June, for example – to Berlin. Despite the mounting evidence, officially it had no knowledge of *Barbarossa*; Hitler had brazenly lied to Schulenburg when the ambassador visited Berlin at the end of April, assuring him, 'I do not intend to wage war against Russia!' The veteran diplomat was not fooled. 'The die is cast, war is a certainty,' he told his assistant Gustav Hilger on his return. For his part, Hilger impressed on Hans Krebs to remind his military masters of the Soviet Union's strength, the vastness of the land, its inexhaustible reserves, the ability of the Russian people to endure suffering and hardship. Russia 'had often been beaten, but never defeated,' Hilger warned the officer. 'I know all this, but I can't use any of it with Hitler,' Krebs resignedly fired back. 'There's nothing we can tell him. We keep our mouths shut unless we want to lose our heads.'[7]

'AN AURA AROUND GERMAN ARMS...'
THE WEHRMACHT, SPRING 1941

Hans Krebs had merely been humouring Gustav Hilger. The colonel had seen nothing during his time in the Soviet Union which would make his superiors in Berlin quake – and told them as much. The Red Army was re-equipping to be sure, but it was in far worse a condition than it had been when the Nazis came to power in 1933. He predicted it would be two decades before the Soviet military was a force to be reckoned with again.

Krebs was merely confirming what most Germans from the Führer down already believed: the Red Army was ripe for the taking. Germany's victories in Poland, Scandinavia and the West had the Russians 'quaking in their boots'. He was convinced an invasion of the Soviet Union would be 'like a child's game in a sandbox' compared with the campaign in the West, famously predicting all he had to do was 'kick in the front door and the whole rotten structure will come crashing down'. His trusted operations officer Alfred Jodl brushed aside the 'Russian colossus' as nothing more than 'a pig's bladder – prick it and it will burst'. And Hans Jeschonnek, Chief of the Luftwaffe's General Staff, rubbed his hands with glee: 'At last, a proper war!'

Such bombast was not confined to the Führer and the senior officers under his spell. To Heinz Guderian, the leading proponent of armoured warfare, it seemed as if his fellow generals were drunk on their successes, the word 'impossible' erased from their dictionaries. Briefing the commanders of Fourth Army, earmarked to advance on Moscow, its chief-of-staff Günther Blumentritt expected '14 days of hard, bloody fighting. Then, hopefully, we'll have cracked it.' The Red Army's leaders were 'to be feared even less than the old, well-trained Tsarist generals'. As for the men they led, they were 'illiterate, half-Asiatic warriors', dogged, impervious to hardship, unafraid of shedding blood or being killed. The average German soldier, the *Landser*, was better trained, better armed, better prepared, more experienced and, of course, better led. Above all, after their many triumphs there was, said Blumentritt, 'an aura around German arms which will soon have an impact'.[8]

The aura was understandable. Poland had been knocked out in the 'campaign of 18 days' (which actually lasted double that), Denmark in one day, Norway in a couple of months, France, Belgium and the Netherlands in six weeks, Yugoslavia in 12 days, Greece in 24 and finally Crete in a fortnight. The speed and ferocity of these victories had given the world a new word, blitzkrieg – lightning war – embodied by the Stuka and the panzer, combining violence with terror. The distinctive Junkers Ju87 or Stuka – short for *Sturzkampfflugzeug* (dive-bomber) – did both brilliantly. Sirens on its fixed undercarriage, 'the trumpets of Jericho', drove fear into the hearts of those being attacked as the aircraft hurtled towards the ground at upwards of 350mph, hurling its bombs onto its target with an accuracy crews of conventional bombers simply couldn't match. The Stuka's payload of one 550lb and four 100lb bombs was tiny and its shortcomings – lack of speed and manoeuvrability – had been ruthlessly exploited by the RAF in the skies of England in the summer of 1940. Against an 'inferior' opponent, more than 450 Stukas would enjoy a new lease of life.

Otherwise, it was down to the Luftwaffe's fleet of 950 medium bombers to destroy Soviet ground forces and infrastructure. None, in June 1941, could reach Moscow, but they could strike at Leningrad, Minsk, Kiev and the industrial heartland of southern Ukraine. The six-man Heinkel He111, in service since the Spanish Civil War, remained the workhorse of the bomber fleet; nearly 300 would be committed in the East. The newer Ju88 carried an almost identical payload and enjoyed similar endurance, but required just four crew and was 40mph quicker. Able to bomb in the dive or in level flight, it was one of the fastest medium bombers in service in any of the world's air forces. Finally, there was the increasingly obsolescent Dornier Do17 with its small payload – half that of the Junkers or Heinkel – and sluggish top speed of only 230mph.

To provide cover for the bombers – either on close escort duties or by sweeping over Russia looking for enemy aircraft on a *freie Jagd* (free hunt) – more than one-third of the aircraft marshalled for *Barbarossa* were fighters. In the Messerschmitt Me109 Germany possessed an aircraft which was a match for, if not superior to, any fighter in the world in spring 1941. The F model – with which most fighter formations were now equipped – could reach a top speed of nearly 400mph, downing opponents with its 15mm or 20mm cannon and two machine-guns. Far less numerous was the twin-engine Me110 *Zerstörer* (destroyer), which possessed twice the firepower of its single-engine counterpart and an increased range of 750 miles, but was slower and less manoeuvrable. Like the Stuka, it had proved a failure over Britain but, armed as a fighter-bomber, the *Zerstörer* would be more than effective in the opening weeks of the campaign in the East.

The men who crewed these machines were all volunteers and among the best-trained fliers in the world's military – most bomber pilots had 250 flying hours under their belt by the time they reached front-line units. To that training was added the experience of combat dating back to the late 1930s in Spain – although more than 3,000 crews had been lost over Britain and in the Balkans. 'The Luftwaffe did not recover from this blow,' fighter commander Theo Osterkamp rued later in the war. Training establishments made good the losses numerically but, 'to fill the enormous gaps, the training was shortened and selection standards lowered'. It remained to be seen whether their enthusiasm could compensate for their inexperience.

Lost crews had been replaced as had lost aircraft. But as it prepared to embark on a campaign of staggering dimensions, the Luftwaffe was no stronger than it had been 13 months earlier at the beginning of the attack in the West. And, unlike May 1940, it could no longer concentrate its striking power in a single theatre; more than one-third of its front-line strength – 1,800 aircraft – was committed elsewhere in the summer of 1941, including some 850 aircraft in the

West to keep the 'beaten' British at bay. That left 3,000 machines to 'paralyse and eliminate the Russian Air Force', give direct support to the army *and*, where possible, destroy rail bridges and strike at the enemy's industrial potential – as laid down in the *Barbarossa* directive. It was beyond the Luftwaffe's means, as commanders supporting the advance through Ukraine warned: the German Air Force simply could not give the ground troops the support it had provided on previous campaigns. The days when soldiers simply called in 'a Stuka attack at the first sign of enemy resistance' were over.

Of its new foe, the Luftwaffe knew alarmingly little. Reconnaissance flights – which had so infuriated the Soviets yet elicited no response beyond protests – helped to build up a comprehensive picture of the Red Air Force's airfields in the zone up to a couple of hundred miles beyond the frontier. Beyond that, however, it relied on outdated information from the war with Finland and whatever snippets its attaché in Moscow, Heinrich Aschenbrenner, and his staff could glean. Rarely were Aschenbrenner's Russian counterparts obliging, but at the end of March he and senior German aero engineers were invited on a three-week inspection tour of the Soviet air industry. At the end, aircraft designer Artem Mikoyan – behind the new MiG-3 fighter entering service – took Aschenbrenner to one side at Moscow's principal Khodynka airfield: 'We have now shown you everything we have and what we can do. Whoever attacks us, we can destroy.' The warning fell on deaf ears. Hitler seized upon Aschenbrenner's report as proof that he had to strike now. 'Well, there you see how far these people are already. We must begin immediately.'

The Luftwaffe's intelligence section largely dismissed Aschenbrenner's findings as Soviet bluff. Indeed, it dismissed the efforts of the Soviet air industry – already outperforming Germany's – convinced it would not be able to meet the demands of war. There was almost total ignorance of new aircraft, and the Luftwaffe fared no better when it tried to estimate the Red Air Force's strength. When there were, in reality, more than 8,500 aircraft in European Russia alone, the Luftwaffe reckoned the Soviets possessed around 10,500 aircraft *in total*, perhaps half of them combat-worthy, and 'only' 2,850 fighters and bombers ready to face it. Even the most pessimistic intelligence report, staff officer Hermann Plocher recalled, regarded the Luftwaffe superior to its new foe in quality *and* quantity.[9]

And then there was the mechanised juggernaut of the German Army which had delivered the Reich's lightning victories hand-in-hand with the Luftwaffe, spearheaded by phalanxes of tanks. Nineteen panzer divisions were committed to *Barbarossa*, each one a 20th-century marvel of around 3,300 vehicles – end-to-end they would stretch for more than 80 miles – supported by a dozen motorised infantry divisions. But for every mechanised formation there were at least three infantry divisions which would rely on feet and hooves to carry them into the depths of Russia. Whatever the image projected by Joseph Goebbels in his weekly newsreels and films such as *Sieg im Westen*, celebrating the triumph over the Western Allies, infantry, not armour, was the backbone of the German Army. More than 100 infantry divisions were deployed in the East, upwards of two million men. Each division averaged around 17,000 soldiers, 9,000 of them pure infantrymen assigned to three infantry regiments. Each man carried more than 30lb of equipment, from his trusty Mauser rifle and stick hand-grenade, to his canteen, bread bag, a small spade for digging foxholes and a canvas strip to cover him in it. He was supported by pioneers – battlefield engineers, clearing mines, barbed-wire obstacles, building bridges or smoking out enemy strongpoints with flamethrowers and explosives; a battalion of machine-gunners with their trusty MG34, capable of spewing out up to 900 rounds a minute; and an anti-tank unit mostly equipped with the obsolete 3.7cm cannon, which had proved all but ineffective against heavy Allied tanks (so much so the men branded it the *Anklopfgerät* – door knocker). A reconnaissance detachment scouted up to 20 miles ahead of the infantry, while to the rear lay four dozen light and medium howitzers of the division's artillery regiment. Behind all of these came the *Etappe*, the rear area troops – vehicle repairers, medics, bakers and butchers, supply teams, nearly 3,500 men in all. The fighting troops required 170 tonnes of supplies a day to sustain them on the field of battle. The bakers obliged with around 12,000 loaves daily, while the butchers slaughtered as many as 120 pigs or 240 sheep. And there were more than 230 officers and men of the veterinary company to care for the 5,000 horses – the infantry division's principal means of transportation; 2,000 of them were needed to haul the artillery alone, the remainder to pull carts of ammunition, food and other supplies.

As for the vaunted panzers, more than 3,500 were being massed for the lunge into Russia, assembled in four mighty tank armies – *Panzergruppen*. The cutting edge was provided by the Panzer Mk3, armed with a 50mm main cannon and the mainstay of the *Panzerwaffe* (panzer force), and just shy of 450 of the latest Mk4s, equipped with a 75mm gun. There were 200 StuG III assault guns and more than 130 tank destroyers – 4.7cm anti-tank cannons mounted on a panzer chassis. All were good tanks. There were just not enough of them – certainly not enough to equip the 19 armoured divisions earmarked for *Barbarossa*. German factories had made good the losses in the West and replaced many older models, but still more than half the panzers about to invade Russia were obsolete or obsolescent models such as the Mk2, suitable only for reconnaissance duties, or the reliable Czech-built *Panzerkampfwagen* 38 medium tank. Not even diluting the strength of each panzer division – from around 250 tanks in May 1940 to just under 200 a year later – sufficed. To provide the divisions with the 5,000 vehicles they required, the

Wehrmacht was forced to raid the armouries of occupied Europe. There were nearly 250 different models of vehicle in one division, 17th Panzer, alone and some 2,000 across the German Army in June 1941. They were, observed the leading proponent of armoured warfare Heinz Guderian, 'markedly inferior in quality to German ones' and 'particularly ill-suited' to a campaign in the East. As a result, there was no such thing as an average or standard panzer division.

Take the 4th Panzer, one of five divisions assigned to Guderian. It would begin its advance on Moscow with 212 panzers and more than 5,000 vehicles. Most of the former were concentrated in 35th Panzer Regiment and its 177 tanks, only 20 of which were the latest Mk4s. Some 105 Mk3s formed the core of the unit, with 44 obsolete Mk2s for scouting duties. What the 35th possessed in abundance was confidence. Its men were the first into Warsaw, had driven the British and French back to Dunkirk, then raced as far south as Grenoble. The men of the 35th felt 'bound with one another through experiences like few other troops', members of a 'panzer family' which officer cadet Richard von Rosen joined in early 1941 when it was stationed in Auxerre in central France. The 18-year-old Württemberger had undergone three months of basic instruction – 16 hours of cleaning the barracks, drill, clothing and locker inspections and exercises each day – which taught him the discipline of being a soldier, but not a *Panzermann*. Next he received his iconic all-black uniform with the death's head emblem on the jacket collar. Rosen and his fellow cadets learned the basics of armoured warfare, such as driving a panzer courtesy of an old Mk1, and were interviewed by the regimental commander, Heinrich Eberbach, one of Germany's ablest panzer commanders. Eberbach impressed the teenage cadet as a warm, friendly leader who would stand by his men, although it mattered little, for Rosen convinced himself the war would be over long before he completed his training. The best he could hope for, he thought, was life as an occupation soldier. But from mid-March 1941, the regiment began shipping east on trains, the men in cattle trucks where they slept on straw and performed their ablutions by simply hanging over the side of the wagons. At the beginning of May, the 35th reassembled on the exercise grounds at Warthelager, just north of Posen, where it received 50 Panzer Mk3s fresh from the factories of the Reich – some with the 37mm gun and others, like Rosen's, with the more powerful 50mm. With his four fellow crewmen – commander, driver, radioman and loader – the newly qualified gunlayer practised manoeuvres in the marshy terrain every day under the direction of his 24-year-old company commander, Hans-Detloff von Cossel, 'who embodied the ideal type of officer', Rosen noted: calm, fair, brave. The young *Panzermann* was equally impressed with his Panzer Mk3. It possessed 'considerable firepower, was well armoured and relatively quick'.

The armoured experts of the Red Army were rather less struck by the Mk3, or indeed any of the *Panzerwaffe*, when they were shown around Germany's tank schools and factories in the spring of 1941. Hitler insisted the Soviet officials were shown *every* panzer. They simply refused to believe that the Mk4 was the German Army's most powerful armoured vehicle. 'It seems,' the Wehrmacht's ordnance office concluded, 'that the Russians must already possess better and heavier tanks than we do.'[10]

LACKING 'THE EXPERIENCE OF CONDUCTING WAR ON A GRAND SCALE...' THE SOVIET ARMED FORCES, SPRING 1941

In spring 1941, no commander in the Red Army had more forces at his disposal than Mikhail Kirponos, a 49-year-old Ukrainian, who had gone from commander of a division to heading the most important – and prestigious – front-line command in the Red Army, the Kiev Special Military District, in little more than a year. It was here that the Soviet leadership concentrated the bulk of its forces in the West – four armies, more than 20 corps, over 900,000 men and nearly 4,500 tanks – for if the Germans attacked, it reasoned, they would focus their efforts in Ukraine.

With more than 450 new heavy tanks, IV Mechanised Corps was by far the most powerful of the eight armoured formations under Kirponos' direction. At the end of May he watched a demonstration by its armour on an exercise area outside Lvov, delighted by the performance of one tank in particular. Nothing stood in its way. 'A great piece of equipment!' he enthused to his adjutant, and offered the tank's commander an engraved watch as reward for his skill.

'And now, show us what your men can do,' Kirponos told the young officer.

The commander clambered back into the turret of his tank and signalled his company. One began to move slowly towards a series of obstacles and struggled to overcome them. Two more followed, and hardly fared any better. Kirponos rubbed his forehead in frustration. 'So it's not working!'

'We shouldn't be surprised, comrade commander,' sighed Rodion Morgunov, in charge of Kirponos' armoured forces. 'The drivers are not familiar with the new tanks yet. In fact, they've not spent more than three hours driving them.'

Gunnery drill went far more smoothly than the driving, but not moving by night in battle order: the lanes of rural Galicia were soon littered with tanks stopped by the roadside. At one halt, the general tore a strip off the commander of an armoured division. 'Why is there such chaos, colonel?' The colonel explained that his older models had broken down. 'They mustn't stop! You've failed to pay enough attention to regular maintenance.'

'We do not have enough spare parts for the old tanks,' the colonel protested.

Kirponos turned once again to Morgunov. 'Bad, general! Think about how you can change the situation – and fast!'[11]

What Mikhail Kirponos saw at IV Mechanised Corps encapsulated the state of the Red Army's armoured forces – men and machines – on the eve of war. The T-34 was the 'great piece of equipment' which had delighted him: simple, rugged, crudely manufactured – and a revelation. Manoeuvrable, generally reliable and better over the rolling terrain than on the road, where it could reach speeds in excess of 30mph, the T-34's mobility was matched by its ability in battle. Its sloping armour – up to 45mm thick – was all but impervious to the standard German 37mm anti-tank and 50mm panzer cannon of 1941 at point-blank range, while no German tank gun could penetrate it at distances over 500 metres. As for its 76.2mm main gun, it was more powerful than any cannon mounted on a panzer.

The T-34 was classed as a medium tank – a mere 26 tonnes. It was dwarfed by the heavy Kliment Voroshilov – KV-1, named after one of the doyens of the Red Army. With armour up to 90mm thick, it was virtually invulnerable, while its 76mm cannon could knock out any German armoured vehicle up to one and a half miles away. But weighing more than 40 tonnes, it was too heavy to cross many Russian bridges, it was underpowered – a top speed of barely 20mph – difficult to drive and prone to breaking down. Its successor, the much less numerous KV-2, was even slower – a paltry 16 or 17mph – and more unwieldy, armed with a monstrous 152mm howitzer. It was more mobile artillery than battlefield tank – and it possessed many of its sister's mechanical shortcomings.

For every KV-1 and T-34 in the armoured divisions mustered in the Soviet Union's western districts in the spring of 1941, there were eight older, lighter models. The backbone of the Red Army's mechanised force was the T-26; there were nearly 4,000 ready to face the Wehrmacht – on paper, at any rate. The T-26 was based on outdated doctrine – providing close support to the infantry – it was weakly armed and armoured. Its 45mm gun might, at close range, achieve a hit on a Panzer Mk3 or 4, but the poorly made shells often exploded on impact rather than punch through the tank's skin. Slow on the roads (20mph) and even slower off them (10mph), it was plagued by reliability problems – as Kirponos had seen during his inspection; at least one-third of T-26s were unserviceable when the Germans invaded.

The average Red Army armoured division – like the German Army there was no such thing as a 'standard' division – possessed twice as many tanks as its German counterpart and was supported by more vehicles, but had 5,000 fewer men on its books – infantry especially – less artillery and one-third of the number of motorcycles. Crucially, it possessed fewer radios. The *Panzertruppe*'s actions on the field of battle were co-ordinated by microphone and headphone. The Soviet tank man was invariably directed by signal flags.

No two sources agree, but the Red Army probably had around 23,000 tanks on its books in the summer of 1941 – although no more than two out of three of them were ready for action. They were being massed in mighty mechanised corps: two tank divisions, 6,000 vehicles, 37,000 men. Nearly 30 such corps were being or had been formed across the Soviet Union, 18 in the West alone. Not one was at full strength. Most possessed half their quota of armour, some only a quarter. On paper XXI Mechanised Corps, forming in rural Russia close to the Latvian border, should have been able to field 1,031 tanks. Instead, Dmitry Lelyushenko commanded just 98 obsolete BT-7s and T-26s. He pleaded with Moscow to send him the equipment needed to complete his corps. 'There's no rush,' he was told. 'You're not the only one in such a position.' Lelyushenko persisted: 'When will the tanks arrive? After all, we get the feeling the Nazis are preparing…' He was told not to worry needlessly. 'According to the plan, your corps should be complete in 1942.' In Ukraine, Konstantin Rokossovsky's IX Mechanised Corps counted only half the men and just three out of the ten tanks it should have had. What armour Rokossovsky did possess was worn out by the incessant training – so much so that he was forced to curb exercises 'for fear that we would find ourselves at war with no tanks to fight in'. At least in the Kiev Military District, IX Mechanised Corps was the exception, not the rule. Further north the Western Military District, based in Minsk, wielded six mechanised corps, 2,250 tanks, nearly half of them – and almost all the new models – concentrated in a single corps, VI. The poor relation was the Baltic Military District, headquartered in Riga in Latvia, responsible for safeguarding the northern part of the Russo-German frontier. Although it possessed upwards of 2,800 tanks in its four armoured corps, barely 100 of them were KVs or T-34s.[12]

More than half the men chosen to command these new mechanised corps had no history in armoured warfare – many were drawn from the cavalry and most were ten years younger than their German counterparts. Their youth and inexperience can be attributed chiefly to the purges which ravaged the Red Army and Red Air Force in the late 1930s. Some 34,000 officers were dismissed. A good third of the leadership cadre, like Rokossovsky, was subsequently reinstated, but still upwards of 20,000 officers were executed. The upper echelons were decimated: most army and corps commanders, two-thirds of divisional commanders and two in every five brigade commanders were removed. The men who stepped into their boots, wrote staff officer Leonid Sandalov, 'did not have the experience of conducting war on a grand scale'. Not only did they lack experience but they were also short on compassion. Most senior commanders were oblivious to losses and the suffering of their men (Konstantin Rokossovsky would prove to be an exception). As a popular song of the day opined: 'The cost did not stop us...' Small wonder, then, that the Red Army suffered 400,000 casualties in the war with Finland over the winter of 1939–40 – double the cost of *all* of Germany's victorious campaigns up to June 1941.[13]

Those losses were made good to some extent by the massive expansion of the *Raboche Krestyanskaya Krasnaya Armiya* – the Workers' and Peasants' Red Army – since the beginning of 1939. Its ranks had been swelled by more than 1,500,000 men, enough to raise more than 100 new rifle divisions. Although Nazi propaganda frequently portrayed them as 'Mongols', 17 in every 20 soldiers actually hailed from the European provinces of the USSR – Russia, Byelorussia, Ukraine. Conscripted for five years following a period of pre-military training, the ordinary Red Army soldier swore an oath 'to be an honest, brave, disciplined and vigilant fighter'. He would be true to his people, his Soviet Motherland and its leaders to his last breath – and would defend all of them 'courageously, skilfully and honourably, sacrificing my blood and my life to achieve total victory over the enemy'. Were he ever to break his oath, he risked facing 'the severe punishment of Soviet law and the undying hatred and contempt of working people'. Gone were tsarist divisions, he was assured; officers and men were now part of 'one toiling family'. It was a family which endured many hardships. Despite the special allowance soldiers enjoyed ahead of the ordinary citizen, food was still poor – so bad that there were regular instances of units refusing to eat. Wages were poor too: the ordinary rifleman barely had enough money to pay for cigarettes, let alone send a contribution home to his family. Barracks were simple, bordering on primitive in many cases. Washing facilities for either the men or their clothes were basic – frequently there was neither running water nor soap. Sanitary conditions in the galleys and toilets were wretched. Officers enjoyed a better standing of living – they were often quartered with their families on or near military establishments, such as the fortress at Brest – and more pay; a junior infantry lieutenant might earn 50 times what a lowly rifleman received.

It was the rifleman – the term was preferred to infantryman – who was the backbone of the Red Army. Dressed in an olive green or khaki jacket with a coloured collar tab – crimson denoted infantry, for example – a rucksack on his back for personal possessions, a soldier relied on the dependable but rather long and cumbersome Mosin–Nagant bolt-action rifle loaded with five bullets and 100 more rounds in the ammunition belt and bandolier slung over the left shoulder. The rifleman's squad of 11 included two soldiers responsible for the sturdy DP-28 machine-gun with its distinctive circular ammunition belt; it could expend all its 500 rounds in under one minute.

His parent unit, the rifle division, was in a state of flux in June 1941, just like the Red Army's tank force. It should have numbered 15,000 men, but only one in five rifle divisions was at full strength. Some possessed just 6,000, most between 8,000 and 10,000 men, and almost all were missing three-quarters of the vehicles they were supposed to have. A German infantry division possessed more men, more horses, more vehicles. Only in two areas – submachine-guns and artillery – did a Red Army rifle division enjoy a marked superiority over its new foe. The artillery – horse-drawn like the Wehrmacht's – was its trump card; a Soviet division was supported by nearly five times as many artillery pieces as a German one.[14]

The Red Army squeezed the bulk of its training into a four-and-a-half-month period spanning May to September; the rest of the year was mostly spent in barracks or conducting small-scale exercises nearby. In the classroom, or in the field, the spirit of the offensive was drilled into every man. Should any foe be foolish enough to attack the Soviet Union, the Red Army would, so its field regulations declared, 'respond with a devastating blow delivered by all the forces at its disposal. The Army of Red Workers and Peasants will be the most eager to attack of any army which has ever attacked. The Red Army will fight until the enemy is destroyed and completely beaten.' The reality did not match the rhetoric. There simply wasn't the time to train the masses being called up, a problem compounded by all-too-frequent 'distractions' as troops found themselves assisting some of the Soviet Union's flagship projects such as collective farms or in one of the new industrial plants, or else they found themselves peeling potatoes in the galley or constructing their barracks. When the men did train, the results were invariably below par. Inexperienced tank commanders committed their armour on the battlefield as they would infantry. There was too little live-firing and almost no training in night fighting. And when the infantry, armour and artillery did combine their efforts, the results could be described in one word: bad. Leonid Sandalov, chief-of-staff of Fourth Army, which would face the brunt of the German attack around Brest, reckoned more than half his men were raw, partially trained recruits who had neither mastered their equipment nor taken part in large-scale exercises. 'A significant number of young soldiers had never even fired their weapons before the war,' he lamented.[15]

If military training was lacking, political instruction was not. Communism and its ideology permeated all aspects of Red Army life, nurtured by a cadre of Party functionaries: commissars in battalions and larger formations, below them political officers – *politruks* – down to company level. The *politruk*, distinguishable from officers of the Red Army by the red star with gold hammer and sickle on the sleeves of his jacket, was the soul of Communism, a member of the Party long before he joined the armed forces, where he enjoyed *at least* equal status with professional military officers. He was to be the first man into battle, prepared 'to fight to the last drop of blood with the enemies of our Motherland and with honour to defend every last inch of Soviet ground'. It was his duty to fill the bellies of his men with socialist ardour, to foster comradeship, love of the Motherland and the Soviet state. As Stalin put it: 'If a commander is the head of the regiment, then the commissar of a regiment should be its father and soul.' But the *politruk* was no father figure, for he also acted as the eyes and ears of the Party. He reported infractions, dissent, bourgeois remarks and activities – making him at best unpopular, at worst hated. He led at least one political lecture every day, encouraged discussions and debate – along good socialist lines, of course – and ensured that the key dates in the Communist calendar, such as the anniversary of the revolution or May Day, were appropriately marked. The *politruk* informed his men of the latest news when there was no radio available – and frequently there wasn't – through posters, leaflets and newspapers. The latter he read out to his unit – rarely were there sufficient copies to go around, and nearly half the Red Army was partly or wholly illiterate anyway – elucidating the speeches and directives of the Party leaders. Explaining, let alone justifying, the Nazi–Soviet Pact had proved beyond his ability. By mid-1941, that was seemingly no longer an issue as there was a distinct shift in the tone of lectures. Commissars and *politruks* began to impress on their men that the German Army was not invincible, that the Nazis were waging an imperialistic war and oppressing the peoples of Europe. The Red Army, the political officers declared, was ready to take on the capitalistic world, waging a 'mighty and just war', accomplishing any mission assigned it 'with honour'.[16]

'IT IS A STRUGGLE BETWEEN TEUTONS AND SLAVS...' GERMANY'S WAR OF EXTERMINATION

The German soldier would be told that he too was about to embark on a mighty and just war. 'The Polish campaign was the prelude, the campaign in the West an enormous affair. The task in hand is a global affair,' Günther Blumentritt told the officers of Fourth Army. 'The world is at stake, the struggle for the world – if we want to be a nation with global ambitions.' The foe the German Army faced would be very different, too. The Soviet soldier was not decent or chivalrous, but underhand and devious. He would use every trick in the book: play dead, then fall upon unsuspecting German soldiers; pretend to surrender, then attack his captors; poison food and wells; drop paratroopers in civilian clothes. 'Be on your guard!' the leaflet '*Kennt ihr den Feind?*' – Do You Know Your Enemy? – urged. 'Be hard and ruthless whenever you come across such methods of fighting, irrespective of whether you are dealing with soldiers or civilians.' Should any Russian step out of line, the men were given virtual carte blanche to act as they saw fit. There was no time – or need – for the military courts to intervene. Snipers would be 'ruthlessly liquidated', armed civilians dealt with 'on the spot' and people rounded up if the perpetrators of an attack could not be identified immediately. And if the German soldier stepped out of line against the civilian populace in the course of his duties, he need not face criminal proceedings, because Bolshevism was the cause of all the Reich's ills since 1918 'and no German has forgotten this fact'. As a series of guidelines for officers explained: 'Bolshevism is the mortal foe of the National Socialist German people. Germany's struggle is against this destructive ideology and those who follow it. This struggle demands vigorous and ruthless action against Bolshevik rabble-rousers, militia, saboteurs, Jews and the complete elimination of all active and passive resistance.'

This was *Barbarossa* as a 20th-century crusade, 'a war of extermination' – exactly as Adolf Hitler had demanded when he stood before his generals at the end of March. Communism was a threat to the future of National Socialist Germany, its exponents criminals. It – and they – had to be eliminated. Commissars and political officers were the torchbearers of Communism, the driving force behind all the Red Army's 'barbaric Asiatic methods of fighting'. They would treat German 'prisoners in a cruel, inhumane, hate-filled manner'. The German soldier had to dispense with any false ideas of upholding international law. If a commissar was captured on the battlefield, he was to be shot immediately. Killing a commissar was made easier by dehumanising him. 'Anyone who has looked into the eyes of a Soviet commissar knows what the Bolsheviks are', guidance issued to the troops stated. It continued: 'No theoretical debates are needed any more. We would be insulting animals if we were to call the features of these slave-drivers – a high percentage of them Jewish – animal-like. They are the embodiment of the infernal, the personification of the insane hatred of all that is noble in mankind.' The advice was unequivocal: *only the sword can help here.*[17]

These instructions would go down in history as criminal orders. There were many officers who were deeply unsettled by them. They feared for the discipline of their men – and the honour of their army. They were determined the German soldier remained 'decent' – *anständig*, which also translates as 'respectable' or 'civilised' – a word which appears frequently in the deliberations of commanders before the attack. 'Russia is ripe for looting after being conquered,' one appalled military chaplain wrote: 'When it comes to sex too, everything is fair game. Political commissars are to be finished off. Dreadful! No investigation of soldiers who commit crimes against the civilian population. I am deeply shaken. Where will it end? Where will all this lead? It means the disintegration of all order.'

Gustav Höhne read out the commissar order to the officers of his 8th Infantry Division – then forbade them from carrying it out. He commanded 'soldiers, not marauders and murderers. I will put anyone who is guilty of attacking prisoners of war before a court martial.' The 32nd Infantry Division's Wilhelm Bohnstedt was similarly offended. 'Gentlemen, as Prussian officers to date we have fought chivalrously and decently,' he told his staff. 'We will do the same on this occasion. I've nothing more to say on the matter.' The 102nd Infantry's John Ansat did pass on the commissar order – but with misgivings. 'The troops are not the hangman's assistants!' he warned his commanders. When Henning von Tresckow, operations officer of the army group earmarked for the march on Moscow, outlined the orders to his incredulous cousin, Alexander Stahlberg, a reservist officer in 12th Panzer Division, the latter protested that executing commissars was 'murder'. Tresckow nodded. That was why it could only be passed on by word of mouth. Stahlberg continued his objections. *From whom had such an order come?* 'From the man to whom you gave your oath,' Tresckow told him. 'As I did.'

But for every Gustav Höhne or Henning von Tresckow, there was an Albert Wodrig or Conrad von Cochenhausen. The former ordered his officers to 'drum into every soldier' of his XXVI Corps 'the need for *furor Teutonicus* to victoriously complete this great mission'. As for Cochenhausen, he insisted, 'Anyone who makes even an attempt to resist – and this includes passive resistance – will be shot on the spot. Every officer can immediately pass the death sentence. This is an order from the Führer which must be passed on to the men.' The 53-year-old wholeheartedly supported it. 'In the old Germany, such an order would never have been possible as no-one would have had the courage to issue it.' And then there was Erich Hoepner, commanding armoured forces aimed at Leningrad. The language of his instructions to his men was straight out of the Middle Ages:

> The war against Russia is an essential chapter in the struggle for existence of the German people. It is a struggle between Teutons and Slavs, the defence against Jewish Bolshevism. The goal of this struggle must be the disintegration of present-day Russia – and there it must be waged incredibly brutally. In its conception and execution, each clash must be guided by an iron will and lead to the ruthless, total destruction of the enemy. In particular, no mercy is to be shown the bearers of the current Russian-Bolshevist system.[18]

Barely more mercy would be shown to the ordinary Russian soldier. As many as 1.4 million were expected to fall into German hands, some in the aftermath of battle, others through desertion. Convinced many men would be eager to throw off the yoke of Soviet rule, the German Army tried to persuade the Russian soldier that it came to their land as liberator, not invader, freeing 'all honest hard-working people from the terrible despotism, from the arbitrary acts of murderers and liars'. As the infantry and panzer divisions mustered in eastern Poland and East Prussia, propaganda units in Königsberg, Warsaw and Rzeszów – serving the armies driving on Leningrad, Moscow and Kiev respectively – began to fill thousands of empty white-red 10.5cm shells with a leaflet written in Russian and Ukrainian. Those who read it would learn that Stalin's 'Jewish-Communist government' had broken faith with Germany and it was time to put an end to its 'criminal wheelings and dealings'. Officers and men of the Red Army were urged to turn their guns and bayonets against the regime they served. Adolf Hitler had driven such 'parasites' from Germany. It was now time for the men of the Red Army to follow his example:

> Down with all Jews and Communists. Let us march on Moscow and Kiev together.
>
> Together with all the peoples of the Soviet Union let's free ourselves from the Communist yoke, from the damned Jews, from the blood suckers and torturers of the peasants and the workers! Peace in Europe and your homeland is only possible if the head of the Jewish Comintern is cut off.
>
> Join forces with the revolutionary German Army!
>
> Rise up for peace and prosperity of your land!
>
> Down with Stalin and the Communists!
>
> Long live freedom for all who work!

Each leaflet was accompanied by a pass for the Russian soldier to present to his captors. 'The bearer does not want any senseless bloodbaths. He leaves the Red Army voluntarily and goes over to the German authorities. He is convinced that he will be treated well.' He would not. The plans to receive the expected mass influx of prisoners were woeful. They would be accommodated in the open and fed 'with primitive means such as horse meat' – no high-quality or scarce foodstuffs and beverages. At best, a prisoner could expect to receive 1,300 calories a day – barely half the normal daily intake for a healthy man. The reality in some camps would be 300–700 calories. One in every two Russian prisoners of war would starve to death. As 134th Infantry Division's commander Conrad von Cochenhausen bluntly told his men on the eve of the invasion, 'The German is a hero in battle – and afterwards a good comrade towards a defeated foe. This time that must not be the case.'[19]

The Soviet civilian populace would suffer on an even greater scale. As Slavs – and therefore *Untermensch*, or sub-humans – they faced a life of servitude. 'Russia,' one SS commander confided in a colleague, 'is to be reduced to the level of a nation of peasants and will never rise up again.' They were to be reduced in number as well as status. German-occupied Europe did not produce sufficient grain, while Ukraine accounted for 40 per cent of the Soviet annual harvest. The invaders would simply seize upwards of three-quarters of it. What happened to the Russian people was inconsequential. 'The Russian people have endured poverty, hunger and frugality for centuries,' sneered Herbert Backe, Hitler's minister for food. 'Their stomachs are elastic, so there's no need for false pity.' And besides, they were Russians. Whether under the Tsar or under the Bolsheviks, the Russian 'at heart is always an enemy not only of Germany, but also all of Europe'. The peoples of the Soviet Union could only be fed 'at the expense of providing for Europe' – and that could not be allowed to happen. As a result, Backe and his staff determined 'many tens of millions of people will be superfluous and will die'. Their blueprint has passed into history as the '*Hungerplan*'.[20]

The *Hungerplan* would take many months, even years, to bear fruit. The Nazi apparatus could not wait that long to pacify the East. Snapping at the heels of the invading German Army would be four killing squads, *Einsatzgruppen*, each one led by an educated man – three lawyers and one police chief. Their mission: to root out all hostile elements from groups and organisations down to individual 'emigrants, saboteurs and terrorists'. With their personnel drawn from the SS, the Security Service, the police and Waffen SS, the four *Gruppen* – from A in the North to D in the south – received orders to execute all senior and middle-ranking Communist Party officials, commissars, any 'Jews employed by the Party or state', and all 'other radical elements – saboteurs, propagandists, snipers, would-be assassins, rabble-rousers'. If there were any undesirable elements left after the *Einsatzgruppen* passed through, they would be mopped up by the (only slightly less murderous) police battalions. They would bring chaos, not order, marching east with instructions to 'act hard, resolutely and ruthlessly'.[21]

'THE EAST WAS ALMOST THE ONLY THING LEFT...' THE GERMAN EAST, MAY–JUNE 1941

On Saturday 24 May, cars pulled up outside the finest stately home in Poland, Łańcut Castle, carrying a succession of corps and divisional commanders and their staffs. They had been summoned to the palace, whose upper storey had been commandeered as the headquarters of Seventeenth Army, for a briefing by the Chief of the German General Staff, Franz Halder. It had been Halder – not Adolf Hitler – who had plans drawn up for dealing the Soviet Union a blow which would remind Moscow that Germany was the dominant power in Europe, *four weeks* before the Führer told his military leaders that Russia had 'to be eliminated' in the spring of 1941. And while the specific details of the operation's execution might change over the intervening nine months, the thrust of the attack never fundamentally deviated: three army groups – North, Centre and South – striking for Leningrad, Moscow and Kiev respectively. Nor did the estimate of the time it would take to crush the Soviet Union. The staff officer Halder picked to draw up the first plan, Erich Marcks, reckoned the Red Army would be finished off inside 12 weeks – although the rump of the USSR might continue to offer resistance 'for an unforeseeable length of time'.[22] By May 1941 Marcks' plan had matured into *Barbarossa*, enormous thrusts into Russia by the three army groups in two stages, with gigantic battles of encirclements in both phases to destroy Soviet forces in European Russia. The first stage would carry the invader to Riga, Minsk and perhaps as far as Kiev, the second to Leningrad, Smolensk and the Crimea. Four armoured armies, *Panzergruppen*, would spearhead the assault: Number 4 in the north racing to the River Daugava, 3 and 2 in the centre, their pincers meeting east of Minsk to trap the bulk of the Red Army in Byelorussia, and finally Number 1 striking south of the vast Pripet marshes straddling the Byelorussian and Ukrainian borders and through the steppe. And Seventeenth Army? Its 11 infantry and *Gebirgsjäger* (mountain infantry) divisions would strike through Galicia, take its capital Lvov, then continue into the Ukrainian heartland and the plains of the Dnieper upland.

The atmosphere in Łańcut's ballroom was electric – 'like before a thunderstorm,' remembered Hans Steets, operations officer of 1st *Gebirgs* (Mountain) Division. Freshly suntanned from visiting victorious German troops in Athens, the Chief of the General Staff told the assembled officers that they faced a difficult task – indeed possibly harder than most anticipated. 'The fighting on the border will probably be bitter and bloody and could last weeks,' he warned. But then the Red Army would collapse. 'And on that you have my word!' Halder was a nervous figure – prone to weeping, outbursts, even the occasional breakdown. Keen observers in the audience at Łańcut noticed that during the pauses in his address, the general's lips trembled continually.[23]

Those called upon to carry out *Barbarossa* were rather more circumspect about the campaign's prospects. 'Do we have to do this as well?' wondered the conservative Wilhelm Ritter von Leeb, whose army group was charged with

The German plan for Operation *Barbarossa*

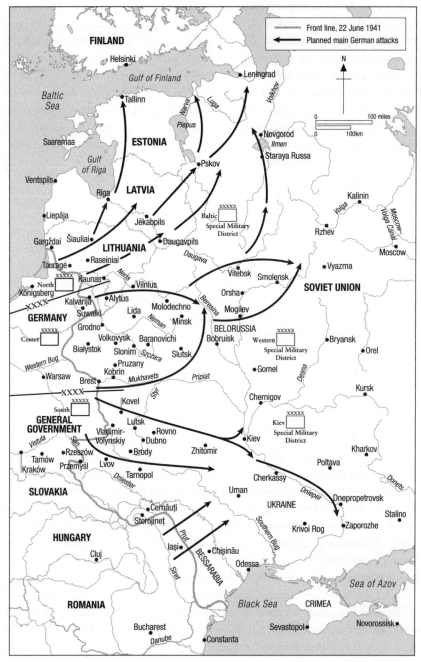

Front line, 22 June 1941
Planned main German attacks

FINLAND

Helsinki

Gulf of Finland

Leningrad

Baltic
Sea

Tallinn

Narva

Luga

Volkhov

N

Piepus

Novgorod

Ilmen

Staraya Russa

0   100 miles

0   100km

Saaremaa

ESTONIA

Ventspils

Gulf
of Riga

Pskov

Kalinin

Volga

Moscow–Volga Canal

Riga

LATVIA

Liepāja

Jēkabpils

Baltic

XXXXX

Special Military
District

Rzhev

Moscow

Gargždai

Šiauliai

Daugavpils

Daugava

LITHUANIA

Raseiniai

Vyazma

Taurage

Vitebsk

Smolensk

North

XXXXX

Kaunas

Vilnius

Neris

Beresina

SOVIET UNION

Königsberg

XXXX

Kalvarija

Alytus

Orsha

GERMANY

Suwalki

Lida

Molodechno

Mogilev

Grodno

Neman

Minsk

BELORUSSIA

Centre

XXXXX

Volkovysk

Baranovichi

Bobruisk

Western

XXXXX

Bryansk

Białystok

Slonim

Szczara

Slutsk

Special Military
District

Orel

Western Bug

Pruzany

Kobrin

Mukhavets

Pripiat

Gomel

Desna

Warsaw

Brest

Kursk

XXXX

Chernigov

XXXXX

Kovel

Styr

South

Lutsk

Kiev

XXXXX

GENERAL
GOVERNMENT

Vladimir-
Volynskiy

Rovno

Kiev

Special Military
District

Vistula

San

Dubno

Zhitomir

Kharkov

Tarnów

Rzeszów

Brody

Poltava

Kraków

Przemyśl

Lvov

Tarnopol

Dniester

Cherkassy

Donets

SLOVAKIA

Uman

Dnieper

Dnepropetrovsk

UKRAINE

Cernăuți

Stalino

Storojineţ

Krivoi Rog

Zaporozhe

HUNGARY

Prut

Chişinău

Southern Bug

Cluj

Iaşi

BESSARABIA

Odessa

Siret

Sea of Azov

ROMANIA

Black Sea

CRIMEA

Bucharest

Sevastopol

Novorossisk

Danube

Constanţa

advancing on Leningrad. 'We don't have the manpower.' After a final conference with Leeb, Army Group South's Gerd von Rundstedt – known for his acidic tongue – parted company with the pithy: 'Well, see you in Siberia.' General Friedrich Olbricht – who would become one of the leading figures in the plot against Hitler three years hence – warned close friends: 'Our army is merely a breath of wind in the wide Russian steppes.' And Carl Heinrich von Stülpnagel, who'd hosted Halder at Łańcut as Seventeenth Army's commanding officer, confided in his riding partner, regimental commander Otto Korfes, during their daily trot: 'We're running towards our ruin.' Korfes, a bitter opponent of the regime he served, urged the army commander to speak out. 'As we've become so closely entwined with Hitler's machinations, unfortunately it's too late for that,' Stülpnagel sighed.[24]

And it was seemingly too late to halt the *Barbarossa* juggernaut. By the beginning of June 1941, divisions were arriving in eastern Poland and East Prussia at the rate of one per day. When units reached their railheads, they moved to the front only by night – with observation towers lining the frontier and Soviet reconnaissance aircraft flying over the border zone, any large-scale movement of troops could easily be seen. Even then, smoking, lights, singing, even issuing orders loudly were banned. The aircraft of the Luftwaffe – camouflaged in a new mottled grey-green livery – remained out of sight on recently created forward airfields. The planes hopped the 1,000 miles from the Channel coast to eastern Poland in a day or two. If they were fortunate, their ground crews might transfer east from Belgium – by road, rail and road again – in just four or five days. Once established in their billets and camps close to the frontier, troops settled into a routine. During the day they attended lectures about the Red Army, learned to identify Soviet tanks and aircraft, familiarised themselves with basic Russian commands such as *Ruki vverh* – hands up. For Luftwaffe engineers and armourers there was work aplenty readying the fighters, bombers and munitions for the coming assault. Along the border, a handful of men watched from their camouflaged observation posts and recorded the precise time and location any Soviet troops or customs officials appeared. On the Bug near Brest, officers clambered into rubber or rowing boats to reconnoitre possible jump-off positions – the only way to move around the waterlogged floodplain on the river's left bank.[25]

The more troops arrived in the towns and villages of East Prussia, the more nervous the populace became, Hans-Günther Seraphim observed. Talking with locals near Insterburg, Seraphim learned they feared the German Army would kill itself advancing through Russia – they even had a word for it, '*totschliegen*'. And once the Wehrmacht was exhausted, the Russians would strike back with terrible fury. 'Memories of a quarter century ago – when houses and farms across wide parts of the land went up in flames – are too deeply rooted. They don't want to live through that again.' Cavalryman Rembrand Elert found the woods around Żuki, on the Bug three miles upstream from Brest fortress, 'full of troops' and the 'colossal' numbers of men and quantities of equipment 'very reassuring'. 'The mood is very good – as before every campaign,' he noted, then added: 'Everyone is a bit tense. Veil of mystery about the future.' It was the mystery and growing tension which troubled Karlernst Malkmus, a radio operator with an anti-tank unit in 9th Panzer Division. He and his comrades had many questions: why the tremendous build-up on the Russian border? Why the many vehicle parks? Why the efforts to conceal vehicles from aerial reconnaissance? Why the lessons on Russian uniforms, equipment and weaponry? But there were no answers. 'I and many others who didn't live for the day just couldn't get it out of our heads!' For 6th Infantry Division, newly redeployed close to the Lithuanian border in eastern Poland from Normandy, life was idyllic – a 'magical world of real, living peace!' doctor Heinrich Haape noted. Reality was just a short distance away in Suwałki, where Poles were frequently flogged in public or had caps knocked off their heads if they failed to salute passing German officers. Otherwise, the men of 6th Infantry kicked their heels, 'patiently waiting for things to happen,' Haape observed. 'We'll be glad when it begins.' Aircrew found the enforced inactivity 'quite monotonous,' as one fighter pilot recorded in his diary. 'We loaf around in our deck chairs and let the sun burn down on our bodies.'[26]

But what were they doing here? No man knew for certain, for there was no official information. 'The fact that no-one can come clean with the truth places an enormous burden on the leadership,' a frustrated Joachim Ziegler, operations officer of 20th Infantry Division, recorded. Everything the division did on the enormous exercise area at Gross Born 'clearly points to a clash with Russia'. All officers could do was to toe the official line. 'Calm down, that's not going to happen,' they assured their men. 'These are all rumours.' And there were plenty to go around. There were warehouses in Warsaw bursting with tropical uniforms and equipment. Soon they would be issued to German divisions billeted around the Polish capital, which would be transported via the Caucasus to the Middle East to attack across the Suez Canal and join forces with Rommel's troops in the Western Desert. Others believed they would pass through Russia and Turkey to attack British interests in Persia, while the men of 110th Infantry Division were convinced they would soon be shipped to India to stir up unrest for the British. Men returning to 1st *Reiter* (Cavalry) Regiment from leave reported that Berlin's Anhalter Bahnhof was festively decorated in eager anticipation of Stalin's visit. Or perhaps Ukraine would be leased to Germany for the next 90 years – a Ju52 transporter with a five-strong delegation had set out from

Munich to thrash out the details with Molotov. 'There's no doubt that we're now on the cusp of a final decision,' a corporal in 269th Infantry Division recorded. 'I would give almost anything to get a peek behind the scenes of the diplomacy.' Heinrich Haape believed 'anything was possible', but deep down knew a storm would soon 'rage eastwards, into the boundless expanses of Russia'. That did not trouble him. 'We are soldiers of the new Germany, who have the confidence that after the hard tasks which must be accomplished there will be the greatest victory.' Infantryman Hartmut Petri remembered maps and charts at his regimental headquarters 'extending beyond Moscow', instantly quashing rumours of a transfer to the Middle East. The tables at 151st Infantry Regiment's headquarters in East Prussia were covered with charts of Lithuania, Latvia and Estonia, while a comrade showed signaller Erhard Steiniger a collection of photographs provided by the Finns of captured Soviet equipment – 'utterly obsolete and primitive,' Steiniger remembered. Fellow signaller Albert Beyer suspected his 121st Infantry Division would soon be marching into Russia; on exercises he repeatedly picked out the names of towns and villages on the other side of the East Prussian border in radio messages. Tank gunner Alfred Opitz remembered 'strange premonitions and doubts', but in the end he and his 18th Panzer Division comrades drew the obvious conclusion: 'Of course after the North, West, and Southeast had been overrun, the East was almost the only thing left.'[27]

'YOU CAN'T BELIEVE EVERYTHING INTELLIGENCE SAYS...' THE KREMLIN, JUNE 1941

The tentacles of Soviet intelligence had come to the same conclusion. Agents reported not merely the arrival of divisions – by early June they reckoned upwards of three dozen were massed opposite the Western Special Military District alone – or columns of panzers and vehicles moving east from Warsaw towards the Bug, but other less obvious signs of German intentions. Hundreds of nurses were gathering in newly created makeshift hospitals across German-occupied Poland. Churches were being turned into depots and warehouses, cemeteries and farms converted into firing positions for the artillery. Thousands of German railway workers from across the continent were waiting at major junctions in eastern Poland, ready to take over Russian stations and direct traffic. Nor did they make any secret of it. 'War between Germany and the Soviet Union,' they told the Polish populace, would begin 'at the end of June'. It was no surprise, then, that the western borderlands of the Soviet Union were awash with rumours 'that the Germans were preparing for war,' one senior Communist Party functionary in

Minsk recalled. 'And these rumours were growing in nature.' Every day there was talk, a major in a rifle division recalled, 'about war with Germany. Not officially, of course.' Oleg Kravchenko's rifle division was transferred to the Bug sector where the 20-year-old artilleryman found 'talk in the new barracks was – quite openly – about the Germans, but was still confident of victory if it came to a fight'. Such talk was not restricted to the ordinary rifleman. Mechanised corps commander Konstantin Rokossovsky and fellow officers were convinced a German attack was imminent. 'The air reeked of war,' he wrote, 'and only the blind and deaf did not notice it or want to notice it.' In some units, men placed bets on the day war would begin: 15 July. Or perhaps at the end of August. Or early September. Once the harvest had been gathered. Or maybe in the autumn.[28]

The prospect of impending war did not seem to trouble the men especially. Faith in the Red Army was boundless – certainly among the Soviet public and ordinary soldiers. It was, one experienced tank commander said, 'the best armed and trained in the world – and hence invincible'. When a captured German spy told the NKVD under questioning that the Germans intended to be in Minsk on the fifth day of their attack, his interrogator was incredulous. 'On the fifth day?' he laughed. Weaned on more than 20 years of Soviet propaganda, the civilian populace believed any war would be swift, brutal but above all victorious. Barely a fortnight before the invasion, Mikhail Kalinin, the titular head of the Soviet Union, rather unguardedly told trainee commissars at the Lenin Political-Military Academy: 'The Germans are going to attack us. And we're waiting for them! And the sooner they attack, the better, as we'll chop their heads off once and for all.' Fourteen-year-old Leonid Rubinstein from Minsk decided the Red Army was 'invincible'; the Soviet Union would defeat any enemy inside a week. 'Our army is disciplined and well armed!' 19-year-old Ekaterina Cirlina proclaimed. 'The USSR is as strong as steel! That's what we were told and that's what we believed.' Besides, any war would be waged, Minsk teenager Michail Trejster convinced himself, 'on foreign soil'. That was self-evident from films such as the ever-popular *If War Comes Tomorrow*, which ended with the Red Army triumphant in Berlin. It was no more jingoistic than other films or songs of the day. Decades later, Trejster could still recall the lyrics of one patriotic tune: 'Our steel shields are bulletproof and our tanks are fast.'[29]

Perhaps. But right now the Soviet Union's military might was impotent. Every day Evgeniy Ptukhin's enraged pilots watched German aircraft fly over the towns, cities, airfields and garrisons of Galicia and Ukraine. They did nothing. Diplomats in Moscow protested to Berlin. The illegal reconnaissance flights not only persisted, but they became more frequent. By early June 1941, Ptukhin could bear it no longer. 'We must bring them down!' he told Mikhail Kirponos, punching his fist in the air in frustration. 'I still remember the Fascists from the fighting in Spain. They're criminals!' Kirponos' hands were tied. He had no authority to shoot down German aircraft. 'Find ways and means to prevent them making reconnaissance flights over our territory without shooting at them,' he suggested to his air force commander.

One word preyed on the mind of Mikhail Kirponos. *Provokatsiya*. Provocation. In the spring of 1941, it dominated Soviet foreign and military policy. No leader or commander wished to give Germany 'the slightest excuse of provocation to act'.[30] When the commander of 125th Rifle Division in Lithuania protested that the Germans would simply steamroller his defensive positions unless proper precautions were taken, all he heard from his superiors were slogans: 'No provocation, cowardice, panic. Show more self-control. You've got the troops and resources. Act firmly. Use everything at your disposal boldly and efficiently, do not be nervous rather make sure you are truly combat ready.' The Germans had invaded Poland after 'attacks' on border posts and a radio station – manufactured, of course. Joseph Stalin had no intention of handing Adolf Hitler a *casus belli* on a plate. Besides, by and large, Stalin was satisfied with the fruits of his pact with Germany. Thanks to the treaty with Berlin, he'd recovered most of the lands lost when the Russian empire collapsed. And so, hundreds of thousands of tonnes of grain, fuel, chemicals and metal continued to roll westwards on trains under the terms of the economic agreement. And when rumours of impending conflict became so widespread, the *vozhd* ordered his official press agency, TASS, to publicly quash them. Both nations were fulfilling their respective parts of the 1939 pact 'to the letter'. Any gossip to the contrary was 'completely without foundation'. Any suggestion that the Wehrmacht was massing along the Russo-German frontier had nothing to do with relations between Moscow and Berlin, while any suggestion that the Red Army was lining up along the same border ready to attack was 'false and provocative'.[31]

Except the Germans *were* massing along the Russo-German frontier, whatever public pronouncement came from the Kremlin. The Chief of the Red Army General Staff, Georgy Zhukov, had even drawn up plans for a pre-emptive strike, launching more than 150 divisions not merely to smash German concentrations, but to seize all of pre-war Poland – and East Prussia as well – all inside four weeks. Stalin turned him down – and the general breathed a sigh of relief. 'Given the condition our troops were in, it could have all ended in catastrophe.' Almost every day in mid-June, Zhukov and Defence Commissar Semyon Timoshenko pleaded with Stalin to at least do *something* along the Soviet Union's western frontier. And almost every day the *vozhd* dismissed their reports out of hand, cursorily flicking through them before tossing them on a table. 'You can't believe everything intelligence says,' he admonished the two generals. 'And I have *other* documents.' He produced a bundle of reports, presented to him by Filipp Golikov, the Red Army's head of intelligence, which contradicted everything Timoshenko and Zhukov had handed him. When the NKVD presented a report from a spy in the Luftwaffe warning that 'the concept of the Soviet Union should be erased from the geographic map', Stalin returned it with a covering note in his own hand: 'You can tell your "source" to go fuck his mother. This is not a "source", but a dis-informer.' At a fractious meeting of the Politburo on 18 June, the *vozhd* exploded in exasperation. Having knocked his pipe against the table the more Zhukov warned of the German build-up – and the need to respond to it – Stalin finally rounded on the general. 'Do you want a war as you are not sufficiently decorated or your rank is not high enough?' Zhukov slumped in his chair, but Timoshenko – bravely – took up the fight in the same vein. He was no more successful. 'So you see,' the dictator told his Politburo cronies, 'Timoshenko is a fine man, with a big head, but apparently a small brain,' holding up his thumb to reinforce the point. 'Germany on her own will never fight Russia. You must understand this.' With that, the three-hour conference was over.[32]

While Joseph Stalin was chastising his senior generals, Ivan Fedyuninsky was being summoned to the telephone at his headquarters in the pleasant, but sleepy provincial town of Kovel. 'Comrade Colonel,' the breathless voice of a border detachment commander said on the other end of the line, 'a German soldier has just come over to our side. He has very important information. I do not know whether to believe him, but what he says is very, very important…'

An hour later the corps commander was face-to-face with the German deserter in the border guards' post. The sergeant – who claimed he had struck an officer while drunk and deserted to evade punishment – repeated what he'd already told his initial interrogator: the German Army would swarm across the border at 4am on Sunday 22 June. 'Soon,' the soldier said, 'war will begin, the German and Russian armies will be enemies.' His story finished, he looked up at Fedyuninsky dolefully. 'Will I be kept alive?'

'Don't worry,' the Russian commander reassured him. 'We don't shoot prisoners, especially those who surrendered to us voluntarily.'

Still the German was uneasy, not convinced – correctly – that his interrogators believed his story. Finally, he composed himself, stood up, and said firmly: 'Comrade Colonel, you can shoot me at 5am on 22 June if it turns out that I've lied to you.'

Wednesday 18 June was turning to Thursday the 19th by the time Ivan Fedyuninsky returned to his headquarters and immediately called his superior. 'No need to believe the provocation!' Fifth Army's Mikhail Potapov said with a calm but confident voice. 'You never know what a German will say out of fear for his own skin.'

Having slept on it, however, Potapov grew increasingly anxious. When brigade commander Kirill Moskalenko called on the general's headquarters in Lutsk, he found him nervously pacing up and down. 'We really must be on our guard,' Potapov warned. 'It looks as if the Fascists will attack us today or tomorrow. And the two of us are not alone in thinking that.' The army commander grabbed a sheet of paper and thrust it into Moskalenko's hands: instructions to begin dispersing tanks and guns.[33]

BY THE BANKS OF THE SVISLACH... MINSK, JUNE 1941

Spring had come late to Minsk. It was well into June, not May, when the smell of lilac and bird cherries filled its streets. Minsk was a city with aspirations – and 1941 was the year to fulfil them. As it began, the city's leaders had agreed to start work on a massive programme of renovation and expansion – building on changes which had swept through the Byelorussian capital over the past two decades and helped to almost double the population to nearly a quarter of a million souls. The next stage of Minsk's transformation would see old wooden houses make way for multi-storey brick apartment blocks; new parks; an extended tram network; the state circus would be given a permanent home by the banks of the Svislach; in time, it would be joined by a botanical garden and a zoo.

As befitted the capital of a Soviet Socialist Republic, it boasted an imposing new government quarter: a sprawling square for parades, rallies and demonstrations – when it wasn't filled with black limousines at the disposal of Party leaders – dominated on two sides by two cathedrals of Communism, the Communist Party headquarters and civic offices, which towered over the city's 'Red Church', the Church of St Simeon and St Helena, now deprived of its religious role and turned into a film studio. There was a new god to worship: Lenin. He stood leaning over a fence, urging on Minskers – even though he never visited the city in person. Nearby, there was another statue of the Communist leader, this time sitting on a bench, with Stalin leaning over him, clearly offering advice.

With the title of capital of a republic came the trappings of a metropolis. The main boulevard, Sovetskaya, boasted the flagship GUM department store. There were state-run shops offering sporting goods, clothes, furniture, pottery, toys and children's garments. There was a network of the government-owned bookshops offering officially sanctioned tomes, while kiosks sold national newspapers such as *Izvestia* and *Pravda* and the regional press such as *Zvyazda*, *Sovetskaya Belorussia*,

Stalinskaya molodozh (Stalin's Youth), the Polish-language *Standar wolnosci* (The Banner of Freedom) and, in Yiddish, *October*.

Cultural life in Minsk flourished. The city's first opera house had been opened barely two years earlier, while for the masses there were at least four large cinemas in the city centre, even one specifically for children. The city's history museum had recently unveiled an exhibition reflecting the 'heroism of the invincible Red Army' in the recent war with Finland, while visitors to the nearby Museum of the Revolution could relive the 'liberation' of western Byelorussia with new displays on the campaign of September 1939. And this summer, the city was awash with visiting theatre groups from across the Soviet Union: at the Jewish State Theatre, the Polish State group from Grodno offered George Bernard Shaw's *Pygmalion*, Schiller's *Intrigue and Love*, Beaumarchais' *Marriage of Figaro*. Its evening performance for Sunday 22 June was a play set in the Imperial Navy during and after the Russian Revolution. The title was prophetic: *Optimistic Tragedy*. The Ukrainian Revolutionary Theatre from Odessa was also in town, its 120-strong troupe offering much of the same across its 16 performances. The biggest draw of all, however, was the prestigious Moscow Art Theatre, which had performed to a full house on its opening night at the Maxim Gorky Theatre. The actors had been a little uneasy about leaving the capital and heading out into the provinces. They found Minsk surprisingly metropolitan. Settled into one of the city's finest hotels, the Belarus, they relaxed in the swimming pool, strolled in Maxim Gorky Park and took in performances of the visiting circus when not rehearsing.

With the school year now over, the 28 pioneer camps for the young Communist movement, peppered in the towns and villages around Minsk, were preparing to receive more than 11,000 youngsters. Their parents might wish to apply for vouchers 'for tours and travel' from the Byelorussian travel bureau, which offered trips to Moscow, Leningrad, Kiev, the Crimea and the Caucasus and perhaps catch such delights as the All-Union Agricultural Exhibition and the Moscow–Volga canal, that triumph of socialist engineering.

The big event this weekend, however, was the dedication of a new lake, a couple of miles north of the city centre. Since Wednesday, the sluice gates had been opened and the waters of the Svislach began to fill the series of channels and ponds which snaked through a large park. Built largely by the city's Young Communists, the lake would be ceremonially opened at mid-day on Sunday, 22 June. The people of Minsk could take to the water in one of 40 pleasure boats, or listen to performances by no fewer than six orchestras. There would be sporting contests, open-air plays, concerts.

The newsreel, *Sovetskaya Byelorussia*, depicted Minsk as a harmonious socialist city. May Day had been a celebration of 'the Party of Lenin and Stalin

– organiser of socialism's victories' with parades championing themes such as 'working tirelessly to bolster the economic strength of the socialist motherland' and 'always keeping the people in a state of readiness'. Otherwise, Minskers in flat caps hurried about the city on trams. The 50 hardest-working employees at the city's railway depot were recognised by the People's Commissariat for Railways for following the example of Ukrainian miner Alexey Stakhanov and vastly exceeding their quotas. The city's inhabitants relaxed by strolling through Minsk's many parks or perhaps they watched one of the demonstrations of mass choreographed gymnastics at the Lokomotiv stadium, where Dynamo had also recently hosted the national football champions, Moscow, and lost 3–2.

But scratch at the surface and Minsk wasn't entirely the workers' paradise portrayed by the Soviet propaganda apparatus. Since June the previous year, a longer working week had been imposed. It had not gone down well, especially with the city's women. They complained that the longer working days left them little time to buy food and cook for their husbands – who expected a meal on the table in the evening. Some workers were overheard by NKVD agents moaning that Soviet rule was no better than 'a return to the old order', even 'a return to serfdom'.[34]

They were fortunate their remarks were only recorded. They could easily have been arrested and imprisoned for subversion. Across Byelorussia more than 16,000 people were incarcerated for political offences – in jails designed to hold barely 10,000. To overcrowding were added inadequate diet, little or no sanitation and the capriciousness of the guards. In Minsk, prisoners on death row awaited their fate in the prison basement. If they were called out of their cells at 4am, it meant they were to be shot; at any other time, their sentence would be commuted. Joanna Stankiewicz-Januszczak, held in for more than a year as a political prisoner, was steeled by her faith and by her belief in the Polish people, recalling the words of Poland's national poet, Adam Mickiewicz: 'We ask you, o Lord, for the war of nations...' And perhaps, she mused this Saturday, 'there'll be the war we long for'. A cellmate had received a food parcel – bacon wrapped in a piece of paper containing the latest news from the outside world: the Germans had delivered an ultimatum to Moscow to abandon the Baltic states, eastern Poland – in short, all the territory the Soviet Union had occupied since 1939. The news seemed to be true. Air defence exercises were taking place in the prison, while blackout curtains had been brought for the windows in the cells.[35]

Air defence drills were taking place too at the city's Loshitsa airfield. The aircraft of 43rd Fighter Division were practising defending the airbase, just three miles south of the city centre. Nimble I-16 Ratas ran rings around the I-153 biplanes above the city. Both were outdated – as were three-quarters of the fighters in the *Voyenno-Vozdushnye Sily* (literally 'military air force') and almost its entire bomber fleet, despite two in every five roubles of the Soviet defence budget being spent on what was already the world's largest air force. Like the Red Army, the Red Air Force was in the midst of an enormous modernisation programme. Scores of existing airfields were being modernised, 150 new ones constructed. Newer aircraft were being introduced to front-line units, but they were few in number and their crews had little time to train in them. Defence of the skies of the western Soviet Union depended largely on the stubby I-16 – dubbed *Ishak* (donkey) by Soviet pilots, *Rata* (rat) by German fliers; except in the turn, where it could outmanoeuvre its German opponent, it was no match for the Me109. The I-153 and I-15 biplanes were being phased out in favour of new monoplanes: the MiG-3, again outclassed by the Me109, except at high altitudes, where the Soviet aircraft came into its own; the LaGG-3, branded a flying coffin by many pilots because it was unreliable, underpowered and handled poorly; and the Yak-1, definitely a match for the best Luftwaffe fighter of June 1941, but available in very limited numbers.

The mainstays of the bomber fleet – the twin-engine SB and DB-3 – were good by the standards of the mid-1930s when they entered service, but increasingly obsolescent by 1941. The lightly protected SB in particular would prove easy prey – and burned horrifically. Even older was the lumbering four-engine TB-3; designed for strategic bombing, it would be pressed into action by day – unescorted – in the opening weeks of the German attack. New models – the fast Pe-2 dive-bomber and the soon-to-be legendary heavily armoured ground-attack aircraft, the Il-2 Shturmovik – were entering service but, as with the new fighters, were in short supply.

And so too were the men required to fly these latest aircraft – from the shores of the Baltic to the Black Sea, there were just 200 qualified crews. This shortage mirrored the situation throughout the Red Air Force in the western districts. A force of more than 7,000 fighters and bombers had been massed, yet there were men to man only six in every seven aircraft. What trained crews there were – all conscripts, unlike the volunteers of the Luftwaffe – had undergone little more than 12 months' training and possessed barely any combat experience. Little more than 10 per cent of the Red Air Force's pilots were qualified to fly the newest fighters; qualification required no more than four hours' flying: a few basic circuits, a couple of flights in formation and a similar number practising gunnery. It was hardly surprising the accident rate was appalling: in three months 141 crew had been killed and 138 aircraft wrecked in crashes.[36]

'I HAVE A FEELING THAT SOMETHING WILL HAPPEN...' MID-JUNE 1941

'We're filled with an unnerving calm, an ominous unrest,' 29-year-old junior officer Hans Schäufler wrote as his 35th Panzer Regiment arrived on the Bug south of Brest. By mid-June 1941, many people in the western republics of the Soviet Union and, to an even greater degree, across Germany were in the grip of almost unbearable tension. 'All of us suspect that we're only separated from an inferno by a matter of hours,' Schäufler continued. 'What will the next few days bring? What sacrifices will they demand from us this time? We don't discuss it. A tightness we've never felt, a chilling cold constricts our chests.' One corporal wrote home from East Prussia: 'I have a feeling that something will happen tomorrow or the day after tomorrow which will leave the world once again breathless.'[37]

The ordinary German was similarly convinced that 'something big will happen' in the coming fortnight. Just a month ago, he'd expected 'a quick war against Russia'. But by mid-June, the German public had for the most part banished the idea of war with the Soviet Union (the exceptions were some well-informed Berliners and the inhabitants of the Reich's eastern provinces). Russia was still a talking point, to be sure – the lack of news from Moscow in particular fuelled rumours. There was talk of an impending conference of European heads of state in Vienna attended by the leaders of every nation save Britain, or a visit by Stalin to Berlin or Munich; flag producers throughout Germany had been running three shifts a day to produce the Hammer and Sickle especially for the occasion.[38] Perhaps the Wehrmacht might strike west. 'Crete as an example' screamed the front page of the first edition of the Nazi Party organ *Völkischer Beobachter* on 13 June – suggesting the invasion of Britain was next. Later editions did not. The article was dropped, replaced by an account of the fighting in North Africa – but not before United Press correspondents had flashed the story around the globe. Propaganda minister Joseph Goebbels saw to that – then cut contact with the outside world. It was all part of an elaborate ruse to divert the world's gaze from the Soviet–German frontier. Wire taps of phone conversations between members of Berlin's foreign press corps revealed the journalists had been 'taken in', Goebbels gleefully recorded in his diary. 'Invasion is once again the big topic in London. The whole thing has been a complete success.'[39]

In Moscow, the official Communist Party mouthpiece *Pravda* sought to put an end to idle gossip, condemning 'chatterboxes and good-for-nothings' and calling on the Soviet people to put more effort into their work and less into passing on the rumours in circulation. And what fantastical rumours they were: ceding Ukraine, perhaps the oil wells of Baku. Some said talks were underway, others that negotiations were imminent, and others still believed Berlin would simply present

Moscow with an ultimatum. Irrespective of what appeared in *Pravda* or came out of the Kremlin, most Muscovites were convinced war was 'inevitable and imminent,' observed Vilhelm Assarsson, the Swedish ambassador in the Soviet capital. A few persuaded themselves that Stalin would somehow strike a deal – at great cost. 'The only certain thing,' the Swede cabled his colleague in Berlin, 'is that we face either a battle of global significance between the Third Reich and the Soviet Empire, or the most gigantic case of blackmail in world history.'[40]

'A CERTAIN NERVOUSNESS IN THE AIR...' SOVIET-OCCUPIED EUROPE, MID-JUNE 1941

In the Lithuanian capital Vilnius, Helene Holzman and her husband Max caught the Thursday evening train back to Kaunas 'very happy and full of plans'. A year had passed since their country had been swallowed whole by the USSR, followed 24 hours later by Latvia and Estonia, after Molotov had 'invited' them to join 'the glorious family of the Soviet Union'.[41] The politicians in Vilnius, Riga and Tallinn buckled to pressure from Moscow – and the Red Army marched in, while the world was mesmerised by the fall of France and the German entry into Paris. The occupiers organised fixed elections inside a month; in all three Baltic states, nine in every ten voters approved the takeover by their so-called 'people's governments'. They did so under duress, for Soviet rule brought with it the apparatus of the Soviet state. Political leaders, army officers and the intelligentsia were the first to be arrested by the NKVD. Over the coming year, more than 11,000 Lithuanians and 26,000 Latvians would be incarcerated or shipped to the Gulag by the Soviet regime. The repression reached its climax on 14 June 1941 in a series of carefully planned and executed mass deportations throughout the Baltic states. Latvian Army officer Osvalds Vanangs managed to throw a note out of a cattle wagon as his train pulled out of Riga station: 'Don't grieve. I am among nice people. Wait for me. I don't yet know where we are going.' Hard labour camps in Siberia and Kazakhstan were the usual destinations. In the space of three or four days, more than 15,000 Latvians and 18,000 Lithuanians were rounded up – not just individuals, but entire families, branded 'class enemies'. It was small wonder Latvians referred to the 12 months of Soviet rule as *baigais gads* – the year of horror.

Yet there was a perception that the Jewish populace had not merely not suffered under the Soviets, but even benefitted. Suddenly, Jews found many of the restrictions on their lives and careers lifted. No longer were they prevented from holding ministerial posts, working in the civil service, in the legal system, in the media, in the police, the new co-operatives and Soviet government apparatus. They could continue their studies at universities and colleges. Such 'privileges' bred at best resentment, at worst hatred. 'The majority of people – certainly the ones I encounter – long for the Germans to march in,' Kaunas historian Zenonas Ivinskis noted. 'Then the slaughter of the Jews would begin in earnest. The anger at the Jews because of their brazen support for Bolshevism knows no bounds.' Another resident of Lithuania's inter-war capital chided the 'arrogant *žydeliai*' – Yids – for siding with the Soviet occupiers. 'The mood is such that the majority of people simply want the Germans to come. And then the killing of the Jews would begin.' In fact, most Jews in the Baltic states did not rejoice at the arrival of the Soviets. They suffered the same arrests and deportations, the confiscation of property, the appropriation of their businesses, the food shortages and endless queues in the shops. They resigned themselves to the lesser of two evils: 'Under Germany we were doomed,' one Lithuanian Jew wrote. 'Under Russia we were free.'[42]

The Holzmans were one Jewish family who had lost out under the Soviets. Over 20 years they had built up a successful bookshop in Kaunas. The Soviets nationalised it. Max found work as manager of a state-run book store in Vilnius, his German-born wife as a German teacher. The weekly commute put a strain on family life, in particular the couple's teenage daughters Marie and Margarete. They didn't want to move, but having found an apartment in the capital, the Holzmans could lead a normal family life again. Throughout the two-hour train journey, the Holzmans excitedly discussed their plans for the future, but the conversation took a more serious turn when a senior police officer entered the compartment. 'We asked him whether he placed any value on the rumours about the concentration of German troops on the Lithuanian border,' Helene recalled. 'He laughed at us.' Neither the Germans nor the Russians were preparing for war against each other, he assured the Holzmans, adding that he was now going on holiday on the Baltic coast. 'This news completely calmed us down,' Helene wrote. 'We turned our thoughts again towards our own affairs.'[43]

———

'Growing danger on the horizon.' Thus did university assistant Stanisław Różycki open his diary chronicling life in the city of Lvov on Friday 20 June. Home to half a million souls, the capital of the ancient province of Galicia was a melting pot of the European borderlands – mostly Poles, then Jews and Ukrainians – which reflected its turbulent history. Like Brest it had traded rulers frequently in its seven-century existence: Poles, Turks, Habsburgs, the Tsar's army for ten months in World War I. At the war's end, Ukrainian nationalists had tried, and failed, to seize control of the city from the fledgling Polish state during a siege over the winter of 1918–19. The defenders were lionised, their triumph celebrated each year with services of commemoration, parades and other events – all to emphasise the Polishness of a city they called Lwów. And, at the same time, Lvov's Ukrainian minority – one in ten inhabitants – became increasingly marginalised: their schools and institutions were closed, their language was banned, and they were dismissed from many civic posts. When the Red Army invaded in September 1939 and Poland was partitioned once again, it was greeted by cheering crowds of Ukrainians, waving flags in the national colours and pumping their fists in their air and crying 'Urra'.

The blue and yellow of Ukraine did not last. Soviet red was soon omnipresent. Red banners. Red flags. Red stars. On façades, poles, street lamps, trams. On a summer's evening, it gave the city the appearance 'of being in Lucifer's living room,' 15-year-old ethnic German Georg Jestadt remembered. With the Soviet banners and flags came Soviet placards, posters and statues: Lenin, Stalin, Commissar for Defence Marshal Voroshilov. The latter stood firm, resolute, his chest bristling with medals, binoculars in his hand and a watch on his left wrist. Underneath, one Leopolitan daubed in paint: 'Seized in Lvov on the black market!'

For the reality of Soviet rule in the Galician capital was rather less impressive than the posters and idols littering Lvov suggested. The queue for a loaf of bread could be a couple of hours long, for sugar double, and for items of clothing all day – if the stores had them at all. The black market flourished. Not just jewellery, watches and clothing, but food, alcohol, soap, better cigarettes. The police occasionally raided such illegal gatherings, less to re-impose Soviet order than to seize the goods being bartered.

Outside the city, collectivisation – mass, state-run farms – was imposed on Galicia's landholders just as it had been introduced across the Soviet Union. It proved no more popular. Worse, Communist officials, however lowly, seized whatever they liked with seeming impunity. For them, this was 'a golden age,' one Polish diarist observed. 'They now have paradise on earth, something which they could never have dreamed of during normal times.' Trains rolled east day and night carrying plunder as Galicia was stripped bare: factories, hospitals, public buildings, military institutions. A good deal of the land and property seized had previously been owned by Poles – just one element of the Soviet policy of 'de-Polonisation'. In a mostly Catholic land, religion was at best discouraged, Polish history was no longer taught, the Polish eagle pulled down, the złoty outlawed, and the Polish language replaced by Ukrainian. But whatever favour such actions gained the Soviets, it was eroded by all the other trappings of their rule. 'Everyone lived, ate, and dressed worse than before,' one Ukrainian complained.

To voice such criticism in 1940 or 1941 would have ended with deportation to the Gulag or incarceration in Galicia's prisons. Arrested individually or in groups, at home, at work, or in the street in broad daylight, there were nearly 21,000 'class enemies' – the middle and upper classes, intelligentsia, teachers, lecturers, clergy, nationalists – held in June 1941. More than 5,000 people were imprisoned in Lvov's three prisons. In the city's largest, Number 1, on Lontskoho Street – built by the Habsburgs but used far more ruthlessly by the Soviets – there were 3,500 inmates aged 13 to 87 in an institution designed to hold 1,500. Each cell held 20 prisoners, all of them standing. There were no beds, just a concrete floor, and only one or two toilets on each of the three storeys. Those condemned to death were held in solitary confinement, waiting between one day and two months for their fate – a shot to the back of the neck.

For the shortages, for the repression, for the incarceration, many Galicians – Poles and Ukrainians alike – held the Jewish populace largely responsible. Like the Lithuanian and Latvian populace, many were convinced that Jews enjoyed preferential treatment, were appointed to senior positions and informed on or denounced them. The Soviets outlawed antisemitism but, as one of Lvov's Jewish inhabitants recalled, 'you could *feel* the hatred of the Jews'. If there was no-one within earshot to denounce them to the authorities, he overheard fellow Leopolitans mutter: 'The Communist Jews have everything and we have nothing. Give us a free hand for 48 hours and you'll see what we will do to these hateful Jews.' Some Ukrainians were even more brazen; a popular song among nationalists proclaimed: '*Smert', smert' Lacham, Smert' zydiwsko-moskowskoiji komuni*' – 'Death, death to the Poles, death to the Jewish-Muscovite commune'. 'If the Germans get here it could become dangerous for the Jews,' Polish priest Józef Anczarski recorded in his diary. 'The Jews really are in a dangerous position.' In June 1941, Lvov's melting pot of nations was more of a powder keg.

And yet for the city's Jews, Soviet rule was still preferable to German. Stanisław Różycki, who had fled Warsaw in 1939, noted that across the border in Nazi-occupied Poland 'war, hunger and sickness prevail, there are shootings, ghettos, armbands, camps and the stripping of all rights'. At least under the Soviets, he reasoned, there was work, food and *some* rights. 'Although Jews have suffered, had their property confiscated and their families have been deported – despite all this, they're banking on Russia, because anything is better than the Germans.'

Russian. Ukrainian. Pole. Ethnic German. Jew. Whatever a Leopolitan's nationality, in June 1941 they noticed 'a certain nervousness' in the air – and a definite cooling in Soviet–German relations. There were no cheers for the successes of Rommel's *Afrika Korps* advancing on Tobruk, while the Wehrmacht's actions in the Balkans were openly criticised in the newspapers and on the radio.

More ominously, throughout April and May, ever more Red Army troops had been seen filing down Lvov's streets. The Ratas at the airfields ringing the city became ever more active, as did the anti-aircraft batteries which were tested weekly. Less frequently, tank columns rumbled through Lvov, Georg Jestadt observed, 'including huge monsters which we'd no idea of until now'.

Most people clung to the official public pronouncements and assured themselves that the Nazi–Soviet Pact was one safeguard of peace, the size and strength of the Red Army another: it possessed more armoured vehicles than all the armies of Europe, a 'world-record number' of aircraft, 'unrivalled' artillery and anti-aircraft guns, and could mobilise 15 million men. Other Leopolitans, fewer in number, were convinced the Germans would be in Moscow within a week; the Soviet soldier would flee or surrender in massive numbers. A few people began hoarding or tried to obtain *putjovki* – travel documents – so they could escape to the Crimea, or even the Caucasus – 'the important thing is as far as possible to the East'.[44]

'STANDING IN FRONT OF A LOCKED DOOR...'
FRIDAY 20 JUNE

Company commander Theodor Habicht was enjoying 'the most wonderful sleep' this Friday morning when he was rudely awakened by a messenger, ordering him to a conference for the officers of 27th Infantry Regiment. Gerhard Kegler was normally a rather cold, brusque figure, but uncharacteristically encouraged his officers to sit or lie down in a meadow not far from the border with Lithuania. 'Now it's war again,' he told them. Beyond telling his men that the invasion of Russia was imminent – he hinted at 23 June – Kegler did not expand on his regiment's combat mission. But he did warn them that the coming battle was unlike any they had ever fought in, 'an out-and-out war of ideologies' between National Socialism and Bolshevism 'waged by the Russians (Jews) with the utmost savagery and treachery'. Germany's response to such savagery would be merciless, Kegler promised. Any civilian bearing arms would be shot on the spot. There was no need for the rigmarole of a lengthy trial, the colonel continued, 'just a brief report to the battalion'. And if the populace offered more persistent resistance, Gerhard Kegler offered a couple of suggestions: reviving the Roman practice of decimation or simply burning down a village. Kegler went on for nearly an hour, interrupted repeatedly by cheers, before concluding: 'I trust that the regiment will live up to its name again!' – 'On that he can rely,' Habicht noted in his diary. 'And now, *meine Herren, Heil* and a soldier's luck!'[45]

The ground crew of *Stukageschwader* 77's I *Gruppe* arrived in the 'endless woods' near Biała Podlaska, two dozen miles west of Brest, more than a month ahead of their aircraft. 'It's quite nice, but far from the town and the beautiful girls there,' *Unteroffizier* Christian Luibl observed in his diary. Worse, the camp was located 'right in the middle of flies'. There was little work for the men; they passed the days sunbathing until the *Gruppe*'s three dozen Stukas arrived on 20 June. Mail was stopped. Above all, it brought an end to the uncertainty. 'Until now, everything has been unclear, no-one knew whether we were coming or going,' the Bavarian wrote in his diary. There was just one unanswerable question left: 'How things will go with Russia, no man knows.'[46]

In the woods outside the town of Vladimir-Volynskiy, barely half a dozen miles from the border with Germany, the technical officer of 41st Tank Division stood in front of crews, an instruction manual in one hand, a pointer in the other as he introduced them to their new weapon, the KV-2. Eighteen of the heavy tanks had been delivered to the town's railway station, from where they were driven through the narrow streets, causing the ground to tremble and window panes to shake, to the division's vehicle park. There they were covered with tarpaulin and prodded and poked by crews. 'Apart from the drivers who'd been sent to the factory to collect them, no-one in our division had seen a KV-2 yet,' the 41st's chief-of-staff Konstantin Maligin remembered. His division was one of the best equipped in the district – more than 300 tanks, most of them outdated T-26s, which now 'seemed like toys' compared with what crews quickly agreed was 'certainly the most powerful tank in the world'. Their initial enthusiasm quickly began to fade. Yes, it was well armoured, but it was slow, cumbersome, not especially reliable – and there were no spare parts – and the steep angle of its mighty 152mm cannon made fighting other tanks difficult (not that any ammunition for the main gun had actually been delivered yet). 'The general consensus was mixed,' Maligin wrote. 'The tank was powerful, of course but ... and there were many "buts"...' The next day, Saturday 21 June, he and his comrades would get their first 'hands-on' experience as they began converting to the new tanks.[47]

On the Bug downstream from Brest, two officers from 17th Panzer Division swam across the river to tap Russian telephone lines on the right bank, smoothing the sand by the water's edge to hide their tracks. Overhead, Luftwaffe reconnaissance aircraft, all armed with bombs, continued to flout international law by flying into Soviet territory – there were nearly 30 violations on the central sector of the front alone this Friday. The Red Air Force reciprocated. Sergei Dolgoushin and a comrade took a couple of Ratas from Novy Dvor near Grodno and headed over the Suwałki 'bulge' – a small German-occupied region of eastern Poland, centred on the town of Suwałki, which protruded into the border with the USSR. They found the makeshift airfields peppering the bulge crammed with aircraft. Nearby, Soviet troops patrolling the frontier outside the town of Augustów found the Germans had removed the wire entanglements along the frontier.[48]

It was past 7 on Friday evening, but still Soviet trade minister Anastas Mikoyan was in his Moscow office. The telephone rang. It was the Riga harbourmaster. 'Comrade Mikoyan, there are around 25 Germans ships, some of them are being loaded, others unloaded. We've learned that they are all preparing to leave port tomorrow, June 21st, even though they will not be finished loading or unloading. Please advise on how to act: delay their sailing or let them go.'

These were tell-tale signs that an attack was imminent. Mikoyan wanted to detain the German vessels. Stalin thought otherwise. Seizing the ships, even temporarily, would be precisely the act of provocation Adolf Hitler was waiting for. The ships could sail.[49]

In the historic city of Jelgava, a couple of dozen miles southwest of Latvia's capital Riga, leave had been restricted for the Soviet anti-aircraft gunners quartered there – another sign of growing tension. After a long, cold winter, Jelgava had come alive with spring; the lime trees blossomed, parks and river banks became lush seas of green enjoyed by the occupying Russian forces. But for two months, German aircraft had impudently flown high over Jelgava with no response either from fighters based at the nearby airfield or the anti-aircraft guns themselves – although battery commanders had been issued Russian–German dictionaries and posters featuring German aircraft photographed from various angles. Jelgava's native population had grown increasingly uncooperative or even downright hostile to Russian troops. Tonight, one of the Soviet Union's most popular singers and actresses, Lyubov Orlova, staged a concert in the former home of Jelgava's guild of craftsmen – commandeered by the Red Army to entertain off-duty soldiers. As they left the show troops were struck by columns of Soviet units unexpectedly passing westwards through town 'in a continuous stream in a kind of ominous silence', Private Ivan Yanson remembered. 'Local residents stood in silence – a silence which seemed somehow eerie, arousing unpleasantly heavy forebodings.'[50]

At the end of a stifling Friday in Berlin, Adolf Hitler was closeted in the Reich Chancellery with Walther Hewel, one of his longest-standing supporters. Hewel, the Führer's Foreign Ministry's liaison officer, found his master in two minds. On the one hand, Hitler was unable to sleep and 'wishing it were ten weeks' time' – for right now he was 'standing in front of a locked door'. And on the other, the German leader was convinced his decision was the right one. He had spent the morning poring over the plans for the campaign down to the smallest detail and had concluded there was 'no way for the enemy to get the better of Germany'. And so he ordered his military commanders to issue the codeword 'Dortmund', setting an unstoppable force in motion. The armed forces of the Third Reich would strike those of Soviet Russia at dawn on Sunday 22 June.[51]

'YOU CAN DRAW YOUR OWN CONCLUSIONS...' SATURDAY 21 JUNE, MORNING

Oblivious to the unstoppable chain of events set in motion by their Führer, Berliners awoke on Saturday 21 June to yet another prediction of the imminent downfall of the British Empire. According to the *Völkischer Beobachter*, 'Jewish capital hyenas already regard the Empire as lost'. Elsewhere, readers were reminded that 12 months had passed since 'the birth of the new Europe' when the French had been forced to surrender at Compiègne. The capital awaited an influx of football fans from Cologne and Dresden, bound for the Olympic Stadium, to contest the third-place play-off of the German championships. (The Saxons would comprehensively defeat the Rhinelanders 4–1.) Berliners looking to escape the oppressive heat headed for the beach at Wannsee, west of the city. While they sunbathed or swam in the waters of the Havel, just a stone's throw away Joseph Goebbels was hosting a reception for Alessandro Pavolini, a former journalist and now Italy's minister for popular culture. Having greeted the Fascist minister at Tempelhof airport and breakfasted with him at the prestigious Hotel Adlon, Goebbels invited Pavolini and his entourage to join him at his villa in Schwanenwerder. He found his guest 'extremely pleasant', but he was unable to devote much time or attention – there were more pressing issues weighing on his mind.[52]

It promised to be a busy Saturday for Leonid Sandalov. Fourth Army's chief-of-staff had a day of inspections and visits ahead of him, beginning with a walk along the bank of the Mukhavets 30 miles east of Brest to inspect work on an alternative command post – several wooden bunkers dug into the ground and covered with earth. Work was progressing well, so the colonel took a staff car to the fighter airfield at Pruzany, 30 miles away. Preparations here were rather less satisfactory; the concrete runway had still not been laid, while the promised new aircraft had not arrived. 'Two days ago the regiment received a couple of new MiGs. All the others – out-of-date fighters armed with machine-gun arms,' the commander told Sandalov apologetically. The flier in charge of the fighter base outside Kobrin, next on the tour, was rather more optimistic. Yes, right now he only had 60 old 'Seagulls' – I-15 biplanes – but 20 new Yak-1s had been delivered the previous day. 'The pilots who can fly these aircraft are arriving by passenger train tomorrow,' the fighter regiment commander told Sandalov.[53]

The crews of 35th Panzer Regiment spent the morning preparing their vehicles for action. Personal effects and coats were stuffed into a crate behind the turret, while bulkier items were handed over to the division's baggage column. A large wooden box in the back of the tank contained blankets and canvas strips. Inside, food was stuffed into any spare space – three tins of rice or vegetables per man, five small bags of bread, three boxes of dark chocolate and a solid fuel stove.[54]

Lieutenant General Dmitry Ryabyshev set out from the small oil town of Drohobycz, 50 miles outside Lvov, to visit the units of his VIII Mechanised Corps, scattered around southwest Galicia. North of Przemyśl, he watched as eight German aircraft broke formation and flew low in pairs, circling over troop concentrations, military installations and main roads. The 47-year-old was enraged by the Germans' arrogance, but 'never imagined that there were hours, not days, before war began'.[55]

Drilling his gunners on ranges outside Vladimir-Volynskiy, Lieutenant Vassili Petrov had also followed the progress of a German reconnaissance aircraft as it circled over the town and the nearby monastery which now served as the Red Army barracks. 'In an hour, the film will be developed and they'll have yet more proof of our "aggressive" intentions,' one of Petrov's comrades mocked. It was such acidic remarks, not the Germans' flouting of international borders, which the 24-year-old officer was expected to react to – as he learned when he was summoned to see his unit's commissar. 'You are forbidden from spreading or commenting on German troops and all we see during reconnaissance,' the political leader impressed on Petrov. 'In conversations you may only refer to official communications. Rumours are rumours.'[56]

In Lvov, Alexander Yegorov reported for duty at the headquarters of 32nd Tank Division to begin his appointment as chief-of-staff of 63rd Tank Regiment. The division was one of the best equipped on the entire southern front – most of its aged T-26s had been replaced by the heavy armour of KVs and T-34s. In two days' time, the young captain would see the regiment 'perform on the range' for the first time. It was none too soon, he told the division's commander Yefim Pushkin. 'There's increasing talk about the imminence of war.' Pushkin nodded. Whatever the TASS communiqué had proclaimed just a few days earlier, all the evidence pointed to a German attack at any moment. Intelligence reports suggested commandants had already been appointed to take charge of Lvov and Przemyśl, while the Germans had stockpiled road signs pointing the way to the Galician capital. 'You can draw your own conclusions,' Pushkin told Yegorov as he offered his hand. 'Good luck and goodbye.' The captain left to join his regiment and begin planning for Monday's manoeuvres.[57]

The trees on the edge of Dzików concealed the mountain infantry of 1st *Gebirgs* Division, who'd spent the past few days reconnoitring the woods, looking for suitable jump-off positions and above all observing the Russians on the other side of the border. Somewhere in the undulating, forested terrain lay the village of Oleszyce and its manor house, headquarters of the local border regiment. Like hunters stalking their prey, the *Jäger* – minus their trademark caps and with windbreaker jackets over their uniforms – counted the changing of the guards in the observation towers, recorded the number of Soviet companies, noted any vehicles coming and going, marked Russian field positions on their maps, and watched the Russian troops and civilians dig trench after trench.[58]

'I PREDICT THE SWASTIKA … OVER THE KREMLIN IN MOSCOW IN FOUR TO FIVE WEEKS…' SATURDAY 21 JUNE, MID-DAY

It was 11am when Major Hannes Trautloft was called to the telephone at the command post of *Jagdgeschwader* 54 in the village of Trakehnen in East Prussia. 'Listen to the following,' the voice on the other end said. 'Dortmund, Mohn, Kresse, Aster, Aster!' Each was a codeword. Collectively they meant that war with Russia would begin in the small hours of Sunday.

A decade earlier, Trautloft had been sent to the Soviet Union when Germany secretly trained its pilots in Russia, but had been too young and obsessed with the idea of flight to make any observations about his hosts. Ten years older, wiser, imbued with National Socialist ardour, and with 13 victories under his belt in the skies of Spain, Poland, France and Britain, the 29-year-old now faced wrestling with 'the demons of Asia'. He dismissed Russia's vastness, the masses of aircraft she possessed; his pilots had a wealth of combat experience and, since returning victoriously from the Balkans, they'd received the latest model of the Messerschmitt Me109. It handled magnificently. 'We have a weapon in our hands with which we can hold our own against any foe.'[59]

Most German commanders reacted with rather less enthusiasm when the confirmation of the attack came through on teleprinters or by radio. Some even refused to accept it. 'Young man, do you believe what you've just been told?' Hans-Günther Seraphim's commander asked with a doleful expression.

'*Nein, Herr Major!*' the 37-year-old adjutant replied.

'Think of me, if you still can. There's a good chance neither of us will see our homes again. All of us will remain there in Russia. How can they make such a mistake? This is the end of Germany.' 52nd Rifle Regiment's Major Hans Treptow shook his head in disbelief. 'It's all propaganda,' he told Walther Nehring, 18th Panzer Division's commander. 'It'll be countermanded during the night.'[60]

More typical, however, was the reaction of 25th Infantry Division's officers. They left the final briefing with their commander Heinrich Clössner in 'no doubt about the difficulty of the fighting which lay in store,' operations officer Major 'Heinz' Gaedcke observed. 'Concern about the outcome of this struggle burdened every man – but he never said so.' The size of Russia terrified Gaedcke. 'Where would it end? At the Dnieper, 500 kilometres away, at the Volga or in the Urals?' he wondered. 'But maybe everything wasn't so bad and much on the other side was just a bluff. Perhaps the war would be decided in our favour by the autumn. Who knew?' This mix of hope and fatalism crops up frequently in the private writings of senior officers. 'None of us knows the political reason why we are supposed to invade and destroy the Russians in complete peace,' Hans Riederer von Paar, commanding an armoured reconnaissance unit, noted. All the former cavalryman could do was reassure his officers: 'The Führer has had wonderful foresight when it comes to the political-military situation up to now. Therefore we have a duty to have rock-solid confidence that this campaign, too, will lead to the great goal we are striving for.' Georg-Hans Reinhardt confided to his wife in a similar vein. 'Sometimes you almost get the impression that we have spoiled those at the top that they think we could do everything,' he wrote in a final letter home before the battle began. 'Hopefully, we can do it all.' Reinhardt had led a panzer division into the heart of Warsaw in September 1939, a panzer corps to the Channel in May 1940 and now would command that same corps again, objective Leningrad. The 54-year-old was convinced of the necessity of the campaign – 'we must attack them and destroy them' – but he was under no illusions about the demands it would place on his men – and the nation. 'It's war again – war not just for parts of, but for the entire great German Wehrmacht and for the entire German homeland! This new theatre of war will be hard, perhaps the hardest, because the Russians know what's at stake – they'll fight.' As he had done in Poland and France, Georg-Hans Reinhardt put his faith in his men, in his Führer, and in the rallying cry of the armoured warriors: *Panzer voran* – panzers in the lead!⁶¹

Whatever their doubts, whatever their misgivings, almost every commander added his postscript to Hitler's appeal: a rousing personal order of the day – all considerably briefer than the Führer's – to spur the men on. Hubert Lanz promised his 1st *Gebirgs* Division would 'drag the Devil out of Hell'. Some generals struck an ideological note, like Erich Hoepner. 'Tomorrow we begin the great struggle which we Germans must wage against the Bolshevik Slavdom to preserve our German people and our descendants.' It was Bolshevism, Joachim Lemelsen reminded his XLVII Panzer Corps, which had caused Germany's defeat in World War I by stabbing the army in the back and causing 15 years of misery in the Reich. 'We should always remember that.' Other commanders tantalised the men in their charge with promises of glory. Conrad von Cochenhausen guaranteed his 134th Infantry Division participation in 'the greatest battle in world history'. In the south, Ludwig Crüwell set his 11th Panzer – the 'Ghost Division' – the goal of reaching the Dnieper. 'Like we were in Belgrade, we'll be the first ones there.' And Walther Nehring offered the men of 18th Panzer the greatest prize of all: 'Our objective is ambitious – it's the enemy's capital: Moscow.'⁶²

So much for exhortations. Alfred Opitz, one of Nehring's gunners, was struck by the 'icy silence hanging over the company' when their commander finished reading the two appeals. As the men were dismissed a handful dared to voice their misgivings. 'As long as it doesn't misfire!' one muttered. 'Well it's goodnight if it does!' a comrade fired back. Radio operator Karlernst Malkmus and his comrades had discussed the idea of war with Russia frequently, but the reality 'was like bad news to us'. His company commander did not sugar coat the coming campaign and the men left the briefing 'in a depressed mood'. A few still refused to believe the news they had just received 'until the first shots have been fired'. Alfred Seidl and his fellow pilots of

Jagdgeschwader 53 returned to their tents outside Suwałki in stunned disbelief. 'Let's hope it all goes well,' they told each other, but with little conviction. Seidl studied a map of Russia. 'How is tiny Germany supposed to cope with this huge empire?' he asked himself.[63]

The majority of junior officers and men, however, were convinced of the cause and convinced of victory. Theodor Habicht's men were itching for a fight – even before he read out Hitler's proclamation. 'They like war, particularly as they can already smell that there is a proper war on the cards again.' Reservist supply officer Erich Maresch studied the faces of his men as first an order of the day from their commander, 45th Infantry Division's Fritz Schlieper, then their Führer were read to them. 'From the enormous preparations, everyone imagined this of course,' Maresch noted, 'and yet every man is utterly surprised. Now everyone, even the ordinary soldier, knows what's at stake. There's a deep, serious look on the young sun-tanned faces.' A non-commissioned officer in 121st Infantry Division observed his comrades 'take in every word of the Führer's order. This is a war on the grandest scale, the likes of which history has never seen. A front from Finland to Romania! How our hearts burned! Didn't the fate of Europe and half the world rest with us soldiers?' Signaller Albert Beyer returned to his company after guard duties near the Lithuanian border to hear his comrades burst into the national anthem after Hitler's declaration had been read out. 'That's all I need to know,' he noted. 'We are delighted that the almost unbearable tension melts away.' A soldier in 296th Infantry Division expected 'Russia's collapse in three weeks', while one SS non-commissioned officer was so confident that 'the destruction of Russia will take no longer than that of France', he was already planning his leave for August. And a junior officer relished 'fire, cordite, iron bombs and shells all raining down on the Russians'. He continued:

> I predict the swastika flag will be flying over the Kremlin in Moscow in four to five weeks and that we'll still have time to give the Tommies a seeing to this year after we have dealt with Russia. It's no secret that we'll reach Moscow in four weeks with our invincible Wehrmacht – it's only 1,000 kilometres as the crow flies. We just need one more blitzkrieg.[64]

'IF IT ALL KICKS OFF AT FIRST LIGHT TOMORROW...'
SATURDAY 21 JUNE, AFTERNOON

Almost ready to unleash that blitzkrieg was the armour of 35th Panzer Regiment. The panzers began to move out of their camp in the middle of Saturday afternoon, bound for woods a couple of miles short of the Bug, just north of Brest. The vehicles passed huge fuel dumps and young men of the labour service, the *Reichsarbeitsdienst*, lining both sides of the road, staring enviously at the panzers. The sluggish journey became more arduous as darkness fell. Despite the stop-start nature of the journey – and the fact that he couldn't sit upright due to his height – Richard von Rosen fell asleep in his gunlayer's seat.[65]

In East Prussia, the commanders of 18th Infantry Regiment put overalls on top of their battlefield grey tunics and threw shovels or pickaxes over their shoulders. Dressed as ordinary labourers, they moved up to the border to select jump-off positions for the morning's attack. While every officer from regimental commander Carl Becker down to platoon leaders surveyed the land west of the small Lithuanian town of Kalvarija, their men laid blankets on the East Prussian grass, stripped down to their gym shorts and sunbathed. 'Hardly anyone was able to sleep any more,' remembered 20-year-old August Freitag, a horse driver with the regiment's artillery. 'There was tremendous tension, naturally, because a good number of us – including me – had not seen anything of war. Everyone talked about what might happen the next morning.' Freitag and his comrades had completed all their preparations for the coming battle: unnecessary baggage was removed from vehicles, rations and ammunition issued, oats for the animals stockpiled. The young driver used the time to write a letter to his family in Westphalia. 'Who knew when we'd get the chance again?'[66]

In Moscow, Stalin's scheming, obsequious head of the NKVD, Lavrentiy Beria, was again machinating against his rivals and seeking to curry favour with his master. In his sights, the staff at the Soviet Embassy in Berlin, especially Ambassador Vladimir Dekanozov and his military attaché, Vasiliy Tupikov. Tupikov – 'a stupid general' – warned Hitler was about to unleash three army groups against the Soviet Union aimed at Leningrad, Moscow and Kiev. As for Dekanozov, Beria complained, 'he is still bombarding me with "disinformation" about Hitler allegedly preparing an attack on the USSR'. The attack would begin the following day, Sunday 22 June. Lavrentiy Beria paid no attention. 'I and my people, Joseph Vissarionovich, firmly remember your wise predestination: Hitler will not attack us in 1941!'[67]

Having finished his inspections, Dmitry Ryabyshev decided not to return to his headquarters, but call on the staff of the Twenty-Sixth Army. The army commander was away. His deputy, Colonel Ivan Varennikov, dismissed the corps commander's reports as Ryabyshev spread out a map marked with German concentrations. 'Your fears are unfounded,' Varennikov said. 'I promise you, we'll still be at peace in a year's time. I'd bet my head on it.' As for the daily violations by German aircraft, perhaps the pilots had acted on their own initiative. 'So should we shoot at them?' the colonel asked Ryabyshev rhetorically. 'Let the diplomats handle such cases.' Disheartened, Dmitry Ryabyshev returned to his headquarters.[68]

The screech of a motorcycle woke cavalry captain Ion Emilian from his afternoon doze on the edge of the Valva woods in northeastern Romania. For the past week, the officer's squadron had occupied a village evacuated by its inhabitants. Barely half a mile away, somewhere beneath the fir and beech trees, lay the border with the Soviet Union – re-drawn 12 months earlier when Moscow annexed the provinces of Bukovina and Bessarabia. Alone, Romania was in no position to recover her lost territories. Germany's impending invasion, however, presented Bucharest the perfect opportunity to strike.

In time, Hungary, Finland and Italy would commit forces in the East, but only Romania was at the Third Reich's side from the very first day of the war. That did not stop German leaders treating their ally with contempt: 'no good at all' was Hitler's terse assessment, while the German military mission, which arrived in the country ahead of the attack, dismissed the armed forces as 'inconsistent, poor and in some cases outmoded'. The Romanian infantryman relied even more than the German on the horse. In divisions of comparable size, there were 1,000 motor vehicles behind every *Landser*, but fewer than 200 supporting his Romanian counterpart. There were, however, more than 7,500 horses in every Romanian infantry division – nearly one beast for every two men. Officers were well trained but in battle lacked the resolve and determination of their German equivalents. As for the men, they were 'undemanding but tough, willing to defend their homeland'.

In Ion Antonescu, Romania had a competent military but uncertain political leader. A career officer and later defence minister, he had been named premier in the wake of Moscow's 'land grab' over the summer of 1940, then relied on German support to overcome his rivals. As a result, the *conducător* – leader – always felt unsure of his position. 'Your Führer – like the Duce – has a great movement behind him, one almost encompassing the entire nation. I have nothing like that behind me,' he told German officials. Of one thing the 59-year-old could be certain: popular support for a war of liberation. The song of the summer opened with the following refrain:

Tonight war began on the Prut
Romanians are marching across

Bringing back under arms
The possessions they lost last summer!

And now the sentiments of the song would become reality. A cavalry officer clambered out of the sidecar and handed Ion Emilian a yellow envelope, whispering as he did so: '*Alea jacta est*' – the die is cast. The contents were Emilian's orders from headquarters: *cross the border and destroy the Russian guard tower and observation post at 3.45am.* 'Now we could finally settle our account with the invaders of Bukovina,' the 34-year-old former lawyer thought. 'Our brothers would be liberated. We would avenge all the humiliation of last year.' But Emilian also pondered questions of fate. How would his trusted horse, Dac, fare? Or the 44 men he led? Would they all survive the night? 'Thoughts of life and death constantly ran through my mind,' he recalled. 'I kept on asking myself questions which I could not answer.' Radiating calmness and hiding his inner doubts, he called together his troop leaders. 'Tonight is the shortest night of the year. It will be one of the longest of your lives in your memories,' he told them. 'My comrades, my friends, tonight we go to war to liberate the provinces taken from us and force Communism into retreat wherever it lies.'[69]

At Radzyń Podlaski, 40 miles west of the Bug, an earnest-looking Fritz Pockrandt spread out a series of maps for his bomber crews. 'If it all kicks off at first light tomorrow, this is our target,' he said, and pointed to a fighter airbase about 40 miles south of Białystok. Pockrandt and the He111s in his *Kampfgeschwader* 53 would attack the ammunition bunkers and runway, another formation the barracks and a third the fighters lined up on the edge of the field. 'I hope that the new and young crews fight as well as the old ones among you and prove themselves in their first and subsequent missions.' The pilots and observers grabbed maps and sketches of the airfield, then left in silence. 'Everybody is stunned,' wrote pilot Arnold Döring – one of those facing his first sortie over enemy territory, 'and then there's excitement.'[70]

Outside the provincial Romanian town of Focșani, a little over 100 miles north of the capital, the bomber crews of *Kampfgeschwader* 27 had been summoned to a briefing by their superior commander, Kurt Pflugbeil, in charge of IV *Fliegerkorps* (Air Corps). The final aircraft had arrived from Belgrade that afternoon. Ground staff, who'd left France three weeks earlier, already had stacks of bombs waiting to be loaded onto the freshly landed Heinkels. There was just time for the new arrivals to receive vaccinations against cholera before gathering around Pflugbeil. The 51-year-old general outlined the political situation, then told crews they would be going into action against Russia that very evening, striking the airfield at Czernovitz in Ukraine, 200 miles away. 'The mood is splendid,' crewman Wilhelm Möller noted in his diary. 'No-one trusted the Russians implicitly since the outbreak of war anyway, although no-one suspected the clash would begin so soon.'[71]

After a full day of inspections, Leonid Sandalov returned to his home, just 300 yards from Fourth Army's headquarters in Kobrin. As they did most evenings, Sandalov strolled with his wife Tanya along the bank of the Mukhavets. When they returned home a couple of hours later, they found the army's commander Aleksandr Korobkov waiting outside. It had been a frustrating day for Korobkov. He'd spoken with the military district's staff in Minsk, raised concerns about the growing German build-up – confirmed by reports from other armies pouring into the headquarters – and requested permission to pull his men back from the border to prepared positions, to withdraw a division from Brest, to disperse the aircraft neatly arrayed at his airfields. Every request had been flatly refused by the district's chief-of-staff Vladimir Klimovskikh.

'So, for a while, we'll forget about business,' Korobkov told his friend. 'I have a nice offer: at 8pm the actors of the Byelorussian Operetta Theatre are performing an open-air concert at the House of the Red Army. Let's have a look.'[72]

'DON'T PANIC... "THE BOSS" KNOWS ALL ABOUT IT...'
SATURDAY 21 JUNE, EVENING

Alexander Poskrebyshev sat by the open window in his office at the Kremlin. It afforded him no cool – it was a hot, stuffy evening in the Soviet capital. Not a leaf stirred on the trees outside. After a busy Saturday, Moscow was beginning to empty as overcrowded trams and trolley buses returned people to the suburbs.

As the head of Stalin's chancellery stared at his large glass of vodka, another Party crony, Yakov Chadaev, secretary of the Council of Commissars, walked into the office.

'Well, what's new, Alexander Nikolaevich?' Chadaev asked.

The normally direct Poskrebyshev stared at his friend for a few seconds, reluctant to respond.

'Something important?' Chadaev prompted him.

'I suppose so,' Poskrebyshev said almost in a whisper. 'The boss' – he nodded in the direction of Stalin's office – 'has just been talking in an agitated state with Timoshenko. Apparently, the Germans are just about to attack.'

'Attack us?' a stunned Chadaev asked.

'Who else?'[73]

For the second time in 12 hours, diplomat Gerhard Kegel was risking his life. A committed Communist since his university days in the late 1920s, the 33-year-old had spied for the Soviet Union as he rose through the ranks of the Foreign Ministry until he was appointed deputy trade secretary at the German Embassy in Moscow. On Saturday morning, he had told his handler, Konstantin Leontiev, that war would begin within 48 hours. It was now 7pm and the two men were meeting again. 'This morning the embassy received instructions to destroy all secret documents,' Kegel said. 'All the embassy's staff have been ordered to pack all their belongings by morning, deliver them to the embassy and remain in the embassy building.'[74]

In the courtyard of an East Prussian farm 20 miles northwest of Grodno, Friedrich Grupe's commander waited until 8pm before calling his men together. All day he had awaited the codeword: *leave the wood for barracks construction behind*. When it failed to arrive, he gathered his battalion as the sun began to disappear behind the woods to the west. The invasion of the Soviet Union was on. Having acknowledged his men with a silent salute, the major began to read Hitler's appeal. 'Soldiers of the Eastern Front...' There was no '*Sieg Heil*' for Hitler, spontaneous or otherwise, at the end. The men moved off to their jump-off positions without a word.[75]

The strains of chamber music followed by jazz poured out of the radios of those Minsk residents who tuned in this mid-summer's evening. In the breaks between the programmes, the announcer encouraged the audience to listen again the next day when there would be a review of the week's military operations abroad and instructions on combating paratroopers.

For the inhabitants of the Byelorussian capital who chose to head into the city this Saturday night, there was varied entertainment. The bill at the city's cinemas was typical Stalinist fare: oil tanker crews striving to improve their output for the benefits of socialism in *Tanker Derbent*; two screenings of *Frontovye Podrugi* (Girlfriend at the Front), the story of women volunteering as nurses in Finland

– but finding themselves also taking up arms against the enemy; a documentary on Maxim Gorky and a biopic of Ustym Karmaliuk, a Ukrainain 'Robin Hood' who became a folk hero for his exploits in the early 19th century. Live entertainment was offered in Gorky Park in the form of an evening celebrating Clara Zetkin – a German Marxist, campaigner for women's rights and the founder of International Women's Day – while the ever-busy touring theatre groups were on stage again: the Poles performing *The Marriage of Figaro*, the Ukrainians *In the Steppe of Ukraine*, while a Jewish group from Vilnius filled the J. V. Stalin Club with an evening of comedy and folk songs.[76]

And in the House of the Red Army, an imposing new neoclassical building just off Minsk's main thoroughfare, Dmitry Pavlov sat down with his senior staff to enjoy the comedic operetta *Svadba v Malinovke* – Wedding in Malinovka. The shaven-headed Pavlov was a brave warrior – and one of the Red Army's foremost proponents of armoured warfare. He'd led Republican tanks in Spain and skilfully commanded a corps in the otherwise inglorious Winter War with Finland. His reward: command of the Western Military District. It was, perhaps, beyond his competency. Subordinates found the 43-year-old general clever and energetic, but also stubborn – he rarely listened to the counsel of juniors and over-compensated for his limited strategic vision with overweening self-confidence. He was not oblivious to the increasingly frantic reports pouring in from his corps and armies about German concentrations in eastern Poland, but chose to brush them aside with a nonchalant: 'Don't panic. Take it easy. "The boss" knows all about it.' Whatever concerns preyed on Pavlov's mind this Saturday evening, he was put at ease to some degree by the presence of the head of the Byelorussian arm of the Communist Party, Panteleimon Ponomarenko, at the performance. As the general enjoyed the operetta – a tale of life in a revolutionary Ukrainian village – from the privileged position of his box, a staff officer burst in and spoke in Pavlov's ear. Chief-of-staff Ivan Boldin could not hear what was said – but he did hear his general's startled response: 'That cannot be!' Pavlov turned to his deputy. 'What nonsense!' he said quietly. 'Reconnaissance reports that there's a lot of unrest on the border, that the Germans have reportedly put their troops on a full war footing and have even begun to shoot in some sectors along our border!' Dmitry Pavlov did not intend to act. He gently held Boldin's hands, put his fingers to his lips, then pointed at the stage, where the actors were playing out a scene from the Russian civil war.[77]

The House of the Red Army in Drohobycz was packed too, the mood feverish, as a concert was laid on for the officers of VIII Mechanised Corps and their families. During the interval, they chatted with their corps commander about how they planned to enjoy the impending day off. 'The concert and the conversations to some extent dispelled my gloomy thoughts and diverted me from worries and concerns,' Dmitry Ryabyshev remembered. 'But only for a while.' A military song and dance troupe provided the entertainment, reaching a rousing climax with the 'March of the Soviet Tankmen':

> With the rattle of gunfire, the glint of steel
> Our machines will go into battle furiously
> When we're called to arms by Comrade Stalin
> And the First Marshal will lead us into action!

How ironic these lyrics seemed to the corps' senior commissar Nikolai Popel. Almost all of VIII Mechanised Corps' armour was obsolete, save for six KV-1s and ten T-34s delivered the previous week.[78]

The last light of a mid-summer's day gave colour and life to Vyacheslav Molotov's otherwise sterile office on the Kremlin's upper floor with its obligatory etching of Lenin and an oil painting of the revolution's leader alongside his protégé Stalin. Friedrich-Werner Graf von der Schulenburg sat uncomfortably in a brown leather chair. Through the early months of the Nazi–Soviet Pact, the 65-year-old ambassador had met the Soviet foreign minister frequently. But as relations between Berlin and Moscow cooled, so the discussions became increasingly sporadic. More than four weeks had passed since they had last conferred. This Saturday night, the German diplomat had been summoned to account for a litany of transgressions: the flagrant and systematic violation of the Soviet Union's borders by German aircraft; the failure by Berlin to respond to the TASS communiqué – or even publish it in newspapers; the growing number of rumours circulating that an attack was imminent; the departure of German officials overseeing the trade details of the 1939 pact; and the fact that the wives and children of embassy staff had packed their bags and left. From tapped phone conversations, Molotov knew the German diplomat believed Hitler was planning to attack Russia. He knew too that Schulenburg had warned Hitler that 'waging war against the Soviet Union is pure madness' – and that his warning had been brushed aside. Tonight, ever the seasoned diplomat, Schulenburg did his master's bidding. He offered no answers to any of Molotov's questions, save for limply remarking that the families of his embassy staff were keen to escape the stifling heat of the Moscow summer. At this, the Soviet foreign minister gave up and Schulenburg was shown the door.[79]

In the small Galician town of Złoczów, 40 miles east of Lvov, Samuel Tennenbaum enjoyed his usual Saturday evening card game with friends. A Polish Jew and a lawyer by education, under Soviet rule the 32-year-old had been appointed technical director of the now-nationalised family pharmaceutical business. Tennenbaum hated the Communists, the dreariness of daily life, the terrible Russian films, the shortages in the government-run stores, the constant harassment of the NKVD. Playing cards was one of the few moments of pleasure in the father-of-two's life, a chance to talk freely with friends. Through the winter and spring of 1941, the conversations had increasingly turned to the subject of Nazi–Soviet relations. 'The question was no longer whether Hitler would attack Russia, but when,' Tennenbaum recollected four decades later. As the talk died out and the guests began to leave, one turned to the host: 'June is coming to an end and the Germans haven't attacked yet.' Tennenbaum was not reassured. He turned on the radio and listened to the BBC's Polish-language service. A German attack could come in a matter of hours.[80]

On the Bug downstream of Brest, the border guards of the 17th Frontier District remained at their posts long after their watches were over. 'No officer went home,' Senior Lieutenant Dzhamankul Dzhenchurayev recalled. The situation seemed too tense. 'Men on duty removed their boots, unbuttoned their jackets and slept on unassembled bunks. Their rifles stood right there, near bedside tables on which lay ammunition and grenades.' Opposite the village of Stary Bubel, Vasily Gorbunov's men watched a figure run up to the Bug, throw himself in the water and swim the 300 or so feet to the Soviet side of the river. The swimmer was a Polish miller, Pavel Dudko. That afternoon he had been informed by his brother that the German officer quartered with them had been boasting while drunk: 'Russians kaput! We'll begin at 4am tomorrow...' While his Uncle Vanya splashed about by the German-occupied bank of the Bug as a distraction, Pavel sought to alert the Russians. Breathless and with tears in his eyes, he told the Soviet border guards: 'Comrades! Tell your commanders that the Germans are preparing to attack the Soviet Union. Be ready!' Gorbunov was sceptical. 'Aren't you lying? Perhaps *they* sent you?' Dudko shook his head. 'I am an old soldier with the Russian army, I fought back in 1914, I want to help you.' Gorbunov reported the incident to his superiors, who made no decision. 'We believe and yet we don't believe,' was their response. 'The facts say: war tomorrow. And our brains: no, this is absurd.' He and his *politruk* made the decision their superiors could not. They put the men in the border outposts on alert from 3am. 'Germany will attack us. We have a task: to defend the soil entrusted to us by the Motherland,' he told his bemused guards. 'To your posts! To battle!'[81]

The Bug at Sokal, 45 miles north of Lvov, is no more than 80ft wide in places. At dusk this Saturday night, a 30-year-old former furniture maker from Bavaria clambered up the right bank and was immediately arrested by the men of the 90th Border Guard Detachment. Alfred Liskow was quickly taken to the local headquarters in Vladimir-Volynskiy, 25 miles away, and interrogated. Around 4am Soviet time, the German Army would attack. 'As a supporter of the Soviet regime, having learned about it, I decided to desert and report it,' he pleaded with his captors. Fifth Army's commander Mikhail Potapov in Lutsk dismissed the news. Border guard commander Major Mikhail Bychkovsky was also sceptical – but he ordered his men along the Bug to be extra vigilant.[82]

Around the same time as Alfred Liskow was swimming the Bug, a deserter crossed the lines of 5th Rifle Division in Lithuania. The Germans were coming, he told his interrogators, and when they did, they would 'finish you off pretty quickly'.[83]

News of *a* deserter reached the Kremlin, where Joseph Stalin had been closeted with a succession of either military or political leaders, or both, since the early evening. As with every other report, the *vozhd* dismissed it out of hand. 'The German generals may have sent this turncoat to provoke a conflict,' he snarled.

'We think he is telling the truth,' Semyon Timoshenko flashed back.

Stalin asked his generals what to do. Silence.

Timoshenko continued. The Red Army numbered more than 306 divisions, 186 of them in the West. It was time to put them on alert – the orders had already been drafted.

'The Germans, to our knowledge, do not possess such numbers of troops,' the dictator snapped. 'And it's too early to issue such a directive.' He was still convinced his army might respond to some act of provocation and invoke a war.[84]

Evening was turning to night by the time the staff of the Kiev Military District had finished loading maps, documents, chairs, typewriters and tables onto waiting buses and trucks. With war clearly imminent, the headquarters had decided to move west to the city of Zhitomir. Among the men, there was no sense of impending disaster, just jokes and laughter. Nor too were Kievans concerned. The military district's deputy chief-of-staff observed life as normal on the streets, in the parks and gardens on the left bank of the Dnieper on a warm June evening. Ivan Bagramyan drove in a staff car at the head of the column, reading the newspapers under the last light of day as the column pulled out of Kiev on its 90-mile journey. 'There was nothing troubling in them,' he wrote.[85]

After a sultry summer's day in the German capital, Berliners were cooling off with a stroll down its most famous boulevard where the linden trees offered a little shade. Women wore brightly coloured dresses, the men accompanying them, dark suits. Boredom, the heat, or perhaps both caused the guard posted outside the Soviet Embassy to lean against the gate post and doze. Inside, almost all the staff had long gone home. But not Valentin Berezhkov. Though just 24, Berezhkov was the embassy's first secretary – the ambassador's deputy – as well as its senior interpreter. All day long his superior had sought an audience with the German foreign minister without success. Berezhkov persisted into the evening. Every 30 minutes he telephoned the German Foreign Ministry, just around the corner in Wilhelmstrasse. And every 30 minutes he received the same response: there was no-one available to receive the Soviet ambassador. Finally, at 9.30pm, the Germans relented and Vladimir Dekanozov was ushered in to see Joachim von Ribbentrop's deputy, Ernst von Weizsäcker. The terse meeting was a near carbon copy of that played out 1,000 miles to the east in Moscow not 60 minutes earlier. The Russian diplomat protested; his German counterpart procrastinated. Dekanozov handed over a note complaining that Luftwaffe reconnaissance aircraft had violated Soviet airspace no fewer than 180 times in the past two months, sometimes flying as deep as 100 miles inside Soviet territory. The Soviet ambassador demanded a response. Weizsäcker could not give him one, but he promised to look into the matter.[86]

In the Crimea, the curtain of night had enveloped the Black Sea Fleet. The big ships rode at anchor in Severnaya Bay; smaller vessels were tied up at the jetties and wharves on the southern shore. It was, remembered Captain A. K. Evseev, on duty in the fleet's headquarters, 'a wonderful Crimean evening'. With the fleet in harbour, there was little for Evseev and his colleagues to do. But elsewhere in the city, life was thriving.

> The streets and boulevards were brightly lit. The white houses were bathed in light, sailors on shore leave were enticed into theatres and nightclubs. Crowds of sailors and the city's inhabitants, dressed in white, filled the streets and parks. The popular promenade was, as ever, filled with people taking a stroll. There was music, jokes and laughter rang out on this evening before the holidays.[87]

'DEATH IS CLOSE AT HAND...' SATURDAY 21 JUNE, LATE EVENING

From the Baltic to the Black Sea, the thoughts of three million Germans under arms turned to home this Saturday night. 'I greet my beloved wife, my boys in spirit,' doctor Hans-Jörg Mauss of 20th Motorised Division noted in his diary.

> I hope that they are spared the horrors of war and can be happy. We willingly put our lives on the line for our loved ones and their future – and will sacrifice ourselves if necessary! We know Germany will continue to live and our children will have a happy Fatherland. For us, there's no more looking back. From now on our watchword is: forwards.

Fellow doctor Heinrich Haape was convinced the coming offensive would determine 'Germany's greatness and future'. 'Totally calm,' Haape pictured his wife at home.

> Right now, she'll be sleeping, like the loved ones and wives and mothers of millions of other men on this enormous front. At home our loved ones have no idea of what lies in store for us. They have no idea of the dangers which the coming hours and days, weeks and months, perhaps even the coming years, will bring their men. For them, it's a night like a thousand others – and we wouldn't want it any other way. We'll march. The names of the towns and villages will change. Some of them will cease to exist, others will be burned into our memories, others still will feature in every history book for a long time to come – right now, we don't know which ones. Villages will be destroyed and towns abandoned by their inhabitants. Anxious people will stand by the roadside, lost, and graves will mark the battlefields and line the main roads. And tomorrow night, where the horizon is aflame, that's where the war will be.

Countless soldiers whiled away these last hours between peace and war penning letters home. Artilleryman Walter Luhan was convinced he would not survive this new campaign. 'God, I reckon that death is close at hand,' he recorded in his diary, before composing a farewell letter to his mother:

> Dear Mutti! Please, please do not cry. Crying has no purpose. Especially not when it's all already over. Things are never as bad as they seem and a shell travels with such speed that you couldn't ask for a more pleasant or quicker death. You still have two children and they will more than make up for my death. Offset your pain through my two sisters, they will ensure you find your joyful nature again in the shortest possible time thanks to their bright, go-getting youthfulness.

A junior officer in 290th Infantry Division felt compelled to compose a poem for his mother:

> Silently the earth all around is lit up
> And the night is bright and clear,
> The playful silver of the moon gently touches
> You and your already-greying hair.
> All the stars which shine here
> Shine on you as well
> And they carry over great distances
> My dear greetings to you.

Several officers were struck by the serenity on the border – fully aware it would be shattered in a matter of hours. In the East Prussian border village of Prostken, 481st Infantry Regiment's Friedrich Weber was mesmerised by railwaymen switching a goods train from Russia onto Germany's narrower gauge. A sign on one of the wagons caught the colonel's eye: *We're bringing you bread*. And Germany was about to bring them death. 'I realised then that we were deceiving them.' XLVII Panzer Corps' commander Joachim Lemelsen watched cows and horses in the meadows and panje horses pulling ploughs to rake the potato fields. 'What will it look like tomorrow morning?' he wondered. 'The bombs and shells will explode everywhere, the houses will burn, the residents flee. The contrast is too unreal.' Manfred *Freiherr* von Plotho was possessed by 'a strange feeling' driving along the frontier, with Soviet border guards oblivious on the other side and, beyond them, farmers toiling in the fields as usual. 'In a few hours a new blitzkrieg will be raging around them,' the 32-year-old officer in 71st Infantry Division wrote to his wife Ingrid.

> When you receive these lines, the days filled with tension will be over. The world is holding its breath, a huge operation is running, a free and independent Europe will emerge from Greater Germany. These are truly exciting hours we are living through. At 7am on the morning of 22 June the armistice came into effect in Lorraine – and with it our division lowered arms. Exactly one year later, almost to the hour, we'll be the first to cross the border. This time there's no Maginot Line in front of us, victorious campaigns under the most difficult conditions have bolstered the confidence of the troops – something which not even the vastness of the East with its unique conditions can shake.[88]

'NOW THE FORTUNES OF WAR MUST DECIDE...'
SATURDAY 21 JUNE, NIGHTFALL

While his Italian guests watched *Gone With The Wind*, Joseph Goebbels was summoned to the Reich Chancellery. As the propaganda minister was driven the half-hour from his lakeside retreat to Berlin's government quarter, Adolf Hitler also took a short ride around the capital. The increasing tension of the past few days had taken their toll on the Führer; Goebbels thought he looked 'utterly exhausted' when he arrived at the imposing new chancellery. For three hours, the two men paced up and down in the parlour. As usual, the Führer talked and his propaganda minister listened. And as Hitler talked, and expanded on his plans – 160 divisions stood ready to strike along a 3,000-kilometre front ('the greatest build-up of forces in history') – he visibly relaxed. 'That's always the case with him,' Goebbels noted. 'The closer the Führer gets to a decision, the more he wakes up from a nightmare.' Having worn out the carpet in the parlour, the two men spent an hour trying out fanfares – every campaign needed one to precede the announcement of another success on the radio and loudspeakers across Germany's towns and cities. In the end they decided upon a short excerpt from Franz Liszt's *Les Préludes*. With that, preparations for the campaign against the Soviet Union were complete. 'Everything which could be done has been done,' Goebbels recorded in his diary. 'Now the fortunes of war must decide.'[89]

Alexander Yegorov returned to his quarters in Lvov and soaked up the atmosphere of a warm summer's evening. 'Lights blazed in the streets,' he recalled. 'The smell of grass and flowers flooded through the open window. It stirred the soul. Had it not been for this new assignment, I would have been on leave now – I'd planned it for June. And now it was difficult to say when I'd get another opportunity.' From a radio speaker somewhere in the same courtyard there was a reassuring, soulful voice:

Favourite city, you can sleep peacefully,
And dream and turn green with spring...

And tonight, Yegorov observed, 'the city slept peacefully'.[90]

Although he had seized the opportunity of a little light relief, neither Leonid Sandalov nor his general felt they could enjoy *Tsyganskiy Baron* – The Gypsy Baron. Sandalov was filled with 'an oppressive feeling'; Fourth Army's commander Aleksandr Korobkov was a bag of nerves all evening, repeatedly leaning across to his chief-of-staff and whispering, 'Shouldn't we go to headquarters?' In the end – and before the operetta had reached its climax – the two men did. At 11pm, Western Military District command in Minsk called and told Korobkov and his staff to be 'ready'. But Minsk went no further. The men of Fourth Army continued to enjoy their evening's entertainment.[91]

It was nearly 11pm when Vassili Petrov and his fellow artillery officers finished dining at a small guesthouse outside Vladimir-Volynskiy and rode back to their monastery barracks. There was the odd melancholic hoot of an owl, the clatter of hooves on the road, the occasional dog barking. Otherwise, the countryside was at peace. The barracks, too, were silent. Only the duty senior sergeant was still awake in Petrov's battery, waiting for the officer to return. All was calm, he reported. With that, Vassili Petrov settled down for the night.[92]

Stalin's generals had not taken their rebuff earlier in the evening lying down. Georgy Zhukov had retired to a room next to his leader's office to re-phrase the instructions he intended to pass down to his commanders in the West. It took him a good couple of hours, even though the finished document only ran to eight brief paragraphs. Forces from Leningrad to Odessa – along the entire Russo-German frontier – were to be brought to full combat readiness 'to meet a possible surprise blow by the Germans and their allies'. Bunkers on the border were to be manned, aircraft at airfields dispersed and properly camouflaged – and all by dawn, not four hours away. Joseph Stalin never put his name to the order – but he did, reluctantly, allow Timoshenko and Zhukov to issue it. 'I think Hitler is trying to provoke us,' Stalin said as the two generals left his study to begin transmitting it. 'He surely hasn't decided to make war?'[93]

'UNLESS THERE'S A MIRACLE, WE FACE THE MOST DREADFUL ADVENTURE IN OUR HISTORY!' SATURDAY 21 JUNE, 11PM

North of Tilsit in East Prussia's borderland with Lithuania, a land at peace for days suddenly came alive. Barriers with the warning sign *Halt! Feindeinsicht!* – Stop! The enemy can see you! – were lifted. Countless columns drove through, rags wrapped around their wheels to deaden the noise. The vehicles of Johann Allmayer-Beck's battery halted on the edge of the village of Jögsden, a couple of miles from the frontier. The 60 inhabitants stood in their doorways watching as hundreds of men from 21st Infantry Division passed through on foot – the noise of engines prevented the vehicles going any further. The moon fleetingly broke through the cloud cover to cast its ghostly light on lively activity: horses tied up in the gardens; messengers dashing around; telephone lines hurriedly being laid. Allmayer-Beck found his command post, a farmhouse from where he could scan the border – here nothing more than a ditch – and the Russian guards in the woods on the other side. With wispy mist hugging the valley floor under the pale light of the intermittent moon, it all looked like a film set to the 22-year-old artillery officer. And just as Allmayer-Beck observed the frontier with binoculars, so he knew the Soviet troops would be doing the same, 'scanning every bush and listening for the sounds of the night'.[94]

The men of the 407th Infantry Regiment packed their kit bags, loaded their vehicles and settled their accounts, handing over valuables and pay slips to company clerks for safekeeping, or asking for wages to be sent home. Shortly before midnight, with the companies ready to move out, non-commissioned officers reminded their men of the need for absolute silence as they marched up to the border with Lithuania. It was a warm night. Haze covered the woods like a veil, while the fragrant smell of lilac filled the air. 'Hardly a word was spoken, the only sound was the crunching of the vehicles' wheels in the sand,' one sergeant recalled. 'The closer we got to the border, the quieter our footsteps until finally we goose-stepped with jerks and pauses.' After a little over an hour, the men halted in a rye field. There they would wait for the attack to begin.[95]

In the Suwałki bulge – 'far removed from civilisation,' as one flak gunner put it, 'pine forests from horizon to horizon, and between them heaths, sand and an infinite number of mosquitoes' – a young medical officer stared at the barbed wire on the border separating 161st Infantry Division from 'the infinity of Russia'. The coming attack filled him with dread. Although he was haunted by the fate of Napoleon, it was his battalion's immediate mission – to force the Neman – which troubled him: his battalion had neither the boats nor the bridging equipment for a river crossing. 'Someone said there was a Knight's Cross hanging on the opposite bank,' he recalled – proof that the men regarded the attack as a suicide mission. The adjutant of the division's senior doctor asked to trade places. He refused. 'Well, you just want to win the Iron Cross, 1st Class,' the adjutant chided. 'You arsehole, that never crossed my mind,' the medical officer snapped back in a flash.[96]

Nearby adjutant Erich Mende and his battalion commander Bernhard Pier could not take their eyes off the grey telephone in their command post, hoping it would carry a coded message from their regiment: *Wood for barrack construction can be chopped down!* Attack cancelled. As they waited in a cold sweat, Pier shared his fears with his staff. 'We'll be swallowed up by this expanse, like Napoleon's soldiers,' he warned. 'More men will be laid low by typhoid fever, spotted fever and other dangers in almost-impassable Byelorussia than in battle! And if we're there in the Russian winter, then God have mercy on us!' As the night drew on, so Pier's pessimism worsened. Mende tried to reassure him that the Red Army would crumble just as the French had done. Perhaps the older Russian soldiers might waver, Pier argued, but not the young ones – 'they know nothing other than their Communism'. And what if the entire nation was called upon to protect Mother Russia? No, said Bernhard Pier, 'unless there's a miracle, we face the most dreadful adventure in our history!'[97]

On the same stretch of front two officers commanding detachments of 5th *Jäger* – light infantry – Division argued. One was convinced the codeword '*Wendeflagge*' – cancelling the attack – would come during the night.

'I don't believe it'll begin tomorrow!' he told his comrade. 'It's all just one huge political demonstration.'

'Don't believe such illusions,' his fellow officer shot back. 'The die is already cast. The momentum of events can no longer be stopped! Just as surely as the sun will rise in the sky tomorrow morning, so we'll attack Russia early tomorrow. Do we want to make a bet? I suggest five bottles of champagne!'

'I'll be shown to be right,' said the doubter, offering a wager. 'Five bottles of champagne that it doesn't kick off – and you'll hand them over at the next opportunity!'[98]

A short distance away on the edge of a cornfield rolled flat to create a makeshift airfield for their Me109s, the pilots of *Jagdgeschwader* 52 stood staring at a starry sky. A few hours before, they'd been ordered to the command tent hidden in the neighbouring woods and been told to escort a Stuka formation attacking Soviet troops garrisoned in Varėna, 50 miles southwest of Vilnius. The pilots smoked, but said nothing until one suddenly broke the silence. 'Napoleon,' he said. 'Napoleon…' He stubbed out his cigarette and vanished into the night.[99]

On the left bank of the San, war correspondent Martin Krieger was struck by the silence of the Galician night. 'Nothing – nothing apart from the lament of a night bird which lands on its nest with a loud flap of its wings,' he recorded. 'Nothing apart from the sound of the breeze which has been stirring for several hours and now moves the tall grass in the woods.' He continued:

> If you couldn't feel the cold metal of the rifle at your side, if you'd not noticed all the unmistakeable signs during the preceding days, if you'd not seen the artillery positions echeloned in depth when driving past, then you might have been fooled. You could sleep on this deceptively peaceful night or perhaps dream with open eyes.
>
> Nothing has happened yet. Our feet are firmly on this side of the border, which separates today from tomorrow. It is a turning point in history from which there is no going back.[100]

'WOULD EVERYONE STILL BE ALIVE TONIGHT?'
SATURDAY 21 JUNE TO SUNDAY 22 JUNE, MIDNIGHT

It was gone midnight when TASS news agency photographer Yevgeny Khaldei returned to his apartment in Moscow. The bright light of the street lamps was reflected by the tarmac and cobbles of streets dampened by the summer rain. As the 24-year-old Ukrainian passed through Pushkin Square, just a mile from the Kremlin, his eye was caught by the glistening billboards on the brutalist *Izvestia* building, urging Muscovites to visit the cinema and theatre. 'Naturally I had no idea, that the lights in the streets of Moscow were on for the last time,' he wrote.[101]

In the good tradition of the Red Army, Dmitry Ryabyshev had invited the performers to dine with him after their concert for his men. It was well past midnight when the party broke up, and 1am on Sunday 22 June before commissar Nikolai Popel reached his quarters. Despite the hour, Popel stepped into the shower – he'd not had time to wash properly all day. 'The warm jets of water washed the tiredness away,' he wrote. 'My mind was clear and now thoughts constantly ran through it: what is happening on the opposite bank of the San right now?'[102]

In Kovel, XV Rifles Corps' Ivan Fedyuninsky had gone to bed late, but found it impossible to sleep, his mind plagued by his interrogation of a German deserter three days earlier. He got up, went to his bedroom window and looked out across a town sleeping under a cloudless sky as he lit a cigarette. 'Had the German lied?' he wondered. 'Is this the last night of peace? Will everything be different tomorrow?'[103]

August Freitag glanced at his watch: *1am precisely*. It had taken a good three or four hours for the driver and his comrades to haul the guns of 18th Infantry Regiment into position, unload the shells and move the empty limbers a couple of hundred metres to the rear. The horses were left to chew the dewy grass while the men waited for the coming day. Around 2.30am, they donned their steel helmets and began to load their rifles in silence. 'The tension was tremendous and even though we had not slept, we were awake as rarely before,' Freitag wrote. 'Suddenly a thought came over me: Would everyone still be alive tonight?' He began to pray quietly: *God, give me a good guardian angel!*[104]

No Soviet commander was more unsettled this night than Aleksandr Korobkov. Still he telephoned Minsk requesting permission to begin alerting his troops and dispersing his aircraft. And still Dmitry Pavlov refused. Only when the telephone lines went dead a little after 1am did the calls cease. Korobkov took matters into his own hands. He sent couriers out with a sealed red envelope containing orders to defend the borders of the Soviet Union if attacked. By the time the messengers had been dispatched, Fourth Army's engineers had restored communications. Almost immediately a message arrived from Pavlov – broadcast *en clair* – ordering Korobkov to begin putting his men on alert.[105]

Alexander Yegorov was roused from a restless sleep by the telephone ringing in his quarters.

'Comrade Captain, report for duty,' a breathless voice said. 'The alert has been sounded.'

Yegorov briefly looked at his children, sleeping calmly, bade his wife farewell and headed through the deserted streets of Lvov. By 2am, 63rd Tank Regiment was ready to move out: two battalions followed by Yegorov and his comrades in the regimental staff. The rattle of armour shook many inhabitants awake. 'Elderly women quickly crossed themselves, feeling something was wrong,' Yegorov remembered. 'Everyone showed alarm in their eyes.'

Outside the city, the columns of armour raced along the lanes of Galicia at 20mph. The drivers had little experience of T-34s, but by 3am they had covered a good 15 miles. The command column was ordered to haul off the Kraków highway and park in a wood. Alexander Yegorov and his deputy, Senior Lieutenant Sizov, climbed an observation tower on the edge of the trees. 'It was dawning and there was a good view of the surrounding terrain,' the tank commander remembered. 'The morning was warm and quiet. The air was filled with the aroma of herbs and flowers. Everything seemed to breathe the joy of the coming summer's day. Only the muffled roar of the tanks, driving deep into the forest, caused some vague anxiety.'

Sizov reported the last vehicles in the column were pulling into the woods, but his words were drowned out by the roar of an engine as an aircraft made a low pass, its machine-gun chattering. As it banked, Yegorov could make out black and white crosses on its wing.[106]

At Dubovo, just south of Suwałki, engineers with dimmed torches clambered over three Ju87 belonging to the staff of their Stuka *Gruppe*, readying the aircraft for flight. As they did, the six aircrew pored over the charts and aerial photographs of Kalvarija, no more than 30 miles away and home to three Red Army headquarters. Across the airfield identical groups – three Stukas, two crew for each – did likewise, before the pilots and rear gunners climbed into their dive-bombers. The darkness and silence were broken simultaneously as exhaust flames flickered, engines roared then settled back to a loud drone, and red, white and green navigation lights blinked. The staff's *Kette* – chain, the V formation favoured by bomber crews – led by Helmut Mahlke, left the ground first, leaving thick clouds of dust swirling around the field. One by one, the groups of Stukas headed northeast over the woods of Suwałki. With their lights still flashing they looked to Mahlke 'like little glowworms'.[107]

Thirty miles upstream of Brest, Hans Reimer reported to the command post of 36th Infantry Regiment, a temporary bunker lit by candles. *Oberst* Ernst Rupp and his officers sat on crates and barrels. All of them were nervous, checking their watches repeatedly, smoking one cigarette after another. The atmosphere in the command post was too oppressive for Reimer. He stepped outside and listened to the frogs on the left bank of the Bug croaking. Otherwise, he remembered, 'there was an eerie silence, like in a cemetery. From time to time, low-lying clouds revealed the shining crescent of the good moon.'[108]

At the command post of 295th Infantry Division, located in woodland outside the village of Plazów in southeastern Poland, General Herbert Geitner constantly stared at the telephone. 'You could tell from his face,' wrote Otto Korfes, commanding one of the division's regiments, 'that he hoped right down to the final half hour that the order would be rescinded.' The telephone remained silent. 'So the dance begins,' Geitner muttered. He walked towards the command post's exit, then turned around. 'The dance of death!'[109]

It was 2.30am when Joseph Goebbels left the Reich Chancellery. The Führer was going to bed, Goebbels back to his office, just two minutes' walk away along pitch-black Wilhelmstrasse. The staff of the Propaganda Ministry were still at work. In three hours' time, the minister told them, Germany would be at war with the Soviet Union. 'All of them are stunned, although most of them had guessed some, or all, of the truth,' Goebbels observed. Now the wheels of his ministry began to turn to mobilise the radio, newspapers and the weekly newsreel. Since the *Anschluss* with Austria in 1938, they'd had plenty of practice. 'Everything,' Joseph Goebbels noted with satisfaction, 'runs like clockwork.'[110]

At his airstrip, 20 miles east of Zamość, Günther Lützow donned his summer jacket while ground crew readied the Me109s of *Jagdgeschwader* 3 for their first sortie of the campaign. 'War against Russia,' he said to his colleague Walter Dahl almost nonchalantly. 'Can you understand this?'

'Actually, I find it incomprehensible. This could become difficult.'

'Now we're saddled with exactly what should be avoided: a war on two fronts,' Lützow continued. 'In fact, we already have a war on many fronts – if we take the Balkans into account. And then there's Africa, of course. I tell you Dahl, we'll really have our hands full with all this.'[111]

The *Landsers* of 121st Infantry Division moved through a field of tall corn to take up their jump-off positions. The occasional helmet bobbed above the sea of corn ears. As the men brushed the stalks, the crickets fell silent. The only other noise at this time of night came from the locomotives shunting in the border station at Eydtkau. As the sky grew lighter and the stars faded, the men's hearts beat faster.[112]

The fast-flowing waters of the San glistened in the moonlight as they were funnelled through the centre of the pleasant southern Polish city of Przemyśl. Nowhere along the entire German–Soviet frontier were the consequences of the Nazi–Soviet Pact more evident than here in the Carpathian foothills. The agreement split the fortress city along the course of the San. On the left bank of the river, *Deutsche* Przemyśl – *German* Przemyśl. Barely 500ft away on the other side of the San, beyond barbed-wire fences and warning signs in German, Russian and Polish, Russian Przemyśl – or simply Przemyśl. Though it was captured outright by German troops in September 1939, the pact gave the Soviets the bulk of the city, including its historic heart, its ruined castle, its medieval town hall, fine Habsburg town houses and apartment blocks, not to mention the many military buildings and barracks from its days as the key Austro-Hungarian fortress. The battles of 1914 and 1915 had left most of the forts which ringed Przemyśl at best obsolete, at worst in ruins. But over the past year Przemyśl's new occupiers had begun fortifying the city afresh with a series of pillboxes, bunkers and casemates. This was the southern end of the so-called Molotov Line: incomplete, hastily built, inadequately equipped, only partially garrisoned. At least eight fortified positions – bunker, watchtower, slit trenches – guarded the San and its crossings, the barrels of 45mm guns and heavy machine-guns withdrawn inside the embrasures for now. In the half-light of night, the pioneers of 101st Light Division could just make out indistinct outlines of these concrete, steel and iron structures from the left bank. Beyond them, the night swallowed up the rest of Russian Przemyśl; for the past week, the city had been plunged into darkness as a blackout was enforced overnight. The once-smart tenements, now plastered with giant portraits of Soviet greats: Molotov, Voroshilov and, of course, Stalin; the town hall square; the now-abandoned Greek Orthodox church and the tree-covered slopes rising above the city – all were lost to the darkness. When they attacked in a few hours' time, the 101st Light Division would stand at the very end of a German front extending all the way from East Prussia and the Baltic shore. After the 101st, as its bespectacled commander Erich Marcks rather dramatically put it, 'the nearest combat-worthy German troops were in Romania' – a good 120 miles away. In between: a couple of security divisions fit only for maintaining order behind the front, the Carpathians and the frontier with neutral Hungary. That worried Marcks' superior, LII Corps' commander Kurt von Briesen, who feared the two Soviet armies deployed around Przemyśl would be a constant thorn in his side. The bespectacled Marcks disagreed; once attacked, the Russians would fall back towards Lvov to prevent being trapped. Right now, however, despite the obvious tension on both sides of the San, the Soviet Union was rigidly adhering to the terms of the 1939 pact. A little after 3am, a lengthy goods train slowly rolled across the San crossing into Deutsche Przemyśl carrying food, fuel and other commodities.[113]

In Vladimir-Volynskiy, deserter Alfred Liskow was still being interrogated. Unhappy with the translation initially provided by the NKVD interpreter, border guard commander Mikhail Bychkovsky had dragged a local German language teacher from his bed for a more thorough questioning. The 30-year-old German corporal repeated the story he had recounted just a few hours earlier. His 75th Infantry Division would attack at 3am – 4am in Moscow. 'I came especially to warn you on my own initiative,' he pleaded. The questioning was still ongoing when an ominous thunder came from the direction of Ustilug, eight miles to the west. Bychkovsky immediately tried to call his men holding the border. The line was dead.[114]

Erich Maresch watched the first larks rise in the gently dawning sky and welcome the coming day with their song. The 45-year-old Austrian had not slept. He lay down briefly, thinking of home and his wife Myria. But only for a few minutes. From 45 minutes after midnight he was in 45th Infantry Division's command post, studying maps, observing the far bank of the Bug. Four minutes before the assault began, he watched as two observation balloons were slowly raised. Would the Russians spot these large 'grey sausages' he wondered? They didn't. He watched too as assault troops stormed the railway bridge spanning the Bug, killed the Soviet border guards and began to cut the demolition cables. Not a shot was fired; not one Russian soldier was alerted. In a matter of seconds the German barrage would be unleashed. 'In Brest they certainly haven't a clue what a tragedy is about to befall the fortress and the city,' he recorded in his diary.[115]

The rattle of an alarm clock woke Gerd Habedanck from a few uncomfortable hours' sleep in his car in Terespol. A correspondent for the armed forces' flagship fortnightly picture magazine *Die Wehrmacht*, Habedanck had spent the final hours of Saturday watching the men of 45th Infantry Division prepare for the assault on Brest fortress: a heavy flak gun hauled into position; sand scattered on roads to absorb the clatter of hobnail boots; assault troops carrying rubber dinghies towards the Bug. He wandered along catwalks through the marshy meadows by the river, where he could clearly hear Russians talking on the opposite bank. As the chatter died down, it was replaced by the song of nightingales and the occasional croak of a toad in the reeds.

Now with a silvery strip beginning to appear on the eastern horizon, the journalist pushed his way past the men in steel helmets with rifles at the ready to reach a battalion command post, where the constant shrill ring of a telephone broke the silence. To Habedanck, it seemed only the battalion commander remained unruffled. He turned to his staff: 'Gentlemen, it's 3.14. One more minute to go.'[116]

2

THE GATES OF HELL OPENED
IN FRONT OF US

Was it just a prelude? Will every day be like this?

Albert Frank, 20th Panzer Division

There's no chaos, no apocalyptic mood, there's tremendous faith in the Red Army, its leadership and the workers of the entire world; they will rise up like one man to eradicate this cancerous ulcer.

Fayvel Vayner

'WE DEFINITELY WOKE THEM UP...'
LITHUANIA, 3.05AM

A light mist blanketed the woodland around Suwałki as *Hauptmann* Helmut Mahlke circled waiting for the rest of his Stuka *Gruppe* to join him. It never did. When the rendezvous time passed, Mahlke took it upon himself to continue with his formation of three dive-bombers to their target just 25 miles away: three army headquarters in and around the small Lithuanian town of Kalvarija. There was no response from the Red Air Force as Mahlke crossed the border – the Soviets 'seemed to still be fast asleep. We were about to give them a proper awakening.'

Helmut Mahlke's Stukas were in the first wave of more than 1,000 aircraft – medium, dive- and fighter-bombers – about to give the most devastating demonstration of aerial power the world had yet seen. In the lead, 150 'pathfinders', bombers flown by specially selected crews, the cream of the Luftwaffe's night warriors who had honed their skills in the near-year-long 'blitz' of Britain. They would 'mark' targets – Soviet airfields and military establishments from the Baltic to the Black Sea – by attacking them, before the main striking force of nearly 900 machines followed a few minutes behind to deliver a paralysing blow to the Red Air Force and Red Army.[1]

One hundred miles to the northwest, just across the Latvian border, Major Manfred von Cossart found Ratas lined up on the edge of the airfield at Liepāja 'as though on parade'. No attempt had been made to camouflage them – and little attempt was made to defend the base from the Ju88s of *Kampfgeschwader* 1; a solitary flak gun and a handful of guns safeguarding the port returned desultory fire.[2]

The Stukas which had failed to join up with Helmut Mahlke's formation were already attacking Kalvarija. 'Pillars of fire flared up.' By the time Mahlke led his three Ju87s into the attack, the defenders had awoken, dotting the morning sky with grey clouds of smoke – flak shells exploding. Mahlke ignored it – 'something like that doesn't put off veteran Stuka crews'. In a matter of seconds, the aircraft were pulling up from their dives having released their payloads. What was left of the headquarters below 'was enveloped by dust, smoke and raging fires'. The Stukas flew the 30 miles back to base at Dubovo, where the aviators were mobbed by excited ground crews upon landing. 'Well, how was it?' 'What happened?' The pilots shrugged their shoulders. 'It was a cakewalk. They were evidently still asleep. We definitely woke them up…'[3]

'SO THEN IT'S WAR!' THE BLACK SEA, 3.05AM

In the headquarters of the Black Sea Fleet, the monotony of the night watch was broken by the sound of the telephone ringing. 'There's the sound of aircraft engines. Aircraft are heading for Sevastopol.' The telephone rang again. And again. The caller always said the same thing. *There are aircraft over Sevastopol.* Searchlights pierced the darkness over the city and Severnaya Bay – dawn was still 90 minutes away – then the anti-aircraft batteries began to shoot at any aircraft caught in the beams.

'But what planes are they?' someone asked.

'Perhaps Ivan Stepanovich [Isakov, the Chief of the Naval Staff] has decided to test the readiness of Sevastopol's defences and these are our aircraft,' his comrade replied.

'No, you're wrong – our anti-aircraft guns are firing live ammunition so it's highly unlikely that these are our aircraft,' a third man said.

Suddenly there were deafening explosions near Sevastopol's famous Primorsky Boulevard on the bay's southern shore and the first houses collapsed.

'So then it's war!' one of the staff remarked.

'But with whom?'

Flying along the Black Sea coast, fighter pilot Georg Schirnböck could see life going on as usual in the towns and villages of southern Ukraine not because it was light – 'it was almost still night' – but because the street lights were still on. 'I must say that Russia really was clearly unprepared,' he remembered. His *Jagdgeschwader* 77 comrade Joachim Diecke watched as 'the Russians came out of their barracks and waved at us' as his formation of Me109s attacked their airfield. 'When we returned to our airfield, we asked ourselves whether or not this attack hadn't been a terrible mistake.' It was too dark for Schirnböck to locate the airfields he'd been assigned to attack. His wing ran into a pair of Ratas, but in the darkness neither side could grapple with the other.[4]

'THE MACHINE OF WAR WAS RUNNING AT FULL SPEED...' LITHUANIA, 3.05AM

Several thousand feet above the East Prussian–Lithuanian borderland, a large blur headed northeast in the half-light between night and day. The Messerschmitt Me109s of three fighter squadrons had lifted off shortly before 3am, forming up before crossing the frontier over the small border town of Kybartai, bound for the Red Air Force bases at Kedainai and Kaunas. As they flew over the border, Hannes Trautloft watched it 'come alive'.

> Muzzle flashes everywhere – from woods, bushes, barns. At this moment, the eastern front is beginning. It's a sublime yet also daunting feeling to be a part of global events! My view covers a vast area from Memel to the Rominten Heath then far into enemy territory, into the tingling uncertainty of war. I must admit that I have a slightly heavy feeling in the pit of my stomach.[5]

Fellow pilot Walter Krupinski watched as the border was suddenly lit up by muzzle flashes and, seconds later, shells landing on Soviet soil and exploding. 'We stared down, shaken but impressed. I'd never seen anything like that.'[6] It was 3.05am precisely.

'I thought my heart would stop for fractions of a second,' an artilleryman supporting 1st Infantry Division recalled as his guns barked and belched along the Lithuanian frontier to the west of Tauragė in Lithuania – Tauroggen to Germans.

> Nature's silence was broken and the air was seized by a maddening shaking. The earth trembled and roared, at that moment it was as if hell had been let loose. Suddenly there was a loud rumble in the air which turned into a deafening noise. Countless squadrons of German bombers flew through the blue firmament, accompanied by our fast fighters. Far beyond them on the horizon a blazing trail of smoke was already visible, mixed with a red tongue of flame.[7]

Just a handful of miles to the east, Johann Allmayer-Beck heard rather than saw the barrage. 'The die is cast!' he thought. 'Now there's no going back, only advancing.' The artillery officer watched two Russian border guards through his scissor telescope. They stood for a moment next to a tree on the border, listening to the distant rumble, before dashing for the cover of nearby woods as rifles and machine-guns joined in the hellish concert. The telephone rang: '*Herr Oberleutnant*, report from 1st Battery's forward observer: The infantry is attacking and has crossed the border of the Reich!'[8]

Fifty miles away, opposite the border village of Kybartai, the men of 121st Infantry Division heard the massed formations of the Luftwaffe overhead – 'a muffled yet distinct roar' – but not did not look up. They were preoccupied, staring at their watches. With the first muzzle flashes of the division's guns, the infantrymen jumped up out of the corn and towards the frontier. The Russians seemed stunned by the barrage – or perhaps there were none there. Not a shot was fired as the troops leaped over the barbed wire which marked the border, then across a stream. The first, brief resistance was offered by a handful of bunkers. It was quickly silenced by rifle fire and hand-grenades before the infantrymen pushed on through the dewy tall grass and fields of corn. Convinced farmhouses had been turned into makeshift strongpoints, the men of the 121st peppered the doors and windows with bursts of machine-gun fire – but found the buildings abandoned. It was like this everywhere, one non-commissioned officer observed. 'We continued past empty positions and overrun anti-tank ditches towards the rising sun. The machine of war was running at full speed.' As Kybartai burned – apart from its tall white church which towered above the flames and dense smoke – white signal flares continually arced through the early morning sky to signal the division's rapid progress.[9]

The blistering barrage from the guns of 161st Infantry Division east of Suwałki largely fell on undefended ground. After setting a farm ablaze, burning some of its livestock in the process – a pig ran around squealing, one side of its body singed – the troops quickly reached the Neman and prepared to cross the river. They swept the right bank with their binoculars and saw recently built earth bunkers, disguised with fresh foliage, but apparently unoccupied. A couple of men were sent down to the river's edge. Nothing. With no assault boats or bridging equipment, the men seized a handful of rafts and began to paddle or punt their way across with whatever they could find. Others simply drifted with the current – in full view of the bunkers – until their rafts struck the far bank on a meander. The men had been told crossing the Neman was tantamount to a suicide mission. Now they were on the right bank and had not lost a man.[10]

'TO ALL OF YOU, *ALLES KAPUTT!*' UKRAINE, 3.10AM

At 86th Bomber Regiment's airfield in Tarnopol, crews watched what they thought were Tupolev SB twin-engine bombers coming in low, at high speed. The men had been alerted for half an hour. Why, they did not know. Perhaps the incoming aircraft were testing their reactions and defences. But as the bombers passed overhead, the men saw black crosses, not the Soviet red star, on the wings; the 'Tupolevs' were Ju88s of *Kampfgeschwader* 51. Bombs were falling before the Soviet crews could react, seven fighters were burned-out wrecks, two of their pilots dead in the cockpits. The defenders were better prepared when the main wave of German bombers came in ten minutes later. Despite the lack of anti-aircraft guns, their small-arms fire brought down at least one Ju88 whose crew bailed out directly over the airbase. '*Stalin kaputt, Heil Hitler,*' one of the captured Germans declared. He was punched twice in the face for his insolence. It didn't seem to work. The German Army would be in Moscow by October, he told his captors. 'To all of you, *alles kaputt!*'[11]

In Lutsk, 90 miles northeast of Lvov, schoolboy Petka Delyatitsky had struggled to sleep. He finally dozed off while reading a book, and woke when it slipped from his hands and onto the floor. As the semi-conscious youngster reached for it, he heard 'several claps, strange noises, like thunder'. His mother admonished him to close the window immediately; his siblings were terrified of thunderstorms.

He did and saw the sky 'black with aircraft'. One bomb landed in front of his home, others on the pilots' barracks and on the army tent. Startled soldiers ran into the open dressed only in their underwear.

'I was fascinated and could not take my eyes off this wonderful and terrible scene of bombs exploding,' Petka recalled years later. 'Messerschmitts flew so low and so slowly that I saw one of the German pilots with his gloved hand waving at me, a boy, standing in a lit window.'[12]

Tank regiment chief-of-staff Alexander Yegorov was standing with his deputy on an observation tower on the edge of woods 15 miles northwest of Lvov, still slightly dazed by the sight of a German fighter strafing the main road to Kraków. The aircraft turned around to make a second run, strafing the highway and littering it with scores of leaflets. The men's attention was immediately caught by a droning rumble which grew ever louder in the west. Transfixed, the two officers watched as an armada of bombers swooped on one of Galicia's numerous woods, shattering the peace of a mid-summer's morning. A few hours before, the trees had shielded the summer camp of 81st Motorised Rifle Division. Like Yegorov's regiment, the riflemen had been alerted. All the bombs did was shred the woodland.[13]

'THE WORLD HAD BEEN LIFTED OFF ITS HINGES…'
BREST, 3.15AM

'It will be like nothing you have ever experienced,' an artillery officer promised war correspondent Gerd Habedanck in a command post in Terespol. Squeezed into two square miles of copses, farmland and overgrown floodplain between the main Moscow–Warsaw–Berlin railway line and the left bank of the Bug were nearly two dozen artillery batteries, their barrels all pointed to the northeast, aimed at Brest fortress. There were light and heavy field guns, nine 21cm mortars, and two weapons being tested for the first time, the *Karl-Gerät* and *Nebelwerfer*. The unassuming names – literally 'Karl equipment' and 'smoke mortar' – were deliberate to hide their true purpose. Karl was a monster which spewed 60cm mortar shells weighing two tonnes apiece out of its barrel at nearly 500mph. From their position on the southern outskirts of Terespol, the 124-tonne mortars could just hit the fortifications of Brest; the shells were designed to smash through concrete more than 8ft thick. The men of 45th Infantry Division could call on two of these beasts for their assault. But Karl was also cumbersome – it travelled on a large, sluggish caterpillar-tracked chassis – not particularly accurate and, at best, could fire six rounds an hour. Firing flat out at Brest, the two giant mortars would run out of ammunition in just three hours, for only three dozen shells had been delivered. Far more numerous were the *Nebelwerfer*, nine batteries of multiple rocket launchers which would hurl 15cm projectiles little more than a mile. Six such high-explosive rounds could leave the barrels simultaneously every 90 seconds. And at 3.15am exactly on Sunday 22 June, this staggering array of firepower was unleashed, concentrated on the square mile of Brest fortress.

It came, as the diarist of the Soviet Fourth Army noted – unusually poetically – 'like thunder from a clear sky'. Gerd Habedanck felt the earth at Terespol shake; 'an infernal buzzing, rumbling, crashing' filled the air. Startled marsh birds and storks fluttered loudly over German positions and headed across the river. The earth on the left bank of the Bug shook so much that soil trickled into the hastily dug foxholes which served as the infantry's jump-off positions. Willow trees were bent almost horizontal as if flattened by a storm. Pioneers, waiting to thrust their boats into the Bug, watched 'dense black jets of smoke rise like mushrooms' on the opposite bank. 'It was as if the curtain lifted on a hellish inferno,' junior officer Walter Loos remembered. 'First we heard the shells leaving hundreds of barrels – from the smallest to the heaviest calibre – then they roared and whistled towards us as they made their way on their devastating journey over our heads towards the opposite bank.' The men instinctively kept their heads down as the barrage 'reached a deafening and breathtaking intensity the likes of which I've never experienced since. Even veterans of the Great War later said that they had not experienced such a concentrated barrage during four years of war'. The sky glowed red, so brightly that the men could see everything as if it were the middle of day, while the trees on the right bank of the Bug swayed wildly 'as if seized by an invisible force'.

Overhead, fighter pilot Franz Schiess looked down on the east bank of the Bug and saw nothing but 'a strip of flame', Brest 'a bed of glowing coals'. Schiess, on his very first sortie, found himself transfixed by a scene which was 'both horrible and beautiful'.

In the middle of this cacophony, some sounds were distinct, above all the peculiar howl of the *Nebelwerfer*. In clusters of six or twelve, they trailed a fiery path across the Bug 'like comets'. The blood-curdling scream the rockets gave as they left their barrels was terrifying, but the effect of their impact, pioneer Helmut Böttcher observed, was far worse than any heavy mortar. 'Everyone within a radius of 300 metres was killed,' he recalled. 'This was caused by a vacuum. It was terrible when you saw people sitting there motionless, as if turned to stone, like dolls. Many of them collapsed, but some were still sitting on a chair or bank. It was a very fast – and quite certain – death.'

Every three minutes there was the particularly jarring crash of the heavy mortars, their rounds so large that German troops could observe the final moments before they impacted. When on target – which was infrequent – the

Karls wrought unimaginable devastation. Their shells brought down two wings of the border guards' quarters at the Terespol Gate on the western end of the citadel island – not merely wiping out many of the guards but also their families and trainees attending a course. The survivors staggered out of the ruins and into the central grounds of the citadel. Those who were not torn apart by the rain of shells stared out on scenes worthy of Dante's inferno: woodpiles, guard posts, shacks, trees all ablaze, walls collapsing, some women and children running about in panic, others pressed to the ground.

To infantryman Hans Wiesinger it seemed 'the gates of Hell opened in front of us'. Austrian Josef Arnreiter and his comrades convinced themselves 'those poor Russians over there are all *kaputt*'. No man who had heard, or witnessed, the barrage at Brest would ever forget it, for they would never experience anything like it ever again. 'We had the feeling,' Walter Loos wrote, 'that the world had been lifted off its hinges.'[14]

'AS IF JUDGMENT DAY HAS COME...'
ARMY GROUP CENTRE, 3.15AM

Nowhere on the fledgling Eastern Front was the barrage as concentrated as it was at Brest, but it was still a mesmerising – and terrifying – spectacle. Just a few miles west of the fortress, 18th Panzer Division's Siegfried Risse watched the right bank of the Bug vanish in 'a sea of smoke and fire' as 'the war took its first, terrible, baleful breath'. Peace, he concluded, was dead. The bombardment a dozen or so miles upstream, outside the town of Koden, seemed no less intense to battalion commander Martin Püschel. He observed 'continuous flashes of lightning along the entire horizon, an endless flickering fiery glow followed by the dull thud of the heavy guns, then the sharp crack of the light guns, and above us a whistling, roaring, howling like flocks of wild geese swooping down'. The transfixed Püschel continued: 'The bang of shells leaving their barrels, the howling, hissing, and wailing of the rounds, their exploding, the clang and clatter of shrapnel, it all merges into one mighty storm and the fury of an earthquake which causes the ground to shake as if Judgment Day has come.'

Seconds later, on the right bank of the Bug, jets of flame and fountains of earth were thrown up, followed by mushroom clouds. Artillery officer Fritz Farnbacher watched some of Püschel's riflemen in rubber boats force their way across the Bug, while on the opposite bank 'heavy grey-black clouds hang in the morning sky – they were born of fire and steam'. Farnbacher felt 'rather ghoulish. We are happy when our fire is accurate and lands where we want it to, where it is needed, spreading death and destruction over there.' Perhaps, he mused, it was a good thing that the artilleryman rarely saw the effects of his fire.

Platoon commander I. Starostin had planned to spend the day resting in the small town of Siemiatycze, 50 miles north of Brest. Instead, the sapper was rudely awakened 'by a roar, whistle and crashing' which flung the door and window of his quarters open. 'For a moment I was stunned,' he recorded in his diary. 'With cat-like agility I got dressed and ran into the street. In the front room was the elderly owner, filled with horror, before an icon, praying to God. He had just managed to get 100 metres from the house when two bombs hit it. The house collapsed, what was left of it burned.' Glancing in the direction of the border, Starostin noticed it was 'lit by thousands of different-coloured projectiles'. He soon encountered his engineering battalion, fleeing from the frontier. 'As we ran, I learned that the Germans had treacherously attacked us.'

More than 100 miles behind the front, the 'ears' of Army Group Centre's intelligence staff in Rembertów on the eastern edge of Warsaw intercepted a brief Soviet radio conversation.

'They are shooting at us. What shall we do?' a beleaguered unit on the Bug asked.

'You must be sick. And why wasn't your message enciphered?'[15]

'WE THINK THESE ARE PROVOCATIONS...'
UKRAINE, 3.15AM

Konstantin Maligin had left his quarters before dawn to go fishing with a friend on the Luga, a tributary of the Bug. With the first light of the new day, the stars began to fade and a blue haze enveloped the villages, meadows and copses around the town of Sokal, 50 miles north of Lvov. 'It seemed that the entire world was enjoying its pleasant pre-dawn slumber,' Maligin wrote, 'the fields and the woods, the birds and the people...' He watched as a flurry of red and green flares rose in the brightening sky. Before they had faded, Maligin heard a far-off thunder, followed by muzzle flashes and tracer rounds. There was the rattle of machine-gun fire, the pop of bullets leaving rifle barrels, the howl of shells as they tore the peace of early morning apart, before they exploded on impact, throwing up columns of earth in the border zone. 'Deep down I still hoped it was an exercise,' Maligin admitted. But when shells began to crash down around Sokal, he dismissed such thoughts.

> We ditched our fishing rods and cans of worms – we didn't need them now – and rushed to the garrison. Above us thick swarms of German aircraft buzzed, flying at various heights. Some were flying high, apparently heading into the heart of the

country, while others were low flying. These formed a circle and swooped one-by-one, dropping bombs on military camps in Vladimir-Volynskiy. As they went into their dive, the pilots used their sirens. A deafening, piercing, blood-curdling howling. And explosions – one after another.

Maligin found Vladimir-Volynskiy emptying. The men of his 41st Tank Division were heading for their vehicles, parked in the woods outside the town. But what were they to do? There were no communications with senior commands.

One hundred and twenty-five miles to the south, Dmitry Ryabyshev was woken by a breathless messenger who implored him to go to VIII Mechanised Corps' headquarters in Drohobycz. When he arrived there a few minutes later, the operations officer of Twenty-Sixth Army was on the telephone, reporting that the Germans had crossed the border in numerous places, were bombing towns and airfields and fighting with border guards. 'But please don't panic,' said the excited voice. 'We think these are provocations. Do not give in to them! Do not open fire on German aircraft! Await further instructions!' Ryabyshev immediately called his three divisional commanders and slipped codewords – 'lightning', 'forest' and 'mountain' – into their brief conversations. Each was a signal to move out.

Ivan Bagramyan was still on the road, somewhere outside the small Ukrainian town of Brody, 70 miles east of Lvov. The journey of his column had been plagued by delays, breakdowns and traffic jams. As dawn broke, the convoy of trucks, buses and cars was stopped once more. Bagramyan was about to order the vehicles to move out when aircraft screamed overhead. 'We knew that there was an airfield nearby,' the lieutenant colonel remembered. 'Our pilots had begun the day's work rather early.' But then there were explosions. Beyond Brody clouds of smoke climbed in the sky. 'It was as if we'd turned to stone,' Bagramyan recalled. 'Everyone was possessed by one thought: *Is this war?*' Any final doubts disappeared when the aircraft made low passes over the vehicle column – the black crosses on the wings could clearly be seen. The men scattered from the convoy, throwing themselves into the ditches at the side of the road as the German aircraft strafed the line of vehicles. When the soldiers had recovered their composure, Bagramyan ordered the column to get under way. 'There was only one thought going around my head: *what was happening at the border now?*'[16]

Seize the bridges... Brest, 3.19am

After four terrible minutes, the barrage at Brest leaped forward 100 yards. It was the signal for the first wave of infantry to leave the relative shelter of their jump-off positions and strike across the Bug in rubber boats. Of the nine craft which attempted this first crossing, three never made the far shore, sunk not by the defenders of the fortress – they had yet to regain their senses and begin offering meaningful resistance – but by mortar shells landing short. The remaining boats reached the Russian bank, their men scaling the embankment before quickly cutting through the barbed-wire fencing. The greatest impediment to their progress was the metre-high grass.[17]

As dinghies and small powered craft churned the surface of the Bug into a white froth, Josef Heinrich Kremers headed downstream, rather than across to the river's far bank, with a mini flotilla of nine assault boats, every man in them a volunteer. Their mission: to seize three bridges spanning the Mukhavets in a surprise attack to speed the advance of the infantry. The omens were not good; four of the nine boats were sunk or damaged by artillery or *Nebelwerfer* rounds falling short, killing or wounding 20 of Kremers' men. The 22-year-old Rhinelander persisted. With six men in each craft, Kremers led his boats down the Bug at nearly 20mph, then turned down one of the arms of the Mukhavets which wrapped itself around the citadel. Once again, the operation faltered. As the boats approached the Kholmsky Bridge, which linked the iconic gate of the same name with the fortress's South Island, they ran aground on a sandbank – directly opposite the fortress citadel. The upper storey of the red-brick structure was already ablaze from the shelling. Troops barracked on the ground floor took aim at Kremers' men – and especially his boats. Under intense fire, the pioneers succeeded in lifting the 20ft boats off the sand and getting them going again. Two of the small boats were so badly damaged that they sank before the now-dwindling group of craft could reach the fork in the Mukhavets, not a quarter of a mile away.

So badly had Josef Kremers' attack miscarried that the first two bridges he'd been charged with seizing had already been captured by the spearhead of 130th Infantry Regiment, which swung around Brest's outer fortifications on the landward side. Kremers' battered unit found them waiting for him and decided to abandon their attack upstream. Instead, the handful of pioneers abandoned their boats and joined the infantry for the attack on the final Mukhavets crossing. Running along a sluice, they swept across the span, killing or capturing the men defending it. Josef Kremers did not end there. Ignoring the advice of a fellow officer, he was determined to show the bridge was in German hands by raising the swastika flag on the parapet. He was felled by a Soviet sniper as he made the attempt and died in the arms of his comrades.[18]

'Damn the manoeuvres, it's war!'
Ukraine, 3.30am

From the left bank of the Bug south of Krystynopol, 40 miles north of Lvov, the guns of 9th Infantry Division hammered Soviet positions on the other side of the river. 'The "voice of the front", which had been silent for a year and now roared with all their might again, made us shudder,' anti-tank gunner Karlernst Malkmus remembered.

> We could clearly distinguish the different batteries – when they fired, when their shells roared over us towards the enemy and when they exploded over there with a rumble. As soon as one salvo thundered overhead, the next one was already on its way, constantly, becoming ever more ferocious. The heavy and light calibre shells turned into a hellish concert. Howling and smoking, they flew across the border and crashed down on the other side.[19]

Kirill Moskalenko was woken by the excited voice of Fifth Army commander Mikhail Potapov. 'The Fascists have attacked us. They are subjecting the troops on the border to artillery fire and bombing airfields and towns.' War had yet to reach Lutsk – it was 60 miles behind the front. But just outside the city, Moskalenko's staff car passed an airfield in flames, every one of the 30 aircraft on it a wreck. In the camp of 1st Anti-Tank Brigade, its 39-year-old commander found his commissar confused.

'What is it? Have the manoeuvres begun? I hear explosions and shooting but the brigade isn't taking part in them,' he asked.

'Damn the manoeuvres, it's war!' Moskalenko snapped. 'The Germans have attacked us. Are you listening? They're bombing the airfield.' He found his camp rather more alert. The men were crawling out of their tents and mounting their vehicles. Moskalenko and his staff gathered in front of them, but before they could begin issuing orders, they heard a muffled noise coming from the west and growing louder. In a matter of seconds, 40 Stukas circled over the clearing where the brigade's vehicles had been neatly parked just two days earlier until Moskalenko had ordered them dispersed. Frustrated at the lack of targets, the German aircraft flew off towards Lutsk.[20]

On the hills on the northern and western outskirts of Deutsche Przemyśl, the muzzles of 10.5 and 15cm guns of 101st Light Division flashed. A few seconds later, the boom of the cannon echoed along the upper San and shells crashed down on the river's right bank around the headquarters of the border guards in Ulica Rokitniańska and the staffs of 99th Rifle Division and 8th Rifle Brigade in

Ulica Mickiewicz. They also reduced the city's courthouse to rubble, as well as an old mill and several tenement blocks.

Under the cover of the hour-long barrage, the assault units began moving through the gardens and past the few scattered houses of Deutsche Przemyśl on the left bank of the San while mortars and machine-guns joined in the onslaught against Soviet positions in places barely 600ft away. Amid the tumult of battle, the melodic peal of bells rang out on the left bank, calling the Polish faithful to early morning prayers. Civilians moved through the streets seemingly untroubled by the shooting. And on the very end of the German line, a small group of pioneers moved across the San unnoticed on three inflatable sacks to begin scouting the outposts of the Molotov Line on the western edge of the city. They found the 1,150ft-high Tatar's Hill, which dominated the valley, unoccupied, and seized three prisoners, including an artillery officer. 'Why didn't you shoot?' his interrogator asked. 'We didn't receive any orders to do so,' he said with a laugh, threw himself on the grass and asked for a cigarette.

Beneath the barrage unleashed on the border village of Ustilug, eight miles west of Vladimir-Volynskiy, two dozen men slipped across the Bug in rubber boats. All dressed in Russian uniforms, eight Ukrainians led the way. Behind them were 16 Germans, their uniforms covered in blood from a slaughtered calf, their faces bandaged to prevent them speaking. The men were Brandenburgers, an elite unit which specialised in raids behind enemy lines. Their mission: to seize two 200-metre-long wooden bridges – one road, one rail – spanning a tributary of the Bug a couple of miles east of Ustilug. The crossings were crucial to the attack by III Panzer Corps.

The group moved forward under the creeping barrage which swept through Ustilug, leaving it in ruins, and moved east. A Russian commissar tried to order the Brandenburgers into a truck to join a counter-attack; the Ukrainians somehow fobbed him off. After an hour they reached the bridges as planned, seized them – and important documents about enemy dispositions in the area from the body of a commissar – and formed a small bridgehead. When Russians approached to blow the crossings up, the Brandenburgers opened fire with machine-guns, which they had hidden under a makeshift stretcher. The demolition of the bridges was prevented – but the Germans had betrayed their presence. They fought off counter-attacks for the next 90 minutes until the vanguard of III Panzer Corps appeared.[21]

Nikolai Inozemtsev's unit was already on the move through the Stryri valley in western Ukraine. The regiment pulled off the main road for a brief rest when someone cried out: 'Look, low-flying aircraft!' Inozemtsev watched as a twin-engine fighter descended towards the column. He could see flashes from the engines' exhausts, but could hear nothing as fountains of earth were flung into the air alongside the highway. The soldiers threw themselves to the ground; the horses ran off. The attack lasted seconds. Some men were convinced it had been an exercise, but they quickly realised otherwise as they collected the wounded, rounded up the horses and righted upturned carts. The main road was littered with the cadavers of horses, while several wounded beasts struggled along by the wayside, nibbling at the grass as they went. Inozemtsev came across numerous corpses, many contorted, and then stumbled across the body of one of his corporals:

> He was hit in the head by several explosive bullets – part of his skull is lying nearby, as if cut off. Nearby there's an infantryman, his machine-gun barrel cut in half. A little further on, our doctor. He was shot in the chest and stomach. When I began to bandage him, he merely said: 'It's useless...', and ten minutes later he died.

Like his comrades, the 29-year-old economist and graduate did not want to believe that war had begun. 'At that moment, it seemed so inevitable and yet at the same time so unexpected,' he wrote. 'I glance at the faces around me: they are so familiar and at the same time there was something new in them. Each man had grown older, become more thoughtful. *Da*, the old world was over. The end of a happy life, the end of dreams and aspirations which were so close a year ago. War!'[22]

'WE RAN TO OUR AIRCRAFT...' WAR IN THE AIR, 3.30–4AM

The clang of someone hitting a steel bar rudely woke Lieutenant Alexander Pokryshkin and his comrades on their airfield outside Tiraspol, some 60 miles northwest of Odessa. The 28-year-old Siberian dismissed the noise as a practice alarm, but there was too much activity, too many engines starting. 'Why don't they let the commanders sleep?' one senior pilot complained.

'Sleep?' a second voice snapped. 'It's war!'

The pilots dressed and made their way out to the field. Some of the MiG-3s were already taxiing. The sky in the direction of Tiraspol was a fiery red. Pokryshkin was discussing what to do with two comrades when they first heard, then saw, bombers escorted by fighters closing in from the northwest. 'Ours or the enemy's?' Pokryshkin wondered. A handful of Ratas lifted off to intercept. As the bombers began to break formation, their outlines became clear: Stukas.

'We ran to our aircraft, without letting the enemy's machines out of our sight,' Pokryshkin wrote. 'We took off and immediately something seemed out of place to me. The MiGs did not have a single round on board.'

The aircraft hugged the terrain for 50 miles until they reached the airstrip at Majaki, still untouched by war. The men set their MiGs down, rolled them into the corn, climbed out and awaited orders.[23]

Armed with 50kg bombs and cannon shells, 23 Me109s of *Jagdgeschwader* 3 were bearing down on half a dozen airfields around Lvov. The sky was overcast, the terrain difficult to follow. As he neared the Galician capital, Hans von Hahn saw nothing but the 'deepest peace below, not an aircraft in the sky and no flak defence'. It was no different at Lvov's airbase.

> We could hardly believe our eyes. The entire airfield was packed full of aircraft – reconnaissance aircraft, masses of fighters, bombers. They were only slightly camouflaged, the fighters in long rows as if on parade. And into these masses we sent our cannon while our 50kg bombs exploded. Down below the silvery grey birds with their glistening red stars burned on a huge scale. Aircraft after aircraft tore the airfield to shreds.

At Kurovitsa airfield outside the city, the crews of 66th Ground-Attack Regiment had been alerted – but dismissed the noise as a practice alarm. By the time they arrived at the base, nearly three dozen of their biplanes had been smashed by the Ju88s of *Kampfgeschwader* 51. The pilots of 164th Fighter Regiment had proved rather more dynamic than their comrades in the bomber force. Several Ratas took off, followed by whatever biplanes were still airworthy. And they avenged their comrades to some degree. Seven of the 28 Junkers which attacked Kurovitsa were brought down by the Ratas and Seagulls. However fast the Ju88 was, without fighter cover its vulnerabilities were ruthlessly exploited.

Only now, with the mauled formations of *Kampfgeschwader* 51 limping for home, did the Me109s appear. Pouncing from above, Robert Olejnik threw his Messerschmitt at the lead Rata, sending it spinning to the ground in flames with a burst of machine-gun fire on his first pass. Olejnik's wingmen Ernst Heesen and Detlev Lüth likewise dispatched Ratas in what was possibly the first dogfight of the campaign. As he came in to land at his airfield, Olejnik waggled his wings

– the sign of a victory. His kill – logged at 3.58am – is often regarded as the first of the new war. The actions of one Lieutenant P. N. Rubstov and his obsolete I-153 biplane which brought down a Ju88 over Kurovitsa several minutes earlier have been largely lost to history.[24]

The He111s of *Kampfgeschwader* 53 left the runway at Dołubowo airfield, three dozen miles south of Białystok, pitted with craters and 15 fighters in the dispersal area – some of them the latest MiG-3s – plus the neighbouring barracks 'burning brightly' as 'fire, mushroom clouds, columns of earth and dirt, mixed with all kinds of debris, are flung into the air', pilot Arnold Döring observed. Dołubowo's defenders fired a solitary anti-aircraft shell in defence – but only as the Heinkels were heading away; it fell more than half a mile short. Only now, with the damage done, did the Red Air Force appear. Someone yelled over the radio: 'Fighters at six o'clock!' The Heinkels closed formation, 'presenting the Russians with an excellent target'. It also meant the bombers could concentrate their defensive firepower. 'The glistening tracer of 27 aircraft is racing past the Russians' noses – they immediately decide to skedaddle by diving,' Döring wrote. Over the Bug again there was still little to see beyond the muzzle flashes of artillery batteries locked in duels. A few minutes later, all 27 aircraft landed safely. The raid on Dołubowo had been so devastating there was no need for them to make a second attack.[25]

War correspondent Egon Kieffer was flying with a formation of Do17s – the oldest of the Luftwaffe's trio of front-line twin-engine bombers – bound for Marijampolė, just inside the Lithuanian border, to attack Soviet troop concentrations. It was impossible to miss the frontier – it was marked by fire 'like a gigantic burning fuse' and columns of smoke rising thousands of feet. The bombers followed the main highway to Kaunas – the main route of advance and retreat in the Lithuanian border zone this Sunday morning. Already Kieffer could see German motorised units 'one vehicle behind another, like on a string of pearls' advancing into enemy territory. In Marijampolė, the Dorniers caught Soviet armour moving through the centre of the city. Only as the last bombers began their attack did the anti-aircraft guns feebly respond; their shells fell far short of the 'flying pencils' which were already turning for home as the wispy flak clouds dispersed. The raid lasted a matter of minutes but left the highway straddled by hundreds of mushroom clouds. 'We see the desperate attempts to extract vehicles from the witches' cauldron we created, until the smoke, which gradually grows thicker, deprives us of our view,' Kieffer noted as his Dornier flew back along the route of attack. Every bomber returned to base unscathed. After refuelling and re-arming, they were airborne again.[26]

Ilya Starinov sat up in his bed with a start. He thought he'd heard an explosion, then dismissed it. There was the monotonous sound of aircraft engines coming through the window of his room in Fourth Army's headquarters in Kobrin, but that was nothing unusual, even at this hour. Another explosion. The building shook, the windowpanes shuddered. Starinov thought it was engineers carrying out early morning demolition work; his roommate was convinced a bomb had fallen from its rack. But then more explosions, merging into a single deafening roar. And Starinov knew the sound of those engines. He'd heard them in Spain. *Stukas*.

There were shouts in the corridors outside: 'Everyone is to leave the building immediately.' Starinov and his comrade hurriedly put on their boots and ran out into the street, still buttoning up their jackets as they went. Someone yelled: 'Air attack!' The men had just enough time to dash across a square and into a ditch before the first 500kg bombs fell, shrouding the building in smoke and dust. Lying in the same ditch as Starinov, Fourth Army's chief-of-staff Leonid Sandalov watched his headquarters disintegrate before his eyes. Nothing challenged the German aircraft – there were no guns defending the site. 'We were lying in a ditch, unable to do anything,' Sandalov seethed, gnashing his teeth in frustration and impotence. When the raid ended, dense black clouds hung above what was left of the headquarters, a felled tree lay across the square and the hysterical voice of a woman screamed. The two waves of attacks left not just the headquarters in ruins, but also wrecked the neighbouring military camp and many family homes as well, including Sandalov's – only the frame was still standing. His wife, daughter and mother-in-law had succeeded in fleeing and caught a lorry to Baranovichi, 90 miles to the northeast. Other families were still cowering in the bushes between the Mukhavets and the main road. 'The faces of the women were haggard, their faces smeared by tears,' Sandalov remembered. 'They spoke softly, most of them dressed in whatever they had to hand. Almost all of them had small bundles in their hands – I didn't see any of them with suitcases.'[27]

At Zhuliany airfield, four miles southwest of the centre of Kiev, 22-year-old engineer Pyotr Shurlakov could hear the distant rumble of aircraft engines. Even at this early hour, the source of the noise was soon visible: a large formation of aircraft, perhaps 50, approaching from the west, moving slowly – so clearly laden with bombs. 'What is this, an exercise or war?' he asked. 'Should we sound the alarm or, like everyone else, calmly observe what's going on?' To sound the alarm unnecessarily meant a court martial. Still, Shurlakov decided to act. He called the local commander. Unavailable. With the bombers now nearing Zhuliany, the engineer struck the alert button and a shrill siren wailed across the airfield. Pilots ran to their machines, gunners to their flak positions. The unknown bombers were now identifiable as German from the crosses on their wings, and it was too late to prevent them wreaking havoc across the base: one hangar destroyed, several aircraft blown up on the ground, the runway ploughed with bombs and a few neighbouring houses. By the time a handful of I-16s had scrambled, the enemy aircraft were long gone – bar one, circling Zhuliany evidently to photograph the results of the raid. Soviet accounts say the Ju88 was brought down, trailing smoke before plunging into the ground west of Kiev, crediting the victory to Ivan Ivanovich Krasnoyurchenko, the 30-year-old inspector of fighters in the district. According to German records, no aircraft were lost in the attack.[28]

Ukrainian actor Nikolai Dupak had not slept all night, rehearsing his lines over and over ahead of a scene to be shot at mid-day by famous director Alexander Dovzhenko in Kiev's film studios. The sound of explosions caused him to rush out onto the balcony. 'Probably exercises of the Kiev military district,' his neighbour said laconically. He had barely finished when an aircraft marked with swastikas banked in front of them and bombed one of the bridges over the Dnieper.[29]

'WE DID NOT DESERVE THIS...' MOSCOW AND BERLIN, 3.40–4.30AM

Georgy Zhukov and Semyon Timoshenko had spent the night in the latter's office on the telephone or radio almost without interruption. They had taken calls from Minsk, from Kiev; they had spoken with Riga and Sevastopol. As the night had drawn on, the reports from the frontier had become increasingly alarming. At 3.30am, Western District's chief-of-staff Vladimir Klimovskikh reported air attacks on towns in Byelorussia. Three minutes later, it was the turn of Kiev's chief-of-staff Maxim Purkayev; Ukraine was under attack. Then, at 3.40am, the commander of the Baltic District, Fyodor Kuznetsov, reported raids in his area of responsibility.

Zhukov called Stalin's dacha in Moscow's western suburbs. It took several attempts before a sleepy official answered. Zhukov demanded the *vozhd* come to the phone.

'What? Now? Comrade Stalin is asleep…'

'Wake him at once. The Germans are bombing our towns!'

For three minutes, Georgy Zhukov waited on the end of the receiver until Stalin came on the line. He said nothing, merely listened to the general as he presented his brief report. Silence.

'Did you hear me?' Zhukov asked.

After a seemingly interminable silence, Stalin demanded the generals and Politburo gather in his office at the Kremlin.[30]

David Ortenberg, the editor of the Red Army's newspaper *Krasnaya Zvezda* (Red Star), was woken by a call from the People's Commissariat for Defence. 'The Germans have begun the war,' the voice said curtly. 'Our trip to Minsk is cancelled. Go to *Krasnaya Zvezda* and publish a newspaper.' The day's edition was already on the presses. It was typical peacetime fare: a mortar platoon on manoeuvres, the tasks of weapons specialists, the self-education of a company of political workers. 'Not a single word about the German invaders, about Hitler's aggression.' There were even reports from German and Italian forces on the march in Africa and the Middle East. The edition would be utterly out of keeping with the mood of a nation suddenly at war.[31]

Outside the Soviet Embassy in Berlin, Valentin Berezhkov found a black limousine waiting as promised. A few minutes earlier he had been woken by the cold, almost hostile voice of German Foreign Ministry interpreter Erich Sommer demanding the presence of his master in the Wilhelmstrasse at 4am. Joachim von Ribbentrop would send his personal car to fetch them.

The journey from the embassy to the ministry took seconds, not minutes. The streets of Berlin were empty – except for the entrance to the Foreign Office, where a crowd of journalists, cameramen and photographers was waiting. The sun was rising over the capital of the Reich. As he opened the car door for Berezhkov's superior Vladimir Dekanozov, Erich Sommer heard the ambassador mutter: 'It promises to be a beautiful day.'

The two Soviet diplomats ran the gauntlet of the media – not just in the street but up the carpeted stairs of the ministry leading to the first-floor office of the German foreign minister. Officials clicked their heels sharply and gave the Nazi salute as Dekanozov and Berezhkov passed. The Soviets walked the length of Ribbentrop's office, watched all the way by a group of Nazi officials, until the foreign minister rose from his desk and invited the two men to sit down.

In the minutes before their arrival, Ribbentrop had excitedly paced up and down his office 'like a caged animal', repeating 'the Führer is absolutely right to attack Russia now' as if, even now, he was trying to convince himself. But when the Soviet diplomats were ushered in, he was nervous, subdued – Valentin Berezhkov was convinced he was drunk: his eyes were red, his speech slurred. The Soviet ambassador tried, as he had done just a few hours before, to protest at the Luftwaffe's constant violations. Ribbentrop cut him off. 'That's not the question now,' he interrupted Dekanozov. 'The Soviet Government's hostile attitude to Germany and the serious threat represented by Russian troop concentrations on Germany's eastern frontier have compelled the Reich to take military counter-measures.' The foreign minister ran through a list of Soviet transgressions – some genuine, most not – 'stumbling over almost every word,' Berezhkov remembered, before presenting the ambassador with the formal note declaring war.

Dekanozov refused Ribbentrop's hand as the two men rose. He was a career Party functionary, not a career diplomat, a short, round 43-year-old Georgian with a receding hairline. A protégé of Stalin's NKVD henchman Beria, he'd overseen the takeover of Lithuania in the summer of 1940 before being ordered to Berlin in December as the new ambassador. Now, his emotions betrayed his background. His face turned red, his fists clenched. 'This is brazen-faced, unprovoked aggression against the Soviet Union,' he snarled. 'And you will pay dearly for it...'

The ambassador and his deputy began to walk out of the office. As they did, Ribbentrop ran after Berezhkov. 'Tell them in Moscow that I was against the invasion,' he said quietly in the young official's ear.

It was broad daylight now in Wilhelmstrasse. The crowd of reporters was still waiting, still jostling for the best photograph or footage of the shell-shocked Soviets.[32]

———

Barely six hours after their last meeting, Friedrich-Werner Graf von der Schulenburg and Gustav Hilger were once again shown into Vyacheslav Molotov's office overlooking St Basil's Cathedral. It was a 'tired and worn-out' Soviet foreign minister who walked in, fresh from a conference in Stalin's study just three minutes' walk away. Schulenburg and Hilger were no less exhausted.

If they slept at all this night, they were woken no later than 3am by the arrival of an important telegram from Berlin. As soon as the cipher staff decoded the instructions, they were ordered to destroy all coded material and smash their radio, while Schulenburg perused the document he was to read to Molotov 'immediately', identical to the one Joachim von Ribbentrop had presented to Vladimir Dekanozov in Berlin. Once again, the veteran German diplomat did his master's bidding. When he had finished, there was an awkward silence until Molotov finally asked: 'Is this a declaration of war?' Schulenburg said nothing; he simply raised his arms. That merely served to infuriate Molotov, his voice becoming ever more shrill as he ran through a list of cities – Odessa, Kiev, Minsk – already bombed by German aircraft, denounced Berlin's betrayal of the pact between the two nations as unprecedented in history and dismissed claims of a Soviet build-up along the German frontier. 'We,' he ended his tirade simply, 'did not deserve this.' The ambassador could say nothing in response beyond assuring Molotov that throughout his six years in Moscow he had striven for friendly relations between the two countries, but could do nothing against Fate. The brief meeting was over. German and Soviet shook hands in silence and departed. As Schulenburg and Hilger left the Kremlin to return to their embassy, they saw limousines pulling in, carrying Communist Party and Red Army leaders.

Vyacheslav Molotov returned to Joseph Stalin's office. As he walked in, he announced: 'Germany's declared war on us.'[33]

'ERASE THE STAIN OF DISGRACE ON THE FACE OF OUR COUNTRY...' PIATRA NEAMŢ, MOLDAVIA, 4.10AM

Two hundred miles north of Bucharest, an armoured train moved slowly through the eastern foothills of the Carpathians. For more than nine hours, *Patria* – Fatherland – had rolled towards Moldavia, giving way at rail junctions to troop trains heading for the border with the Soviet Union. Waiting at the station in the medieval town of Piatra Neamţ was General Eugen Ritter von Schobert, commander of the Eleventh Army and the senior German officer in Romania. Standing in the doorway of his carriage, Romania's leader, General Ion Antonescu. The two men greeted each other warmly, before Antonescu invited von Schobert to join him. The men talked for 20 minutes before an ice-filled bucket was produced and the *conducător* – leader – rose to address his guest and staff. '*Herr* General Schobert, gentlemen, today I can announce that the hour has come to erase the stain of disgrace on the face of our country and the standards of the Army,' Antonescu told them. 'In just a short while, the nation's Army will receive orders to cross the River Prut to make the country whole again after Bessarabia was taken away. In this struggle for justice and our sacred right, we honour the bravest army which has come to our land to fight for our justice. We know we will be worthy of this honour.' The general raised his glass. 'Let us toast victory and the triumph of justice over injustice and violence, the triumph of light over darkness.'[34]

'Cities are burning, people are dying...' Army Group Centre, 3.45–5am

On the Bug a dozen miles downstream of Brest, opposite the village of Ogrodniki, the first wave of infantry threw their assault boats into the river, their bows rising high in the water. Behind them inflatable sacks and rubber dinghies, crammed with men, rowed hurriedly. One overturned, throwing five soldiers into the dark waters of the Bug. Weighed down by their uniforms and equipment, they drowned. It proved to be the only mishap in 315th Infantry Regiment's crossing. On the right bank of the Bug they found only a solitary wounded Russian soldier. There was sporadic fire from a couple of enemy batteries, soon neutralised by German gunners. Otherwise, the infantry were advancing so quickly they were outpacing the curtain of protective fire from their own artillery; German shells were now beginning to crash down on German infantry. *Gefreiter* Max Schricker was able to fire a red flare – 'move fire forward' – and the barrage shifted. His actions earned him the Iron Cross, 2nd Class, although he never received the medal; he was killed the next day.[35]

Vasily Gorbunov's decision to put his men on alert from 3am had been vindicated a couple of hours later when the German barrage was unleashed against his border posts and trenches outside the village of Novoselki, 20 miles northwest of Brest. 'The village went up in flames,' he recalled. 'People ran from one end to the other – crying, screaming, not knowing what to do.' Decades later, remembering the bombardment still made his hair stand on end. The sight of dense smoke rolling across the Bug and red flares rising above the smog announced the German assault. The guards in the bunkers by the river opened fire. After a while a dog trotted into the command post, a short note in a capsule fixed to its collar penned by Gorbunov's friend Ivan Sergeyev: 'The Germans deployed a large number of troops on the border and are crossing the Bug in two places. We have entered battle. We will fight to the last bullet. Don't think ill of me. Sergeyev.'[36]

Northwest of Grodno, the men of 8th Infantry Division dashed over wooden bridges which pioneers had thrown across a stream and up a hill where a series of Red Army bunkers faced the border. 'Not a single shot has been fired from the Russian bunkers,' wrote junior officer Friedrich Grupe.

> Surprise is complete. German shells are still exploding up ahead; the enemy's artillery is silent – if it still exists at all. Our machine-guns rattle to our left; somewhere a man cries out for a medic.
>
> We continue. Flame-throwers spit their raging flames through the bunker embrasures. The screens are still in front of the concrete blocks – there was probably no time to remove them. Luftwaffe squadrons – Stukas, fighters, bombers – roar towards the enemy.
>
> The first Russians appear with their hands raised in front of us. They are without exception very young, the terror is in their wide eyes. The hellish fire has torn them from their sleep; most are still in their nightdress... Ahead of us a deserted camp is in flames, in the middle, lost and abandoned, a white horse.

Now came the first resistance as Soviet soldiers emerged from a burning house. To Grupe, they seemed more determined to escape than fight. 'They come out in droves, run away, throw away their weapons; one of them gives his rifle to one of our soldiers and then runs away as well,' he wrote. The fleeing Russians were shot in the back.[37]

Ninety minutes after the initial barrage, the infantry of 18th Rifle Brigade had forged a bridgehead on the right bank of the Bug at Pratulin, a dozen miles downstream from Brest, deep and secure enough for Panzer Mk3s and 4s to plunge into the river, hauling fuel bowsers. Specially modified for one abortive invasion (England), they were needed now for another. Completely sealed apart from tubes which fed air to both the crew and the engines, the panzers could drive through water 15ft deep. They found the Bug was not even half that. After the first *Schwimmpanzer* were on the right bank, the regular armour of 18th Panzer Division began to roll across the river bed, their turrets open.[38]

At Communist Party headquarters in Minsk, Panteleimon Ponomarenko took a telephone call from an angry Joseph Stalin. The war was not two hours old and the *vozhd* had evidently already found a scapegoat: he was dissatisfied with the information he was receiving from Dmitry Pavlov. He demanded his lackey clear up matters immediately – 'without succumbing to panic'. Ponomarenko headed to the Western Military District's headquarters. He didn't find any signs of panic, but he found little in the way of information either. Pavlov was almost entirely cut off from his front-line units, with most of his telephone and radio communications down.[39]

While the general was closeted with the Party chief, his deputy Ivan Boldin took a call from Semyon Timoshenko. Boldin could offer only bad news: airfields and bases being bombed, communications cut, German troops crossing the border. But Timoshenko urged caution.

'Bear in mind, Comrade Boldin, no actions are to be started against the Germans without our consent.'

'What?' Boldin screamed down the line. 'Our troops are forced to retreat, cities are burning, people are dying...'

'Iosif Vissarionovich – Stalin – thinks that these may possibly be provocations on the part of some German generals.'

Ivan Boldin was dumbfounded. 'Comrade Marshal, we must act. Every minute is precious. This is no provocation. The Germans have started a war!'

About the only concession Boldin was able to wring out of the People's Commissar for Defence was permission to fly to Białystok – all communication with Tenth Army had been severed.[40]

In the immediate aftermath of the devastating raid on its headquarters in Kobrin, the surviving staff of Fourth Army began to relocate to the temporary command post at Bukhovichi, five miles outside the town. Ilya Starinov, visiting the army to observe its summer manoeuvres, decided to head in the opposite direction. He grabbed a ride on the first truck driving west for Brest, 30 miles away. The vehicle fought against a stream of traffic fleeing the border zone: officers and men trying to re-join their units and, already, long lines of refugees, mostly women with children in tow, carrying bundles and blankets. The truck drove through the centre of Kobrin, which was filled with the acrid stench of fires. The tinny, childlike strains of *Shiroka strana moya rodnaya* (Wide is my Motherland) suddenly came from loudspeakers in the main square, the signature of Radio Moscow. 'It is 6am, Moscow time,' the voice announced. Everyone stared at the speakers. Starinov's driver stopped the truck and opened his door to listen. But the only news this morning was the usual fare: more outstanding achievements by workers, the prospects of an excellent harvest, some celebration in an obscure Soviet republic 400 miles east of Moscow. Then came news from Germany: air attacks against Britain, the sinking of ships by U-boats, fighting in Syria. With that, the broadcast ended and the morning's programming began with the usual daily gymnastics. It was a surreal scene. Here were refugees, some on foot, some in trucks, desperately trying to escape Kobrin, and the voice from the loudspeaker was encouraging people to bend, stretch, raise their arms, jump up and down. Ilya Starinov's driver slammed his door in anger and re-started his truck. There seemed little point continuing to Brest. The vehicle turned around and headed for Minsk.[41]

'I CAN HEAR THE BREATH OF HISTORY...'
BERLIN, 5.30AM

There were few people on the streets of Berlin at 5.30 on a Sunday morning. The odd person heading to work. A guard doing his rounds or policeman on patrol. The milkman making his daily deliveries. Suddenly loudspeakers across the German capital came to life: a 20-second fanfare, a drum roll, the final few bars of Liszt's epic *Les Préludes* – 'powerful, loud, majestic', chosen by Hitler and Goebbels as the signature theme for the burgeoning campaign. When the music faded, those Berliners awake at this hour heard the voice of their propaganda minister. Joseph Goebbels had not slept. The day was too momentous, his mind too active. 'I can hear the breath of history,' he confided to his diary later in the day. 'A great, wonderful age, in which a new empire is born.' On the table in front of him in an office in the Propaganda Ministry, two microphones and several pieces of paper. For the next 20 minutes he worked his way through those sheets; they bore Adolf Hitler's appeal which, until now, only the soldiers of the new Eastern Front had heard. When he finished, Joseph Goebbels felt 'totally liberated. The burden of many weeks and months disappears.'[42]

'WE HAVE DREAMED FOR A LONG TIME OF DOING
SOMETHING LIKE THIS TO THE BOLSHEVISTS...'
SKIES OVER ARMY GROUP CENTRE, 5–6AM

Within two hours of his first sortie of the day, Helmut Mahlke was airborne once more, heading for the main roads leading to Grodno, 35 miles to the south. His

Stukas were to cause chaos at the Neman crossings – but they were to ensure the bridges themselves remained intact. The crews had a few minutes to study maps and aerial photographs of the approaches to the city, before strapping themselves into their dive-bombers once more. They found opposition slightly more determined than at Kalvarija, but not enough to prevent their attack. Their bombs funnelled deep craters in the roads leading to the bridges; houses by the roadside collapsed, spilling rubble across the tarmac, blocking the road. The bridges over the river were undamaged.

An excited Heinz Knoke touched down back at his airfield in the Suwałki salient, his first sortie – just 56 minutes long – complete. His Me109 – and those of three comrades in *Jagdgeschwader* 52 – had been equipped with 100 5lb fragmentation bombs to cause havoc in a Red Army camp at Druskininkai, two dozen miles north of Grodno. And cause havoc they did. Not a soul could be seen in the huts as the Messerschmitts arrived over them. The fighters released their bombs almost in unison. Great fountains of earth were thrown up as the small bombs impacted – there was so much dust in the air the pilots struggled to see. When the columns of dirt collapsed, they revealed overturned vehicles, blazing barracks and scores of soldiers – most of them dressed only in their underwear – running around in confusion, mostly looking for cover in the neighbouring woods. One tried to manoeuvre a light anti-aircraft gun into position. He was shot dead. Heinz Knoke made several passes as the German fighters buzzed around the camp 'like a swarm of hornets'. To the 20-year-old this was less war, more sport, even fun. He brushed the ground – claiming he flew as low as 6ft – strafing the 'Ivans' and 'Stepsons of Stalin' with cannon and machine-gun fire. Trucks and huts were left in flames; a good number of Soviet soldiers were left lying on the ground. 'We have dreamed for a long time of doing something like this to the Bolshevists,' Knoke recorded in his diary at the end of the mission. 'Our feeling is not exactly one of hatred so much as utter contempt. It is a genuine satisfaction for us to be able to trample the Bolshevists in the mud where they belong.'[43]

'EVEN THE BRICKS BURNED...' BREST FORTRESS, 6–8.40AM

The staff of 45th Infantry Division believed the battle for Brest fortress won not three hours after it had begun. The South Island had already been captured; the men were clearing up the North Island. The citadel, the division's diarist confidently predicted, would 'soon be firmly in our hands'. He was being wildly optimistic.

When the Germans struck at 3.15am this Sunday, there were an estimated 9,000 troops in Brest fortress, 5,000 of them in the citadel: elements of two rifle divisions – the battle-hardened 42nd, which had fought in Finland, and the untried 6th, very much its poor relation – a detachment of border guards, a battalion of NKVD troops, a regiment of engineers and an assortment of ancillary formations. Many of the guns lacked shells, many of the men were short of ammunition, but what they lacked above all was leadership. Most of the fortress's commanders died with their families as shells rained down on their quarters. That same barrage also prevented the survivors from crossing the bridges to reach the citadel. There was little, if any, co-ordination of the defence of the central island. Many men fled, crossing the Mukhavets, making for the outer walls – not through cowardice but following the pre-war plan to rally outside the fortress. Most were cut down by the terrible combination of artillery, mortar and machine-gun fire. Others resolved to fight and die. At the shattered Terespol Gate, the western entrance to the citadel, border guard Lieutenant Andrei Kizhevatov received orders to fall back and regroup with his men.

'Are you with us, Comrade Lieutenant?' one asked.

'I have nowhere to go,' Kizhevatov replied. 'This is our outpost and I am its commander.'

It was a dilemma for captains, lieutenants and sergeants cut off from their leaders across the fortress complex: to stay and fight or to leave and regroup outside the fortifications. The decision was made for many of them by the attacker, who had already cut off most lines of retreat. But having reached the edge of the vast fortress – and advanced beyond it in places – the Germans found fighting flaring up in their rear. For a start, the North Island, home to anti-aircraft and artillery barracks, several rifle regiments and housing for 300 families, was proving far tougher to pacify than the terse entries in 45th Infantry's divisional log suggested. The home Nadezhda Gribakina shared with her husband, a lieutenant colonel, her mother and the couple's daughter had been damaged with the first shelling. Despite being wounded, she fled the building. 'We ran out into the street. Shrapnel and bullets were whirling around everywhere,' she recalled. An officer told them to take shelter in a partially collapsed house where the Gribakinas found upwards of 30 other people hiding. They spent three hours listening to the terrible sounds of battle, interspersed with occasional voices – first German, later Russian. Gribakina studied a man sitting in a corner 'with tears in his eyes, staring.

I thought he had a letter, but it was actually a Party membership card.' A friend advised him to destroy it. One after another, four Communists went up to the sink, tore their cards and stuffed the pieces down the pipe. 'The fourth man stared at his card for a long time, smiled and even kissed it before ripping it,' Gribakina observed. The men then made a break for freedom. Minutes later German troops entered the house and took the women prisoner. Passing one row of houses, 21-year-old Austrian infantryman Josef Arnreiter and his comrades were suddenly subjected to grenade and small-arms fire. 'One after another' one of Arnreiter's comrades 'rolled in his own blood. The cry: "Medic, help!" became more and more terrible.' Arnreiter was shot in the head – but the bullet missed his skull somehow after piercing his helmet. 'A stroke of luck? Or would it have been better had it gone through?' he wondered. Having fought his way through the citadel and across the compound in the centre of the fortress – by now 'filled with dense smoke, partially ripped up by shells and strewn with rubble from walls' – *Gefreiter* Hans Teuschler reached the gate to the North Island. 'Who will volunteer to go with me?' Teuschler asked his group. Six men raised their hands and joined Teuschler in racing over the northern arm of the Mukhavets and on to the island. German infantry grappled with Russian anti-tank guns; anti-aircraft gunners were engaged in fighting on the ground amid 'a huge town of tents'; and, worst of all, Russian snipers 'enjoyed organising a rabbit shoot during which death had a rich harvest'. Having captured an enemy flak position, Teuschler tried to bring every weapon to bear on the sharpshooters, scanning the island with his binoculars. In doing so, he made himself the perfect target. One of his machine-gunners urged him to get down, but it was too late; he was hit in the chest. 'I was just able to give my hand to my comrade at my side and bade him farewell,' he recalled. 'Then I collapsed, prepared to die, thinking of God and my home.'

Nor was the West Island, swiftly captured in the opening minutes of the assault, safe any longer as scattered Soviet troops regrouped and began to pick off advancing Germans. The South Island, equally lightly garrisoned, was home to the fortress's new 150-bed hospital. The red crosses painted on the roofs of its three dozen buildings had offered them no protection during the initial bombardment. 'Everything burned,' nurse Praskovuya Tkatshova recalled. 'Houses, trees, even the bricks burned.' Medical officer Boris Maslov ordered the patients moved to the relative safety of the nearby casemates under an earthen embankment which ringed the island. 'Dead and wounded lay on the ground everywhere,' remembered fellow nurse Katshova Braskova Lesnevna as she helped evacuate the hospital. Facilities in the casemates were non-existent.

The assault on Brest fortress, 22 June 1941

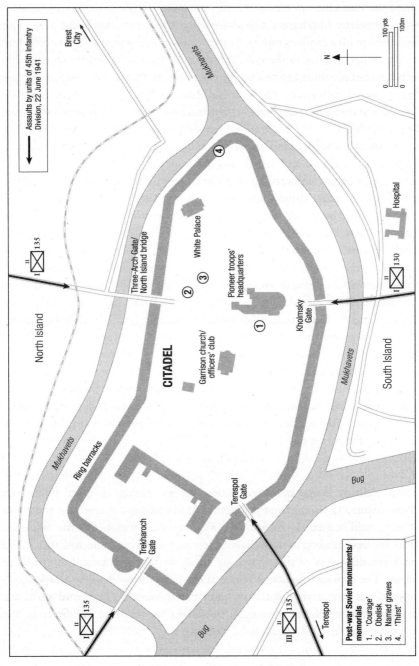

First the bandages ran out. Nurses improvised by ripping up their underwear. Then the medicine ran out, and finally the water. The only source of the latter was the nearby Mukhavets. One nurse, Rovnyagina Dussya, crept to the river and tried to fill a canister, only to be shot. It was too dangerous for her colleagues to get to her. She lay in the grass for more than a week. Despite Dussya's fate, other nurses continued to risk their lives, crawling down to the river, small cans hung around their necks. They wriggled back and passed the canteen around – 'only a few drops for everybody,' said Tkatshova, 'just enough to wet the lips of the wounded'.

From the South Island it was no more than 50ft over the river to the citadel, the physical and visual embodiment of Brest fortress, the zenith of mid-19th-century military engineering. When constructed, the two-storey red-brick structure ringed almost the entire island – well over one mile in diameter. The only way in or out of the citadel was through four imposing gates, which led to bridges linking the central island with the outlying fortifications. Outer walls 7ft thick overlooked the water, those facing the inner courtyard were a 'mere' 5ft thick, while embrasures lined the innards of each gateway should attackers get this far. If the invader did reach the centre of the island, he would find stables, vehicle workshops, a parade ground, artillery pieces, in the centre the former garrison church which now served as an officers' mess, and towards the eastern end of the compound, which was nearly 300 yards wide and 750 across, the famous White Palace where the Bolsheviks had signed a peace treaty with the Germans a generation before. By 1941, the palace – it took its name from the white paint which hid its red brickwork – had become an officers' mess, while much of the eastern portion of the citadel ring had been flattened, probably destroyed during the three-day battle for the fortress in 1939.[44]

From 7.30am onwards, disconcerting reports began to filter through to 45th Infantry Division's headquarters across the Bug in Terespol. The enemy was offering stiff resistance. And all the artillery and mortars at Fritz Schlieper's disposal were as good as useless. With his men locked in hand-to-hand combat with the defenders of the citadel, he could no longer bombard it to support them. The ordinary *Landser* too was starting to realise that the attack on the fortress was miscarrying. Radio operator Hans Wiesinger overheard a panicked message from a neighbouring regiment: 'Help, we are encircled!' Seconds later, the same unit pleaded: 'Help, help, we're burning!'[45]

'WHAT JOY, WAR...' LITHUANIA, MORNING

The inhabitants of Kaunas woke to the sound first of aircraft engines, then explosions, followed shortly afterwards by the sight of dense smoke rising above the suburb of Aleksotas on the south bank of the Neris – home to the city's airfield. 'That's where Soviet aircraft are burning on the ground,' one excited Lithuanian nationalist wrote. 'I grab the hands of my friends and shake them: war!' Elena Kutorgienė-Buivydaitė's terrified lodger burst into her room and blurted out: 'It's war.' The 52-year-old doctor simply laughed and sent her back to her room. Kutorgienė-Buivydaitė decided to stick to her plans for the day, starting with a visit to her hairdresser. She found the streets deserted and smiled to herself: *How easily people lose their heads and panic.* The city's archbishop, Juozapas Skvireckas, led Mass as he did every Sunday at the city's red-brick Catholic cathedral – despite the crash of bombs and repetitive boom of anti-aircraft guns. Afterwards, the cleric drank tea with members of his congregation. These were just the Red Army's summer manoeuvres, some argued. More astute worshippers surmised that war had begun. Back at his official residence on the northwestern outskirts of the city, Skvireckas talked with some of his employees. 'There's a couple of Bolsheviks among them,' the archbishop noted in his diary. 'They earnestly hoped that it was not war, and then, when there was no doubt, these Bolshevik fools tried to persuade themselves that even though war had begun, the Bolsheviks would nevertheless be able to rule for a long time to come.'[46]

In historic Trakai, 15 miles west of Vilnius, people at first feared a second wave of arrests and deportations was under way. 'Suddenly, like a thunderstorm, the sound of war across Lithuania. What joy, war,' one inhabitant recorded. 'Everyone is of the same mind: congratulating each other, tears of joy in their eyes. Everyone feels that the hour of liberation is near with the German Army beginning to drive the Reds out of Europe. NKVD officials and other Chekists run through the streets, gnashing their teeth that not everything was going to plan.'[47]

Just east of Trakai, in the small town of Rubežius, a young Red Army soldier wrote a few excited lines to his parents in the Soviet Union before his unit moved out to meet the invader.

> Life is perfect. I'm looking forward to it getting even better. I'm leaving for [censored]...
>
> Today war broke out. German Fascism won't reach us, we'll beat them on their soil. We've prepared for them. If I die at the hands of a Fascist bullet, I will die honourably and bravely. Our dreams have come true. We will carry out the

orders of the government and Soviet people honourably and courageously. Let us smash the snakes into the dirt so that they no longer live on this earth. They will not pass. That is all.

I want to announce: I am married, my wife is Lithuanian – she's on the photograph. If you would like to write, please write to: Lithuanian SSR, Jonava… I hope you'll write to her…

The soldier never posted his letter. It was found a few days later in the burned-out ruins of the town of Jonava, 20 miles northeast of Kaunas.[48]

'What kind of war?' Soviet Union, morning

In Lvov, there were already long queues outside the grocery stores. 'The Russians do not believe that it's war,' polytechnic assistant Stanisław Różycki, a Polish Jew, observed. 'They indulge in illusions, believe the official version of manoeuvres, yet flee in panic from the bombs into the bunkers, pale and frightened, soldiers and civilians, young and old, to the delight of the inhabitants of Lvov, the old-timers, who don't mind the bombs because they are used to it.'[49]

In Moscow, Yevgeny Khaldei was enjoying a free Sunday with family. The rain of the previous night had passed and it was a fresh, fine morning in the capital. Over breakfast, the photographer thumbed through the day's edition of *Pravda*: the lead story focused on the state education system; the Germans were giving the British a drubbing in North Africa; scientists in Leningrad had built the first cyclotron in the Soviet Union so they could smash the nucleus of an atom; and, 100 years since his death, one article paid tribute to 19th-century romantic poet Mikhail Lermontov, who had penned celebrated lines about Russia's showdown with Napoleon in 1812: 'Not in vain does all Russia remember the day of Borodino!' The ringing of the telephone interrupted Khaldei's leisurely reading. TASS's editor wanted to see him at mid-day. Five minutes later, another call. Another family member was called back into work – to a factory. As Khaldei headed to the TASS offices, he passed the German Embassy in Leontievsky Lane, barely a mile from the Kremlin. The building was heavily guarded. 'Suddenly, everything became clear.'[50]

By the time he arrived at the editorial offices of the *Krasnaya Zvezda*, David Ortenberg found most of his reporters waiting for him in uniform with suitcases packed, ready to head to the front. Some men even had compasses in their hands. Each writer wanted to go where the fighting raged. Not all could leave, Ortenberg ruled, for someone had to produce a newspaper. His staff argued and pleaded: Why should I stay here? Am I not as good as the others? Why am I suffering this insult? 'I had to remind them immediately of military order and discipline.'[51]

Military police stood on the main streets of Złoczów in Ukraine, directing the movement of army vehicles, while soldiers stood around with all their equipment packed. Officers bundled their wives, children and whatever possessions they'd had time to grab into waiting trucks; tears streamed down the women's faces. The civilian populace stood on corners, discussing the lively goings-on until they were dispersed by NKVD officers or soldiers. Samuel Tennenbaum headed to his factory. It was September 1939 all over again, he thought. Jewish employees were huddled together discussing what to do – 'fear was in their eyes and faces'. The Ukrainians were brash, 'hardly disguising their glee'. Tennenbaum's Polish staff were quieter, but seemed pleased with the course of events. 'For them throughout their history, there was always the choice between these two neighbours, two evils, if you will, between hatred of the Russians and fear of the Germans,' he wrote. 'Evidently at this moment they hated the Russians more than they feared the Germans.' Tennenbaum himself was more concerned with the fate of his immediate family. He got through on the telephone to his parents in Lvov, who told him the city had been bombed repeatedly. His mother was calm, his father sobbed.[52]

In Leningrad, the morning sunshine streamed through the windows of Elena Skrjabina's apartment. Her eldest son was about to head out to the Peterhof to see the refurbished fountains in the palace grounds switched on. Having breakfasted, Skrjabina too planned to head out of the city, visiting a sick boy in Pushkin, south of Leningrad. But then the telephone rang. It was her husband, normally calm, but this morning extremely agitated, begging his wife to stay at home with their sons.[53]

Thirteen-year-old Katya Korotayeva left home to buy some fresh rolls to take to the opening of Minsk's Komsomol lake. A keen swimmer, the schoolgirl wanted to be the first to take a dip in it. It was a beautiful summer's morning and the houses along her street in one of Minsk's more affluent suburbs 'drowned in a sea of flowers'. On the way to the bakery she bumped into a friend who told her war had begun. 'I thought: What kind of war? What is she talking about?'

Pravda correspondent Peter Lidov also planned to spend the day at the new lake with his family. What would they wear? Should they pack blankets for the children? Should they take a picnic or eat out? In the middle of the Lidovs' deliberations, the telephone rang. The secretary of *Pravda* was on the line; his voice stressed. 'I don't think the lake is all that important,' he advised Lidov, who guessed immediately that war had broken out. He put on his shirt and boots and headed to the Party offices. Minsk was calm – news of the invasion had yet to filter through. People headed for the lake, the many public parks, or even for the countryside beyond the city. When he reached the gleaming new Communist headquarters at the end of Sovetskaya Street, he was immediately shown into the Party committee room. Normally it was deserted on a Sunday, but today, Panteleimon Ponomarenko was closeted with senior Communist officials. 'There you are,' Ponomarenko said as he rose to greet Lidov, an old friend from their days in Moscow. 'War's begun! There's fighting on our soil.' Brest had already fallen. The German Army was advancing southwest of Vilnius, Białystok had been bombed, enemy aircraft had been sighted over Baranovichi just 90 miles to the southwest.

The telephone interrupted the two men's conversation. Stalin was on the line again, demanding to know what Dmitry Pavlov was doing – and especially how he was coping. Ponomarenko had seen the general just once that morning, but already he felt qualified to tell his leader that his commander was not up to the task at hand. He begged Stalin to send one of the Soviet Union's fabled marshals to take command. The *vozhd* agreed.[54]

Inhabitants of the Ukrainian capital, like those in Minsk, were preparing for a set-piece Communist Party spectacle this Sunday. For days posters all over Kiev had urged city folk to attend the opening of the rebuilt main sporting arena, renamed in honour of Party leader Nikita Khrushchev. Perhaps now only Leningrad and Moscow had finer stadia; there was seating for 50,000 spectators, terracing for 20,000 more, while the pitch – 'a lush green carpet' – was up to international standards. The turf would be 'christened' in an exhibition match between Kiev's much-loved Dynamo and a select Red Army XI. The game was a sell-out.

From his flat in a tall apartment block just off Kiev's main boulevard, four-year-old Dmytro Malakov watched Russian biplanes surrounded by exploding clouds of flak. His father assured him it was a rehearsal for the opening of the nearby stadium – such events were always accompanied by a military demonstration. But then the telephone rang. It was a family friend. The suburb of Podil, two miles to the north, was being bombed.

More than just Podil came under attack in Kiev on 22 June in a series of five raids. Half a dozen airfields were bombed, as were barracks, the main railway station, factories and power stations. Some Kievans were convinced the enemy was dropping poison in the Dnieper to infect the city's water supply. To children this was all great fun. Dmytro Malakov's brother rushed to a bomb site and stared at 'ruined buildings, huge bomb craters, with feathers from ripped pillows still flying around'. The raids killed 16 people – one 'victim' rose from the dead at his subsequent funeral, having merely been concussed by the bombing of his foundry – and wounded nearly 40.[55]

'THE BLOOD OF INNOCENTS FLOWED...' THE EASTERN FRONT, MORNING

Twenty miles downstream of Brest, border guard Sergeant M. A. Paschenko scanned the Bug floodplain in front of his strongpoint. German troops were swarming across the river but, annoyingly, Paschenko's commander demanded restraint from his men. 'Don't shoot without orders!' The wait was 'excruciating', Paschenko remembered. The enemy was no more than 200 metres away, the plain already littered with Russian dead and wounded from the initial bombardment. 'We understood that war had begun,' he wrote, 'but we did not want to believe it. Murder was not our profession.' But when his commander ordered 'Fire at the invaders!' Paschenko pressed the trigger, and the attackers were cut down as if a scythe moved over the lowland. The Germans fell back to the water's edge, leaving dead and wounded behind. While Paschenko's commander and political instructor moved up and down the trenches congratulating the men, the Russian dead were loaded onto carts and sent to the rear while a few Soviet soldiers crawled out onto the floodplain and deprived dead Germans of their automatic rifles as bullets whistled past their heads.[56]

By 9am, the frontier defences at Sokal had been overrun and the first German armour was rolling into the town itself. The command post of the border guards had been reduced to rubble – with women and children still sheltering in its cellar. As a panzer drove over the ruins, Jaroslav Branko watched border guard V. P. Karpenchuk dowse a dressing gown in petrol, put it on, then set it on fire and 'charge at the armoured monster. He tore off his burning gown and threw it on to the grill of the engine cowling, then rolled like a blazing torch under the tank. There was a huge explosion and the Germans turned around.' Elsewhere in Sokal, a young border guard officer from a village west of Kharkov in Ukraine, Lieutenant Nikolai Sinekop, penned a short note to his family and slipped it into one of the pockets on his uniform, a final, brief note to his family: 'I will die for the Motherland rather than be taken alive.' The note was later found on Sinekop's corpse.[57]

Germany and the Soviet Union had been at war more than five hours, but in Przemyśl the border guards on the right bank of the San had made no attempt to blow up the railway bridge spanning the river. On the opposite bank, pioneers had waited impatiently for the moment to storm the crossing, convinced the Russians would demolish it before they attacked. Under a renewed barrage which pummelled the railway embankment, a platoon of pioneers stormed the bridge. For several hours, Lieutenant Oleksandr Patarikin had observed German shells crashing down on Przemyśl – near the post office, in the hospital and signal box at the railway station. He had not responded. Nor had he demolished the river crossing – he had no such orders and no intention of acting on his own initiative. He was, however, prepared to defend himself. He observed the Germans crossing the railway bridge 'as if on parade' and, as the pioneers approached the guards' barracks, fire was finally returned. Soviet troops in the nearby houses joined in. The pioneer lieutenant leading the attack was cut down. The cries of wounded men drifted across the San; a few succeeded in crawling back over the railway bridge, among them a corporal, one of his arms in tatters. He had succeeded in cutting the fuse wire to the explosive charges under the railway bridge before he was shot.

Alexander Yegorov's 63rd Tank Regiment raced along the Shklo valley a good 30 miles west of Lvov. German aircraft circled overhead constantly, the bitter fruits of their labours lining the road: burned-out trucks, exploding ammunition carts, wrecked and abandoned tanks and armoured vehicles. Suddenly, the column halted. The regimental commander climbed out of his tank to question retreating Red Army infantry. Yegorov only heard a snatch of the conversation: 'German tanks broke through…'

At that moment an armoured car appeared. Its commander, his face flush, the strap of his leather tank helmet unbuttoned, ran to Yegorov's superior, battalion commander Major Zheglov.

'Comrade Major,' he reported, 'the reconnaissance platoon captured a prisoner.'

'What have we learned?' Zheglov asked impatiently.

The detachment had captured a soldier from the 68th Infantry Division near the border village of Krakovets.

'What else did you learn?' Zheglov pressed.

'Nothing more, Comrade Major. He doesn't want to answer questions. All he does is repeat: "*Russia kaputt*" and "*Heil Hitler*"…'

Zheglov gritted his teeth, then continued his questioning. What else had the reconnaissance found in Krakovets?

'Germans advancing,' the platoon leader replied hesitantly. 'Tanks, artillery, infantry…'[58]

The air in the woods west of Drohobycz was filled with exhaust fumes and petrol vapour. After five hours of waiting for orders, VIII Mechanised Corps finally had them: it was to drive some 20 miles to the west to the town of Sambor as the newly renamed Southwestern Front began massing forces for a counter-attack. In view of Germany's 'unprecedented attack', Georgy Zhukov had ordered forces along the entire frontier to destroy the invader wherever he had crossed the border (at the same time the Red Air Force was to locate and destroy enemy troop concentrations and Luftwaffe airfields, as well as bomb Memel and Königsberg).[59] The crews of 34th Tank Division had no doubt they would succeed, daubing their vehicles with slogans – even though it was against orders: 'For the motherland'; 'Death to Fascism'; 'On to Berlin'; 'Long live Communism'; 'Raise the flag of the Red workers all over the earth'; and 'Proletariat of all nations unite'. The corps' senior commissar Nikolai Popel was impressed by the morale of the men. They wanted to act. 'We'll deal with Hitler, then occupy Berlin,' one declared. Others wanted to know if Germany's workers had risen up against their Fascist rulers. They debated how long the war might last. When one soldier suggested 'half a year', he was laughed at and shouted down. Popel finally brought the animated discussion to a close, ordering the men to mount their vehicles and move out. As one, the tank crews cheered a hearty 'Urra!'

The 40-year-old political officer shared their optimism. He too had laughed at the soldier who'd guessed the war might last six months. In fact, deep down, Popel reckoned it might last 12 months. But he was in no doubt that the battle would soon be carried into occupied Poland and then on into Germany. Two decades later, he conceded how wrong he had been. 'We didn't have the slightest idea about the scale and nature of the test facing us at the time,' he wrote. 'And when I say "us", then I mean both the ordinary Red Army soldier and the commanders. This also applies to me.'

The tanks rolled down the main road to Przemyśl, leaving the symmetrical impressions of their tracks and streaks of oil on the hot asphalt. Soon they encountered an endless column of trucks fleeing the border zone, looking for safety further east. Each vehicle told a different story of suffering and misery. Some carried women and children, sitting on suitcases, carrying bundles of possessions. Others carried wounded soldiers. 'Some were unconscious,' Nikolai Popel observed, 'others were possessed by tragedy, others still silent, as if turned to stone by their pain. Blood seeped from the hastily-applied bandages.'

The nearer the 34th Tank Division got to the frontier – Sambor lay only two dozen miles from the border – the louder the rumble of artillery. Finally, a shell crashed down on a cottage next to the road. Nikolai Popel climbed out of his armoured car and went inside to rescue the inhabitants. There was no-one left to save. The body of one young girl had been blown out of the house by the blast and impaled on a fence. Her sister, aged about 12, dressed in a green dress, white knee socks and sandals, was crushed by joists in her bedroom. There was no sign of their parents. A veteran of the fighting in Finland, Popel had seen death many times, but never a child killed or a woman wounded – or so he claimed in his memoirs. 'And now, before one day had passed, the blood of innocents flowed,' he wrote. 'Here was a war being waged against the entire people.'[60]

Along the entire front, men on both sides were discovering the misery war had visited upon soldiers and civilians alike. When Friedrich Sachsse's reconnaissance unit ran into heavy artillery fire outside the Galician village of Tartakow, he sent a handful of men ahead to find out what was happening. As they moved forward, a shell crashed down. A corporal was killed instantly – a piece of shrapnel pierced his steel helmet and drove into his head. 'The first dead man – I had to fight back the tears,' Sachsse admitted as his men buried their comrade in a simple grave. Passing through the villages of Lithuania, August Freitag was accosted by local women who ran into the street 'screaming and begging, telling us in their language – which we didn't understand – and gesticulating that the Russians had robbed them or set their homes on fire or kidnapped their husbands and sons or even killed their children,' Freitag wrote. 'So on the very first morning we got an insight into how much misery war brings – especially in the country over which it rages. But we had so little time to think about such things. Our mission was to pursue the fleeing enemy and inflict losses.' The men of 121st Infantry Division torched any farm or cottage which offered shelter to the Red Army, although most Lithuanians wanted to help the invader, not the occupier. Teenagers offered to carry their machine-guns for several miles. Farmers placed pails full of water by the roadside or handed cups to the passing soldiers. And yet the villages of Lithuania burned. Signaller Albert Beyer marched towards dense smoke hanging over the small town of Vilkaviškis, a dozen miles inside the border. He passed a burning Russian staff car. 'The driver's clothes are burned from the body, leaving him with red-roasted skin,' the 26-year-old wrote. 'Not a pleasant sight!' In the fields flanking the main road lay the dead and wounded of both sides. A brief, but bitter street fight raged through Vilkaviškis as the 121st cleared out the last Soviet stragglers, leaving the town in ruins.[61]

There was little new in such wretched scenes. They had been played out in France or East Prussia in 1914. Poland in 1939. The West in the spring and summer of 1940, the Balkans as recently as this spring. But from the very first hours of war in the East there was a brutality, an inhumanity, which set it apart from previous conflicts.

Shortly before 6am a Red Army truck bumped down the rutted tracks and lanes which ran through the plains southwest of Marijampolė. With its brightly painted wooden cottages – yellow, white and green – with their steep roofs, Lakštučiai was a typical Lithuanian farming settlement, home to barely 100 souls. The lorry pulled up in the middle of the village and five men in olive-green uniforms climbed out. In a matter of minutes, the soldiers had arrested Lakštučiai's three priests, bundled them into the back of the truck and driven off, heading south towards Bartininkai. In the woods on the edge of that village, the clergymen were ordered to strip, while the soldiers deprived them of all their valuables. The three men were then shot, and stabbed with bayonets to make sure they were dead.[62]

Around the same time, the gunner of a Ju88 jumped from his burning aircraft after bombing the station at Kėdainiai, 30 miles north of Kaunas. On the ground, he was quickly captured by Soviet troops. Stripped of all his clothes and equipment apart from his shirt, underpants, socks and a scarf, he was stabbed in the thigh before a gold cap was prised out of one of his teeth. He may have been dead at that point – but to make sure, he was thrown face down into a drainage ditch, which was then hurriedly filled in with soil. For good measure, the earth over his head was weighed down with large stones.[63]

At least ten wounded – or hitherto-unharmed – German soldiers fell into Soviet hands during fierce fighting in woodland on the road to Kovel in Ukraine. Each man was executed by a rifle shot to the chest – as if he had faced a firing squad.[64]

Killing prisoners was not a Soviet preserve, however. Border guard M. A. Paschenko was appalled by what happened to his captured comrades after a dogged defence of the Bug. 'The cruelty of the enemy was simply inhuman,' he wrote. 'Even wounded comrades who fell into their hands were first beaten and then shot. This awful spectacle aroused our indignation and strengthened our determination to fight them unto death.' The *Landsers* of 35th Infantry Division were outraged by their enemy's method of fighting – allow the vanguard to pass, then ambush the main body following behind, shooting at them from houses, fields, often while dressed in civilian clothes. 'Such methods of fighting caused tremendous bitterness among our men,' the operations officer recorded in the division's war diary. 'As a result, few prisoners were taken.' 20th Panzer Division's ranks were similarly angered by the defenders of Kalvarija on the main highway to Kaunas, who not only knocked out two German tanks but shot two non-commissioned officers in the back in an ambush. 'The Bolsheviks are wiped out. These are soldiers who do not fight fairly,' machine-gunner Kurt Pfau noted cryptically in his diary. His comrades took just two enemy troops prisoner; the remaining 150 members of the garrison were all killed. A few miles downstream from Brest, border guard Ivan Belyaev had almost single-handedly defended his position for several hours. He was wounded at least six times before he was captured and taken to Rudavets where the Germans forced villagers to dig a hole. 'This Russian commissar is worthy of a good grave,' the German officer said in broken Russian, before turning to Belyaev. 'Good, brave warrior, remove your belt, cap and stand up against the wall!'

'No, I will not!' Belyaev responded.

'Face the wall!'

'I will not! I will not take off my belt and cap! Are you afraid to look me in the eye and shoot?'

As a local peasant clawed at the soil at Ivan Belyaev's feet to complete the grave, the bruised, battered and bleeding border guard remained defiant. 'I know you will kill me, you reptiles, but you will not kill the cause for which I fought,' he told his captors. 'Farewell, comrades! We will return to the Bug!'[65]

'TO BATTLE! TO THE FRONT WITH GOD!'
ROMANIA, MORNING

'You have just heard the bells of our captive churches and cathedrals – the bells of Chișinău, Cernăuți, Hotin, Cetatea Albă.' Thus spoke a Romanian radio announcer, who told listeners they would now hear an appeal from Ion Antonescu, at that very moment attending a church service in Piatra Neamț. The *conducător* promised to 'erase the stain from our history' and liberate sacred Romanian territory. The Romanian people could not 'idly stand by' at a time when other nations were forging history. They had a duty to join 'the honourable struggle for civilisation on the side of the great German nation'. Antonescu turned to his soldiers.

I order you: Cross the Prut! Smash the enemy from the East and North. Free our oppressed brothers from the red yoke of Bolshevism. Bring the ancient soil of

Bessarabia and the royal forests of Bukovina, their fields and meadows, back into the bosom of the nation.

Soldiers!

You will fight shoulder-to-shoulder and heart-to-heart with the strongest and most glorious army in the world. Prove that you are worthy of the honour, which history, the army of the great Reich, and its unique leader Adolf Hitler have given you.

Soldiers! Forwards! Fight for the liberation of our brothers in Bessarabia and Bukovina. Fight to avenge your humiliation and the wrong inflicted upon us.

'Soldiers!' Ion Antonescu concluded. 'Victory will be ours. To battle! To the front with God!'

Civilian or soldier, the Romanian people welcomed the war almost to a man. This was a war not of conquest, but of liberation. 'We were all convinced that we would liberate the precious soil of Bessarabia and Bukovina and our brethren under foreign occupation,' one infantryman recalled. 'Some thought that some of us would not live to enjoy seeing these wishes fulfilled.' War correspondent Virgil Gheorghiu was 'drunk with joy' at the news that four million Romanians would now be liberated. 'Nothing under the sun is more beautiful than the liberation of prisoners and captives,' he wrote. 'The very earth, trees, rivers and angels in heaven – all rejoice and celebrate when chains are broken, when prison walls crumble, when prisoners regain their freedom.' 13th Infantry Division's commander General Gheorghe Rozin told his men: 'The country summons us to a sacred struggle for the liberation of our brothers in Bessarabia and Bukovina.' Called up to join 1st Guards Division, junior officer Victor Comşa left a note for his father.

I'm leaving tomorrow, I'm healthy and happy that I can go back to where my place is today – with my company on the border.

You have to stay – for the good of the country, for the family, for all of us. They cannot do without both of us. You did your duty.

I am ready to fulfil it. I will be able to face the miseries and hardships more easily knowing that I will not have to take care of those left behind at home. I would be a cowardly father if I stayed. There are no reasons today. You know. Do you understand me? Before you are widower or husband, you are a soldier. That is why I have your assent, now that I am leaving to return with eyes filled with victory, if God wills it.

In the provincial town of Brad, 250 miles northwest of the capital, peasants from the surrounding area descended on the police station demanding to join Romania's 'struggle for justice'. The streets of Braşov in Transylvania echoed to the sound of 'endless cheers from thousands of throats. Soldiers were deluged with flowers.' With tears running down their cheeks, people sang the Romanian and German national anthems. In Arad, close to the border with Hungary, the main square was filled with a crowd which sang nationalistic and patriotic songs.

Nowhere was the patriotic fervour greater than in the capital. From mid-morning, people streamed through the streets 'like a torrent', hugging each other, tears running down their cheeks. They grabbed newspapers from the hands of sellers, or gathered on corners where proclamations were posted. Shops, businesses and public buildings hoisted the national colours. Military bands struck up the national anthem in Bucharest's many public squares, where they vied for space with clergy organising mass prayer sessions. At the Cathedral of the Holy Patriarchs, the elderly Metropolitan of Bessarabia, Gurie Grosu, blessed a 'holy struggle to liberate our brothers from Bessarabia and Bukovina and crush the Red beast from the east, which has tortured part of Europe's soul for a quarter of a century'. Trainee infantry officer Ion Şuţa marched through the city with his comrades, singing patriotic tunes – *They were heroes!*, *Advance Carpathian battalions!* As the cadets approached the city centre, all traffic stopped as the streets filled with cheering and applauding civilians. A shower of flowers rained from the windows of buildings lining the main roads as people cried: 'Long live the Romanian Army!' The largest crowd gathered in front of the Royal Palace. 'I could only make out the words: "Romania, Army, Antonescu",' Şuţa recalled. The square disappeared, replaced by 'a sea of heads'. A young woman from Bukovina, dressed in the national costume, appeared next to the statue of King Carol I and began to perform a folk dance. It left the crowd enraptured. The mood changed when the strains of *Te Deum* came from loudspeakers and the radio broadcast the bells of Chişinău. Everyone knelt. A 'deep silence' suddenly descended on the square, which left diplomat Gheorghe Barbul deeply moved. 'People fell to their knees in prayer,' he wrote. When they got to their feet again, they chanted in unison: 'Long live the holy war! Victory to the crusade! Out with the Asiatic barbarians from Europe!' Amid the tumult, the sight of an elderly man scaling the palace railings caught Barbul's eye. 'Forward,' the man shouted, 'may the Bolsheviks not celebrate a year's occupation of Bessarabia.'[66]

'VICTORY WILL BE OURS...' MOSCOW, 12.15PM

The faces of Muscovites were stony. Workers in caps and boiler suits, office workers in suits, working women wearing headscarves, bearded old men lifting their grandchildren up. All stopped and stared up at the half million loudspeakers across the Soviet capital. Ever suspicious, the country's leadership shunned personal radio sets – listeners might be able to tune into news from outside the USSR – and instead used an extensive public address system in large towns and cities to impart the news. It was the voice of their foreign minister, not their leader, that the citizens of the Soviet Union heard, speaking from Moscow's central telegraph office. With little fanfare – there was a brief introduction from the announcer – Vyacheslav Molotov addressed the nation for eight minutes. Despite the best efforts of his immediate entourage, Joseph Stalin had proved immovable. 'I have nothing to say to the people,' he snapped. 'Let Molotov speak.' The foreign minister was a wooden orator at the best of times. Today strain and nerves made his delivery even more hesitant.

> Citizens of the Soviet Union! The Soviet Government and its head, Comrade Stalin, have instructed me to make the following announcement:
>
> At 4am today – without making any protests to the Soviet Union or issuing a declaration of war – German troops attacked our country, violating our borders in many places and subjecting our cities of Zhitomir, Kiev, Sevastopol, Kaunas – and others – to bombing, killing or wounding more than 200 people.
>
> This perfidious aggression against our country is a betrayal without precedent in the history of civilised nations.

Molotov protested innocence on Moscow's part – 'full responsibility for this predatory attack upon the Soviet Union rests entirely upon the German Fascist rulers'. But now it had been attacked, the USSR would respond by driving German soldiers from the earth of the motherland. The valiant Red Army and Navy and the 'daring hawks' of the Red Air Force would deal the attacker 'a crushing blow'. Only towards the end of the address – drafted jointly by the foreign minister and Stalin – did Molotov's delivery become impassioned, his voice almost breaking at times.

> This is not the first time that our nation has had to deal with an attack by an arrogant foe. Back when Napoleon invaded Russia, our people rose to the challenge in the Patriotic War. Napoleon suffered defeat and met his doom. The same fate will befall Hitler who, in his arrogance, has proclaimed a new

crusade against our land. Once again the Red Army and our entire nation will wage a victorious Patriotic War for the motherland, for honour and for freedom.

Now the many peoples of the Soviet Union would rally and join forces 'as never before', devoting all their energies to supporting the armed forces, rallying behind the Communist Party. 'Our cause is just. The enemy will be defeated. Victory will be ours.' The closing sentences had been added by Stalin, who damned his foreign minister with faint praise at the end of the address. 'Well, you sounded a bit flustered, but the speech went well.'[67]

Schoolgirl Gena Yushkevich didn't think so. The people of Minsk wanted Stalin. They got Molotov. Where, inhabitants of the Byelorussian capital asked themselves, was their leader? Elsewhere in the city, a 13-year-old boy went out onto his porch and called to neighbours hanging washing out to dry. 'War's begun!' he yelled. The women ignored him. It was another children's game. It wasn't an uncommon reaction. One 11-year-old girl urged her mother, 'War's started, we must do something!' Her mother continuing sewing a dress, before calmly hanging it on the back of a chair when she'd finished. 'I am not worried about the Germans,' Kiva Palej, a former leather trader, told his grandson Joseph. 'They were nice people during the occupation in 1918, certainly better than the Communists.' None of the family considered fleeing Minsk – they hated Communism. 'The Germans can't be any worse,' they told themselves, 'probably a great deal better.' The family of one schoolgirl decided things 'were not so serious'. There'd been war before – with Finland and the 'liberation' of western Byelorussia. The grandmother suddenly chipped in, 'No, my children, this won't be a war like that…'[68]

Now Elena Skrjabina knew why her husband had implored her to stay at home. When the foreign minister finished speaking, Skrjabina stepped out into the streets of Smolny district. Leningrad was in uproar, the shops crammed with customers eager to hoard anything they could get their hands on. The panic seized the housewife as well. She rushed to the bank to withdraw her savings. Too late. The bank had no money left to give. 'People clamoured, demanding,' she wrote. 'The June day blazed on with unbearable heat. Someone fainted. Someone else swore vehemently.' A city official responsible for issuing ration cards studied the reaction of women waiting in a queue as Molotov spoke. 'Alarmed faces, horror in their eyes, and in the midst of an eerie silence, an unexpected heart-rending cry,' he observed. A mother of four was appalled: 'Oh, my dear sons!' she cried out sobbing, wringing her hands. Other women in line bluntly silenced her. 'You're not the only one with sons,' one snapped. Teacher Elena Mikhailov had spent an idyllic morning in Nevsky Forest Park with her husband Dmitry, a lecturer in German at the city's state university. Returning home on the tram, she noticed Dmitry turn pale. Leaning across the carriage, he said simply: 'War!' 'With whom?' his incredulous wife asked her. '*Da*, the Germans attacked,' a passenger scolded her. 'Wake up!'[69]

Actor Nikolai Dupak listened to Molotov's speech with the cast and crew of the historical epic *Taras Bulba*. The 19-year-old had been startled by the first attacks on Kiev at dawn, but still took a tram as planned to the Ukrfilm studios. When the foreign minister finished, director Alexander Dovzhenko addressed everyone. Instead of 18 months, they would finish their production in just six. 'And we would beat the enemy – on his territory,' Dupak remembered. 'That was the mood.'[70]

At the All-Ukrainian Academy of Sciences, 'everyone listened in silence, then went home,' diarist Nina Gerasimova noted. 'I'm not worried, I'm very calm, even though the city is in danger and the night will not be calm,' she tried to convince herself before adding: 'Will Kiev be destroyed?!' The German attack was 'an unprecedented atrocity,' 23-year-old cadet Leonid Krasikov fumed to his family. 'The enemy has miscalculated, however. The battle will rage on his territory. Mama, I plead with you not to be upset, to remain calm and also to calm down those who panic. Our Red Army has repeatedly shown its strength to the whole world. It is invincible.' And one Kiev schoolteacher felt compelled to write to his son:

> My dear son Vasya! Today I experienced a few very difficult seconds. This was when I saw enemy aircraft flying over us. We were frightened. Bombs were dropped, there were victims in Solomianka. At mid-day they announced war with Germany. People stopped everything to stock up on food...
>
> I, my son, am completely calm, I'm calming others down... Naturally, you know all the details about the beginning of the war. I cannot convey to you this feeling of hatred for the German clique which started this slaughter...
>
> My son, remain calm and firm, you know what you are protecting. I hope that our valiant army will not allow the defeat of Kiev.[71]

Yevgeny Khaldei had been sent to photograph the reaction of Muscovites and headed to Nikolskaya Street – linking Red and Lubyanka Squares – where he found people gathered around loudspeakers. 'I heard the first words and lines: "Our cities of Kiev, Sevastopol and Kaunas have been bombed…",' he recalled, 'and felt the cold spread through my body. After that I didn't hear anything else.'[72]

'THIS IS FORTRESS! WE ARE FIGHTING…' BREST, MID-DAY

The voice of Vyacheslav Molotov carried as far west as Brest. Though faint – the battery on the set was running low – the men of 333rd Rifle Regiment heard it, clustered around one radio in the citadel. Sending messages from the fortress, however, was proving considerably more difficult. There had been no acknowledgement, let alone response, to the coded messages 84th Rifle Regiment's signallers had sent to higher commands. The airwaves, it seemed, were German. Frustrated, the regiment's commissar Yefim Fomin ordered a message broadcast en clair: 'This is fortress, this is fortress! We are fighting. Ammunition in good supply, losses slight. Await instructions. Over.'

And how the fortress was fighting. The *Reichskriegsflagge* may have been hoisted above the South Island in the middle of the morning, but it was merely an outpost. The heart of the fortress was being contested to the death. Near the western exit, the Terespol Gate, frontier guards and a mishmash of infantry, NKVD soldiers and transport troops were doggedly holding out – it would take flamethrowers and pioneers with demolition charges to finally bring their resistance to an end. Attempts to forge a link between Germans striking south from the North Island and those, like Hans Teuschler's squad, driving north through the heart of the citadel, had all been cut down, again by ad hoc groups of Soviet troops led by energetic junior officers. By late morning, the attackers only really had a firm foothold at the western end of the citadel, from where they directed 20mm anti-aircraft gun rounds at the red bricks of the circular barracks, and Church of St Nicholas, where elements of one infantry regiment and a battalion of pioneers were holed up. Sitting on a mound roughly in the middle of the citadel, the gold-domed house of worship had been stripped of much of its white plaster by the bombardment, revealing the red brick beneath – now rapidly being scarred by rifle and machine-gun fire. Once the church of the fortress garrison, under Soviet rule all religious activity had ceased; the building was turned into a mess for the officers of a rifle regiment. The struggle for it would embody the battle for Brest fortress in microcosm.

Around mid-day, under covering machine-gun and rifle fire, a concerted effort was made to dislodge the invader. Russian troops swept across the centre of the citadel – ground occupied only the night before by tents and field kitchens – up several steps and burst into the church. After the bright daylight of a mid-summer's day, the darkness was a shock to the eyes of the entering Russian troops. Ivan Dolotov could see only the muzzle flashes of automatic weapons at first as German troops in the balcony, once occupied by the church choir, poured down fire. When his eyes adjusted, he realised there were 'just five or six submachine-gunners' holding him and his comrades at bay. A few Germans tried to force their way out, smashing the windows, jumping down onto the parade ground and running for cover across around 300ft of the courtyard. Most were cut down as they fled. But the attackers attempting to drive the Germans from the church fared no better. Two in every three men became casualties. All they had achieved for their efforts was a foothold just inside the church.[73]

The Red Air Force was able to offer little relief to the defenders of Brest. While Luftwaffe bomber and Stuka squadrons thundered eastwards 'in formation, as if on exercise', Lieutenant Walter Loos watched the Messerschmitts of Werner Mölders' squadron pick off Russian aircraft 'by the dozen'. Reservist officer Erich Maresch counted at least 14 enemy aircraft brought down in flames. The blue sky above Brest was quickly dotted with 'snowballs' – parachutes. As the aircrew descended to earth, some shot at German troops on the ground with carbines. 'One lands near us, draws his pistol, fires three shots at us, then shoots himself,' Maresch wrote. Russian pilots, Walter Loos concluded, 'were carved from hard wood'. German medics rushed with a stretcher towards another Russian airman who parachuted to safety, only to be driven back when he fired his automatic weapon.[74]

Walter Loos watched the dogfights from Brest itself, rather than the fortress. The main German ground assault had simply skirted around the fortress and pushed into the city. Resistance was sporadic at best, but where the Russian soldier stood firm, he fought bitterly. 'We came under fire from cellars, windows, skylights, from trees, new buildings, bunkers,' Loos complained, as he watched colleagues fall to the ground hit. 'In the smoke, fug and dust generated by shells impacting and burning houses, it was very hard for me to identify enemy sharpshooters.' A few tanks tried to break through the city to the fortress but were driven back, while trucks packed with Russian riflemen sent to reinforce the citadel garrison were shot-up at point-blank range by machine and anti-tank guns. When Josef Arnreiter moved into the city, 'there was no sign of the Russians'. There were plenty of civilians in the streets – 'busy looting', the Austrian noted. 'They made every possible gesture of subservience. They all came out of their houses, apparently delighted by our appearance.' Young Polish girls presented the soldiers with posies; their parents brought tea, eggs, butter and sweets. There was little resistance because no-one was co-ordinating the defence of Brest. 'With the very first shots, panic broke out among the troops' – and not just the ranks, but officers, colonels, majors, even commissars, Brest Communist Party functionary Mikhail Tupitsyn complained. Some sought to evacuate their families; most simply fled – 'many half-dressed, without almost any weapons'. The flight was only stopped 100 miles from Brest on the main Minsk highway – and even then only for a matter of hours. Brest's Party leadership also chose to flee, rather than direct the battle. Nor did Tupitsyn and 100 other senior Communists have any intention of remaining in the city. They fled east, for Gomel – 350 miles away. Those Communists left behind in Brest – there was no formal order to evacuate the city – destroyed their Party membership cards, military passes and other official documents, then began creeping through the side streets, hiding in cellars to avoid the invader.

In the chaos of the retreat from Brest, at least three Party members were shot by their comrades, 'mistaken for saboteurs'. Fourth Army's Leonid Sandalov fought against a torrent of vehicles and trucks as he tried to reach the fortress from Kobrin. Every time an aircraft appeared, there was a desperate thump on the cab of a truck, and the vehicle hastily pulled off the road and tried to hide in the trees; the forest tracks and side roads of western Byelorussia were full of lorries and carts carrying the archives, documents, safes and money of government institutions and the Communist Party. Just as common a sight was refugees, 'all carrying bundles, wallets, bags,' Sandalov remembered. 'Exhausted, with haggard faces, they moved silently towards Kobrin, taking cover under trees and bushes when enemy aircraft appeared.'[75]

'SALVATION IS COMING...' PRZEMYŚL, MID-DAY

It was noon before 101st Light Division made a renewed attempt to seize the railway bridge at Przemyśl. Artillery and 3.7cm anti-tank guns concentrated their fire on the houses on the right bank of the San, reducing them to rubble one after another. They also set the fuel depot next to the bridge on fire. 'Huge black clouds darkened the heavens,' battalion commander Hans Kissel recalled.

Even though the 150ft river was easily fordable – the water came little higher than a soldier's waist – the pioneers, now bolstered by infantry, struck out across the San on inflatable sacks and rubber boats. They were met by only the occasional shot as the railway bridge was finally secured. Soviet accounts claim the man commanding the bridge detachment, one Lieutenant Nechayev, was the last to die; fatally wounded, he blew himself – and several Germans – up with his last grenades.

The attackers now began fanning out into the houses, combing through each one, but failing to find any Red Army soldiers until they pushed into the city centre where Soviet troops were holding out. The workers of the power station, dressed in their overalls, fought to the death in the generator hall; it took a field gun to end their resistance. Otherwise, Russian resistance on the right bank of the San broke rapidly. By early afternoon, most of Przemyśl had been captured by 101st Light Division 'without suffering noticeable casualties'. From the windows of the Franciscan monastery, Father Rafał Woźniak watched 400 German soldiers file past. 'So,' he recorded in his diary, 'salvation is coming.' Another priest urged caution: 'Let's just hope that the Bolsheviks do not return…'

COMPLACENCY… BYELORUSSIA, MID-DAY

By mid-day, the truck in which Ilya Starinov hitched a ride in Kobrin had reached Pinsk, 70 miles to the east. The town was spared war until 9am, when the men of *Schnellkampfgeschwader* (Fast Bomber Squadron) 210 pounced on its airfield. They found no opposition in the air or on the ground – the only response to the 1,000kg bombs impacting below were the balls of fire and smoke billowing across the base. The dark swathes left by the initial attack made the fighters' second run – strafing the aircraft on the edge of the field – more challenging, but the Russian SB and Pe-2 bombers were neatly arranged and had no dispersal pits to protect them. One by one, the Messerschmitts lined the aircraft up in their crosshairs and sent 20mm cannon shells tearing into them at point-blank range. Still there was no response from the defenders – seemingly the only dangers to the Me110s were colliding with comrades or shrapnel hurled up by the explosions. After wreaking havoc for 30 minutes, the Messerschmitts turned for home.

The airfield was still burning when Starinov's truck passed. As for the town, there was lively activity in the centre, especially outside the conscription office where Byelorussians were being enlisted. In the Communist Party offices, Starinov was questioned by the local committee. The 41-year-old engineer could offer no answers, but the Party officials did not seem perturbed. The border was 100 miles to the west. The Germans would never reach Pinsk.[76]

Such confidence – or complacency – was shared by Party grandees in Minsk, who resumed their deliberations after listening to Molotov's address. What, Party secretary Panteleimon Ponomarenko wondered, would happen if the Germans bombed the dam on the Komsomol lake? Would the city be flooded? 'We should have experts look into this.' A specially equipped air-raid shelter with telephone lines was needed urgently – an engineer suggested the cellar beneath the city's Proletarian club. A comrade suggested changing the date of the annual central committee congress, planned for 3 July. Panteleimon refused. Plans were made to prepare a special train to move the families of Party officials to safety if necessary. Otherwise, there was no talk of retreat, no thought of abandoning Minsk or evacuating civilians. Any such measures would demoralise the populace and probably provoke panic.

Not ten minutes' walk away, the Moscow Art Theatre's matinee performance of *School for Scandal* went on as planned before a full auditorium. During the interval, a military figure strode onto the stage and told a stunned audience and performers that war had begun. A few people left; most stayed. The play resumed. The actors of the Ukrainian Revolutionary Theatre found the stalls in the House of the Red Army empty. They were supposed to perform *In the Steppe of Ukraine* for the men of the Minsk garrison. There was no explanation for the soldiers' absence. The actors drew their own conclusions – anything from a sudden departure for summer camp to manoeuvres – but not once did they guess that war had begun.[77]

'HITLER WILL BE HERE BEFORE LONG...'
LITHUANIA, MID-DAY

In Vilnius, poet Abraham Sutzkever had spent the morning with his friend Nojech Priluzki, professor of Yiddish at the city's university who was engrossed in his work, *The Phonetics of Yiddish*.

'With the first bomb on Russian soil Hitler has dug his own grave,' Priluzki prophesied. He did not seem troubled by the outbreak of war; he was more concerned about finishing writing his tome.

When Vilnius came under attack around mid-day, Sutzkever decided it was time to return home. The bombs shattered most window panes in the city centre, began a few fires, burned out a small number of homes and the former Polish theatre, but killed few Lithuanians. Sutzkever fought his way past fire-fighters dealing with a conflagration around the historic Green Bridge. His mother was delighted to see him, smothered him in kisses and assured him everything would turn out well. As the two ate a lunch of sorrel in milk sauce, bombs fell continually. A gasometer on the other side of the Vilnia was hit.

Acrid smoke drifted across the river and into the Sutzkevers' apartment, tickling the diners' throats.

'Come, Mama, we'll save each other together!' Sutzkever urged.

His mother stroked his head, kissed him and looked at her 27-year-old son with an unforgettable, painful expression: 'My child, I'm not going anywhere. My life is in you. You go and save your young self.'[78]

In Kaunas, inhabitants had responded to the day's first air attacks by hurriedly sticking strips of paper to their windows to prevent shards of glass being flung around the rooms. When the sirens sounded the all-clear, people rushed into town to buy food and withdraw their savings from banks – even though most of the latter were closed as it was Sunday. Shops could not cope with demand and lengthy lines quickly stretched out into the streets. And there the shoppers were caught when German aircraft returned. They pressed themselves against the walls of houses to protect themselves as clouds of smoke spiralled through the streets and shrapnel was flung through the air.[79]

Forty-five miles to the northeast, war had yet to reach the provincial centre of Ukmergė. Many inhabitants had spent the morning picnicking in the surrounding countryside with baskets of buttered bread. A group of young Jewish Communists and pioneers marched through the city centre carrying Red Flags and singing the Lithuanian translation of *If War Comes Tomorrow* – as they headed to the neighbouring pine forest in Dukstynos. Only when they returned at mid-day and heard Molotov's speech over the loudspeakers did Ukmergė's citizens realise they were at war. Party officials immediately began burning documents; the wives of officers started to pack their belongings 'as rumours spread that the entire exercise area where their husbands were had been overrun,' one Lithuanian nationalist observed.[80]

Few Lithuanians expected the Red Army to stop the invader, dismissing the Soviets' antiquated 'tanks of 50'. 'It took one man to steer, we joked, and 49 to push,' one teenager recalled. No, the Germans would soon come and most of his fellow countrymen, lawyer Avraham Tory observed, 'saw their place on the side of the swastika'. Jews like Tory immediately realised the danger. Lithuanian nationalist Kęstutis Miklaševičius noticed Jewish neighbours in Šančiai were packing their possessions in preparation to flee 'as if sensing their end'. A chronicler in Ukmergė relished the sight of the town's Jewish populace 'putting bags on their backs and running where their feet can carry them'. With the outbreak of war, antisemitism in Lithuania became blatant, not latent. 'Hitler will be here before long and will finish you off,' one group roaming Kaunas sneered at Tory. Nationalists seized the moment to stoke such hatred. 'The fateful hour of final reckoning with the Jews has come,' the Lithuanian Activist Front proclaimed. 'Lithuania must be liberated

not only from Asiatic Bolshevik slavery but also from the age-old yoke of Jewry.'
Jews had enjoyed the right to live in Lithuania since the days of Vytautas the Great
500 years before. That was now revoked. They were to be made foreigners in their
own land. For those who had sided with the Soviet regime, 'betraying the
Lithuanian state' and 'persecuting, torturing or abusing' fellow Lithuanians in the
process, even worse was to come. It was the duty of 'all honourable Lithuanians to
take their own measures to apprehend such Jews and, if necessary, carry out the
punishment'. The appeal concluded:

> The Jews are to be expelled completely and for all time... In the newly-restored
> Lithuania not even one Jew will have either the rights of citizenship or the means
> of earning a living. In this way, we will rectify past mistakes and repay
> Jewish villainy.
>
> Let us all prepare for struggle and victory – for the freedom of the Lithuanian
> nation, for the cleansing of the Lithuanian nation, for an independent Lithuanian
> state, for a bright and happy future.

There would be no independent state, no bright and happy future for Lithuania.
But there would be cleansing on a terrible scale.[81]

It began long before the nationalist appeal was spread through the land. Just
seven hours into the war, the small border town of Lazdijai was in German
hands. Barely 40 of its 1,200 Jews – nearly half the population – had managed
to flee in time. Those who sought refuge in the outlying villages and crofts
rarely found shelter, for few farmers were willing to house them. Some refused
to even offer sustenance, slamming their doors in the Jews' faces: 'Go to your
father Stalin!'

Fifteen minutes after German troops marched into the border village of
Kudirkos Naumiestis, butcher David Gladnikov opened the door of his house. He
was shot on the spot by a German soldier who yelled at him: '*Verfluchter Jude!*' –
'Damn Jew!' A Jewish teenager and a coachman were also immediately executed.
When a German soldier was found dead in the street, two Jewish barbers were
hauled out of their homes and put before a firing squad in full view of villagers.[82]

'TANKS AHEAD!' THE FIRST CLASHES OF ARMOUR,
EARLY AFTERNOON

A Lithuanian serving in the Red Army ran through the small town of Butrimonys.
Alytus, just a dozen miles to the southwest, was being bombed, he cried. 'I

thought it was a joke,' 53-year-old Khone Boyarski wrote to relatives; Alytus was 30 miles inside the border. The soldier tried to commandeer Boyarski's truck, but he refused. 'We thought he was pulling our legs. So he went on his way.' Soon others came from Alytus – Jews, women, children. 'They said it was true – all of Alytus was on fire, there were many dead lying in the streets.' German aircraft flew over Butrimonys. They did not drop any bombs, but their appearance provoked widespread panic. 'Everybody started to pack and to look for carts,' Boyarski wrote. 'The Russian Army was beginning to fall back on Vilnius and we did not know what to do.'

By the time the German vanguard reached Alytus around mid-day, more than 350 homes and buildings had been reduced to rubble, while a haze from the still-raging fires shimmered over the town. Albert Frank steered his motorcycle past burning, collapsed houses and buildings, downed telephone poles – the lines they once carried lay tangled in the road – abandoned weapons, vehicles, household goods. 'And among it all,' he wrote, 'the dead. There's a foul smell of burning pervading everything.' Machine-gunner Kurt Pfau watched 'civilians in poor clothes look for something to save amid the ruins. War has shown how cruel it is on the very first day.'

The town was key to the German advance because of two bridges spanning the Memel – the Nemunas to Lithuanians, Neman to Russians – on the eastern outskirts, one to the north, the second four miles upstream. Twenty panzers safely rolled over the northern crossing. The 21st, a Czech-built 38(t), never made it to the right bank, wrecked by a well-hidden T-34. Having achieved a kill, the Russian tank quickly withdrew – defeating every attempt by the 37mm guns of Panzer Mk3s to knock it out.

The solitary T-34 – the first encountered by German armour this day – was the vanguard of the 5th Tank Division, thrown into the battle with little ammunition or fuel, its crews possessing almost no experience of their new tanks. They fought valiantly. Three times they counter-attacked 7th Panzer's bridgehead, three times they were held off by the Germans; 25th Panzer Regiment's commander Karl Rothenburg called it 'the hardest battle of his life'. His division lost 11 panzers this Sunday afternoon, the 5th Tank Division more than 70 vehicles, including more than two dozen T-34s.[83]

Ninety miles upstream, and still on the left bank of the Neman, Horst Slesina checked the map: Koniuchy. 'An insignificant village on a country road ten miles west of Grodno,' he thought. Suddenly a cry passed through his armoured reconnaissance unit: 'Tanks ahead!'

Vehicles and men spread out around Koniuchy, foxholes were hastily dug, anti-tank guns moved into position while troops not involved in the action took shelter behind cottages and houses. The scouts pushed on – running straight into Major Josef Cheryapkin's 57th Tank Regiment outside the village. 'The Germans came on with their sleeves rolled up and collars unbuttoned, firing machine-guns, shooting from the hip. I have to say that it was impressive,' Cheryapkin recalled. 'I let them get closer and then opened fire. They did not expect us to offer serious resistance and were stunned when they encountered a hurricane of fire from the tank cannons and machine-guns.' The scouting party turned and fled. To a soundtrack of the high-pitched whistle of anti-tank shells and the crack of small-arms fire, they ran through Koniuchy yelling: 'They're coming – 20 to 30 tanks up ahead!' *Sturmgeschütze* rattled through the village led by a monocled junior officer who called out to Slesina: 'Are you coming with us? I think there's a lot happening up ahead!'

Soon there was the sound of engines and caterpillar tracks approaching the village, followed by the sight of earth-brown vehicles with long barrels, at least six light and medium tanks, plus several armoured cars. The turrets on the tanks turned, then the Soviet armour opened fire. Slesina, a radio reporter who had covered the 1936 Berlin Olympics, watched as anti-tank tracer rounds reached for the Russian tanks 'like glowing fingers' before the assault guns entered the fray.

> The first two shells from the two *Sturmgeschütze* hit the heavy tank in the lead, simply tearing its turret off with terrible force, hurling it several metres away. Tall tongues of flame, the bursting and crashing of exploding ammunition, fuel tanks go up in the air – in one minute five smoking, burning turrets lie in front of us, five Soviet tanks have literally been ripped apart.

Friedrich Grupe's attention was seized by the cry: 'Tanks on the heights over there!' He looked in the direction of an outstretched arm and saw 'dark shadows' advancing slowly.

> The eyes of hundreds of *Landsers* are fixed on the rolling fortresses drawing ever closer, the guns on the tanks in the lead are already clearly visible. Our hearts are pounding because there's another cry: 'Tanks also on the heights to the north – next to the factory chimneys!'
>
> To our right, a *Sturmgeschütz* rumbles forward, its cannon already roaring – over there a loud crash. Hit! Dark clouds of smoke billow from the tank. Now the anti-tank guns are also firing. The next Russian tank is left standing after being hit, its crew – black dots against the terrain – jump out and disappear in the grain fields. Our heavy machine-gun group peppers the area.

The battalion has formed a hedgehog. Below us, to our right, outside a small village, there's a battery of light field howitzers. Dark monsters appear on the horizon around it too – tank formations from the barracks in Grodno. They are surrounded by accompanying infantry.

Shell after shell leaves the barrels of the field howitzers, the first houses in the village over there go up in flames. Again, several tanks remain motionless, shrouded in smoke and flame.

Our anti-tank guns fire continuously. Soon the terrain in front of us is littered with burning wrecks.

This first encounter had revealed alarming shortcomings with Soviet armour. 'The T-26 and BT tanks had petrol engines, weak armour and went up in flames when the first shell hit,' a worried Josef Cheryapkin wrote. It was only the beginning of a terrible clash Horst Slesina called the *Panzersterben* – the death of the tanks.[84]

Another Soviet unit making a desperate stand west of Grodno was 213th Rifle Regiment, which had already lost half its men trying to defend the border. As it fell back on the fortress city, messengers were dispatched; they either failed to return or brought only bad news: 'The road is blocked by German motorcyclists'; 'The Nazis have seized the crossing over the Neman!'; 'Our 184th Rifle Regiment withdrew from the village of Gozhi!' An energetic artillery major resolved to fight rather than retreat. When one of his gunners was killed, he moved the body out of the way and took the dead man's place. By the time the fighting ended in the late afternoon, just two of the regiment's guns – one 76mm and a 122mm howitzer – were still capable of firing; the rest were shapeless metal. Corpses with the horror and terror of the men's final seconds permanently carved on their faces stared from still-smouldering shell craters. The major mounted his horse and rode up and down what was left of his regiment. A German shell knocked him from his steed and killed him instantly.[85]

Grodno itself was partially cloaked by smoke and fug from fires caused by Luftwaffe raids. The city had been formidably defended by 36 anti-aircraft guns. They claimed they downed 16 German aircraft – a claim not supported by Luftwaffe records. More importantly, they failed to prevent bombs raining down on Grodno. By mid-morning, at least 17 major fires were raging and more than 150 people were dead. One Communist Party officer bemoaned, 'there was no firm leadership'. Troops were confused, had no communications, little food, fuel or ammunition, while the crews of anti-aircraft guns and KV tanks could not operate them properly. Perhaps his description was accurate. Perhaps he was looking for scapegoats. If nothing else, later this afternoon the tank crews would at least show they knew how to die.[86]

In the Shklo valley in western Ukraine, elements of 63rd Tank Regiment finally encountered the enemy. They thwarted the first German attack but lost three tanks and a battalion commander. Unable to establish contact with the rest of the regiment, the battalion fought alone, waiting for the next enemy assault. 'Ahead we could already hear the loud roar of tank engines,' Alexander Yegorov recalled. 'Ten more of Hitler's panzers were advancing along the valley.' The battalion's temporary commander ordered the tanks to halt and let the Germans close to within 500 yards, whereupon the Soviet cannons thundered. In an instant, three panzers were knocked out. 'Leaving a few burned-out and immobile tanks, the Germans withdrew.'[87]

'SEND NOTHING MORE INTO THE CITADEL...'
BREST FORTRESS, MID-AFTERNOON

For all he had captured the bridges spanning the Bug and the rest of the army was now making use of them, Fritz Schlieper was not master of the situation in Brest fortress. The Russians were defending themselves far more doggedly than he ever imagined – especially after the ferocious artillery barrage. Belatedly, he acknowledged that the defenders knew every inch of the complex – and his men did not. As far as Schlieper's superiors were concerned, Brest was already a sideshow. It was not worth wasting the lives of German soldiers to seize it. Corps commander Walter Schroth ordered his divisional commander 'to send nothing more into the citadel'. The troops were to pull back, the island sealed off and levelled by artillery.

With men still trapped in the garrison church, Fritz Schlieper rolled the dice one last time. Six *Sturmgeschütze* were committed against the citadel from the north and began pummelling the barracks in the hope that their barrage might offer some relief to the beleaguered troops, firing into the masonry and a few workshops in wood huts at a range of no more than 200ft. Hand-grenades and charges were hurled from the upper floor of the barracks block, inflicting heavy casualties on the assault-gun crews – inexplicably they had left their turret hatches open. Nevertheless, their shells took their toll of defenders, who retreated to the basement. Perhaps a relief party might force their way over the north bridge onto the island and reach the church, not 250 yards away. But no. No matter how much fire the *Sturmgeschütze* brought down on the barracks, they could not subdue the Soviet defenders. The handful of infantry who tried to cross the bridge were either mown down or wounded. Still, at least two *Sturmgeschütze* forced their way over the north arm of the Mukhavets, through a gate and into the centre of the citadel. Without accompanying infantry, they were sitting ducks. One was knocked out, every one of its four crew killed. The second was hit by a shell from a Russian gun and quickly returned whence it had come.[88]

'PERHAPS ONE MADE IT HOME...' THE RED AIR FORCE COUNTER-ATTACKS, MID-AFTERNOON

At Majaki airfield in Moldova, Alexander Pokryshkin was sitting in the cockpit of a now-armed MiG-3. A squadron of enemy bombers had been reported approaching the airbase, but for ten minutes the increasingly impatient Siberian had been waiting for the signal to take off. By the time it came – three flares arcing over the field – the bombers were already in sight.

The single-engine aircraft flew past the airfield in a strict 'wedge' formation. They were unlike anything Pokryshkin or his wingman had seen. Pokryshkin intercepted the closest bomber and fired a short burst from his machine-guns. 'I couldn't miss – I was so close to him that the turbulence from his propeller shook my plane.' As he pulled away and began to climb above the bomber formation, he looked down and noticed the red star on their wings. As the rest of the fighters moved in to finish off the rest of the squadron, Pokryshkin intervened, manoeuvring his MiG-3 in front of them and waggling his wings to warn them off. Some still shot, but only the aircraft Pokryshkin had hit went down.

His 55th Fighter Regiment had encountered the Su-2, a new reconnaissance/light bomber – so new that there were only 75 in service, and so secret that most Soviet aviators knew nothing of its existence.[89]

At 17th Fighter Regiment's airfield between Kovel and Lutsk, engineers readied Fyodor Arkhipenko's Seagull biplane for the only sortie he would make this day. The base suffered the first of four raids before 3.30am and never recovered. As duty officer, the 19-year-old Arkhipenko had tried, in vain, to organise some form of response and clear the wrecks off the field and, while his comrades took to the sky to grapple with the Luftwaffe, he was kept on the ground to act as assistant to his commander. Finally, early in the afternoon, the impetuous Arkhipenko was allowed aloft. In company with another formation, he flew along a 150-mile stretch of the Russo-German border from Rava-Ruska, near Lvov, to Brest. The controls of his I-153 fighter demanded almost his entire attention, but when he looked out of the cockpit, 'it seemed the entire border was on fire and the earth itself was burning'.[90]

While Fyodor Arkhipenko was mesmerised by the frontier, Ivan Boldin was heading into the inferno. From his twin-engine SB bomber he could see the horizon glowing red, the sky filled with enemy bombers. His pilot had followed the main railway line southwest from Minsk for nearly 100 miles until Baranovichi, where the railway station, trains and warehouses were ablaze. From there, the two bombers, carrying a handful of staff officers for Tenth Army, turned west, flying as low as their pilots dare take them. It quickly became apparent that they would never reach the army's headquarters in Białystok. A couple of dozen miles east of the city, they spied an airfield, its aircraft burning on the ground. Boldin demanded they land – a timely instruction for a Messerschmitt appeared on the bombers' tails and began to loose several bursts of machine-gun fire. The SBs landed safely; the passengers and crews abandoned them swiftly. They had got no more than a couple of hundred yards before the airfield came under attack once again. The ground shook; the two SBs burned.[91]

One hundred miles to the south, Herbert Pabst watched as half a dozen Soviet bombers approached *Stukageschwader* 77's base at Biała Podlaska, only to be intercepted by Me109s. Hit by a burst of fire, the first bomber began to roll on its side, plunging to the ground, its engines screaming. 'A huge tongue of flame shoots up!' Pabst wrote excitedly in his diary.

> The second bomber turns a bright red, exploding as it plunges – all that's left are a couple of bits of wing which spiral to the ground like large leaves. The next one flips over on its back in flames. And another one. The last one crashes in a village, the fire rages for a full hour afterwards. There are six columns of smoke on the horizon – all six have been shot down!

It went on like this all afternoon. Soviet bombers approached; German fighters intercepted them. Christian Luibl, one of the squadron's ground crew, saw no more than 16 'eggs' dropped on the field, causing negligible damage but making 'a terrible noise'. Of the Russian bombers, Luibl reckoned 'perhaps one made it home'. Herbert Pabst counted each enemy aircraft downed: 21 in all.[92]

Ivan Kopets never learned of the massacre of his bombers over Biała Podlaska. Sometime on Sunday afternoon officers of the NKVD escorted the general, commander of the aerial forces of the Western Special Military District for the past 12 months, out of his office in Minsk. Since the end of May, half a dozen senior Red Air Force commanders had been picked up in a purge provoked by high accident rates among crews and the shock appearance of a Ju52 over Moscow undetected by Soviet air defences. The air force's deputy chief-of-staff Yakov Smushkevich had endured 12 days of torture before offering up Kopets' name. The 33-year-old Hero of the Soviet Union – he'd commanded fighters in Spain, downing a couple of Nationalist aircraft – was never seen again.[93]

'NOW WE ARE FIGHTING OUR REAL ENEMY...'
GERMANY, AFTERNOON

American reporter Harry Flannery watched Berliners grab newspaper extras from the hands of vendors 'almost as fast as they appeared'. No-one was interested in the lead story in the first edition of the flagship Nazi newspaper *Völkischer Beobachter* – 'Churchill is now personally admitting: British figures relating to sinkings in March and April were forged' – or the reception for the Italian culture minister. The extras hurriedly produced this Sunday carried no news as such, just Hitler's declaration and Ribbentrop's statement reprinted over several pages. Even so, Flannery noticed that, for the first time in this war, there was momentary enthusiasm, even excitement. 'The war against Russia was the first popular campaign,' he noted, chatting with the capital's news-hungry inhabitants. 'Now,' they told him, 'we are fighting our real enemy.' The agents of the secret service, the SD, were equally eager to discover the reaction of citizens of the Reich. They observed shock and surprise initially. But as the German people read the Führer's lengthy explanation, or heard it repeatedly read out on the radio, shock and surprise gave way first to calm reflection, then acceptance, above all relief, summed up by the monitors in one sentence: 'Now everything is out in the open.' As one soldier's wife in a village outside Hamburg wrote to her husband: 'At least there's a clear line again and that means we can breathe a sigh of relief. Everything is in order again.' The Russians would be dispatched just as swiftly as the Poles, the Norwegians and Danes, French, Belgians, the Yugoslavs and Greeks. To be sure, there were a few 'anxious types' worried about the vastness of Russia, there was widespread concern that the war would now clearly continue, and wives especially feared for their men grappling with the Red Army and its 'Asiatic methods'. But there was, the eavesdroppers of the German security service noted, 'extraordinary faith in the Wehrmacht, and in its leadership by the Führer'. Now, 'when the best-trained soldier in the world faced Russia, victory was assured'. People debated the length of the campaign in the East. No-one estimated more than three months.

Otherwise, it was a typical Sunday in a National Socialist Germany at war. In Leipzig, home of the German publishing industry, senior Party functionary Philipp Bouhler opened an exhibition celebrating Gutenberg. In Breslau's Jahrhunderthalle, an impressive cathedral of concrete and steel beloved by the Nazis for hosting rallies, Hitler's labour leader Robert Ley addressed a rabid audience of thousands. 'The faith of Adolf Hitler has moved mountains and I believe that this faith in the German people is stronger than the world of plutocracy and Bolshevism,' he told them. 'Germany does not wait. Adolf Hitler strikes when the time is right.' Ley's words were drowned out by rapturous applause.

The main public event of the day, however, was in Berlin's Olympic Stadium: the final of the German football championship, watched by a near-capacity crowd of 95,000 people, as favourites Schalke – they'd won the title for the past two years – faced Rapid Vienna. Many of the women dressed in their Sunday best, the men in shirts and ties – the latter were quickly loosened in the summer heat – while some donned paper hats, quickly fashioned from newspapers, to shield their heads from the sun. The grandee of Nazi sport, Hans von Tschammer und Osten, was joined in the VIP box by the political leaders from the teams' respective regions, Baldur von Schirach from Vienna, Alfred Meyer and Josef Wagner for Westphalia. Despite events in the East, there was a good smattering of military personnel – senior and junior – on parade, not least a band for the half-time entertainment. By the time the musicians performed, Schalke were 2–0 up courtesy of the quick Heinz Hinz and German international Hermann Eppenhoff. When Hinz grabbed a second and Schalke's third on 58 minutes it looked all over. But then striker Georg Schors pulled a goal back for the Viennese, before the tall Franz 'Bimbo' Binder scored a hat-trick in just nine minutes: a penalty (he'd already missed one in the first half) sandwiched between shots from open play. Schalke had nothing left to give. The championship went to Rapid – the only time an Austrian team lifted the German title.[94]

'THE WRATH OF THE SOVIET PEOPLE IS TERRIBLE...' SOVIET UNION, AFTERNOON

The only public spectacles across Russia this Sunday afternoon were hastily arranged rallies. In every city, every town, every collective farm, every factory, citizens of the Soviet Union affirmed their love for their motherland – and their readiness to defend it.

'Our place is in the ranks!' students at Minsk's dental school declared, volunteering for the front. More than 2,000 metalworkers at Moscow's Hammer and Sickle foundry heard their deputy director proclaim: 'If we have to go to the front with rifles, we are ready for it immediately! If we have to work for 24 hours – we are ready for it!' After a rally at the Kirov machine-tool factory in Minsk, the workers returned to their machines. Some doubled or even trebled the output of a regular shift. The 1,600 employees of the Kaganovich shoe factory promised similar superhuman feats of production. Every employee of Leningrad's Zhdanov works took an oath – voluntarily or not. 'We will place ourselves at the disposal of the Communist Party and the Soviet government and will fight for our motherland to the last drop of blood!' The employees of one collective farm outside Kiev vowed themselves 'ready to respond to the first call from the Communist Party and government to defend our motherland, to protect our peaceful work and to help the glorious Red Army – without sparing our strength and our lives – to achieve victory over the enemy'. In Moscow, the workers of one factory simply declared: 'The wrath of the Soviet people is terrible.'

These were official pronouncements, meant for the pages of the official Soviet press. At one rally in Minsk, a Communist Party official asked *Pravda* correspondent Peter Lidov how strong his rhetoric about Hitler and the Germans should be. 'Anything is possible,' Lidov told him firmly. 'The stronger, the better.' Yet the indignation and patriotic fervour which seized most Russians was genuine – it did not need whipping up by Party propagandists. Moscow's Communist Party and draft offices were swamped by people – men *and* women – volunteering for the front. Party officials in the western suburb of Kuntsevo, home to Stalin's dacha, reported 50 people coming forward; in the east in Sokolniki the number was 200. And in Sverdlovsk, just northwest of the city centre, the recruiting office dealt with 188 applications to join the Red Army in one morning. Communists, Komsomol members, ordinary citizens, former soldiers – too old or too infirm to fight – workers, engineers, writers, students, teachers and veterans of the fighting in Finland and Spain all tried to volunteer. 'I'll go off to beat Hitler,' said one miller, 'and I won't come back without a medal.' One student in Kiev put his studies on indefinite hold. 'I'm going to the recruitment office now. You know, I'd love to go to the front and kill at least one German. I'll graduate from university in a few years' time.' A warehouse worker in Moscow longed to join his son serving in the Red Army. 'Right at this moment I am very sorry that I'm not his age and able to take part in driving the German fascists beyond the borders of the USSR.' In Novgorod, 120 miles south of Leningrad, workers at the Stepan Khalturin timber mill vowed to 'produce as much lumber as our country needs for its defence'. They would also turn their workplace into 'an impregnable fortress. We are ready to take up arms at any moment to destroy the enemy.' And a worker in the city hospital told his colleagues to stay at their posts. 'I am off to the frontier to fulfil my duty to my parents. I assure you that I will be a worthy Soviet patriot.'

As with their counterparts in Germany, so agents of the Soviet security service, who moved around Russia watching, listening and observing their fellow citizens, found almost unanimous relief that the unholy alliance between Nazism and Communism was over. 'The Treaty gave the Germans food, we fed them, even gave them some of the things which were denied to us, and in the end they ignored us and began to bomb us,' a shop worker in Kiev seethed. One academic no longer found himself tormented by an inner conflict. 'We in our country had certain feelings about Hitler but officially said nothing. Now everything is clear. We'll beat them and we will win.' And here was another similarity with Germany. Confidence in victory. Confidence in a *Soviet* victory. 'Our men will hit them so hard, it will all be over in a week,' one Muscovite observed. 'Well, it won't necessarily be finished in a week,' his colleague pointed out. 'They've got to get to Berlin. It will take three to four weeks.' Miner – and committed Communist – Fayvel Vayner found the mood in the small town of Postaway in northern Byelorussia 'extremely calm. There's no chaos, no apocalyptic mood, there's tremendous faith in the Red Army, its leadership and the workers of the entire world; they will rise up like one man to eradicate this cancerous ulcer, which threatens humanity in the 20th century, in battle.' In the Siberian city of Omsk, nearly 1,400 miles east of Moscow, Aliaksandr Ulianavich, a 20-year-old gunner and radio operator in a bomber, felt aggrieved at being so distant from the fighting front – as did his comrades. 'We were afraid of missing the opportunity to become heroes.' A female employee of a Kiev clothes factory was convinced that having 'bathed in the blood of others', this time Hitler would 'drown in his own blood', while a Jewish performer predicted the attack on the Soviet Union was 'the beginning of the death of Nazi Germany'. And this from the mouth of a junior Communist Party official: 'There will be many victims, but no matter what Hitler will be smashed, our army always wins.'

But not every Soviet citizen thought so. 'It's good that the war has finally begun,' one Moscow factory worker muttered. 'Life in the Soviet Union has become unbearable. Forced labour and everyone exhausted by hunger. Better to put an end to it.' A few Kievans contemplated the city's fall and life under the

Nazis, but even if that happened, one publishing firm director reasoned, 'the Germans are not the barbarians that people describe them as'. A former industrialist blamed the Soviet leadership for repeatedly provoking Hitler, including occupying the Baltic states and supposedly massing 160 divisions along the Russo-German frontier. 'The Soviet government was not elected by the people, and now they will pass judgment,' he predicted, comments which led to his arrest. 'Finally we can breathe easily,' one loose-lipped official remarked. 'Hitler will be in Moscow in three days.'[95]

Having wandered the streets of Minsk and attended a patriotic rally, it was a little after 6pm by the time Peter Lidov filed his first war dispatch over the telephone to Moscow. Across the Soviet Union the reporters of *Pravda* were doing likewise for an article capturing the nation's mood, whose tone was set by the headline: 'Huge patriotic enthusiasm'. 'Life in the streets continues in complete calm,' Peter Lidov reported, not entirely inaccurately. Everywhere the same topics of conversation came up: the treachery of the Germans, faith in the Red Army, determination 'to put an end to bloody Hitlerism once and for all. The first day is coming to an end. Complete tranquillity reigns in the capital of Byelorussia. The people are alert, confident, self-assured. Such people are invincible.'

While Lidov dictated, trucks and cars brought Svoboda Square, one of Minsk's principal intersections, to a standstill. The vehicles carried women and children – all of them distraught, panicky, dirty, some with torn, even blood-stained clothes, and hardly any possessions. They were the families of the garrisons of western Byelorussia and Lithuania, sent into the hinterland. They told Minsk's military commandant Fyodor Bagreev a pitiful story of the surprise attacks on the towns and bases on the border, of panic. They begged Bagreev for help. The only help the commandant offered was to refuel the vehicles – then send them back to the units to support the fighting troops. The refugees continued their journey on foot, heading for Mogilev and Orsha, nearly 150 miles to the east.[96]

Refugees were streaming through the capital of Galicia too: some on foot, some with horse-drawn carts, a few in vehicles. Communists had tried to spread rumours that the Red Army had already occupied Przemyśl, Rzeszów, Tarnów and even Kraków and Warsaw. No-one in Lvov believed them. All the refugees came from towns near the border with Germany. 'Everyone – without exception – is already expecting the Germans to arrive inside a few hours,' polytechnic assistant Stanisław Różycki noted. Schoolboy Georg Jestadt found most of Lvov's inhabitants 'seized by an inexplicable happy, yet tense, mood.

Our Polish neighbours smiled expectantly and looked at each other tellingly.' The 15-year-old had also noticed that the tone of the Soviet news broadcasts had turned virulent in the wake of Molotov's address. 'Someone who just yesterday or a few days ago had been talked about in almost friendly terms became the most hated enemy in a matter of hours.' Now there were tirades of abuse, curses and threats against the barbarian invaders.

And while the radio spewed invective, Lvov's anti-aircraft guns were spewing shells at German twin-engine bombers. It did not stop the Luftwaffe dropping their bombs 'like a chain of black dots', Georg Jestadt saw. 'Then a wall of black smoke spread in the distance.'[97]

'GIANTS MADE OF STEEL...' GRODNO, EARLY EVENING

Horst Slesina watched with alarm as a wall of dust was thrown up by Red Army tanks rolling down the narrow lanes and tracks west of Grodno: the bulk of 29th Tank Division. Despite the broiling heat, the war correspondent turned cold. Fountains of earth were hurled up between the zig-zagging advancing tanks as the German guns opened fire. Racing ahead of the heavy tanks, armoured cars and light tanks tried to draw the German fire – and succeeded as heavy machine-guns and light flak concentrated on them. The Red Army responded in kind. Machine-gun bullets danced around the German positions, while those who dared raise their heads were treated to 'an insane firework display of tracer rounds'. Slesina provided a vivid description of the battle:

> The roaring hurricane rages around us without a break – orders are hollered through the hellish noise, the screams of the wounded. Explosions here and there, shaking the earth, then tongues of flame shoot up and black clouds of smoke roll across the sky. Tanks stop, burn out, go up in the air with an awful roar. One fewer, then another, two more, there's a mass of them meshed together, shells crashing into them, tearing them apart, destroying them! And still more and more tanks continue to push through the wall of earth, smoke and dust...
>
> Russian anti-tank shells crash into houses, here and there dry wood burns like tinder. Flames in front of us, between us, behind us. The pioneers' ammunition vehicle runs into an uprooted, burning tree. The truck catches fire. Mines, explosive charges, hand-grenades explode, throwing up a raging

wall between us. The surrounding houses and dried-out trees catch fire – they go up like blazing torches. The very air seems to burn, forcing its way into our panting lungs like red-hot lead, singeing our hair, burning and irritating our eyes. In the midst of it all, death dances and howls in a thousand pieces of red-hot steel… All around us there are blazing turrets aflame and giving off smoke. The losses are too heavy. The following waves lack the same impetus – first individually, then in closed formations, the tanks turn around, disappearing into the low ground and hollows. We break out in wild cheering!

It was not the end of the battle, merely a lull. With the sun low on the horizon, muzzle flashes in the distance announced the arrival of a fresh wave of Soviet tanks. For now, Slesina and his comrades were convinced enemy artillery had joined the battle as heavy-calibre shells rained down, churning up the soil. But then they saw the unmistakeable outline of a tank turret. 'Tanks! Giant tanks like we've never seen!' Horst Slesina wrote. 'Giants made of steel rumbling towards us on the slope! Russian 52-tonne tanks with 15cm cannons! We're seized by paralysing terror.' Slesina had come face to face with the KV-2. He watched, horrified, as anti-tank shells bounced off the hulls of these tanks 'like rubber balls'. Every possible German gun was brought to bear on the Russian 'monsters' at point-blank range. Only now did the KV-2s prove vulnerable. 'Hit after hit strikes the steel boxes, rips apart their sides, tears tracks to pieces, rips the roofs off the turrets,' wrote Slesina. The three beasts were only wounded. They continued to advance – and shoot. An entire corner section of the lead *Sturmgeschütz*, its armour 3in thick, was torn away. The second assault gun was running low on ammunition. It loosed its final rounds at a range of just 50 metres. Three of the four shells scored direct hits, but the KV-2s kept coming, rolling over the German anti-tank gun positions. Men climbed out of foxholes and onto the slow-moving Soviet tanks, stuffing hand-grenades down the 15cm gun barrel. Pioneers laid mines in their path and tried to fix explosive charges to the hulls. 'If God had given them the strength, they would have torn them apart with their bare hands,' Horst Slesina observed. It was a final desperate act and it worked.

It was dusk by the time the fighting subsided. The meadows and roads west of Grodno were littered with burning and smouldering Russian hulks, perhaps as many as 150.[98]

Nearby, infantry officer Erich Mende watched a similar – or possibly the same – death ride of Soviet tanks. There was little rhyme or reason to the enemy's tactics – they roamed around the countryside seemingly without any plan and were picked off accordingly. Anti-tank guns and panzers 'seemed to vie for target practice' as the Russian armour was 'shot up one after another'. Soon the sky was scarred with dozens of mushroom clouds and a pungent stench – 'a mixture of burning wood, red-hot iron and oily smoke,' Mende remembered. 'It truly smelled of war.' He was also struck not by the sight of 'old, clumsy models with box-like turrets', but the handful of new tanks, one in particular with wide tracks and angled armour: a T-34. 'The turret had been blown to the side by exploding ammunition, and not far from it lay a singed book, the manual.' The booklet was still largely intact. It was immediately sent to headquarters.[99]

'THE HARDEST AND BLOODIEST DAY...'
THE BATTLE FADES, EVENING

In his command post in Terespol, Fritz Schlieper was briefing General Günther von Kluge. Thirteen hours had passed since the Fourth Army commander had watched the opening stages of the assault on Brest's fortress. Now, Kluge had seen enough. He ordered Schlieper to call off his attacks and starve the defenders into submission. 'No useless blood' was to be spilled capturing a citadel whose relevance was superseded by events. Fritz Schlieper breathed a sigh of relief. The first day of battle had cost him more than 300 men killed.[100]

After nearly 12 hours on the roads and tracks of Lithuania, anti-tank gunner Helmut Martin had seen no fighting and little sign of the enemy, apart from a few prisoners – 'brown figures with shaven heads, they gave the impression of being scruffy'. Kalvarija, hammered by Helmut Mahlke's Stukas in the first minutes of the war, bore traces of heavy fighting, however. 'Smashed ruins, blackened gables and chimneys alternated with houses that rose almost intact from the rubble,' he remembered: 'Broken telegraph poles, fences in splinters, wires and shot-up carts were lying in the streets. From dark window frames, abandonment and emptiness. The smell of burned and still-smouldering wood hung over this place of desolation. This warlike scene of destruction was imprinted on my mind. Only the dead were missing.'[101]

In the Lithuanian border village of Kudirkos Naumiestis, a dozen border guards had stubbornly held out all day long in their command post against successive German attacks. In the late afternoon, two panzers and several guns were brought up to finally end the dogged resistance which was led by Captain I. G. Bedin. An inveterate Communist and Civil War veteran, Bedin rejected German calls to surrender: 'As long as our hands can hold weapons while we are alive, we will fight to the last drop of blood.' The attackers placed explosive charges beneath the building and withdrew. According to Soviet accounts, the strains of the *Internationale* and a defiant final cry – 'Farewell, comrades! We have honestly fulfilled our duty.' – were heard before the charges exploded.[102]

Vasily Gorbunov's border guards had held out near Novoselki for nearly 12 hours before deciding that defending the bunkers and posts on the Bug any longer was pointless – the Germans had long since passed them. Besides, the men were almost out of ammunition. They had begun the day with 35,000 rounds. By evening, they had no more than 700 left. They decided to make for the village of Volchin, three miles to the rear, in the hope of catching up with their retreating comrades.[103]

On the road to Vilnius, a junior signals officer felt thoroughly satisfied with 7th Panzer Division's progress this Sunday: 'We have maps far to the east, and if you think that Napoleon's Army did that on foot, we who are motorised will do it in 14 days,' he recorded confidently in his diary. Others were less sure. 'The Russians defended themselves like devils and never surrendered,' Heinrich Haape noted. His 18th Infantry Regiment lost more men this day – 21 dead and 48 seriously wounded – than it had in the entire campaign in France. 'It's a hard day that's behind us,' the doctor recorded in his diary as night fell. The fighting had ended at dusk – the final four Russians holding out in a border bunker 'were slain with rifle butts'. The chronicler of 77th Infantry Regiment, advancing on Marijampolė, felt 'officers and men were probably still too heavily influenced by the final, relatively easy days of battle in France. That could come back to haunt us.'[104]

It took the mountain infantry of 1st *Gebirgs* Division until 7pm to finally silence the defenders of Oleszyce, especially those holding out in the grounds of a country house. Nowhere, with the exception of the fortress at Brest, did Soviet troops fight more bitterly this day. The mountain infantry found themselves fighting with pistols and entrenching tools at times. It seemed as if every Soviet soldier had to be killed three times. 'They shoot at the wounded, medics and doctors from treetops, bushes and hedges, from every cellar,' one German soldier wrote indignantly. In the end, it had taken flamethrowers, their jets of flame incinerating treetops, bushes, hedges, spilling through cellars. It was too late for German ski champion Willi Walch, killed by a shot to the head while being treated at a first-aid post, or for three officers shot by snipers as they flung open the hatches of their assault guns. Their bodies – and others – were carried in blankets and strips of canvas to the roadside in the village, where the Polish inhabitants were digging a large pit. There was still the occasional crack of rifle fire as the men of 13th Company, 98th *Gebirgsjäger* Regiment, their faces dirty, covered in sweat, their uniforms filthy, torn, stood by the grave and removed their caps. As they did the division's commander, Hubert Lanz, suddenly appeared. The first day of battle had left its physical and mental scars on 1st *Gebirgs* Division's 45-year-old leader. Like his men, the general had been on the go for 16 hours, never stopping, dashing from one unit to another to ascertain the situation, restore order, give fresh instructions. While sheltering behind a wooden fence during one enemy counter-attack, his shoulder was grazed by a bullet which hit the man next to him. Despite bleeding profusely, Lanz refused treatment until he collapsed from exhaustion. A doctor said he should return to the division's command post to recover. The general spent no more than an hour there before returning to the front. Now he clambered down into the open grave, took off his cap and, for a minute, silently stood face to face with a dozen or more dead. This was not what Hubert Lanz wanted. He accepted the need for sacrifice. But he led mountain infantry and the rolling landscape of Galicia was not their natural element. Before the battle he had pleaded with his superior for 'a different, better mission' – and he had been turned down. And this was the price. Yes, his men had largely wiped out the 97th Rifle Division. But the fighting had been bitter – far more ferocious than anything Lanz had seen in Poland, France or the Balkans. There had been few prisoners taken – the enemy fought to the last, the feet of the ordinary Red Army soldiers had been tied together by their commissars so they could not flee from their foxholes. But losses among the mountain infantry had been correspondingly heavy – 18 officers alone were dead on the field of battle. 'The first day of fighting in the eastern campaign,' the division's war diarist observed, 'was the hardest and bloodiest day the division has known.'[105]

Despite the day's events Dynamo Kiev's players mustered at their new stadium for the inaugural match as planned. Even after the large crowd gathered outside the ground for the occasion listened to Molotov's address, people had refused to accept either that their country was at war – or that the match was cancelled. Nor too the players. The team sheet to face Moscow CDKA was drawn up – the only shock was the rookie Oleg Laevsky in goal rather than the trusty Kolya Trucevich. Kick-off time – 3pm – passed before the decision was taken to cancel the match. A sign was hung on the gates: *postponed until after the victory*. The crowd outside the stadium finally dispersed, but the players hung around until 7.30pm, when the air-raid siren sounded again. The footballers said their goodbyes and went home.[106]

At 41st Tank Division's headquarters outside Vladimir-Volynskiy, chief-of-staff Konstantin Maligin was under siege, surrounded by the anxious wives and frightened children of officers. The youngsters wanted to sleep, but Maligin didn't even have any blankets to offer them. Eventually 20 trucks arrived to ferry the families to Kovel, three dozen miles to the northeast. Otherwise, the 35-year-old staff officer was reasonably pleased with the course of the first day of war. Shoulder-to-shoulder with the infantry of 87th Rifle Division, the tank men had doggedly defended Vladimir-Volynskiy all day. The riflemen had been fired up by their commissar, Bystrov, who moved among the ranks before leading them in a counter-attack. 'All of our land is now rising up to fight the enemy,' he assured them. 'We will wipe these Fascist bastards from the face of the earth. Our motherland is mighty. Our people are united. We are led by the great Communist Party.' Such courage did not save Vladimir-Volynskiy. The Germans captured it late in the evening. The cost was fearful. In one of the 41st's battalions, 30 out of 50 T-26 tanks had been knocked out. One of its commanders – 'his face smeared with sweat and blood' – showed Maligin the cause of such losses: a captured German anti-tank gun. 'What a pity our infantrymen had no such weapon,' Maligin thought.[107]

Dmitry Ryabyshev had suffered punishing losses too – a quarter of his armour out of action – and his VIII Mechanised Corps had still to engage the enemy. The lanes of western Galicia had crumbled under the weight of more than 900 tanks and armoured vehicles; bridges had given way. The roadside and ditches were littered with broken-down and abandoned vehicles, which whittled down Ryabyshev's paper strength to 700. Some units had travelled no further than Sambor, just 20 miles from the corps' headquarters in Drohobycz; others were closing in on the frontier with Germany. As his men cleaned and refuelled their vehicles ready for the coming day of battle, Ryabyshev reported, with some pride, that his corps was ready to carry out the mission assigned to it. But now he was told of new orders. His corps was to turn around and regroup northeast of Lvov – a march of nearly 100 miles. It was to be ready to go into battle by noon the following day.[108]

Outside an estate in the Lithuanian village of Putinai, a captured Soviet soldier was taken aside by the staff of the 123rd Infantry Division. While various seized Red Army documents were dispatched to the intelligence officers of XXVIII Corps, a solitary shot echoed around the Lithuanian countryside. The prisoner fell to the ground. The 123rd's operations officer punctiliously noted the time in the division's official war diary: 8.35pm. Kusma Sarin, political commissar of the Red Army's 178th Construction Battalion, had been executed 'according to martial law'.

Sarin was not the only commissar executed in line with Adolf Hitler's orders this evening. After being ambushed during a brief rest in a village, the troops of 5th Infantry Division quickly smoked out the Soviet troops responsible, among them one commissar. He was forced to accompany the division all day until evening, when he was led into a meadow and shot dead.[109]

North of Grodno, 59th Tank Regiment briefly held off the German assault before leaving the hills strewn with blazing vehicles as it fell back on the city. 'There was no-one in command in Grodno,' the regimental deputy commissar fumed. Establishing contact with the parent 29th Tank Division proved impossible. The 59th's remaining vehicles re-filled their fuel tanks while their crews restocked ammunition and fuel from abandoned warehouses before following the tide of Red Army units heading for Lida – 70 miles to the east.

In fact, there were still Soviet leaders in Grodno – military and civilian – but both were preparing to abandon the city. Grodno was aflame – firefighters toiled until the last of their engines was knocked out – and there was chaos in the streets. Communist Party leader Ivan Poznyakov had been ordered to have all 3,500 'counter-revolutionary elements' in the city prison executed. Perhaps he might have succeeded, but the jail fell victim to the air raids as the guards began shooting the inmates, who now swarmed through Grodno. Some even took up arms against their oppressors. That and the crumbling front served as the cue for Poznyakov to summon all Party members left in the city, arm them, then strike out for Lida. Third Army commander Vasily Kuznetsov was also preparing to abandon Grodno. He ordered 85th Rifle Division to destroy anything of value: the fuel depots which had proved such a blessing to 59th Tank Regiment, the ammunition dumps on the city's southern outskirts, the bridges over the Neman. As they went up in flames and German shells crashed down on Grodno, the staff of Third Army moved out, leaving the men of the 68th Fortified District to their fate in the pillboxes and bunkers scattered in and around the city. Still expecting to be relieved by the divisions of Third Army, the men sang folk and patriotic songs long into the night.[110]

General Aleksandr Korobkov spent the final hours of Sunday visiting the divisions of his Fourth Army, keen to see how they had fared on this first day of battle. After the strictly regimented peacetime regime, they had been unable to adjust to the sudden shock of war. Korobkov found many men – staffs especially – physically and mentally exhausted, unfed and often asleep.[111]

Having narrowly escaped first being shot down and then blown up on the ground, Ivan Vasilevich Boldin was still a good 20 miles from his destination: the headquarters of Tenth Army in Białystok. He commandeered a truck and headed into the city. The fuel tanks and grain warehouses on the outskirts were already burning, while a good portion of the city had been evacuated, including Tenth Army's command post. Boldin eventually found the army's commander, Konstantin Golubev, on the edge of a small wood to the south. The temporary headquarters was a simple affair: a couple of tents, a telephone and a radio truck. Golubev explained that two of his corps had virtually ceased to exist. His obsolete T-26s were 'only good enough for shooting at sparrows'. His fuel dumps had gone up in flames during the first wave of Luftwaffe attacks. His communications were disrupted. 'It's hard, very hard, Ivan Vasilevich. My men are fighting like heroes, but what can you do against a tank or a plane?' A strong, imposing figure with considerable experience, Konstantin Golubev now gave the impression of a broken man. The German advance seemed inexorable. They were already strutting around, 'behaving like conquerors. And that's on the very first day of the war! What'll happen after that?' A signals officer interrupted Golubev's litany of woe. Contact had been made with Pavlov in Minsk. Boldin reported the gravity of the situation, but the Front commander was not listening, merely demanding a counter-attack. Golubev protested. Pavlov was unmoved. 'That's all I have to say. Get on with the task that I've given you.' It was clear to Ivan Boldin that Dmitry Pavlov was living in a world of his own – 'but what could we do? Orders are orders.'[112]

The telephones at Minsk's Communist Party headquarters had barely stopped ringing all day. Reports from its tentacles in western Byelorussia were alarming:

air attacks here, elsewhere German paratroopers or panzers rolling through. Minsk promised help. It would send troops to relieve threatened towns and villages. In the meantime, it ordered local party leaders to begin distributing weapons. But now, as the day drew to a close, the phones were quieter. There was no longer any contact with many of the border districts.

Still, no-one thought to cancel the evening performance by the Moscow Art Theatre – or if they had, they had been unable to inform the actors; telephone and telegraph lines out of Minsk were unable to cope with the demand for their services. Maxim Gorky's *The Lower Depths* began half an hour later than scheduled due to an air-raid warning and played to a half-empty theatre.

The chilling sound of sirens echoing across their city prompted some Minskers to leave their homes and apartments and take refuge in parks and woods. Perhaps thousands of people congregated in the Jewish cemetery, clinging to the gravestones or hiding behind them. 'No-one used the word "war",' remembered Gena Yushkevich, 12 years old at the time. 'I heard another word in its place: "provocation".' A rumour quickly spread: the Red Army would counter-attack at any moment – Stalin himself had given the order. 'And everyone believed it,' Yushkevich recalled.[113]

'Quite incredible numbers...' The destruction of the Red Air Force

There was still sufficient daylight for Heinz Knoke to head off on his sixth and final sortie of the day. He was more exhilarated than exhausted, thrilled by a day of unprecedented success. He had seen nothing of the Red Air Force all day. He had seen plenty of the two warring armies though. The contrast between them could not have been greater. German soldiers waved as Knoke's Messerschmitt Me109 made its low passes. Soviet soldiers scattered, 'stumbling and bleeding as they flee from the highway'. Every road and lane on the Russian side of the front was clogged with vehicles, presenting an unmissable target. As he dropped fragmentation bombs on a column of horse-drawn artillery, Knoke almost felt pity for his foe for the first time this Sunday. 'I am thankful not to be down there myself.'[114]

Heinz Knoke encountered no Soviet aircraft on his last flight of the day. His squadron had brought down 16 enemy fighters and bombers this Sunday. On the airfields of East Prussia, eastern Poland and Romania, Luftwaffe commanders were sifting through the combat reports filed by their pilots and poring over reconnaissance photographs from more than 60 airfields hit during the day's attacks. Werner Mölders was tallying 'quite incredible numbers': 132 aircraft shot up on the ground, 69 kills in the air by his *Jagdgeschwader* 51. In the north, Hannes Trautloft's *Geschwader* downed 45 Soviet aircraft in the air, 35 on the ground for just one loss. And *Jagdgeschwader* 53 claimed an unprecedented 75 aerial victories. By sundown on Sunday 22 June 1941, the Red Air Force had suffered a defeat unparalleled in history. In all, 1,811 Soviet aircraft were destroyed this day, all but 322 of them on the ground; the Western Military District alone lost 738 aircraft – three in ten of them shot down – and the Kiev District 277 aircraft. The Luftwaffe had lost 61 aircraft on combat missions, another 17 in accidents. Its bomber formations suffered most. *Kampfgeschwader* 51 counted 15 crews – 60 men – missing or dead, among them some of its best and most popular men, like 'old pig fiddle' von Wenchowski, while half the Ju88s in one unit were either total losses or needed extensive repairs. 'We felt really depressed that night,' Klaus Häberlen recalled. 'This feeling could be relieved only through some bottles of wine.'[115]

At least some of these losses had been inflicted by Soviet pilots taking desperate measures. Lieutenant Ivan Ivanov failed to stop a raid by Heinkel 111s of *Kampfgeschwader* 55 on the airfield at Dubno in Ukraine, but his Rata succeeded in catching up with Werner Bähringer's bomber as it returned to base. When his guns ran out of ammunition – or jammed – Ivanov crashed his fighter into the bomber, sending both tumbling towards the ground, killing all the occupants. Ivan Ivanov's deed would enter Soviet folklore as the *taran* ('battering ram'). It would earn him, posthumously, his nation's highest honour: Hero of the Soviet Union. And it would be repeated several times this day. Mid-morning, Dmitry Kokorev's formation of MiG-3s and Ratas intercepted Messerschmitt Me110s near Zambrów. In the ensuing dogfights, three Soviet and two German fighters were shot down. Out of ammunition, Kokorev used the propeller of his MiG-3 to smash the rudder of an Me110, causing it to crash, while the Soviet pilot succeeded in bringing his damaged fighter back to his airfield. Lieutenant Leonid Butelin lost his life when he drove his propeller into the rudder of one of several Ju88s which had attacked his airfield at Stanislav in Ukraine.[116]

Their names – and others – would be entered in the annals of Soviet history. Focusing on individual acts of bravery helped to gloss over the cataclysmic losses the Red Air Force had suffered. But not every pilot was an Ivanov, Kokorev or Butelin. The airfield at Wysokie Mazowieckie, 30 miles southwest of Białystok, was hit during the first hour of the German attack –

and attacked repeatedly during the rest of the day by Me110s. They left more than 40 blazing and smashed hulks. No Soviet aircraft took off from Wysokie Mazowieckie on Sunday 22 June. But they could have. The airfield's commander lost his head in the first minutes of the opening attack and fled to the neighbouring woodland. When the Luftwaffe had passed, he continued fleeing eastwards.[117]

Most Red Air Force crews, however, responded bravely and selflessly. The 55th Fighter Aviation Regiment claimed more than ten kills over Moldova and Ukraine: Lieutenant Konstantin Mironov had downed a Henschel 126 reconnaissance aircraft near Bălţi; Captain Atrachkevich had apparently downed an Iron Cross recipient. Captain Karmanov scored three kills defending Chişinău, while Captain Morosov had rammed a German fighter in the same dogfights and his MiG-3 had largely come through unscathed. 'After this, we grew more confident,' Alexander Pokryshkin remembered. 'So, we were able to challenge the enemy a little. And tomorrow we would be smarter.'[118]

Today, however, they had impressed their foe. 'Russian fliers fight toughly,' the adjutant of *Jagdgeschwader* 51 wrote, 'more doggedly than the French and even the English.' And they responded en masse. When his advance was halted by a traffic jam, radio operator Frank-Rudolf Averdieck looked up and saw three dozen Soviet bombers flying west. *Which city in the homeland would they visit?* he wondered. The bombers visited towns across East Prussia – among them Gumbinnen, Ebenrode, Tilsit, Sudauen, Lyck – killing more than two dozen people. The port of Memel suffered by far the worst damage – and the heaviest death toll: more than 40 civilians, prisoners of war and German soldiers. 'That was something we were not used to seeing during our previous campaigns – we'd hardly ever seen anything of an enemy air force,' Averdieck wrote. He did not have time to chew over such thoughts. His infantry column was pounced upon by three Ratas.[119]

After his flight along the burning frontier, during which he'd come under fire from Soviet anti-aircraft guns, Fyodor Arkhipenko brought his Seagull back down safely at Wieliczka airfield between Kovel and Lutsk. It was no longer deemed safe to stay on the base. The men ate supper in nearby woods. There were not many of them and, the young pilot observed, 'all were tired and shaken by the painful impressions of the day'.

Following the evening briefing at Majaki airbase, a truck pulled up to take Alexander Pokryshkin and his comrades back to their quarters. 'It was war, and yet everything was like it was yesterday,' the 28-year-old Siberian observed. 'The one and a half tonne truck, the shoulder of comrades, the evening meal we could expect.'[120]

On the airfields of *Kampfgeschwader* 51 in southern Poland, engineers bathed in sweat, their upper bodies naked, patched up bullet holes with metal sheets, cleared away aircraft which had made emergency landings, replaced frayed cables or damaged plexiglass cockpit panels and tuned engines. While they toiled throughout the night, the aircrews returned to their quarters. 'Dead-tired, the men fell into their bunks towards midnight,' the unit's chronicler wrote. 'Their last thoughts were: What happened to our missing comrades? Are they still alive? Hopefully. But what will the coming day bring? How will it all end? What are our relatives at home thinking?'[121]

'WHERE SHOULD WE FLEE?' LITHUANIA, LATE EVENING

The streets of Kaunas were filled with overcrowded vehicles carrying Red Army families and buses whose windows were lined with appeals for blood donations. Kęstutis Miklaševičius and other nationalists met at a friend's house, gathering around a battery-powered radio to listen to an appeal from their countrymen exiled in Germany. 'Even your heart trembles when you hear a fatherly, free, promising but honest voice speaking to you.' But there were also disquieting rumours circulating in Kaunas that night that the Red Army intended to seize able-bodied men as it withdrew. For safety, Kęstutis Miklaševičius and his colleagues decided to spend the night sleeping on hay in a barn.[122]

While Miklaševičius and most Kaunas inhabitants awaited liberation, the city's Jews faced a terrible dilemma as Sunday drew to a close: to stay or flee. All manner of rumours were circulating. Some said the Red Army had captured Memel, others that the Germans were in Marijampolė just 35 miles away. The Holzman family believed the latter (it wouldn't actually fall till the following day) – and debated their course of action. 'Now it had come, that anxious moment which for years we had believed possible and discussed with friends a hundred times over, without seriously believing it would come,' Helene Holzman recalled. Yesterday's plans – the move to Vilnius – were 'in tatters'. Avraham Tory's telephone rang incessantly. 'Colleagues and friends wanted to know: "What should we take with us?" "Where should we flee?" The Ganor family had resolved to leave the city. 'As frightening as the Russian police were,' 13-year-old Solly Ganor reasoned, 'the Nazis were scarier.' Before departing, his mother insisted on a family ritual. The Ganors sat around a mahogany table as she served dinner on her finest china, which sparkled beneath the lights of the crystal chandelier. 'It all felt eerily unreal to me, and sad,' Solly recalled, 'like the last meal of the condemned.' Having eaten, the family quickly packed whatever belongings they could realistically carry; Solly had time to take a final look at his bedroom – and slip a copy of Jules Verne's *The Mysterious Island* into his rucksack.

The Ganors found the streets of Kaunas were already hostile. Gangs of Lithuanians, armed with rifles and revolvers and calling themselves 'patriots', roamed the city, occasionally taking pot shots at retreating Soviet troops, more frequently attacking and robbing any Jews they encountered. 'Our neighbours had turned against us, and the Germans hadn't even arrived,' Solly Ganor wrote.

Some made for the railway station on the southeastern edge of Kaunas, but most trains were reserved for military personnel. A few civilians managed to find space in the carriages. Others threw bundles over their shoulders and, hand-in-hand with their children, headed down the road to Ukmergė, 40 miles to the northeast. It was 'choked with refugees and retreating Soviet troops,' Solly Ganor remembered. 'An endless variety of vehicles, horse-drawn wagons, motorcycles, and bicycles threaded their way through a huge swarm of people on foot. Although ragged columns of Soviet soldiers mingled among them, most of those on foot were civilians, and most of them were Jews.'

Yet the majority of Kaunas' Jewish population stayed. They stayed because, for now, they feared punishment by the Soviet authorities more than they feared the German invader. They feared being imprisoned for up to six months for deserting their place of work. They feared being separated in the chaos of the columns and retreating Red Army. 'We wanted to stay, above all to stay together, not to be parted under any circumstance,' Helene Holzman and her husband Max decided. 'So we too would endure hard times.'[123]

'WAS IT JUST A PRELUDE?' NIGHT

As the sun set over the Carpathian foothills, the outlines of German infantry could be seen filing across the railway bridge in Przemyśl. When they reached the right bank the soldiers turned to the northeast, following the course of the river downstream towards the heart of Galicia. They left behind just a single company guarding the bridgehead over the San and the rest of Przemyśl. That night they – and the rest of the city – were subjected to constant disruptive fire from Soviet artillery.[124]

With nightfall, 'a solemn silence' descended on the undulating countryside of western Galicia, *Gebirgsjäger* Hubert Hegele observed. And yet he could not sleep. The fighting this Sunday had been too bitter. 'In the cloudless night sky above us millions of stars glisten,' he noted in his diary. 'On Earth the white flares of the Germans and the red of the Russians; they create the "magic of the night". And tomorrow?'[125]

Covered in dust from the day's exertions – 8th Infantry Division had advanced more than 20 miles, fighting some of the way – Friedrich Grupe and his comrades settled down in foxholes outside Grodno. The sky above them was blood red. 'This time it's not the uplifting sight of a sunset, but the eerie backdrop of burning ammunition dumps,' the officer wrote. 'It's a hellish concert, exploding, banging and crackling. In the face of this inferno, we fall asleep, exhausted and aware that we have survived this day.'[126]

In Brest, Dr Hermann Türk and his medical company occupied the officers' mess in a barracks in the city. So hastily had the Russians abandoned them, there were still rolls spread with butter in the canteen. Otherwise, the 32-year-old assistant doctor was impressed by the facilities: the barracks were modern, the tank workshops every bit as good as those in German bases. The men seized everything they could use – leather goods especially. That wasn't the biggest, surprise, however. 'We find perfume and powder next to foul smelling, dirty things in every room,' Türk observed. 'Unlike in France, here there's no smut, no lewd pictures or magazines. On the contrary, it seems that many women sleep with the officers and Party functionaries.'

Elsewhere in Brest, soldiers found bottles of wine and champagne outside homes and apartment blocks – put out by the city's inhabitants as a gift. 'Not having eaten or drunk all day, we grabbed them, of course,' Hans Wiesinger recalled. 'I drank a bottle of champagne as if it were water.' Officers put a stop to it almost immediately; the men had to pour their precious bottles into the gutters of Brest. The intervention came too late; convinced they were being shot at from cellars, the soldiers fought drunken skirmishes with foes real or imaginary long after dark before settling down for the night in the Communist Party headquarters. Josef Arnreiter and his squad were directed to a brewery which locals were looting. They found beer sloshing on the floor several inches deep as people eagerly filled pails. The soldiers rolled three barrels back to their positions – but had no chance to enjoy their booty. They were ordered back to the fortress to form a security screen around the citadel to prevent the garrison breaking out.

Erich Maresch was also on his way back to the fortress after visiting the city centre. 'I've never seen scenes like it!' the supply officer recorded in his diary: 'War and peace at the same time. There was intense fighting at the railway station when I drove over the crossing. The dead were lying around – civilians, women, children and our soldiers. People pass the bodies without paying them any attention, as if it were nothing.'

Maresch had left the fortress around 6pm, convinced it was all but in German hands. 'We were fooling ourselves,' he wrote as he returned after dark, 'there are masses of Russians still inside.'

The citadel after nightfall with its fires and smoke presented 'a tragic, yet beautiful view'. Shadowy outlines moved in front of the flames – Soviet troops attempting to break out, as predicted. They caught Josef Arnreiter and his comrades off guard, overrunning the embankment the Germans held. One non-commissioned officer cracked, threw all his equipment away and ran off, hiding in a railway goods wagon. When he was found, he claimed the Russians had hunted him down and shot him in the stomach. His comrades branded him 'the hero of Brest'. They rallied and drove the Soviet troops back. 'There was no thought of sleep, even though we hadn't closed our eyes the previous night either,' an exhausted Arnreiter noted. 'We had to be alert.'

Throughout the night flares arced above the central island as German troops still trapped in the garrison church signalled for help. Lying on his back on the North Island surrounded by the dead, the wounded Hans Teuschler watched the hypnotising light show. Since being shot in the chest by a Russian sniper, Teuschler had spent the day passing in and out of consciousness. He was able to grab bread and cheese from the backpack of a dead comrade, carefully dividing the rations to last him four or five days – 'after this predicament I didn't want to die of hunger,' he reasoned. The heat of the day gave way to the desolation of night and a soundtrack of never-ending artillery fire and the shrill sound of rifle shots echoing around the fortress walls. 'Never have I longed for the coming day as much,' he wrote.[127]

Sergeant M. A. Paschenko held out in his strongpoint on the Bug 20 miles downstream of Brest for nearly 12 hours. But by mid-afternoon German troops were filtering past on both sides, leaving the two dozen or so surviving defenders cut off. They vowed to break out when night fell, exploding in small packets with cries of 'Urra', which pierced the darkness and unnerved the Germans. But once through the rear German units, the border guards soon found out that wherever they went, the enemy had occupied all the villages behind the Bug front. In Volchin, five miles from the river, the Germans were 'running amok ... looting the shop, climbing over houses and barns, chasing birds'. Again a sudden charge by the border guards caught the Germans by surprise, but once they regained their composure they chased the Soviet group towards a nearby forest. The Russians' horse and cart became stuck in a bog, but concerted machine-gun fire from Paschenko and his comrades forced the Germans to break off their pursuit. The guards saved both their horse and cart and sought shelter in the woods where they collapsed, exhausted. 'Thus ended the first day of the war,' Paschenko wrote. 'There were seven of us left. What happened to the rest is unknown.'[128]

Not 24 hours had passed since Yevgeny Khaldei had walked through Pushkin Square, lit up by neon signs. Now, it was plunged into darkness. 'Not even any of the older residents of Moscow remember it so dark and gloomy,' he wrote. Despite the blackout, Khaldei could see motorised troops scurrying westwards and anti-aircraft troops setting up their guns to defend the capital.[129]

It was late in the evening when a signals officer handed Ivan Bagramyan the latest instructions from Moscow at the Kiev Military District's field headquarters in a village just outside the Ukrainian city of Tarnopol. The 43-year-old quickly scanned the document. 'It took my breath away,' he admitted. The district's forces were expected not merely to smash the German units which had violated Ukrainian soil in a great battle of encirclement, but also drive into occupied Poland. Just two days hence, the Kremlin expected Soviet troops to stand in the city of Lublin, 60 miles beyond the frontier.

Bagramyan breathlessly read the order to his master, the district's chief-of-staff, who snatched the document from his hand – he simply could not believe what he was hearing. A stern figure, with pince-nez and wiry, thick jet-black hair, Maxim Purkayev was prone neither to emotional outbursts nor rash actions. 'What should we do, Mikhail Petrovich?' he asked as he burst into General Kirponos' office. 'They're asking us to take Lublin the day after tomorrow!'

Kirponos, like his deputy, was not someone to react impetuously. He read the order carefully, then showed it to the district's senior commissar, Nikolai Vashugin.

'Well, what it is comrades? We've received an order and we'll carry it out.'

'That's just it, Nikolai Nikolaievich,' Purkayev responded, 'we are not prepared for it right now. We must think about defence, not attack.' Kirponos' chief-of-staff ran through a long list of reasons why the instructions from Moscow could not be carried out. The corps and armies were still mobilising, on the move, or regrouping and wouldn't be ready for up to a week. He had no idea where one armoured division was – it had moved out from Vladimir-Volynskiy in the morning and that was the last anyone had heard of it. Anything he could throw at the Germans right now would be committed piecemeal – and crushed. No, the only solution was to fall back to defensive positions 70 miles *east* of Tarnopol – more than 200 miles behind the frontier with Germany. It meant surrendering the entire western Ukraine to the enemy. 'There's nothing left for us to do, Comrade General, but to report the situation to the People's Commissar and request a change of mission urgently,' Maxim Purkayev told Mikhail Kirponos. 'In our situation, this is the only sensible decision I can see.'

Silence descended on the room. Kirponos was lost in thought. Nikolai Vashugin weighed in. 'You're thinking purely as a military man,' he admonished Purkayev. 'Don't you also have to take the moral factor into account? Did you just once consider the moral damage we're inflicting? We trained the men of the Red Army to carry high morale into battle and now, from the first day of the war, we're being passive, going over to the defensive, and handing the enemy the initiative on a plate.' The commissar paused briefly, before delivering his final blow. 'You know, Maxim Alexeievich, you are our comrade in arms, and if I didn't know you were a trusted Bolshevik, I would think you'd panicked.'

Only now did Mikhail Kirponos speak, agreeing with both his deputy and his commissar. Withdrawing was the wise thing to do. But he simply could not ignore instructions from Moscow. 'Of course there's almost no chance of taking Lublin by the evening of June 24th,' he admitted, 'but orders are orders. We must carry them out.'[130]

It had been a frustrating first day for gunlayer Richard von Rosen. The pioneers of 4th Panzer Division had thrown a bridge across the Bug south of Koden by mid-day, even though the river and marshy floodplain was 500ft wide. Impressive though the feat of military engineering was, it could not cope with the volume of traffic impatient to use it. Rosen's Panzer Mk3 had reached the approaches to the crossing at 3pm. It was another 90 minutes before the tank was on the right bank of the Bug – the sheer number of troops using the bridge had damaged it and forced repairs. As Rosen's panzer rolled onto the boggy Russian terrain, he took 'a healthy gulp' from a bottle of cognac passed around the crew. Having come through the marshes and woods of the Bug valley, the company, bolstered with the arrival of three Panzer Mk4s, regrouped for the advance on Kobrin, which finally got under way at twilight.

The commander of Rosen's panzer stood in his turret, directing his driver by microphone along the pitch-black lanes which cut through the copses and woods southeast of Brest. The crews had been told to expect enemy resistance. There was none – fortunate, perhaps, for Richard von Rosen could see nothing through his sights in the darkness. With little to do, Rosen and the gun's loader fell asleep. They awoke around midnight as their tank pulled onto the Brest–Moscow highway. There had been no contact with the Russians.[131]

Midnight found poet Abraham Sutzkever debating what to do with his friend, newspaper editor Dowid Umru. The Germans decided for them. Flares lit up Umru's apartment as bright as day as the Luftwaffe subjected Vilnius to a pounding which caused houses to collapse and fire and smoke to spread through the streets. It also caused an exodus as the inhabitants of the Lithuanian capital fled their city, among them Sutzkever and his wife Freydke. They joined a group of Jews in an endless column heading along the road to Minsk, 120 miles away. Other refugees had piled carts high with possessions. Freydke Sutzkever took with her only the diary which she had been compiling since the age of ten, her husband the manuscript of his poem *Siberia*.[132]

A light mist began to blanket the Lithuanian landscape, dampening the grass. The field kitchen finally caught up with Johann Allmayer-Beck's battery in woods somewhere north of Tauragė. 'Now we can remove our pistol, belt, map case, gas mask and all the other stuff and sit alone under a tree, just a very short distance from the command post,' he wrote. The gunners ate their meals staring into the growing darkness. 'In the east, something is on fire – all you can see is a reddish glow on the horizon. A vast and mighty starry sky arches over everything.'[133]

One hundred and twenty miles to the southeast, Albert Frank and his fellow motorcyclists from 20th Panzer Division were reliving the day's events outside Alytus. 'Was it just a prelude?' he wondered. 'Will every day be like this?' The Russians did not allow him to answer, for suddenly the nearby woods came alive as every possible heavy weapon – panzers, anti-tank guns, flak, light and heavy machine-guns, mortars – opened fire. The tracers united, forming glistening rays which pierced the night and exploded among the trees. 'Everyone is standing there, silently watching this drama. No-one speaks – in this tumult no-one can understand a word,' Frank wrote. 'But each man thinks the same thing: now these woods belong only to us. There is no Russian alive there any more. Now we can sleep calmly until the approaching morning. Our mission has been accomplished.'[134]

3

TO LENINGRAD

We fled from the plague and the plague caught up with us. Tank after tank
after tank.

The entire road was a row of tanks. They rumbled, rattled, roared, deafened.

Abraham Sutzkever

'A PEACEFUL MARCH...' LITHUANIA, 23 JUNE, MORNING

A few miles southeast of Tauragė, Eberhard Raus surveyed the landscape before
him: a land of green fields bordered by woods, bathed 'in the soft light of the
morning sun'. The columns of 6th Panzer Division moved relentlessly along
every road heading east, the vanguard – including the regiment of motorised
infantry Raus commanded – trailing a huge cloud of dust on the horizon. 'Rather
than the second day of a great war,' the 52-year-old former Austrian Army officer
mused, the advance 'resembled a peaceful march.'

The peace of Raus' morning was rudely shattered by the crash of artillery.
Black mushroom clouds replaced the dust on the horizon. The spearhead of
6th Panzer had run into Soviet troops outside Raseiniai, an insignificant small
town – insignificant with the exception of the two bridges spanning the Dubysa
river to its east, the division's objective for the day.[1]

Having punctured the frontier defences and cleared the border zone on the first
day of battle, the moment had come for Army Group North to turn the screw
and drive deep into the Soviet hinterland. Its commander, Wilhelm Ritter von

Army Group North – the drive through Lithuania and Latvia, 22–27 June 1941

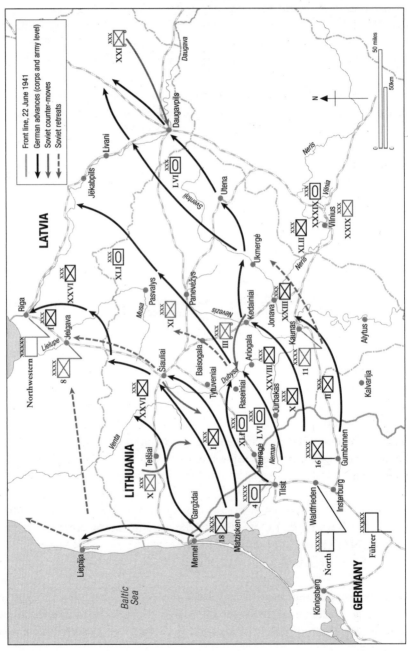

Leeb, aristocratic, elderly – he would turn 65 in a couple of months – and cautious; Leeb was, famously, the German Army's leading tactician and strategist on defence. In the campaigns of 1939 and 1940, his army group had played second fiddle to its counterparts. But no longer. What a prize awaited it: Leningrad, birthplace of the Russian revolution. Nevertheless, it remained the smallest of the three army groups striking into the Soviet Union – 650,000 men, 29 divisions, just three of them armoured, shared among two infantry armies and one *Panzergruppe*. The tanks were aimed at the River Daugava, 160 miles away, Pskov, another 140 miles, and a final 160-mile push to Leningrad. Guarding the panzers' left flank, the infantry of Eighteenth Army, advancing on the naval base at Liepāja, Courland, Riga and ultimately Estonia, while the Sixteenth Army would protect the right wing by seizing Kaunas, Vilnius and southern Lithuania, southern Latvia and Russia's northern provinces.

Standing in Leeb's way, the Baltic Special Military District – immediately renamed the Northwestern Front when war broke out – under Fyodor Kuznetsov. A committed Bolshevik from peasant stock, Kuznetsov was more than 20 years younger than his German opponent. He had no experience of leading anything larger than a regiment in battle – and that had been two decades earlier during Russia's civil war. His predecessor – relieved at the end of 1940 – had done practically nothing to prepare the Baltic for a German attack, failing to either train the troops or build adequate fortifications along the border. And the three armies at Kuznetsov's disposal were smaller than their counterparts in the centre and south of the front: 25 divisions in all, numbering 370,000 men, with the infantry in particular under strength. The trump card was the two mechanised corps: 60,000 men with more than 1,350 tanks at their disposal, over 100 of them the new 'heavies'. With these forces, Kuznetsov was expected to hold the Baltic coast, smash German forces around Kaunas and push into German-occupied Poland. The order reached Northwestern Front headquarters at 10 on Monday evening. Kuznetsov was given until midnight on Tuesday to accomplish his mission.

'BETTER TO DIE OF EXHAUSTION AND HUNGER THAN BY THE HAND OF A GERMAN...' KAUNAS AND VILNIUS, 23 JUNE

Around the same time that the spearhead of 6th Panzer Division ran into the Red Army in Raseiniai, Kaunas was rocked by a series of explosions as withdrawing Soviet forces blew up the warehouses on the left bank of the

Neman. The power of the blasts caused objects to be thrown across rooms in homes nearby and scarred a 'clear, glistening sky' with flames and eerie swathes of thick black smoke.[2]

Eleventh Army's commander Vasiliy Morozov had been given strict orders to hold the city 'stubbornly'. But with what? On paper, Morozov could call on one mechanised corps of 630 tanks and eight rifle divisions. His armour – as we shall see – would acquit itself with valour. The same could not be said of his infantry, whose lower ranks were characterised by men like Vladimir Nevidomski. Two weeks before, Nevidomski had been living in Sochi, nearly 1,400 miles away on the Black Sea coast. Drafted into the Red Army, he found himself in Kaunas a week later, and at war four days after that. He received a uniform, rifle and five rounds – but no training. The only instruction from his commanders: 'We should always keep two rounds for ourselves because we should not fall into captivity.' His officers vanished. Nevidomski and his comrades joined the torrent of Soviet troops streaming through Kaunas, heading east. With the tide of war seemingly against him, Vasiliy Morozov took the only course of action left: he prepared Kaunas' bridges for demolition, ready 'to destroy everything, leaving nothing for the enemy'.[3]

After spending the night hiding in a barn, Kęstutis Miklaševičius awoke to find the streets of Kaunas 'full of starving, yellow-faced, dusty, barefoot "invincibles"' – the retreating Red Army. Some soldiers gulped at water from the fountains; others slept on the pavements. Few had guns. 'It is sad and at the same time unfortunate when you look at them,' Miklaševičius observed. 'After all, they are partly innocent. Communism is guilty, the Jewish Kremlin is guilty and the Jewish government is guilty.'

With Soviet rule in Kaunas visibly crumbling, Lithuanian nationalists seized the opportunity – and seized the airwaves. At 9.30am, those who had their radios switched on would have heard the strains of '*Lietuva, tėvyne mūsų*' (Latvia, Our Dear Homeland), the national anthem, for the first time in more than a year, followed by the voice of Leonas Prapuolenis proclaiming: 'This is Kaunas speaking, this is the free and independent Lithuania speaking.' Prapuolenis, the underground movement's leading figure in Kaunas, read the words of 'prime minister' Kazys Škirpa – who was actually under house arrest in Berlin: 'After the torment of the Bolshevik terror this new state will rise afresh on national and social foundations and be ready to defend itself.' Škirpa called on his fellow countrymen to harry the retreating Soviets and support the advancing Germans, reputedly closing his appeal: 'Long live Adolf Hitler.' Some Lithuanians listened to Škirpa's words with tears streaming down their faces and hastily flew the national flag outside their homes. Some felt the proclamation was a call to arms.

Elena Kutorgienė-Buivydaitė peered through the window of her home in Kanto Street, just off Kaunas' main boulevard. She saw a company of Russian soldiers exchanging shots with armed Lithuanians who fired at them not merely from the road, but from the windows and rooftops of houses. Others took it upon themselves to protect key infrastructure. The Metalas factory in Šančiai on the southeastern outskirts became the focal point of the uprising. What started as three men armed with a solitary pistol and a couple of hammers expanded throughout Monday as Lithuanian nationalists 'seized by enthusiasm and bravery' learned of the rebels' actions – initially centred on defending the factory and surroundings from being sabotaged by the retreating Soviets. But as Monday progressed, their actions became bolder – and their cache of weapons and ammunition grew the more retreating Red Army troops were picked off. Šančiai's main street was soon littered with 'heaps of corpses and the cadavers of horses', then abandoned carts. On the rare occasions the street was empty, nationalists rushed out, moved the corpses, seized what booty they could and carried any wounded comrades back to a makeshift first-aid post set up in the factory. To compound the chaos, Kaunas was rocked repeatedly by explosions both from German air raids – at least one bomb landed near the Catholic cathedral and shattered windows across the city's old town – and Soviet demolitions. Huge fuel tanks, stores of firewood, military depots went up in flames.

'The Bolsheviks have apparently decided to leave causing as much destruction as possible,' Archbishop Juozapas Skvireckas noted in his diary. Appalled though he was by the devastation, the cleric was secretly pleased. 'It was only the second day yet our liberation was already certain.' Near Kaunas railway station, nationalist Kęstutis Miklaševičius had come to the same conclusion. Miklaševičius was enjoying 'a pleasant reunion' with acquaintances when 'there was a tremendous, indescribable explosion' which seemed to knock the three men off their feet: the Soviets had demolished Kaunas' famous Green Bridge, carrying the rail line over the Neman. It was a terrible moment, but it also convinced Miklaševičius that the Russians were leaving. 'Full of hope, I waited for the hour of freedom to come.'[4]

Kaunas' Jews took the torrent of Red Army troops wearily retreating through the city as the signal to flee – men and women who just 12 or 24 hours before had resolved to stay, fearful of punishment by the Soviets if they left. 'Jews were trying to escape the black fate that had more than once descended upon them like a dark cloud,' one chronicler of Jewish life in the city wrote. 'When we attempted to look ahead, we shuddered from the blackness and envisaged terrible things.' There was no order, no direction. Just bewilderment and panic. People grabbed and stuffed possessions into whatever was to hand

– baskets, prams, carts, suitcases – then scurried through the streets with frightened, pale faces. A Jewish neighbour asked Elena Kutorgiené-Buivydaité to look after his family while he fled. The Germans, he told the 52-year-old eye doctor, 'would probably not kill women and children'. Jewish lawyer Avraham Tory made for the railway station with his sister Batia and her husband, a senior official in the Soviet government; all three faced almost certain persecution under Nazi rule. The trio fought their way through streets crammed with civilians and Soviet troops determined to get away. They found the station ablaze, the tracks filled with wagons packed with Russian soldiers going nowhere. Avraham Tory seized a bicycle and headed northeast out of Kaunas, towards Ukmergé, 40 miles away.[5]

The chaos at Kaunas' station was mirrored in Lithuania's capital. Officials had locked the iron gate leading to the platforms, probably fearing a stampede. When the crowd began to scale the fence, the gate was opened and people spilled onto the platforms. There were two trains waiting on the tracks, a short one of half a dozen carriages, reserved for senior Bolshevik functionaries, and one of more than 50 goods wagons but with no locomotive to haul them. The civilians clambered aboard regardless, until it was soon overcrowded. A solitary German aircraft circled overhead, causing people to shelter in the subways linking the platforms. Soviet troops took pot shots with rifles and pistols, even though the enemy plane was far too high. When it disappeared in the direction of Kaunas, having dropped no bombs, railway officials reluctantly coupled a locomotive to the long goods train. It pulled out of Vilnius, followed by the special train carrying the last Soviet administrators.[6]

By the time she, her mother, two sisters and brother reached the station, Marija 'Masha' Rolnikaité found no trains running. Her father, a Communist lawyer who had worked for the Soviet regime, had gone on ahead of his family to buy tickets. In the tumult at the station, on the edge of Vilnius' old town, he was nowhere to be found. Masha's mother took firm action. She joined the throng leaving the Lithuanian capital on foot. Carrying bundles of clean clothing, shoes and winter overcoats, the Rolnikaités were barely beyond the city limits before they were worn down by the punishing heat. The two youngest children cried and moaned. Their mother encouraged them to continue. Finally she gave up and stopped by the roadside. Other exhausted families did likewise, pondering their course of action, as 13-year-old Masha observed.

> Some of us are for going on – better to die of exhaustion and hunger than by the hand of a German. Others think that the Germans are by no means as bestial as they're accused of being. We don't need to bother with politics. Simply just sit it

out calmly and wait for liberation. At any rate, we can't get to Minsk on foot, certainly not with small children.

The little ones want to go home. Mira says we should go on. I am silent. The children cry. Mummy turns around. We are not the only ones who are returning to the city.[7]

Solly Ganor was still on the road, perhaps 12 hours ahead of Avraham Tory, and yet his family had not reached Jonava, halfway to Ukmergė. The trek was repeatedly strafed by the Luftwaffe, causing the column to scatter and leaving the main route through the Neris valley strewn with corpses. During one rest, Solly was sent to fetch water from a nearby pond. He struggled through thick undergrowth to reach the water's edge, where he froze in his tracks. At the other end of the pond a group of Jews stood in the water, among them Solly's history teacher, stripped naked. In front of them were several armed men, dressed in old Lithuanian Army uniforms. There was a curt order and the crack of rifle fire echoed around the countryside. Only the teacher's five-year-old daughter did not fall down. She stood petrified, her thumb in her mouth. The militia leader ordered his men to shoot her. They refused. He carried out his own orders, walking up to the child, striking her with his revolver. With blood streaming down her face, she fell into the water without making a sound. 'I couldn't believe what my eyes had seen,' Solly Ganor recalled. 'The retreating Soviet Army was only a few hundred yards away and the Lithuanians were murdering Jews under their very noses.'[8]

'COMPEL EACH SOLDIER TO FULFIL HIS DUTY BEFORE THE MOTHERLAND...' LITHUANIA, 23 JUNE, AFTERNOON

In the meadows outside Raseiniai, Erhard Raus' spearhead tried to smoke out the Red Army rearguard which had suddenly held up its advance. The fields and thicket were still littered with scattered Red Army troops – individuals and groups, largely the remnants of the unfortunate 48th Rifle Division, which had only taken up its positions that morning ... and had largely ceased to exist as a fighting unit by the afternoon. The riflemen were left behind; 6th Panzer Division simply did not have the time to deal with every last enemy soldier – the timetable for seizing the Dubysa crossings did not allow it.

'All eyes remained focused on Raseiniai, which lay on the ridge in the bright noonday sun like a fortress dominating the surrounding countryside,' Raus recalled. As shells rained down on Soviet positions on the high ground south of Raseiniai, Raus' armour first drove through the town, then seized one of the river crossings to the northeast, while half a dozen miles upstream, Raus' comrade Erich von Seckendorff pushed a small detachment of anti-tank gunners and motorcyclists across the river. By early afternoon, both bridges over the Dubysa were in German hands, the Soviet troops on the high east bank dislodged, and small bridgeheads had been forged ready for the push on the Daugava, 130 miles to the east.[9]

By ignoring Russian troops either side of the Vilnius highway, Hans Riederer von Paar's armoured reconnaissance unit was just 30 miles from Lithuania's capital by mid-afternoon.

> The Russians are still in all the woods we pass through. A few bursts of machine-gun or half-track fire quickly bring them to their senses. The custom is quickly established: Every time you enter a forest, you shoot into it, then the Russians run out, like in a vending machine. There are already hundreds upon hundreds moving back along the road. Motor vehicles, guns, equipment and a few tanks also line the advance route. The pace picks up on the main road. There is a terrible dust. Our black uniforms turn grey, our faces black. Guns, trucks and passenger cars are left on the road as our prey, columns of prisoners move to the rear, and like some hellish hunt, it is on to Vilnius.[10]

From what scant information reached his headquarters in woods outside Panevėžys, barely 60 miles north of Kaunas, Fyodor Kuznetsov realised that Lithuania's two largest cities were in danger of falling to the enemy. His instructions to Eleventh Army were less orders, more exasperated admonishments. Eradicate, eliminate, destroy – these were the words the Front commander used, convinced Vasiliy Morozov had weak German forces before him. 'Take control in your hands,' Kuznetsov demanded. 'Where is 5th Tank Division? Establish what the situation is in Vilnius. I order you to restore order, urge on and compel each soldier to fulfil his duty before the Motherland.'[11]

For the Soviets, the situation in Vilnius was desolate. The national uprising in the capital began when the yellow-green-red of the Lithuanian tricolore was raised above Gediminas Tower, one of the symbols of the city – and country – around 4pm, only to be torn down by the occupiers. A few hours later the national colours appeared once again – this time over Vilnius' university. As night fell, the city was again lit up by German flares, signalling another night of bombing. Streets were almost deserted – most Soviet troops had already fled. The occasional army truck raced through the capital, only to be ambushed by armed Lithuanians. The clashes reached their climax in the small hours of Tuesday. 'Whistling bullets peppered the walls, smashed windows, knocked soldiers off their feet,' Vilnius resident Algirdas Gustaitis wrote. The 24-year-old was impressed by the determination and bravery of Vilnius residents who picked up arms against the retreating Red Army. 'They had tanks, trucks, machine guns, cannons, grenades, a large number of automatic rifles and shotguns,' he recalled. 'Lithuanian guerrillas – just rifles and Browning pistols, occasionally a few grenades and machine-guns.' The odds seemed against the nationalists: outnumbered, outgunned, with no information when – or even if – German troops would reach the capital. 'Many people were unsure whether our partisans would survive or be slaughtered by the brutal Bolsheviks.'[12]

Early in the evening Hans Riederer von Paar threw his vanguard of motorcycles over the Vokė, an otherwise insignificant river sluggishly meandering towards the Neris no more than eight miles from the centre of Vilnius. Here the Red Army was determined to make a stand. As the light began to fade, Paar's meagre bridgehead came under ferocious enemy fire: heavy artillery, machine and anti-tank guns pinned his men down around the village of Kazbiejai for 90 minutes until the first armour of 7th Panzer Division appeared. Using the smoke and flames of the burning village as cover, the panzers manoeuvred into a position behind Soviet lines – and then engaged in a duel with the enemy's artillery. 'It's the most incredible thing I have ever experienced,' Paar wrote. 'The noise is so loud that you can't hear a word.' He hunkered in a foxhole and waited for the panzers to prevail as Kazbiejai burned to the ground. He did not have to wait long. Before midnight the battle of the Vokė crossing had been settled in Germany's favour.[13]

'HOLD LIEPĀJA. DO NOT LEAVE IT UNDER ANY CIRCUMSTANCES...' 23 JUNE, EVENING

In the fading light of Monday evening, the naval infantry of the *Marine Stosstrupp Abteilung* mounted trucks and headed along the main Riga road, determined to storm the port of Libau – Liepāja to Latvians. In 12 months of Soviet rule, it had been turned into the Red Navy's principal Baltic harbour – and was protected accordingly; in the spring of 1941, two coastal batteries armed with 130mm guns had been installed, while a couple of anti-aircraft units and the 67th Rifle Division – admittedly at three-quarters strength – had arrived to defend the port. The latter had been given unequivocal orders from Nikolai Berzarin, the youthful commander of Twenty-Seventh Army: 'Hold Liepāja. Do not leave it under any circumstances. You have sufficient forces.'[14]

The Germans' dusk assault came to a halt after barely a mile; enemy armour was reported advancing towards them. Anti-tank gunners took up position, but the progress of the 'monster' was stopped only when it ran into a ditch and went up in flames. Packed with wood and hauling a field kitchen filled with flammable liquid, it had been intended to block the road. It did not. The marines re-mounted and resumed their advance on Liepāja – running into, and destroying, an almost-identically booby-trapped Soviet tank. Finally the lorries could go no further. The marines continued on foot along the roadside ditch until they came under fire from Soviet troops in a farmhouse. Mortars were brought up. Their rounds quickly set the building on fire – and the arms stored there. For several hours, the bangs of exploding ammunition shook the summer night. The German attack was suspended.[15]

'NOW YOU KNOW WHAT THE SOVIET REGIME MEANS...' SOVIET ATROCITIES IN LITHUANIA, 23–26 JUNE

Within hours of the German attack, the NKVD received orders to evacuate all 5,900 inmates of its prisons across Lithuania. The speed of the enemy advance – and Red Army's collapse – would allow them to ship no more than a quarter of those incarcerated eastwards. In many cases, extermination proved easier than evacuation. At Rumšiškės labour camp, a dozen miles southeast of Kaunas, around 300 prisoners were ordered to fall in for roll call in the courtyard. Instead, they were scythed down by a machine-gun on an armoured car. For good measure, the NKVD tossed in several hand-grenades. As men and women – including one nine months pregnant – lay dying on the ground, their executioner moved among the bodies and ever-growing pools of blood. 'Now you know what the Soviet regime means,' he snarled. The troops of 27th Infantry Regiment came across another camp outside Vilnius; the inmates – men, women and children – had been machine-gunned to death. In the northern town of Panevėžys, 50 miles east of Šiauliai, doctors and a Sister of Mercy in the city hospital were tortured and at least three surgeons killed, while 19 prisoners – hastily brought in from outlying villages – were shot and their bodies tossed into a pit near the town's sugar factory. At Pravieniškės prison, 15 miles east of Kaunas, the NKVD shot dead 230 of the 444 inmates. Just for good measure, they finished off 31 prison employees. It was the largest – and most high profile – single massacre carried out on Lithuanian soil in the wake of the German invasion, but it was not the most gruesome. That took place outside the small town of Telšiai, roughly halfway between the Baltic and the provincial capital of Šiauliai, before dawn on Wednesday 25 June. After dark the previous evening, several trucks had pulled into the courtyard of Telšiai prison, a rather unassuming two-storey brick building which looked more like an institute or college. Inside 162 people were incarcerated – farmers, workers, labourers, teachers, Lithuanian citizens of every social class. They had celebrated when most of the guards ran away on the 24th, shouting that 'Hitler would liberate them', but as prison official Domas Ročius later testified, 'under no circumstances could we release these bloodthirsty Fascists to kill our comrades'. The 'worst' counter-revolutionaries among them, 76 prisoners in all, were bundled into the trucks and driven to the woods around Rainiai, which took no more than 15 minutes. Waiting for them under the canopy of trees was a specialist NKVD 'punishment squad' and four freshly dug mass graves. What occurred before the sun came up on Wednesday morning almost defies description: tongues, ears, scalps, noses, genitals were cut off – the latter were then stuffed in the victim's mouths. Eyes were gouged out, fingernails pulled out, skin peeled off, bodies burned with boiling water, acid or torches – all while the prisoners were still alive – before the fatal blows were finally delivered, probably with maces. Throughout, the engines on the trucks were gunned to drown out the screams. Later that morning, the prison – and Telšiai – were abandoned by the Communists. The city, Ročius recalled, was 'lifeless'. When the victims of Rainiai were exhumed three days later with Telšiai under German rule, barely two dozen could be identified. All were subsequently laid to rest after a mass funeral service in the city's cathedral.[16]

'INSTANCES OF NEAR PANIC...' RASEINIAI, 24 JUNE, DAWN

The first rays of light on Tuesday 24 June were accompanied by the sudden crash of artillery fire – the opening barrage from the guns of 2nd Tank Division, shaking the window frames of homes in Raseiniai. 6th Panzer Division responded, followed shortly afterwards by the distinctive 'crack' of tank cannon exchanging blows.

Major Dmitry Osadchy, commanding a platoon of four KV-1s, led the charge, the vanguard of upwards of 250 Soviet tanks. There was nothing subtle about his tactics – 'shooting continuously, we simply drove straight at them,' he recalled. The bridgehead precariously held by 6th Panzer's motorcycle battalion was crushed, literally, for the 'monster tanks' simply 'ground into the dirt everything in their path – guns, motorcycles and men'. Any man left behind by the battalion on the steep right bank of the Dubysa – wounded or not – would later be found dead, many of their bodies mutilated.

The shallow river proved no obstacle to the Soviet tanks' progress and, as he crested a hill on the left bank, Dmitry Osadchy found the terrain in front of him 'literally filled with enemy tanks and armoured vehicles'. Osadchy ordered his platoon to smash its way through the enemy's lines at full speed – which it did, but at a fearful price. Burning BTs and T-26s soon littered the landscape. 'There were so many tanks in close proximity that almost any shell fired hit a target,' Osadchy remembered, although 'the KV was invulnerable with its mighty shield of armour – the shells merely left dents in its armour'. A 15cm howitzer fired directly at one KV at point-blank range, causing it to stop 'as if hit by lightning'. The German gunners cheered – but only momentarily, for the Soviet monster resumed its journey, ramming the howitzer and crushing it 'as if it were nothing more than a toy', 6th Panzer's operations officer Johann Adolf Graf von Kielmansegg observed. A 'tornado of fire and smoke' enveloped the Dubysa valley as the 2nd Tank Division rolled westwards, seemingly unstoppable. Small wonder, then, that there were 'instances of near panic' in 6th Panzer's ranks.

Perhaps 11th Panzer Regiment might blunt the Red Army onslaught. Moving up the line, platoon leader Wilhelm Sander's Panzer Mk3 passed a string of 'German vehicles, flattened motorcycles, staff cars completely crushed, overrun by the gigantic Russians without firing a shot – they look like crushed tin cans – and tractors whose tracks have simply been torn off'. Away from the road, the abandoned tanks of 11th Panzer's 2nd Platoon littered the landscape. 'Every man tells himself we're not going to repeat such a scene!' Sander recorded in his diary. 'If we do not remain firm in the face of the Reds' attack and do not sacrifice ourselves, if that's what it has to come to, then there's nothing stopping the riflemen and all the other troops and our line, our front will collapse as far as the rearward services. Every *Landser* knows what that means.'

Sander manoeuvred his Panzer Mk3 into position on the crest of a hill and waited for the enemy tanks to appear. Amid the tumult of battle – Soviet soldiers emerging from the high corn and hurling hand-grenades at panzers at point-blank range, heavy batteries hammering away, the crack of rifles, the sustained bursts from machine-guns – the panzer platoon commander was struck by the sight of a pair of blue butterflies flying around his vehicle. 'They know nothing about the war, just like the larks in the sky above us whose pleasant sound we can hear when the artillery isn't shooting.'

When the Red armour came into view, Sander's platoon opened fire, 'sending one salvo after another over'. Several T-26s went up in flames. But not the KVs. 'From time to time all of us cheer: hit! And then: crap! Despite very clear hits, the tank continues to calmly, slowly, and stubbornly roll.' Wilhelm Sander reckoned every third round which left the barrel of his 3.7cm gun hit its target – but simply ricocheted off the Soviet tank 'in a wonderful curve'.

'IT'S THE BEGINNING OF A NEW ERA...' VILNIUS, 24 JUNE

There was no such resistance on the approaches to the Lithuanian capital. The deep, sandy banks of the Vilnia, which gave the city its name, were covered with abandoned equipment. No attempt had been made to build a makeshift bridge, let alone save the light and heavy guns and armoured cars, now all stuck in the quicksand. 'Lying next to them,' 27th Infantry Regiment's commander Walther Seydlitz remembered, 'were red flags and large red banners bearing Communist fighting slogans, all in an indescribable mess.' At least someone had thrown a pontoon bridge over the Neris upstream of Vilnius, though it aided the retreating Soviet troops and refugees, driving their cattle in front of them, little; the Luftwaffe pounced on the makeshift crossing. 'People on the road ran to the edge of the forest to seek cover, they jumped off the road into the river, but death caught up with them everywhere,' Red Army man Georgy Bekasov remembered:

One bomb exploded in the heart of the seething masses. I was knocked to the ground by something slightly warm and sticky. When I regained consciousness, I noticed that I was lying under the tattered parts of something which had once been a human body. Even the soil burned, boxes with cartridges and shells flew into the air and the bridge which we had striven so hard to build was destroyed. After the bombers had departed, it took more than an hour to restore order among our men, to rescue those buried alive and to give first aid to the wounded. With heavy hearts we buried the dead pioneers by the river and erected a modest monument for them.

Civilians and soldiers alike were fleeing the German vanguard: motorcyclists of 7th Panzer Division. They simply rode into Vilnius, capturing 50 aircraft at the airfield and rich booty at the now-deserted railway station, food especially. After two wheels came four as the division's motorised infantry rolled into the city. To journalist Grigory Shur, they never seemed to stop: large tanks, endless columns of infantry – 'almost all of them in vehicles' – motorised artillery, motorised flak rolling through his city 'like a steel avalanche'. They were greeted 'with tears of joy and flowers' by a city dressed in the national colours and Lithuanian inhabitants 'dressed in national costumes, offering flowers, cold water, and papyrus' as nationalists endeavoured to give the city 'a pure Lithuanian stamp'; as Wilno it had belonged to Poland for two decades until 1939, and only three in every ten inhabitants were ethnic Lithuanian; the rest were Jews or Poles 'who lurked in their apartments'.

Most of Vilnius' Jewish inhabitants remained out of sight, nervously observing their new masters from behind twitching curtains. 'Unless some miracle happens, everything really is lost,' Herman Kruk observed. A 44-year-old librarian and Polish Jew who had fled to Vilnius from Warsaw at the outbreak of war, Kruk had decided not to run a second time but remain in Lithuania's capital to chronicle daily life, even though he had no doubt about the fate awaiting his people. 'It's the beginning of a new era, perhaps the hardest in my life.'

Eight-year-old Shoshana Rabinovici was already learning how hard. Rifle butts thudded against the door to her family's apartment. *Offnen! Schnell! Schnell!* The elderly Polish janitor opened the door and several German soldiers burst in, moving quickly between the rooms before halting in the lounge where the officer told the concierge that he wanted the occupants evicted within 24 hours. The old Pole did not understand and when he tried to ask a question, was struck in the head with a rifle by one soldier. 'The soldiers left the apartment as fast as they had come in, leaving the old man lying in his blood,' Shoshana remembered:

> The sound of their boots could still be heard in the stairwell when my mother closed the apartment door and got the old housekeeper back on his feet. Dolka brought water and a towel for him, but he didn't want her help. Filled with hatred, he cried out '*Zydówka*' – Jewess. Dolka had been injured, was frightened and started to cry. She'd lived in this house for years and until that moment she'd regarded the janitor as a good friend.

In the coming hours and days, concierges would betray Jewish families across Lithuania.

For now, the Rabinovicis had lost only their home. In the suburb of Šnipiškės – just over the Neris from the city centre – a mob set several synagogues on fire, then dragged the rabbi and some elderly Jews out of their homes by their beards and forced them to dance around the Torah scrolls before the sacred documents were tossed into the flames. Other Jews were ordered to remove all their clothes, hold hands and sing a Soviet tune. The grounds of the Church of Our Lady of the Assumption, one of Lithuania's oldest houses of worship, became a site of both horror and spectacle. Nationalists set up a machine-gun in the garden, then gunned down any Jew or Red Army straggler unfortunate enough to stray past. Jews rounded up across the capital were brought to the church, searched, deprived of any personal belongings, mocked, beaten and finally shot. In a matter of hours, the bodies of several dozen people were piled up in the garden. 'The bodies lay on the earth in full view – their burial was not permitted,' Grigory Shur recalled. In the heat the cadavers quickly began to decompose and a foul stench soon hung over the church grounds. The city's firefighters dowsed the corpses with water, but still no effort was made to bury the dead. 'All day long people – mostly Lithuanians and Poles, women dressed in their finest clothes – flocked here to have a look, as if it were some amusing spectacle,' Shur continued. 'The "audience" expressed their satisfaction in various ways. People competed to see who could swear the most at the Bolsheviks and Jews.' Only when night fell were the bodies removed and taken out of the city for burial.[17]

The best that could be said about the killings in Vilnius this Tuesday is that they were spontaneous acts. Not so the murders taking place 200 miles away along Lithuania's coastal strip.

'A GENERATION HAS TO GO THROUGH THIS SO THAT IT'S BETTER FOR OUR CHILDREN...' GARGŽDAI, 24 JUNE, MID-DAY

In a field outside the small town of Gargždai, Werner Schmidt-Hammer raised his sword and addressed ten men and women lined up on the edge of a hurriedly expanded pit by a half-destroyed stable. 'You are being shot on the orders of the Führer because of crimes against the Wehrmacht.' With sweat pouring down his face, the 33-year-old optician and police reservist lowered his blade, and the sound of volleys echoed around the Lithuanian countryside. The firing squad had spent the morning honing their marksmanship in the courtyard of Memel's police headquarters, a dozen miles away. Still it required Schmidt-Hammer to deliver the *coup de grâce* to a couple of the victims. He strode over and emptied his pistol into them.

The prisoners had been rounded up the previous day, part of efforts to create a 15-mile-wide 'security zone' along the border with Lithuania. There was no place for undesirable, suspicious or dubious elements in this zone. No resident of Gargždai – Garsden to Germans – had offered resistance, but authorities in Memel had been ordered to arrest every Jew and Communist in the town on the pretence that they had. Werner Schmidt-Hammer embellished the lie, telling his men that these prisoners had attacked an ambulance.

Having spent the night under the stars in the municipal park, the prisoners were marched to the site of their execution – an abandoned defensive ditch – on Tuesday morning. Most were then put to work deepening and widening the pit, while others buried dead Russian soldiers whose cadavers still scarred the terrain. One young, well-dressed Jew did not work hard enough for the liking of the Gestapo and was shot in the neck.

When the firing squad arrived, a Gestapo officer hurried the prisoners into position on the edge of the pit, ten at a time, striking them with a club: 'Faster, faster, then we can call it a day earlier!' Each fresh group of victims was forced to toss the corpses of those just shot into the pit, which was soon swilling with blood. Then they stood or, occasionally, knelt as they stared down the barrels of 20 carbines and submachine-guns aimed at them 60ft away. A few, including a 12-year-old boy, pleaded for mercy, a handful cried and groaned, but most were stoic, praying, holding hands; they knew the fate which awaited them. 'Gustav, shoot well!' one soap manufacturer called out to his former neighbour and friend-turned-executioner. Another young Jew who wasn't killed instantly called out: 'One more!' It was all too much for a handful of men in the firing squad, who broke down and had to be replaced.

When the shooting was done, 201 men, women and children were dead. While Gestapo and Security Service personnel filled in the mass grave, the policemen posed for a group photograph, before climbing into vans to return to Memel. The journey was short – a drive of no more than half an hour – but interrupted by a Soviet air raid. 'You see,' one police officer remarked to his colleagues, 'punishment is following us on foot.' Some of his comrades shared his misgivings, demanding to know from Werner Schmidt-Hammer why they had been ordered to execute women, children and the elderly. 'I don't know either, I'm just a small fry who is given orders.'

This was as far as criticism of the massacre at Gargždai went. Most men justified their actions with a dismissive: 'Well, damn it, a generation has to go through this so that it's better for our children.'[18]

'The crisis is overcome...' Raseiniai, 24 June, late afternoon

Dmitry Osadchy's platoon of heavy tanks continued to encounter elements of 6th Panzer Division on the road to Raseiniai, but German counter-measures were finally beginning to take their toll. Three KVs were immobilised, but their turrets still turned, so they continued to fight while the platoon commander's lone KV-1 pushed ever westwards. It too was eventually knocked out; a hit from one enemy shell jammed the turret, another the 76mm gun. When the fuel tank ruptured, petrol poured into the interior, caught fire and threatened to detonate the shell fuses.

With revolvers in their hands, Osadchy and his surviving crew – his radioman and gunloader – climbed out of an escape hatch and crawled along a drainage ditch, where they extinguished their smouldering overalls. 'I didn't have time to catch my breath before there was the stamping of boots on the road,' Osadchy recalled. The three men made for an adjacent rye field, using the tall grass as cover. German troops fired bursts from their machine-guns into the field, then set the rye alight, but the tankmen reached the relative safety of nearby woods before the flames reached them.

Dmitry Osadchy's lunge deep into German lines this Tuesday deeply unsettled the Germans. But his actions were also typical of the uncoordinated nature of 2nd Tank Division's counter-attack. The Soviet armour failed to concentrate their strength, heading off in opposing directions, while foot soldiers of the Red Army were unable to exploit the chaos raging in the German line. Moreover, by late afternoon, the men of 6th Panzer Division were beginning to get the measure of their foe as they discovered the KVs' Achilles heel: their tracks. If the Soviet tanks could be immobilised – through shell fire or pioneers bravely placing charges on the caterpillars – flak or artillery could finish them off. Word quickly spread. 'In a flash it gets around the division that these tanks can be destroyed after all,' 6th Panzer's operations officer noted. 'At a stroke – albeit right at the last moment – the panicky mood vanishes, the crisis is overcome.' Overcome with emotion, Graf von Kielmansegg broke down in tears, throwing his arms around a junior officer in relief.

'Now you'll suffer...' Kaunas and Vilnius, 24 June, evening

At 5.15pm the vanguard of Sixteenth Army, a makeshift detachment under Colonel Norbert Holm, reached Lithuania's second city. The retreating Russians had blown the bridge over the Neman in the small hours – while their artillery was crossing it. It did nothing to impede the German advance; by the early afternoon, Lithuanian nationalists had a ferry running. Ninety minutes after setting foot in Kaunas, Holm's men raised the swastika.

The first Germans in Kaunas found an uneasy calm over the city. Save for the militia swaggering around, firing their rifles in the air in celebration, the streets were largely empty. All day long, however, a constant procession of trucks had ferried Jews of all ages towards the city prison. In their wake, ambulances and nurses collected the corpses from the streets. The militia were the only authority in Kaunas on Tuesday 24 June, as Helene Holzman discovered when she accompanied her daughter Marie, who was determined to visit the mother of a friend who'd fled the city. The Holzmans were accosted by one nationalist as they walked down Green Hill into the heart of the city. 'Aren't you the Communist?' he snarled at Marie. 'Now you'll suffer.' At the bottom of a flight of steps, another militia man blocked the two women's path. They decided to return home. They would stay there until order returned to Kaunas.[19]

Abraham Sutzkever and Avraham Tory had also resolved to return home. Tory found himself harried constantly by German aircraft on the Ukmergė–Utena road – as did other refugees and the retreating Red Army. 'I felt,' he recorded in his diary, 'like a hunted animal in a forest going up in flames.' On bicycle and on foot, with no food and virtually no sleep, Tory continued along a road of desolation and ruin – destroyed homes, wrecked telegraph lines, wrecked vehicles, the cadavers of soldiers, civilians and animals. Finally the road ended, blown apart by German bombs. There was only one course of action left for the lawyer: to go back to Kaunas.

After a day and a half Abraham Sutzkever had covered three dozen miles along the road from Vilnius to Minsk. His progress had been slowed by the burden of carrying his friend's child – separated from its father and mother. It longed to feed from the latter. All Sutzkever could offer were a couple of berries he'd picked. And now, outside the village of Ashmyany, the 27-year-old poet heard the clatter of tanks. 'We fled from the plague and the plague caught up with us,' he wrote. There was no point continuing. He headed back for Vilnius, taking shelter in barns whenever the enemy appeared. 'Tank after tank after tank,' he observed. 'The entire road was a row of tanks. They rumbled, rattled, roared, deafened.' Somewhere outside the capital, he and his wife somehow ran into the father of the child they had taken under their wing. When they reached the Vilnia, the Sutzkevers washed and tore up their identity papers. 'My wife kissed her diary and cast it into the water, page by page.'

In Vilnius, the Sutzkevers found the swastika now flew above the Royal Palace, while armed figures wearing white armbands led a group of 20 men at rifle point up Castle Hill. They returned not to their apartment but that of Sutzkever's mother. Her face was stained by dried tears. 'Yesterday an eager messenger had told her he'd seen me lying on the ground, dead, ripped apart by a bomb.'[20]

'A WILD SCENE...' RASEINIAI, 24 JUNE, DUSK

By the time 2nd Tank Division commander Igor Soliankin launched his sixth and final assault on German lines at Raseiniai at last light, 6th Panzer had finally brought up its 88mm flak guns, as well as 10cm howitzers, to blunt the Soviet attack – which they did, coupled with the continuous intervention of the Luftwaffe. The scene in the Dubysa valley described by Wilhelm Sander was hellish:

> The barns and huts 600 to 700 metres ahead of us are in flames. Russian riflemen have set up machine-gun nests there and are strafing us from the right. They've been driven away by the fires, however. The flames of the Christie tank next to us on the hill and the burning buildings over there create a wild scene. To cap it all, Red artillery – probably a self-propelled gun – is also hammering at us. An 88mm flak anti-tank gun battery sets up behind us and sends several quite-well-aimed greetings the way of Soviet tanks disappearing in the distance.

When night descended, the Soviet counter-attack petered out. It would not resume, for while Soliankin had spent the day battering 6th Panzer, 1st and 8th Panzer Divisions had driven deep into his flanks. By the end of 24 June, what was left of his armour – just 30 tanks, two-thirds of them KVs – was threatened with encirclement.

'I AM DYING, BUT NOT GIVING UP...' LIEPĀJA, 24–25 JUNE, MIDNIGHT

Anyone still awake in the vicinity of Liepāja at midnight would have been treated to the horrifying – yet mesmerising – spectacle of the naval base going up in flames: five submarines, an icebreaker, gunboat, fuel tanks, ammunition dumps, food warehouses and lastly the destroyer *Lenin*. Just a few hours before, her stokers had her boilers producing steam for the first time in more than six months; the 1,400-ton warship had been in refit in the Tosmare shipyard since before Christmas. The naval base's commander Mikhail Klevensky had given *Lenin's* commander Yuri Afanasiev clear instructions: the destroyer was not to fall into enemy hands; she should be scuttled. Afanasiev's crew begged him to try to break out. 'Comrade Captain, let's risk it.' Afanasiev agreed and let his men ready the ship for sea. But by the time *Lenin* was able to move under her own power, the situation around Liepāja had changed dramatically. There was now shooting close to the Tosmare yard. Crews of some of the five submarines in harbour appeared to be preparing to scuttle their boats. The men of the 67th Rifle Division were streaming back into the city. Afanasiev tried to ring Klevensky, but there was no answer from the naval base commander. He acted according to his final instructions. Shortly before midnight on 24 June, Yuri Afanasiev ordered a signal hoisted: 'I am dying, but am not giving up.' It was the order to blow up anything in the yard which might be of use to the enemy.[21]

'A FUNNY OLD WAR...' KAUNAS, 25 JUNE, MORNING

Kaunas was still smouldering when 121st Infantry Division filed through it at first light on Wednesday. Its soldiers found the approaches to the city lined with birch crosses adorned with steel helmets. No such courtesy was afforded Soviet dead – their corpses littered the landscape – nor the cadavers of horses, now emitting a foul stench as they decomposed. During the night pioneers had thrown a pontoon bridge across the Neman – here 700ft wide – under the glow of flames from the old town, where inhabitants tried to rescue possessions from their burning homes.

Despite the pall of smoke hanging over the city, Kaunasians felt secure enough to hail the German invader. 'We're greeted by inhabitants clapping their hands and celebrating, adorning us with flowers, welcoming us as liberators from Bolshevism,' a battalion adjutant in 121st Infantry Division noted. 'A funny old war,' he mused. 'Flowers and lead in turn.' Harry von Kirchbach's infantry regiment was greeted with 'flowers and cries of "*Sieg Heil*".' The men of 89th Infantry Regiment found 'tables laden with milk, coffee, eggs, cake and bread', inviting them to eat. Adorned with a flower in their buttonholes, the soldiers marched through Kaunas 'in perfect order, singing loudly' accompanied by the applause of inhabitants. 'Many *Landsers* thought that the campaign in the East would be another *Blumenkrieg*,' wrote the regimental historian, 'but the Russian soldier soon put them right.' Even Elena Kutorgienė-Buivydaitė could not help admiring the discipline of the Germans – 'well-clothed, well-fed, precise' – as they marched down streets now dressed in Lithuania's national colours. 'They leave a completely different impression from the Red Army which marched in a year ago – overly-tired, scruffy, ill-fed.'[22]

Certain the Red Army was gone – and would never return – the people of Kaunas now began to rid themselves of all vestiges of Soviet rule. Shop windows were smashed and books, photographs, displays – anything featuring the hammer and sickle – destroyed as 12 months of pent-up anger erupted. At her eye clinic, Kutorgienė-Buivydaitė watched as a nurse tore down a portrait of Stalin and trampled on it. 'The Lithuanian people had acted obediently, but thought otherwise in secret,' she observed. 'They stored up their hatred, and the more this happened in secret, the more violently it was unleashed now when it was no longer necessary to keep it in check.'[23]

Kaunas' residents soon turned their attention away from the inanimate trappings of Communism.

'THINGS HERE MUST HAVE BEEN AWFUL...' RASEINIAI, 25 JUNE, MID-DAY

Having spent the night concentrating what was left of its forces in woodland northeast of Raseiniai, the remaining armour of 2nd Tank Division burst from cover shortly after dawn. They found the Germans waiting for them, subjecting the Soviet vehicles to punishing fire at point-blank range. The Red Army men responded in kind. 'Our tanks crushed his guns and machine-gun positions, quickly bursting into an open field filled with enemy tanks and other military equipment,' Dmitry Osadchy recalled. Nevertheless, the gallant 2nd Tank Division was surrounded. At the headquarters of 1st Panzer Division, a desperate Soviet radio message was intercepted: 'Enemy is plastering us with howitzer fire. We're completely encircled. I'm asking for help.' But finishing off the Soviet division proved no easier than blunting its counter-attack 24 hours earlier. 1st Panzer Division reported that one KV-2 was hit 70 times – yet not a single shell penetrated its armour. Only at point-blank range – 100ft – did armour-piercing shells seem to have any effect on the Soviets' 'big old lumps'.

By nightfall, the division had been reduced to a dozen tanks. Out of fuel, their ammunition expended, they were blown up by their crews.

'I will never forget how crews parted company with their tanks with tears in their eyes,' remembered Pavel Rotmistrov, chief-of-staff of III Mechanised Corps.

His commander, Alexey Kurkin, gathered surviving officers and commissars, ordered small arms, grenades and ammunition distributed, made provision for the wounded, then ordered his men to strike out to the east. Some – on foot like Dmitry Osadchy, or in the occasional vehicle – slipped through the weak ring of encirclement around them and fell back towards Riga. But not Igor Soliankin. He put a revolver to his head, telling his commissar: 'No division – no commander', before pulling the trigger. Just 400 of his men and a solitary tank escaped annihilation.

Thus ended the battle of Raseiniai – a battle XXXXI Panzer Corps' commander even went so far as to label 'a mini Tannenberg' after Germany's momentous victory over the Russians a generation earlier. Hans Georg Reinhardt's panzers had smashed 'the elite of the Russian armoured force', wrecking 150 enemy tanks in the process – 'including some proper monsters,' he gleefully told his wife.

Those at the sharp end were rather more sober. Raseiniai 'was one of the greatest strains on my nerves I experienced throughout the war,' Johann Graf von Kielmansegg recalled, 'and, measured against the many battles later in the Russian campaign, was one of the hardest which we ever had to survive.'

Trapped in their steel hulls, few tank men on either side grasped the scale of the encounter. Through the visors in their vehicles they saw only the action immediately in front of them, perhaps a shot-up vehicle sporadically, the odd dead body, burned-out tank. Raseiniai was a huge, terrible battle. 'It is a scene of devastation and destruction, stretching 30 or 40 kilometres into the land,' a stunned police officer from Bremen wrote a week later as his unit crossed the battlefield, still scarred by burned-out, shot-up or abandoned tanks. A good few were left seemingly intact, out of fuel. Others were ripped to pieces. Occasionally there were German and Russian graves: four panzer gunners buried together, the black caps of the *Panzerwaffe* hanging on the wooden crosses instead of steel helmets. 'You can't describe the devastation – you have to see it with your own eyes,' the policeman continued. 'Things here must have been awful.'[24]

'SENTENCED TO DEATH FOR INSULTING THE GERMAN ARMY...' KRETINGA, 25 JUNE

Having eradicated 'threats' in Gargždai, security services creating a 'safe zone' along the German–Lithuanian frontier moved to the market town of Kretinga, a dozen miles north of Memel. Local police had rounded up more than 200 Jews on the first night of the German occupation in response to the shooting of three officers. A solitary Jew who'd served in the German Army as an officer in World War I and earned the Iron Cross was dispatched to Memel to face an uncertain fate. The rest were now packed into trucks, driven to the village of Pryšmančiai, then forced to build a makeshift embankment along an abandoned Soviet anti-tank trench. The prisoners worked too slowly for the 20 or so Gestapo, German police and soldiers guarding them and who repeatedly lashed out with rifle butts and boots. When the embankment was finished, the prisoners were shot ten at a time – 'sentenced to death for insulting the German Army' – their bodies rolling down the freshly built mound into the trench below.

And still the deaths of 214 men and women did not satiate the bloodlust of the killers. When Kretinga's synagogue was set ablaze and fire raged through part of the town, more than 60 Jews were arrested and locked in a cellar – even though the arsonist was a Lithuanian policeman. When drunken German police turned up armed with wooden clubs, they forced the Jews first to jump into a fish pond, then pretend they were swimming in sand as they crawled up and down the embankment. Their amusement complete, the police murdered every one of the Jews.

The third and final act in creating the 'security zone' was completed two days later in the dunes outside the small coastal resort of Palanga, where 111 men were executed by a firing squad of Luftwaffe cadets and Lithuanian police – the victims were again Jews or supposed Communist sympathisers. While they were executed, their homes were plundered by their neighbours. 'They looted, looted, looted,' a 16-year-old girl recalled. 'German soldiers stood by the way and merely laughed – loudly.'[25]

REVENGE... KAUNAS, 25–26 JUNE

Unlike his wife Helene, Max Holzman had not been able to sit in his home and await developments. From rumours, he'd heard that mixed marriages were permitted in Germany and Jews had been left in post in the Netherlands. Once he'd been a respected international bookseller. Perhaps his connections might allow his family to remain together. Accompanied by his daughter Marie, he headed into the city to make his case to the new authorities. In Laisvės Alėja, Kaunas' main boulevard, they were accosted by a militia man who recognised the girl. 'You're a Communist – you're getting your just deserts now,' he sneered. He stared up and down Max Holzman. 'Who's the gentleman? Your father? He can come along too.' The pair were led to the police station where they were separated.

As his daughter was led away, Max Holzman called out: 'The first of us to be freed is to strive to free the other!'

Back at the Holzmans' home, Helene found two elderly friends, the Zinghauses, standing before her front door. After a day in hiding near Kaunas' railway station – they had sought shelter in the cellar of a house when the Luftwaffe attacked – the couple had decided it was safe enough to return home. They found their apartment had already been commandeered by the Germans, but bribed their janitor to allow them in nonetheless. The flat had been plundered, stripped of everything: clothes, shoes, furniture, crockery. The Zinghauses were still searching their apartment when the caretaker burst in and subjected them to an antisemitic tirade. At that point the couple left and sought refuge with the Holzmans, pleading with Helene: 'We used to be wealthy people, now in the space of a day we've become beggars.'[26]

***

As darkness fell on the first full day of Kaunas' liberation, a seething mob began to move through the city towards the opposite bank of the Neris and the suburb of Slobodke, the heart of the city's Jewish community for a good six decades. Jews, proclaimed the inaugural edition of *Į laisvę* – To Freedom – the first newspaper published since the end of Soviet rule, were Communism's 'best weapon for exploiting and controlling others'. 'Bolshevism and Judaism,' it concluded, 'are one and the same, inseparable.' But it pleaded with Kaunasians not to take the law into their own hands; those who had committed crimes against the Lithuanian people would face justice.[27]

Kaunas' citizens were not prepared to wait for the wheels of justice to turn. Armed with rifles, pistols, knives and axes, hatchets, the mob moved systematically along streets 'from house to house, apartment to apartment, from room to room and killed every Jew they found, old and young – it didn't matter,' one rabbi who survived this night recalled. Harry von Kirchbach watched militiamen 'drag the Bolsheviks and Jews from their hiding places' and 'numerous synagogues' set on fire. Gangs burst into homes and hacked their occupants to death, rounded up residents of apartment blocks in courtyards and shot them against the walls. Other homes were set ablaze, their occupants burned alive inside. 'The cries,' one survivor remembered, 'could be heard for miles.' The last act of one dying Jewish locksmith was to write in Yiddish on his door in his own blood: *nekome* – revenge. Decapitation was a favourite method of execution; the head of one rabbi was chopped off and hung out of the window of his apartment, while looters raided and plundered his possessions. Elsewhere severed heads were sometimes put on display in the windows of Kaunas' shops. Otherwise, the corpses of Jews were mutilated hideously: breasts cut off, bodies sawn in half.[28]

Dawn on Thursday put an end to the mob's violence – even they shunned committing their bloody acts quite so openly. The respite was short-lived. An hour or so after first light, policemen began banging on the doors of Jewish homes. The inhabitants were forced into the street, then sent into the homes of murdered neighbours to recover their corpses and haul them to a mass grave dug by the waters of the Neris. Other Jews were force-marched to the pit, forced to dance, recant Jewish prayers, sing Russian songs and perform gymnastics, before they were shot to the sound of cheers and applause from watching Lithuanians.[29]

One group of militia led by the former army officer and nationalist Algirdas Klimaitis was particularly sadistic. More than 30 dying or dead Jews were found in one garage. Some were unrecognisable, others were covered with bloody footprints, one had a rubber tube for petrol in his mouth. Every one of the bodies had been mutilated in some form.[30]

At least 800 Jews died during this first wave of violence – perhaps as many as 1,500 were killed. 'Any non-Jew could do with us as he pleased,' one Jewish chronicler recorded. 'We were plundered, beaten, raped, shot, slaughtered. Dark powers assumed authority, the slumbering demon awoke.' Elena Kutorgienė-Buivydaitė was horrified by what she had seen – 'infamy, hatred, emptiness, the murder of Jews, robbery of their property. Doom, fear, tragic human fates. How gladly I would have run away from this accursed city, these people were alien to me!' Kaunas' new masters did nothing to stop the pogrom. 'Our soldiers were quiet spectators,' one German staff officer noted. 'In any case, they had no orders to stop this blood court.'[31]

'WON'T YOU RETURN?' THE RED ARMY LEAVES LITHUANIA, 25–27 JUNE

Following defeat at Raseiniai, it was as if Eleventh Army, defending central and southern Lithuania, simply melted away. 'The troops are out of control,' one senior Soviet intelligence officer fumed. 'They are retreating by themselves. There's trouble.' Newly arrived reinforcements such as the 11th Rifle Division were unable to restore order, let alone grapple with the enemy. The division arrived piecemeal from Estonia. 'The battalions and regiments arrived little by little, day after day, and the enemy massacred us little by little, battalion by battalion,' one of its commissars complained. The signals battalion was attacked by the Luftwaffe the moment it disembarked – and promptly ceased to exist, leaving the division without communications. 'The divisional commander ordered us to retreat towards Riga,' the political officer continued in a report intended for Stalin's eyes. 'We were told that we were surrounded, that it was every man for himself.' What was left of 11th Rifle Division would eventually reach the city of Pskov amid a torrent of soldiers and civilians from the Baltic states and northwest Russia. 'No-one took charge of them,' the *politruk* fumed. He sought out the staff of Eighth Army. Where should the division regroup? 'I don't know,' the chief-of-staff told him.[32]

After Kaunas, German troops pushed northeastwards along the highway which led, eventually, to Leningrad, more than 450 miles away. Resistance was uneven. When Germans soldiers on bikes rode into Jonava, Soviet artillery subjected it to a two-day hammering, destroying much of the centre, including the town hall. 'The town turns into a blazing cauldron,' one inhabitant wrote. Lithuanian doctors and nurses continued to tend to wounded Soviet soldiers in the civic hospital; their commander refused to allow the men's evacuation. Only when flames raged through the building as it fell victim to the bombardment did he relent.

Jonava's two-day ordeal came to an end when an attack by Soviet armour was halted 'in the nick of time' by German anti-tank guns near the railway bridge spanning the Neris. The town, one soldier observed as his 122nd Infantry Division marched through, had been reduced to 'one big smouldering pile of rubble... Hardly a building has been spared by the fire. A couple of civilians apprehensively creep around the burning ruins. Shot-up Soviet tanks are lying in the road. Burned tank gunners are hanging from the hatches.' With defeat at Jonava, 'the strongest Soviet resistance in Lithuania has been crushed,' one Lithuanian nationalist celebrated. 'Only 100 mounds with wooden crosses are left behind in the fields...'

Ukmergė, two dozen miles along the highway, had been subjected to a succession of unopposed German air attacks to unnerve the defenders. It worked. '*Gdie jest widy samalioty*,' one junior political officer screamed – 'Where are our aircraft?' – as he fired his pistol in desperation at a low-flying German bomber. He was one of the last vestiges of Soviet rule in the city; many Party officials, military families and Communist supporters had fled Ukmergė on Monday, leaving the jail unguarded – though not before killing half a dozen or more political prisoners.

German troops marched into Ukmergė the next day – according to one eyewitness at the cost of just one soldier, 'whereas the roadside ditches were filled with Russians corpses'. The people of Ukmergė county offered the Germans –

the wounded especially – eggs, milk, sour cream, butter, bacon and cheese, while partisans and militia units began sweeping the countryside around Ukmergė for 'Reds'. 'Every day,' wrote the chronicler, 'they come across dozens of starving and exhausted Red Army soldiers.'[33]

Lithuania's forests still offered sanctuary to Soviet troops left behind by the war's rapid progress. On the 26th – when German soldiers were already in Jonava and Ukmergė – an advance detachment of 405th Infantry Regiment left Kaunas on bicycles along the same highway. They got no further than the small town of Karmėlava, just four miles away, where they were ambushed. A few hours later, 26-year-old Albert Beyer marched past the site. 'Now they lie on both sides of the road, some with rifles still in their hands, their suntanned faces yellow and drained of blood,' he noted. 'Around 70 comrades lost their lives.' Such attacks, the division's doctor Hans-Jörg Mauss noted, 'provoke a certain degree of nervousness among the men, of course. It leads to unnecessary shooting – often on both sides.' It wasn't just the occasional Red Army soldier cut off from his unit, but Soviet armour roaming around behind the motorised division's vanguard. They wiped out a baggage column and ambushed troops as they marched through the 'charmingly situated' village of Aukštadvaris, 30 miles west of Vilnius, where just a short time beforehand inhabitants had welcomed the entering Wehrmacht. The German response was unequivocal: they razed Aukštadvaris to the ground.[34]

The woods and copses provided refuge, too, for Lithuanians who had sided with the Communist regime and who now sought to flee to the Soviet Union. Vytautas Naktys, who'd left Kaunas with a 150-strong group of students and young Communists, was warned not to attempt reaching Utena, despite avoiding major roads. Friendly villagers warned him that a group of Communists had already tried to slip through the woods only to be surrounded, caught and slain to a man by partisans. Naktys was frequently received 'with great warmth' by peasant families – particularly those who'd been given land under Soviet reforms. 'Won't you return?' some begged, with tears in their eyes. But there were countless more – especially those wealthier peasants who'd suffered at the hands of the Communists – who refused to give them even a glass of water. Vincas Poderis found no road, no town, no village was safe. German air raids he could endure – although he did his best to avoid them by moving along country lanes – but the methods of nationalist partisans appalled him. Frequently they pretended to be Communist sympathisers, or members of the Komsomol youth organisation, sometimes wearing the uniforms. They let genuine Communists get within a few yards before opening fire. As he and his comrades made their way towards Latvia from Kaunas along the Ukmergė–Utena highway, Poderis was repeatedly ambushed by groups of partisans. He survived a succession of skirmishes – but anyone who lagged behind the group of Communists gingerly making their way east across Lithuania and fell into the nationalists' hands faced a gruesome death. The secretary of a Soviet International Red Aid group – 'a peasant, a calm, hard-working man' – was killed and thrown into the ditch, his eyes stabbed, tongue cut off, his body peppered with knife marks. Two Komsomol members were captured by partisans on the road to Trakai; their decapitated corpses were later found in a ditch. 'These thugs acted in the most brutal manner, killing innocent people, even women and children,' Poderis lamented. The editor of Kaunas' socialist newspaper *Darbininko* – The Working Man – became separated from his colleagues on the road to Utena. They went in search of him, convinced he had fallen asleep through exhaustion. Instead they found him lying in a pool of blood, his throat cut.[35]

'LIBERATION' AND DEVASTATION – THE GERMAN EXPERIENCE OF LITHUANIA, JUNE 1941

Just hours into the advance through Lithuania, a German Army doctor recorded with some surprise in his diary: 'Here we truly seem to have come as liberators.' For the first time since he had marched into the Memel two years earlier, the German soldier was not faced by a hostile populace on his conquests. 'We never ceased to be amazed,' a trooper in the 3rd SS Division wrote home. 'People stand in front of their houses, wave at us, bow deep down and tug their caps at the cars rolling past. It dawns on us: here we are not enemies but liberators of a small, powerless people from Bolshevism's reign of terror.' Rarely did a unit pass through a town or village without offerings of flowers, food and, occasionally, cigarettes. Lithuanians regularly gave the Hitler salute while the Nazi flag frequently flew alongside the national colours of yellow, green and red. 'The village inhabitants and their clerics cheered and prayed for God's blessings on the German colours,' Hans Lierow, a doctor in 6th Infantry Division, remembered. There was a formal thank-you from the inhabitants of historic Trakai, near Vilnius. 'The community is grateful for its liberation by the mighty German Army and the leader of the German people, Adolf Hitler.' Troops passing through Dusetos in northeastern Lithuanian were showered with flowers – 'not a single red flower,' one nationalist observed, 'all white like snow.' When German troops entered the small town of

Alanta, two dozen miles east of Ukmergė, they were greeted 'enthusiastically', one inhabitant noted. 'Young girls handed out bouquets of flowers to German soldiers. There wasn't a dry eye.'[36]

The *Landser* struggled with the Lithuanian language and the unpronounceable village names, all seemingly ending in kiai, ciai or niai. He found the Lithuanian landscape 'often dreary, uncultivated, a lot of scrubland', its buildings poor – 'no more stone buildings, nothing but pathetic wooden huts,' Hans Pichler, serving with an SS medical company, observed – its people 'filthy and scruffy'. To Rolf Hocker of 77th Infantry Regiment the Lithuanians were poor, but a 'clean and pleasant people'; their homes 'had no floors, no cupboards, no tables, no beds or stools, just an oven, a large pot, frying pan and a few items of crockery. The inhabitants possessed nothing but the clothes they wore.' The German soldier, panzer commander Wilhelm Sander rued, 'cannot live as he did in France'. By the standards of Western Europe, Lithuania was backward, its men 'dirty and ragged', its children 'squalid'. But it was the women of Lithuania who disappointed the German soldier most. He drew unfavourable comparisons with the ladies of France 12 months before. 'This bunch look untidy,' Sander noted.

> You see women going to church in dirty grey-coloured clothes. The women usually run barefoot – you rarely see clogs. And when they're going to church, they carry these shoes in their hands. There are no hats here. If there's anything on the head, then it's white headscarves worn by the women, but these are usually grey and dirty.

They were, however, exceedingly helpful. The newly 'liberated' Lithuanians provided the entering German troops with information about Red Army troops hiding in the countryside – or the militia rounded up the scattered enemy troops for them. Farmers put their horses and carts at the disposal of the Germans, joining the long baggage columns which trailed behind the fighting troops. Armed Lithuanians guarded roads and bridges, or stood guard in front of makeshift prison camps and public buildings.[37]

It was all going exactly as the German propaganda machine hoped. From the transmitter in Kaunas – now in German hands and whipping up not merely Lithuanian nationalism, but also Latvian, Byelorussian and Estonian – the German Army was hailed as a liberating force, behind which would come rebuilding the country's economy and infrastructure, cultural and religious freedom. But on the key subject of independence, the airwaves were silent. And therein lay the problem. The more perceptive German soldier realised the euphoria of late June would not last. To 281st Security Division's commander Friedrich Beyer, the sight of the national flag everywhere 'showed the dream of their former independence' was alive. Lithuanians longed for 'the restoration of how things used to be'. And that Nazi ideology would never allow to pass.[38]

To 'liberate' Lithuania, the Wehrmacht had to destroy it. Villages and small towns in the path of the German advance were left in ruins. Johann Allmayer-Beck passed through the small town of Kelmé on the main road which eventually led to Riga – 'or rather what is still left of Kelmé, and that's not much. The fiery breath of war has reduced this small town to empty, burned remains of walls. In the market square, only the church steeple rises from the ruins.' The market square, where life had thrived just three days earlier, was a desolate sight. 'On one wall still standing, a sheet of metal rattles in the wind and the breeze drives clouds of dust from the piles of rubble. There's a pervasive stench of gangrene. The columns shuffle through the ruins.'

The German soldier quickly grew accustomed to such sights and smells. Wilhelm Sander stopped to refuel his panzer in a cornfield next to the corpses of four Russian tank men. The stench from the bodies was dreadful, but not as bad as the sights and smells emanating from a Soviet tank found lurking in a barn which the gun of Sander's Czech-built panzer destroyed, throwing pieces of tank, its crew and the building in every direction for 500 yards. 'The crew were completely burned and torn to shreds,' Sander recorded in his diary. 'The stench of burned rubber mixed with the smell of the corpses and I made sure we didn't hang around.'

Rarely were the Russian dead lining the routes of advance permitted any dignity. Most were stripped of their possessions, especially their boots, which the marching *Landsers* eagerly seized. Besides, to many German soldiers, the enemy deserved no respect given the manner in which he fought. As early as the second day of the war, 20th Motorised Infantry Division warned its rear columns to beware Russians hiding in the woods and grain fields: 'They enjoy attacking resting troops, individual messengers and vehicles.' Outside Raseiniai, German dead were found 'with swastikas or the hammer and sickle carved into their chests,' one policeman 'mopping up' behind the front with his battalion told his wife. He made no secret of the treatment of Soviet prisoners – snipers and women with guns. 'Snipers are finished off there and then,' he wrote home. 'These beasts shot at German soldiers in an ambush. They had to dig their own graves.'

If they survived initial contact with their captors, Soviet prisoners lived up to every Nazi preconception. A soldier in 23rd Infantry Division found them 'half ape-like' and 'on a low cultural level'. This was a foe unlike any the *Landser* had faced before. Erich Kuby and his 3rd Infantry Division comrades came across the uniformed corpse of a woman. Kuby's officers were convinced she'd been in charge of a unit whose personnel had all committed suicide when surrounded. 'If the Soviet leaders can whip up their Party members to such acts of fanaticism,' Kuby noted with concern, 'they'll make things terribly difficult for us.' North of Vilnius, the vanguard of 253rd Infantry Division lost 46 men in ferocious fighting with a Red Army rearguard – but at least 30 of the dead had fallen into the Russians' hands alive, if wounded. 'Every wounded man was killed, usually with a shot to the head, some with blows from a rifle butt which smashed the skull in,' battalion commander Major Richard Schmidt reported. 'Some of the dead held their hands in front of their faces to protect them, their forearms or hands were shot to pieces.' Though none of the corpses had been mutilated or abused, the scene left a deep impression on Schmidt. When he attended the burial of his men the next day, he reminded his battalion never to forget what they had seen and to act 'without any reservations' in future. Inveterate Nazi, Reichstag deputy and company commander Theodor Habicht had no time for any Russian who ambushed his men – they deserved to be shot on the spot. But he grudgingly admired Red Army units 'cut off from their own troops and surrounded by united enemy divisions' which continued to resist. 'I cannot help myself, these folk impress me,' he conceded in his diary. 'The Russian soldier,' one company commander noted, 'fights bravely and doggedly – much more spirited than the French.' A few days after a bitter first encounter with Russian troops which lasted more than 14 hours, one man in the 3rd SS Division wrote home:

> The soldiers of the Red Army are no longer the Russians of the World War. They are the bravest and finest soldiers we've ever fought. In no way can they be compared with the French or even with the British, who do nothing but run – and keep on running – when we attack. They do not move an inch from their foxholes, even when they were almost being drowned in them. Only bodies were left. They continuously made counter-attacks, hammered our routes of advance with their artillery and at times made our lives really rather unpleasant. The troops were mostly Siberians with Mongol characteristics, small, dogged chaps. We only took two prisoners. These were badly wounded and no longer able to shoot themselves.

The crew of one Soviet tank were brought before Army Group North's commander; they had continued to fight even when their predicament was hopeless. They had not surrendered, they explained to the field marshal, because they would have been shot by their officer in the tank. The Russian soldier of 1941, Wilhelm Ritter von Leeb realised, was not the Russian soldier of 1914. 'He is very tough, bitter and, at times, underhand and fights better than he did in the Great War. He does not surrender, rather he fights to the last man, even when the situation is hopeless.'[39]

'THE NAME OF DÜNABURG HAD BEEN FOREMOST IN THE MIND OF EVERY OFFICER AND MAN...' DAUGAVPILS, 26 JUNE, 6.40AM

Beyond the occasional brief but ferocious encounter with the enemy, 8th Panzer Division had endured little of the pain its counterparts suffered at Raseiniai. Thanks to the impetus of its motorcycle detachment, it had secured two crossings over the Dubysa, before dusk on the very first day of the war, spent the second consolidating its position, and, after *Panzergruppe* 4 commander Erich Hoepner had contemplated, then rejected, sending the division to help its comrades at Raseiniai, the third and fourth days making for its first major objective of the campaign: the Daugava at Daugavpils – the Dvina at Dvinsk to Russians, the Düna at Dünaburg to Germans. By nightfall on the 25th, 8th Panzer was poised barely a mile from the west bank – but it would not lead the assault on the two bridges spanning the river. To improve the chances of seizing either, or both, crossings intact, the division was assigned a company of Brandenburgers, a specialist unit which exploited captured equipment, captured uniforms and men fluent in the enemy's tongue to seize strategic points such as road and rail junctions, and bridges.

Shortly after 6am on Thursday, the crews of 8th Panzer watched with bemusement as a rag-tag group of men with Red Army trucks began to change into Russian uniforms and put on Russian helmets; there were too few of either to go around, so some Brandenburgers simply hid under tarpaulin thrown over the back of the trucks. The column moved off, and after climbing a hill for a little more than a mile reached the top, from where the Daugava valley and Daugavpils itself lay below them. The Brandenburgers' view was obscured by the blinding sun and the morning mist. They could see the river, 'meandering through a sea of houses', and the two bridges spanning it: upstream, the road bridge, and a short distance downstream, the railway bridge – crossed at that very moment by a train. The men blanched at the sight before them. 'We knew we faced a suicide mission,' remembered Sepp de Giampietro, an Austrian from South Tyrol. 'We had a feeling that this time we were riding into Hell and needed luck, a lot of luck, to come through it alive.'

As the four trucks entered Krivas, the suburb of Daugavpils on the left bank, the road became clogged with refugees and even some Russian infantry, all struggling east. The Brandenburgers waved at the Red Army men as the wagons forced their way through the crowds to reach the riverside road, where the column divided: three trucks turned right, towards the road bridge, the fourth left, towards the railway crossing. Russian traffic police with red flags in their hands urged soldiers and civilians to hurry along, determined to get as many people, troops and as much equipment as they could over the river. The Germans were determined to exploit the chaos, as de Giampietro recalled:

> Russian soldiers cling to our vehicle, ask us something which we don't understand, so we just point to the rear and shout: 'Germansky, Germansky' – a word which struck fear in to the heart of many Europeans. Trams, crammed with people hanging off the footboards like grapes, ride alongside us. Light artillery, drawn by horses, marches towards the bridge, [and] soldiers push their way between our trucks.

The surprise attack on the railway bridge almost succeeded. The Brandenburgers overtook five unsuspecting Soviet armoured cars before they became engaged in a firefight with others as they began to cross the bridge. Enemy artillery fire joined in the skirmish. A shell smashed into the structure, detonating some of the explosive charges, blocking the crossing.

Around the same time, military police waved driver Willy Acherer in the first truck onto the road bridge. As Acherer drove across the 650ft span, he passed crates connected by cabling fixed to the metalwork – clearly demolition charges. On the far bank he turned onto the riverside embankment and halted, his passengers immediately leaping out and taking cover.

As they did, the second truck tried to cross. Its impatient driver did not wait for permission from the traffic policeman; he revved his engine and began to roll across. The guard was livid and fired several warning shots. The ruse was over.

While his men sought cover between the walls of houses and the embankment on the right bank, the man leading the *coup de main*, Hans-Wolfram Knaak, spent a few more seconds surveying the scene from the roadside. It cost him his life. Willy Acherer watched the officer fall to the ground, felled – depending on different accounts – by two rifle shots, a bullet to the stomach or shrapnel from a Soviet anti-tank gun round. His actions would earn him Germany's highest decoration, the Knight's Cross. The plight of his men was desperate. 'Our situation was quite simple,' Acherer wrote bluntly. 'Twenty men armed only with sidearms in the middle of 8,000 Russians.'

On the bridge, the Brandenburgers in the second truck began throwing out grenades, before dismounting and firing their pistols and machine-guns into the crowd indiscriminately. Sepp de Giampietro began cutting the wires to the demolition charges. His sabotage was halted by fierce machine-gun and anti-tank gun fire from trenches overlooking the river on the far bank. As he scrambled for cover, he scanned the crossing: the bridge and its approaches were now filled with the dead and dying.

Worse was to come as cries of 'Urra!' pierced the clatter of pistol and machine-gun fire. Soviet troops – 'arms linked together to form a solid mass' – bore down on the few Brandenburgers. 'The entire boulevard along the river was full of them,' an alarmed de Giampietro recalled. They never stopped screaming and never stopped advancing – until the Germans brought their machine-guns to bear. The attacking Russians were mown down, row by row, until the German barrels glowed, the gunners ran out of ammunition and the yells of 'Urra!' faded.

The second truck evidently exploited the confusion caused by the counter-attack to drive over the bridge. But as it began to move along the embankment it either ran over a mine or detonated an explosive charge. The blast blew the vehicle – and all its occupants – down the slope onto a road below, where it burned out.

In the meantime, heavy shells began raining down on Sepp de Giampietro on the left bank. He rolled down the embankment to escape the barrage and ended up next to a house by the Daugava – with a wire leading from an upstairs window to the bridge. De Giampietro tossed in a grenade and forced his way in. The blast wrecked most of the ground floor, upturning furniture and leaving a portrait of Stalin askew on the wall 'like in some tacky film'. A terrified Russian soldier cowered in one corner, his head between his knees, rocking uncontrollably and covered in blood and dirt. De Giampietro let him live. A comrade raced up the stairs, firing his machine pistol as he went. In the upstairs room he found two Red Army troops: one, his hands raised in surrender, the other repeatedly pushing the arm on a detonator. But nothing happened. De Giampietro's frantic sabotage efforts on the bridge had worked. As he looked out of the window onto the river, the first armour of 8th Panzer Division was approaching.

The sound of caterpillar tracks of 10th Panzer Regiment was 'heavenly music' to Willy Acherer. The panzers directed their guns at the embankment on the right bank and opened fire on the move. The road running along the right bank of the Daugava 'was like hell's kitchen,' tank commander Hellmut Schmid recalled. Acherer watched with satisfaction as the Russians 'fled from their foxholes'. It was not quite as easy as that, as Schmid reported. 'You had to shoot into every hole – and then it was re-occupied time and again.' The defenders would have disabled several panzers but failed to set the fuses on their grenades correctly as they attached them to the caterpillar tracks; the devices merely 'fizzled'.

The whole action lasted no more than 20 minutes – 'an unbelievable 20 minutes accompanied by unprecedented carnage,' de Giampietro wrote. Only 15 of the 50 Brandenburgers were unscathed. Five were dead. Willy Acherer walked past the burned-out second truck. 'We stood shaken in front of the half-baked corpses of our comrades and felt the misery of this murderous war surge inside.' After shepherding a few Russians into captivity, Sepp de Giampietro sank to the ground and watched the advancing German Army pass. He felt not euphoric but 'detached and apathetic'.

The panzers began to fan out through the streets of Daugavpils while one group headed upstream to seize the damaged, but still standing, railway bridge. By 8am, both crossings over the Daugava were in German hands.[40]

Six hours passed before the Red Army responded. Lieutenant General Stepan Akimov tried to re-take the crossings with a scratch force supported by just half a dozen artillery pieces. Small groups penetrated Daugavpils' northern suburbs, then pushed on towards the centre. Discarded clothes – underwear, cardigans, socks – and all manner of personal items, dumped by inhabitants as they sought to catch the last train out of the city the previous evening, were strewn in the streets. 'The town was one huge inferno of burning houses and exploding shells,' Soviet soldier Georgy Namsayev recalled. In the middle of chaotic street fighting, a woman suddenly appeared with a baby in her arms, screaming for someone to take the child off her hands. A young lieutenant, no older than 20, ignored the bullets whistling around the narrow streets, grabbed the child and ran with the woman to her apartment block. When he returned to his platoon a few minutes later, a German shell landed in the street, depriving the young officer of his leg below the knee. Namsayev removed his belt and tied it above the wound to stem the flow of blood, though both men knew it would help little. 'This isn't important,' the lieutenant smiled. 'What matters is that I've saved this woman and her baby.' After three hours, Namsayev and the rest of Akimov's scratch force were forced to fall back from Daugavpils' northern suburbs under concentrated artillery and machine-gun fire, leaving upwards of 50 wrecked armoured vehicles, and three dozen field and anti-tank guns in their wake. The German Army had a foothold over the Daugava. The bridgehead held.

Corps commander Erich von Manstein was delighted. He had set his armour a deadline of four days to capture the bridges – otherwise the Soviets would surely demolish them – and it had accomplished it 'because the name of Dünaburg had been foremost in the mind of every officer and man,' he wrote. 'It gave us a tremendous feeling of achievement to drive over the big bridges into the town. It was an added satisfaction to know that we had not had to pay too high a price.'[41]

THE DEFENDERS OF LIEPĀJA BREAK OUT...
26 JUNE, LATE EVENING

Two hundred miles away, the resolve of the defenders of Liepāja was crumbling. One Communist Party functionary wrote a scathing indictment of the port's defence, claiming sailors and soldiers 'considered it their duty not to defend the city, but to break the siege... Everyone is saving themselves as best they can,' he reported. The criticism was unfair – and largely unfounded. The garrison had held out for three days against the German onslaught. But now the two coastal batteries which had kept the Germans at arm's length were down to just ten shells per gun and pounded repeatedly by the Luftwaffe. In trying to defend them – and the city – the anti-aircraft batteries fired two-thirds of their ammunition. The Red Air Force could offer no relief; Liepāja's airbase had been wiped out on the first day of war.

With the skies undefended, Liepāja suffered terribly under German shells and German bombs. Perhaps as many as 77 civilians died when one of the newest, best-equipped shelters took a direct hit. Almost the entire length of Vitolu Iela – a residential street on the edge of the city centre – was flattened. From the relative safety of a neighbouring shelter, one householder watched 'huge columns of dust and splinters of wood thrown up in the surrounding houses'. After the bombs came the artillery. 'The howling of shells was unbearable, but even more horrible were the faces and screams of the wounded,' the anonymous resident wrote. When there was a lull, around 250 people emerged from the shelter. 'I went to our home,' the diarist continued. 'Only the foundations remain. I can't make myself understand – I don't even mourn the loss of my belongings.' Twenty-one-year-old Valija Imbovicas volunteered to help Liepāja's wounded, accompanying medics after such air raids. 'During the raids, the city was in panic – people were running, screaming for help. We didn't ask anyone who was injured if they were a Communist or anything else, we just did what we could to save them,' she recalled. 'When I went to the ambulance after an air raid, people looked at me with horror, because my whole gown was soaked in the blood of the wounded.' There were many beyond saving. Liepāja's streets were littered with 'people's heads, feet, hands, even whole families were lying on the ground'.

Even now, as Soviet authority in Liepāja waned, its *apparatchiks* sought vengeance. Kārlis Siljakovs – who would go on to head the secret police in Liepāja under the German puppet regime – claimed the NKVD roamed the streets of the port, arresting political opponents according to a prepared list. But they also seized any Liepājan who ventured into the city – some out of curiosity, some looking for food. Anyone carrying binoculars or observed on a rooftop was regarded as a German spy. All were taken to the NKVD headquarters, the basement of an imposing five-storey apartment block known as *Zilo brīnumu* – the Blue Miracle – due to its paint scheme. And there they were executed, 18 souls on one day alone (five wounded prisoners survived by hiding beneath the bodies of the dead). 'It was not the danger of war that we feared. But the city was threatened by Communist terror, and the population could be forcibly involved in the defence of the city,' recalled writer Arturs Plaudis, who somehow escaped the Stalinist dragnet. But it was also clear to Plaudis that the days of Soviet rule in Liepāja were numbered as he walked through the city centre 'sensing the mood'. Many of his fellow inhabitants had already abandoned the city, fleeing via the popular cycle path to the village of Grobina, four miles to the east. The defenders they left behind – soldiers, sailors, marines, militia and Liepāja residents unwillingly forced to fight – were 'shabby, sweaty, huddled in dense rows'.

With such men, Twenty-Seventh Army's commander Nikolai Berzarin – completely out of touch with the situation on the coast – intended to carry out an orderly withdrawal towards Riga, more than 130 miles away, even taking along the families of Party leaders and valuable port infrastructure. Liepāja's last defenders drew up more practical plans – an escape by land and sea. Having fired their last rounds, the coastal batteries were blown up – the signal for the defenders to begin their breakout along the coast towards the port of Ventspils, or Windau to the Germans – 70 miles to the north. The transporter *Vieniba* slipped away from the naval base carrying the families of soldiers and the wounded, escorted by three torpedo boats. They were barely a dozen miles from their destination when they were pounced on by the Luftwaffe. The *Vieniba* was sunk, taking with her an estimated 800 souls. Six German *Schnellboote* clashed with the Soviet torpedo boats, sinking one and damaging another. Naval base commander Mikhail Klevensky and his staff escaped in the third, eventually reaching the island of Saaremaa in the Gulf of Riga. The short, determined, but fruitless defence of Liepāja cost the Soviet Navy one destroyer, five submarines, around 15,000 tonnes of fuel, 146 torpedoes, 3,532 mines and about 3,000 depth charges destroyed or captured in the port itself.

The breakout on land was even more bloody. It should have been a co-ordinated affair, but 67th Rifle Division's commander had been killed in an artillery strike and communications across the city had been cut. Two groups – one fighting its way north through the sand dunes, the other striking out to the northeast – attempted to force their way through the German ring of encirclement. At 10am on 27 June, after a 15-minute barrage, the assault began. Pushing east was a motley assortment: a few tanks, trucks, guns and several hundred troops – riflemen, border guards, sailors from the scuttled submarines and ships, and naval cadets. They were poorly armed – the men had no grenades and only a couple of light machine-guns, the cadets were restricted to 60 bullets, the artillery barely any shells – and poorly led. The cadets were cut down almost immediately by a wall of machine-gun fire, while the columns got no further than the highway running out of Liepāja to the northeast – dubbed the 'Red Road' by the besiegers – where they too ran into enemy fire. 'A shell hit one of the lead tanks which exploded and set several more on fire,' Major General Ivan Blagoveschensky recalled. 'There was terrible chaos when the ammunition began to detonate.' Those Red Army soldiers who did make it through enemy lines did so on foot. The Red Road was littered with the detritus of cut-down Red Army units: half a dozen tanks, more than 40 trucks, heavy artillery pieces, and especially the dead. 'They had all taken off their uniforms – something which was a novelty to us,' marine infantryman Fritz Dallmeyer recalled. And there was something else unique: dead female soldiers. 'We had to steel ourselves for the enemy's completely new way of fighting: women with weapons, that didn't exist in Germany yet and it wasn't easy for us to deal with.'

Ivan Blagoveschensky told his captors that 'most of the breakout succeeded, but in complete disarray'. In fact few, if any, of Liepāja's defenders escaped along the Red Road. The breakout along the coast proved more successful. Perhaps 2,000 men reached Russian lines.[42]

'THE HOUR OF RECKONING HAS COME…'
POGROMS AND ANTI-JEWISH ACTIONS AGAINST
LITHUANIA'S JEWS, 26–28 JUNE

'I see war, the murder of the innocent, destruction, death, hate, fear, brutalisation, simplification, hardening, intellectual decline, fires, corpses, malice,' Elena Kutorgienė-Buivydaitė recorded in her diary on Thursday 26 June. Through the window of her apartment at her eye clinic in Kaunas' Kanto Street, the 52-year-old doctor continued to cautiously observe the pogrom raging through her city, now into its third day. The masses acted just as they had done 12 months previously when the Soviets marched in – only then the armbands on their sleeves were Communist red, not the yellow, green and red of Lithuania, and their victims were the country's ruling classes. Now it was the city's Jews, more often than not betrayed by caretakers and concierges, who were at the mercy of the mob. Trucks drove down streets, screeched to a stop, and the militia poured out, smashing down the doors to apartment blocks. Seconds later the street was filled with screams and cries in Yiddish before several shots rang out, the militia returned to their vehicles and drove on. An armed raider who plundered the apartment of Don Levin's grandfather 'boasted about how many Jews he had killed – and to prove it he showed us their blood-stained passports'. And when they didn't shoot Jews, they bundled them into vans and drove them to the city's prison, or else a baying mob hounded them through the streets. Some Jews chose suicide over the horde. At least two doctors Kutorgienė-Buivydaitė knew took their own lives – one killing his entire family. A Jewish Merciful Sister carrying a briefcase was shot dead; inside, supposedly, were bullets and grenades. In Šilainiai, on Kaunas' northwestern fringes, a handful of Jews were arrested dressed as nuns and carrying ammunition. One group of Jews was forced to haul a tank from the bank of the Neman to Kaunas' historic town hall; others were forced to lie in the streets and clear up manure – by nudging it along with their faces. Their fate thereafter was invariably death. So numerous were the corpses in the city's streets that the provisional government belatedly took action; it took on extra staff to bury the dead. 'The executions are heartbreaking and almost unbearable: every family member – young and old – is shot,' Archbishop Juozapas Skvireckas observed. Yet he too shared many of his compatriots' antisemitic tendencies, continuing in his diary: 'But then their crimes are inhumane: they had lists of Lithuanians who had to be shot or killed somehow compiled. Jews possess a good deal of sadism.'

And after the killings and roundings up, the plundering. 'All day long people with victorious faces and armbands in Lithuania's national colours hurried through the streets, forcing their way into houses, taking away Jewish possessions in broad daylight – even down to the last piece of junk,' Kutorgienė-Buivydaitė wrote. 'It is like an epidemic, an outbreak of greed.' One of her friends, appalled by the murderous rampage, nevertheless believed her fellow Lithuanians were seeking revenge for 'Jewish "domination"'. Kutorgienė-Buivydaitė witnessed plenty of vengeance, but little justice, merely 'blind hatred – a hatred which is obviously nurtured and stoked by base and selfish motives and makes me shake.' That blind hatred was about to reach its bloody climax not a mile from Kutorgienė-Buivydaitė's clinic.[43]

There was no such pogrom in Lithuania's capital, but the Jews of Vilnius felt the hatred of their countrymen all the same. They faced abuse as they stood in line outside shops with Poles and Lithuanians, who pushed them to one side, and frequently beat them, screaming: 'Dirty Jew!', 'Communist!' or 'Get your bread from Stalin!' When restrictions were imposed, shopping was limited to two hours in the late afternoon – by which time the shelves were largely empty. As for Jewish stores, they were immediately raided by the police, their wares seized. Officers did not stop there. They confiscated Jews' bicycles, telephones and radios. Jews were barred from almost every public institution – swimming baths, hospitals, cinemas and theatres – dismissed from the university, forbidden to travel by train. And they were forced to wear a *Schandzeichen* – a sign of infamy – in the form of a small yellow circle on the front and back of their coats bearing the letter 'J'. Nationalist Algirdas Gustaitis did not believe the branding, the curfews, the restrictions went far enough. 'Jews and Bolsheviks are one and the same,' he wrote. 'Vilnius has so far shown too much tenderness towards Jews. They were spared bullets to the forehead, even though in a number of cases these hideous creatures shot at Lithuanian or German fighters.'

Journalist Grigory Shur was struck by the plight of Jewish orphans, thrown onto the streets when children's homes were closed – the youngsters had practised pro-Soviet songs during Communist rule, according to one denunciation. 'These children wandered through the streets with their little bundles, asking passers-by where they should go,' he observed. 'But who was prepared to open their door to an orphan when the entire city had been turned to stone by fear?'

Vilnius' new German military authorities seized at least 60 Jews – plus 20 Poles for good measure – as hostages in a bid to ensure the obedience of the city's inhabitants. The Jews were held in a single cell in the city's infamous Lukiškės prison for nearly a month with no news from the outside world. On 22 July, all 80 hostages were ordered into the jail courtyard. Six doctors and engineers were singled out. They would be the only people released. The rest were executed.

Worst of all, however, were the packs of militia dubbed *chapunes* – grabbers – who 'lacked any scruples' and whose sole mission it was to hound the Jewish populace. Any Jew found on the city's streets without a work permit was promptly dispatched to Lukiškės prison. Few returned. And so, as Shur observed, 'Jews crept away like mice into their holes. No-one dared to leave their homes out of fear of being arrested and shot.'

Not that staying at home offered any protection. The concierges of Vilnius proved every bit as willing as those in Kaunas to betray Jews in their apartment blocks. During one raid, the grabbers found a friend of Abraham Sutzkever hiding in a cupboard and hauled him out into the courtyard. 'The Jew tried to buy his freedom – but he did not have enough money,' wrote Sutzkever. 'He asked his grabber, whom he knew as a student from university, "Knock out my gold teeth but let me live."' The grabber did as Sutzkever's friend pleaded.[44]

Across Lithuania, the void between Soviet and German rule was quickly – and bloodily – exploited by nationalists who visited 'revenge' upon the country's Jews. Outside towns and cities nationalist partisans – never entirely supressed during the year of Soviet occupation – were now the only law, issuing bloodthirsty proclamations urging their countrymen to join them. 'The hour of reckoning has come,' one appeal declared. 'Let us wreak hundredfold vengeance on the Jews and Communists for shedding the innocent blood of our countrymen. *Our fellow Lithuanians: if you are among the living, join the struggle against Jewry.*'

'Let us pay the Jews back in kind – in blood,' another poster proclaimed, while a third warned the Jewish populace: 'After being ravaged and mauled by you, *Lithuania is ready to rise up.* Freedom will come to us over your corpses.'

These were not idle threats. Outside Šiauliai, partisans – distinguishable from the mob by their white armbands – drove a group of naked Jews into a river and shot them. In the village of Ramygala, 50 miles north of Kaunas, one Jew was buried alive upside down, leaving only his feet sticking out of the ground, while the rabbi was tied to a cart and driven around the countryside until he died of exhaustion. A dozen or so miles away in Šėta, Rabbi Yehoshua-Aharon Levi was ordered to tear up the Torah scrolls. He refused – and was shot on the spot.[45]

On Friday morning 44-year-old Lothar von Bischoffshausen drove through the streets of Kaunas. His master, Wilhelm Ritter von Leeb, wanted a field headquarters closer to the front than the health spa near the East Prussian town of Insterburg which the staff of Army Group North currently occupied. As von Bischoffshausen moved down Vytautas Prospekt – the main road linking the city centre with the railway station – he saw a large crowd gathered around a petrol station. Children rode on shoulders or else stood on wooden crates for a better view of the spectacle. With the wall of applause and sound of laughter coming from the garage forecourt, the German officer was convinced they were watching some sort of victory celebration, or perhaps a sporting contest. Von Bischoffshausen asked one of the bystanders what was taking place and was told the 'Death-dealer of Kaunas' was at work, delivering justice to Lithuanians who had collaborated with the Soviets. The officer climbed out of his staff car and walked towards the filling station, used until a few days ago by the Lietūkis Co-operative Society. What he saw next, he testified two decades later, was 'probably the most gruesome spectacle that I saw in two world wars'.

In the middle of the courtyard a youngish man with striking blond hair, a jacket over a white shirt with sleeves rolled up in the June heat, and trousers pulled up high around his waist, rested on a stocky club, at least 5ft long. At his feet, perhaps 20 corpses, their blood gently swilling into the gutter courtesy of a hose which was left running constantly. In the corner of the courtyard, armed men wearing the armbands of the Lithuanian militia guarded about 30 prisoners – every one of them Jews.

The victims awaited their fate silently, with dignity, calmly stepping forward when the 'Death-dealer' ushered them onto the forecourt. He swung his club over his head and beat them to a pulp to a soundtrack of approval from the crowd. Other militia joined in with cudgels and iron bars. A handful of prisoners were forced to smear a cloth in the blood of the dead, then dance around this makeshift red flag – until they too were killed.

A few bystanders voiced their disgust. 'A disgrace for Lithuania!' someone cried out before the crowd silenced him. A Lithuanian professor protested to a junior German officer 'at this bestial murder run riot'. He did nothing. Nor did von Bischoffshausen, or any of the German soldiers milling with the crowd – 'they had no orders to stop this blood court'.

'The behaviour of the civilians present – women and children – was unbelievable; after each killing, they began to clap,' a member of a German Army bakery company recalled. 'I stayed at the scene of this crime for around a quarter of an hour, long enough for the murderers to beat the victims until the last man was dead.' Upwards of 60 people died at the Lietūkis garage, among them a soap factory employee, musician, plumber, shopkeepers, even two schoolchildren.

Satisfied with their morning's work, the militiamen sat on a pile of bodies. Someone fetched a concertina and began to play the Lithuanian national anthem. The crowd sang and clapped along.[46]

'A BLOOMING TOWN TURNED INTO A FIELD OF RUINS...' LIEPĀJA, 28 JUNE

The war was on its seventh day before German troops finally moved into the heart of Liepāja. A Stuka assault 'clobbering' enemy positions preceded the advance by marines and soldiers through the goods yards in the south of the city to the suburbs, where they came under sustained fire from enemy soldiers occupying houses, cellars and rooftops. Light flak guns poured rounds into apartments occupied by Soviet snipers, hand-grenades were tossed into nests of resistance, houses burned furiously and thick smoke spilled into the streets where Russian shells fell 'like raindrops'. Red Army troops held out in a sausage factory until a field gun was brought up and aimed into the building. The defenders soon streamed out of the burning structure and were taken prisoner.

The advance stopped again at the canal linking the Baltic with the lagoon which separated Liepāja from the mainland; the only bridge spanning the waterway was rigged to explode, the detonator controlled by troops occupying houses on the far side. Pioneers refused to risk trying to cut the cable, forcing the army to move up heavy mortars. The marines on the south bank were worried – the targets were barely 400ft away and mortars were an imprecise weapon at best. 'We hear them wailing over us terrifyingly and everyone wonders whether they're going to fall short,' wrote Fritz Dallmeyer. 'No, not this time. The earth trembles from the tremendous explosions, smoke and dust spreads out and nothing can be seen of the enemy.'

When the smoke cleared, the marines could make out animated voices across the water; the defenders were evidently quarrelling over whether to surrender. The Germans used loudspeakers to encourage desertion, broadcasting repeatedly in Russian and Latvian: 'We won't do anything to you. We're only killing Jews and Communists.'

As it was, with the bridge now crossed, resistance quickly crumbled. By mid-afternoon, the old fortress and main post office were in German hands. Surveying 'liberated' Liepāja, a German war correspondent found 'a blooming town turned into a field of ruins. Dead Bolsheviks – mostly sailors and armed civilians – lay everywhere.' Entire streets had been flattened south of the canal which split Liepāja in two. Barely any structure from the 18th or 19th centuries in the city's historic heart was left intact, while two in every five buildings city-wide were destroyed – some German officers referred to the devastation as 'the second burning of Rome'.[47]

Although the city had been captured, there were still Soviet forces in outlying military installations such as the barracks, airfield and coastal batteries. Petrol was poured into some pillboxes and set alight to force the defenders to surrender. 'But even after this the enemy ran out of the burning pillbox, attacked and inflicted losses on us,' one German report noted. 'This is evidence of the Bolsheviks' exceptional stubbornness in battle.' Other isolated groups made a final, desperate attempt to break out. They were cut down mercilessly. Germans justly dubbed the main route leading out of Liepāja 'the road of horror', as war correspondent Walter Melm noted:

Exploded ammunition trucks which tore apart the vehicles following them, burned-out tanks, medium flak which had tried to take up position. All around the column of vehicles, which stretches for more than a kilometre, dead Bolsheviks. Many drivers were killed behind their steering wheels, others while they tried to get out and others in the roadside ditch where they sought cover. There must have been wild panic – some of the vehicles tried to reach open ground by driving over the dead and wounded. They did not succeed.

The Courland countryside was littered with abandoned ammunition and weapons, shot-up tanks, radio trucks, searchlights, cars, buses, anti-aircraft guns, even rubber pontoons and bridge-building equipment. And there were bodies: cadavers of horses and corpses of soldiers. 'And above everything,' Melm observed, 'there's the foul, sweet smell of decomposition beneath the radiant sun.' German reporters touring Liepāja's smouldering ruins claimed they found 17 civilians tortured to death – noses and ears cut off, eyes gouged, tongues and fingernails ripped out – in one former barracks, while upwards of 500 local inhabitants were reportedly executed by the Soviet authorities in the final three days of their occupation.

Arturs Plaudis welcomed the invaders as liberators. 'Foreign soldiers met strangers in a foreign land and behaved like human beings towards fellow human beings,' he wrote. 'German soldiers, offered festive goodies, became even more talkative, took out their wallets and showed family photos. None of the furtiveness, mistrust, brutality, stupidity of the Russians.' Valija Imbovicas remembered simply: 'As soon as the Germans appeared, we could breathe…'

But Liepāja's new masters proved just as ruthless as its former overlords. Within hours of entering the city, Germans in uniform – eyewitnesses were unable to distinguish between soldiers and the security services – shot seven Jews and 22 Latvians next to a bomb crater which then conveniently served as their grave, while the Jewish émigré composer and director of the town's opera, Walter Hahn, was roused from his apartment, shot in the courtyard and buried next to rubbish bins.

The bitter six-day struggle for Liepāja turned out to be even bloodier for the attackers than the assault on Brest fortress: more than 850 men killed and total casualties well in excess of 1,600. It was the only concerted effort by the German Army to defeat Red Army forces in Courland during the first week of the invasion. The peninsula's defenders would simply be cut off, trapped by a bold dash for Latvia's capital.[48]

'No Russian must be allowed to save himself by crossing the Düna...' The drive on Riga, 28–29 June

For five days, the East Prussians of 1st Infantry Division had marched swiftly, if unspectacularly, across Lithuania. By nightfall on the 27th they were the very tip of Eighteenth Army's spear impaling the Northwestern Front, barely ten miles from the Latvian border and little more than 50 from the capital Riga. The moment had come for a daring lunge along the main road to seize the city and trap the remnants of Soviet Eighth Army. It was, remembered Otto Lasch – the man chosen to lead the thrust – a mission 'which suited the bold East Prussian soldiers down to the ground'. Just turned 48, Lasch had fought on the Eastern Front a generation before as a junior officer, then re-trained as an aerial observer. After 15 years as a policeman, he re-joined the army when it emerged from the shadow of Versailles in 1935. Now the Silesian was put in charge of a scratch force of infantry – roughly two regiments strong – bolstered by several assault guns. As 27 June turned to 28 June, *Kampfgruppe* (Battle Group) *Lasch* began its march on Riga.

By mid-day on Saturday Lasch's men were in Bauska, 40 miles from the capital. That afternoon they forced the Mēmele nearby, prompting a determined response from the Soviets, who were finally stopped by a combination of Lasch's *Sturmgeschütze* and the end of daylight. The group rested briefly before resuming its advance at 3am on Sunday, brushing aside disorganised enemy resistance which crossed its path, including two batteries of motorised artillery. One after another small towns on the road to Riga were passed. Iecava. Misa. Kervaka. A Red Air Force reconnaissance aircraft flew over Lasch's formation and dropped orders: *Return to your winter quarters immediately!* 'So onwards,' wrote Lasch. 'The surprise had succeeded!' At 10.20am on 29 June, the first of his vehicles were rolling through the outskirts of Riga and making for the three crossings over the Daugava – the pontoon, road and rail bridges.

Lasch's vanguard of assault guns drove straight over the road bridge while pioneers edged along the railway line, cutting the cables to the demolition charges as they went. Five assault guns, a handful of mobile flak guns, an anti-tank gun and a mixed group of infantry and pioneers, some armed with flamethrowers, reached the opposite side of the Daugava before the Soviet rearguard defending the crossings woke up. The pontoon and road bridges collapsed into the fast-flowing waters as the explosive charges were detonated, but, thanks to the disruptive efforts of the pioneers, only some of the spans on the rail crossing tumbled into the Daugava; troops could still file across, albeit hazardously, but not vehicles.

Not that Otto Lasch could spare any men to send over the river, for as his column reached the approaches to the road bridge, it ran into Soviet troops also making for the Daugava – hoping to flee over the river. The resulting fighting, Lasch reported, was 'wild' and 'hand-to-hand', with every man reaching for his weapons; he claimed he personally knocked out one Soviet vehicle using his carbine. Russian snipers picked off his men from cellars and rooftops. Several tanks succeeded in smashing their way into the heart of Lasch's detachment. They were stopped only by his men fixing shaped charges to their hulls or tracks.[49]

Precarious though the German position was, the lunge towards Riga had caught the Soviet Eighth Army entirely by surprise, as 21st Infantry Division discovered marching on the Latvian capital to reinforce Lasch. Three vehicles suddenly pulled onto the main road and tried to slip into the German column as it moved off following a brief halt – convinced they were re-joining Red Army units falling back on Riga. The cars carried the staff of a Soviet corps, who now fell into German hands. 'We never captured Russian generals so cheaply again,' company commander Udo von Ritgen wryly observed.[50]

Although he'd already moved his Northwestern Front's field headquarters to woodland 150 miles to the east, Fyodor Kuznetsov was determined to hold Riga. He blamed neither the Germans' rapid advance, nor his own ineffective leadership, but the Eighth Army's commander, Petr Sobennikov. 'You criminally left forces to the mercy of fate and covered your own hides,' he rebuked Sobennikov, listing a litany of failures by his subordinate: failing to plan the withdrawal, failing to co-ordinate it, failing to lead it, failing to maintain radio communications 'because you know nothing and do not wish to know about your forces'. Kuznetsov demanded Sobennikov save all his men, regroup and stand firm in Riga; an umbrella of Soviet fighters and bombers would shield the retreat. Fyodor Kuznetsov had lost touch with reality.

There was, however, some justification to his criticism of Eighth Army's commander, as the Red Air Force's Andrei Rytov discovered when a military truck pulled up at his airfield near Riga. A tired but cheerful and suntanned Petr Sobennikov climbed out of the vehicle and presented himself, holding out a dry, sinewy hand: 'What do you know of the enemy and have you seen elements of my army?' he asked.

'I saw a small group of people and individual vehicles, but I did not ask where they were heading,' Rytov responded.

Aircraft were dispatched to reconnoitre the roads leading to and from the Daugava. When they returned, Sobennikov studied the photographs taken and the map, then muttered: 'It's bad.'

'Where are you going to make a stand?' Rytov asked.

'Oh, my friend, do you think I know?' Eighth Army's commander glibly replied. He ate a quick meal and continued on his journey out of the city.[51]

It wasn't only Petr Sobennikov who left Riga at the mercy of the Germans. Gone too was the Communist Party. It fled Latvia's capital on the night of 27–28 June and attempted to re-assert its authority over the country from the town of Valka, 100 miles to the northeast on the border with Russia. The defence of the city rested upon the shoulder of Latvian Communists, the Workers' Guard, established the previous year supposedly to restore public order. Three battalions were hastily mobilised, issued a variety of rifles – almost all of them obsolete – grenades and ammunition, and began to occupy key points around Riga. Few men had served before. Now they had a matter of hours to learn how to handle arms. Joining them were the remnants of Sobennikov's army – if it could reach the right bank of the Daugava. 'We'd not eaten for more than a day,' one of them remembered, 'but the hope that we would re-join our units or join the partisans gave us strength.' Yet at every homestead they came across on the left bank, the stragglers of Eighth Army learned that the German Army had already passed through – after warning the farmers that 'anyone who helps or hides Russian partisans will be shot'. The only salvation lay in reaching the opposite bank of the Daugava.[52]

By late Sunday afternoon, Otto Lasch's scattered groups began to notice Soviet troops moving into Riga's western suburbs, feeling their way towards the river 'in endless columns'. The Germans barricaded the two main roads, but the Russians simply spilled through the houses and apartment blocks. 'Every house is occupied. There's shooting from windows and cellar windows,' Lasch wrote. 'What matters now is offering the most dogged resistance against the far superior enemy who's pushing from the west. No Russian must be allowed to save himself by crossing the Düna.'

German soldiers carrying demolition charges knocked out heavy Soviet tanks – killing themselves in the process. One attempt to break through to the river faltered near the Lutheran cemetery, straddled by the main railway line and road leading to Jelgava, 'leaving masses of dead Russians in front of German lines'. The final assault at dusk was supported by three dozen tanks and armoured vehicles – all of them picked off by Lasch's anti-tank gunners. The streets of Riga's suburbs were filled with abandoned and burned-out tanks, armoured cars and trucks, their crews lying dead or dying by the road. As far as Otto Lasch was concerned, the crisis had been overcome.

Not so on the right bank of the Daugava. Despite being wounded three times, Gottfried Geisler and a handful of his men somehow crawled across the remains of the railway bridge under the cover of growing darkness to report the annihilation of the spearhead which had tried to force the river. First the flak guns were knocked out. Then most of the infantry. Next came the pioneers. And finally, after several hours of bitter fighting, all the assault guns were eliminated. There was now no German alive on the opposite side of the river.[53]

'THE GERMAN PEOPLE ARE SENDING YOU THEIR SOLDIERS TO FREE YOU FROM THE BOLSHEVIK YOKE...' JELGAVA, 29 JUNE

This Sunday German arms proved more successful in Latvia's fourth city, Jelgava, a couple of dozen miles southwest of the capital. Jelgava had been bypassed by Otto Lasch's dash to Riga, but it was events further upstream on the Daugava which brought the war to the city in earnest. When German forces crossed the river at Krustpils, all Soviet forces in Latvia west of it were in danger of being cut off. Eighth Army began falling back pell-mell towards Riga. For many, the routes of retreat converged on Jelgava. Having assured the city's residents through the Party organ *Zemgales komunists* that the German attack had not merely been stopped 'but the insolent, uninvited guest has been driven back to where he came from', most Communist authorities had abandoned Jelgava on the night of 26–27 June. The next morning, the militia of the Workers' Guard battalions followed them. Soviet accounts claim the roads out of Jelgava were lined with tables, laid with bread and milk, as Latvian civilians cried. The recollections of Paulis Cukurs, serving with the Communist militia, seem more accurate. 'We marched in columns on both sides of the road,' he recalled four decades later. 'Weapons at the ready, barrels pointed at house windows – in case saboteurs opened fire on us.' The procession of Soviet units passing through Jelgava – 23rd and 28th Tank Divisions, 10th Rifle Division, XII Mechanised Corps – became increasingly dishevelled and disorganised, the Riga highway a road of death as the Luftwaffe hounded the unmissable, endless column of tanks, trucks, and tractor- and horse-drawn artillery. The last train pulled out of the city late on 28 June. It had barely crossed the Lielupe, which split Jelgava, when pioneers blew up the bridge. Their comrades only succeeded in damaging the road bridge, but they did destroy classified documents and cipher machines, rendering communications between Eighth Army and its units impossible. Its headquarters sent a reconnaissance aircraft over Jelgava to ascertain the situation – only for Soviet gunners to open fire despite clearly visible Red Stars on its wings.

Twenty-year-old Artur Nepart – volunteering with nationalist Latvian partisans – had watched Soviet rule in his city collapse. He'd observed 'widespread nervousness in the police headquarters'. Telephone lines were down so motorcycle dispatch riders constantly arrived from or set off for Riga. When several trucks appeared, police officers fought for spaces in them. A senior figure fired two pistol shots into the air in a vain attempt to restore order. As the Communists and Soviet forces departed, the partisans temporarily filled the void. They urged food stores to open for at least a couple of hours every day, bakeries to continue to operate, farmers to bring milk, meat and vegetables into the city. They took over policing duties – a white band on the left arm proof of their 'authority' – and conducted patrols, guarding key institutions and buildings. They recovered a rich haul of Russian weapons from the abandoned airfield, although there was little ammunition, and dug out the red-white-red flags of independent Latvia, banned for more than a year, from attics and basements. On the morning of the 27th, a group of armed youths sought to liberate political prisoners. The NKVD had fled, taking all but around 100 prisoners with them. The corridors were filled with smoke from burning papers as the boys opened the cell doors and the inmates 'rushed out into the street like animals'. Yet Soviet rule in Jelgava had not entirely ended. A few hours later, trucks arrived to remove the last batch of prisoners only to find the prison empty. They did, however, find two drunken former inmates with a Latvian flag who were promptly executed.

And all the while 'hungry, ragged and tired' Red Army troops continually trudged through Jelgava from the south or west 'in a disorderly manner in small groups, even one-by-one'. Desperate for food, some exchanged their weapons for food from Jelgava's inhabitants. There was a final surge of Russian soldiers marching through during the night of 28–29 June, then no more. By 11am on Sunday the city was under German artillery fire. Around three hours later the first German troops cycled into Jelgava. Artur Nepart seized the opportunity to raise the national flag at the teachers' institute he was guarding with other youths. The boys chanted 'God Save Latvia' heartily. Soon every house in Jelgava was bedecked in red-white-red. Curious residents stepped out into the streets for the first time in days to welcome their 'liberators', while a small crowd gathered outside the Hotel Cera – commandeered as the new German headquarters, marked by a hastily produced swastika flag – in the market square to hear an officer address them. The new newspaper *Nacionālā Zemgale* – published under Nazi supervision – gushed: 'We salute the army of Great Germany – the liberator of the people of Latvia.' It also proudly reported that 'no excesses were noted when Germans entered Jelgava'. Perhaps it was true – but an appeal from Jelgava's new rulers, reproduced in the same edition, warned that a reckoning was coming:

> Latvians! The German people have no hatred towards Latvians. The German people are sending you their soldiers to free you from the Bolshevik yoke…
>
> The deceptive socialism of slavery under the Bolshevik tyrants has come to an end. The end of the Jewish exploiters!
>
> Western European culture is returning to you!
>
> Do not let the traitors of your people destroy your bridges, railways, towns and villages.
>
> Latvians! Down with the Bolshevik yoke!
>
> Long live our common cause and the well-being of your people!

Two days later the same newspaper published orders aimed at Jelgava's Jewish inhabitants. They were to be dismissed from their places of employment with immediate effect and, from 5 July, barred from a dozen city centre streets – if they lived there, they would have to abandon their homes – as well as all theatres, cinemas, museums and parks.[54]

'A SMOKING AND BURNING HEAP OF RUBBLE…' DAUGAVPILS, END OF JUNE

Four days after it had stunningly seized the bridges over the Daugava following its pell-mell dash to the river, 8th Panzer Division was still deployed around Daugavpils – much to the chagrin of Erich von Manstein. The LVI Panzer Corps commander was determined to push on, to continue driving into the Red Army's rear, to continue causing panic and confusion. Leave the scattered Soviet troops spread across southern Lithuania and Latvia to the infantry, he urged his masters; the panzers should continue along the road to Leningrad immediately.

Manstein's masters disagreed. Both Army Group North's commander Wilhelm Ritter von Leeb and *Panzergruppe* 4's Erich Hoepner favoured consolidation. Once *all* their armour, not just one solitary division – short of fuel, many of its panzers in need of repairs – was ready, they fully intended resuming the attack. It was, Manstein fumed, 'the safe decision. And so, for the immediate future, the goal of Leningrad receded into the distance, leaving us to mark time at Dünaburg.'[55]

But perhaps the safe decision was the correct one. At first light on 28 June, 46th Tank Division thundered down the highway to Leningrad, the vanguard of Dmitry Lelyushenko's under-strength and ill-prepared XXI Mechanised Corps. Despite its weaknesses, the corps smashed its way into Daugavpils' eastern suburbs, where its armour engaged panzers at point-blank range. When low on ammunition, Red Army crews resorted to attempting to crush and ram their foe. One Soviet soldier, Ivan Sereda, jumped onto a panzer and hacked its crew to death with an axe before using an anti-tank mine to destroy a second German tank. He would be named a Hero of the Soviet Union for his actions.

When the spearhead of 42nd Tank Division finally arrived, Lelyushenko threw eight tanks over the Daugava to strike into Manstein's rear. According to the Soviet corps commander, this surprise blow destroyed three dozen enemy vehicles, an entire company of infantry and part of LVI Corps' headquarters. German prisoners were sent back across the Daugava and paraded through villages still in Soviet hands. 'Let the people see that we are able to beat the Fascists,' detachment commander Aristarkh Goryainov declared.

In his memoirs, Dmitry Lelyushenko hailed his counter-attack as a victory. 'The outskirts and streets of Daugavpils were littered with hundreds of enemy corpses,' he recalled with relish. 'Fascist tanks were ablaze, the barrels of broken guns stuck out, and wrecked cars lay around.' Contemporary records describe his raid as a failure, one which dealt a severe mauling to his corps. Manstein dismisses Goryainov's raid as a minor attack which got close to his field headquarters but never seriously threatened them. Certainly by evening, Daugavpils was firmly in German hands – though some districts had changed hands three times. German aircraft hounded Lelyushenko's divisions. Fuel and ammunition ran low – supply columns could not get through – and the 39-year-old corps commander decided his position was untenable. He ordered his divisions to fall back three dozen miles to the east, convinced his day-long counter-attack had dealt his opponent a serious blow.[56]

The fighting reduced Daugavpils to 'a smoking and burning heap of rubble through which what is left of its intimidated inhabitants wander,' adjutant Hans-Günther Seraphim recalled. Barely a quarter of the peacetime populace remained, understandable for most of Daugavpils had been razed – burned down *after* the fighting; rumours circulated that the town's Jews, their numbers swelled by an influx of refugees from Lithuania, were to blame (five were supposedly 'caught in the act' and shot on the spot). Such arbitrary 'punishment' was followed by an organised round-up of every Jewish male aged between 16 and 60. Some were promptly marched off to prison – more than 1,100 would subsequently be shot by the SS and Latvian police; others were ordered to bury the dead from the recent fighting. And that was no small task, for the plains on both sides of the Daugava were strewn with the dead, as Gustav Klinter, a company commander in the newly arrived SS *Totenkopf* Division, discovered:

> Transports of prisoners, overturned enemy baggage vehicles, dead horses with the usual smell of decay, and abandoned field kitchens alongside our units racing for the front at high speed dominated the view.
>
> Over everything the sun blazing down mercilessly and clouds of dust. The air was filled with the battlefield's stench of decomposition and burning – all our senses and nerves already felt the breath of the front. To the right and left of the road there were steep embankments littered with abandoned enemy equipment. Suddenly all heads turned to the right. Like a symbol of all the destruction of war, the first dead of the Russian campaign lay before our eyes. The skull of a Mongol, distorted in its death throes, torn uniform, a naked abdomen shredded by shrapnel. The column continued, sped up, leaving the scene behind.

There were still injured and dead lying in the streets of the town itself. 'Intimidated civilians crawled out of their cellars, trying to scoop water from still-intact wells, staring with eyes still filled with horror at the panzers and motorised columns racing through the streets of the town,' Klinter wrote.

At least the Red Army depot in the citadel was intact – and now readily plundered by the advancing German soldiers. They grabbed rubber boots with their red lining – they would make ideal slippers to wear in some Moscow hotel. But they left the cotton jackets and trousers, perfect winter wear, for the war would be over long before then.[57]

'RALLY UNDER THE RED-WHITE-RED FLAG OF LATVIA...' RIGA, 30 JUNE–1 JULY

Otto Lasch spent the whole of the last day of June consolidating his position, driving the Red Army from Riga's western suburbs. The hastily formed Workers' Guard crumbled at the first sight of German troops. 'Dozens of vehicles carrying workers' units sped down the Pskov highway,' one Soviet officer fumed. 'The men yelled that they had been smashed to pieces and so on – they were in a state of complete panic.' Blocking detachments detained up to 300 of the fleeing militia, who were immediately sent back into Riga led by an NKVD officer. The stragglers of Eighth Army offered rather more determined resistance. They threw barricades of vehicles, carts and limbers across the street. They shot at the advancing Germans from cellars and roofs – and kept on shooting when the attackers had passed. To prevent Riga's populace joining in the fighting, every male of military age was rounded up by the Germans and sent to the rear. Houses and apartment blocks were set on fire to smoke out the Red Army, but few men gave themselves up – even as buildings threatened to collapse on top of them. And when the Germans finally reached the Daugava at dusk, 'liberating' 120 wounded men in one of Riga's hospitals along the way, they found themselves having to return to streets already swept to clear up nests of resistance which had resumed fighting. 'The few Russians who did surrender either gave the impression of being fanatical – or utterly apathetic,' one combat report observed. Otherwise, the main roads leading to the Daugava, the goods yard and the Martinya cemetery were filled with the detritus of a destroyed army: shot-up vehicles, abandoned weapons, the cadavers of horses, wrecked carts and bodies piled high.[58]

Nightfall this Monday brought no darkness to Riga. The ornate 418ft spire of St Peter's – the very symbol of the city – burned, then the rest of the church, for the third time in its 732-year history. The Germans would – wrongly – blame the retreating Red Army for torching the iconic building, rather than their own shells, for Red Army troops started numerous fires across the city, hampering the efforts of Riga's overwhelmed fire brigade. Fires in the western suburbs raged unchecked. Flames from blazing houses lit up the left bank of the Daugava – and prevented scattered groups of Russians reaching the opposite shore unseen; silhouetted against the glow of fire as they tried to make their way across the wooden bridge, still passable for those on foot, or using rubber dinghies, they were mown down or taken prisoner.[59]

While Otto Lasch slugged his way towards the left bank of the Daugava, pioneer commander Wilhelm Ullersperger had sent detachments across the river a few miles upstream – and found the opposite side devoid of the enemy. He began to ferry men across the river in small assault boats and an old Latvian steamer. It took all night, but by 7am on 1 July, Ullersperger decided the time had come to take Riga. His makeshift group of infantry, pioneers, a couple of 2cm flak guns and two assault guns cautiously edged into the capital's Moscow suburb – largely home to Russians, but also a substantial proportion of the Jewish populace – just south of the city centre. Moscow's inhabitants were as nervous as the invader. They offered no resistance. Nor did anyone else, until Ullersperger's men were just a few hundred yards from the main railway line – not half a mile from the heart of Riga. Here a small, forlorn group of Red Army troops – probably forgotten as their comrades pulled out – briefly held up the German advance until the assault guns and flak were brought to bear. Now the attackers came across the remnants of Lasch's spearhead – '69 dead German soldiers, tightly packed behind each other and on top of each other, and a line of shot-up cars, motorcycles and damaged assault guns on the road and rail bridges'. There was a sole survivor, a wounded man, stuck on the ruins of the railway crossing. All in all, Ullersperger wrote, it was 'a devastating sight'. No German soldier had advanced more than 100 yards beyond the end of the bridges before being cut down.[60]

For the first time in two days, the strains of '*Riga dimd*' – Riga Resounds, a 19th-century folk song – suddenly sounded over loudspeakers dotted around the capital. The signature tune of Radio Riga was quickly followed by another popular theme, and then the national anthem. The voice Rigans now heard was unfamiliar. 'Latvians, young and old unite. Greet the German soldiers with gratitude and joy and give them a helping hand wherever you can. Each Latvian is master in his own land. Rally under the red-white-red flag of Latvia.' The broadcast urged soldiers and public-spirited Latvians to report to Riga's central post office. The man behind the microphone was probably sound engineer Alberts Jekste. Pro-Soviet radio station personnel and NKVD officials had tried to destroy the broadcasting equipment before they fled Riga, but Jekste and his colleagues quickly repaired their rather amateurish sabotage. The brief broadcast brought the city to its feet. The peal of church bells echoed across the city. The streets filled with women and children, who assured Wilhelm Ullersperger that Riga was free of the enemy. It was not. As his group advanced on the main square, half a dozen Soviet soldiers hiding in one of the pontoons on the wrecked bridge opened fire. The cannon of an assault gun blasted the pontoon to bits. The corpses of the Russians were carried by the Daugava into the Gulf of Riga.

As Wilhelm Ullersperger's men combed through Riga, another 15 men from Otto Lasch's advanced detachment were discovered in a barracks, all dead, their corpses mutilated. They – and the rest of the ill-fated assault group wiped out on the east bank of the Daugava – were laid to rest in Riga's war cemetery with full military honours. The dash through Latvia and lunge across the Daugava cost Lasch 91 dead, just shy of 300 wounded and nearly 150 men missing – many of the latter murdered after they had fallen into Russian hands.

While his men cleared out any last pockets of resistance, Ullersperger was ushered towards Riga's finest hotel, the Hotel de Rome, where he was hailed as a 'liberator' by a civic representative and encouraged to address the city's inhabitants in the hope of restoring order and reopening stores and businesses. Put on air, the colonel declared 'ancient Riga free of the Bolshevik yoke' and assured Latvians the German Army would fight 'shoulder-to-shoulder' with them 'until the last Bolshevik is driven out of this land'. Ullersperger's address was brief and entirely in German, save for his final three words: '*Dievs, sveti Latviju*' – 'God bless Latvia', also the title of the country's national anthem, which was played after the German officer finished speaking.[61]

What followed went beyond anything witnessed in Kaunas or Vilnius; celebrations in Riga over the coming hours were more akin to those experienced in Austria, the Sudetenland or Danzig. As in Lithuania, the Germans were greeted by the Latvians as liberators. 'The soldiers hardly make progress through the streets,' one German war correspondent wrote. A passing motorcyclist was dragged from his bike, garlanded with flowers then thrown up in the air by a jubilant crowd crying 'Hurrah!' His comrades were showered with roses and cigarettes.

> Girls and women hand them tomatoes, cucumbers, bread and butter, beer, in short anything they can lay their hands on. There's no end to the applause, cries of '*Sieg Heil*', '*Heil* Hitler' and 'Bravo'. More and more people flock together. They come running wherever our *Landsers* are marching, wherever there's the clatter of caterpillar tracks. Men leap onto the vehicles and hug the soldiers. Buses and trucks adorned with the national flag drive down the wide streets and along the magnificent green gardens, past the wonderful buildings, and cries of sheer jubilation resound everywhere. Our vehicles are overflowing with flowers and gifts; but new gifts are constantly thrown our way.

To Walter Hubatsch, a signals officer with the 151st Infantry Regiment, the celebrations seemed macabre with the city in ruins. Fires still smouldered; the streets were littered with wrecked and burned-out armoured cars and tanks, abandoned guns. The bridges over the Daugava were in ruins, the old town, including the medieval House of the Blackheads and town hall burned out, and the ornate tower of St Peter's Church, the city's symbol, was now 'nothing more than a stump, towering above the fire-blackened façades of narrow lanes'. But then, as one Latvian eyewitness observed: 'Few cities had ever welcomed their own bombing as eagerly as Riga.'[62]

Away from the crowds, former policeman Viktors Arājs was attempting to establish order out of the chaos in Riga's police headquarters. The 31-year-old nationalist, anti-Communist and antisemite had spent the year of Soviet rule in hiding. Now he seized his chance. He and his band of like-minded partisans would put an end to any looting and arson. But above all, they would exact revenge against Latvia's oppressors.

Sometime that Tuesday afternoon, Arājs found Walter Stahlecker standing before him. The commander of *Einsatzgruppe* A – the SS task group charged with 'pacifying' the occupied territories – had sought out the police headquarters to begin his mission of ridding Latvia of undesirable elements. As Arājs explained what he intended to do with his small band of supporters, Stahlecker realised he was exactly the man he needed. Arājs was given a free hand to act against Jews and Communists as he pleased, with one proviso: they should look like spontaneous acts of revenge by the Latvian people.

As the celebrations continued, young Rigans ran through the streets thrusting copies of a newspaper into passing hands as they shouted: 'Free land for a free land.' While their compatriots partied, enterprising journalists Arturs Strautmanis and Adolfs Mežmalietis had started the printing presses of a journal for farmers for the first time in more than a year. *Brivais Zemnieks* (Free Peasant) became *Brīvā Zeme* (Free Land). There was little news in the first issue – it was just a single sheet of paper. There was a small portrait of Hitler, whose soldiers were hailed as 'our heroic liberators! Under the mighty blows of the German Army, the walls of the Kremlin are crumbling.' Now, 'after a year of darkness and slavery we are again a free nation, Latvians in beloved Latvia'.[63]

It was the only edition of *Brīvā Zeme* to appear. The German authorities refused to tolerate an independent newspaper, however pro-German the first edition had been, and published their own organ, *Tēvija* – Fatherland. 'Liberated' Latvia was no more a 'free country' than Lithuania before it.

For now, however, Rigans considered themselves liberated, and the city's Freedom Monument, spared demolition by the Soviet occupiers, became the focal point of celebrations. A Latvian soldier maintained a guard of honour in front of it, while a flood of Rigans placed flowers at the foot of the statue to Liberty. 'Today in Riga – and probably throughout Latvia – the spirit of freedom is characterised by the flying of our flags,' one contemporary Latvian account stated. 'There was no swastika flag to be seen, as it was when German troops marched into Vienna and Prague.'[64]

A crowd gathered too about half a mile further down Brīvības Street outside the former headquarters of the NKVD on the edge of the city centre. A young Latvian, armed with a pistol, called on his countrymen to fight alongside their 'German friends against the internal enemy – Communists and Jews'. The cells were empty – Stalin's police had succeeded in evacuating most of Latvia's prisons before fleeing, transporting more than 3,700 opponents of the regime to a hellish existence in the Gulag. And as elsewhere in Eastern Europe that week, when the means to move prisoners were lacking, they simply executed them: 78 in Riga on 26 June alone. Some were executed in the courtyard, others in the woods outside the city. The bodies of 98 victims were subsequently exhumed from the prison grounds; two dozen were never identified.[65]

Otherwise, Latvia's capital 'had a Sunday air about it,' junior doctor Bernhard Press noticed. Friends greeted each other with a mixture of relief and joy 'as though they had just survived a great danger together'. Teenager Valentīna Freimane noticed that Latvians cast aside their long-standing hostility towards Germany – 'all was forgotten in the shock felt during a single year of Soviet rule' – convinced their new rulers would allow them to turn the clock back 12 months and 'start life anew'. But as Jews, Bernhard Press and Valentīna Freimane sensed only danger. Freimane instantly regretted not fleeing with the Soviets and now was seized by 'feelings of doom and apprehension'. Henceforth, her life 'began to resemble a claustrophobic nightmare'. Bernhard Press at least enjoyed the 'protection' afforded by the small medicine kit he carried and the red cross on his sleeve. The 24-year-old had responded to the radio appeal to head to the right bank of the Daugava and made his way across the city, against the flow of German troops – 'strong, tanned fellows with rolled-up sleeves'. As he passed the Freedom Monument, his attention was seized by the sound of applause from a neighbouring street. Armed militia were leading a group of more than 30 Jews towards the river, where they would fill in the trenches dug by the Red Army. Riga's inhabitants evidently approved. 'I stood there as though in a daze,' Press remembered. 'What would these people do to me if they knew who I was?'[66]

'PLACE OF HORROR...' FORT VII, KAUNAS, 30 JUNE–6 JULY

For four or five days, Helene Holzman had made the forlorn trek from the family home in Kaunas' northern suburbs down to police headquarters. Both her eldest daughter Marie and husband Max had vanished in the chaos of mob rule on 25 June. Marie returned home after three days in custody having convinced a German official she was German. But not Max. Each day Helene stood before a different German official. Each day a different excuse. Sometimes they demanded a form filling in; on other occasions her pleas were dismissed out of hand. Helene Holzman presented her husband's World War I records and medals. 'We're not interested,' the SS official snarled. 'Jews are Jews.' Another day, the custody officer told the teacher to return in 24 hours; her husband would be waiting for her. He was not. She scanned the faces of Jews silently and sullenly trudging through the streets, escorted by rifle-wielding militia 'with hard cruel faces and arrogant steps'. Again and again, Max

Holzman was not among them. Finally she decided to head to the destination of these columns: Fort VII.

Built in the late 19th century as one of a series of fortifications ringing what was then Kovno in Tsarist Russia, the red-brick structure with its 200-strong garrison was intended to guard the main road to St Petersburg, yet fell to the Germans in 1915 without a shot being fired. They stripped the fort of almost all its weaponry so that when the war ended the army of a newly independent Lithuania turned it first into a depot, then into a repository for their archives. During the year of Soviet rule, the fort had been occupied by troops again, Red Army pioneers who left a hole 12ft deep and 30ft across in one of the ramparts after blowing up one of the five ammunition dumps before fleeing. On the last day of June, the Lithuanian Provisional Government decided to put the fort back into use as a concentration camp; Kaunas' prisons were overcrowded – there were at least 3,200 people in custody, more than half of them Jews – and the pogrom could not be allowed to continue unchecked. To bring order to the killings, and to do so out of sight, two companies from the newly formed labour battalions were charged with guarding – and executing – the arrested Jews.

The first prisoners were delivered to Fort VII shortly after mid-day on the 30th. Anyone wearing glasses was led away immediately and shot in one of the inner courtyards, while women and small children were separated from the men and locked in the casemates. The remaining prisoners milled around on the embankments or on the cobbles in front of the main barracks, while the labour companies stood guard above on the grassy embankments. Groups of five or ten prisoners at a time were led away and either forced to dig their own graves, or stand on the edge of the huge crater left by the Red Army pioneers. And there they were shot, all through the afternoon until the early evening.

Perhaps as many as 500 Jews were killed before a young Lithuanian dressed in a dark-blue air force uniform appeared and immediately took charge, ordering all those arrested to lie down in the courtyard. 'Everyone fell down on the spot where they'd been standing and most fell on top of one another,' remembered Yitzhak Nemenčik, one of the few eyewitnesses of the horrors played out at Fort VII.

> In a high-pitched voice, the officer yelled that every mangy Jew must lie there like the dead and must not move. Anyone who dared to move would get a bullet in the head. After he gave this order, he vanished. The Lithuanian guards who stood on the embankments all around followed the officer's order to the letter and carried it out. The densely packed crowd – lying on top of each other like herring in a barrel – could not remain like this for a long time.

People slowly began to straighten and stretch their limbs which were tensing up. There was an immediate hail of bullets into the crowd from the embankments and they were hurt. The groans of dying and moans of the wounded passed through the crowd. Then the murderers descended from the mounds to have those lying down dragged away with the order: Carry the wounded and dying away with your hands! So all night long from Monday into Tuesday bullets rained down on the crowd.

In the casemates, where temperatures rarely rose above 10°C and the walls were constantly damp, there was neither food nor water for those incarcerated. Occasionally, the doors would be opened and someone allowed to crawl out to the well only to be shot after taking a sip. Bread was provided only on the fourth day, but even then it was mouldy. And at least 30 women were raped by guards, who were drunk most of the time, then murdered.

German medic Heinrich Hippler was drawn to the fort by curiosity sparked by the constant shooting. He and several comrades scrambled up the earth-covered ramparts and witnessed the aftermath of one killing spree. Newly arrived Jews were made to bury those just shot, tossing their corpses into mass graves then covering the bodies with sand. Suddenly a Jewish woman, aged about 30, rushed up to him. Shot in the cheek, she saw the red cross armband on Hippler's sleeve and begged for help. He tried to pull a bandage from his pocket only to be halted by an armed German, a member of the security services. The Jewess didn't need the bandage, he told Hippler, driving the woman back into the fort. The medic was shocked, but did not intervene. 'Rebelling against the SS would have made no sense,' he testified two decades later. 'He'd have threatened to turn me to dust if I didn't leave.' Heinrich Hippler left Fort VII. He never returned. 'I did not want to go back.'[67]

The executions continued for at least five days. Priests attending to German wounded at a nearby military hospital heard 'the continuous fire of machine-pistols or machine-guns from sunrise until sunset' and even visited 'the place of horror', where they found open graves carved out of the ramparts and masses of Jews of all ages awaiting their fate in the courtyards. One chaplain was so horrified that he pleaded with his superior to intervene. The bishop merely told him to drop the matter. Nevertheless, one Austrian soldier succeeded in freeing five Jewish women and four men on the pretext that they were needed for a labour detail. And around 70 men were spared execution on the orders of Kaunas' commandant Jurgis Bobėlis because they had previously served in the Lithuanian Army.

Even after a week of killing, there were still 2,500 prisoners at Fort VII – the Lithuanian labour companies could not physically, or mentally, cope with killing more than 500 people a day.[68] The executions had to come to an end. They did. Bloodily, over the weekend of 5 and 6 July. The remaining prisoners were herded into the courtyard once used by the artillery and mown down by machine-gun fire, while guards tossed grenades down from the ramparts. When the shooting stopped, the men of the labour company moved among the bodies, delivering the *coup de grâce* to the wounded, while their comrades prised gold fillings from the teeth of the dead, removed gold rings and watches and stripped the corpses of clothes. When the few survivors left or hiding in the casemates crawled out on Sunday evening, they found the courtyard littered with bodies.

With the massacre at Fort VII over, the Kaunas pogrom came to an end. The fort served as a concentration camp for another month before being officially closed down in favour of another of the city's old fortifications, Fort IX, situated further out of town. The stench from the decomposing corpses lingered for weeks.

Some 6,000 Jews died during the first ten days of German rule in Kaunas, 1,000 or so during the anti-Jewish actions in the city itself, the rest in Fort VII. Only 93 of the victims in the fort were ever identified, for the men of the National Labour Protection Battalion kept no formal records. At the ages of 74 and 67, Yaakov Yaakov Rucheiski and Elchonon Wasserman were the oldest to die. Three members of the Wolpert family – Khaia Ana, Khana Khane and Aide Yehudit – perished alongside six-year-old Zlata Shapiro and Josef Yosef Brojda, not yet two.[69]

No-one made their way down the wide, poplar-lined avenue which led to Fort VII voluntarily. For most families it was an act of last resort to find their relatives. Some had even been able to talk to them, though few had succeeded in negotiating their release. Now, one evening in early July 1941, Helene Holzman stood in front of the main gate. She bribed the guard to look for her husband. He disappeared for what seemed like an eternity. 'No,' he told her, 'there's no Max Holzman.'

As she walked away, Helene Holzman passed a small store which was full of guards from the fort flirting with the attractive young owner, Wanda. Perhaps they might help.

'You should have told us that earlier,' one of the guards told Helene. 'Now many of them are already no longer there.'

'No longer there?' she asked. 'Where are they now?'

The guard was silent.

'I often went down the avenue, along which hundreds of Jews had been driven, most of whom were "no longer there",' Helene Holzman wrote in her memoirs. 'One of them was Max Holzman. He was my husband.'[70]

'SCREAMS WERE HEARD FROM EVERY DIRECTION…' POGROM IN RIGA, 2–4 JULY

Just three days after the fall of Riga, an artilleryman in 1st Infantry Division found 'normal city life pulsated again'. Yes, there were wrecked bridges and the blackened façades of houses and rubble, obscured to some degree by a 'colourful sea' of red-and-white national flags, but 'the people of Latvia truly breathed a sigh of relief – you could see it on their faces'. The gunner was struck by large numbers of 'student volunteers marching with fixed bayonets through the streets, ensuring order and peace'.

The first night of German rule in Riga had indeed passed relatively peacefully, thanks largely to a curfew in force from 10pm until 6am. But come daylight on 2 July, Jews felt themselves at the mercy of the city's new masters. For a start, they were banned from standing in line with fellow Rigans in front of the city's stores; they could only shop where there were no queues … and in July 1941, there were always queues. Far worse was befalling Jewish families across the city this Wednesday, however, as young Latvians, armed and with red-white-red armbands on their sleeves, forced their way into the homes of Jews – in places systematically, house by house – and led the inhabitants away to prison. Jewish families who lived in the apartment block at 19 Gogol Street, just south of Riga's central station, were betrayed by the building's concierge, who'd reported their presence to German authorities immediately. Groups of students rode up in horse-drawn carriages, burst into the property and drove 36 men, women and children into the street, where they were shot. All but two of the Jews died. In the Moscow suburb one SS officer ordered groups of Jews to march through the streets with portraits of Lenin and Stalin tied to their faces. Rifles were then thrust into the arms of Latvian youths. 'Shoot at the Bolsheviks!' Any youth who refused to fire was ordered to join the group of Jews. Elsewhere, one SS non-commissioned officer forced Jews to dig their own graves and lie in them to take the measurements. Only when they were entirely to his satisfaction did he shoot those condemned to death.

The atrocities continued after dark. Some Germans celebrated Riga's occupation with an orgy on the edge of the old town. Several dozen Jewish girls were brought along, forced to completely undress, then dance and sing. Many were raped before being led out into a courtyard and shot. One junior officer devised a 'game', tying girls to chairs with a small stove placed beneath the seat. As the girls writhed in agony, the soldiers danced around the chairs in glee. Whenever the victims tried to scream, filthy rags were stuffed in their mouths.[71]

The German soldier passing through the Latvian capital saw only 'righteous justice' applied. 'The atrocities we were told about by people in and around Riga and what we saw with our own eyes simply cannot be described,' one machine-gunner told his family. 'Children and old people were no exception to the crimes committed by these scoundrels. Many a mother stood in front of her son or husband who had been horribly mutilated and buried somewhere by the beasts.' Wherever caught, the soldier assured his parents, 'the Asian rabble were ruthlessly cleaned up'.[72]

The militia had already arrested Max Kaufmann's brother and son-in-law. On the second day of the round-ups, it was the turn of the 44-year-old businessman as armed youths burst into his apartment. Kaufmann and his son were hauled to Riga's police headquarters. On the way, the Kaufmanns – and other Jewish inhabitants of the same tenement – were beaten and abused by a mob screaming: 'Jews, Bolsheviks!'

In the police courtyard, Jews were led in naked, bleeding, beaten. Some were dragged around by their beards, women were stripped then taken down to the cellars and raped. Elderly Jews were subjected to jets of water, Jews with long beards were made to polish the shoes of Latvians with them. 'Screams were heard from every direction,' Max Kaufmann remembered, 'so horribly were the Latvian murderers tormenting their victims. Their sadism knew no bounds.' The Kaufmanns were somehow spared, but held overnight, then sent onto the streets of Riga in forced labour groups, made to fill in trenches or load tyres from a warehouse onto waiting trucks. And all the time they were at the mercy of their Latvian guards who struck out at random or made their Jewish prisoners sing the *Internationale*. It would, the police officers reminded them, be the last time they performed it.[73]

So far – and despite the authority given them by Walter Stahlecker – Viktors Arājs and his men had played no part in the round-ups. At dusk on Friday 4 July, they were unleashed with full fury against the capital's synagogues. It was time, Arājs told his men, to deal with the Jewish 'parasites' and their houses of worship. He plied some of his men with vodka before sending his wrecking parties into the Jewish district. At least three synagogues and prayer houses had been set ablaze – in the case of the building in Elijas Street, with worshippers still inside – before attention turned to the focal point of Riga's Jewish community. For 70 years the Great Choral Synagogue had dominated Gogol Street, the main road running though the Moscow suburb. For the past few days it had sheltered Lithuanian Jews, fleeing both Germans and their fellow countrymen. And, over the past 48 hours, Riga's Jews had also sought refuge there. But at sunset on the eve of the Sabbath, more than a dozen of Arājs' men suddenly pulled up outside the building, emptied the petrol from the fuel tanks of their vehicles, and doused the interior as they smashed it up, before Viktors Arājs himself gave the order to set everything alight. Having been released from police custody thanks to the intervention of a friend earlier in the day, businessman Max Kaufmann returned to his plundered apartment in time to watch from the balcony as flames engulfed the building. The Torahs, the holy scrolls, were dragged into the streets, defaced and defiled, then tossed into the flames. Jews, dressed in their prayer shawls, tried to save the scriptures, only to be shot in the attempt. Inside the blazing synagogue, Rabbi Kilov continued to read prayers, his voice audible above the roar of the flames. There was little such composure from those trapped in the cellar. 'The screams of the burning victims could be heard over a great distance and filled the souls of the people in the neighbouring houses with horror,' Bernhard Press remembered. A grenade was hurled in to silence them. Riga's firefighters looked on, ready to intervene only if the blaze threatened surrounding buildings, while any Jews who tried to save the synagogue were held back by Arājs' policemen.

Of some 40 Jewish sites across Riga, only the Peitav synagogue was spared this night – it was in the heart of the old town and a fire might spread. It was spared outwardly only. Like the capital's other Jewish prayer houses, its innards were plundered.

Thus ended Riga's three-day pogrom. Between 300 and 400 Jews had been killed. But there had been no 'spontaneous' uprising of the Latvian people. Almost every man had died at the hands of either the Latvian or German authorities. A few Rigans had joined in the Jew-baiting and taunting. Most simply wanted to resume their lives.[74]

'KEEP THE KNIFE AT THE ENEMY'S THROAT...' DAUGAVPILS BRIDGEHEAD, 1 JULY

At his new field headquarters hidden in the woods outside Rastenburg in East Prussia, Adolf Hitler was delighted with the success of his invasion – and impatient. In just one week, his soldiers were 'one-third of the way to Leningrad'. If they continued at the same pace they'd reach their objective inside a fortnight. Except that they weren't maintaining that initial tempo. Five days had passed since 8th Panzer Division's stunning coup at Daugavpils and still its armour lay within a stone's throw of the ruined town. Day after day, Erich Hoepner consolidated his position on the right bank of the Daugava, first Manstein's corps then Reinhardt's 50 miles downstream at Jēkabpils. It took four days for XLI Panzer Corps to extract itself from the chaos around Raseiniai and forge a bridgehead over the Daugava. Both bridgeheads had to endure determined Soviet counter-attacks and air raids, but even the cautious commander of Army Group North, Ritter von Leeb, was growing concerned at *Panzergruppe* 4's seemingly sluggish build-up. He sent his operations officer Helmut Staedke to light a fire under Erich Hoepner. 'Keep the knife at the enemy's throat,' Staedke reminded the *Panzergruppe* commander. Hoepner got the message. On 1 July he let his panzers off the leash at last. The advance would resume the following morning. The goal was 300 miles distant: Leningrad. 'Let this objective fire our spirits,' Hoepner exhorted.

'So tomorrow we're off again,' wrote 6th Panzer Division tank commander Wilhelm Sander. 'Who knows if the Russians will still make a stand.'[75]

The first stage of Army Group North's campaign was over.

4

TO MOSCOW

We are for peace!
We are not afraid
But if someone should strike a blow
We will respond

Slogan painted on a Stalin Line bunker

Racing through the night along the Brest–Moscow highway, gunlayer Richard
von Rosen cursed the road. It was marked on his map as a highway, but it wasn't
'even remotely like our autobahns'. Just an ordinary asphalt road. Still, by Russian
standards, it was good – and there was no straying from it, for to the left and
right lay the Pripet marshland where his Panzer Mk3 would quickly become
bogged down. In the half-light between night and day, Rosen could just make
out the triumphal arches at village entrances and exits, each adorned with the
obligatory portrait of Stalin, still standing seven weeks after 1 May celebrations
and still dressed with fir. It was evidently just for show – villagers lined the route
of advance, 'waving enthusiastically' and offering butter and eggs to the passing
panzer crews.

For Rosen, the advance was as frustrating as it was exhilarating. Yes, his
company was making excellent progress – nearly 40 miles in one night, without
any sign of the enemy. But it was trailing in the wake of 3rd Panzer Division.
Having captured two bridges intact, the Berliners had not spent the bulk of
Sunday waiting for a crossing to be built over the Bug.

By 9am, Rosen's 4th Panzer Regiment was moving through Kobrin. German
armour crossed the square where barely 24 hours before Ilya Starinov had been
struck by the surreal contrast between war raging and the loudspeakers urging

residents to conduct their morning gymnastic routine. The huge statue of Lenin still stood, but now was flanked by two abandoned Red Army tanks. A large fuel tank in a goods yard on the edge of town burned, but otherwise Soviet Fourth Army had left its warehouses intact. The booty was rich: luxury soap, shirts, underpants, underwear, blankets, sleeping bags, canteens, trousers, boots. There were Communist Party badges for souvenirs and, best of all, Dutch cheese. The tank men had no bread. It didn't matter. They ate the cheese all the same. With the men satiated, and with fuel tanks re-filled at a Red Army depot, 4th Panzer Regiment turned back onto the Moscow highway and continued eastwards.[1]

Richard von Rosen's unit was just one regiment in a huge armoured arrow which had punctured the Soviet defences around Brest on the first day of the war and were now driving deep into the Red Army's rear. If the campaign followed the *Barbarossa* plan, this armour – massed in Heinz Guderian's *Panzergruppe* 2 – would meet the tanks of Hermann Hoth's *Panzergruppe* 3 around Minsk, trapping the bulk of Soviet forces in Byelorussia. Behind them, two infantry armies – Ninth and Fourth – would meet east of Białystok and then begin the act of crushing the two gigantic pockets. While they did so, the panzers would repeat the manoeuvre, crossing the Dnieper, one of the great natural barriers of European Russia, before the armoured pincers met once again, this time around Smolensk.

The two *Panzergruppen* – soon to be renamed *Panzerarmeen* (Panzer Armies) – were the mailed fist of Army Group Centre, the strongest force the German Army wielded in June 1941: four armies, eight infantry corps, six panzer and motorised corps, more than 30 infantry or motorised infantry divisions, and nine panzer divisions with nearly 1,800 tanks – in total more than one million men under arms, led by a seasoned campaigner, Fedor von Bock: aristocratic, cool, serious, uneasy with the 'political' orders given to his men, and convinced the Red Army would never allow itself to be caught in the enormous trap his armies were about to spring.

His opponent was nearly 20 years his junior, possessed none of his airs and graces and, beyond command of an armoured brigade and a brief, unsuccessful few weeks leading a makeshift force in the war with Finland, little of Bock's front-line experience. The shaven-headed Dmitry Pavlov had fought bravely against the Germans a generation before as an ordinary soldier. But as commander of the Western Front – the Special Military District was immediately renamed with the outbreak of hostilities – Pavlov showed himself overwhelmed by events from the outset. His army group was two-thirds the strength of Bock's: 678,000 men. He had possessed 1,550 aircraft 24 hours before. Now that figure

Army Group Centre – smashing the Western Front,
27 June–8 July 1941

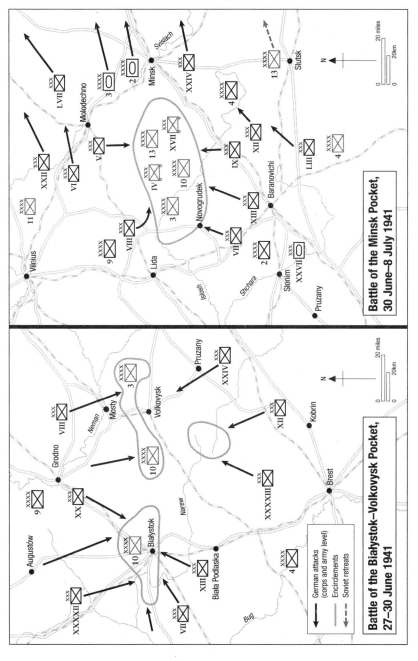

Battle of the Minsk Pocket,
30 June–8 July 1941

Battle of the Białystok–Volkovysk Pocket,
27–30 June 1941

had been halved. He still possessed more tanks than Bock: 2,200, nearly half of them – including 350 new T-34s and KV models – massed in the mighty VI Mechanised Corps which had yet to enter battle.

From the outset, Pavlov was hampered by the deployment of his forces: two armies – the Third and Tenth – and three mechanised corps were committed in the Białystok salient, protruding more than 80 miles into German-occupied Poland between Grodno and Brest. A rapid advance by German troops from Brest and Grodno could easily trap them. German armour had already brushed Fourth Army aside around Brest – with one eye on any future court martial, Pavlov had found a scapegoat in its young commander, Aleksandr Korobkov, who had 'lost control' of his men and then 'lost his head'.[2] In the coming days, the same could be said of Dmitry Pavlov.

GRODNO, 23 JUNE

A bold dash by cyclists at first light had caught the defenders of Grodno off guard and led to the stone bridge over the Neman in the city centre falling into German hands, opening the way to Białystok for Ninth Army. The Soviets tried – and failed – to re-take it, then tried – and failed – to hold Grodno itself. By mid-day German armour was rolling through the streets and over the Neman. So swift was the fall of Grodno that Soviet Third Army had no time to evacuate their headquarters. Gotthold Rhode, an interpreter and intelligence officer with 8th Infantry Division, found 'piles of excellent-quality maps of East Prussia, much better than our own'. Why, he wondered, did the Red Army need 'hundreds of maps of a neighbouring country?'

When Erich Mende's regiment marched through the city in the early afternoon, he found Grodno devoid of men – Party leaders and the garrison, plus all men of military age, had fled during the night. Women came out of their homes and handed the passing soldiers fruit and cigarettes, even cans of beer. The only disorder in Grodno was at the city's food depot, abandoned, unguarded, and now subjected to widespread looting. 'Anyone who could run, did so, panting with bags of flour and sugar, tins and boxes, dragging them, falling, yelling and cursing – a sight we'd not experienced before,' the officer recalled. Mende's commander Bernhard Pier immediately put a stop to the plunder.

Otherwise, Grodno was largely calm and intact. Most of its inhabitants – mainly Poles, but also many Jewish families – had stayed behind. Jewish youths in particular offered their services to the invaders: 'Good gentlemen from Germany, can I help you, what do you want?' they asked.[3]

'WE DIE WITHOUT DISGRACE...' BREST FORTRESS, 23 JUNE, 5AM–9AM

Daybreak at Brest found the men of 133rd and 135th Infantry Regiments pulling back from their exposed – and untenable – positions in the citadel and the fortress's West and South islands. In doing so, they immediately abandoned the hard-won ground to the garrison – and left behind their 50 or so comrades still holding out in the old garrison church. As the troops fell back, the citadel was subjected to a ferocious artillery barrage. 'Many of the soldiers were bleeding from the ears and nose,' one defender remembered. Some men lost their nerve and had to be restrained by their comrades. The White Palace, site of the 1918 peace negotiations with Germany, was flattened by a shell, burying alive around 50 men. Trapped in the ruins of the basement, one soldier used his knife to carve his final words in the brickwork: *We die without disgrace*. The barrage also subdued the snipers hiding in the trees – but only while the shelling lasted. When it stopped, the excellently camouflaged sharpshooters once again began picking off any German soldier in the open. The intermittent barrage wasn't a total failure, however, for at least some Germans trapped in the church used the shellfire as cover and somehow slipped through the Terespol and Kholmsky gates, over the bridges and back to their own lines.[4]

'EVERY PICTURE OF THE SORROW AND HORROR OF WAR...' MINSK, 23 JUNE

Monday began in Minsk seemingly like any other Monday. The radio urged people to remain calm, to go about their regular business. Shops, factories, schools and public institutions all opened. Except that it wasn't a regular Monday. The usual hustle and bustle was punctuated by frequent air-raid alarms – the first had sounded at 4.30am – which served only to anger the female populace who were deprived of the opportunity to go shopping. Military vehicles sped through the streets with soldiers, rifles over their shoulders, clinging to running boards. To one of the citizen's inhabitants it seemed as if people were 'waiting for something to happen. Everyone thought that there would soon be dogfights as there had been over Madrid,' he recalled. Yet only the visiting actors from Moscow seemed to take the sirens seriously. Each time they sounded, the troupe hurried to the basement of the Belarus hotel. The staff did not. They merely poked fun at their guests.

The frequent alarms were irritating the Communist Party's Central Committee – the sirens were making Minsk's citizens 'unnecessarily nervous'. Like the people of the city they supposedly served, the Party leaders seemed either complacent or paralysed. When news reached them of the airfield being strafed and columns of civilians attacked on the main road coming into Minsk from the west, leaving several wounded and dead cows and horses in the carriageway, the committee's only action was to order the cows sent to the abattoir.[5]

In fact, few of Europe's cities were less prepared for war in 1941 than Minsk. Unlike elsewhere on the continent over the past decade, there had been no large-scale civic defence exercises. Factories, public utilities, railway stations – all were unready. The provision of shelters was woeful: for Byelorussia's 14 cities and their 1.2 million inhabitants, there was protection for just 18,300 souls. There was not a single adequate shelter in Minsk. Eight weeks before the German invasion, Party leaders agreed to build six shelters across the capital to accommodate 15,000 people; they would be ready by mid-August. The blackout system was imperfect at best – and it was impossible to turn off all of Minsk's street lights at the flick of a single central switch. It mattered little. The Germans would attack by day. With impunity.[6]

It was 11am before the first German aircraft appeared over Minsk itself. The regular radio broadcast suddenly stopped and a single announcement sounded from personal sets and loudspeakers: *Air-raid warning for the city of Minsk.* Newsreel cameraman Jossif Veinorovich – filming a policeman dressed in his white shirt and spiked white helmet directing traffic to show the rest of the Soviet Union that life in Minsk continued as normal – suddenly noticed around 20 aircraft appear in his viewfinder, 'flying like at an air display'. As they drew closer, 'huge black objects' began falling to the ground. He realised they were bombs – yet continued to film, until the policeman grabbed him. 'Your papers, or I'll shoot you.' Veinorovich handed over his identity card. 'You swine, they're dropping bombs on us and you have nothing better to do than film the people's misery!' And Veinorovich continued to film. Every ten minutes, enemy aircraft appeared over Minsk. He recorded each wave of bombers, each fresh wave of destruction. And none of his footage would ever be used. 'The Red Army was retreating, cities burning, the Fascists were taking Red Army men prisoner,' he recalled. 'Every picture of the sorrow and horror of war – this misery should not be shown on film.' When the footage reached his editors in Moscow, it was simply thrown in the rubbish bin.

With few public shelters, the city's inhabitants headed for hurriedly dug slit trenches, foxholes, or simply remained in their homes and apartments. But some caught in the streets found themselves mesmerised by the spectacle. Peter Lidov was struck by the impressive formation maintained by the German bombers as they dropped their payloads, somewhere near the central station. 'The sound of their engines was indelibly imprinted in my mind – a brash, jarring, defiant noise.' The Red Air Force belatedly rose to intercept them, downing the final bomber in the formation. Whenever an aircraft plunged to the ground, people applauded – convinced the victim was German.[7]

THE ROAD OF VICTORY... *PANZERGRUPPE* 2 TURNS THE KNIFE, 23 JUNE

With the border battles behind it, Heinz Guderian's armour was now racing through western Byelorussia, a path cleared for it in part by the Luftwaffe. 'You could have called the route of advance *via triumphalis*,' wrote a gun loader with 4th Panzer Division. He continued:

> Vast numbers of light Russian tanks, T-26s, were shot up, stuck or abandoned in panic by the side of the road. Brand-new artillery, flak, tractors, anti-tank guns stare at us, overturned, pushed into the ditches by our panzers. We often come across the results of our air raids. Men, animals and equipment lie there, mown down, in a chaotic mess, on top of each other. Dead horses, their stomachs bloated from decomposition, stick their legs in the air. The sweet smell of decay lingered on the highway. The trunks of trees, chopped down and ripped apart by bombs, stick out amid the branches of fallen crowns.

4th Panzer was still following in 3rd Panzer's wake – and it had been a spectacularly successful day for the Berliners. By dusk, their spearhead was across the River Szczara, outside the town of Bereza Kartuska. In two days, the division had advanced nearly 90 miles. Whatever counter-attacks XIV Mechanised Corps had been able to mount were smashed; 36 T-26s were finished off in a single action by 6th Panzer Regiment in the mid-afternoon, 12 of them dispatched by just one company in a matter of minutes. By the time a small bridgehead had been forged over the Szczara, the main road all the way back to Kobrin was littered with the burned-out and abandoned hulks of more than 100 tanks and other armoured vehicles.[8]

At his headquarters in Minsk, Dmitry Pavlov tried to follow the German advance as best he could. Reports were patchy, contradictory. Communications with his commanders were even worse – orders were delivered by hand, sometimes by aircraft. The Luftwaffe was systematically knocking out his rail junctions – as far as 250 miles behind the front – and wiping out his already-mauled air forces; one airfield was subjected to a dozen attacks this Monday. He knew that Fourth Army had collapsed in the face of Guderian's *Panzergruppe*, and Tenth Army was threatened with encirclement. Far from warning Konstantin Golubev of the impending threat, he rebuked Tenth Army's commander for his apparent inaction. 'Why did the mechanised corps not attack, who is guilty?' he demanded. VI Mechanised Corps, Western Front's strongest striking force, had not attacked because it had exhausted three-quarters of its fuel on the first day of the German attack. There was no chance of resupply – the nearest dump was in Baranovichi, more than 100 miles behind the front. With rail lines smashed and roads jammed, it would never reach the corps. Pavlov continued to chastise the harassed Golubev. He should have a better grasp on his divisions, where they were, what they were doing. And above all he should commit his armour. 'Remember,' Pavlov ended threateningly, 'if you do not operate dynamically, the military council will lose its patience.'

In fact, Dmitry Pavlov scolded every one of his senior commanders. They failed to care for the wounded ('not a single wounded soldier should be left behind for the enemy'); they evacuated families rather than organise the timely resupply of ammunition and supplies when units ran out; the dead were being left behind ('the memory of those who perished for right and for the Motherland should be revered'); and the retreating troops were leaving cattle and food behind for the enemy. He reserved his strongest threat for the disintegrating Fourth Army, dispatching an envoy to Aleksandr Korobkov's headquarters with strict orders to stop it withdrawing any further; anyone who failed to comply would be shot.[9]

'YOUR SITUATION IS HOPELESS...' BREST FORTRESS, 23 JUNE, AFTERNOON AND EVENING

A largely fruitless day for the attackers at Brest fortress ended with Soviet soldiers suddenly deserting in their hundreds. Attempts to persuade the garrison to surrender by sending captured Russians forward under a white flag had invariably failed – and not a few of the negotiators were shot at by their former comrades. The Germans made no distinction between civilian and soldier in the fortress. When Heinrich Ebenseder and his comrades hauled a handful of civilians out of the rubble, a non-commissioned officer said gruffly: 'Shoot these dogs,' then led them to one side. 'He put a pistol to the back of the head of the first one and pulled the trigger,' Ebenseder noted. The gun misfired. 'Then a second shot rang out, the first civilian collapsed, followed by the second and third.' A short time later another 13 male civilians were captured. With groups of women and children, this time Ebenseder's sergeant baulked at killing them in cold blood. 'We reported this to the battalion commander, he said: "Execute".' A junior officer carried out the murders instead.

Around 5pm, a newly arrived *Propaganda Kompanie* van moved towards the central island after a particularly savage barrage of the citadel. The van's occupants translated an appeal into Russian, urging the defenders to give themselves up 'for reasons of humanity'. General Mikhail Puzyrev, the commander of the Brest district, was already in German hands, the loudspeaker claimed – falsely – drinking vodka with his captors 'while you're continuing senseless resistance': 'Your situation is hopeless. Don't spill your blood in vain, since there is no way out of the siege. You've been cut off from the others. More than 100 kilometres separate you from them. No-one will come to your relief.'

The men were given an hour to consider their decision. Hundreds chose to surrender. Several trapped pockets of German troops and at least one Red Army officer exploited the confusion caused by the mass surrender, the Germans to break out of the fortress, the officer to break *in*. Stuck in the city when war broke out, Vasily Bitko had spent 36 hours evading German troops, patrols and finally slipped past German troops surrounding the citadel. The 34-year-old veteran of the Winter War with Finland felt duty bound to re-join his unit of non-commissioned officers from 44th Rifle Regiment. In full dress uniform, Bitko threw himself into the Mukhavets, swam the few yards to the central island, and staggered into the northern section of the circular barracks. 'Don't shoot!' he pleaded. 'I'm Soviet.' He brought no news from the outside world, but his appearance was a brief fillip to morale, especially in his regiment.

By nightfall, 45th Infantry Division counted 1,900 prisoners. Perhaps, the division's diarist mused, 'the fighting morale of the Russian garrison has been decisively weakened'.[10]

'OF ALL THE TERRIBLE THINGS I'VE SEEN IN MY LIFE ... THIS WAS THE WORST...' MINSK, 24 JUNE

It was mid-morning in Minsk when the air-raid sirens sounded warning of approaching German aircraft, and another hour – 9.40am – before the first enemy aircraft appeared over the city. Peter Lidov and his family were sitting down to breakfast in their apartment having spent the night sheltering in the cellar of their seven-storey block. The journalist tried to cheer up his daughter.

'Lucky you, Svetlana,' he said reassuringly. 'None of your schoolfriends have been bombed. They'll envy you in the autumn!' The breakfast table conversation was interrupted by the rumble of engines. The Lidovs rushed to an open window. Directly overhead 'an entire armada of bombers' – his daughter counted 27 before Minsk's anti-aircraft guns opened fire. Lidov continued in his diary:

> There was that howl of terrible force, whistling, screeching, gnawing. Explosions somewhere nearby: one, two, three – a lot of explosions. A storm burst into the room, the door was flung open and I could clearly feel the whole house shaking. Then everything passed and explosions could be heard somewhere far away. I went down to the basement, where everyone had now gathered. I tried to cheer up the depressed women with jokes. One of them rushed around, wailing, panicking. I tried to persuade her to be quiet, then I seized her and threatened to throw her out.

Every half hour formations of 35 to 40 German aircraft attacked the city – at least 18 waves in all. No-one had experienced anything like it. 'To anyone who was in Minsk that day and night, of all the terrible things I've seen in my life, I could say this was the worst,' Ivan Krupeni, deputy chairman of the Byelorussian Soviet Social Republic, recalled.

> Tram lines were damaged – pitted by bomb craters, fragments of rails and sleepers, electricity wires torn down. Paving stones were scattered. At the junction of Soviet and Uritsky Streets, overturned trams became a mass grave of people of all ages. Chaos reigned in the city's finest shops: counters and walls pierced by bomb splinters. Products strewn with fragments of glass from chandeliers and windows, lay on the floor, on the pavements.

Teenager Katya Korotayeva watched individual houses, then rows, then entire streets and finally the entire city burn. 'You enjoy looking at fire, watching a camp fire, but when it's a house that is burning, that's bad, and here the fire raged from all sides, the sky and streets were full of smoke,' she remembered. The incessant raids were too much for one woman queuing for bread. 'Just give us a break!' she screamed at the heavens. Others were haunted by the sight of the dead. One inhabitant came across the body of a boy lying under a tree, a few feet from a main road. 'Facing upwards, his glassy eyes were wide open,' he recalled. 'Murdered! The first dead person I'd seen. I knew this boy's face. His open eyes shook me to the core – I'd always believed that the eyes of the dead were closed.'

Student Maria Korbut was being treated for scurvy in a hospital on the outskirts of the city. Fellow patients and staff fled when the first bombs fell, but Maria was too weak to move. The persistent air raids terrified her. A nearby building collapsed, the window panes in her ward shattered, a mirror fell off the wall. It was the signal for her to leave and make her way out into the street. 'There I saw nothing but flames and black smoke – you couldn't distinguish between heaven and earth any more.' A couple of men from a neighbouring hostel saw the distraught teenager and helped her to escape until they reached the outskirts of Minsk, where they realised they would have to go back through the burning city to reach their hometowns – in Maria's case, Gomel, nearly 200 miles to the southeast. The student was haunted for the rest of her life by what she saw as she passed through Minsk: 'We did not see a living soul, no authorities, no-one. Everyone had fled. The streets were full of corpses, some of them terribly bloated. The smell of burned flesh pervaded the entire city. We saw torn arms and heads – a terrible sight. You never forget something like that.'

The succession of raids destroyed Minsk's power stations. Cobbles in the streets were scattered as if they were pebbles. Entire rows of houses were flattened, including most of the streets surrounding the new opera house, while the Kirov machine-tool works, a power station, the Kommunarka sweet factory, the KIM sewing machine plant, the *Zvezda* printworks, the central post and telegraph office, both of Minsk's maternity hospitals, two children's hospitals, four cinemas, the six-storey Europa hotel, one of the finest pre-revolutionary structures in the city, and the nearby Belarus hotel were in ruins. One bomb landed next to the House of the Soviets where women and children had taken refuge in the basement. More than 100 of them were killed. Even the headquarters of the Western Front were badly damaged.

'WE'LL HAMMER THE NAZIS...' VI MECHANISED CORPS AT GRODNO, 24 JUNE, AFTERNOON

It was late on Tuesday morning before the much-criticised VI Mechanised Corps was finally in a position to intercept the invader east of Grodno. Mikhail Khatskilevich wielded a mighty force of more than 1,000 tanks, a good 100 of them KVs, plus double that number of T-34s. Its opponent, the infantry of XX Corps, possessed little in the way of armour. The outcome of the encounter should not have been in doubt. Except that the Germans were not where Khatskilevich thought they were. His tanks ran out of fuel as they continued their advance. The corps' stretched rear services could not cope; petrol tankers reached the front, but not the diesel, so the heavy armour could not be refuelled. It was mid-afternoon before Khatskilevich was finally able to grapple with his foe, but the Germans had had time to prepare, while the formation of hundreds of tanks had not escaped the prying eyes of Luftwaffe reconnaissance. Every available aircraft in *Fliegerkorps* VIII was thrown against the Soviet armour. By dusk, the airmen alone claimed 105 Russian tanks destroyed or abandoned, while riderless horses roamed the battlefield.

At Tenth Army's headquarters, Pavlov's special envoy Ivan Boldin took a desperate radio call from Khatskilevich.

'Comrade General,' his voice said excitedly, 'we are running out of fuel and ammunition. The tank crews are fighting bravely, but without fuel and ammunition our vehicles are helpless. Please give us everything we need and we'll hammer the Nazis.'

Boldin knew Mikhail Khatskilevich was not a man prone to idle boasts, rather a commander with 'deep faith in his men, confident that the enemy could be beaten'.

'Listen to me, Comrade Khatskilevich,' Boldin replied. 'Hold on! I will immediately take every step to help you.'[11]

In fact, Mikhail Khatskilevich's assault deeply unsettled the Germans. 8th Infantry Division, committed around the town of Skidel, 20 miles southeast of Grodno, reported that the situation 'quickly became critical'. Its artillery took up position in the open terrain and fired directly into the dense columns of advancing Soviet armour. One battery fired half as many shells as it had done in the entire campaign in the west one year earlier, while the guns in a company of howitzers shot so rapidly that their barrels began to melt. The division held its line – just. Dogged fighting in Skidel – reduced to rubble by the day's battle – continued into the small hours of the 25th when the Russian troops finally withdrew.[12]

SUCCESS AND FAILURE, BREST FORTRESS, 24 JUNE, MID-DAY

Inspired by the impressive haul of prisoners the previous evening, 45th Infantry Division waited until the middle of Tuesday before repeating the tactic. For 15 minutes shortly before mid-day, 48 guns and mortars in every artillery battery fired at the fortress's central and northern islands, before the *Propaganda Kompanie* was sent in with its loudspeakers. The results were discouraging: a measly eight deserters, one of whom was interrogated by Dr Leo Losert. 'He told me that the remainder in the fortress would not surrender, but continue to fight.'

The barrage was not entirely without success, however. A small raiding party exploited the shelling to force its way into the heart of the fortress. The stormtroops found the central island largely abandoned, apart from a handful of houses in the centre, and began to clear out the last pockets of resistance, 'liberating' cut-off troops such as the wounded Hans Teuschler and the 50 men – 'some of them wounded, all utterly exhausted' – trapped in the garrison church, and taking 1,250 prisoners in the process. Once again, Fritz Schlieper sensed success and headed to the centre of the citadel. He was quickly disappointed. Despite the stream of prisoners filing past him, resistance in Brest fortress was far from broken.[13]

'BEHIND US RUSSIANS, IN FRONT OF US RUSSIANS...' *PANZERGRUPPE* 2, 24 JUNE

The tentacles of Heinz Guderian's *Panzergruppe* now reached more than 120 miles into Byelorussia, past Kobrin, past Pruzany, past Slonim. They prodded and poked at Baranovichi, the last major town before Minsk. Electrifying as the dash from the Bug had been, there had been more advancing than fighting. Most Soviet units in the way of Guderian's armour had been swept to one side or simply bypassed, not least the unfortunate XIV Mechanised Corps, more than 500 tanks strong – but not one of them was a new T-34 or KV. In one encounter, three dozen T-26s were knocked out, 26 of them by the nine vehicles in a single company of 3rd Panzer Division. 'Is this war?' motorcycle messenger Peter Stölten asked himself. The 18-year-old was soon reminded it was. 'No Russian aircraft, no artillery, just scenes of destruction: prisoners, dead horses – and men, occasionally, a bombed-out Russian tank every 100 metres – I only saw the first German one recently,' he wrote in his first letter home to his family near Weimar. 'The tremendous, bold advance is great fun. This campaign in Russia will become as famous as the previous ones. Will we need 18 days again?' But in lunging deep into enemy territory, the panzers left scattered and dispersed Red Army formations on their flanks, units which could – and would – try to break out. On the third day of the invasion, the area around the town of Slonim – roughly halfway between Brest and Minsk – became the focal point for such efforts. 'Behind us Russians, in front of us Russians,' Erich Hager, a radio operator in 17th Panzer Division, recorded tersely in his diary. 'An unpleasant feeling.' Things became even more unpleasant when the surrounded panzers were attacked from behind by numerous Soviet tanks and vehicles attempting to break out. Every one was shot up by the Germans, but that did not put an end to the fighting, for the wounded tank crews and riflemen continued to fire. The tall fields of corn came alive. 'Anything that came into view was shot.'[14]

As his armour raced along the lanes and highways of Byelorussia, carving up the Red Army, Heinz Guderian was in his element. 'He's one hell of a guy,' his admiring Luftwaffe liaison officer Karl Henning von Barsewisch gushed. 'A bull full of energy, clever, with a good memory, but also likeable.' Guderian's superiors might not have agreed. The 53-year-old panzer general was bull-headed, fiery, insubordinate. He clashed repeatedly with his seniors, determined to advance when they urged halting – not, he claimed 'for personal glory, but for the glory of the German Reich'. Serving on his staff was exhausting, but also exhilarating. 'When Guderian makes a decision, it's as if the God of War himself is riding across the battlefield,' Barsewisch wrote. 'When his eyes flash it's as if Wotan is hurling bolts of lightning or Thor is swinging his hammer.' And he was prepared to face the dangers his tank crews encountered. While visiting 17th Panzer Division's command post on the edge of Slonim shortly before mid-day, Guderian was forced to throw himself to the ground when enemy tanks burst through 'with cannons and machine-guns blazing'. Panzer Mk4s drove the intruders off, but not before two lieutenant colonels had been mortally wounded. Undaunted, the *Panzergruppe* commander continued his visit to the front, heading down the road to 18th Panzer advancing on Baranovichi. Guderian succeeded in conferring with the division's commander Walther Nehring, but on his way back his Panzer Mk4 ran into a column of Russian motorised infantry. The riflemen were preparing to dismount. Guderian ordered his driver to simply pass between the enemy vehicles at full speed. The bluff worked. Before the Red Army men had time to react, the general was through. Russian newspapers later declared Guderian had been killed in the encounter. 'I felt bound to inform them of their mistake by means of the German wireless,' he noted laconically.[15]

'A PROPER DOGFIGHT RAGED...' RED AIR FORCE ATTEMPTS TO STOP THE GERMAN ADVANCE, 24 JUNE

Despite the slaughter in its ranks on the first two days of the German attack, the Red Air Force still strove to halt the enemy's advance. Twin-engine SB-2 and DB-3 bombers were repeatedly thrown against Army Group Centre's axes of advance, increasingly without fighter cover. Over *Panzergruppe* 2, they ran into the Me109s of Werner Mölders' unforgiving *Jagdgeschwader* 5. The squadron did not down a single Soviet fighter on 24 June. It did, however, bring Soviet bombers down by the dozen: 80 aircraft this Tuesday alone, all but 17 of them SB-2s. Among their victims was Evgeni Borisenko, pilot of one of nine DB-3 bombers from the long-range 212th Bomber Regiment ordered to strike at German columns advancing along the Brest–Minsk highway. The dense traffic was unmissable. At 5,500ft above the Byelorussian countryside, Borisenko could clearly see the lines of vehicles carving routes through fields or throwing up clouds of dust on the roads. The acting regimental commander ordered his men to make a low-level attack. After the first pass, clouds of smoke rose above the German armour, but there were simply too few bombs and too many vehicles to wipe them all out in one go. The commander led his bombers in again. The flak, which had fired wildly but largely ineffectively during the initial attack, fell silent. 'German fighters – roughly double our number – suddenly pounced on us from behind,' Borisenko recalled. 'A proper dogfight raged.' The Soviet bombers formed around their leader and persisted with their attack. The DB-3s in the lead dropped their bombs. Those at the tail of the formation 'went up in flames one after another and fell like burning torches, leaving black trails of smoke in the sky'. As the heavens filled with aircrew bailing out, German troops peppered their parachutes with machine-gun fire. Evgeni Borisenko succeeded in making his bombing run only to be attacked as he pulled away. His gunner claimed one Luftwaffe fighter downed before he was killed, leaving his bomber defenceless. The port engine went up in flames, followed shortly afterwards by the starboard. Borisenko's wounded navigator was determined to jump. The pilot urged him not to – 'the Germans would turn him into Swiss cheese'. He was proved right. The navigator plunged to earth in a hail of fire from an enemy fighter, leaving Borisenko to put his bomber on the ground on his own.

One hundred miles away to the north, on Army Group Centre's left wing, Heinz Heppermann watched an almost identical one-sided encounter over his 6th Infantry Division. 'Nine Russian bombers appeared,' the non-commissioned officer wrote to his wife.

> German fighters were there in a flash: and then a drama unfolded, so fast and magnificent, that it took your breath away. The fighters fell upon the Russians, a short burst of fire, and the first was already burning brightly – it fell to the earth around 100 metres in front of us, producing an enormous column of smoke. Within five minutes seven Russian bombers were trailing smoke in a one-

kilometre radius! Three Russian airmen were taken prisoner. One fell to his death – his parachute did not open. We screamed with enthusiasm.

When he eventually returned to his regiment, Evgeni Borisenko learned his had been one of 26 aircraft shot down. A sole DB-3, its fuselage riddled with bullet holes, returned to base. The Red Air Force lost more than 550 aircraft this Tuesday. In three days of war, nearly 4,000 of its machines had been destroyed.

Yet the skies of Russia were too vast, the Red Air Force too numerous, the German fighter umbrella too small for the Luftwaffe to be dominant everywhere. When they did evade the enemy's fighter cover, Soviet bombers proved they could be effective – and hamper the German advance. The cavalry of 1st *Reiter* Regiment were on a 40-mile advance along the dry, dusty, monotonously dead-straight highway running southeast from Brest. The exhausted riders had just passed through the village of Mokrany when they heard the sound of aircraft engines. 'Let them buzz – we're too tired to care,' a dismissive Rembrand Elert recorded in his diary. But when they heard explosions in Mokrany and turned around to see thick black clouds of smoke above the village, they realised their mistake – too late. Before the men could give orders, machine-gun bullets were strafing the road. Elert paints a vivid picture of the ensuing chaos:

> Excited by the roaring and shouting, the horses can hardly be held back any longer, and then comes total disaster: riderless, frantic horses from behind, ammunition pack horses, six-horse teams harnessed to limbers and cannons ... Now no horse can be held back, like a rolling stone everything gains momentum, 1st Platoon is already galloping, then 2nd, the entire squadron ... everyone. Whoever leaves the road will sink into the swamp. Just reach the forest! Poor riders fall off the rushing horses, others are swept off by passing riders. Bursts of machine-gun fire whistle over our heads. Finally the forest – now off the road – under the trees! Pine trunks hit me. In front of me, someone loses his steel helmet and is separated from his horse. Finally, some of us manage to tame the horses. We try to bring them to a standstill and create order on the road. We're not especially successful because the airmen turn back, chase the riderless horses back to Mokrany and from there back again.

It was nightfall before the cavalry regiment had regrouped. The cadavers of 60 dead horses, plus the bodies of 47 men were scattered along the highway and adjacent terrain. 'We have to do without food today, the field kitchen can't get here,' a bitter Elend continued in his diary. 'The thirst is even harder to bear. We go to sleep on the spot. Morale is at rock bottom.'[16]

BREAKOUT AT BREST FORTRESS, 24 JUNE, 6PM

Under the cover of machine-gun fire, and with cries of 'Urra!' echoing across the limp waters of the Mukhavets, a scratch group of Soviet troops charged across the northern bridge leading to the citadel. During the preceding few hours, 29-year-old Lieutenant Anatoly Vinogradov had mustered what men he could, determined to make a concerted attempt to break out of the central island and reach Soviet lines – unbeknownst to them already more than 100 miles away. Vinogradov would lead a spearhead of 120 men, drawn from the 44th and 455th Rifle Regiments, over the Mukhavets – via the bridge, or wading, swimming and on rafts – paving the way for the bulk of the garrison to follow.

There were 700 yards of mostly open ground to cover just to reach the outer walls of the fortress. Many men never reached the opposite bank of the river, cut down by German fire as they thrashed around in the water or clambered down the bank. Anatoly Vinogradov succeeded in forcing his way across the bridge where he waited for the majority of the breakout troops to join him. They never did. They were too busy dealing with a renewed barrage against the citadel. The junior officer continued alone. His group moved out at a moment when the fortress's North Island was largely devoid of German troops – they were busy smoking out the last resistance in the barracks, casemates, cellars and passages with a specialist flamethrower unit. Perhaps as many as 100 men reached the edge of the fortress. They barely got beyond it. The main roads were filled with German vehicles, German troops and German guns. When an artillery unit opened fire on the escaped troops around dusk, Anatoly Vinogradov surrendered.[17]

'LIT BY THE CRIMSON GLOW OF FIRES...' MINSK, NIGHT OF 24–25 JUNE

It was dusk when the air raids ceased and people nervously crept and crawled out of Minsk's basements and shelters. 'And what did we see!' historian Vladimir Romanovski recalled. 'Burning houses, rubble, ruins. And corpses everywhere in the streets. People tried to flee the city during the bombing, but they could not get away quickly enough because the streets were blocked. And those who were outside were mown down by low-flying German aircraft.' Despite the day's horrors, machine-tool designer T. P. Mickiewicz was struck by the confidence of his fellow citizens. 'In spite of the fact that Minsk was burning and possessed almost no defences, I did not meet one person who believed that Minsk would be occupied by Germans.' But thousands of his compatriots *were* convinced – and took the end of the bombing as the cue to flee their city. In the morning, Inna Levkevich's mother had gone to work as a bookkeeper to pay her colleagues their wages. By the evening, the family were refugees, fleeing Minsk. Something of a tomboy, ten-year-old Inna had been awestruck by the air raids initially, trying to follow the bombs as they whistled their way towards the ground. But she wailed when she saw her school ablaze and the destruction the bombing wrought. 'Everything which happened before our eyes was terrible and incomprehensible,' Inna remembered. 'Above all, death: kettles and pots were lying around between the dead bodies. Everything burned. It was as if we were walking over burning coals.'

As a trusted Communist, transport was provided for Peter Lidov and his family. Their Chevrolet joined the torrent of people heading out of the city towards the highway to Mogilev 'like streams running off a mountain, rushing in one direction'. From the Svislach onwards, Minsk was 'one great raging inferno'. The roads running east were overcrowded; the car struggled to make progress. Lidov observed:

> Children are in their mother's hands and on their father's shoulders. Some carry children in their carts, others hold the very small ones in their hands. They also take goats and cows with them. In their hands and on their backs, everything they could get their hands on at the last moment: fur, cats, a sack of provisions, a pot of flowers. Some haul their personal belongings on carts. Trucks only slowly overtake the crowd. They are besieged, people ask to be taken along, hang on to the back, fall down. Some trucks are packed with people to breaking point. They are glad that they don't have to walk.
>
> A half-tonne truck carrying people tries to squeeze through the narrow gap. Our driver brakes, but the Chevrolet continues to skid on the wet tarmac. Collision. The truck runs off the side of the road and people fall out of the back. We hear the screams. Some are hurt, someone has been killed. Water pours out of the wrecked radiator with its broken pipes. It took two hours to fix it.

Most Minsk residents lacked Peter Lidov's privileged status. They left their city on foot, as one boy recalled:

> There were four of us with mother – three of us walked, the youngest was in mum's arms. My sister was seven years old, she was carrying a kerosene stove and

my mother's shoes, terrified of losing them. The shoes were new… Mummy had her key but forgot to lock our apartment. She was trying to stop vehicles, crying and begging: 'Take our children and we will go to protect the city!' She did not believe that the enemy would enter Minsk.

The city's Party leaders did. Between 2 and 4.30am on Wednesday 25 June – with Stalin's permission – they deserted the city en masse. In darkness, anxious officials, commissars and militia stuffed sacks with documents as they sought to empty the Party archives before a cavalcade of cars and trucks joined thousands of citizens on the road to Mogilev. As far as many of Minsk's inhabitants were concerned, their leaders simply 'got in their cars' and 'shamefully fled the city'. Even Dmitry Pavlov deemed the moment had come to abandon the Byelorussian capital. His staff packed their papers and belongings in the basement of the House of the Red Army and made for the village of Borova, five miles outside the city, before deciding it too was under threat, to join the rest of the republic's leaders in Mogilev.

As the night drew on, Peter Lidov was struck by the apparent calm of Minskers. They were walking, almost marching, in an orderly fashion. They strode purposefully without hurrying. 'They talked about ordinary everyday things – in short, they'd already got over the danger and put the horrors of yesterday far behind them,' Lidov observed. Their backs were lit by the 'crimson glow of fires from burning Minsk' while in the east there was the first glimmer of the coming day on the horizon.[18]

THE SHORTEST – AND LONGEST – NIGHT…
BYELORUSSIA'S PRISONS ARE EVACUATED,
NIGHT OF 24–25 JUNE

Minsk's prisons were already empty. As soon the bombing stopped on Tuesday evening, the NKVD began evacuating them, assisted by the Red Army. Inmates had cheered at the sound of the first bombs exploding, convinced that liberation was at hand. But in the small hours of Wednesday, militia armed with pitchforks appeared at cell doors and ordered the prisoners to march east through the still-burning city. The columns marched in silence. The only sound came from the hooves of mounted soldiers on the cobblestones. The prisoners' eyes smarted and stung as they were driven on 'like cattle', Polish nationalist Joanna Stankiewicz-Januszczak wrote.

All the time you can hear shooting – they kill those who try to flee. And yet escaping seemed so easy because we were being driven in the middle of a crowd of free people. I guess they too were killed by these shots if they got too close to us – that wasn't hard, because we were walking among the ruins, unable to see where the road was, where the pavement was and where the ruins of the houses began. The city was being ploughed by bombs so we continued, stumbling over the rubble, jumping to one side to avoid the fires and if the entire wall of a building collapsed, then many people died under the rubble.

Estimates vary, perhaps as many as 20,000 prisoners were on the move, more likely around 6,000 – including those evacuated from Kaunas – girls as young as 12, elderly men and women, almost all of them 'counter-revolutionaries'. Their numbers were ever dwindling. Anyone who fell by the wayside during the march was finished off, while the NKVD led groups away at every halt and shot them. 'The shortest night of the year,' Stankiewicz-Januszczak wrote, 'was probably the longest for us.'[19]

It wasn't just prisoners from Minsk on a death march along the lanes of central Byelorussia. The warden of the prison in Glubokoye, a town of just 10,000 souls 100 miles north of the capital, had taken it upon himself to march his 916 inmates – 500 of them 'counter-revolutionaries', the rest 'burglars' – to Vitebsk. The column halted at least three times on the 100-mile journey and prisoners were shot at each stop. A revolver in his hand, the warden joined his guards in executing 110 prisoners. When he reached Vitebsk at the beginning of July, he claimed the prisoners had tried to escape, screaming: 'Long live Hitler!'[20]

'THE FRANTIC WHIRLWIND OF BATTLE...'
GRODNO, 25 JUNE, DAWN

As day broke on Wednesday, VI Mechanised Corps renewed its attack outside Grodno. The Germans fended off two waves of Soviet tanks, but it was only in the final wave of the assault that Mikhail Khatskilevich committed his heavy armour. Boris Borodin led a platoon of T-34s from 13th Tank Regiment into action near the Białystok–Grodno railway line.

The entire area as far as the eye could see was filled with swirling trails of dust behind tanks on the move. Black plumes of smoke rose through this fog of grey. Against this backdrop, the flash of muzzle shots, exploding shells. To the left and right there was the frantic whirlwind of battle. Tanks shooting, running into each other, separating, re-forming in columns and, all of a sudden, turning around, already in battle formation, going past each other, halting briefly, moving to the left or right, throwing up clouds of black dust, shooting continuously as soon as they catch sight of the enemy.

In a duel with one panzer, Borodin's turret was grazed by an enemy shell. He responded by sending a 76mm round in the opposite direction. 'Flames and smoke come from the turret of the enemy tank,' he wrote. 'Victory! But there was no time to rejoice.' He disabled a second panzer by shooting off its caterpillar track, before his radio operator gunned down every member of the crew who leaped out of the crippled vehicle. Hit by a German shell, Boris Borodin withdrew from the field of battle. 'Thank you for the T-34 tank,' he wrote. 'How many lives it has saved! This is not a T-26, BT-5 or BT-7, whose armour can be pierced by heavy machine-guns. Surrounded on three sides by petrol tanks, they burned like matchboxes.'

The appearance of KV-1s was a shock to the defenders, as a soldier in 8th Infantry Division described:

Directly in front of us suddenly there's the roar of heavy shells. We can see the gun barrels with the naked eye: heavy Russian artillery! But then these gun barrels advance from the horizon, we can see tank turrets, enormous tanks the likes of which we've never seen. They rumble over the slope towards us, 52-tonne tanks with 15.2cm cannons. We're seized by paralysing fear. The anti-tank guns shoot from every barrel, but their shells bounce off the thick armour on the tank like rubber balls. The giants continue to roll. Our assault guns roar into action at the decisive moment. It's over in seconds. They shoot as if they're on the exercise area. Their hits tear the steel crates to bits, they tear open the armour, rip the roofs off tank turrets. It's a gruesome duel. We shoot faster and better, but where heavy Russian shells strike, there's death and destruction. One assault gun is paralysed. Over there, three giant tanks are aflame. But three more continue to stubbornly roll towards us. The second assault gun has used up all its rounds. One of the crew jumps from the gun, races through the hail of fire, dashes back making huge leaps, with two shells under each arm. The three Russians have closed to within 50 metres. Seconds later, four shots are fired. Three direct hits have set these last three gigantic tanks on fire.

Further to the right an anti-tank gun company tries to move its guns into a favourable position. Two motor-cycle despatch riders race ahead to occupy a hill. Suddenly a 52-tonner stands in front of them. They run into the tank at full speed, there's a squelching crunch and crump; the tank rolls over them. The horror of it all leaves us unable to speak. Then both of them jump up again behind the tank, pale, but unharmed. They lay right in the middle between the two caterpillar tracks.

By late afternoon, 8th Infantry Division's position along the Neman – here obstacle to neither vehicle nor man – was beginning to crumble. The weight of a Soviet armoured corps, bolstered by motorised infantry and riflemen, was simply too great. But then *Fliegerkorps* VIII joined battle again. Its commander, Wolfram von Richthofen threw more than 450 aircraft and was delighted when the first reports came back from his airmen; the enemy had been 'successfully slaughtered'. The railway line to Białystok, just 50 miles southwest of Grodno, was littered with burned-out Soviet tanks, many of them shot up by German assault guns. Beside the track, individual German and Russian graves; the former were marked by a cross and steel helmet, the latter with a cross primitively made from tree branches and no inscription. The fields, lanes and villages south of Grodno were also strewn with destroyed tanks, guns and vehicles 'and between them, dead Russian soldiers and horses on both sides of the road,' infantryman Heinrich Boucsein remembered. 'Civilians were on hand to bury the dead. They were in a hurry for the sun was blazing.' To the southeast of Grodno, the anti-tank gunners of 256th Infantry Division – which evidently had not faced heavy armour – counted 250 tanks destroyed.

Not every Soviet tank left behind on the battlefield at Grodno was wrecked by German hands. At the height of battle, an anxious Mikhail Khatskilevich had appeared at Tenth Army's headquarters. 'We're down to the last rounds,' he told Ivan Boldin. 'Let's use them to destroy the tanks.'

Boldin agreed. '*Da*, perhaps there is no other option. If the vehicles can't be saved, it is better to destroy them.'

With the counter-attack at Grodno thwarted and, more worryingly, the first signs of the German Army threatening to encircle Soviet forces between Białystok and Minsk, Western Front ordered the assaults halted and the armour to lead the withdrawal of all Red Army units out of the nascent pocket.[21]

Chaos and plunder, Minsk, 25 June

Without rulers, Minsk descended into anarchy. 'No-one was in charge, there was chaos and confusion,' wrote one resident documenting the downfall of their city. 'We were left to our fate,' junior accountant Ekaterina Zirlina bitterly recalled half a century later. 'The city government quickly fled – they all climbed into cars and drove away with their families. There was only an organised escape for those in high positions.' When Minsk's remaining citizens awoke on Wednesday and realised the Soviet authorities had fled, they began to raid the city's surviving shops and food warehouses, convinced that the Germans would provide them with nothing when they came. Unguarded, they became easy prey. Schoolboy Leonid Bulat was astonished to find the window of a grocery store smashed, the door wide open and looters inside. 'What are you standing there for, boy?' one asked him. 'Help yourself.' One student watched her neighbours return with flour, cereals, sugar, treacle, yeast, salt, vegetable oils, salted fish, cod, soap and matches.

> Not everyone could carry off sacks weighing 50 to 70 kilogrammes. They were cut open and the contents stashed in sacks, bags and buckets. The rest was trampled beneath their feet. Treacle poured out of holes punched in huge vats. It slowly flowed into bowls held out [by looters]. So a lot of holes were punched. At night, the syrup poured onto the ground. Solid bars of soap melted in the fire and ran in streams. In short, people stocked up with as much as they could...

Schoolgirl Gena Yushkevich watched people rushing past her home carrying whatever they could grab:

> A white man is running, completely white from his hair to his shoes. Covered in flour. He carries a white bag. Another one runs past. Jars of food peek from his bags – he's also holding jars in his hand. Confectionery... Packets of tobacco. Someone carries a cap in front of them, full of sugar. A pot full of sugar. Indescribable! Someone hauls a roll of cloth, another has wrapped themselves in blue cotton. Or red. It's enough to make you laugh. But no-one laughs.

The temptation was too much for the 12-year-old, who made her way to the warehouse, overtaken by a woman who was running. 'She had nothing with her, no bag, no net – but she had taken off her underwear. Her knickers, panties. She crammed them with buckwheat, then made off with it.'

Anything and everything was prey to the plunderers. They emptied the Lenin library – the city's finest – and the art gallery. At the Kommunarka market, some tried to scoop syrup from huge vats. They fell in and drowned.[22]

'THE IMPORTANT THING WAS NOT TO FALL INTO GERMAN HANDS...' REFUGEES ON THE ROAD, 25 JUNE

After two and a half days on the road, forester Fayvel Vayner had hoped to find rest in Glubokoye when he reached the town on the evening of 25 June. Instead, he found chaos. Glubokoye had been repeatedly bombed that day; its inhabitants were 'planning to flee'. The 43-year-old had set out with his wife and two children from the small town of Postawy, 80 miles east of Vilnius, on Monday morning. 'Anyone who has the chance gets away – or to be more accurate, flees – it doesn't matter where,' Vayner noted. 'Workers building the airfield leave, the banks pull out, all government institutions do the same. Those who cannot leave, who have no chance of leaving, run around depressed, their eyes red from crying, because everyone knows what's coming.' Communist officials condemned their actions: 'why did we want to leave the town, it would only cause panic and so on.' Fayvel Vayner ignored them, fully aware of the risks he was taking. 'I know that hunger and sorrow lie ahead – not just for me, but for my entire family.' Twenty-four hours later, he reluctantly abandoned them after walking just 18 miles. He scoured the deserted town of Dunilovich in vain for some form of cart to transport his family. 'My wife began to convince me that I should flee on foot and leave her with the children,' he wrote. He agreed, 'knowing all too well that I was leaving my family in the talons of a beast of prey, the German soldiers, and their atrocities'.

David Klementinowsky, one of nearly 50,000 Jews in Białystok, watched as lawlessness and racial hatred almost instantly replaced Soviet rule. 'Anyone who could fled with the Russians,' he wrote. 'The streets are full of tragic sights. Families which have lived together for dozens of years are being forced to separate. The Soviet warehouses are being looted for food, and the Poles are attacking the Jews. We are afraid to leave the house, because there is no-one around to keep law and order.'

Klementinowsky chose to remain. Hundreds of thousands, perhaps millions, chose to flee. An official historian later estimated that more than half the populace of Minsk – over 100,000 people, including most of the intelligentsia: scientists, artists, writers, doctors and at least 7,000 teachers – abandoned the city. It seemed as if all of western and central Byelorussia was on the move, a sorry tide of humanity struggling eastwards. 'Whatever town I passed through, I came across agitated, dejected and broken people asking the same questions: "What will happen?" "What should we do?" Our only answer was silence – what could we have told them?' Fayvel Vayner recalled. There was no order to the retreat – civilians simply fled on their own initiative, sharing the main roads in carts, vehicles, or simply on foot with the troops of the Western Front. Traffic jams took as long as six hours to clear as columns of retreating soldiers stretched for more than two dozen miles. 'Senior officials, police and the NKVD were the first to leave towns and cities,' the deputy head of political propaganda of the Western Front complained in an official report:

> After the first bombing raids life in several cities came to a standstill, the city emptied. The evacuation of food, equipment, factories, money and other valuable

property, or the populace, was not organised, nor was assistance for the wounded and fire-fighting. After the bombing of Minsk on 24 June, all the senior officials left the city, all the property was abandoned, the entire city was on fire – and it was not put out. The wounded and burned died beneath the rubble from loss of blood. All this led to a stampede by the populace, clogging the roads, and they were shot in large numbers by the Germans… Panic set in among the populace and leaders as well, not only in cities close to the front but in others such as Orsha, Mogilev and more. Unfounded rumours about paratroopers often caused the panic. In Baranovichi, there were rumours that there would be a landing during the night which led to senior officials, police and the NKVD fleeing. Police arbitrarily seized a train and fled to Minsk.

Any column still on the road when day came was subjected to ferocious Luftwaffe attack. Ditches straddling the main road to Mogilev were soon lined with corpses. According to one account, an enemy fighter even landed on the Moscow–Minsk highway and shot at refugees while it taxied along the asphalt. And while German bombs and bullets accounted for many of the dead, far more of Minsk's citizens were killed by their compatriots, according to one official report: 'Vehicles crashed into each other, pedestrians were killed because shots were fired from the cars, mostly involving the military, police and NKVD. Sometimes they threw civilians who did not obey out of vehicles, striking them with a pistol or rifle butt.' Army doctor Vladimir Tolkaczov was led about 100ft from the Borisov highway where he waited to be shot by the NKVD, having been unable to produce any papers. Tolkaczov had reported for duty in Minsk, only to find the city in flames and people advising him to turn around and head for Borisov. He did, but was soon stopped by military police. 'They took my rifle and ammunition pouch from me and ordered soldiers to shoot me as a deserter,' he recalled. But no-one fired. After a while his rifle and ammunition pouch were returned and he was taken to an assembly point for refugees.

The merest rumour could provoke panic. 'When someone provocatively cried out that the Germans were near, the retreat of the populace took on a chaotic, panic-stricken character,' Fayvel Vayner wrote. 'Those who previously walked now began to run with their last ounce of strength. Those who'd previously driven now began to toss baggage out of their vehicles. Bedding, suitcases with their contents, clothes, shoes and so on lay in the roads.' Few knew their destination, but every man, woman and child was possessed by a single thought. 'The important thing was not to fall into German hands,' one Minsk inhabitant recalled. 'We were all convinced that our lives as "refugees" would only be brief. A few weeks, a month at most!' Unaware of the exodus from Minsk, refugees from western Byelorussia believed that once they reached *true* Russian soil – the pre-1939 border of the Soviet Union which ran just to the west of Minsk – they would be safe. 'Fear of the Germans, fear of atrocities and suffering, ended at the border,' Fayvel Vayner recalled. 'It wasn't just me who felt like this, but everyone who ran foaming at the mouth, people who kept asking all the way to the border if they weren't already on the other side of it.'[23]

'DO NOT BE DISCOURAGED...' BREST FORTRESS, 26 JUNE

Only on the northeastern side of the central island, at the beginning – or end – of the ring barracks, was there still determined resistance in the citadel. Led by 32-year-old Byelorussian Yefim Fomin, a regimental commissar now without a regiment, perhaps 700 or 800 men stubbornly clung on in a two-storey red-brick building, 450ft long, 60ft wide, and which the attackers branded 'The Officers' House'. After four days of constant fighting, the defenders' strength, if not resolve, was fading. Ammunition was running low. There was little food, and less water. The encircling ring also ruled out any thought of a breakout from the citadel; Yefim Fomin had forbidden an attempt in the small hours because it held no prospect of success. All that was left for the defenders of the Officers' House was to sell their lives as expensively as possible. When some of the men vowed to save their last bullets to take their own lives rather than fall into German hands, Fomin stepped in. 'No, friends, you must use even your last cartridge on the enemy,' the commissar urged. 'Every cartridge must be for them, for the Fascists alone.'

By the morning of 26 June, it was clear to every man in the citadel that resistance probably wouldn't last more than 24 hours. There was no food, no electricity, no contact with the world beyond the red bricks and concrete. Windows were barricaded with mattresses, furniture and bricks. In the still air, the stench of decay from bloated corpses decomposing in the open lingered and gently drifted through the cellars and passageways. It mixed with the brick dust, which grew thicker with each bombardment, and the foul smell of burned flesh and gangrenous wounds. There was no medicine to treat the injured, nor even any bandages. Clothes, pillow cases, bedsheets were ripped and wrapped around wounds. Grigori Makarov remembered a female medic who stayed with the men to tend to them. 'There were many wounded, but no disinfectants so that gangrene spread very quickly and many men died of their injuries.' Worst of all, there was no water. There were no wells in the citadel; it drew its water from the

Mukhavets and Bug. The pipes were shattered in the opening minutes of the German assault and, once the central island was surrounded, any hope of filling pails or cans in the river was ruled out; the slightest movement, day or night – for the entire battlefield bathed in the ethereal light of star shells throughout the hours of darkness – resulted in furious German fire. The bodies of Germans were raided for their canteens and whatever iron rations were carried. If water was found, the wounded took priority – it was about the only relief their comrades could offer them, beyond false assurances that the Red Army was counter-attacking and would soon relieve the beleaguered fortress. The last defenders snatched no more than a few hours' sleep, drank urine, even blood, passing in and out of consciousness from exhaustion. The stronger ones bade their comrades goodbye, promising to write to their families if they survived – and if they could remember the address. And they vowed to fight on, to the last round. As they faced their final battle, they carved pithy messages in the plaster and masonry of the fortress. 'On 26 June 1941 there were three of us. It was hard for us, but we did not lose courage and die like heroes.' Or: 'There are five of us. We will die!! For Stalin.' In the officers' mess: 'There are three Muscovites – Ivanov, Stepanchikov, Zhuntiaev – who have defended this church and we have sworn that we will not leave here.' At the Terespol Gate: 'We've not lost courage and we'll die like heroes.' In the officers' club: 'One grenade left, but no surrender. Avenge us comrades.' On the wall of the casemate near Brest Gate: 'We will die but we will not abandon the fortress.' In the cellar of the ruins of the White Palace: 'We are dying without disgrace.' And found scratched in the plaster in the main barracks: *'Ya umirayu no ne sdayus'! Proshchay, Rodina'* – 'I am dying but will not surrender. Farewell, Motherland'. The note was dated 20 July 1941.

The troops of 45th Infantry Division had spent the past 24 hours systematically sweeping through the buildings and houses in the fortress. Nothing frightened the Austrians more than combing through the underground passageways and dormitories beneath the casemates. Infantryman Josef Arnreiter found them 'all topsy-turvy, like a pigsty'. There were blankets, pillows, officers' and commissars' coats on hooks on the walls, burned secret documents and papers, musical instruments, boots, shoes, belts. The canteen and armoury had been hastily abandoned: ammunition was piled up; light and heavy machine-guns, mortars, rifles were stacked up unused. The floor of the mess hall was littered with salt, flour, sugar, rice and coffee granules; on the tables: bread, tinned foods, sausages, fish, a large barrel of butter. 'Occasionally a Russian jumped out,' Arnreiter wrote. The defenders hid themselves under rags, in tubs, beds and blankets. They lunged at their attackers with knives or fired their rifles. 'There's a Frenchman!' one of his comrades yelled; the *Landser* had yet to grow accustomed to his new foe, let alone give him a nickname. 'We were not yet familiar with the fact that our opponents were Russians, no longer the French of the campaign in France,' the young Austrian noted. 'And the Russians wore the same brown-coloured uniforms as the French and Belgians.' Clearing out an underground passageway after one particularly heavy bombardment, the attackers urged the garrison to give themselves up. The response came in German: *Kiss our arses!*

Above ground, 'houses had to be searched two, three times until we had found out that apparently dead bodies had come back to life overnight and were shooting in the area again,' officer Günter Baumgartner wrote. Pioneers scrambled along rooftops with explosives on metal poles which they used to fix the charges to windows and embrasures. 'Even then only a few Russians surrender,' exasperated junior officer Franz Schneiderbauer wrote. Flamethrowers were employed. There was enough fuel in the heavy backpack for just ten seconds of flame. But ten seconds of flame was enough to wipe out everything and everyone in a cellar. Tongues of fire extended 100ft, reaching temperatures of 4,000°C, sucking the oxygen out of confined spaces, scorching lungs, burning eyeballs and leaving men blind – if they survived. 'Everything burned,' Georgii Karbuk recalled. 'Even the bricks melted.' At night there were attempts to slip over the waterways and break out of the encirclement. 'Fire from every weapon and a terrific artillery barrage – which fell just 50 metres in front of our own troops – repulsed every one,' an impressed Günter Baumgartner noted.

Among the most desperate resistance was offered by the wounded abandoned in the hospital on the South Island – captured on the first day of the attack. But now German troops combing through the three dozen buildings suddenly found themselves attacked by wounded men who 'pulled pistols from under their bandages and shot'. In another ward, where empty beds and surgical equipment had been pushed aside, the Germans were surprised by 'a Russian, hidden under the blankets, who flailed around wildly with a knife'. Nurse Katshova Braskova Lesnevna had managed to evade the Germans as they swarmed over the island during the initial assault, hiding in the casemates where she attempted to care for the wounded. The Germans eventually found the refuge. 'Before our very eyes they shot everyone – all the wounded, children, women, soldiers,' she recalled 40 years later. 'We nurses wanted to hurry to them – we were wearing our white overalls marked with the Red Cross, and our nurse's bonnets. We thought they would respect this. The Fascists shot

Barbarossa unleashed, 22 June 1941

(Above) A 5cm Pak 38 fires at a Soviet bunker on the far bank of the Bug at first light on 22 June.

(Left) A horse-drawn 7.5cm infantry gun crosses the border near Sokal, north of Lvov, as 57th Infantry Regiment advances into western Ukraine.

'Now we are fighting our real enemy…'

(Above) Troops of 101st Light Division cross the railway bridge over the San at Przemyśl.

(Right) German troops comb through the ruins of the citadel in Brest fortress.

(Below) A motorised German column pauses on the outskirts of Grodno.

'Cities are burning, people are dying…'
Elements of Otto Lasch's advanced detachment moves through the burning suburbs
of Riga on the left bank of the Daugava.

Armour of 4th Panzer Division moves through the outskirts of
Minsk at the end of June.

'Our heroic liberators…' Oppressed nations welcome the German Army
'People were wild with enthusiasm…' Ukrainians give the Hitler
salute to passing motorcycle troops of 12th Panzer Division.

Rigans salute the arrival of German assault guns on the edge
of the old town.

'A scene of unimaginable horror…'
Tank warfare, June 1941

(Top) A Red Army truck burns next to a knocked-out OT-130 flamethrower tank and T-34 at Jeziornica, near Slonim.

(Above) A German 3.7cm anti-tank gun takes up position at Dubno while (left) nearby a German soldier inspects a disabled T-34 as a column of trucks files past on the embankment.

'The German is a hero in battle – and afterwards a good comrade towards a defeated foe. This time that must not be the case…'

(Above) German troops stare at the corpses of murdered Soviet prisoners at Varėna in Lithuania, 24 June.

(Right) Russians captured in the Białystok–Minsk pockets await their fate in a makeshift camp on the edge of the Byelorussian capital.

'The war assumes bestial forms…'

(Above) 'The most gruesome spectacle…' A crowd of Lithuanians and German soldiers watch Jews bludgeoned to death at Kaunas' Lietūkis garage.

(Left) 'A dark chapter of human history was written here…' Lvov citizens file past corpses in the grounds of Zamarstynów prison.

'War also numbs the senses…'

(Above) The mental and physical strain of holding the line on the edge of the Volkovysk–Minsk pocket is evident in these German infantrymen awaiting another Soviet breakout attempt.

'Think of the worst exhaustion you've felt…'

(Below left) Weariness is written on the faces of 5th Infantry Division's ranks moving through the steppe and (below right) endless lines of German infantry move down a dusty Byelorussian road.

28 wounded in my section alone. And if they weren't killed immediately, they tossed hand-grenades at them.' On at least one occasion, captured women and children were driven towards the Kholmsky Bridge by the Germans in the hope that the defenders would surrender. Instead, they opened fire. The hostages threw themselves to the ground. 'With every shot, it seemed as if my brain would seep out of my head,' Arshinova Anastasia Antonovna recalled 40 years later. 'Blood streamed out of the ears and mouths of the children. My daughter died. My five-year-old son has been deaf since then.' The ruse failed. The German attackers fell back.

What prisoners were taken often preferred to be 'shot on the spot' rather than taken into captivity. When one group of wounded Red Army troops and their families was being led over one of the central island bridges, the senior officer among them, battalion commander Captain Vladimir Shablovsky, handed his daughter to his wife, kissed her, then jumped over the guard rail crying: 'Follow me!' Several of his men did. Every one of them was killed by German bullets as they flailed in the shallow water of the Mukhavets.

By mid-day on the 26th, the attackers had reached the Officers' House. German pioneers detonated a series of charges they had placed at strategic points around the barracks. The first explosion brought down most of the western end of the structure – a 150ft section of the building caved in. When they recovered from the shock, 80 men staggered out of the rubble and were immediately taken prisoner. Over the next couple of hours further charges were set off, finally bringing the last resistance in the citadel to an end. At least 200 bodies were later recovered from the ruins and cursorily buried in nearby shell holes by some of the 450 Red Army men taken prisoner. As was now becoming routine, Jews and commissars were singled out. Yefim Fomin was both. He was betrayed by one of the men he had led just minutes before. Fomin was taken aside at the Kholmsky Gate and shot as Soviet soldiers filed over the bridge and into captivity. His last words were aimed at them. 'Do not be discouraged,' he shouted. 'Victory will be ours.'

With the citadel finally subdued, Fritz Schlieper turned his attention to the last substantial outpost of resistance at Brest: the North Island. Its defenders showed no signs of giving up. 'The only decision left,' 45th Infantry Division's commander decided, 'was to force the Russians to surrender through hunger and especially thirst and use all means to speed up wearing them down.' He would use mortars, tank guns and bombing raids to keep the defenders hunkered down in their vaults, bunkers and casemates, megaphones would blurt out demands to surrender, while leaflets would urge soldiers to desert. The last defenders of Brest fortress were to be ground down, physically and psychologically.[24]

'There is no way to oppose them...'
Panzergruppe 3, 26 June

Even though Heinz Guderian's armour was carving up his left wing, it was the threat from the north which perturbed Dmitry Pavlov. 'Up to 1,000 tanks are enveloping Minsk from the north-west,' he alarmingly reported to Moscow. 'There is no way to oppose them.' In fact, the three armoured divisions bearing down on the city – 7th, 12th and 20th Panzer – possessed a little more than 600 tanks when the invasion began, fewer than 100 the latest Mk4s. And their commander, *Panzergruppe* 3's Hermann Hoth, was sending his panzers to Minsk against his better judgment – not for fear of being dragged into street fighting, but because he was convinced a much greater opportunity was slipping through German hands. Hoth wanted the jaws of his and Guderian's armoured pincers to close much further east than Minsk, perhaps as far east as Vitebsk, 150 miles northeast of Byelorussia's capital. For Hitler and the Army High Command – 250 miles behind the front amid the forests and lakes of East Prussia – the risk of the Red Army escaping from such an enormous pocket was too great. They ordered the jaws closed at Minsk.[25]

The ordinary *Landser* at the tip of Hoth's spear cared little for such considerations. The advance was breathless, exhilarating, as Gerhard Möws, a motorcyclist scouting ahead of 12th Panzer Division, described:

> Suddenly there's shooting from a farm on our left. Several tracer rounds from the machine-guns set the dry straw roof on fire and silence the snipers. We wind our way through the countryside, avoiding Russians in a position, and cross a railway line. The town [Molodechno, 45 miles northwest of Minsk] lies in front of us. We dismount and approach the houses. Darkness has fallen. At the entrance one of those wooden triumphal arches burns eerily. There's deathly silence, just the crackle of the fire. There's no-one to be seen and no sound of engines from any unit following us. Have we pushed so far ahead? We come to an empty square with a church. Quiet. We're lit up by the fire – it makes everything seem so strange. Shooting could break out at any moment...
>
> In the distance, far to our rear, we hear a train puffing along the line. And suddenly we hear lively shooting there. Machine-guns rattle, panzer cannon roar. The train gives a loud, constant whistle which penetrates the night. We later learn that a Russian troop transport has been attacked. On the northern edge of the town there must be Russian tanks, we can hear them drive up and stop, the sound of engines and caterpillar tracks. Then the sound of motors coming from the

south. Some armoured vehicle advances into our square. At first we think it's an Ivan. 'Men, it's a half-track.' We breathe a sigh of relief.[26]

At times, the defenders resorted to desperate means in the hope of halting the enemy advance. When a DB-3 bomber was engulfed in flames while attacking German armour on the Vilnius–Minsk highway, its pilot chose to crash his stricken aircraft into the advancing column. He killed himself and three crewmates, but destroyed a dozen German vehicles in the process. During a period of catastrophic collective failure by Soviet arms, individual acts of bravery and sacrifice were seized upon by the Communist propaganda machine. The actions of 33-year-old Captain Nikolai Gastello became the stuff of Soviet legend. The jug-eared bomber pilot was named a Hero of the Soviet Union. His face adorned stamps. His name was given to streets. Party activists read out details of his deeds to inspire their comrades. Other aviators would repeat Gastello's actions – now given a suitably heroic name, *ognenniy taran* or 'fiery ramming' – performing 'unforgettable feats in the history of human daring, bravery and selflessness…' Stephan Zdorovtsev, Mikhail Zhukov and Piotr Kharitonov, who all rammed German aircraft on the approaches to Leningrad, were suitably decorated by the Soviet leadership and eulogised by one of the regime's most famous young poets, Aleksandr Tvardovsky:

And how many more Soviet people
Will show themselves
in dashing battles!
We'll glorify many,
but these three
We'll never forget.[27]

Yet such actions drew not admiration from the Red Air Force's foe, but rather contempt. This wasn't bravery, wrote fighter pilot Erbo von Kageneck, but 'blindness, imbecilic stubbornness'. A veteran of almost every theatre of war to date, the 23-year-old had spent the majority of the opening days of the campaign in the East bombing and strafing enemy ground units. He yearned to grapple with 'enemy aviation worthy of the name', but the Red Air Force, he told his parents in the Rhineland, was 'practically non-existent'. 'You've got to hand it to them, they're fighting to the death, but you wonder whether it's for an idea or out of sheer stupidity. Half the way to Moscow is behind us, and we are still advancing…'[28]

'SHOTS DROWNED THE CRIES AND GROANS OF THE VICTIMS...' CHERVYEN, 26 JUNE, EVENING

After 36 hours being force-marched, prisoners evacuated from Minsk had covered about 45 miles, reaching a jail on the outskirts of the small town of Chervyen. At least 600 corpses were scattered in the roadside ditches of central Byelorussia – prisoners murdered by their guards on the journey. But in Chervyen, the marchers were permitted not merely a rest, but a cup of water and 200g of bread for the first time since early on Wednesday. A nurse even applied some Vaseline to Joanna Stankiewicz-Januszczak's sore leg. 'I smeared it and went to sleep against the wall,' she remembered. 'Aircraft continued to fly and drop bombs, but we were deep in our dreams and were not disturbed.'

The bombing, however, was the catalyst for a fresh wave of killings. Around 700 prisoners were marched to woods a couple of miles outside town. There was no order to halt; no instructions were given. The guards simply opened fire on the final rows of the column – from the side, as if the prisoners were running a gauntlet. 'Run into the woods, otherwise we'll shoot,' they encouraged those still alive. Most stood up, only to be gunned down. 'The shots drowned the cries and groans of the victims,' remembered Janusz Prawdzic Szlaski, who stayed on the ground with another Polish insurgent. 'We crept into the roadside ditch, where we remained during the worst of the shooting. Then we crept slowly into the woods and escaped.' For the survivors, the death march continued towards Mogilev.[29]

'WHEN WAR KNEW NO LIMITS...' BIAŁYSTOK, 27 JUNE

While Guderian's and Hoth's panzers cut through hundreds of miles of Soviet territory, Army Group Centre's two infantry armies were still bludgeoning their way across western Byelorussia. The armour was advancing upwards of 30 miles a day. The ordinary *Landser* could count his daily progress on both hands. After five days of marching and fighting, Fourth and Ninth Armies were closing in on their objective – the town of Volkovsyk, 50 miles east of Białystok. When they met, the trap would close on the bulk of the Russian Tenth Army, now desperately streaming eastwards to escape encirclement. At the western edge of the nascent pocket, 221st Security Division began moving into the outskirts of Białystok. The 221st was never intended for front-line combat: a mish-mash of a regular infantry regiment, reservists and police officers, it was meant to restore and enforce order behind the front, to root out partisans, to secure the fighting troops' lines. It had already been thrown into the fighting outside Białystok. At dawn on 27 June, it began moving into the city.

Only scattered troops and a few rearguards were left behind, as infantry officer Wilhelm Müller quickly realised scouting the outskirts of Białystok, where elderly people hid in the cellars of 'wretched timber-framed houses', terrified by the noise of battle. There was a skirmish for the city's barracks and occasional house-to-house fighting, but by 7am, helped by Poles acting as guides, the first German soldiers had reached the city centre. Here there was a short, but vicious, battle for the central post office, an imposing four-storey building where the Russians had established several machine-gun posts. An anti-tank gun was wheeled into a bar which overlooked the market square and post office. 'The concussion and sound of the gun firing caused the plaster to fall from the ceiling. It was a good job that the front window had been removed,' Müller recalled. 'There wasn't the tiniest cloud in the sky, just puffs of black smoke from timber houses which had been set on fire by hand-grenades or anti-tank shells, occasionally darkening the sun. We'd reached the point when war knew no limits, ruthlessly destroying everything to achieve its goals.' The rounds from the anti-tank gun silenced the machine-guns, but there were still Soviet troops holding out in the post office who refused all calls to surrender. Müller's company was forced to take the building room by room, floor by floor. Burning furniture gave off acrid black smoke, which filled the building and provided cover for 30 Russian troops to escape. After killing 19 of the post office's 'garrison', Müller's group eventually reached the attic, where ten enemy soldiers surrendered.

Ignoring the fighting in the suburbs, 221st Security Division's commander Johann Pflugbeil drove to the city centre in time to see his operations officer Karl Hübner raise the *Reichskriegsflagge* on the tower of the 200-year-old town hall and hear him give a hearty '*Sieg Heil!*' for Hitler and his victorious armies. It was barely 8.30am. The short battle for Białystok cost the division just 46 dead and a similar number of wounded and missing. Russian casualties numbered 300.[30]

While the German standard was being hoisted in the centre of Białystok, the Rhinelanders of 309th Police Battalion were still combing through the suburbs, rooting out Red Army stragglers and 'inhabitants hostile to the Germans'. How the policemen acted this morning set the tone for the rest of the day.

Białystok's Polish inhabitants welcomed the policemen as liberators, offering the Germans flowers, sweets and drinks. But this was the battalion's first action and its men were wary. The previous day they'd come across the mutilated corpses of two dozen German soldiers cut down by a Russian ambush; genitalia had been cut off some bodies, the swastika was carved in the chest of one, while nails forming the hammer and sickle had been driven into the skull of another corpse. One company commander told his men that the Soviets were sub-humans and they were to take no prisoners.

When he found one Russian straggler, a policeman forced him to walk ahead as cover, while the prisoner's partner ran behind him, moaning. After a while, the police officer simply pulled the trigger on his rifle. The soldier fell to the ground dead; the woman fell on top of him in tears. Other Soviet soldiers found by the battalion as it combed through Białystok's western suburbs were simply lined up against walls and shot in a 'clearing' action which became increasingly undisciplined. In the broiling heat of a June day, the men smashed their way into drink stores and quenched their thirst with red wine, champagne and vodka. They took their lead from their commander, Major Ernst Weis, who encouraged his men: 'Grab yourselves a little booty, lads!'

When the battalion reached the city centre around mid-day, Weis reckoned his men had already finished off 200 enemy soldiers. But the 'pacification' of Białystok was far from over, for Weis now switched his attention to the Szulhojf district – the city's Jewish quarter – as he dispatched his squads to round up any man of military age.

The battalion moved with brutal purpose through the narrow streets of one- and two-storey wooden houses. Any door not opened immediately was blown open using hand-grenades. The inhabitants were then forced into the road, where they were either driven in the direction of the city's main synagogue with kicks or blows from rifle butts, or executed on the spot. Elsewhere in the densely populated quarter, which covered no more than a fifth of a square mile, the Germans 'went on a shooting spree, without any reasonable justification, clearly to terrify people,' one Jewish resident testified a quarter of a century later. 'They shot blindly through windows and into houses – without giving a thought to whether someone was standing there.' When one platoon found a prayer room, their commander ordered it destroyed. His men obliged, swinging on the chandelier to bring it down. Some policemen set fire to Jews' beards and forced them to dance or yell out 'I am Jesus Christ'. Their relatives begged for an end to the torment, offering gold or jewellery, but the torture continued. To Jewish historian Szymon Datner it was as if 'scenes of Dante's Hell' were being recreated on the streets of his city.

Some groups of Jews were led to a disused gravel pit on the edge of Białystok, where they were shot – though 30 prisoners were let go when the Germans were startled by the sound of Russian military marches and men singing, and fell back in panic, yelling: 'Every man for himself!'

Not every member of the police battalion agreed with what was happening this Friday afternoon. One policeman refused to execute more than a dozen women and children supposedly found with weapons in their hands, while the pitiful story of one Jewish father of three persuaded his captor to let him go. Some men even went so far as to protest – without effect. 'Shut your mouth,' one comrade snapped at a disapproving veteran police officer. 'You've probably not received the correct ideological education yet.' An army officer told one of the ringleaders of the massacre he would do better 'risking his life at the front than killing defenceless civilians'. He received no response. Martin Ronicke, commander of 2nd Security Regiment, was equally unsuccessful. The colonel and his staff had established themselves in the Hotel Ritz, Białystok's grandest hostelry and a favourite of Poland's pre-war elite, where staff welcomed their new masters 'with the customary salt and bread'. When he saw smoke rising above the city centre, he went to investigate and was appalled by the scenes. He screamed at the policemen, even threatened to shoot one of them. The German Army, he told them, waged war. It did not commit murder.

That was as close as anyone came to putting a stop to the atrocity. 221st Security Division's spineless commander certainly wasn't going to intervene. When one elderly and one young Jew threw themselves at Johann Pflugbeil's feet at his headquarters, pleading for an end to the killings and arrests, he turned his back on them. He did nothing when one member of 309th Police Battalion urinated on the two prostrate Jews. But he did protest when some of the executions took place in front of the windows of his quarters. The shootings were promptly moved.

Those Jews not shot – most estimates suggest 800 people – were led to Białystok's Great Synagogue, an imposing two-storey red-brick building on a small hill just a couple of minutes' walk from the city's main square. As the police formed a double cordon around the place of worship, the prisoners were forced inside to enthusiastic taunts from a growing crowd of Poles: 'Hurrah, the Jews are kaput!' First the side doors were locked and barricaded with furniture, then a machine-gun was placed in front of the main entrance. As the final victims of the round-up were forced kicking and screaming into the synagogue, police carried in cans filled with petrol. Realising their fate, the Jews inside began to sing in unison; their chants carried across the city centre. They only stopped when one of the police officers tossed several hand-grenades into the synagogue; the singing turned to screams first as the explosives detonated and then as the petrol canisters went up in flames.

The police in the cordon took aim at anyone who tried to climb out of the windows, even women and children. Some Jews appeared at windows in the hope a German bullet would end their lives, rather than be burned alive; at least one man hanged himself in the rafters to spare himself the same fate. Half a dozen men, some with their clothes on fire, succeeded in forcing open the front door to reach the square, only to be cut down by machine-gun bullets. Others sought salvation by moving to the ante rooms, hoping to escape through the side doors. Some even succeeded, aided by the synagogue's Polish caretaker, Jozef Bartoszka. Most were trapped between German bullets and the flames, burned or, worse, even baked alive.

It lasted perhaps an hour. The Great Synagogue was nothing but a charred shell, its great dome reduced to a twisted metal frame. But at least the screams had faded. The sights, the sounds, the smell of burning flesh now carried across the square around the synagogue, causing some police to vomit, others to turn to alcohol. One platoon leader, Heinrich Schneider, was so inebriated that he collapsed in the street and was run over by a vehicle, while a sergeant on guard duty had to be tied to a post to prevent him from falling down.

The conflagration did not end with the Great Synagogue, however. The flames spread to neighbouring wooden buildings, then through the entire Jewish district and across the market square. 'On the horizon, the red flames of burning Białystok glow,' reservist officer Fritz-Dietlof Graf von der Schulenburg observed as his 9th Infantry Regiment marched towards the city at dusk. The city burned all night. The flames only died out around 8am on Saturday thanks to fire breaks created by German troops. By then the fire had reduced a dozen streets, the fish market and main square to rubble and charred timbers, and claimed perhaps as many as 1,000 lives.

The Germans were well satisfied with their work. They posed for snapshots in front of the synagogue's ruins. After all, Friday 27 June 1941 was, the diary of 221st Security Division recorded, 'a proud day in the division's combat history'. The Jews of Białystok called it *Royter, Blutiker* or *Shvartser Fraytik* – Red, Bloody or Black Friday. One in every 20 of the city's Jews – between 2,000 and 2,200 men, women and children – died during the day-long massacre. For several days horse-drawn carts pulled through the heart of the city to the old Jewish cemetery. In the synagogue, the burial parties found contorted naked corpses piled up, or bodies 'burned beyond recognition – there was nothing left to bury'. Some remains were simply scraped off the floor and shovelled into sacks. They were still recovering the dead – and tearing down statues of Lenin and Stalin and any other vestige of Communist rule on the instructions of their new masters – two days later when Białystok's churches held services of thanksgiving for the city's deliverance from the Soviet yoke. 'The populace breathes a sigh of relief,' 221st Security Division's intelligence officer noted smugly. 'Whether Pole or Byelorussian, they warmly welcome the German soldiers. We are liberators from a seemingly almost impossible terror.' Swaths of central Białystok were still smouldering.

As 9th Infantry Regiment marched through Białystok after dark on the 27th, its men found 'slain Jews lying in the streets'. But otherwise, Ernst Weis and Johann Pflugbeil succeeded in covering up the massacre rather neatly. Newspapers attributed the city's destruction to the work of the Luftwaffe. In his official report, Ernst Weis – who'd spent most of the afternoon and evening of 27 June in a drunken stupor – blamed the inferno on fire from an enemy anti-tank gun. He made no mention of the round-up and execution of Jews carried out by his men. In fact, his actions in Białystok were even seen as exemplary. One week after the massacre, he was recommended for the Iron Cross for pacifying the city 'in a relatively short time'. 'He – and his battalion – were always on the spot, ready to intervene,' the citation read. 'He is worthy of the award.'[31]

'AND THEN A YOUNG GERMAN LED OUT THE JEWS ... PUT THEM AGAINST THE WALL AND SHOT THEM...' WESTERN BYELORUSSIA, 24–28 JUNE

The Białystok massacre was the first major atrocity committed by German forces in the East, but not the first crime against the district's Jews. Within days, if not hours, of the invader's entry into the towns and villages of western Byelorussia, Jews who stayed realised that they could no longer trust their neighbours. As in Lithuania, the Polish populace blamed Jews for the injuries suffered during nearly two years of Soviet rule. The mayor of the village of Tykocin, 20 miles west of Białystok, drew up a list of supposed Communists – which just happened to correlate with a list of almost every Jew in the village. A dozen miles away in Trzcianne, Meir Markowicz watched as Poles helped German troops single out 'Communists' from the village's Jewish community. 'And then a young German led out the Jews with his short carbine, put them against the wall and shot them.' Twenty miles away in Radziłów, the minority Polish populace showed their hand immediately, hastily erecting a triumphal arch adorned with a swastika and portrait of Hitler. Every male Jew was ordered to report to the village synagogue where German troops made them remove holy books, papers and scrolls, which were then piled up, doused in petrol and set on fire. Jews were forced to dance around the pyre as they were beaten by Polish villagers. When the fire died down, the torment continued as Jews were harnessed to carts and made to haul them around the village – dragging the delighted Poles and Germans. The torture ended in the swamps outside Radziłów; the exhausted Jews were driven into the water up to their necks – or deeper. And in the town of Grajewo, close to the East Prussian border, Poles not only identified 'Communists', but meted out the punishments as well, 'furiously beating Jews with truncheons, sticks, anything which they had to hand'. The Germans did not join in, according to one eyewitness. 'They stood around, watched, laughed and encouraged the participants of the pogrom.'

The Polish inhabitants of Rozanka, 20 miles southwest of Lida, welcomed German soldiers when 56th Infantry Regiment finally 'liberated' the village after several days of see-saw fighting. The final hours of Soviet rule had been characterised by treachery and murder as Jewish inhabitants supposedly betrayed the hiding places of Polish nationals, plus five German soldiers left behind as a rearguard during the previous day's skirmishes. All were assaulted or tortured before being shot, their bodies kicked into a rapidly filling mass grave beneath a cluster of trees on the edge of Rozanka. Surviving Poles quickly drew the attention of the entering German infantry to the mass grave, then began to inform on the village's Jewish populace. Their 'testimony' fell on fertile ground; the 56th's commander Helmuth Thumm had 50 of Rozanka's Jews arrested and shot in retaliation – all played out in full view of Rozanka's remaining inhabitants. When the shooting stopped, one inhabitant moved through the sea of bodies, removed the boots of a dead man and put them on with a grin.[32]

THE STALIN LINE, ZASLAVYE, 27–28 JUNE

About 40 minutes' drive northwest of Minsk, troops in bunkers scanned the gently rolling countryside for the enemy from first light on Friday. The first four days of the invasion had passed in peace. But on the afternoon of the 26th, the bunker and casemate garrisons of the Stalin Line around Zaslavye had been put on alert: the Germans were approaching.

Never continuous – it comprised a series of 'fortified zones' defending major towns, cities and routes into the heart of the Soviet Union from the Baltic to the Black Sea – the Stalin Line should have presented a daunting barrier to any invader. In the early 1930s, nearly 300 pill boxes, 242 machine-gun bunkers, over a dozen 76mm gun emplacements, anti-tank ditches, the turrets of T-26 tanks buried in concrete, had been built in the zone protecting Minsk – one of four in Byelorussia. Gunners shielded by 3ft of concrete and 3in-thick steel doors stooped to load shells weighing 17lb into their barrels, aiming their fire based on directions from the battery commander over a voicepipe. Once closed up in their position, the men lived off rations and performed their ablutions in buckets. When battle came, the artillerymen were expected to hold their positions for up to 15 days – as long as food and ammunition lasted. Slogans on machine-gun posts proclaimed 'The border of the USSR is sacred and inviolable', while above the entrance to the artillery bunkers, a red star and words in red paint declared:

We are for peace!
We are not afraid
But if someone should strike a blow
We will respond

The sector centred on Zaslavye alone comprised nearly 250 bunkers, pillboxes and emplacements. It should have been a formidable obstacle. But when machine-gun battalion commander Arseny Sugakov arrived in April, he found the fortifications in a sorry state: fewer than half the guns were still installed and those left were rusty, their sights broken. The power supply in the casemates cut out frequently and the ventilation system had failed; as soon as troops began operating the machine-guns, they began choking on the gases produced. Barbed wire barriers had frequently been torn up; lights, telephones, radios were all out of order, and there were no fire tables, charts or instructions to assist the gunners. Nor was the personnel situation any better. There should have been six battalions guarding the Minsk sector of the Stalin Line – five machine-gun, one artillery. Sugakov found just machine-gunners – and they were barely fit for guard duty. When he protested about the state of his sector, Dmitry Pavlov slapped him down: 'Captain Sugakov does not know that we've built another line of defences on the new border. Collective farmers will pour potatoes in the old pillboxes.' Irrespective of Pavlov's put-down, Sugakov brought his sector up to strength, guns restored and repaired, gaps in personnel filled.

Now in a bunker position armed with four 76mm guns on the right wing of Sugakov's positions, deputy commissar Filipp Ryabov waited for the German onslaught with 19 comrades – some veterans of the war with Finland – and two women, wives of officers. 'I can see Fascist tanks on the old Minsk–Vilnius highway,' the private manning the periscope reported.

'Load guns one and two – armour-piercing shells,' the battery commander ordered.

'Fire!'

The bunker shook and filled with powder fumes. When they cleared, the soldier looked through his sight again.

'Well done!' he shouted. 'Two hits.'

Two more panzers were swiftly knocked out – one lost its turret, the other was set ablaze.

'We repulsed several Fascist attacks,' Ryabov recalled with pride. 'Not one enemy tank passed down the road to Minsk.'

The Soviet positions were subjected to Luftwaffe attack, which knocked out the bunkers' water and electricity supplies, hit fuel for the generator and wrecked the galley. Gunsmoke filled the casemates, suffocating the gunners. They kept shooting, however, until their shells ran out.

Frustrated by their losses on the 27th, the Germans renewed their assault at dawn on Saturday. Gun emplacements were knocked out by heavy mortars and 105mm field guns before anti-tank and rapid-fire 20mm flak guns were brought up to pour fire into the embrasures. Assault pioneers mounted on Panzer Mk4s now rolled up to finish off the final positions – and the garrisons holding them – hurling explosive charges through embrasures and finishing off the garrison in hand-to-hand fighting; one company alone knocked out 22 bunkers. Some bunkers fought to the death; the garrisons of others preferred to fight in the open. All, 12th Panzer Division reported, fought with 'extraordinary tenacity'. Bunkers believed to be neutralised or which had shown no signs of life suddenly began to pour fire on their attackers. One machine-gun crew emptied 25 entire cartridges before abandoning their position. Such doggedness caused 'no end of trouble and slowed the division's attack'. Slowed but did not stop. The battle had turned in the Germans' favour.

With Zaslavye on the cusp of falling, a handful of troops volunteered to remain behind to destroy its most valuable asset: military depot No.11, a complex of Red Army magazines and warehouses. There were no explosives or petrol left. Instead, the demolition party soaked soldiers' uniforms and underwear in oil, placed artillery rounds on top and set them alight.

Having lost contact with his superiors and with one casemate after another being knocked out, Arseny Sugakov decided the time had come to abandon the line. He and the last five men still fit in his bunker withdrew to a farm, which acted as a rallying point for many of the survivors from the sector. Surrounded, the troops tried to break out. Most were mown down by German guns. Sugakov survived, but decided the time had come to ditch his uniform, bury his Party card and personal documents, and slip away in civilian clothes. He made for Minsk but ran into a German patrol and was taken prisoner.

After bludgeoning their way through the Stalin Line, the motorised infantry of 12th Panzer Division paused on the north bank of the Svislach, awaiting orders. The men could see the spires and onion domes of Minsk in the distance. A signaller picked up a radio message with orders for the battalion: attack Minsk and seize every bridge. 'In an instant, the company mounted up, engines growled, motorcycle despatch riders dashed to and fro, the men had their weapons in their hands at the ready,' a junior officer recalled: 'We drove through a ford and reached the broad, unpaved road which led to the city. Forwards, forwards! The engines pounded. Thick clouds of dust swirled over the grey column of army trucks, panzers and vehicles pulling the heavy weapons. We were going to Minsk!'[33]

'A CITY SCARRED BY WAR...' MINSK, AFTERNOON, 28 JUNE

With the Stalin Line punctured, there was nothing to prevent the Germans entering Minsk. Through the late afternoon and evening of 28 June, they moved through the city, clearing out final pockets of Soviet resistance. They found 'a city scarred by war,' one junior officer wrote. All that remained of the large brick buildings lining the streets were burned-out façades. Air attacks had brought down the tram wires in a tangled knot and lifted the tracks themselves from the asphalt, bending and contorting them in the process. The sights – showers of ash, chimneys and burned joists rising from ruins – reminded war correspondent Rasso Königer of Pompeii. 'There's an acrid smell of burning in the air which makes you cough,' he wrote. 'Flames still lick from some of the naked skeletons of houses. A ceiling beam falls down with a crash and crackle, throwing a shower of sparks into the air. Plumes of smoke rise above the seats of countless fires and merge high in the sky, turning into black clouds hovering over the city.' To 23rd Infantry Division's supply officer, Minsk appeared 'completely burned out – probably like no city before it'. The destruction was neither total nor consistent, however. The opera house, theatre, the ten-storey House of the Soviets with a huge statue of Lenin in front of it, the central railway station, where empty trains still stood on the tracks, and the House of the Red Army had largely survived the Luftwaffe onslaught unscathed. Pretty much every German who saw them contrasted these 'showpiece Bolshevik buildings' with the 'wretched shacks and cottages' of the city's inhabitants. The streets of Minsk were strewn with rubble, gas masks, steel helmets. On some street corners and bridges there were sandbag barriers and abandoned machine-gun posts. And there were the dead. Dead soldiers. Dead civilians. No-one attempted to bury them, not even the decaying corpses which emitted an awful smell. 'As if to add insult to injury, a kitten sits on the face of a dead Russian and cleans itself,' machine-gunner Kurt Pfau observed. The living were too busy either rescuing their possessions or looting the abandoned Soviet warehouses to trouble themselves with the dead. 'These poor people, starving, in ragged clothes, sheepishly pounce on these marvellous things,' wrote Pfau, 'unless the German soldiers take them away from them.' He watched people haul sacks of grain and flour back to their homes. 'They look at us filled with fear when we find seven or eight of these sacks in their apartments,' he wrote. 'An elderly woman tenderly strokes the contents and, in poor German, says: "Bread, at last bread." Tears stream down her withered face.' Rasso Königer watched women, bent and silent, standing next to rubble which was once their home. What possessions they had rescued were stuffed into baskets or wrapped up in large, knotted bundles, which they dragged through the streets. There was sporadic fighting with Soviet rearguards: they dug in on the banks of the Svislach, retreating Russian troops in trucks tried to force their way through to the east near the railway station, a few die-hards held out in cellars and amid the rubble. Otherwise by nightfall on the sixth day of war, the capital of Byelorussia was in German hands.

The entering Germans struck many of Minsk's inhabitants as 'well-groomed, well-fed, cheerful'. They were well disciplined, singing as they marched in unison. And their hobnailed boots made an unforgettable sound as they came down on the cobblestones. One youngster watched a column of armoured vehicles, their bonnets marked with the swastika flag, roll into the city. 'Although I was small I realised that something was not right,' he remembered.

> The armoured cars drove as far as the bakery and fired several bursts of machine-gun fire to see whether there was anyone in the city or not. The response? Total silence. Not a sound…
>
> After 20 minutes, the column continued… Tanks, armoured troop-carriers with infantry. They entered without any shooting. Our first impression was that they were not hostile – they treated kids to sweets. I didn't take any – it was disgusting to take something from foreigners, from the enemy…[34]

'Hecatombs of human sacrifices...' The Białystok–Volkovysk pocket, 27–28 June

As German troops swept through the suburbs of Minsk, 150 miles to the west 137th Infantry Division forced their way into Volkovysk, an insignificant town of 20,000 souls who worked in its tanneries and canning factories. Barely a building was still standing in the town centre – 24 hours before it had been subjected to a savage Stuka attack. The 137th narrowly missed capturing Tenth Army's commander Konstantin Golubev, but did capture his cook and his personal papers. More importantly, by capturing Volkovysk at dusk this Saturday, 137th Infantry Division had closed the inner ring of encirclement around thousands of Red Army troops in the woods and swamps of Byelorussia.[35]

Trapped in the 50-mile-wide pocket between Białystok and Volkovysk were around a dozen divisions and brigades – infantry, armour and cavalry. Nature favoured the defender; the landscape was flat but often swampy, criss-crossed with water-filled ditches, and littered with copses and woods, mostly comprising tall, spindly pines. They would prove to be excellent hiding places – and sites of unimaginable horror. While combing through woods east of Grodno, the Silesians of 7th Infantry Regiment were surprised by a breakout attempt. 'Every wounded soldier who fell into Russian hands was murdered,' they reported, 'in some cases they were found hideously mutilated.' Their opponents had been a construction detachment, Mongolians 'who had no idea where they were or about the wider surroundings, no heavy weapons and evidently no officers'. Spurred on by commissars, they had fought until captured. To the Silesians, their prisoners seemed unable to grasp their plight. 'They sit silently, crouched down, cautious, they don't complain, they seem numb, apathetic and motionless,' 7th Infantry's historian recorded. 'And they don't speak at all, not with each other, not with their wounded.' The regimental history is silent too when it comes to the prisoners' fate.

In many cases, it was less a matter of combing out the pocket than preventing a Soviet breakout. The 261st Rifle Regiment looked for a way out of the pocket north of Białystok. Progress was slow as the Luftwaffe targeted any movement on any road. 'The road which we marched down presented a terrible sight,' one company commander wrote. 'On it and by the roadside were the corpses of soldiers and civilians, the cadavers of horses, wrecked vehicles and carts.' With enemy motorcyclists constantly snapping at their heels, the regiment's luck ran out in the woods southwest of Augustów when it stumbled into a German column. The Russians gave battle. In the resulting fighting, 261st Rifle Regiment ceased to exist.

At first light on 27 June, a truck carrying 23 Russians drove straight for 445th Infantry Regiment's lines near Nowy Dwór, roughly halfway between

Brest and Białystok, overrunning the command post, where officers, messengers and drivers grabbed side-arms and tried to defend themselves. The wild ride ended only when a 2cm flak gun caused the truck to explode, but even then the Soviet troops fought on until there was nothing but 20 Russian corpses in the burned-out wreckage of the vehicle. It was the curtain-raiser to two days of desperate breakout attempts which left parts of 134th Infantry Division cut off for hours on end. The division's supply column was blown up to prevent it falling into Soviet hands, which meant by the afternoon of the first day, ammunition was running low – or had already run out. Several German battalions were simply bypassed in the dense woods of Nowy Dwór as elements of six Russian divisions – one cavalry, five rifle – streamed eastwards. A Luftwaffe reconnaissance aircraft dropped a message to the trapped troops. 'Full of concern, we're thinking of you. Escape to the east or southeast.' On the late afternoon of 28 June, the cut-off German troops decided the moment to escape had come. The omens were not good, however. The men's morale was low, having barely eaten or slept for days and with ammunition down to a few rounds. They avoided all contact with human life, a column more than a mile long snaking through the pine forest. Some of the men had given up hope of making contact with friendly troops again. Others robotically followed their leaders. After occasional and brief skirmishes with Soviet troops – just as scared and uncertain in the terrain and situation – the Germans decided the only way to reach friendly lines again was to break through the Russian front. At dusk on the 28th, they stormed and overran a Red Army battery and headed towards where they thought the German front line was. White flares – 'German troops are here' – lit up the woodland. The men broke out into strains of *Deutschland über alles*, but there was no sign of friendly troops. Only after struggling through the swamps and marshes were the cut-off Germans reunited with their comrades.

134th Infantry Division weathered the storm at Nowy Dwór, but at a cost. It lost a dozen artillery pieces, a couple of anti-tank guns, two dozen trucks and 16 machine-guns. It counted 1,610 enemy dead, but its own losses 'were no less,' the division's chronicler lamented. 'The troops had to pay a heavy price in blood.'[36]

The fighting at Nowy Dwór was a shock to the men of the 134th Infantry Division – at least one officer was hospitalised after suffering a mental breakdown during one Soviet assault. For the first time an encircled enemy had not surrendered, despite the leaflets raining down on him:

Comrades of the Red Army!
You are encircled on all sides.

Your situation is hopeless.

Any resistance is pointless.

Why should you shed your blood in vain?

It's not true that Germans mistreat their prisoners or even kill them.

That's an impudent lie. German soldiers treat prisoners well.

Occasionally, such exhortations bore fruit. But most Red Army soldiers fought to the last round 'even in desperate situations', 7th Infantry Division – squeezing the north side of the pocket – reported, convinced by their commissars that they would be shot as soon as they entered German captivity. 'This is the main reason why he doesn't surrender.' In the face of such obstinacy, there could be only one outcome, Gotthard Heinrici wrote home: 'hecatombs of human sacrifices'.[37]

'THE RUSSIANS AT BREST-LITOVSK FOUGHT WITH EXCEPTIONAL DOGGEDNESS AND DETERMINATION...' BREST FORTRESS, 28–29 JUNE

There were still nearly 400 men holding out in Brest fortress's North Island. They were short of water, but little else. Food, weapons, ammunition, all were in plentiful supply. They were in no mood to surrender, even when captured Russian and French tanks were driven up to the edge of the fort and pounded the remaining strongpoints. A few defenders surrendered – and were put to work burying German dead in a cemetery in the city – but most did not.

The Luftwaffe proved no more successful initially either. At 8am on Sunday – seven days after the initial assault – German aircraft dropped half a dozen 500kg bombs on the eastern fort. Two failed to explode, another two missed the target. But two of the cluster bombs at least hit the bullseye. They made no impression on the casemates and vaults, nor the men inside, who continued to shoot at their attackers. Yet conditions in the fortification after a week of battle were becoming unbearable. Only one of the vaults was still intact. It was no place for soldiers, to say nothing of the women and children trapped there. In the middle of Sunday afternoon, they were led out under a white flag. The men, however, resolved to fight on.

In his desperation to bring the siege to an end, 45th Infantry Division's Fritz Schlieper was considering medieval methods, filling the moat with a mixture of petrol and fat and setting it alight. The acrid fumes would spill through the embrasures and fill the congested underground passages and magazines and force the garrison to give up.

Brest's last defenders would never have to endure such horrors. Around 5.30pm, the Luftwaffe returned. Yet more 500kg bombs. And one Ju88 carrying a 1,800kg explosive – the largest available in the airfield's armoury and, at 13ft long, among the largest and heaviest used by the Luftwaffe. The men called it the 'Satan'. The smaller bombs shook the fort. The 'Satan' hit the moat wall and detonated. The blast wave shook not merely the eastern fort or even the North Island, but much of the city of Brest. It was more than most of the defenders could take. 'Long ranks of Russians came out of North Island, their hands in the air, carrying white cloths and scraps,' Josef Arnreiter wrote. A large crowd gathered on the ramparts – not just men of the 45th, but also construction battalions, Luftwaffe ground troops, members of the national labour service, the *Reichsarbeitsdienst*. They watched men covered in red brick dust emerge after a week in hiding. 'They were not at all shaken, looked strong, were well-fed and gave the impression of being disciplined,' 45th Infantry Division's somewhat surprised diarist noted. He also observed that the major and commissar who had been leading the defence of the fort were not among those captured. Prisoners told their captors their leaders had shot themselves. That didn't trouble the Austrians. As far as they were concerned, the battle for Brest fortress was over.[38]

After the week of unforgiving fighting, the new masters of Brest fortress inherited fortifications hardly worthy of the name. Collapsed casemates and cellars, the northern section of the ring barracks, the White Palace, the commandant's headquarters – all reduced to rubble. The Terespol Gate barely stood. Courtyards and parade grounds were pockmarked by shell craters and littered with abandoned vehicles, discarded ammunition crates and shell canisters, melted bricks, twisted metal and charred wood from doors blown apart.

Josef Arnreiter retraced his route on the first day of the assault. His bugle and assault pack, cooking implements and his wallet lay where he had abandoned them. So too were the German dead – now 'quite black, bloated and unrecognisable' after a week lying in the heat. Arnreiter gathered his possessions and the dog tags and paybooks of fallen comrades, collected machine-guns and rifles. And in the charred remains of a timber house in a corner of the North Island he came across the burned body of his battalion commander, 41-year-old Friedrich Oeltze. 45th Infantry Division's Catholic priest Rudolf Gschöpf oversaw Oeltze's burial and the interment of 481 comrades in the grounds of Brest's southern church. The corpses of more than 2,000 Russians were also recovered. Recognition was almost impossible – the bodies had decomposed terribly in the summer heat. There were no wooden crosses erected, no markers. The corpses were tossed into the nearest crater or shell hole.

The division counted just 7,223 prisoners, including 101 officers, but reckoned two Soviet divisions had been wiped out in the fortress. The booty was vast: nearly 15,000 rifles, 400 side-arms, over 1,300 machine-guns, a couple of dozen mortars and nearly 100 field or anti-tank guns and howitzers, and nearly 800 horses (plus the same number killed). The Germans also found a rich harvest of food and provisions: tonnes of tea, pasta, peas, barley, enough flour for ten days' bread, enough soap to meet the entire division's needs for two months, and three-quarters of a million litres of vodka. Few vehicles had survived the eight-day maelstrom, perhaps three dozen obsolete tanks and tractors. The remaining 1,500 cars, trucks and tanks had either been wrecked by the fighting or sabotaged by the defenders.

'The Russians at Brest-Litovsk,' Fritz Schlieper wrote in his concluding report, 'fought with exceptional doggedness and determination, demonstrated excellent infantry training and a large proportion showed considerable fighting spirit.' Nevertheless, his division of Austrians – 'which draws its replacements from very close to the home of the Führer' – had prevailed. In honour of his men's achievements the main road to the fortress was subsequently renamed: Strasse der 45 Division – Road of the 45th.[39]

'They are making a show of this war…' Germany, 29 June

The German people learned of Brest's fall that very Sunday. Indeed, they learned of it several hours *before* the 'Satan' bomb brought an end to organised resistance. In fact, they learned that the fortress had been entirely in German hands for five days – all part of an orchestrated propaganda campaign.

For the past week, the daily official military communiqué had talked about every front other than the Russian. Newspapers had carried a few first-hand reports of heroic deeds – 'Sweeping thrust by our panzers', 'Across the Bug in inflatable boats and assault craft', 'This is how the first town was taken' or 'A corporal knocks out six Soviet tanks' – but otherwise the German people had been starved of concrete news from the new front. Deliberately. Hitler had insisted.

Sunday 29 June was a wet day in Berlin, but the cafés and pavements of the Kurfürstendamm, the capital's most elegant shopping and entertainment street, heaved. Jostling with the crowds, Harry Flannery, a 40-year-old CBS Radio correspondent, noticed an air of unease. The German public craved news. At 11am, the loudspeakers on the K'damm, as Berliners knew it, came to life and the new fanfare selected for the Russian campaign suddenly blared out. Diners rose from their café tables. Strollers stopped in their tracks. They looked up at the loudspeakers and listened. '*Aus dem Führerhauptquartier das Oberkommando der Wehrmacht gibt bekannt...*' – 'The High Command of the Armed Forces announces from the Führer's headquarters...' Twelve times this Sunday the excerpt from Liszt's *Les Préludes* would sound, each time introducing a *Sondermeldung*, special report, from the Russian front: the fortress of Grodno had fallen on the second day of the invasion; the citadel of Brest-Litovsk – 'the last enemy strongpoint' – stormed the next; German troops had forced the Daugava and seized Daugavpils; they had reached Minsk, while a gigantic pocket was developing around Białystok, trapping two Soviet armies; in the south, panzers had smashed 215 Russian tanks in a mighty battle around Dubno and were now bearing down on the Galician capital, Lvov; in seven days of fighting, German arms had captured or destroyed 600 guns and 2,233 tanks 'including 46 52-tonners', while 4,107 enemy aircraft had been shot down or wrecked on the ground for the loss of just 150 Luftwaffe planes. 'The numbers,' the announcer told listeners, 'grow by the hour.' As each special report ended, the national anthem sounded.

The assault on German ears was incessant. At 2.30pm, people heard the new, hastily composed *Russlandlied* – Russia Song – for the first time. Theme tunes had accompanied the campaigns against France and Britain. It was only logical one was written for the advance into the Soviet Union:

> We stood on guard for Germany
> And kept the great watch
> Now the sun is rising in the East
> *Chorus*
> From Finland to the Black Sea
> Forwards, forwards!
> Eastwards, you attacking army!
> Freedom your goal, victory your banner!
> Führer, give your orders! We will follow you!
> The march that Horst Wessel began
> In the brown cloth of the SA
> Will be completed by the grey columns:
> The great hour has come!
> *Chorus*

Now the armies roar eastwards
Into the heart of Russia.
Comrades, now to arms!
Victory will be ours!

At first people were stunned, then impressed, and finally angry. Harry Flannery caught the initial reaction of Berliners. 'Fantastic! Unbelievable! Wonderful!' But as this rainy Sunday passed, loudspeaker wagons rolled through the streets of the capital repeating the original reports and broadcasting a seemingly endless succession of additional announcements. There was no escape. 'It is obvious that they have saved these communiqués for today,' one Berliner complained. 'Why didn't they tell us during the week how the war was progressing? They are making a show of this war.'

What happened in Berlin was repeated across the Reich. Whenever there was a drum roll on the radio, people rushed to turn up the volume. Some Germans were disappointed that more Soviet soil had not been captured. Others were convinced German troops would be marching through Moscow in a week's time. But a dozen bursts of Liszt, a dozen special announcements, was simply overwhelming. By early afternoon, many Germans had grown bored of the fanfares, the statistics, the list of cities now in German hands. The effect of the day-long propaganda campaign was, Joseph Goebbels conceded, 'not what we'd hoped for'. The never-ending announcements left people 'slightly numb'. They realised that their government had deliberately withheld news from them purely for effect. 'The Russian war was being presented as a spectacle, but, as might have been expected, the people began to react against it before the day was over,' Harry Flannery observed. 'It was not long before the men and women of Germany knew that the whole thing had been planned, and they resented it.'

There was still a huge appetite for news from the new campaign. There was a rush for maps of Russia in the nation's bookshops – one cartographer in Karlsruhe sold 8,000 in a matter of days. Carefully selected images of Soviet prisoners, Jews and commissars in the daily newspapers and weekly pictorial magazines had fallen on especially fertile ground. 'You only have to see these hideous criminal faces, then everyone knows that this war against the Soviet Union is a just cause,' one Königsberg resident commented, while an inhabitant of Posen remarked: 'We never imagined the Bolsheviks to be so tattered and unsoldier-like.' The German people had to wait until Sunday evening for the first moving pictures from the East. The first newsreel since the invasion 'tormented audiences a little'. Cinemagoers had to sit through footage from the thrilling cup final, and the rather-less-thrilling visit by the Japanese ambassador Oshima to Hannover,

Croatia joining the Axis, the Italian popular culture minister in Berlin and a lively segment on artillery pounding the British garrison at Tobruk before the first glimpse of fighting on the new Eastern Front appeared: the muzzle flashes of guns at dawn, soldiers pushing border posts aside, German forces advancing on Kaunas, shaven-headed Russian prisoners being rounded up and, finally, He111 bombers plastering Soviet lines of communication to the rousing finale of *Les Préludes* once again.

If the dozen *Sondermeldungen* had been a disappointment, not so the 11 minutes of rather disjointed film, especially the first footage of Germany's new foe. 'People were thoroughly shocked by the appearance of these prisoners,' the compilers of the German security service's regular reports on public morale reported. Audiences branded the Red Army soldiers 'savages', 'sub-humans', 'convicts'. Wives were horrified that their husbands had to fight such 'animals', then consoled themselves with the conviction that 'soldiers dressed like that could hardly be serious opponents for the disciplined Wehrmacht in the long run'.

And so, as he recorded his thoughts on the day, Joseph Goebbels was convinced that, 'despite the clumsy timing of the numerous special announcements', the German people retired to bed ready for the new week filled with 'pride and enthusiasm'. He continued: 'It's a wonderful Sunday, a rainy day brightened up by the light of victory.'[40]

'THE WAR ASSUMES BESTIAL FORMS...'
BYELORUSSIA, LATE JUNE/EARLY JULY 1941

The German soldier did not dismiss his new foe as readily as newsreel audiences. Within hours of joining battle, Gotthard Heinrici had decided the men of the Red Army were 'much better soldiers than the French. Exceptionally tough, devious and crafty.' 15th Infantry Division's first encounter with the enemy 'put anyone who expected an easy fight firmly in their place and made the seriousness of the clash with Bolshevism obvious'.[41] Time and again, German troops reported enemy units wiped out rather than surrender.[42] 125th Infantry Division blamed 'the old fairy tale which had persuaded the Russian soldiers that they would be shot dead in captivity'.[43]

It ran much deeper than that. Most Russian soldiers felt genuinely aggrieved that Germany had invaded their country. They believed that Russian soil had been violated. And they believed in their cause; more than two decades of Soviet propaganda had left its mark. This was not the Russian soldier Germany had faced a generation before. 'What has become of the Russian of 1914–17, who ran away or approached us with his hands in the air when the firestorm reached its peak?' one World War I veteran asked himself. 'Now he remains in his bunker and forces us to burn him out, he prefers to be scorched in his tank, and his airmen continue firing at us even when their own aircraft is set ablaze. What has become of the Russian? Ideology has changed him!' Battalion commander Hans Schulze, who also fought against the Tsar's army, agreed. 'The Russians fight completely differently than in the World War. They fight until the last moment, even when the situation is utterly hopeless.'

For veterans of the campaigns in Poland, the West, and the Balkans, too, the tenacity of the Russian soldier was a shock. He simply ignored German machine-gun, mortar and artillery fire and attacked, one wave after another. 'Anyone who expected the Soviet soldiers to desert en masse or surrender once they were trapped or surrounded was bitterly disappointed,' Erich Mende recalled after fending off Red Army breakout attempts at Grodno. 'For the first time we realised the sheer cruelty of hand-to-hand fighting, the penetration of our positions at night and the effect on morale of Soviet companies attacking as they yelled "Urra!"' The 24-year-old battalion adjutant was left deeply shaken by the experience. 'We knew we couldn't expect anything good from the coming battles. The campaign in the East had shown its true character and the horror of Grodno weighed heavily on every man in the coming weeks.'

It was no different in the skies of Byelorussia. 'The Russian is a foe!' Paul Wenzel, the adjutant of *Jagdgeschwader* 51, wrote to a friend in the Luftwaffe High Command. 'Russian fliers fight toughly – more doggedly than the French and even the English. They carry out bombing raids which leave us stunned.' His commanding officer Werner Mölders – who'd fought in the skies of Spain, France and Britain – described it as 'the most incredible war which I have ever taken part in'. The Russian airmen, he told his fiancée, 'defend themselves desperately. You can't believe the ruthlessness with which they throw their aircraft and men at us time and again.'[44]

A terrible fate awaited any German soldier or airman who fell into Soviet hands in these opening days of the campaign. Outside Slutsk, south of Minsk, three Me110s pounced on a halted goods train as the evacuees on board sought water from a pump in the stifling heat. 'The earth was littered with the corpses of women and children,' pioneer Piotr Palii remembered 40 years later. Anti-aircraft gunners brought down one of the aircraft; the pilot and gunner bailed out. The train passengers wanted to lynch the two Germans, but Palii's commanding officer organised a court martial in the field. The airmen were tried, found guilty and shot for the murder of 41 people, including 16 children and 21 women. Two German aviators shot down near Slobodka northwest of Minsk were found stripped of their clothes and shot dead in the cells of the town's prison.[45]

Contemporary accounts frequently talk of German soldiers 'enraged' by the Red Army's 'insidious fighting methods'. One soldier came across dead comrades in a bomb shelter. When he turned their bodies over he saw that 'someone had cut off their genitals, gouged out their eyes, cut off their tongues'. He informed his company commander, who was infuriated. 'That's it – the war stops for me now!' he declared. His men understood him to mean: 'If just once we see a Russian, that's the end of them.' Another man found the corpses of his comrades tied together, dowsed in acid and then ripped apart by hand-grenades. 'It was so awful that any qualms we had about dealing with the Russian people were brushed aside in an instant,' he wrote. He observed the reactions of the other men in his company. A philosophy and theology student who'd seen his brother among the dead exacted revenge for several days afterwards. 'He had a word with any Russian he saw, forced him to dig his own grave at pistol-point and then shot him in this grave.' The staff of *Fliegerkorps* VIII were quartered in an orphanage outside Minsk. 'The Reds just ran away and the small children had simply starved,' the usually unmoved Wolfram von Richthofen noted. 'The majority of the two to nine-year-olds were locked in a hut and half starved. These Reds are nothing but animals!' The war, wrote journalist Benno Wundshammer, accompanying a reconnaissance unit, had assumed 'bestial forms'. The 28-year-old Rhinelander barely saw a prisoner of war – they were almost always 'bumped off'. When Kurt von der Chevallerie learned men of his 99th Infantry Division had been executed when they'd fallen into Soviet hands, he immediately ordered the 45 Red Army soldiers taken prisoner that day shot. Six men from 23rd Infantry Division were shot dead by enemy soldiers pretending to surrender under a white flag. Their commander, Heinz Hellmich, ordered his troops to ignore such signs of truce in future. 'There will be no mercy!' Berliner Robert Rupp saw a group of German soldiers standing around the fresh graves of two Russian prisoners. Both men had continued to resist after being taken prisoner. They were shot for their trouble. 'One of them remained alive for a long time, even as a thick layer of earth lay on top of him,' Rupp wrote home. 'He still wheezed, causing the earth to rise, and tried to lift his arm.'[46]

There was a fine line between justifiable revenge and arbitrary murder. It quickly blurred. Robert Rupp heard rumours German soldiers had executed every woman and child in one village after a unit of motorcyclists suffered heavy casualties. The corpses were reportedly tossed in a mass grave, which the inhabitants had been forced to dig minutes earlier. The ordinary soldier was acting as judge, jury and executioner. 'There's a danger to discipline if our men start "bumping people off" on their own initiative,' Fritz-Dietlof Graf von der Schulenburg, a 38-year-old reservist officer serving with 23rd Infantry Division, recorded in his diary on just the seventh day of war. 'If we allow this to happen, we'll descend to the level of the SS.' Schulenburg was delighted when the division's parent Fourth Army ruled that 'only those in battle who bear arms, those who shoot from an ambush, who offer resistance as a prisoner of war or flee' could be shot. 'Everything else simply removes all inhibitions and leaves no possibility of keeping basic instincts in check once they've been unleashed.' One of the few senior officers who tried to curb the excesses was XLVII Panzer Corps' Joachim Lemelsen, infuriated by 'senseless shootings'. His troops took no notice. 'Once again, no yield of prisoners due to incorrect actions by the troops,' his intelligence officer fumed the next day. Appalled by the common sight 'of countless corpses of Soviet soldiers, lying next to the route of advance, without weapons, hands in the air, clearly killed by a shot to the head from point-blank range', Lemelsen felt impelled to reissue his instructions more forcefully.

There have been repeated shootings of prisoners, deserters and defectors, which occur in an irresponsible, senseless and criminal way. This is murder! The German Wehrmacht is waging this war against Bolshevism, not against the united Russian peoples. We want to restore peace, law and order in this land which has suffered badly through years of oppression at the hand of a Jewish-criminal gang.

Russian prisoners were 'entitled to honourable, good treatment and food' – as long as they fought fairly. 'Harsh measures against partisans and civilians who fight will save the German armies a lot of blood, as will the good treatment of prisoners and deserters.'[47]

Joachim Lemelsen's instructions did not extend to the political officers captured on the field of battle. The commissar would continue to be singled out and executed. Benno Wundshammer watched as one *politruk* was picked out among a group of Soviet prisoners and immediately led away. 'The commissar,' Wundshammer noted, 'did not live to see the coming day – there was the commissar order.' Theodor Habicht's regiment captured a commissar and a Russian civilian, both armed. The political officer spoke fluent German – he was almost certainly a German Communist who had fled to the Soviet Union. Habicht's superior ordered both men shot. 'The Russian maintains a stoic calm, the commissar goes down on his knees and whimpers,' the Reichstag deputy recorded in his diary. 'But that doesn't help him.' Robert Rupp offered a drink of tea to a wounded commissar – the last act of kindness the man would enjoy. The Russian was forced to lie down in a freshly dug grave where he was shot by a non-commissioned officer. German soldiers did not stop with commissars and politruks. Prisoners with Komsomol tattoos – the sign of membership of the Communist youth organisation – had supposedly 'sworn an oath to kill every German as long as they could'. They too were executed. It helped, of course, that they apparently 'looked like criminals'.[48]

Senior officers either endorsed these killings – Fourth Army's Günther von Kluge called them 'necessary executions' – or turned a blind eye. In his unpublished memoirs, Maximilian von Weichs claimed just a single commissar was shot by the men under his command – a bold claim to make with eight infantry divisions in his Second Army – and that was when the Communist tried to strangle his interrogator. In fact, von Weichs' men murdered at least 35 Soviet political officers. Army Group North's intelligence officer, Rudolf Christoph *Freiherr* Gersdorff, was similarly convinced that the 'shooting of Jews, prisoners and even commissars has been rejected by almost the entire officer corps. They are viewed as an insult to the honour of the German Army – and especially the German officer corps.' Insult or not, in June 1941 alone the soldiers of his army group shot 70 commissars. Along the entire Eastern Front, nearly 400 commissars were shot during the first nine days of the invasion. In July 1941, political officers were executed at the rate of 25 every day.[49]

The commissar was the torchbearer of an ideology the German soldier had, until now, only learned about from books, newspapers and propaganda films. The reality, one former waterworks employee wrote to his old colleagues back in Hamburg, was 'far worse'. 'I've been moved to the core by what I've seen so far and, if in the past I'd thought our propaganda was a little over the top, then I can say today that it actually put a gloss to its description of conditions.' For while Hanns-Adolf Munier, a 19-year-old junior officer, found the Russian people friendly, their living conditions in their wooden huts were squalid. 'When you go through the entrance, you find a large stove on the right, leaning against it as far as the wall a simple bunk,' he noted.

> The left corner of the room is the so-called 'golden corner' where pictures of saints and crucifixes hang. To the left of the entrance there are pots of milk, honey and eggs on a shelf. In the middle there's a table with a bank. The whole room is full of flies. Piglets and chicks are locked up under the stove and make a noise.

There were none of the attractions – or amenities – of France, a junior officer in 20th Panzer Division bemoaned, just a 'never-ending expanse, monotony in form and colour'. In every substantial town, the main square was invariably dominated by tawdry statues and murals of Lenin, Stalin and other Soviet leaders. And every church in the land had been closed, left to descend into ruin, or else put to other uses. Fritz Gercke, 23rd Infantry Division's supply officer, found one church which had been turned into a garage. 'Where the high altar had once stood, the inspection pit for vehicles. Next to neglected holy pictures, typical cheap and kitschy images of Stalin, Molotov and other Soviet grandees stare down from the walls. Everything of value was taken away.'[50]

In letters home there was widespread praise for Hitler; his actions had spared the Reich from being overrun by a barbaric, godless Bolshevik horde. 'Germany can only count herself lucky to possess a leader who will rid us of this spectre once and for all,' soldier Albert Stahl declared. The former waterworks employee wrote home to Hamburg that 'every man who sees the Soviet paradise must stand next to his Führer with all his heart', while one Berliner gushed: 'The Führer has grown to become the greatest human being of the century.' And one corporal assured his father:

> This struggle was absolutely necessary. The German Armed Forces have the fate of all of Europe and the entire civilised world in their hands. It's a great mercy that in this age when Europe was threatened, the Führer came along and forged a strong Germany which alone is capable of averting the danger. One day maybe even England and France will thank us.

Here was another recurring theme: Germany as defender of Western civilisation. 'Our task is to eradicate the Red subhumanity,' the first edition of *Mitteilungen für die Truppe* – Information for Troops – published after the invasion reminded its readers. 'The German people face the greatest task in their history. The world will see that this task is carried out to the letter.'

Panzer company commander Helmut Krause 'knew that sooner or later there would be a conflict with the Jewish-Bolshevik poison in the East'. The people of Byelorussia were little better than robots – 'the soul and the spirit count for nothing,' he fumed. 'The bourgeoisie at the beer table and inhabitants of the Western nations cannot imagine the enormous tasks Germany is currently dealing with in the East,' Krause continued in a letter home. 'Once again there are casualties and many of the best will not return. But Germany can only live, if these few repeatedly step to the fore, even if the masses will never understand this.' An officer in a *Propaganda Kompanie* was convinced 'if the civilised world is to continue to live, we have to wipe out this criminal system'. Germany would inflict 'the greatest defeat there has ever been in the history of the world. The hour of the greatest court on Earth has dawned – German soldiers are its executors!' A Berliner wrote to his brother in a similar vein: 'May the Führer's clean sword crash down on this devilish monster. I am fortunate that I am taking part, albeit as a very small cog in this war of light against darkness.'

A war of light against darkness? Catholic lawyer Arnold Brinz serving with 132nd Infantry Division went further. 'Is this a holy war which we are embarking upon?' the 40-year-old from Munich asked himself. 'They talk of the struggle against Bolshevism like it's a crusade. Will our victory – which I do not doubt – re-open the doors of churches and chapels? Will it make the resurrection bells sound once again in a land which has turned godless?'

No man embraced the idea of a crusade against Bolshevism more than the German Army's Catholic bishop, Franz Josef Rarkowski. The peoples of Europe were yearning to banish 'Bolshevism from history for all time,' he proclaimed on the second Sunday of the campaign in the East. Now Germany was the 'saviour and champion of Europe', its soldiers on a mission 'just like the German knights from an era far behind us, a task of unique significance, whose impact on our people, *ja*, on Europe and all of humanity cannot be overlooked.'[51]

Certainly the peoples of western Byelorussia – the territory occupied by the Soviets in 1939 – welcomed the 'German knights' as liberator, not occupier. Motorcyclist Albert Frank was 'warmly received by the populace, in fact with jubilation'. Inhabitants even gave the German greeting – the Hitler salute – and offered the 20-year-old and his 20th Panzer Division comrades flowers and cigarettes. Mirroring scenes in Lithuania and Latvia, German soldiers were frequently showered with flowers as they marched, rode or drove through the villages and small towns of western Byelorussia, while jugs of milk or water were put by the roadside. The populace offered 20th Infantry Division 'a hearty welcome,' its doctor Wilhelm Mauss noted. 'Young girls, many of them very pretty, dressed in white blouses with colourful embroidery, threw mountains of flowers at us, often birch leaves as well – or whatever they had just found. So by driving Bolshevism away we really seem to have given them cause for joy.' Hans von Luck, 7th Panzer Division's adjutant, spoke Russian and conversed with the local populace, who were all too willing to offer their new masters eggs and pieces of bread. 'We are still Christians. Free us from Stalin who destroyed our churches,' one woman holding an icon beseeched him.[52]

In Białystok services of thanksgiving were held. 'Never, one German-speaking woman told me, have the churches been as full,' 23rd Infantry Division's supply officer, Fritz Gercke, recorded in his diary. Few, if any, shed tears for the end of

Communist rule. In Slutsk, Fritz Farnbacher watched householders tear down portraits of Stalin and Molotov, then smash them. Hurriedly put up in their place: holy images, crucifixes and icons, all hidden during the long years of Bolshevik rule. 'When it comes to religion, people really do breathe a sigh of relief,' the artillery officer recorded. 'They apparently regard us as liberators. From signs they make and so on we notice that under Bolshevik rule holy images were tossed on the ground and destroyed.' The people, one Berliner serving with a signals unit wrote to his family, 'are delighted that we've come. They want to see Stalin on the gallows.'[53]

Rarely has an invader occupied such fertile ground. The inhabitants of Byelorussia 'have had their fill of Bolshevism', Johann Hamm, a Catholic priest with 31st Infantry Division, observed. 'If we could guarantee them religious and economic freedom, the war would soon be over. They would all come over to our side.' But Hamm was not convinced the German Army had entered this land to liberate it. In fact, having been assured for years that the Russian was an inferior being, the invader invariably acted as lord, not liberator. 'Every little rear area formation, *ja* every little soldier, imagined that they had "conquered" this territory, and therefore they could act as they wanted,' Minsk's freshly installed German mayor Wilhelm Janetzke observed. Byelorussia simply exchanged one authoritarian ruler for another. Clocks were immediately set back an hour to German time, the Reichsmark replaced the rouble – at a punishing exchange rate – while any weapons and radio sets had to be surrendered to Byelorussia's new rulers, who imposed a curfew between 6pm and 6am, demanded every inhabitant register, and forbade them from going within 100 yards of any railway line or installation and threatened any transgressions with immediate execution. Round-ups began almost immediately. In Slutsk, every Communist or member of the Komsomol was ordered to register. 'Of course, anyone who went kissed goodbye to their lives,' Sonja Davjidovna Burgovno remembered. 'Anyone who provided a Soviet soldier or partisans with food was shot immediately.' The town's prison was 'filled afresh every three days' as suspects were brought in from across the district and, invariably, executed within 72 hours. Daily life in Minsk, historian Vladimir Romanovski remembered, was punctuated by constant patrols by the SS and police and sudden house searches. 'People were arrested for the slightest reason, disappeared into the Gestapo cellars, were taken away for shooting,' he recalled. 'There was a constant state of fear in the city.'

A prison camp was established in a sandy field by the right bank of the Svislach at Drozdy on the northern edge of Minsk. Alexander Tolstik was one of an estimated 40,000 'suspicious' civilians sent there at the beginning of July. 'When darkness fell, the Germans would suddenly fire a submachine-gun just over our heads,' he remembered. As a new arrival he did not understand the warning, but fellow inmates cried out: 'Get down!' Thirty seconds later, the guards fired another burst. Anyone still standing was immediately cut down. The rest of the prisoners remained lying on the ground until dawn. In a matter of days, numbers at Drozdy reached perhaps 150,000 as prisoners of war from the battles of encirclement were brought in by the thousand. War correspondent Rasso Königer watched prisoners file through the heart of Minsk 'like some wide, brown flood wave. Beaten men. Dragging their feet. Emaciated, sullen,' he observed. 'In the West we'd seen large columns of prisoners, but never on such a scale.' There was no fence, no barbed wire, just a few German cavalrymen 'on small, shaggy Cossack horses' guarding the dejected Red Army soldiers 'like sheep dogs watching over a herd'. Among the thousands of troops – held separately from the civilians – was Nikolai Semyonovich Saporoshez, captured during a failed breakout attempt. 'We had nothing to eat for a couple of days,' he remembered. 'When we protested, they brought us a couple of sacks of barley and dried fish. Those who were strong got hold of something, the rest stayed hungry.' Rafael Bromberg, one of thousands of Jewish civilians sent to Drozdy, watched as a German car drove up and hurled biscuits in the direction of the prisoners. 'The starving pack fell upon them and there was a scuffle which the Germans photographed,' Bromberg recalled. 'Many people were unable to pick the biscuits off the ground, chased after the vehicle and were beaten on the arms and head. If that didn't scare them off, the Germans shot at them.' Though the camp was located by the Svislach, prisoners were forbidden from drinking from it – though this was perhaps wise, for mountains of corpses began to pile up on its bank; a terrible stench of decomposition pervaded the camp. There were no toilets – prisoners performed calls of nature on the spot, standing up – and no medical care. The ground was stripped of any vegetation – it was ripped up, cooked if possible and eaten. Many prisoners resorted to drinking urine. Some went more than a week without eating. Those with relatives in Minsk were more fortunate. During the day, family members came to the camp, laden with supplies for their loved ones. They were wise to eat almost immediately, for after dark starving prisoners pounced on any man who still had food. Animal instincts took over. Prisoners killed each other over pieces of bread. And 'everywhere and at every step, we were beaten with batons,' a Communist Party official from Grodno who escaped from Drozdy later testified. 'We quickly forgot that we were still alive, that we were human beings.' Despite the few guards, there was little fear of a breakout. The prisoners were too weak and apathetic, their jailers too quick to act ruthlessly with the rifle and pistol if any man stepped out of line. A *Reichsbahn* inspector sent to oversee the repair of Minsk's smashed railway infrastructure watched 'men fighting over bread and old scraps of clothing which had been tossed at them'. These were fights to the death; the corpses were buried 'on the spot, by Jews, like dead dogs'. The inspector felt no sympathy. 'The Russians have been governed by fear and that can't be any different now. They are no longer human but bestial hordes.' The only concern of Minsk's new masters was the possibility of an epidemic – beginning to fester in the camp's unsanitary conditions – spreading to the city. With public utilities smashed, disease would spread rapidly.[54]

'A SCENE OF UNIMAGINABLE HORROR…' THE BIAŁYSTOK-VOLKOVYSK POCKET, END OF JUNE

By the end of June, mass breakouts in the woods between Białystok and Volkovysk were giving way to individual skirmishes or even silence. Just 48 hours after the horrors of Nowy Dwór, battalion commander Hans Schulze was struck by the silence of the former battlefield. 'I sit in the small front yard of my quarters which are filled with the sweet smell of jasmine,' he wrote. 'Bees buzz around me. We can see our men in their positions in the corn fields on the hills in front of the edge of the village. Cornflowers are in bloom. Horses graze in the meadows. Above everything, a clear blue sky and white clouds.' Robert Rupp, a Berlin schoolteacher, found no beauty or peace in the woods of western Byelorussia, only desolation. 'We hear terrible cries for help from the woods,' he wrote, 'terrible cries which suggest boundless loneliness.' Wounded Soviet soldiers, abandoned to their fate by their comrades and often plagued by flies, lay in foxholes, at the foot of trees, or on the ground. Some even crawled along on all fours. At the war's outbreak the Western Front had possessed impressive medical services. The whole apparatus collapsed almost immediately. Medical companies were destroyed as they formed – if they formed at all, as rail lines and highways were interdicted. In the first eight days of the invasion, at least 60 military or field hospitals – capable of accommodating 17,000 patients – were captured by the Germans or destroyed, three motorised medical companies and 35 other units wiped out. Occasionally, Soviet casualties were tended to by passing Germans who replaced bandages, or offered cigarettes. Some held out hope of being rescued. 'Unfortunately, I don't believe it,' wrote Rupp. 'I imagine their terrible end.' Medic Max Dörfler accompanied doctors as they conducted rounds at one of 167th Infantry Division's first-aid stations in the woods south of Białystok, when a patrol brought in a wounded Soviet general, shot in the lungs. Dörfler applied an air-tight bandage while the doctor gave the Soviet commander, 113th Rifle Division's Major General Khristofor Nikolaevich Alaverdov, tetanus and morphine injections. The bearing of the 44-year-old Armenian impressed Dörfler. Alaverdov was a tall, imposing figure, wearing his camouflage jacket over his dress uniform. He pointed to the three medals on his chest and repeated: 'I'm a general, I am a big man.' He spent several hours at the first-aid post until he was taken away for interrogation. Khristofor Alaverdov was sentenced to death *in absentia* for betraying his Motherland. He did nothing of the sort. A committed Communist, he incited his fellow incarcerated comrades in captivity. The Germans executed him for it in April 1942.[55]

Khristofor Alaverdov was one of more than 100,000 prisoners to pass through Ninth Army's processing stations in just one week of fighting in the East. It never counted Soviet dead, nor the 'inestimable mass of abandoned equipment', only destroyed tanks (1,400) and guns (550). Its commander, the fearsome Adolf Strauss, was delighted with his men's achievements. 'Forget any hope of going into action again in this struggle against Russia,' he told the ranks of 87th Infantry Division, who had seen nothing of battle, only its aftermath: collecting scraps of old weapons, counting, stacking, writing lists and reports. 'If you were to add up all the units the Russians still possess capable of delivering a powerful blow, then you'd come to a figure of barely more than seven or ten divisions!'[56]

Fritz Gercke, 23rd Infantry Division's supply officer, was similarly impressed by the scale of the Red Army's defeat. He passed barracks in Białystok which had been bombed by the Luftwaffe – probably on the first day of the war. One bomb had penetrated the roof of the building and passed through several floors of dormitories before exploding in the basement. The blast tore the barracks apart: the beds and their occupants were thrown out of the building 'in their hundreds', ending up in craters outside. There they were buried, a thin layer of earth thrown over the corpses. After a few days the soil settled. Now 'boots, uniforms, legs and arms protruded from this thin layer of earth'. Leaving the city, Gercke drove for a dozen miles down a highway. 'There's probably never been a road like it in the history of warfare,' he wrote. The officer tallied the number of wrecked vehicles he passed: 138 tanks, 65 of them heavy, 54 heavy guns. He lost count when it came to trucks and cars, while men and horses were shot or shredded to pieces, or hideously burned. The highway was 'a scene of unimaginable horror'. Hartmut Petri's infantry company encountered a large wheat field 'strewn with corpses', Russian troops mown down by German machine-guns. 'It's a terrible sight,' he wrote, 'a dead man at every step' –

mostly, he claimed, 'Chinese and Mongolians', but also 'the shredded bodies of female soldiers'. And above everything, 'the disgusting, nauseating stench of unburied Russian dead', a vile smell spread with every breath of wind across the field. And yet, as Petri's company moved through this field of the dead, the field kitchen arrived and served the infantrymen a hot meal 'which we quickly gobble down – we're so hardened already'. Even the normally restrained Fedor von Bock was moved by a 'desolate' landscape – 'a scene of total destruction'. The enemy, he concluded, 'has been very badly beaten'. Gotthard Heinrici concurred. 'The enemy has suffered losses on a scale not seen in this war to date,' he told his family. 'The Russians have been badly beaten, but they're definitely not defeated yet.'[57]

'MUCH WORSE THAN DUNKIRK...' THE VOLKOVYSK– MINSK POCKET, END OF JUNE 1941

By far the greater prize – elements of three Soviet armies (Third, Tenth and Thirteenth) and two mechanised corps – lay in the much larger eastern pocket: 125 miles long, a couple of dozen wide, stretching from Volkovysk to the western outskirts of Minsk. Not only was it much larger, but the ring around it was much more porous – the 15 encircling divisions were too few, the trapped forces too determined to break out. They concentrated their efforts on the southern end of the pocket and the 50 miles of woods and fields between the small town of Zelva and the city of Baranovichi.

At last light on 28 June, with the jaws on the pocket barely closed, the noise of an approaching train alerted the ranks of 29th Motorised Infantry Division of an impending Red Army attack. An armoured train supported a mass breakout attempt by Russian infantry, cavalry and tanks outside Zelva. As the train started to cross a bridge, the track was blown up, derailing the forward carriages – mostly empty goods wagons. It served as the unofficial signal to begin the attack. Troops jumped out of the train and stormed towards German lines, supported by the train's guns and tank cannons. Shells crashed down on the 29th's lines, now manned by every available soldier. Field guns, heavy machine-guns, anti-tank guns. All sent their shells into the Russian ranks. Suddenly, there was a jet of flame followed by a tremendous explosion as the armoured train exploded. 'Again and again columns of fire rose into the heavens after ammunition wagons exploded one after another, giving the sky a blood-red glow,' a non-commissioned officer recalled. 'The Bolshevik advance was thwarted. Only a few escaped our murderous defensive fire.'

The next morning, the 29th lined up more than 1,000 vehicles, neatly arranged in columns 'as if on the parade ground', waiting for panzers to join them before moving off to the northeast. The sudden sight of two large black clouds of smoke rising above the neighbouring woods announced a fresh breakout attempt; Russian cavalry had overrun the baggage column of the division's reconnaissance and motorcycle battalions. As enemy troops prepared to swarm out of the woods, the 29th's field guns engaged them in direct fire, causing the Soviet soldiers to scatter. The Germans believed the crisis had been overcome when two heavy tanks appeared. They got to within 100 yards of the German positions before they were stopped by the concerted fire of every field and anti-tank gun. The encounter lasted less than an hour. By the following day, 30 June, the only enemy troops approaching the division's lines were 'demoralised and exhausted deserters' – but it had cost the 29th dearly: in just seven days it had lost 1,171 men – heavier casualties than during the six-week campaign in France.[58]

A little to the east, anti-tank gunner Erich Bunke was moving along the Brest–Slonim road when terrified German infantry ran towards him 'yelling like madmen'. The officer immediately deployed eight guns along a lane by the River Zelvianka. The first Soviet tank, a clumsy, multi-turreted T-28, was picked off at 800 yards as it scouted ahead of the main body: several battalions of Red Army infantry, cavalry and more T-28s. The infantry emerged from the woods first and was mown down by machine-gun fire as it stormed the road with cries of 'Urra!' By the end of the second wave of attacks, there was no Russian still standing. The cavalry was no more successful. At least 100 men on horseback rode straight at Bunke's guns and paid a terrible price for their folly. A few horses, most without riders, jumped past the gunners and through the German lines.

At dusk, more Red Army regiments sought to bludgeon their way through to Slonim. 'With a wild chorus of cries of "Urra", which cut right through us, they swarmed towards the road,' Bunke remembered. Three attacking waves were scythed by the German guns. 'This meadow of death by the Zelvianka was strewn with Russian dead,' Bunke wrote. 'In the twilight, we could still make them out through our binoculars. Many were calling for medics.' Another Red Army regiment swarmed out of the woods. It suffered the same fate.

Finally, came the tanks. Ten T-28s. Again, they proved sitting ducks for Bunke's gunners. Every one was knocked out. Convinced the crisis had been overcome, the anti-tank men were surprised by the roar of an engine as 'a monster the likes of which we'd never seen before' appeared:

It shot at us with machine-guns from its turret and nose and also with its long barrel. Eight of our anti-tank guns fired at it and we watched as the shells struck the armour plate and bounced off. One round after another bounced off and spun through the air. A blood-curdling sight – particularly for us. We shot continually and sometimes had the impression that the tank almost stopped under the impact of so many shells. But it drew closer and closer. Now it reached our line and went straight through it, right into the rear area, and began to shoot wildly. That was where our limbers were. Our men took cover. The infantry staffs in the rear were also threatened. Trucks carrying mounted infantry which followed the tank did not get far. They burned and the Russian soldiers jumped down, taking cover on both sides of the road.

The chaos caused by the 'monster' – a KV-1 – ended only when it became stuck on the sandy road as it roamed at will behind the German lines.

And still the Red Army continued to emerge from the woods by the Zelvianka. Five T-28s. Knocked out. More riflemen screaming 'Urra' as they swept along the road to Slonim. 'They ran into very strong defensive fire again,' Erich Bunke recalled. 'Individual waves got up repeatedly. But the infantry evidently had enough ammunition to knock all of them out.'[59]

West of Baranovichi, the elite *Grossdeutschland* Infantry Regiment defended a sector far too extensive for its size. A gunner with an anti-aircraft company wheeled a 3.7cm flak gun into position and sent six rounds at a time into the oncoming Russian lines:

Our cannon had to be fed continually… The hot barrel raised blisters on the hands. Hands were in motion here and there, calls for full clips of ammunition, half deaf from the ceaseless pounding of the gun. The Russians were unmistakably gaining ground. They stuck to their guns, although we kept up a continuous fire on the edge of the wood and any groups of Russians that sprung up. Our supply of ammunition was also running low.

The company's infantry comrades eventually arrived to relieve them – the gunners were unsure whether minutes or hours had passed. The ground around their position was littered with empty shell casings and ammunition clips.[60]

There was no co-ordination directing any of these breakout attempts, no central leadership, no direction for men inside the pocket. Individual units fought individual actions – if they fought at all. For every Red Army company, regiment or division which fought to the death, there was another which capitulated or simply melted away. Georgy Semenyak's 204th Rifle Division was trying to reach

Minsk with 'virtually no commanders – lieutenants, captains, second lieutenants took rides on passing vehicles,' he recalled. 'Without commanders, our ability to defend ourselves was so severely weakened that there was really nothing we could do.' Semenyak was taken prisoner near Minsk on 6 July, bitter that his officers 'used their rank to save their own lives – but every man has his weaknesses'. 208th Motorised Division, deployed around Hajnówka near Białystok, was reduced to just 60 officers and men after only a few days of war; the rest had 'slipped away for various reasons'. By the end of June, 86th Rifle Division, stationed nearby, numbered a mere 300 men. When XXI Rifle Corps tried to break out in one of the last acts of the battle, all that remained of three divisions were a few hundred infantrymen and officers. NKVD sergeant Mikhail Ermakov complained that leaders fled the field of battle, leaving their men to fend for themselves while Byelorussian soldiers complained about Soviet rule, about their leaders who sent them to fight panzers armed with rifles and about the Red Army which was no match for its opponent. It was hardly surprising, then, that many Byelorussians trapped in the pocket 'willingly went into captivity'. What happened to Oleg Kravchenko, a 20-year-old gunner with 75th Rifle Division, was symptomatic of hundreds of thousands of ordinary soldiers trapped at Białystok. By the time Kravchenko and his comrades realised they were encircled, their divisional commander had disappeared along with most of his senior officers. Hiding in a wood, a group of junior officers tried to rally what was left of the division. 'The talk was of holding out and breaking out,' Kravchenko remembered. 'But then the horses were rounded up so they could be shot and it was clear to everyone that that was no longer the intention.' Instead, the remaining officers took aim at their own men so that no man fell into German captivity. 'So desperate were those trapped men that they broke out of the ring like wild animals, shooting wildly in every direction and fleeing in panic,' Kravchenko subsequently told his German captors. 'Many died in the marshes, shot by their own side.' Oleg Kravchenko emerged from the woods on a road east of Rozana, between Brest and Slonim. It was teeming with advancing German soldiers. Kravchenko surrendered immediately. He was treated 'very amicably'.[61]

With its burning villages, blazing trucks, and corpses on a scale like never before, the Białystok–Minsk pockets presented 'a true picture of war', one *Landser* wrote. 'But war also numbs the senses so that you can witness such scenes calmly.' Twelve months earlier in France, he had been deeply affected by the sight of dead bodies. 'Now you gradually become indifferent or hard. War makes you hard and that means it's a good school.' War correspondent Hans Bayer, a veteran of the

French campaign, confided in his diary in a similar vein: 'By day I'm bombarded by many images. In the evening I lie awake and think about everything I've experienced. The only thing which surprises me is how I can see all the things I do and not be shaken to the core. How cold-blooded and hard you have to act when it is necessary.'

Harald Henry, a 21-year-old former PhD student from Berlin, marched for 15 miles past 'terrible scenes of devastation': all manner of tanks upturned by the force of bomb blasts, wrecked guns, field kitchens, anti-tank guns, a sea of weapons, helmets, military equipment, pianos and radios, cinema trucks, medical equipment, crates of ammunition and books, shells, blankets, coats, backpacks. And then there were the corpses, almost all turned black by the June heat. 'The horses were dreadful,' Henry wrote in a letter to his family which left nothing to the imagination. 'Utterly torn to shreds, bloated, their intestines hanging out, their muzzles bloodily torn away. They give off an overwhelming smell of decomposition – something terrible, half-way between being butchered and rotting – which has a paralysing effect on our columns. The worst sight was a pig which noisily – and greedily – ate some of this horse flesh.'[62]

Amid the horrors, strange episodes, too. Thirty miles north of Slonim, the Polish inhabitants of Zdzieciol – women in white headscarves and men in their Sunday best – were determined to celebrate Mass on 29 June for the first time since the Soviets had occupied the town in 1939, even though fighting raged on the outskirts. Townsfolk even sent a delegation to the command post of 14th Infantry Regiment on a hill above Zdzieciol to offer the Germans the traditional greeting of salt and bread, and to thank them for liberating the town from the Communist yoke.[63]

To fighter pilot Walter Krupinski it seemed as if 'the entire *Fliegerkorps* VIII was in the air' over the pocket. The risk of colliding with comrades was far greater than being shot down by Soviet fighters or flak. Anything which moved on the ground was attacked. The Messerschmitts' 20mm cannons tore horse-drawn carts apart. Less effective, however, were the low-level attacks on Soviet armour. 'I don't remember how many shot-up tanks we reported,' Krupinski recalled, 'but we were extremely disappointed the next morning when most of our supposed victims had vanished into thin air.' Crews suddenly realised that in the face of heavy Soviet tanks, 'our ammunition was good for knocking on someone's door at best'. The corps' commander, Wolfram von Richthofen, revelled in this new Armageddon, ignoring the awful stench as he flew 200ft above it. The battlefield was strewn with vehicles, tanks and guns, 'some of them destroyed or damaged by us, some of them shot up by the army, some stuck without fuel, some stuck attempting to ford rivers where we've destroyed the bridges'. There were dead soldiers, dead cavalry, dead mules. He estimated 25 divisions had been wiped out, and with it 'the bulk of the offensive Red Army has been destroyed'. It was, he decided, 'much worse than Dunkirk'.[64]

The woods of eastern Poland and western Byelorussian teemed with cut-off Russian troops, desperate to escape the encirclement. No road running through this terrain was safe. Vehicles travelling on their own were frequently ambushed. Gotthard Heinrici was driving along an embankment through marshland when more than half a dozen Russian soldiers crossed it barely 100ft in front of his staff car. 'It would have been child's play for them to shoot at us in our car,' Heinrici wrote. 'There were about ten of them and three of us.' Both sides were equally startled. Before either could react, the Russians were gone, disappearing into the impenetrable marshes. A Berliner with a signals unit told his wife he had 'daily brushes' with Russian stragglers hiding in the copses. 'From morning to night, always outside, our nerves always tense, rifles always at our fingertips.' Radio operator Erich Hager's panzer was ambushed outside Slonim, hit three times in rapid succession at a range of no more than 100ft. The driver was killed instantly – he never even made a sound. 'I can only speak of luck that I didn't get hurt,' he recorded in his diary later that day. Four men succeeded in scrambling out of the Panzer IV, but they left all their weapons and possessions behind as flames raged. It took three days for the fires inside to die down so the crew could bury their comrade. All they found was a solitary body part. The fire had devoured everything else.[65]

Every wood, copse and country lane around Slonim bore the scars of battle as Dr Jürgen Nicolas, a 21-year-old sergeant with 29th Motorised Infantry Division, found when he drove around the battlefield barely 24 hours after the fighting had died down. 'Everywhere there are trees cut to pieces by shells and bursts of machine-gun fire and individual Russian tanks scattered around the terrain,' Nicolas observed. 'Light, medium, heavy. *Ja*, we even see 52-tonne tanks.' Nicolas dubbed the highway to Slonim 'the road of horror'. Accompanied by armour, the trapped Soviet troops had tried to force their way through to Slonim. The men of 15th Infantry Regiment stood firm in their foxholes. 'Everywhere Russian corpses, tanks, charred Russians hanging out of hatches, anti-tank guns shot to pieces, destroyed motorcycles and time and again trucks with bullet-riddled sides and wrecked engines.' Nicolas passed a heavy tank. 'All around it – and also on it – lie charred Russians, infantry who mounted the tank and were unable to jump off when it received a direct hit,' he wrote. 'All the time we're driving over Russian corpses – soon they're quite flat. We have no time to clear them to one side – and nor do we possess the will after the horrible sight we saw.' That sight was a

German medical company overrun by Soviet troops along the Slonim road. 'The vehicles were riddled with rounds from Russian tank guns,' Nicolas noted. 'No wounded – each vehicle was loaded with four injured Germans – was left alive. They were beaten to death in a bestial fashion. We're filled with such anger at this sight that we intend to repay the Russians in kind for this brutal cruelty!' Just two ambulance drivers survived the massacre.[66]

Not every infantry division endured the horrors of clearing out the Białystok pocket. Many simply traipsed eastwards in the wake of the motorised divisions. Highways – marked with an 'R' for 'Rollbahn' – were reserved exclusively for the panzer divisions and motorised infantry; any horse-drawn unit was banned from using major roads – identified with a 'P' for 'Panzer' – leaving the infantry to trudge along the secondary roads and country lanes, for the most part dirt tracks. Baked dry by the June heat, the soil crumbled to fine dust under the German soldier's jackboots – fine dust which was whirled up into suffocating clouds which also stung the eyes. 'Coughing and spluttering, with some lively swearing, the oppressed infantrymen put one foot before the other – almost automatically,' the chronicler of 315th Infantry Regiment noted. 'The monotony of the march matches the landscape. The space seemed endless, the horizon blurred. The repetitious landscape and the immensity of the woods, marshes and steppes depressed us.' The men might set off marching, even singing, but after five or six miles they stopped and continued almost in silence in the hope that the occasional sight of an onion dome suggested 'a vibrant town' ahead. 'But when we get there,' a soldier in 8th Infantry Division lamented, 'it's the same wooden huts as before, half falling down, occasionally interrupted by a flat-roof stone building of the Party and a plaster statue of Lenin'. So the men dreamed. Or hallucinated. 'Our imagination runs riot,' the infantryman wrote. 'The cool of shady woods, girls in colourful dresses, freshness in their happy faces. And then a glass filled with cold lager…'

More than anything, however, the infantry yearned for a taste of glory. After nearly a fortnight on the march, a platoon leader in 7th Infantry Division snapped. 'I'm filled with unspeakable anger,' he wrote. 'We're nothing but a marching regiment. It's now the end of the second year of the world war and all we ever do is march! Today I can barely sleep. All I can think of is that we don't have a mission, we simply have to march, march through Russia. That's hard!' The operations officer of 87th Infantry Division was equally exasperated. 'There's nothing left to do than to move your hand across the situation maps, following as the front line of the panzer armies advances further and further,' he sighed.

'As a result our last hope of going into action again soon lessens by the day.' And the men of the 258th Infantry Division felt they were only involved 'on the fringes of success' as they chased after the motorised units along 'the worst roads' and 'unimaginably thick dust – unless it rains and it all turns to mud'. 'There's no contact with the enemy and no feeling of success.'[67]

'A DEATHLY SILENCE EVERYWHERE...' BREST, 1 JULY

There was no fighting in Brest now, but little peace either. The streets were littered with unexploded shells and bombs – they would still require clearing away a month later. Dysentery was rife. There was no regular water supply to many parts of the city. Communist and Jew Solomon Ioffe spent the first week of the German occupation in hiding: in a cinema, a synagogue, a shed and a shoemaker's shop, from where he observed 'the Fascist gangsters' at work. Commissars and Red Army officers were forced to pull heavy German guns through the streets. 'Seeing all this, the populace is afraid to appear in the streets,' Ioffe noted. 'Jewish inhabitants are particularly scared – they barely venture into the streets at all.' Two out of every five inhabitants of Brest were Jewish. They began to suffer as soon as the first German security forces entered the city on 24 June. One teenager was shot when he entered his home as Germans troops searched it, while an elderly Jew was stabbed with a razor by a drunken German soldier purely because he did not want to cut off his beard. Far worse was to come.

Brest's new masters looted at will – ostensibly searching for weapons. Their army commandeered the food warehouses, while the ordinary soldier seized boots, trousers, watches and bedding from the local populace. Most of the city's inhabitants remained indoors, but after several days without food – shops had been closed since Saturday afternoon – they responded in force to a placard posted in German, Polish, Byelorussian and Russian promising bread for Soviet roubles. People queued in their thousands outside bakeries and stores – despite the punitive exchange rate of ten roubles for a single Reichsmark. A propaganda photographer recorded the first loaves being handed out, then left. The distribution of bread ended with his departure. The majority of those queueing went home empty-handed.

Red Army troops tried to take advantage of the chaos, discarding their uniforms and trying to slip through Brest dressed as civilians. A dozen were caught and put in front of a firing squad. The men pleaded – in vain – for mercy before they were shot, yelling '*Heil* Hitler!' and even '*Heil* Himmler!'

Otherwise, captured Red Army troops were held in the former barracks on the edge of the city. Turned into a processing camp, it was quickly overwhelmed by the number of Soviet troops captured. Families came in search of their relatives, giving the Germans food to hand to the prisoners, 'but the Germans took the best for themselves,' Brest citizen Alexander Khromov recalled. 'And when food was brought, everyone rushed to the wire. They were beaten or even shot on the spot.'[68]

Early on Tuesday evening, the decimated ranks of 45th Infantry Division gathered in the grounds of Brest's southern church. The infantrymen had spent the day sorting through the knapsacks and laundry of the dead so personal effects could be sent to families back in Linz, before packing to move out for Pinsk, 100 miles to the east, later that night. Over the past few days, the churchyard had been turned into a cemetery as the bodies of 432 German dead were recovered from across the fortress and city and laid to rest. 'There were long freshly-dug graves all around the church and if you moved along them, you could say to yourself: "I knew him too…"' wrote Josef Arnreiter, whose battalion had received just 22 soldiers from the Reich to replace the fallen. Divisional commander Fritz Schlieper gave a short address; the division's Protestant and Catholic priests led prayers before the men sang the soldiers' hymn, '*Ich hatt' einen Kameraden*'.

Before nightfall, Josef Arnreiter returned to the citadel to take some photographs for his album. The fortress was a forbidden zone, its ruins cleared by Brest's Jews during the day and patrolled by guards at night. The young Austrian bluffed his way inside and took several snapshots. 'Now there was a deathly silence everywhere.'[69]

'WE WILL BE IN MOSCOW IN FOUR WEEKS…'
GERMANY'S LEADERSHIP, LATE
JUNE/EARLY JULY 1941

For the first ten or so days, Adolf Hitler had followed the progress of the campaign intently but had not, by and large, interfered in the conduct of operations. He had spent 22 and 23 June in his chancellery, his only official duty a meeting with Alessandro Pavolini on the Monday. But shortly after Italy's culture minister left, the Führer made the five-minute drive from his official residence to the Anhalter Bahnhof. From there his special train – 15 carriages hauled by two locomotives – headed east via Posen (where Hitler woke and boasted to one of his servants: 'Now we'll crack open this hollow shell'), Thorn and Preussisch Eylau. At 1.30am on Tuesday, after a 450-mile journey, the train pulled up at a new station in the Forest of Görlitz, 15 minutes' drive outside the pleasant small East Prussian town of Rastenburg. This was *Wolfsschanze*, the Wolf's Lair ('The name,' Hitler told the Foreign Ministry's Walther Hewel proudly, 'was my idea'), the field headquarters from where the Führer would preside over his victory in the East.

The complex had been built over the winter and spring of 1940–41 at around one-third of the cost of Hitler's new chancellery, though it lacked any of the grandeur. More than 4,000 employees of the Organisation Todt – the official labour for public projects – had erected ten bunkers and barrack huts, some for working and conferences, a couple for dining, several offering rudimentary accommodation. Individual cabins – about the size of a sleeping compartment on a train – were furnished simply: a bed, wash basin, wardrobe, mirror, radio and a telephone. Military and civilian staff alike hated them. The ventilators which protected them from chemical agents were noisy, the rooms damp, humid, windowless. Clothing – underwear and uniforms – was always damp. Inhabitants understandably suffered from all manner of ailments. 'We shiver wretchedly,' Helmut Greiner, the Wehrmacht's official chronicler, wrote to his wife. 'There's the constant loud rattle of the electrical ventilation system which creates a dreadful draft, causes you to sleep restlessly and wake up in the morning with a headache.' Camouflage netting and the dense forest canopy shielded the headquarters from the prying eyes of aerial reconnaissance, but they also meant the site was gloomy and cool. Above all, the Wolf's Lair was plagued by mosquitoes. Veils and nets were a necessity; otherwise the merest hint of bare flesh became a feeding ground for insects. 'They could hardly have picked a more stupid location,' Greiner fumed. 'Deciduous woods with swamp-like ponds, sandy soil and stationary lakes – the ideal breeding ground for these vile creatures.'

Conditions at the Army High Command's field headquarters, half an hour's drive away by the western shore of the Mauersee, were similarly dark, damp and oppressive. Beneath a canopy of 60 and 70ft-tall pine trees – so dense that no natural light penetrated after nightfall, bunkers and barracks huts were scattered around; no path linked them and only a barely legible number on the structure gave any clue to its occupants. This was *Mauerwald* – Mauer Wood – larger than Wolf's Lair, and also much busier as the principal recipient of signals and reports from front-line units and commands along the entire Eastern Front. The first comprehensive reports of the day's fighting arrived from the army groups at 10pm – and were immediately typed up while operational situation maps were updated. The rest of the night was spent relaying the information to Hitler's headquarters before terse morning reports from the front-line units began to filter through after first light to add the overnight picture. At 8am, Adolf Heusinger, the army's operations officer, was briefed on the night's reports so he, in turn, could outline the situation for the Chief of the General Staff, Franz Halder. Mid-morning the two would drive to the Wolf's Lair for the daily conference.

Adolf Hitler would also survey the overnight situation reports in the map room at the Wolf's Lair before a simple breakfast – a glass of milk and an apple – in a rather spartan dining room, decorated with a couple of paintings and a freshly captured Soviet flag. Opposite the Führer's seat was a large map of Russia. Staring at it, he would frequently launch into monologues about the dangers of Bolshevism. 'Had I waited another year,' he told his captive audience, 'it would probably be too late.' At 1pm, the military staff mustered for the situation conference. Reports of staggering enemy losses were read out repeatedly, as were accounts of dogged Soviet resistance and inhuman acts by 'wild beasts'. The briefings lasted upwards of two hours before Halder and Heusinger returned to *Mauerwald* with fresh instructions for the front-line units, while Hitler occasionally had duties to perform for the newsreel cameras, such as presenting decorations to military heroes. Otherwise, the soporific afternoons were broken only by afternoon tea and cakes with Hitler, which might drag on for a couple of hours, before the evening meal. For women like Christa Schroeder, one of the Führer's secretaries, it was a monotonous existence. 'I sleep, eat, drink and strike up conversations – if I can be bothered,' she wrote to a friend after just a few days at the Wolf's Lair. Hitler, meanwhile, would retire with his entourage, who listened with awe and reverence to their Führer's ramblings on diverse subjects – the origins of mankind, religion, the Nazi Party – until 3 or 4am.

Aside from grumblings over the living conditions, the mood in the hidden headquarters of East Prussia was euphoric. After receiving the daily reports from Friedrich Paulus, the German Army's head of operations, its Commander-in-Chief Walther von Brauchitsch enquired, 'How long do you think we'll need this time, Paulus?' *Probably take six to eight weeks*, was the response. '*Ja*, Paulus, you're right. We'll probably need eight weeks in Russia.' With German soldiers having covered one-third of the distance to Leningrad and Moscow already, 'at this rate we'll be in both cities in 14 days,' Helmut Greiner predicted. His Führer was only slightly more cautious. 'We will be in Moscow in four weeks,' he declared after one situation conference. 'Moscow will be razed to the ground.' On another occasion he boasted: 'I will go down in history as the destroyer of Bolshevism.'

And after poring over the number of tanks and aircraft destroyed, Hitler bragged to his staff: 'I am always trying to put myself in the enemy's shoes. He has practically lost this war already.'[70]

'THE WAR DEMANDS WE STRAIN EVERY SINEW...' THE SOVIET UNION, LATE JUNE/EARLY JULY 1941

Perhaps – for a few hours at least – Joseph Stalin agreed with his adversary. For a week, the *vozhd* had maintained a punishing schedule. Like Hitler he had remained out of public sight. Unlike Hitler he did not gather his *apparatchiks* and subject them to endless monologues into the night; the Soviet leader was either at work in the Kremlin – on one occasion for more than 22 hours without a break – or resting at his dacha on the western outskirts of Moscow. By late evening on Saturday 28 June, he was both exhausted and, above all, exasperated. Desperate for information from Byelorussia, Joseph Stalin was convinced his generals were holding out on him. Dissatisfied with the information he was receiving over the telephone, he decided only a visit in person to the People's Commissariat of Defence – a ten-minute drive from the Kremlin – would give him a true picture of the state of affairs in the west. Accompanied by his security chief Lavrentiy Beria, Vyacheslav Molotov, one of his closest Party comrades Georgy Malenkov and trade minister Anastas Mikoyan, the Soviet leader found Semyon Timoshenko, Georgy Zhukov and his youthful and relatively inexperienced deputy Nikolai Vatutin discussing the situation.

The unplanned conference ran deep into the night. The mood was tense, at times heated. At one point, Vatutin took the floor to describe the situation in Byelorussia. Stalin interrupted him. 'What was that you said, what's happening at Minsk? Have you got this right?'

'No, Comrade Stalin, I'm not getting mixed up,' the petrified Vatutin stuttered. 'The Western Front has virtually collapsed.'

Georgy Zhukov stepped in. He had dispatched officers to re-establish communications but could not say when – or even if – they would.

Having remained calm throughout, Stalin suddenly 'exploded' and rounded on Zhukov. 'What kind of a General Staff, what kind of Chief of the General Staff – someone who lost his head on the first day of the war – has no communications with his armies, represents no-one and commands no-one?'

After the strains and exertions of the past week, this final insult was more than Zhukov could take. 'He cried like a woman and quickly went into another room,' Anastas Mikoyan witnessed. Molotov followed him. 'After five or ten minutes Molotov came back in with Zhukov, who was calm outwardly, but his eyes were still moist.' The conference was over.

It was a depressed *vozhd* and entourage who left the Commissariat in the small hours of Sunday. 'Lenin left us a great legacy,' he told his cronies as he climbed into a limousine to take him to his dacha. 'We, his heirs, have pissed it all away.'[71]

In the dark days of late June and early July it seemed as if the Communist Party and Red Army were in their death throes throughout Byelorussia – and beyond. The Red Army streamed through the city of Pinsk without stopping, continuing eastwards – even though the Germans were a good 25 miles away. Worse, soldiers and Party officials blew up the ammunition and fuel depots. They ended up in the small town of Luninets, three dozen miles east of Pinsk, where they did little but spread panic. 'People are wandering around aimlessly, there are no weapons and uniforms to issue,' one Communist official fumed. 'The town is full of Red Army officers from Brest and Kobrin who don't know what to do, continually heading east in cars without any orders.' The chaos, confusion and disintegration extended 150, 200, 300 miles behind the front, to Vitebsk in northeastern Byelorussia, Gomel in the southeast, and the Smolensk district of Russia. In Vitebsk, soldiers' wives beseeched the commandant to allow them to leave – Communist Party officials and their families had fled. Life in the city fell apart. No public institution operated. The prison had been abandoned. The few remaining officials hurriedly burned the archives. 'Work and normal life in the city is completely paralysed,' the Vitebsk garrison's military prosecutor fumed. Airfield personnel abandoned their posts and ran through Gomel – more than six weeks before the city was actually captured by the Germans. 'It has a corrosive effect on the populace and wreaks havoc in the rear,' Gomel's Party Secretary complained. 'Things like this make it impossible to deliver a devastating blow to the enemy and repulse him.' There was similar panic in the small town of Yelnya, southeast of Smolensk, and 'cries that the enemy is marching towards Orsha', barely 100 miles away. People were already passing through Yelnya having abandoned Smolensk. And the Party did nothing.[72]

Even the normally dependable NKVD was beginning to falter. Prisoners hurriedly evacuated from Byelorussia's jails and marched eastwards were now abandoned by their guards and left to their own devices. The survivors of Joanna Stankiewicz-Januszczak's column from Minsk decided to head west into the arms of the advancing Germans instead, pretending to be reinforcements for the crumbling front. 'We're fighting, our enemies are running away,' they told the torrent of refugees streaming eastwards. They were not always convincing. Despite their weeks or months in prison, they looked like *zapadnikov* – people from the West – as Soviets called Poles from western Byelorussia and Ukraine, and were treated with suspicion. Still, some villagers offered the marchers bread and bacon as they moved ever closer to the front line. 'Germans one way, the Soviets the other,' Stankiewicz-Januszczak pondered. 'Hell. Hell which only the Mother of Mercy led us safely out of.' Just 18 months before, Russians had mocked Poles for their nation's swift defeat at German hands: 'You were dancing the tango while we built tanks and you lost the war!' they snarled at Joanna and her compatriots. 'Now they'd lost the war faster than we had – after just four days the Germans were in Minsk,' she wrote. 'You can imagine our joy and satisfaction, our *Schadenfreude* – to use the German word.'[73]

Too many arms of the Party had 'failed to grasp the seriousness of the danger', Communist leadership in Moscow conceded at the end of the first week of war. The moment had come to impress on them the gravity of the hour. On 29 June, Party leaders proclaimed:

> In this war forced upon us by Fascist Germany, the life or death of the Soviet state is at stake, namely whether the peoples of the Soviet Union will be free or be enslaved. The enemy is strong. It would be reckless to underestimate his strength. The war demands we strain every sinew, iron perseverance and manly cold-bloodedness. We must not become intoxicated with the thought of easy successes.[74]

No cinema, theatre, restaurant or bar was to remain open beyond 10.45pm. Employees of major state enterprises were expected to be at their places of work by 8.30am, 9am for lesser institutions and organisations. In Leningrad every able-bodied man aged between 16 and 50 (45 for women) was expected to devote at least three hours daily – in addition to their regular job – to assisting in the defence of the city. Failure to comply ensured a fine of 3,000 roubles – or six months in prison. Every citizen was ordered to surrender their radios – 'transmitters might be used by hostile elements to harm the Soviet government' so the sets would go into 'temporary storage until the end of the war'. Henceforth, the only news – or entertainment – the Russian people would hear would come through the public loudspeakers, at work or in clubs and institutions.[75]

It would take more than confiscations, threats and admonishments to defeat the Fascist invader. Most citizens of the Soviet Union had reacted with rage and indignation to news of the German invasion. It was time to harness that anger and turn it to the USSR's advantage. After the awkward two-year courtship with Nazi Germany, the Soviet propaganda machine was now unleashed with full force against the invader. Newspaper articles and radio broadcasts might spew invectives, but posters and patriotic tunes sought to inspire the Soviet people. No song would become more associated with the Soviet Union's struggle than the hurriedly written 'Svyashchennaya Voyna' – Sacred War. It took lyricist Vasily Lebedev-Kumach two days to come up with the words, composer Aleksandr Alexsandrov – the man behind the Soviet Union's national anthem – another two days to provide the music. Hastily mobilised troops bound for the Western Front heard it for the first time at the waiting room of Moscow's Byelorussky station on 26 June. An improvised dais had been erected for choristers who were uneasy at performing in such surroundings; the hall was noisy, with frequent announcements over loudspeakers. But when Alexsandrov raised his baton and the men began singing, silence descended. 'When we got to the second verse, everyone had stood up as if the national anthem were being played,' one of the choristers recalled. 'Many people were in tears – we were too.' At the request of the audience, they performed 'Sacred War' five times in succession:

Arise, vast country
Arise, for a fight to the death
With the Fascist force of darkness,
With the accursed horde.
Let our noble rage
Boil over like a wave!
There is a people's war,
A sacred war![76]

It took a few more days for the USSR's printing presses to run off the first posters to rally the public. These early efforts were simple, even crude affairs. 'For the Motherland, for Stalin!' urged one depicting a soldier, rifle in one hand, red banner in the other, advancing under the guns of T-26s and Rata fighters. A similar effort, featuring phalanxes of tanks supporting advancing infantry, echoed Molotov's radio address: 'Our cause is just! The enemy will be smashed!' The cartoonists Mikhail Kupriyanov, Porfiri Krylov and Nikolai Sokolov – better known as the Kukryniksy team – quickly sketched a soldier bayonetting a crazed Hitler as he tore the Non-Aggression Pact apart as a banner encouraged: 'Ruthlessly crush and destroy the enemy!' Few of these appeals are remembered today, save one. On the first day of the war, artist Irakli Toidze had been so startled by the sudden appearance of his wife bursting in on him at work with news of the conflict that he ordered her to stand still while he sketched her expression. Within a fortnight, her face would appear on one of the most iconic posters of the war as a defiant Mother Russia, beseeching her countrymen to rally to the cause and read the military oath to defend the nation. It was a theme Joseph Stalin would soon return to.

For at least 24 hours, the Soviet Union was leaderless. After the disastrous conference in the small hours of 29 June, Joseph Stalin retreated to the dacha built for him in the woods at Kuntsevo in the early 1930s. He did not emerge.

By dawn on the 30th, Molotov, Beria and other senior Party figures had decided that the nation needed firm leadership, it needed a committee to seize the reins of government and direct the war effort. The only problem was the *vozhd*. 'Molotov said that over the past two days, Stalin had been so low that he was not interested in anything, showed no initiative, and was in a bad way,' Anastas Mikoyan recalled. The cabal decided to confront their leader.

After a 15-minute drive, a limousine pulled up to the gate outside the lawn-green-coloured single-storey dacha. Seeing Beria, the guards immediately waved the vehicle through. Its passengers found their leader in a small dining room sitting in a chair. At the sight of the doyens of the Communist Party, the *vozhd* froze. He tucked his head into his shoulders and, with eyes filled with consternation, asked: 'Why have you come?' Mikoyan was convinced Stalin believed they had come to arrest him.

Molotov stepped forward and explained that the Soviet Union desperately needed to concentrate power in the hands of a new State Committee for Defence. 'Stalin literally changed before our eyes,' Mikoyan recalled. The *vozhd* sat up, his shoulders straightened. Still, there was an awkward silence before Stalin finally spoke. 'And who is in charge?' he asked.

'You are, comrade Stalin,' Molotov told him.

'Good.'[77]

Dawn on the first day of July found Dmitry Pavlov breakfasting in his tent at the headquarters of the Western Front, now located in woods outside the city of Mogilev, 100 miles east of Minsk. Each day conduct of the battle had slipped increasingly from the front commander's hands. He had become a slave to rather than master of events, cut off from his corps and armies for hours, even days at a time – he blamed saboteurs, spies and paratroopers dropped behind his lines for cutting telephone lines. His units tried to stand fast on lines already long-since bypassed by the enemy. In places, his men fought with skill and determination, claiming they had knocked out 50 panzers here, 100 there. One anti-tank unit reportedly fell back across the Beresina without a single shell left; it had fired every round before withdrawing. Relations with his chief-of-staff, Vladimir Klimovskikh, had completely broken down; Pavlov double-checked every order issued in his name, even sending commissars to check his instructions were being carried out.

The sudden, unexpected appearance of his old friend Andrey Eremenko this Tuesday was a welcome surprise. It had taken the 48-year-old general three days to find Pavlov's headquarters, the end of a nine-day, 6,000-mile odyssey from the Red Army's headquarters in the Far East. As one of Russia's most experienced commanders, Eremenko had been recalled immediately. Out of contact on the six-day rail and air journey from Khabarovsk to Moscow, Eremenko refused to believe what he could see on the map spread out on a table in the Kremlin office of the People's Commissar for Defence. Semyon Timoshenko outlined the situation – far graver than Eremenko could have imagined – blaming front-line commanders, Dmitry Pavlov especially, for the Soviet Union's plight. 'Now you know the state of affairs,' he concluded.

'It's a sad state,' Andrey Eremenko agreed.

The marshal nodded, then told Eremenko that he was to replace Pavlov.

'What is the specific assignment?' Eremenko asked.

'To stop the enemy advance,' Timoshenko responded bluntly.

Now Eremenko stood before his friend. Pavlov perked up visibly and asked the general to join him for breakfast. Eremenko declined. He handed Pavlov his orders. 'The People's Commissar instructs you to go to Moscow,' he told the Western Front commander coolly, then asked him to outline the situation.

'The enemy has driven deep into our territory,' Dmitry Pavlov lamented. He blamed enemy superiority and Moscow's shortcomings for his plight. Pavlov's staff merely mirrored his state of confusion and bewilderment. The decision to replace the Western Front's commander was the correct one, Eremenko quickly concluded. 'I had to whip the Front into shape.' His first task: to hold the line of the Beresina river.[78]

'I CAN STILL KILL A FEW FASCIST SCUM...'
THE BERESINA, 1–3 JULY 1941

As July 1941 began, three German armoured divisions were converging on the Beresina around Borisov: 7th Panzer upstream, 10th downstream and 18th in the centre, along the Moscow highway. The defenders positioned tanks on either side of the main road running into the town, hoping to set an ambush. Each one was picked off by 18th Panzer's vanguard. The bunkers in the woods straddling the route proved rather more difficult to subdue, neutralised 'at the point of a bayonet'. Upwards of 20 light tanks of 1st Moscow Proletarian Rifle Division – regarded as an elite unit by the Germans – burst out of the woods and advanced in two rows down the highway. They caught the spearhead off guard. One tank succeeded in ramming Walther Nehring's command panzer, tearing the front wheel of the caterpillar track away. Another Soviet tank, already in flames, turned its cannon at Nehring's crippled vehicle. An artillery officer saw it and warned his divisional commander at the last moment. Nehring jumped out of the way. His driver was wounded. Yet 18th Panzer's commander seemed unperturbed. Though executed with 'admirable élan and the greatest audacity', the enemy's attack was uncoordinated and badly led. Half the tanks disappeared into the nearby woods, tried to turn around but became bogged down among the trees and were knocked out one by one. Even when ablaze, their crews ignored pleas in Russian to surrender and continued to shoot. The remainder were dealt with by Nehring's panzers and anti-tank guns. As one junior officer put it: 'With engines roaring, the Russians drove to their doom.' The last one was finished off as it was about to overrun the divisional command post.

Overhead, the Red Air Force was no less determined to prevent the Germans crossing the river. One of Nehring's non-commissioned officers watched the dogfights, spellbound:

It was as if the aircraft were locked together. They tore through the sky, circling each other, turning sharply, gliding low over the countryside, pulling up and flying in such chaotic formations that you didn't know where to look. Some of the fat Russian biplanes fell from the sky, their fuselages burning, before exploding on the other side of the field.

But then a shiver ran down our spines. A Messerschmitt fighter hissed over our position trailing smoke. It crashed into a small hill and went up in flames. Immediately afterwards another one of our fighters plunged straight into the ground, and blew up in our faces. And then I saw another German fighter explode in mid air. Just a few seconds later, a flaming Messerschmitt drilled itself into the ground a few metres from the highway. The fuel poured out. It ran burning across the road and onto a half-track. The crew, poor devils, ran across the road as if they were living torches. Another Messerschmitt made an emergency landing ahead of us. But one of those fat beasts with the Red Star loitered behind the Messerschmitt and shot it to pieces just as it touched the ground.

The bravery of Soviet aircrew and tank men was unable to prevent 18th Panzer Division forcing the Beresina. Despite heavy enemy artillery fire – and a demolition party trying to blow it up – the Germans seized a road bridge over the river. By nightfall, 18th Panzer had a viable bridgehead on the river's right bank. The division's supply officer handed out bottles of champagne – freshly looted from warehouses in Borisov – to the exhausted troops. As Walther Nehring acidly observed: 'To be able to think clearly now and possess the imagination to take fresh decisions, we already needed champagne.'[79]

Forcing the Beresina at Borisov gave 18th Panzer a springboard for the drive on Smolensk and brought in a rich haul of six dozen enemy tanks, 40 trucks, a smattering of guns, 'several hundred prisoners' and even an armoured train. At dusk on 2 July it was deeper inside the Soviet Union than any other German unit. But it paid a high price for its success, as its rifle regiment commander, Erwin Jollasse lamented: 'You could rightly say that the flower of our young Officer Corps fell or was wounded on the Beresina on 1st and 2nd July.' The division's Catholic priest, Heinz Wolf, visited the main first-aid post, located in a half-destroyed building marked by a large Red Cross flag just behind the front line. 'Ambulances come and go, offloading their tragic cargo, disappearing back to the front,' he recorded in his diary.

> I move from room to room. All words fail me here. Here you have to provide physical assistance: A slight groan, a slight whisper, most are silent, with large eyes wide open. Occasionally someone gives me a tired smile. Behind the house in a shaded corner lie the dead, officers and men. Their numbers grow. There are some friends among them. Silent and dumb, their hands stiff as they struggled to make their final movements. These are young men – they've barely come of age.[80]

The first-aid post was the 'principal place of work' for the Wehrmacht's military chaplains accompanying the armies into Russia. It wasn't the priest's first duty, chaplain Josef Obmann acknowledged, but he felt compelled to remain with his men. 'Wounds, misery, dying – I experience them in this form for the first time,' he recorded in his diary. 'Men dying has a tremendous effect on me time and again.' 31st Infantry Division Catholic priest Johann Hamm, who would end the war in Dachau for his outspoken criticism of the Nazi regime and the war it waged, felt it was his duty to care for the wounded and dying and give their comrades spiritual support. 'Their comrades cannot stick it out without the comfort of religion, they cannot be surrounded by death and pain without the comfort of Christ.'[81]

3rd Panzer Division's drive on the Beresina – another electrifying thrust by armoured forces focused on a single objective – brought it to Bobruisk, where hastily posted placards on the sides of buildings depicting Hitler as a baby Napoleon being beaten by the butt of a Russian rifle promised 'Napoleon suffered defeat. The arrogant Hitler will suffer the same fate'. By 5am on Sunday 29 June, the *Reichskriegsflagge* was flying over the citadel – the only part of Bobruisk to offer the vanguard of 3rd Panzer any substantial resistance.

Fourth Army commander Aleksandr Korobkov proposed throwing a rag-tag collection of student battalions armed with grenades, infantry and tanks to re-take Bobruisk, only to abandon the idea almost immediately. But the Soviet general was determined to hold the right bank of the 300ft-wide Beresina on the eastern edge of the city. Throughout the day, artillery rained shells on the citadel and German positions on the left shore. 'The howl of incoming shells, the crash as they impacted, the screeching of shrapnel and the shattering of windowpanes, mixed with the roar of vehicles seeking cover somewhere at full speed, were the sounds echoing around the old citadel,' war correspondent Günter Heysing wrote. Sheets of metal were ripped off the roofs of barrack blocks and tumbled through the air before crashing onto the pavement. In the oppressive heat and humidity, rivers of sweat flowed down the faces, arms and backs of the fighting men. A mid-afternoon thunderstorm added to the hellish concert in the Beresina valley, as lightning alternated with muzzle flashes and thunder with the boom of howitzers and field guns. A Red Army assault party tried to exploit the fug hugging the valley floor to cross to the left bank but were cut down by German machine-gunners. 3rd Panzer Division was more successful. In the evening a battalion of motorised infantry finally reached the opposite bank in inflatable boats and by scrambling over the ruins of the road bridge. By the small hours of 30 June, 3rd Panzer had a toe hold on the right bank of the Beresina, though not a single vehicle was over the river.[82]

The division's engineers spent the rest of the night throwing a pontoon bridge across the Beresina. As soon as it was completed, motorised infantry rolled across, but no panzers, even though Red Army resistance on the right bank of the Beresina was beginning to weaken. For at dawn, a specially trained assault group had headed in the opposite direction on boats and rafts. It had slipped into Bobruisk, seized the historic citadel and from there continuously harried the Germans. The defenders of Bobruisk were a rag-tag group – staff of the Automobile and Tractor School, soldiers from the garrison, Party members, students. A platoon of young Communists fought valiantly. When their leader was gravely wounded, he rejected all offers to treat him. 'I can still kill a few Fascist scum and request permission to remain with my men,' he told his commander. However hard they fought, their numbers were small and getting ever smaller. A counter-attack by a mechanised corps to re-take Bobruisk never materialised. The only relief came from the heavens. The Red Air Force dominated the leaden skies over the river. It repeatedly struck German concentrations on the left bank, the bridgehead on the right and the makeshift bridge linking the two sides of the river. 'The enemy is offering dogged resistance,' armoured car commander Hanns-Adolf Munier wrote. 'One squadron of Russian bombers after another approaches Bobruisk.' Low cloud prevented the Luftwaffe joining battle in earnest, but the skies cleared mid-afternoon and *Jagdgeschwader* 51 entered the fray. 'Mölders has a great day with his fighters,' Munier continued. And how. Werner Mölders downed his 82nd enemy aircraft this Monday, making him the most successful fighter pilot in history – surpassing the great Red Baron. His squadron brought down 110 Red Air Force planes, raising their total of 'kills' since the war began to more than 1,000. 'Many bombs are dumped, many bombers plunge to the ground like torches,' Munier noted. The sky over the Beresina valley was filled with the parachutes of Soviet aircrew, while tall black clouds of smoke rose where the aircraft, their bombs and fuel had impacted the earth. And on the ground, search parties dashed to and fro in staff cars and on motorbikes to arrest the downed fliers and take them to their headquarters for interrogation.[83]

Over two days, what was left of Western Front's air power was thrown at the still-weak German bridgeheads on the right bank of the Beresina. The bombers went in first and, while the Messerschmitts grappled with them, formations of Soviet fighters suddenly appeared en masse – up to two dozen at a time. Eremenko claimed the tactic cost the Luftwaffe an improbable 60 aircraft, for the loss of just 18 Red Air Force planes. The fighting also gave Russia her first double Hero of the Soviet Union, Stepan Suprun. Already an ace thanks to clashes with the Japanese in the Far East, Suprun was also one of the USSR's most experienced test pilots – he had flown more than 100 different models and earned a Hero title as a result. Suprun and his elite regiment of fighter test pilots were sent west with their Yak and MiG fighters and thrown into battle immediately to bolster Western Front's depleted air force. 'Today I am flying to the front to defend my Motherland, my people,' he wrote home enthusiastically. 'I will do my utmost to prove to the Fascist bastards what Soviet pilots are capable of.' On its first day of battle, his pilots clocked up half a dozen sorties each. Suprun alone claimed four kills. But the brightest star burned out the quickest. Stepan Suprun lasted no more than four days in combat with the Luftwaffe. When faced with two Ju88s and four Me109s, he characteristically elected to fight. He brought one of the bombers down, but superior numbers told. His MiG was hit and plunged vertically into the ground. Within three weeks, Stepan Suprun was a Hero of his nation once more. The actions of his regiment perhaps bought the men on the ground a little time, but above all they were a fillip to the Red Air Force's shattered morale. 'Soviet fliers took heart,' Eremenko wrote. 'They saw the enemy could be beaten if they fought skilfully and in organised fashion.'[84]

'NO RESTING UNTIL WE HAVE TOTAL VICTORY...'
THE MINSK POCKET, 1–8 JULY 1941

And still there was fighting in the Minsk pocket.

Though the smaller pocket had been eradicated, not so the larger encirclement of Red Army forces to the north and west of Minsk. Perhaps as many as a dozen Soviet divisions – or, more accurately, the remnants thereof – were trapped by a similar number of German infantry and panzer divisions in a pocket still covering 1,500 square miles of Byelorussian countryside. But by early July co-ordinated resistance was becoming infrequent. There was the occasional mass surrender; 12th Panzer Division seized 52,000 prisoners in a single day. More typically, the encircled Soviet soldiers threw away their uniforms and tried to slip through the German cordon dressed as civilians. Some succeeded. Some were shot. Most were captured and sent to processing camps behind the front.

Some trapped Red Army troops made determined final attempts to break out, as one company of pioneers deployed 100 miles north of Minsk discovered on 5 July. While the Germans were occupied searching and interrogating a small group of deserters, the trapped Russians launched their bid for freedom 'by heavy fire and yells'. Four companies – mostly comprising officers and commissars wearing the uniforms of ordinary soldiers – swept through the pioneers' lines and a mile into their rear, where they fell upon its vehicles, shooting up radiators and dashboards and, tellingly, plundering food. The pioneer company counted 40 casualties. Its outposts had fought to the last man or last round – or both. 'The wounded were maltreated in an inhuman manner, especially non-commissioned officers and soldiers who wore the Iron Cross or other decorations,' an after-action report stated. 'They were mutilated with bayonets until they were no longer recognisable and robbed of all possessions, even dog tags, so that later identification was difficult.'[85]

Nearby the motorised infantry of 5th Rifle Regiment held off one of the most determined last efforts to escape the pocket. 'Countless masses of Russian soldiers came towards us, through hollows and over the hill,' a junior officer recalled.

> Our fire inflicted a terrible massacre in their ranks. The initial chaos prevented them from correctly identifying our platoon. Two hours later we knew that we lay at the centre of the breakout attempt. There were only a few rounds of ammunition left for the carbines and pistols. The Russians regrouped for their next assault – their fourth.

A lance corporal, one Friedrich 'Fritz' Reken, was dispatched with a motorcycle and sidecar to fetch ammunition and returned a few minutes later as the Russians emerged from cover to begin their attack. Reken zig-zagged between the German positions, hurling ammunition belts to his comrades. As he made his final 'delivery', the sidecar was hit by enemy fire. Reken waved his hand: 'It went past me!' before toppling off his motorcycle. His comrades fed the belts Reken had given them into their machine-guns. With the usual cries of 'Urra', the Soviet attack faltered under the murderous automatic fire. When the assault ended, the men of the 5th recovered their dead comrades and buried them. They found a farewell letter on Fritz Reken's corpse:

> Dear comrades,
>   If a bullet hits me and I have to cross over to the other side, then send greetings to my mother and tell her that I suffered a quick death and was glad to die for Germany. Take good care of our lieutenant because I cannot any more.
>   Your comrade Fritz[86]

There was no heroic last stand, no final dramatic act of surrender or action. The Battle of the Białystok–Minsk Pocket, as it has come to be known, petered out in skirmishes or scattered groups of exhausted and emaciated Russian soldiers surrendering at the end of the first week of July 1941. 'Prisoners constantly emerge from the woods and fields along the route of advance, most of them without weapons,' Dr Karl Mauss, a dentist serving with 10th Panzer Division, noted. 'They're exceptionally ragged figures from all sorts of races.'[87]

Pausing briefly to eat after eight days continuously in action, Major Werner Heinemann, commanding a battalion in 23rd Infantry Division, was suddenly struck by the 'profound image of peace': 'Only the continual appearance of Russians from out of the cornfields and the bushes is a reminder of the collapse of two huge armies. Whenever possible, they are shot dead because they have murdered Germans who fell into their hands in the most bestial manner.'[88]

You did not have to wander far from such idyllic sites to discover a truer picture of the Białystok pocket. Priest Johann Hamm found the main Minsk highway near Slonim littered with every conceivable trace of battle, above all 'the pungent stench of corpses'. The road was lined with wrecked tanks and trucks 'for kilometres on end'. Friedrich Hossbach's 31st Infantry Division marched along the same road near Baranovichi, past 'flattened cornfields, destroyed vehicles, useless anti-tank guns, and a number of shot-up tanks, most of them German'.[89]

By 8 July, with his infantry units still combing out the forests and copses of central Byelorussia, Fedor von Bock felt secure enough to declare the battle won. Never had an army suffered a defeat on such a scale in modern history. It was, a special announcement from Hitler's headquarters trumpeted, a battle of annihilation 'of global-historical significance'. Army Group Centre reckoned it had smashed 22 enemy infantry divisions, seven armoured divisions and six mechanised brigades. His men had captured 287,704 Soviet soldiers, 'including several divisional and corps commanders' and captured or destroyed more than 2,500 tanks, to say nothing of the trucks, cars, guns and rifles seized. 'Now we have to exploit this victory!' Fedor von Bock concluded his order of the day. 'I know that my army group will continue to give its all. There can be no resting until we have total victory!' Even as the field marshal issued his exhortation, the number of prisoners passed the 300,000 mark. According to official Soviet records, based on a paper strength of 625,000 men on 22 June, in just two weeks Western Front had lost more than 400,000 men killed, captured or wounded. Of the 44 divisions which began the battle for western and central Byelorussia, 24 ceased to exist. The rest were sorely mauled – some had lost as much as 90 per cent of their men and materiel. Over 9,000 artillery pieces and mortars were lost or destroyed, 4,700 tanks, over 1,700 aircraft. More than 60 depots – food, fuel, vehicle and ammunition – were now in enemy hands, as well as 50,000 tonnes of fuel (half the front's reserve) and 2,000 ammunition trucks. Nine in every ten medics were dead or missing. Four corps and three divisional commanders were dead; ten had been taken prisoner.[90]

The scale of the Soviet defeat was – for now – unparalleled. But not every German was as bullish as von Bock or the official communiqué. 'Someone said he had the feeling that we'd experience a trench war here in Russia,' 23rd Infantry Division supply officer Fritz Gercke recorded as his staff surveyed the devastation outside Białystok. 'I regarded this prophet as a killjoy and rejected such a possibility, even bearing the infinite expanses here in Russia in mind.'[91]

'How endlessly vast Russia is...' Army Group Centre, beginning of July 1941

After several days' rest, 134th Infantry Division followed the path of the Moscow highway towards Minsk. As the soldiers approached Baranovichi, they passed a small graveyard for German and Austro-Hungarian soldiers killed in the fighting of 1915. Now German trucks and troops rolled past the cemetery, while in the sky there was the constant sight and sound of the Luftwaffe. 'What a tremendous roar of victory by the young Wehrmacht of the Greater German Reich descending on the last resting place of old comrades from 1915,' battalion commander Hans Schulze wrote. His men marched on side roads and summer tracks through the woods, down the main railway line and, finally, on the Moscow highway itself, normally reserved for the panzers. In the roadside ditches there were still burned-out and wrecked Soviet tanks and vehicles, plus the occasional German vehicle marked with a white G – *Panzergruppe* Guderian. Above the highway, no higher than 250ft, there was an almost endless succession of three-engined Ju52 transporters heading northeast with fuel, ammunition and other supplies for Guderian's spearhead, or heading in the opposite direction carrying the wounded to the Fatherland. 'This highway is possibly the clearest demonstration of modern warfare,' Hans Schulze noted. 'And it's aimed straight at Moscow!'[92]

With the Białystok pocket eliminated, 12th Panzer Division was at last released to resume its advance. As its armoured and motorised columns thundered along the main road running east out of Minsk, motorcyclist Gerhard Möws paused briefly. 'The highway vanished far away, on the horizon,' he observed. 'How endlessly vast Russia is. What a small piece of this gigantic empire we've occupied, what still lies ahead of us? The tremendous size, the tremendous distances are thoroughly depressing.' Where would the German Army be in winter? he wondered.[93]

5

TO KIEV

The thunder and roar of the guns, the shots bursting as they land, the trails of tracers from the flak, the burning houses in the town. It's frightful – and beautiful.

Wilhelm Prüller

'WHAT HAPPENED TO THAT SUPERIORITY OVER RUSSIAN TANKS?' GALICIA, 23 JUNE, MORNING

By 5.30am on Monday 23 June, the armour of 11th Panzer Division was already on the move again, spurred on by the rallying cry of its commander Ludwig Crüwell. 'Our watchword is attack, our goal the Dnieper,' he told his men. 'As in Belgrade, we want to be the first ones there.' On the first day of war in the East, the ghost division had lived up to its name, capturing the bridge over the Bug at Sokal intact before advancing 20 miles, mostly brushing aside Red Army resistance. The short night – barely four and a half hours – had passed peacefully. Now the division's vanguard, 15th Panzer Regiment, was moving on Radekhov – aerial reconnaissance had reported Soviet tanks advancing on the village. The German armour rolled in, overrunning Soviet infantry. But in the centre of Radekhov, some panzers encountered elements of 10th Tank Division: 30 light tanks and half a dozen new T-34s. Three Red Army BT-7s were destroyed and one panzer knocked out, its turret shot off with its commander still inside. The Russians withdrew; the Germans continued. The mood of the panzer crews was 'fantastic,' gunlayer Gustav Schrodek recalled. 'After all, what could happen to them given their tremendous confidence in their panzers?'

The formation advanced as far as a country lane when there was the sound of engines coming from a nearby copse. In the platoon commander's panzer, Schrodek counted one, two, three, four 'monsters' with red stars on the turrets moving along the track at 50-yard intervals. They failed to notice the Germans, who opened fire at point-blank range. Every round hit its target, but the only effect the shells had on the Russians was to make them speed off into the distance. 'For God's sake, what happened to that superiority over Russian tanks?' Gustav Schrodek wondered, while his superior reported the one-sided action to the regiment's commander, Gustav-Adolf Riebel: 'We've just been in action with four enemy tanks. Type not determined as they're not listed in our intelligence cards. Despite multiple hits from our fire no effect. Impression that our shells simply bounced off. Enemy tanks turned and drove back without offering resistance.' Thus ended the first encounter with the T-34 on the Southern Front. It was the precursor to ten days of titanic clashes of armour unparalleled in the history of warfare.[1]

No-one was in a better position to crush the German incursion onto Soviet soil than Mikhail Kirponos and his newly designated Southwestern Front, a mighty force of just under 900,000 men, massed in four armies and eight mechanised corps, equipped with nearly 4,500 tanks – almost 800 of them KVs or T-34s – and supported by a good 2,000 aircraft. If only the front commander had the means and ability to lead them. The 49-year-old Ukrainian was typical of the men who led the Red Army in the summer of 1941: a committed Communist and long-time servant of the Red Army, he had fought bravely for his Tsar, then for the Bolshevik cause in the Civil War. By the time of the Winter War with Finland, Kirponos was commanding a rifle division. His skilful leadership of it in the capture of Vyborg led to rapid promotions. In April 1940 Kirponos was in command of a rifle corps, by July the Leningrad Military District and, in February the following year, he was put in charge of the Kiev District where the usually caustic Nikita Khrushchev surprisingly took a liking to the new general: 'a good commander and an honest man', but one also clearly out of his depth. To the Party leader, it was all too evident that Mikhail Kirponos 'didn't have the experience of leading such a large number of troops'. His relations with his staff were fractious from the outset; they favoured holding the border, while the new commander preferred to hold at least some of his 61 divisions in reserve to deal a devastating counter-blow should the Germans attack.

The man Mikhail Kirponos faced was arguably the Third Reich's most famous military commander. Revered within the Officer Corps before the war, Gerd von Rundstedt had led German arms to victory over Poland and France, earning him a fearsome reputation around the globe. Such triumphs masked the 65-year-old field marshal's shortcomings. He was conservative in every sense of the word: dependable,

Army Group South – the advance through Ukraine, 22 June–3 July 1941

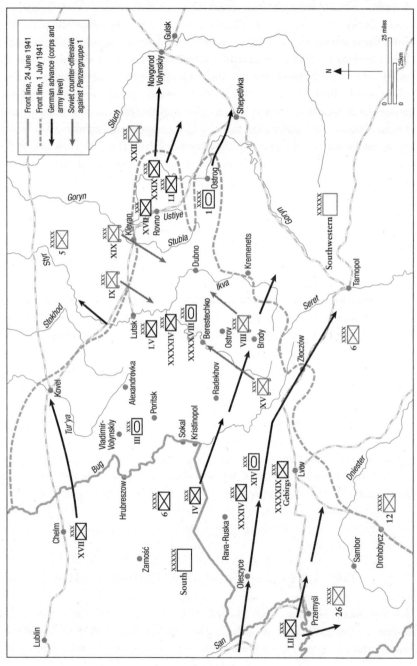

but also stolid and unimaginative. He possessed an acerbic tongue, was prone to sarcastic outbursts, frequently dismissing Hitler in private as 'that Bohemian corporal', yet he loyally served the Führer and his regime. The German leader frequently repaid Rundstedt's loyalty and always treated him 'courteously', even making his deputy Hermann Göring stand while offering a seat to the field marshal on one occasion. His Army Group South was a powerful force: just shy of 800,000 men in 41 divisions spread among three armies and one armoured group. The panzers would strike south of the Pripet marshes across the plains of Galicia, heading almost directly eastwards towards Kiev. Army Group Centre and the inaccessible marshland would safeguard the armoured lunge's left wing, Sixth and Seventeenth Armies its right as they battered their way through southern Ukraine, seizing cities such as Lvov and Tarnopol. And on the very end of Rundstedt's line, Eleventh Army and two Romanian armies would march into Bukovina and Bessarabia, 'liberating' lands snatched from Bucharest the previous summer. In the documents and on staff charts, the mission appeared relatively straightforward. But the distances were vast: Army Group South's front stretched for 450 miles to the northern shore of the Black Sea. Kiev lay 300 miles away, Rostov, gateway to the Caucasus, more than 800. The distances – three times greater than his drive to the Channel in the spring of 1940 – troubled Rundstedt, who warned his wife that this new campaign would not run 'as quickly as hoped and as we've grown used to in the past'.[2]

The commander of Rundstedt's armour shared his master's misgivings – and many of his master's characteristics. Six years younger than the field marshal, Ewald von Kleist was conservative, critical of the Nazis – in private – but had always answered the call to serve his country. It was Kleist's armour which had overrun France and then Yugoslavia. Now, in the renamed *Panzergruppe* 1, the 59-year-old was given five armoured divisions – 730 vehicles, two-thirds of them the Mk3 and Mk4 models – but feared his foe possessed 'more than twice or three times the forces at our disposal'.[3]

In fact, Mikhail Kirponos enjoyed a sixfold superiority in tanks, but in the coming week's battle that advantage would be frittered away by poor leadership, dreadful communications, disjointed counter-attacks and outdated tactics.

'OUR PLACE IS AT THE FRONT...'
THE GERMAN–SOVIET BORDER, 23 JUNE

Kirill Moskalenko's day began reconnoitring the terrain near Vladimir-Volynskiy where his 1st Anti-Tank Artillery Brigade had taken up position. A handful of miles from the border, Moskalenko's armoured car halted on a hill from where he surveyed the scene. 'There it was, the notorious panzer wedge which would smash the defences,' he wrote. In the lead were Panzer Mk4s, protected by Mk3s and Mk2s, behind them motorcyclists, then motorised infantry and finally artillery. Possibly blinded by the rising sun at Moskalenko's back, the vanguard of 14th Panzer Division failed to spot the Soviet officer, who now fell back to his prepared position and waited for the enemy to attack. The brigade commander was confident: his men were dug in on ground of their choosing, there was plenty of ammunition and gunners had an excellent view of the approaching German armour as it moved through the fields in close formation, flattening the corn. Moskalenko ordered his men to hold their nerve until the enemy tanks were barely 300 yards away. 'At that moment the enemy faced a firestorm,' he remembered. The crews opened fire on the advancing panzers at point-blank range, 'certain of a hit'.

The German armour broke formation and tried to outflank Moskalenko's position, only to run into more Soviet anti-tank guns on each flank. Repulsed, 14th Panzer Division fell back, regrouped and attacked with supporting infantry after a Luftwaffe raid had pulverised the Red Army lines. Once again the German onslaught failed. After ten hours of battle, the attackers broke off their assault, leaving 'around 50 burning or disabled panzers and armoured cars as well as many dead on the battlefield'.

To the northwest of Vladimir-Volynskiy, 41st Tank Division was finally in a position to support the infantrymen of XV Rifle Corps, having been hounded since dawn by German aircraft. The division's chief-of-staff Konstantin Maligin marvelled as two tank companies bore down on the German positions, carrying the Red infantry with them as they went. Maligin's mood quickly changed. After initial success, the armour fell back in disarray. Just three tanks from one company returned and two from a second.[4]

It took the pioneers of 295th Infantry Division until the middle of Monday afternoon to eradicate a bunker complex built into the hillside on the road to the division's first objective, the town of Rava-Ruska. They needed seven attempts to reduce the field fortifications, finally neutralised by a combination of heavy artillery, explosive charges and hand-to-hand fighting. Just nine prisoners emerged from the shattered bunkers – their officer chose to take his own life.[5]

Accounts of the heroism and doggedness of Soviet soldiers holding the border fortifications can be found repeatedly in contemporary reports and diaries and in post-war histories. Wounded Russians were hauled out of captured bunkers only to seize any weapon to hand and resume the battle, while bunkers long-since subdued suddenly sprang back to life after hours or even days as dispersed Red Army troops re-occupied them. 'Some Russians with several chest wounds and fist-sized exit wounds who'd lost a lot of blood and not received a bandage in ten to 15 hours were observed reaching for their weapons again.' The Bavarians of 296th Infantry Division had to smash their way – there was no other word for it – through a chain of 34 bunkers. It cost them 200 dead and double the number in wounded. 'When we think they're finished,' regimental commander Heinrich Thoma complained, 'they spring back to life because the garrisons can simply go down to a lower level.' It wasn't simply skilful bunker construction which held up the 296th, however. 'Even when badly wounded they continued to shoot until they were completely dead,' artillery officer Hans Reinert observed. 'You can only talk of heroism if you want to do justice to the soldiers' honour.'[6]

Vassili Petrov's artillery battery still hoped to reward such heroism by joining up with the 87th Rifle Division near the village of Ustilug, before throwing the invader back across the Bug. The first day of war had cost Petrov's platoon four dead and five wounded, yet it had seen little action. 'Our place is at the front, that's where the enemy must be made to halt,' the battery commander told his men, who almost disappeared as they trudged through fields of tall grain – at times, only their olive green helmets were still visible. The setting – a river valley, with clear skies, fresh air, rich fields and the carefree twitter of birds – could not have been more idyllic. In the occasional village the gunners passed through, residents came out of their houses and offered milk and bread while the women stood silently and dried their tears with cloths. The sight of the troops – their uniforms muddied, their boots sodden – cannot have been inspiring, but Petrov ensured the men at least maintained discipline. 'We went on like this for two days, tortured by thirst, the heat was unbearable, everyone was tired,' he later wrote. 'But no-one gave in to weakness, even though each man had to carry a coat, gas mask, canteen, flask, carbine and ammunition pouches.'

No-one told Petrov's battery that the division it sought to help was already falling back towards Lutsk.[7]

'ENEMY TANKS KNOCKED OUT EVERYWHERE...' RADEKHOV, 23 JUNE, AFTERNOON

Gustav Schrodek had caught a few minutes' sleep after his brief encounter with 'unknown' enemy tanks only to be woken by the crash of shells on 15th Panzer Regiment's positions in the fields west of Radekhov. A tiny Fieseler Storch reconnaissance aircraft passed low over the panzer of Gustav-Adolf Riebel, dropping a message for the regimental commander. Riebel immediately signalled his men: *Prepare for battle!* 'Soon everyone – down to the last man – knew that beyond the hill outside Radekhov there was a large concentration of enemy tanks, advancing towards the regiment; they could appear at any moment,' Schrodek wrote.

Fifteen minutes passed before the first Soviet armour appeared: 10, 20, 30 tanks rolling over the crest of a hill, shooting the moment they did. The shells fell short. The oncoming armour momentarily disappeared from view in a shallow hollow, before clattering over the undulating terrain. At a range of 400 yards it made a perfect target for the panzer gunners. 'Shell after shell flew towards the Russians,' Schrodek remembered. 'Most of the first shells hit, some even scored direct hits. Others still tore entire chunks of armour plating from the enemy tanks. Already we could see enemy tanks knocked out everywhere and their crews clambering out – if they could still do so.'

Schrodek's regiment had run into the 10th Tank Division – or rather elements of it. The Soviet armour entered the action without any reconnaissance, without artillery and without one of their tank regiments. 11th Panzer Division would report that the enemy fought 'very skilfully and stubbornly'. Stubbornly, certainly, for the 60 or so tanks committed attacked in several waves, never varying their tactics. One T-34 took at least 30, possibly even 50, hits from German cannon or anti-tank guns but was still not knocked out. The battle of Radekhov lasted perhaps a couple of hours. When it was over, more than half the Russian tanks lay burning or knocked out in the fields beyond the village. German losses were not inconsiderable: seven panzers, 13 crew killed, another 50 wounded.[8]

'BLOOD FLOWED IN RIVERS...' UKRAINE, 23 JUNE

As in Lithuania, Latvia and Byelorussia, the German onslaught prompted the immediate evacuation of Ukraine's prisons. Most NKVD commanders determined there was neither the time nor the means. They chose execution over evacuation or, in some cases, simply fled their posts.

In Lutsk, 2,000 inmates rioted in the aftermath of an air raid on the prison on the first day of war. They armed themselves with axes, razors and knives but never got beyond the courtyard as guards threatened to shoot them. Order was finally restored on Monday morning when prisoners were returned to their cells – but only briefly. At mid-day, on the warden's orders, all the inmates were led to the exercise yard. Forty-four prisoners were released. The remainder were separated:

Ukrainian prisoners were ordered to gather with their possessions in one yard, Poles in another. They thought they were being shipped out, but the guards had other ideas. Using tank machine-guns and hand-grenades, they began murdering the Ukrainians first, before shifting to the neighbouring yard to finish off the Poles. 'Blood flowed in rivers and body parts flew through the air,' one survivor recalled.

> The spots where most people had been killed and where the lower part of the walls was spattered with blood and bits of brain were dowsed in thick liquid lime. It all dried – blood and lime – because it was a hot day. A foul smell of blood and lime – hard to describe – spread. The inner courtyard was a pure charnel house. They'd not only shot people with machine-guns but tossed hand-grenades as well. On the ground which was covered with lime, we saw shallow shell craters. Amid the blood and lime there were still small body parts, mostly shredded fingers and skull fragments.

Upwards of 370 prisoners survived the massacre. 'Those still alive, get up! We won't shoot anymore!' the guards urged, but this was no act of mercy; the living were now forced to bury the dead. 'We dig graves and clear the yard of corpses, suitcases, personal belongings, clothing and body parts which had ripped off,' Polish prisoner Mieczyslaw Ogrodowczyk wrote. 'All this is tossed on to a pile, soaked in petrol and set alight. The smell of burning human flesh is dreadful.' When all the bodies had been recovered, the guards forced the prisoners back into the cells. Ogrodowczyk again: 'Half drunk, they brandished their pistols and yelled: "*Bystrej, bystrej*" [Faster, faster]. After the work was complete, we too would be killed. Now the end had come: emptiness, hopelessness, fear of death. It was as if I was paralysed. In just a few minutes, I would no longer be alive. This was the end of our lives.'⁹

Ninety miles away in Lvov, the sentences on all 108 prisoners on death row were carried out before 22 June was over. As for the 4,591 remaining inmates in the city's jails, transport east was arranged for just 500. The rest would suffer a terrible fate. At the NKVD's main interrogation centre in Lontskoho Street on the southern edge of the city centre, prisoners were hauled out of their cells on the upper floors and led to the ground floor where they were ordered to lie on the ground. '"Get down, you whores!" they shouted at us,' remembered Omeljan Matla, arrested the previous summer as a Ukrainian nationalist. 'Immediately after shooting began. Twelve men were killed, two badly wounded, three, including me, were not hit. I escaped the bloodbath because someone who was fatally shot fell on top of me.' He smeared himself with the blood of those shot to avoid detention, then fled from the prison during the night, by which time perhaps 280 inmates, including upwards of 30 women, had been shot.

At Brygidki prison on the main road to Lvov's central station, inmates realised the guards had fled in the small hours of 24 June and decided to make a bid for freedom. 'I wanted to go out into the courtyard but first cautiously peered out, as if warned by a premonition,' Pole Zygmunt Cybulski later testified. 'At that very moment a soldier shot at me from the courtyard. The bullet whistled past my nose and struck the wall.' As gunshots echoed through Brygidki, Cybulski cowered in a cell on the second floor and awaited his fate. An officer with a pistol entered accompanied by three soldiers with rifles. They screamed: '"Lie down!" We lay down and they went away.'

The returning jailers at Brygidki were the vanguard of 233rd NKVD Regiment, dispatched to Lvov to put an end to the disorder. It did so, driving some 'counter-revolutionary elements' who had dared to leave their cells back inside – 13 were killed at Brygidki – before reporting: 'Order has finally been restored.'[10]

'THE ENEMY ... WON'T KNOW WHAT'S HIT HIM...' SOUTHWESTERN FRONT, 23 JUNE

In an unassuming cottage in a village northwest of Tarnopol which served as the hastily created headquarters of the new Southwestern Front – the only defensive precaution was a ditch hurriedly dug all around the building – Mikhail Kirponos presided over an acrimonious council of war as dusk fell on the second day of war.

Kirponos and his senior commissar, Nikolai Vashugin, favoured holding the frontier. For more than 36 hours, troops had been trying to defend the border without any support from the mechanised corps. 'There'll be nothing left of them in a few days,' he fumed.

The front's chief-of-staff, Maxim Purkayev, was still determined to deliver the enemy a decisive blow with massed armoured formations rather than squander the mechanised corps. 'That's exactly what the enemy is dreaming of,' he snapped at Vashugin. 'Smashing our corps one by one...'

Kirponos sided with Vashugin. 'We really cannot wait for divisions to die before our eyes,' he told his chief-of-staff. 'Can't you grasp this?'

But Maxim Purkayev stuck to his guns. 'We mustn't sacrifice the big units to save the little ones,' he told his colleagues. 'In two days' time we'll have formed strong formations and then we'll attack the enemy from various directions. He won't know what's hit him. Five mechanised corps, that's a force!'[11]

'It does not correspond to our concept of the war...' Western Ukraine, 24 June

Other Red Army tank units were being wasted in piecemeal actions. XXII Mechanised Corps was meant to blunt the panzers' advance and press on to the border around Vladimir-Volynskiy. Instead, 14th Panzer Division steamrollered 135th Rifle Division, then, when the armour of 19th Tank Division entered the fray in the early afternoon, it did so piecemeal. In two and a half hours of unequal battle, more than half the T-26s were knocked out. It was the beginning of a terrible 36 hours for 19th Tank's commander, Kuzma Semenchenko, at the hands of 14th Panzer. By dawn on the 26th, the Soviet armoured division ceased to exist. The Germans claimed 156 tanks destroyed. The now-wounded Semenchenko commanded just four tanks, his corps commander was dead, and the man who had led the initial ill-fated counter-attack on Tuesday afternoon was a German prisoner.

The light infantry of 97th *Jäger* Division were attacked by heavy Soviet tanks around the village of Magierów, 30 miles northwest of Lvov. Having crushed the Germans' baggage column, the 'rolling monsters' simply drove over most of the 97th's anti-tank detachment, crushing guns and crews in the process and encircling the *Jäger*. Flak and artillery were brought up to smash a relief route into the village. Magierów was reduced to ashes. And the armour which had been invulnerable to the German anti-tank guns now fell victim to the shells raining down on the village. Soon the roads leading out of Magierów were clogged by 'shot-up tanks with broken caterpillar tracks and wrecked gearboxes,' wrote a war correspondent accompanying the *Jäger*. 'Fire emerges from the turrets... We jump on the monsters and very soon know where they can be fatally hit.'

Ivan Czernov and several hundred newly qualified officers were thrown into battle outside Lutsk. Straight out of training, the men were made platoon leaders – and infantry regulations dictated that Soviet officers lead their men into battle. 'And so the Germans calmly slaughtered our freshly trained second lieutenants in their berets as if on the shooting range,' he bitterly remembered. Czernov reckoned half his class was wiped out in the first encounter with the enemy. He survived only because he ignored regulations. 'I threw my officer's cap away and "commandeered" the field cap with the steel helmet from a soldier in my platoon who was killed.'[12]

Kievans struggled to understand why the Red Army was retreating, not attacking. 'It does not correspond to our concept of the war, namely fighting the enemy on his territory, not on ours,' librarian Irina Khorochounova recorded. Her neighbours had already begun to stockpile food. They dug slit trenches in open spaces – even in Mariinski Park, where the roses seemed more colourful than ever. They covered their windows with masking tape. They withdrew their savings from banks, had briefcases and bags at the ready containing money and key papers. Vehicles camouflaged with mud and branches rolled through the streets by day and night. The academics in charge of Khorochounova's library scrapped plans for an exhibition devoted to 19th-century romantic poet Mikhail Lermontov; instead, they would stage a hurriedly arranged celebration of Napoleon's defeat in Russia in 1812 – something Kievans could rally around. There was now a section in the daily newspapers for anti-Nazi propaganda, while hastily drawn posters depicting a wounded German dictator in the form of a swastika appeared on every street. 'We'll smash the mouth of Hitler the bandit!' they promised. Ordinary citizens tried to continue their pre-war lives as best they could, but the constant strain of taking to the makeshift shelters or cellars quickly took its toll; the people of Kiev were soon 'dying of fatigue'. Toviy Kriger, a Jewish engineer from Siberia, was amazed to see 'people running from their homes to watch the bombing raids' and the anti-aircraft guns pounding away, rather than take cover. He felt compelled to join them. 'What a beautiful and joyful sight it is and how pleasantly blood pulses through your whole body when you see a burning aircraft marked with the cursed swastika falling to the ground,' he wrote. 'It makes you want to fly with the shell if only to ensure that it does not miss.' Children thought it was all a game, dashing into the streets as soon as the all-clear sounded to pick up the anti-aircraft shell shrapnel peppering the city. The raids were, in fact, somewhat sporadic and not especially effective, save one attack which wrecked an armaments works and an aircraft factory. Upwards of 200 people were killed; rumours circulated that they'd been ordered to remain at their posts throughout the bombing.[13]

'SO DREADFUL THAT IT DEFIES DESCRIPTION...'
WESTERN UKRAINE, 25 JUNE

In Dubno, a rumour spread through the small town that German motorcycle troops had reached the outskirts. For a brief moment, it put an end to the slaughter in the prison, where the NKVD were systematically murdering the remaining inmates. Located on the Lutsk–Tarnopol highway, Dubno counted no more than 10,000 inhabitants yet its three-storey jail had held 3,000 prisoners. Most had been transferred to Gulags in Siberia on the eve of the German invasion, but an estimated 600 were left behind. With the Germans at Dubno's gates, evacuation was impossible. The guards ordered inmates, including children, to face the walls of their cells, then began to butcher them using rifles, bayonet stabs and hand-grenades. When the scare of approaching Germans passed, the murders resumed on Wednesday in a morning of frenzied killing. Just four prisoners survived, though only three were able to recount what happened; the fourth lost her mind – and her right arm. She lay apathetically in her sickbed. Aged just 23, she looked 'like a mad 50-year-old woman'.

Dubno's new masters soon discovered these horrors. 'The sight in the cells,' investigators from XLVIII Corps reported, 'was so dreadful that it defies description.' Some tried. 'Every cell was occupied with six or more people – men of all ages, old women and young girls,' one junior officer found. 'Almost all the inmates were shot. The corpses were literally piled on top of each other, hideously contorted. From the position in which the corpses were found, you could tell that many of the women had been raped in their final moments.' Curiosity drew a flak gunner from East Prussia to the prison, but he was only able to stand visiting a couple of cells before 'shrinking back. Now you understand the misery of the people waiting outside who want to get to their daughter who's been raped, to their father who's been shot, to the son who's been assassinated,' he wrote. Nothing surpassed the 'ghoulishness' female prisoners suffered, 'young girls, 18 years old at best, their abdomens torn apart, breasts cut off and skulls smashed in!' And amid the horror of Dubno's prison, amid desperate families seeking their relatives, townsfolk in their hundreds took anything they could from the building, such as furniture.[14]

'Now Lemberg belongs to us...' On the road to Lvov, 25–26 June

After three days of marching and fighting, the mountain infantry of 1st *Gebirgs* Division were halfway towards their goal of Lvov, a city they had fought for not two years previously, only to be forced to hand it over to the Soviets under the Molotov–Ribbentrop Pact. They did not relish seizing it a second time. Their commander, Hubert Lanz, had repeatedly pleaded – in vain – for 'a different, better mission'; attacking Lvov in the summer of 1941 would undoubtedly pit the mountain troops against Soviet armour – something for which they were ill-equipped. Outside the village of Jażów Stary, 30 miles from his objective, Lanz's fears were realised as Soviet tanks – the vanguard of IV Mechanised Corps – emerged from woodland on the early evening of 25 June. Lanz himself directed the defence from the front lines. 'Our anti-tank gunners are ready to fire,' he wrote.

> When the steel crates, which rumble towards us with a lot of noise and smoke, are about 600 metres in front of us, the anti-tank guns suddenly open fire. Bursts of tracer race towards them – and bounce off. We do not believe our eyes. Everywhere hits and each time a ricochet. Of course our artillery is ready to fire and now opens fire. Given the unexpected ineffectiveness of our 3.7cm anti-tank shells, around 30 tanks advance unstoppably and break into our positions, unless they get stuck in the large marshy hole on the road.

The Germans let the enemy tanks roll over and past their foxholes, then struck from behind, clambering onto the armour and hurling hand-grenades through the turret hatches. The tanks had no infantry support, and their uncoordinated attacks fizzled out as they became bogged down in the marshy terrain or were held up long enough by Lanz's men for the Germans to bring up their artillery. By nightfall, the fields around Jażów Stary had become the graveyard of 32nd Tank Division: German sources suggest as many as 80 tanks and heavy guns were destroyed or abandoned, Soviet accounts a mere 15. There was no dispute over the outcome; the mountain infantry had stood their ground. 'We've done it,' an ecstatic Lanz exclaimed. 'My men have banished their tank terror. From now on they'll not have any more fear.' His men entered the burning ruins of Jażów Stary. Hubert Lanz pleaded with his superior, Ludwig Kübler, to allow them to press on. The corps commander relented, prompting Lanz to remark: 'Now Lemberg belongs to us.'[15]

'IT WAS HARD TO TELL WHO WAS SHOOTING AT WHOM...' DUBNO, 25–26 JUNE

As he readied his corps for the coming battle in the woods outside Brody, Dmitry Ryabyshev lamented the toll four days of rumbling around the lanes of western Ukraine had taken. Not a single multi-turreted T-35 had survived the chaotic 300-mile march – almost every one a victim of mechanical failure. Many of his KVs were struggling – their brake belts had overheated and failed. A good proportion of his battalion of flame-throwing T-26s had been left by the wayside. The men, too, were exhausted. This was their fourth night without sleep. 'No-one complained,' Ryabyshev remembered. 'Knowing that they would go into battle in a few hours gave the men and commanders double the strength. All night long, they worked hard: they made sure their weapons and equipment were in order, filled the fuel tanks, topped up their ammunition. Everyone was eager to make the enemy feel the strength and might of our arms.' The front's political department urged the tank crews to take heart from small groups of Soviet troops who'd held off entire enemy regiments, from a Red Air Force squadron which had supposedly downed 22 German aircraft in the first two days of combat, or from a formation of nine bombers which had allegedly fended off 15 enemy fighters, bringing six of them crashing down, and one pilot had rammed a Nazi bomber, 'killing its crew of four and dying a brave death himself'. The implication was obvious: men going into battle at Dubno were expected to sacrifice their lives if they could not halt the German onslaught. 'Comrades!' the appeal closed. 'Our cause is just. Let us avenge the Fascist bastards for the blood of our comrades, our wives and children… Death to the enemy, death to bloodthirsty Hitler! Forward! For the Motherland! Victory will be ours!'

Mid-morning on 26 June Dmitry Ryabyshev's tanks began moving on Berestechko, 30 miles west of Dubno, to drive into the southern flank of *Panzergruppe* 1. His corps, plus XV Mechanised, would form the southern arm, IX, XIX and XXII Mechanised Corps the northern. Should the two pincers meet, they would cut off the bulk of two panzer divisions, 11th and 13th.

'The earth shuddered and groaned,' Ryabyshev recalled. 'The silence was ruthlessly shattered by exploding shells. Everything was in motion.' The attack soon began to miscarry. German guns brought 12th Tank Division to a standstill. Then the Luftwaffe joined battle – a factor Dmitry Ryabyshev had either discounted or simply somehow forgotten when he drew up his plans for the attack. Now, in groups of 50 or 60 at a time, German bombers attacked the Soviet armour. No Russian fighters challenged them.

Still the Soviet spearhead bludgeoned its way northwards. Soviet accounts describe heroic individual soldiers smashing their way through the German lines 'with bayonet and rifle butt', their deeds spurring their comrades on, or else encouraging near-suicidal charges with cries of 'For the Motherland! For Stalin!' VIII Mechanised Corps drove through the village of Leshnev, then over the Sytenka – one of half a dozen watercourses which ran through the battlefield. German guns targeted Ryabyshev's rear services – fuel tankers, ammunition trucks, repair vehicles, even the corps' command post were wrecked or damaged.[16]

Mid-day had long passed before the northern pincer of the great attack stuttered into action. Konstantin Rokossovsky's orders were unequivocal: deliver a powerful counter-blow into the flank of the enemy group which has broken through, to destroy it and to restore the situation. And his IX Mechanised Corps may have delivered a powerful counter-blow had its actions been co-ordinated. But they were not. The three corps entered the battle piecemeal – as soon as they reached their jump-off positions after hours, if not days, on the march. In fact, Rokossovsky had no idea where Nikolai Feklenko's XIX Corps, on his left, or XXII, on his right, were. His corps possessed no heavy and not that much light armour after four tortuous days vainly moving around the Galician countryside. He was given no time to regroup his divisions, rest them, or reconnoitre the terrain. He simply threw them into the battle. 'Time was pressing, the hardships exceptional, surprises arose everywhere,' Rokossovsky lamented.

As Rokossovsky's corps moved off, so Feklenko's tanks lumbered into action, spearheaded by Colonel Ivan Tsibin's 43rd Tank Division, arguably delivering the most successful attack on this first day of the counter-offensive. Lacking any information about its foe, short of spare parts and lubricants after its aimless three-day drive around western Ukraine, Tsibin's armour entered the fray five hours late and spasmodically – only one-third of the division actually joined battle. The Soviet tanks smashed into the tail of 11th Panzer Division. With two T-34s and two KVs in the lead, the attack at first appeared invulnerable as German shells bounced off the Soviet heavy armour. So hastily had the Russians entered battle that their tanks did not have armour-piercing shells; the only way to knock out German vehicles was to ram and crush them. 'It wasn't a retreat, rather a proper flight,' V. S. Arkhipov, commanding the division's reconnaissance battalion, recalled. The Germans were 'seized by panic. I only saw German troops in such a psychological state of depression and panic after Stalingrad and the Battle of Kursk.' Towards dusk eight medium panzers even joined the Soviet column, convinced it was their own; they surrendered when they realised it wasn't. Arkhipov claimed taking scores of prisoners, who proved to be garrulous although not one among them admitted to being a Nazi, and a rich booty of German vehicles. His commander, Ivan Tsibin, would go even further, reporting that his men rode on the coat-tails of the retreating Germans as far as the outskirts of Dubno, where the advance stopped only because the enemy blew up several road bridges. In fact, his division got no closer than ten miles from Dubno, the attack blunted, as so often, by a failure to reconnoitre, co-ordinate and provide infantry support. The two KV 'heavies' leading the assault were left burning on the field of battle, as were 15 T-26s. In just a few hours' battle, Tsibin's division had lost one-fifth of its strength.

Still, the Germans breathed a sigh of relief. The attack unnerved 11th Panzer – the Russians never realised the chaos they had caused in its ranks, especially when the main advance route to the east was temporarily severed, let alone exploited it.[17]

The southern pincer of Southwestern Front's great counter-attack was faring no better. The men of XV Mechanised Corps yearned for the chance to get at the enemy, but their actions this Thursday were, at best, impetuous, at worst, reckless. At 10am, on the personal initiative of its commander, 19th Tank Regiment struck on the very left wing of the attack at Radekhov – the same village where its parent 10th Tank Division had clashed with the Germans on the second day of the war. Except now Radekhov was fortified. The advancing Soviet tanks ran into a wall of co-ordinated fire from the heavy and light guns of 297th Infantry Division. 'Enemy shells cannot penetrate our armour, but they can break the caterpillars and wreck the turrets,' battalion commander Zakhar Slyusarenko wrote.

> The KV on my left goes up in flames. A plume of smoke rises up into the sky above it, with a thin jet of fire at its core. 'Kovalchuk is on fire!' – my heart misses a beat. There's no way I can help his crew: 12 vehicles are advancing with me. Another KV stops: the shell knocked its turret off. The KV tanks are very powerful machines, but they are clearly not fast or manoeuvrable enough.

Company commander Bruno Gebele saw the same jet of flame shooting out of the first Soviet tank to be hit, then watched two more enemy vehicles explode in quick succession. Panic seized the remaining tank crews, who drove wildly around the terrain as they sought to escape from the German guns' field of fire. They finally found cover behind a road embankment and in a hollow, while one of the three tanks hit in the initial encounter was torn apart by a terrible internal explosion. 'With binoculars pressed to their faces, standing up, of course, the gun commanders or platoon leaders directed the fire,' Gebele wrote. 'Wherever a tank, a turret or a barrel appeared, the position was immediately plastered with shells.'

Zakhar Slyusarenko watched as his deputy's tank was knocked out – the commander clambered out of the burning machine, jumped onto another and directed the battle sitting on the armour. Over the radio came encouragement from the regimental commander who had ordered the precipitous attack: 'Good, good, keep it up! You've already knocked out eight panzers. Fires, real fires. Forward!' The Russians sent around 30 tanks forward again. But the attack was not pressed home. 'Either they heard the sound of battle in their rear or saw several clouds of smoke and feared their retreat route had been cut off,' Gebele noted as he watched most of the formation turn around. In doing so they presented themselves to the German gunners. When the shooting ended, the Germans had just nine rounds left for their heavier 5cm anti-tank gun. The Soviet attack had gained just a couple of kilometres of ground in six hours of fighting.

19th Tank Regiment left nine KVs and five BT-7s behind on the battlefield, yet Zakhar Slyusarenko was not disheartened. His men, he believed, had shown themselves to be tougher than their foe. 'But we, the commanders, made a number of grave mistakes and we paid for them with our equipment and the blood of our men,' he conceded. The tanks had entered battle knowing nothing of the terrain or the enemy and with no communications. And, not least, it was clear the crews' training was inadequate.

As night fell on the fields around Radekhov, the fires of seven blazing Russian tanks cast the battlefield in a ghostly light. 'Despite receiving no food, despite a strict smoking ban, despite the fact that it was highly likely we were surrounded by strong enemy formations, the mood was joyful and confident,' Slyusarenko wrote.[18]

Twenty miles to the east, commissar Nikolai Popel watched the light tanks of 7th Motorised Rifle Division cross the Styr on a makeshift bridge north of Leshnev. The armour spread out on the left bank in full view of 16th Panzer Division, prompting a furious duel with an ever-dwindling number of Soviet guns. 'Only two could still shoot,' Popel wrote. 'A third had just been overrun by a panzer, which only survived its victim by a few seconds. Emitting a narrow cloud of smoke, the monster lay immobile in front of a 76mm gun which looked like a toy and which two soldiers fearlessly crewed.' Observing the battle through a pair of scissor binoculars, VIII Mechanised Corps' senior commissar counted nine knocked-out enemy tanks – and another 15 Panzer Mk3s emerging from woods as Stukas circled ominously overhead, before diving on the Soviet guns. 'Everything was hidden by smoke and dust,' Popel recalled. Clumps of earth were thrown up in the air and rained down on the commissar, sheltering in a ditch. One of the two remaining guns was blown into the Styr. But perhaps four panzers were immobile – knocked out either by mis-aimed bombs from the Stukas, or the last firing 76mm gun. As the smoke and dust cleared, Popel observed Red Army men pushing charges down the panzers' stubby barrels.

The encounter had sorely shaken 16th Panzer's anti-tank gunners, encountering KV and T-34 tanks for the first time. Some Russian vehicles received 21 or 23 hits, but the only damage they suffered was that their turrets were unable to turn. 'The men cried with rage,' 16th Panzer's chronicler noted. 'The anti-tank gunners were only able to take out the light tanks.' And how. A single company finished off 16 Soviet vehicles that Thursday.

And so the German advance on the Styr continued. The Russians fell back, the weak beams of the temporary bridge sagging as they ran across it, before they took up position in a shallow ditch on the right bank. Popel wrote:

The air in the bridgehead was filled with the smell of burning, plus another, indefinable sweetish smell which made you feel sick. On top of the usual noises of battle there was the obtrusive rattle of submachine-guns and the howl which accompanied the explosions of the rocket projectiles – this was the first time we encountered this enemy weapon. Beforehand, we'd known little about it.

Submachine-guns and mortars continuously peppered each metre with shells and shrapnel. The shells were impacting very close to each other. The howling of shrapnel and shells paralysed the men. You could hardly raise your head. Every man pressed against the earth as if he wanted to burrow into it. It was impossible to aim your fire, no mission could be accomplished here. You were at the mercy of the curtain of fire, were small and helpless, cut off from the rest of the world. I believe you would have needed superhuman strength to rise and attack.

The dead, Popel noticed, 'were lying everywhere'. The wounded were abandoned on the field of battle. Just a few were carried across the engineers' bridge to the right bank. 'And the Germans shot and shot, they spared neither bombs nor shells.'[19]

Dmitry Ryabyshev was roaming the battlefield in his T-34 determined to see what progress 34th Tank Division was making. The tracks carved in the black Ukrainian earth by the division's heavy armour pointed the way to the front – as did the horrific sights of battle. 'Everywhere there were corpses of crushed Fascist machine-gunners, twisted and flattened motorcycles with sidecars,' the corps commander recalled. Engineers toiled on broken-down tanks by the roadside, but there was no sign of the 34th's commander or any of his staff. Night was beginning to fall when Ryabyshev's tank approached the village of Khotin. The fighting had reduced the wooden cottages to little more than 'charred stoves and still-smouldering embers'. It was here that Ryabyshev's staff ran into 34th Tank Division's commander, an excited Colonel Ivan Vasiliev. 'Comrade General!' he reported breathlessly. 'The division under my command successfully broke through the enemy's defences, completely destroying three motorcycle battalions, ten panzers and 12 guns. We've captured 200 Fascist soldiers and officers.'[20]

Sixty miles south of the battlefield, at Southwestern Front's headquarters, Mikhail Kirponos was far from impressed with the actions of his armour, chastising Rokossovsky and his neighbour, XV Mechanised Corps' Ignaty Karpezo. Both,

Kirponos claimed, had attacked 'half-heartedly'. True, the attacks had been disjointed, but that was as much the fault of the senior commands which provided little, if any, information about Red Army forces, let alone enemy dispositions. And whatever influence Karpezo had on the day's fighting, it ended abruptly around 6pm. His command post was bombed by He111s of *Kampfgeschwader* 55. When the Heinkels had passed, Karpezo was found near his headquarters tent, covered in blood. A junior doctor pronounced him dead and Karpezo was buried with full military honours: eulogies, a rifle salute, even a bouquet of wild flowers on the freshly dug grave. A short while later, the corps' commissar Ivan Lutai returned from a visit to headquarters. He refused to believe Karpezo was dead, reached for his pistol and began to threaten the surviving staff. 'Karpezo dead? It can't be. Hero of the Civil War, a man without fear. Dead? No!' He ordered the terrified staff to dig. They did – and found Ignaty Karpezo was still breathing, if unfit to command.[21]

The Luftwaffe was the scourge of Soviet tank commanders this Thursday. 12th Tank Division suffered particularly badly, reduced to a mere 40 vehicles by the day's end. Its commander deemed it no longer combat-worthy and hauled it out of the line on his own initiative. Nikolai Popel was caught on the open road outside the village of Baranne, northeast of Brody. His tank was rocked three times by the blast wave from bombs before stuttering to a halt: both tracks had fallen off. One of the crew put a smoking object on the track guard. From afar it looked like the tank was burning – 'another vehicle among the many knocked-out tanks and motor vehicles which could be clearly seen in the glow of the flares,' the commissar wrote. Dmitry Ryabyshev and his staff parked their armour for the night on the main Brody–Dubno road. There was no peace this evening. Haystacks in the fields and roadside cottages burned. Light machine-guns chattered. Bullets whistled in every direction. 'It was hard to tell who was shooting at whom,' the general wrote. 'Overhead Fascist aircraft buzzed incessantly. Wave after wave headed east to bomb our peaceful towns and villages.' His attack had unnerved the Germans, but not beaten them. Only they knew how close their foe had come to success on 26 June: had Ryabyshev concentrated his attacks and supported his tanks with infantry, he could have cut off the bulk of XIV Panzer Corps.[22]

'THE WAR HAS SHOWN US ITS TERRIBLE FACE...'
DUBNO, 27 JUNE

Friday 27 June dawned warm and cloudless in western Ukraine. In Tarnopol, Mikhail Kirponos had barely digested the news that the attacks by VIII and XV Mechanised Corps had failed to make the expected inroads when his head of intelligence reported that panzers had broken through at Dubno, brushed aside a rifle corps and were racing towards Ostrog, 40 miles to the east.

'We've got to stop them at all costs,' Kirponos warned his staff, 'otherwise the enemy will not merely cut off our right wing, but advance as far as Kiev.' He looked at the map laid out before him, then turned to his chief-of-staff. 'Give our mechanised corps new missions. Turn VIII Corps to the northeast, head directly for Dubno. When Ryabyshev links up with Rokossovsky and Feklenko, the formations which have broken through will be caught in a trap.'[23]

However much Kirponos wanted to attack, his mechanised corps were in no position to launch a fresh assault until long past mid-day. Konstantin Rokossovsky spent most of the day on the defensive, fending off 299th Infantry and 13th Panzer Divisions. The latter conceded that the day's fighting had been 'very hard', but the Magdeburgers nevertheless brushed past IX Mechanised Corps. 'It's only down to the fact that all commanders did not lose their nerve that we succeeded in fighting our way through – and thus were spared even greater losses,' the division's chronicler noted. 13th Panzer was now the spearhead of German armour cutting through Ukraine, 25 miles east of Dubno. Despite the tumult in its rear, come first light on Saturday it would resume its lunge 'with unshakeable faith in victory'.[24]

At least on the Southern Front Soviet armour made significant inroads into the right flank of *Panzergruppe* 1 as VIII Mechanised Corps surprised infantry and panzer crews, caught sunbathing in just their swimming trunks in the village of Granovka. They were wiped out before they had time to man their guns or armour. Next, the Soviet tanks smashed into 16th Panzer Division's rear services 'leisurely driving down the road'. They never suspected enemy forces were roaming around far behind the supposed front line – the division's vanguard was more than 30 miles to the east. Men in the trucks rolling down the highway at regular intervals 'slept, read newspapers or quietly played the mouth organ', VIII Mechanised Corps' commissar Nikolai Popel wrote. 'They felt they were far behind the front.' Soviet motorcyclists caused the initial confusion, pouring machine-gun fire into the columns. 'Anything that was left was thrown into chaos, burned or crushed by the tracks of our tanks,' Popel recalled. 'The dead in their jackets, their sleeves rolled up, lay covered in flour, sugar, macaroni, in the middle of newspapers and colour magazines, between crushed cardboard boxes and parcels, in bluish puddles of petrol which seeped across the tarmac.'[25]

For Soviet tank men and many rookie panzer crews, the fighting around Dubno – the battle was subsequently given several names, but Dubno seems the most fitting as it was in the centre of the battlefield – was a terrible baptism of fire. Willi Kubik, a tank gunner with 13th Panzer Division, passed a column of death and destruction which seemed to stretch for miles. His comrades told him there were 200 wrecked enemy tanks in all, destroyed at a cost of only five German dead and 11 damaged panzers. The Soviets had evidently been caught on the road either by the Luftwaffe or panzers and scattered immediately; they got no more than 300ft from the highway before they were knocked out. Curiosity got the better of the young gunner and he inspected a couple of shot-up Russian tanks. 'In one the dead driver looks out of the hatch – one hand is outside. The fatal bullet struck him as he was clambering out,' Kubik wrote. 'The remains of burned Russians stare at us in another tank. This scene of gruesome destruction is imprinted on my memory. During the first few days, the war has shown us its terrible face.' The sight of German positions overrun by Soviet tanks was no less awful. A non-commissioned officer in 125th Infantry Division marched past at least 60 shot-up Soviet tanks – including 'four of the super heavies' – on a four-mile stretch of road. 'You can't imagine what behemoths they are,' he wrote home. 'Utterly incredible brutes.' His division's anti-tank guns and flak had finally ended their rampage – but not before the Soviet tanks had smashed through houses and driven over some German gun positions, 'crushing them to pulp'. Nikolai Popel remembered that 'the dead lay everywhere – on the road, the seats and bumpers of the burning vehicles, or in the sidecars of upturned motorcycles. There were even limbs in the shreds of *feldgrau* uniform hanging from trees. In the midst of this chaos there was groaning, some barely-distinguishable words in a foreign language.'[26]

The villages and countryside around Dubno were littered with wrecked tanks, some with the charred remains of their crews still inside, ammunition crates, burned-down cottages, shot-up guns and cadavers of horses. Personal papers were strewn across the battlefield, as were hurriedly dug graves: '16 Russian soldiers rest here'. 'No names – not like our graves which are carefully recorded,' junior officer Walter Melchinger wrote home. 'Wives and children will hear that their husbands and fathers are missing in this terrible war. They won't know whether they're coming back.' The 32-year-old realised his wife might find her husband's observations harsh, even brutal. 'I do not feel it is hard,' he told her. 'The further east we advance, the more we are filled with tremendous pride about being German, about our great culture, our clean, decent lives.'[27]

Like hundreds of Kirponos' tank men, Alexander Golikov's first battle proved to be his last. In a disabled tank south of Rovno, the 24-year-old penned a final letter to his wife Tonya – a letter later found on his body by the Germans.

Dear Tonetshka!

I do not know whether you will ever read these lines. But I know for certain that this is my last letter to you. A bitter, fatal fight is raging right now. Our tank is shot up. There are Fascists all around. All day long we've been trying to fend off their attacks. The road to Ostrog is littered with corpses in green uniforms – they look like large lizards which don't move. Today is the sixth day of the war. Pavel Abramov and I have stayed together. You know him, I've written to you about him. We are not thinking about saving our own skins at all – we're soldiers and not afraid to die for the motherland. We're simply thinking about how we can make the Nazis pay dearly for our lives. I'm sitting in a tank which is peppered with holes and twisted. The heat is unbearable. I am thirsty. There's not a drop of water. Your picture lies on my lap. I'm staring at your blue eyes and feel better – you are with me. I would like to talk with you for a long time, sincerely, like before in Ivanovo. I have thought about you since the first day of war. When will I return to you and press your head against my chest? Perhaps never. That's war.

When our tank ran into the enemy for the first time, I fired the machine-gun at them to wipe out as many Nazis as possible, to make the war end more quickly, so that I could see you sooner. But my dreams were not fulfilled. Our tank has been shaken by enemy shells, but we're still alive. We do not have any shells left, just the cartridges. Pavel shoots at the enemy with precisely aimed fire and I 'recover' and talk with you. I know that this is the last time. I would like to speak with you for a long time, but there's no time for that. Can you remember how we said goodbye at the station? You doubted my words when I said back then that I would love you forever. You suggested getting married at the registry office so I would belong to you alone all life long. I joyfully fulfilled your request – now we have documentary proof that we are man and wife. That's good. It is good to die if you know that there is a person somewhere far away who is thinking of you. 'It is good to be loved.' Through the holes in the tank I can see the road, green trees, colourful flowers in the garden. Life after the war will be just as colourful and joyful as these flowers. I'm not afraid to die for this. Do not cry. You probably won't be able to visit my grave. In fact, will there be any grave?[28]

By now, stragglers and the lightly wounded were filing through Kiev, where transit camps had been established to care for soldiers for a couple of days before returning them to their units. 'We are supposed to read to them, set up exhibitions and organise board games, but we don't do anything like that,' wrote librarian Irina Khorochounova, volunteering at a centre set up in the grounds of a school.

'They only want to sleep and eat. They are covered in mud, hungry and exhausted. The supply chain has not got going yet and the soldiers are malnourished. To rest and sleep, they have only benches and tables, some lie on the ground.' There was no space to move between the sleeping soldiers, still less to play board games and nothing the volunteers could do for the more serious burns cases delivered to the centre. 'Our presence is useless,' 28-year-old Khorochounova concluded. 'We cannot provide any assistance. Everywhere there's always indescribable chaos – and the war has only been raging for a week.'

Some of the Soviet wounded were transported to hospital at Proskurov, where recently mobilised medics like Alexander Vishnevski struggled to cope with the influx. It took at least three days to deliver casualties to the temporary hospital – wounds were already festering and the stench was foul – and several more to transport them by truck or train to Kiev, should they survive surgery. Rarely was there enough anaesthetic. Vishnevski amputated one tank crewman's leg below the thigh due to horrendous burns; the patient woke halfway through the operation. And all the time, Proskurov came under air attack. The Red Army medics toiled by candlelight and to a soundtrack of screams and the bark of anti-aircraft guns. They operated on casualties almost robotically, treating men with stomach wounds reluctantly, despite being convinced that most would die anyway. 'Eventually we succeeded in saving the odd one or two condemned to death,' Vishnevski recalled.[29]

Tank battalion commander Ivan Bokov was wounded outside Rovno, but dismissed his knee injury. 'I'm not leaving the front line – there's no need to go to hospital with such a trifling injury,' he told his wife and daughter in Zhitomir, 100 miles behind the front.

> I've never been a coward and I'll never be one and you should remember this: it is better to be a widow or a daughter without a father who is a hero than to be the wife or daughter of a coward and traitor.
>
> We were in action on four occasions, surrounded on four occasions and heroically broke off the action on four occasions.
>
> Do not give in to the general panic. The Germans are scoring a temporary success – an insignificant one at that – and will never crush the heroic spirit of our people and defeat them…
>
> You cannot imagine what these Red Army heroes do when they yell: *For the Motherland!*[30]

Desperate tank crews resorted to *taran* – ramming – to stem the enemy's advance. The leader of one tank platoon claimed to have knocked out at least two panzers before a hit from the third jammed his turret in desperate fighting south of Dubno. With his driver and gunlayer dead, Lieutenant N. F. Kravez moved the body of the driver aside, seized the control column and drove his tank at full speed at the advancing German armour.[31]

Across the battlefield there were similar acts of bravery: one young Russian lieutenant stalled an attack by elements of 14th Panzer Division with four men and three machine-guns for four hours. A group of soldiers from 131st Motorised Infantry Division 'defended themselves bravely' when their truck accidentally ran into German motorcyclists. But there were plenty of instances of cowardice too. In the course of just three days, 131st Mechanised Division rounded up nearly 200 'stragglers' from other divisions. Seventy of them were thrown immediately into the front line with the rest of the division; the remainder were returned to their units. One soldier in 685th Rifle Regiment was stabbed with a bayonet for failing to carry out an order from a non-commissioned officer. His comrades approved the punishment: 'That's how all traitors to the Motherland will be treated!'[32]

Somehow, as ordered, VIII Mechanised Corps re-took Dubno before 27 June ended. It was pitch black when Nikolai Popel entered the outskirts shortly before midnight. Clouds obscured the moon and stars. 'No lights flickered in windows,' Popel remembered. 'The street was desolate.' There was the constant chatter of machine-gun fire coming from the northwest; according to the map, it meant there was fighting in the civic cemetery.[33]

Determined to exploit this apparent success, XV Mechanised Corps on Ryabyshev's left hoped to smash through German lines and link up with the northern arm of the great pincer movement. Now led by Georgy Ermolayev in place of the 'resurrected' but gravely wounded Ignaty Karpezo, the corps' threw more than 200 tanks — mostly light BT-7s — and 5,000 men into a lunge at Berestechko. The anti-tank gunners of 57th Infantry Division proved all but immovable. Having forced the Styr, the Russian armour ran head-first into the Germans on the left bank and was decimated. Its supporting infantry fared even worse. The banks of the Styr were strewn with the dead and wounded of 37th Mechanised Infantry Regiment as three in every five riflemen became casualties. Their comrades who survived fell back in disorder, demoralised.[34]

Neither they nor their commander knew that there was no armour bearing down from the north to shake hands with them. Far from advancing, Rokossovsky's and Feklenko's corps were, at best, holding their lines, at worst falling back. Nikolai Popel's charge into the suburbs of Dubno marked the high-water mark of Southwestern Front's attempt to blunt the panzers' thrust through the heart of Ukraine. Instead of cutting off the head of *Panzergruppe* 1, Ryabyshev's counter-attack on Dubno now threatened his own corps' very existence: four German infantry and panzer divisions were closing in on the spearhead, which was separated from the bulk of VIII Mechanised Corps. Breaking through to the east rather than linking up with the Soviet armour in the north was now the only option.

Outside Tarnopol, Southwestern Front's staff had been starved of reliable information from the Dubno battlefield for nearly two days. It was only when two of 12th Tank Division's staff appeared at the front headquarters late on the 28th and reported that Ryabyshev's corps was largely cut off that the scale of the counter-offensive's failure became apparent. As the two emissaries outlined the situation, the front's commissar Nikolai Vashugin strode in. He visibly blanched as he listened to the report and left the room.

With one of his best armoured corps encircled and another, XV Mechanised, exhausted, Kirponos decided to fall back, regroup and launch a fresh attack on 1 July. His decision made, the front commander asked Ivan Bagramyan to inform the rest of the military council. The Armenian found a depressed Khruschev and made his report. The Party leader gave his approval. But when Bagramyan told him he next had to find Vashugin, Khruschev responded: 'Don't bother. You don't need to report to him any longer. Nikolai Nikolaiyevich's battle is over.'

A few minutes earlier, the commissar had entered Khruschev's office distraught. 'It's all lost, it's France all over again. It's over. I'm going to shoot myself,' he said. Khruschev called his bluff. 'Why are you talking foolishness? If you've decided to shoot yourself, what are you waiting for?' The commissar immediately drew his revolver, put it to his temple, pulled the trigger and fell down dead at the Party leader's feet.[35]

'EACH TIME I USED THE WORDS "ADOLF HITLER", PEOPLE APPLAUDED...' WESTERN UKRAINE, END OF JUNE 1941

One by one the towns and villages of western Ukraine were being abandoned as the Red Army fell back. It did so not merely surrendering sacred Soviet soil to the enemy, but also leaving cut-off units and outposts behind – even some border fortifications. After five days of unequal battle, the junior officer commanding one strongpoint in Dęby, ten miles northwest of Rava-Ruska, pleaded for help from his superiors in 36th Machine-Gun Battalion – if the battalion still existed. The neighbouring rifle regiment had deserted the bunker garrisons and retreated. 'With help like that, everything will be pointlessly lost,' the strongpoint commander seethed. His last message from his bunker was a strange mix of desperation and determination:

> There must be some radical intervention. There simply can't be a situation like this in the USSR. No field artillery, not enough tanks, no aircraft, abandoned to our fate and all this on Soviet soil. We are facing total annihilation here...
>
> The garrisons of the bunkers fight heroically, but the outcome is grim. We will die here like flies because there's nothing more we can do about it.
>
> And should we all go under then even so long live the victory of the Red Army.
>
> Long live Communism.
>
> Long live Comrade Stalin.[36]

No troops were more exposed than those gamely holding out in Przemyśl six days after the initial German attack. On the 23rd the defenders – forced out of the town on the first day of war – struck back, re-capturing most of it and driving the Germans back across the River San, leaving 300 dead behind. For the next five days, rather than re-cross the San, the attackers chose to subject the Soviet side of the town to artillery bombardment, each battery sending up to 750 shells a day into the city – and the Soviets responded in kind. 'On both sides of the river columns of smoke rose in different places and at night the ruins glowed,' one Przemyśl resident recorded.

> From the windows of the attic I watched the cathedral burn and several houses in the market square. The Jewish quarter was completely destroyed. On our side, the school buildings and the Benedictine monastery – all occupied by troops – were completely destroyed. The roof of the church also burned down.
>
> The barracks were still on fire. One well-aimed shell smashed through the window and into the crypt of the Orthodox Church, where the Ukrainian police were gathered and were ripped to shreds.

The barrage and counter-barrage reached its peak on the night of 25–26 June. Inhabitants cowered in their basements as entire streets were flattened. The

Benedictine church and school burned down. The pharmacy was destroyed. Two more schools were damaged. The scarred cathedral now burned, as did the Church of the Sacred Heart. And, just for good measure, the Soviet defenders torched the Benedictine monastery.

By late morning on 26 June, however, the bastion on the San was 40, even 50 miles behind the front line. Kirponos ordered the remnants of 99th Rifle Division to fall back, leaving just a few engineers behind to destroy the remaining warehouses and military installations. They did so – and partially demolished the railway crossing. Then silence. 'Something has happened,' one Polish chronicler recorded. For days the town's inhabitants had shunned life outdoors, 'overwhelmed with fear', threatened with being shot if they appeared at the window. But no longer. '28 June is a very important day in the history of Przemyśl,' delighted priest Rafał Woźniak wrote. 'The Bolshevik occupation of Przemyśl has ended. May it be for ever.' German troops crossed the river almost without opposition and fanned out through a deserted town. They found Przemyśl almost half destroyed – the streets around the market square had suffered especially. They did not find many Russians, beyond the occupants of bunker No.8813, overlooking the San on the western outskirts of the town. Despite being occupied by only a dozen men instead of the requisite 32, the strongpoint held out for six days, surviving upwards of 500 direct hits from German guns. Only when flamethrowers were brought up were Lieutenant Pavel Czaplin and his men subdued. Each man was burned alive. For their dogged resistance, the defenders would posthumously receive the Order of the Red Banner.[37]

In northern Ukraine, 41st Tank Division was retreating through the village of Kostopil. It had only been involved on the fringes of the Dubno battles yet it was barely a combat-ready unit any more – there were just two working anti-aircraft guns and 20 T-26 tanks still running, and the heavy tank battalion existed in name only – reduced to a solitary, damaged KV-2 and a repair truck. There were, however, 500 tank crews without vehicles, armed with the machine-guns stripped from wrecked or abandoned armour, revolvers and rifles. And accompanying the division as it filed wearily through Kostopil was an equally dejected civilian populace carrying small bundles of clothes and food. A boy of about ten angrily buttonholed the division's chief-of-staff, Konstantin Maligin.

'Uncle soldier! Where are you going? Are you leaving us to the Germans?'

Maligin nodded.

'But you've got guns!' the youngster pleaded.

'We'll come back and we will avenge everything,' the officer told him without daring to look in his eyes. The boy gave Maligin a look of disapproval then turned around.

Maligin was crestfallen. 'What I would have given for the lives of the dead, for the tears of the women, for the reproach of this boy which was seared into my heart for many days and nights!' he wrote.

> Evidently, I was not alone in feeling this way. When we regrouped in the woods east of Kostopil in the evening, grief over the death of comrades, all the pain for people's suffering and torment was reflected in the faces of the soldiers and officers. Men angrily threw down their overcoats, lay on the grass and were silent. But fatigue was taking its toll, and they fell asleep.

Southwest of Lvov, Nikolai Inozemtsev and his comrades pulled out of Drohobycz as an enormous column of smoke began to rise over the town and fill the pale blue sky. 'Smoke swirls in clusters – like a giant waterfall – and the width of the column of smoke grows and grows,' he noted in his diary. 'When it reaches a specific height, the smoke spreads, forming a giant umbrella. A magnificent, unforgettable sight. They're burning the huge reservoirs of oil and petrol around Drohobycz.' The 29-year-old Muscovite's division withdrew through Boryslav, half a dozen miles to the southeast, where the scene was the same. 'Everywhere burning oil wells, tanks, machinery,' Inozemtsev noted. 'Many of the sappers have burned hands and faces, but selflessly continue their work.' As the troops marched through the town centre, a shower of sparks rained on them, threatening to set the homes of Boryslav alight. Many of the town's inhabitants had decided to flee to the surrounding woods, driving cattle along the road, scooping children up in their arms. 'Many people have abandoned all hope and stare at us from the pavements, with tears in their eyes,' Inozemtsev observed. 'What misery! And no-one screams at or curses us. On the contrary, many stretch out their hands and shout: "Comrades, come back soon!"'[38]

Maligin's and Inozemtsev's accounts are at odds with the contemporary observations of German soldiers – entering Ukraine not as invaders or occupiers, it seemed, but as liberators. As he drove through the towns and villages of western Galicia to impose order and discipline on the conquered territory, Karl von Roques, commanding Army Group South's rear area and security detachments, was celebrated as 'a victor and liberator from the Bolshevist yoke'. His car was covered in flowers in every village. 'If you stopped in a square somewhere to ask for directions, you were immediately surrounded by hundreds of helpful people clapping their approval,' he wrote. The greeting in the border town of Dobromyl surpassed them all. 'A crowd in festive clothing awaited me,' von Roques noted. 'When the vehicle stopped, I was surrounded by a dozen Ukrainian women in their picturesque national dress. Everyone presented me with a bouquet of flowers – I've never received so many flowers in my entire life as I did when I was in Dobromyl!' After a gushing welcome from the mayor and Ukrainian nationalists, von Roques watched as the town's inhabitants headed to church for the first time in more than 20 years. The houses of worship were unable to cope; queues stretched into the streets, and people prayed where they stood or knelt. Later, von Roques was invited to attend a rally in front of the town hall. The 61-year-old stood on the balcony of the town hall and soaked up the applause and gratitude of the small town's inhabitants, who filled the main square: the women in their festive dress, young girls in colourful traditional costumes, clergymen in all their regalia. After several speeches, Roques addressed the crowd with the help of an interpreter. 'Each time I used the words "Adolf Hitler", the people were filled with enthusiasm and applauded.'[39]

Engineer Richard Zajac remembered being presented with garlands 'more than once' as his unit marched through a village.

> Women, men and children stood at the roadside. Girls with flowers brought us water and milk to drink and handed us eggs. We felt as if we were marching through Germany after a dance. Gramophones were often fetched out of homes and we danced with girls in the middle of the village or in the small crofts.
>
> When we entered one of the small Ukrainian villages we were often greeted with a table of food. When we went into a cottage, on the left there was a large wooden barrel of pickled cucumbers, plus a barrel of pickled tomatoes. In the main room where the ground had been stamped down, there was a table. There was usually a fine blanket on the table, plus bread, salt, a glass of milk and a bouquet of wild flowers.[40]

Artilleryman Rolf Reichold was struck by the 'triumphal arches with swastika banners and Ukrainian flags, with inscriptions in German and Ukrainian: *Heil* Hitler, long live Germany and so on'. The entering soldiers were greeted with applause from villagers. 'All of them are delighted that the Russians, who deprived them of everything, have gone.' Non-commissioned officer Emilian Hindelang remembered 'a number of nice young girls came towards us, singing. There had been a thanksgiving service for being liberated from the Soviets. People everywhere are so happy that we have come and driven the Russians away.' A Norwegian Waffen SS volunteer felt like he was serving in 'an army of liberation. People were wild with enthusiasm, flowers were being thrown up to us in the vehicle we were sitting in.' Clergy held services of thanksgiving where, in halting German, they praised their 'liberators' and prayed for the wellbeing of Germany and her army. Fighter pilot Heinz Sannemann found the Ukrainian people not just friendly, but willing collaborators, happy to hide German fliers forced to make emergency landings behind enemy lines, 'in bales of hay or under piles of manure', before 'smuggling them through Russian lines in civilian clothes'. Male inhabitants often marched alongside the Germans, offering to act as ammunition carriers. They stayed with the invaders until nightfall and only returned home after a good deal of persuasion from officers. Despite the danger they faced accompanying the Wehrmacht, infantryman Karl List was convinced that many a villager 'would have immediately followed us if we'd have armed them'. One non-commissioned officer was greeted by a sea of 'happy faces – people who are delighted that they've escaped the Bolshevik yoke and terror!' Yet there was also palpable tension in their voices. 'Will the Bolsheviks come back, will you stay, will you drive those in power – mostly Jews – even further away?' In pidgin Ukrainian the soldiers replied that they were advancing on Moscow. '*Dobrze, dobrze*,' villagers nodded. 'Good, good.'[41]

The populace's apprehension was perhaps understandable, for as the Soviet authorities fled, their crimes were uncovered. In Dobromyl jail, 82 inmates were 'killed by blows to the body with a device used to stun cattle', shot in their cells or on the stairs. 'The floor and walls of the prison were spattered with blood, the stairwell entrance too,' recalled Pole Tadeusz Pstrąg, who was searching for family members. The floors of the cells ran with blood, while in the courtyard, 30 bodies were piled up in a bricked-up chamber 'above which thousands of flies buzzed. It was a horrible sight that I will not forget until I die.' Far worse prevailed outside Dobromyl, where the bodies of more than 500 prisoners were tossed down the shafts of an abandoned salt mine, every one of them killed by blunt instrument. The NKVD's victims in Boryslav were disinterred – they'd only been covered with a couple of inches of soil – and laid out in the prison courtyard. There was a teenage girl, her nipples torn out as if with pliers, her face burned. Her brother was also among the dead, missing one eye, his lips sewn together with barbed wire, his hands crushed, his skin peeling off as if they poured boiling water over it. Around 2,800 of the 4,000 inmates of Lutsk prison were murdered by the NKVD in the final days of Soviet rule. 14th Panzer Division's legal advisor was led to a freshly filled-in grave in the prison courtyard, where he ordered the bodies exhumed. Digging revealed the corpses of four German aviators, each one mutilated. One lacked a lower leg, another had both legs cut off. A soldering iron had been driven 4in into the chest of a third men, while there was a plate-shaped cut on an officer's abdomen.[42]

In the vacuum between Soviet and German rule, the mob briefly ruled, their wrath fanned by inflammatory leaflets distributed by the Ukrainian nationalist movement, the OUN. It laid the blame for these atrocities – indeed all the misfortunes and maltreatments of Soviet rule – at the doors of the Jewish populace. 'You welcomed Stalin with flowers, we'll lay your heads at Hitler's feet as a greeting.' Having been 'the most devoted supporters of the ruling Bolshevik regime and the vanguard of Muscovite imperialism in Ukraine', there would be no home for Jews in an 'independent' Ukraine; they would be handed over to the militia and liquidated 'for the slightest offence'. The citizens of Dobromyl set fire to the synagogue in revenge, then killed 132 Jews for good measure. Over three days, more than 300 'Communist functionaries, NKVD agents and snipers' and 'Jewish Communists' were shot in the border town of Sokal. Another 500 Jews were rounded up in the streets, forced to strip off all their clothes, then were marched to the town's seminary; several were beaten to death on the way. Moses Brüh watched as a kangaroo court was established in a school courtyard – there were even stenographers and a Ukrainian lawyer assigned to the defendants. It did not help them. The sentence was always the same: death by shooting. The condemned were led to the nearby brickworks. As they were, fresh defendants were brought before the makeshift court. In all, 117 Jews were shot.[43]

'THE NEED TO RID OURSELVES OF THIS SCOURGE IS OBVIOUS...' IAŞI, 28 JUNE–5 JULY 1941

The wave of brutal antisemitism sweeping through the borderlands of Eastern Europe increasingly worried playwright and novelist Mihail Sebastian. The 33-year-old barely dared to leave his home in Bucharest any more. 'I am worried about the antisemitic tension that is being fuelled by the press, radio and posters,' he recorded in his diary. Jews accounted for barely one-fiftieth of Romania's population, yet were widely distrusted and openly maltreated by most of society. Barred from countless occupations – government posts, the law, journalism – forbidden from speaking Yiddish in public, Jews had even been denied Romanian citizenship until the 1920s. The evacuation of Bukovina and Bessarabia in the summer of 1940, when Romania was forced to cede territory to Moscow, provoked a wave of atrocities against the region's Jewish populace, sometimes committed by the mob, mostly by the retreating Romanian Army – at least

450 Jews were killed, especially those who tried to seek sanctuary in the USSR. The seizure of power by Ion Antonescu a few weeks later ushered in a fresh wave of official limitations, humiliations and discrimination, as well as unsanctioned – and unpunished – pogroms. Antonescu was determined to rid Romania of its *jidani* – Yids. The invasion of the Soviet Union offered the perfect pretext 'to carry out the purification of the population'. And so, in the week after 22 June, the propaganda campaign intensified, and the restrictions on Jewish life tightened. 'Yids to labour camps!' one newspaper screamed. Jews were forbidden from flying the national flag, while Jewish inhabitants in the small Moldavian town of Huşi, close to the Soviet border, were forced to wear distinguishing yellow badges. And on the last day of the month, Sebastian read a terse official communiqué: 500 Jewish freemasons had been executed in Romania's second city, Iaşi, for collaborating with Soviet paratroopers.[44]

Built on seven hills 230 miles north of Bucharest, Iaşi was no Rome, but it was the heart of Romania's cultural and academic life, home to *fin de siècle* buildings – Gustav Eiffel had built its grandest hotel – the country's first university, fine theatres, squares and parks. It was also home to more than 45,000 Jews – one in three of the city's populace – who had lived in Iaşi for more than 400 of its 500-year existence. The city was also a hotbed of antisemitism, birthplace of two violently antisemitic political parties (one of which chose the swastika as its emblem). And, with war now declared on the Soviet Union, Iaşi was a front-line city, a springboard for the Axis armies to 'liberate' Bukovina and Bessarabia and push along the Black Sea coast. At the end of June 1941, the city teemed with Romanian and German troops, plus hundreds of police. That made it a prime target for the Red Air Force.

The first air raid on the 24th was largely ineffective. Two days later, Soviet bombers returned and hit the headquarters of 14th Infantry Division, a telephone exchange and a hospital. It was Iaşi's Jewish quarter which suffered the most: at least 100 homes were damaged and 38 people killed. Yet somehow Jews were blamed for their own – and their city's – misfortune. Posters began to appear in the streets: 'Romanians! One dead Jew equals one fewer Communist! The hour of revenge has come!' Or: 'Kill the Jews! Each Jew is a Communist. Let all of us exterminate what threatens us!' At the very least, Jews were ordered to surrender any torches, several men were arrested for 'signalling' to Soviet aircraft, while one family was seized for hanging out a red blanket to dry. One antisemitic soldier went further. Sergeant Mircea Manoliu brought in three 'suspicious' Jews. His senior officer released the men immediately – but ordered Manoliu to escort them. None returned home. Two were shot dead; the third ended up in hospital, badly wounded. Some police advised the city's Christians to paint crosses on their doors and windows so they would not be targeted. Elsewhere hurriedly written placards could be seen in apartment block windows: '*Aici locuiesc Creştini. Nu sunt jidani în curte*' – 'Christians live here. There are no Yids in this courtyard.' These were ominous days for Iaşi's Jews. 'They sat in fear next to their doors,' recalled one of them, lawyer Beno Beer, 'as if waiting for something, something hovering in the air.'[45]

At 9pm on Saturday 28 June, the air-raid sirens sounded across Iaşi once again, followed shortly afterwards by the drone of aircraft engines. In the fading light of a mid-summer day, one aircraft fired a blue flare – the signal for various gunmen spread across the city to begin shooting at passing Romanian and Germans troops. Not one was hit; the sharpshooters either fired into the air or used firecrackers to simulate automatic fire. The panic the 'shooting' caused, however, was very real. The troops fired back, even wheeling up field guns in their 'battle' with the insurgents. To help them, more than 700 police and gendarmes were sent onto the streets of Iaşi. Almost immediately, Beno Beer realised what was afoot. 'I expected to see dozens of dead and wounded,' he later testified. 'No casualties among soldiers or animals. Not even one wounded.' The shots fired were blanks; the 'uprising' was really an act of provocation by Romanian antisemites and nationalists. It worked. As Iaşi's citizens took refuge in its air-raid shelters, Beer eavesdropped on conversations. 'Did you see?' one Romanian asked. 'The Jews rebelled. They are attacking the city.'[46]

By the time the people of Iaşi emerged from their shelters, a pogrom was in full swing. Groups of nationalists, police and soldiers, as well as a seething mob – as one observer noted, at the heart of the pogrom were 'ordinary Romanians who had been waiting for the right moment to rob and kill' – were moving through the city, hunting down Jews.

No attempt was made to hide the pogrom. Round-ups were conducted in the streets – and were recorded by curious photographers, who went on to follow columns of unfortunate Jews, their hands raised in the air, through the heart of the city to the police headquarters. Scores never made it. One man tried to save his Jewish friend; both were gunned down by a Romanian police officer who snarled: 'Die, you dog, with the Jew you're protecting.' In some cases, senior police officers intervened and ordered the maltreatment and shooting to stop, the groups of prisoners released. The Romanian owner of a mill refused to relinquish the 100 Jews working for him. But other cityfolk were all too eager either to betray Jewish friends or neighbours to the authorities, or worse, take matters into their own hands. 'Our Christian neighbours, whom I considered my friends, came out of their homes with iron bars, hoes, spades and guns and began to hit us,' Lazar Leibovici recalled. 'Dozens of people fell down without the possibility of defending themselves, guilty only of being Jews.' One 14-year-old boy armed with an axe gleefully led German troops to Jewish apartments, pointing out: 'Here live Yids.' Tax inspector Silviu Luca drew up a list of Jews in his block, then showed Romanian soldiers and police where his neighbours were hiding. 'This is what you deserve,' his wife hissed as the Jews were led away. Three gendarmes, two police officers and two civilians armed with clubs banged on the door of the Zwieback family in Ştefan cel Mare Street, one of Iaşi's main thoroughfares. Room by room, they emptied the house and ordered all the Jewish inhabitants to muster in the courtyard. With their hands on their heads, they were marched off, continuously beaten by clubs and iron bars. They passed at least two corpses, a teenage girl and the father of young Jacques Zwieback's schoolfriend Lică. And with hundreds of Jewish apartments now lying empty or 'inhabited only by frightened women and children', the basest urges seized many of Iaşi's residents, who plundered at will. There was little order or organisation to the attacks; Jews were singled out at random, save for one incident near the national theatre in Brătianu Street, where a tank – it has never been determined whether it was German or Romanian – supposedly came under fire. Upwards of 20 Jews were quickly seized in surrounding buildings and businesses, forced to lie on the ground, then machine-gunned by the tank. By mid-morning on Sunday, Iaşi, one German observer wrote, had become 'one big battlefield where soldiers from both armies, gendarmes and Romanian police and civilians – organised or otherwise – hunted down Jews, robbed them and killed them'. The cobbled streets and pavements were strewn with corpses. People made no attempt to remove them. Some stared. Others strode past the bodies as if they were a normal part of city life. Leon Haimovici found a still-conscious rabbi lying in the road in a pool of blood, having been shot twice by a soldier who told him: 'This is what we will do to all the Yids!' Railwaymen picked up revolvers; shopkeepers and shoemakers seized iron bars. They shot at Jews or bludgeoned them to death. One tram worker beat an entire family to death with a metal bar, but few could match the bloodlust and brutality of university laboratory technician Ioan Ştefănoiu. He killed more than a dozen Jews and stole from many more in a two-day rampage at the head of a mob. Ştefănoiu behaved like a 'wild animal', Salomon Reinharz observed as he was being led away in a column. Seeing a Jewish woman on her own, Ştefănoiu attacked her. She fell to her knees and begged to be allowed to return home. 'Then this beast clubbed her on the head and she collapsed.'[47]

The destination for those Jews who survived the gauntlet of being marched through Iaşi's streets was the police headquarters in Strada Vasile Alecsandri, just one block east of the main square. Beno Beer, who arrived at the police station around 9am, found conditions unbearable. The heat was stifling, the stream of fresh prisoners never ending – 'old people, young people, women, children, cripples ... all covered in blood, having been savagely beaten on the way by the guardians of law and order.' A cordon of German and Romanian troops, plus civilians armed with metal bars, stood at the entrance. They rained blows on the unfortunate Jews, stabbed them with bayonets, smashed rifle butts in their faces. Some fell to the ground dead – there was soon a pile of corpses with broken arms, legs and feet, eyes gouged out, covered in blood at the entrance to the courtyard. Lawyer Mayer Juhr forced himself to his feet and stumbled into the yard. He found no sanctuary, just thousands of Jews 'mashed into one another, wounded, and waiting to die'. At one point during the morning, General Gheorghe Stavrescu, 14th Infantry Division's commander, appeared in the courtyard to address those arrested. He promised the firing squad for anyone found guilty of shooting at Romanian troops. Worse, if attacks on his men persisted, 'the entire Jewish population will pay for it with their lives'. If calm and order prevailed in Iaşi, however, the prisoners would be discharged, women and children first.

At least one senior police officer was sceptical about the 'criminals' and 'spies' being brought into the headquarters and ordered women, children and the elderly released immediately. They were even given a pass bearing the word '*liber*' – free. Yet many more police took advantage of the prisoners' plight. They beat back anyone who tried to reach a tap in the courtyard, but were prepared to sell water for 100 lei. By early afternoon, the price had climbed to 5,000 lei – the equivalent of one month's salary for a police officer.

There were now thousands of prisoners crammed in the headquarters courtyard, its cells and outbuildings – some eyewitnesses claim the figure was as high as 20,000 Jews. To make space for the constant stream of new arrivals, troops fired into the crowd. The air-raid siren sounded to drown out the noise of rifle and machine-gun fire being poured down on the unfortunate prisoners. Police officers and German and Romanian troops took aim from every vantage point – not just in the headquarters, but from the rooftops, windows and balconies of surrounding buildings. 'The bullets flew past my ears, but the screams of pain of the wounded were much more shrill,' Jacques Zwieback recalled. The schoolboy scrambled over a wall and spent the rest of the day hiding in abandoned chicken sheds, abandoned courtyards, empty houses. Only when darkness fell did he feel it was safe to move about the streets of Iaşi once more. 'In each courtyard, there were bloody naked corpses of old people, some shot, others with their skulls smashed in,' he remembered. He'd always imagined death to be peaceful. 'But the corpses of these murdered people had distorted faces, of pain, hatred and disgust. Angry faces which demanded revenge.'

Eventually it all became too much for the captured Jews. In a mass breakout from the prison headquarters, they spilled out of the courtyard into neighbouring streets. Some fled; others tried to hide in the alleys and outhouses off Alecsandri Street. But most got no further than the street itself, where they were cut down by rifle and machine-gun fire. One elderly Jew, wounded in World War I fighting for Romania, was shot in the throat. 'He lived his last moments on a garbage can like a dog,' one survivor recalled. The same observer heard the fatally wounded son of a leather merchant crying out for his family. 'Mother, father, where are you? Give me some water, I'm thirsty.' All he received was a bayonet to the chest as Romanian troops moved among the dying and finished them off. The cobbles of Alecsandri Street ran red with blood which stained hundreds of discarded identity cards, now no longer needed, for their owners were dead.

Engineer Israel Schleier, who had been released earlier in the day with a '*liber*' pass, was re-arrested by Romanian troops who forced their way into his apartment. He arrived at the police headquarters with a column of prisoners around 6pm. The killings had stopped – the executioners were seemingly tired. Instead, they ordered the bodies in the police courtyard collected and piled up to create space. The dead were seized by their hands and feet, one Jewish eyewitness recalled, 'and thrown onto the mound of corpses, which had turned red from blood, to make room at the entrance for fresh victims'. Some of the 'corpses' heaped on the pile were still alive, 'but suffocated as they were tossed one over the other'.[48]

Israel Schleier was among the last Jews to be delivered to Iaşi's police headquarters. As afternoon turned to evening, prisoners arrived in a trickle, not a flood. The pogrom had run its course. Almost. The Romanians had one last torment in store for the surviving Jewish populace.

'What has happened gives us a sombre insight into the nature of the Romanian people,' wrote the horrified German consul in Iaşi, Dr Fritz Schellhorn. He pleaded with the local German commander, XXX Corps' Hans von Salmuth, to intervene – but Salmuth was absent and his staff were powerless, admitting 'that they had lost control of the troops' passing through the city. Salmuth's superiors at Eleventh Army were even less inclined to intervene. In fact, they supported the pogrom. Convinced German soldiers had been shot at by 'Jewish spies', the army dispatched troops to help the Romanians to put down a Jewish uprising. They arrived in the early evening to find the pogrom was largely over. Instead, they set about disarming any civilians with guns and oversaw the burial of the dead. The corpses were afforded no dignity. They were thrown into garbage trucks.[49]

At Iași's police headquarters, columns of Jews were now leaving, rather than arriving. Since 8pm, trucks had been pulling into the courtyard and the surviving Jews forced to climb into them – those not fast enough for the guards' liking were bayonetted to death. They were then driven to the city's railway station one mile away where two trains were waiting to transport them supposedly to a special camp in Călărași, 230 miles to the south. Between 80 and 200 prisoners were packed in each wagon. Wooden boards were nailed over large holes or ventilation ducts – ostensibly to prevent anyone escaping. The doors were locked. The sides were daubed with graffiti: '*Jidani-Comuniști*' or '*Ucigași ai ostașilor Germani și Români*' – 'Communist Yids' or 'Killers of German and Romanian soldiers'.

The first train, hauling around three dozen goods wagons, pulled out of Iași in the small hours of Monday. First it headed west, then east, then south, and finally north, pulling into the small town of Târgu Frumos, just 30 miles west of Iași, around 9pm on Monday. The train had been on the move for 17 hours and travelled 125 miles. Israel Schleier reckoned there were at least 100 fellow Jews in his wagon. The weak and wounded slumped on the ground; others grasped at two skylights – the only source of light and fresh air. People stripped off their clothes in the heat, became delirious or were simply baked alive. Others paid 100 lei for wet rags from gypsies at the many stops – or 1,000 lei for a cup of water, if they could afford it. Or perhaps they surrendered their jewellery to the train's engineer, who offered buckets of water from the locomotive to anyone who might pay his extortionate price – upwards of 20,000 lei. He was bartered down to 17,000 lei. The prisoners doused their clothes in the foul water, then sucked at their shirts until they were dry. Some Jews were hauled off the train and marched through Târgu Frumos. Out of thirst, many tried to drink water from puddles by the roadside, only to be shot by a police officer. The remainder were taken into a house, ordered to surrender their money and valuables, and were then frogmarched back to the train. The carriages stood for 19 hours in Târgu Frumos, but no-one made any attempt to help the passengers. No food or water was given to them. Only the dead were removed, unceremoniously tossed onto the side of an embankment. Howling peasants scolded the passengers – and the handful of guards. 'Shoot them!' they urged. 'Why are you dragging them around in a train?' When the corpses had been recovered, the train resumed its tortuous journey. During one prolonged halt near a river, a boy made a dash for the water only to be shot by one of the guards. 'Water, water!' he pleaded. 'You want water?' the guard snarled. 'Well, drink all you want.' He drowned the youngster head-first in the river. Elsewhere, one Romanian soldier took pity on the Jewish prisoners, grabbed a few rags, dipped them in a puddle and handed them, plus a rusty can filled with water, to Israel Schleier. 'Being able to refresh ourselves with the wet cloth and soak our lips revived us a little,' the engineer later testified. 'After that, the doors and windows were sealed again and the train continued its wretched journey.' Some Jews sensed the end and committed suicide, using their belts to hang themselves. The corpses quickly inflated in the heat, while bodies on the floor of the wagons burst open when anyone stood on them trying to reach pockets of air near the roof. 'Inside, the smell was unbearable – a mixture of blood, decomposing bodies and faeces,' Schleier remembered.

The thirst, terror and heat were such that the passengers went mad. The scenes of horror resumed. A chorus of complaints demanding 'drink, drink' was heard continuously, both during the journey and when we stopped. Some tried to ask for water from those standing near the carriage through the skylight, sometimes managing to get a bottle of water in return for a wedding ring, a pair of shoes or money which they'd succeeded in hiding despite the searches. But some bottles were filled with petrol or some other infected, undrinkable liquid. When a bottle appeared in the wagon, there were clashes which quickly turned into a fight to the death. As a result, the bottle eventually shattered and its contents spilled on the floor.

Many were reduced to drinking their own urine, but this soon proved inadequate. From then on, people used their urine to apply wet compresses to each other's heads and chests.

One after another, people died, suffocated; many killed themselves. We grew fewer and fewer in number – this was the good fortune of those still alive: we had more space and could even sit in the middle of the bodies lying on the floor.

In the town of Roman, prisoners were forced to remove their clothes, which were burned in a giant pyre. They remained naked for two more days until the train finally pulled into Călăraşi. Of the 2,530 people loaded into the carriages on 29 June, just 1,101 were alive seven days later. The survivors – sunburned, dehydrated, emaciated, covered in dried blood, their uncleaned wounds seeping pus, 'had lost all human appearance,' Israel Schleier remembered. The local populace fled at the sight of the column, terrified.[50]

The journey of the second 'train of death' was much briefer but no less dreadful. It crawled out of Iaşi with 1,902 prisoners on board around 6am on 30 June and moved at a snail's pace through the valley running west of the city. The horrors of the train to Călăraşi were played out all over again: the struggles for fresh air and water, countless cases of heat stroke, men hanging themselves, soldiers offering water at unimaginable prices. When the train finally halted in the small town of Podu Iloaiei early on Monday afternoon and the wagon doors were opened, the survivors tumbled out and ran to the nearest ditch where they drank bog water. As they did, they watched Romanian troops rifle the bodies of the dead for valuables. 'We were living corpses,' survivor Leizer Finchelstein later testified. 'We looked as though we were from another planet.' The train had been on the move for no more than eight hours and covered no more than a dozen miles. In that time, 1,196 of those on board died.[51]

In Iaşi, the first victims had been delivered to the Jewish cemetery, high on a hillside on the northwestern edge of the city, even as the pogrom raged. But it was Monday before Iaşi's sanitation chief Vlad Marievici set about clearing the dead in earnest. He began with the police headquarters where he found 'corpses piled up like lumber' in the courtyard, where blood perhaps an inch deep ran along the cobbles. Marievici immediately dispatched four refuse trucks and two dozen carts to begin removing the bodies – the living as well as the dead. They were transported to the Jewish cemetery, where youths rounded up by the police acted as gravediggers and pallbearers. Already decomposing in the heat, the corpses were tossed into mass graves. It took four days, a 160-strong army of diggers, rubbish lorries and trucks. At first the bodies were unloaded at the cemetery entrance, then carried by stretcher to the grave. This time-consuming process was soon abandoned, and rubbish carts simply drove up to the graveside and tipped their loads – led by a wave of blood – into the pit. Romanian soldiers inflicted one last insult on the dead, moving through the burial pits, depriving the corpses of watches, gold teeth and other valuables.

In the city, police stations were besieged by anxious wives and children. Enquiring about the fate of her husband, brother, father and father-in-law, Lilly Moscovici was told – like everyone else – that her relatives had been sent away from Iaşi by train. Moscovici was not convinced – she had seen the corpses in the streets as well as the rubbish carts crammed with bodies. At the wheel were refuse collectors, now attired in clothes they had robbed from the dead. They showed no remorse. 'So shall be done to all the Yids,' they yelled as they drove by.

There was no hurry to bury the dead in Podu Iloaiei. For three days, the corpses of Jews on board the second 'train of death' were left in the open. They decomposed terribly in the summer heat – some bodies were inflated five times their normal size; others fell apart when lifted and had to be loaded onto carts piece by piece. The Italian war correspondent Curzio Malaparte was one of the few foreigners to witness the 'field of the dead', accompanying the Italian consul in Iași on a visit. He watched as peasants and gypsies systematically moved along the rows of corpses, stripping them of clothes. 'Clutched between his mother's knees, a few months' old baby was still alive. It had fainted, but was still breathing. One of its arms was broken,' the journalist observed. He estimated there were 2,000 corpses in all 'stretched out under the sun' on the railway embankment.[52]

The official communiqué talked of 500 casualties. Fritz Schellhorn reckoned 4,000 dead. The Romanian security services estimated the death toll in the city and on the trains to be as high as 13,266. Romanian Jewish historian – and most comprehensive chronicler of the pogrom – Jean Ancel goes even higher, perhaps 15,000 in all: 8,000 killed in Iași, the rest in the trains.[53]

There were no Romanian and German wounded, let alone dead. Investigators didn't find a single bullet hole in walls or windows shattered by shooting. They never found a single weapon or any 'foreign shooter'. Iași's police chief General Emanoil Leoveanu decided the 'attack' was a ruse 'carried out with replica weapons and a network of firecrackers'. Its perpetrators were ultra nationalists who deliberately chose the city's Jewish quarter and quickly slipped into the night. Civic authorities tried to blame the Germans for the atrocities. 'Infuriated' German troops had scoured the streets, rounding up Jews and mistreating them, Iași's prefect Dumitru Captaru reported to Bucharest. They had even shot 'some Jews' and been assisted in their work by Romanian soldiers and 'gangs of civilians, who plundered the homes of Jews who were arrested'.

Ion Antonescu was not fooled. The rioting in Iași had shown the world Romania was 'an undisciplined and uncivilised nation… Such crimes are a shameful stain on the entire nation.' It wasn't the pogrom which troubled the *conducător*, it was the manner in which it had been carried out: by a seething mob of soldiers and civilians, not an orderly round-up conducted largely in secret. The Jews would be dealt with, he promised, but there must never be a repeat of the public pogrom. 'The disturbances which occurred a few days ago in Iași put the army and the authorities in a thoroughly unfavourable light,' he warned.

During the evacuation of Bessarabia, the Army was truly shamed when it was insulted and attacked by Jews and Communists – and could not defend itself.

But the shame is even greater when individual soldiers randomly attack and murder the Jewish populace at will, often purely to loot and maltreat, as happened in Iași.

For centuries, the Jewish race has sucked the Romanian people dry, exploited them and impeded their development. The need to rid ourselves of this scourge is obvious, but only the government has the right to take the necessary measures.[54]

'WHEREVER YOU LOOKED, THE DEAD...'
DUBNO, 29 JUNE–1 JULY

Three hundred miles to the north, the trapped Soviet forces corralled by Nikolai Popel southwest of Dubno were determined to break out. A reconnaissance patrol from 16th Motorised Infantry Division stumbled into the cut-off Russians in the woods. Radio transmissions ceased and thin columns of smoke began to appear over the detachment's last reported position. The reconnaissance company's commander, Robert Borchardt, drove forward and found his men's vehicles burned out and still smouldering. He watched his anti-tank gunners engage heavy Soviet tanks, but their shells failed to penetrate the enemy's armour – 'it was like using a film prop'. Only when a flak battery was brought up and its 88mm guns trained against Soviet tanks, not aircraft, did the fighting turn in the Germans' favour. In half an hour 44 Russian tanks – including several T-34s and KVs – were shot up, some at point-blank range. The fighting continued through the night of 29–30 June, when 'hand-grenades, Molotov cocktails and flamethrowers played a big role' as Soviet infantry tried to punch through the German lines, followed by two waves of armoured attacks which were finally driven off when mortars smashed the road and made it impassable. Shortly after first light, it was the turn of the Germans to attack, moving on the village of Ptycha. 'Our foremost positions vanished in smoke and dust,' Popel wrote. 'The clouds of smoke and earth thrown up blotted out the sun.' The enemy's fire shifted from the outposts to the heart of the makeshift force. Now the Luftwaffe entered the fray. Popel had nothing with which to oppose German air superiority – 'not a single barrel'. The bombardment continued, with the occasional pause, for two hours. It was the prelude to a series of attacks on Ptycha by the Viennese of 44th Infantry Division.[55]

Battalion commander Eberhard Pohl provides a breathless account of the ferocious fighting:

> We unlimbered a gun from the car. Assisted by the crew I pushed the easily manoeuvrable gun down a path through a field to the edge of a copse and, well camouflaged, took up position in a roadside ditch. An observer, around 150 metres ahead of us, used signals to report if the noise of tanks getting ever closer was actually heading our way.

I lay behind the gun, my right hand on the handwheel, my gaze fixed on the observer. The crew lay beside me, their bodies on the spars so they wouldn't have to jump up when the gun fired. Then came the agreed signal. My heart was in my mouth. The moment was already exciting! Then it appeared, its hatches closed, slowly, carefully, its barrel pointed slightly towards the ground. The clanking tracks dug themselves into the sand. I targeted just below the turret. The sound of the shot leaving the barrel and hitting the target was a sharp, deafening crash. The shell bounced off the turret at a sharp angle and flew off as strangely like a blazing round of tracer. Now to make a quick getaway – into the cover of the wood! The tank's driver had already spotted our gun and was driving at full speed towards it. There wasn't much left of 'my' gun. I got my men to safety – the tank did not want to pursue us into the wood.[56]

Eberhard Pohl did not destroy a single Russian tank. But his division did. It claimed 106 enemy armoured vehicles destroyed during the two days it was in action at Dubno.

Nikolai Popel's troops fought off five or six assaults on Ptycha before the lines buckled. The centre of the village changed hands several times until the Germans finally had a firm hold. When panzers threatened Popel's makeshift force, he committed the last of his KV tanks. The Germans had no heavy armour to counter them. But then the Soviet tanks were almost out of shells. In desperation, they rammed the enemy, or used their wide chains to literally crush the German infantry. The brutal tactics worked. 'Vehicles burned, the barrels of guns flattened into the soil pointed skywards, overturned personnel carriers were scattered around,' Popel wrote. 'And wherever you looked, the dead.'

By mid-afternoon, however, German pressure was beginning to tell in the north where Popel's friend and fellow commissar Ivan Gurov was leading 67th Tank Regiment. Gurov had some good news – he claimed to have captured 44th Infantry Division's commander, Friedrich Siebert. Popel climbed into his T-34 and hurried to the scene. As he neared Gurov's lines, Stukas appeared and hammered the Soviet armour – the curtain-raiser to an attack by numerous Panzer Mk3s and Mk4s. When Popel arrived, he found his friend's tank smouldering. Peering inside, he saw three charred skeletons. His driver climbed into the wrecked tank and found one of the Soviet Union's highest decorations, the Order of the Red Banner, stripped of its enamel by the heat of the fire which raged inside the T-35; it had been awarded to Ivan Gurov for his service in the Winter War against the Finns.

Popel's force was now down to just 80 tanks, each with perhaps two dozen shells and half-empty fuel tanks. The infantry only had a few rounds left. Five minutes after a reconnaissance aircraft appeared over the formation, the first German bombers began to attack. Only six dropped their loads, but that was sufficient to disorientate the Soviets, as Panzer Mk3s and Mk4s emerged from the surrounding woods to attack. In an instant, one T-34 was tearing across the terrain like a burning torch. Popel watched as the tank commanded by his friend – and one-time tank regiment commander – Peter Volkov was set ablaze. Volkov struggled out of the turret, only for his legs to give way, causing him to fall off and lose consciousness. None of the remaining crew escaped.

With little ammunition left, Soviet tank commanders waited until the Germans were within point-blank range. When the shells ran out, the Russians turned to ramming. A major commanding one of the few remaining KVs smashed into several Panzer Mk3s, reducing his tank to 'nothing but a shapeless heap of metal'. As the blood-red sun began to slowly disappear beyond the horizon, the acrid smoke from the battlefield tainted the lush grass a foul yellow. 'Constant thunder fills the air, echoing off the forest,' Popel wrote. 'It's impossible to determine where our and where German tanks are. Steel boxes from which flames lick lie all around.'

It was impossible to tell when night fell, for the red glow of the last light of day blended with the fires raging on the battlefield. Popel's men had little more to give. 'We've been fighting since dawn,' the brigade commissar wrote. 'Our nerves are paralysed, the instinct of self-preservation has gone. Some men no longer even react to bombs and shells exploding. They leap from their tanks, out of their trenches, stumbling forward but failing to keep their heads down, until they're hit by a bullet or shrapnel.' All that remained of his command at the end of the last day of June were a small group of battered tanks, an ambulance and three staff. The surviving crews of wrecked tanks and remaining infantry mounted the last armoured vehicles or moved wearily eastwards. But the Germans did not hound them. When the Russians entered the woods southeast of Dubno, the panzers broke off the pursuit.[57]

At dawn the next day, 1 July, trapped Russian troops burst out of woods and tried to break out along the Dubno–Rovno road, where they ran into the rear columns of 25th Infantry Division. 'It was all but a miracle that our column only suffered a few wounded, even though it was caught napping, so to speak,' wrote one German supply officer. The fighting raged for eight hours. 'Ammunition exploded, columns of fire and smoke climbed skywards,' the officer continued in his diary. 'The fire of heavy weapons then mixed with the yelp of machine-guns and side-arms: an anti-tank gun and flak had finally intervened, after which the Russians fell back, leaving behind many dead.'[58]

While the bulk of Soviet forces trapped at Dubno were attempting to break out, 41st Tank Division was still trying to puncture the German armoured bulge which now stretched for more than 150 miles through the heart of Galicia. The division waited until dusk on 30 June to make its move northwest of Rovno, 'as it would have been senseless during the day when enemy aircraft dominated the skies,' its chief-of-staff Konstantin Maligin wrote. At 9pm two flares rose over the battlefield – the signal for 150 tanks, supported by two dozen howitzers and a regiment of motorised infantry, to move out. Despite the lack of anti-tank guns and mortars, the division smashed its way through the thin German lines covering the left wing of Kleist's *Panzergruppe*. The town of Olyka, 30 miles north of Dubno, was soon liberated and, with the first rays of light on 1 July, the vanguard of 41st Tank Division pushed its way into the village of Petushki, six miles to the south. There it ran into 14th Panzer and 111th Infantry Divisions and faced the full wrath of the enemy: tank, artillery and mortar fire. 'The battlefield became sheer hell,' Maligin recalled.

> The smoke of burning German and Soviet tanks was choking, flakes of ash floated through the air. Howling, explosions, shooting which drowned out the words of commanders, the faces of tank crews turned black. Men jumped from burning and smashed-up fighting vehicles and fell, cut down by rifle and machine-gun fire, shrapnel, mortars. The counter-attack did not reach its objective. The enemy had suffered considerable losses, but we could not stop him.[59]

A circling Luftwaffe reconnaissance aircraft dropped a message to the men of 530th Infantry Regiment northeast of Dubno: 'Tanks advancing!' The troops dug in and waited. And waited. It was early evening before they first heard, then saw, Russian armour coming towards them – upwards of 40 vehicles. 'Tank after tank and between them infantry mounted on trucks roll towards our position,' one German infantryman wrote. 'The tank shells pass over our foxholes by a hair's breadth. Still, no man leaves his post. Fingers on the trigger, everyone waits for the most favourable moment.' The defenders let the enemy tanks close to within 50 yards before opening fire. Anti-tank rifles blew up the trucks, and bursts of machine-gun fire cut down the Soviet troops as they jumped off to escape the inferno. Self-propelled anti-tank guns joined in and the Russian armour went up in flames or fled the battlefield. Nearly three dozen burned-out tanks and trucks were left behind.[60]

The Russians got to within ten miles of Dubno before receiving orders to fall back as the front in Galicia threatened to cave in. As 41st Tank Division withdrew, the Germans gave chase. Polkovnik Pavlov, the divisional commander, committed his flame-throwing T-26 tanks and KV tanks as his rearguard to cover the withdrawal. The flamethrowers were wiped out to a man, while just one of 18 heavy tanks survived the German onslaught. Their sacrifice saved the rest of the division. After the battle, an appreciative Maligin thanked the sole-surviving KV commander. 'The vehicle looked like a wounded beast,' he wrote. 'Its armoured turret was scratched, the armour plate of the howitzer had armour-piercing shells sticking out of it, the engine hardly ran.' With tears in his eyes, its commander, a young lieutenant, lovingly patted the armour. 'This beauty saved us!' he said.[61]

The failed charge by 41st Tank Division was the last significant action of the battle of Dubno. There had never been a tank battle like it. A Norwegian volunteer with the freshly committed *Wiking* Division was struck 'by the stench of all the horse cadavers' as his truck drove across the Dubno battlefield. 'The bodies were inflated and bloated by gases. Next to them, I saw all the shattered corpses of Soviet soldiers and burning T-34 tanks.' In the space of one week, more than 4,400 tanks – just 600 of them German – had clashed in an area roughly eight times the size of Berlin. And when it was over, Mikhail Kirponos had frittered away two-thirds of his armour and lost western Ukraine. Three mechanised corps had been smashed; three more fell back towards the Stalin Line, having lost half their tanks – mostly to breakdowns, lack of fuel or inexperience – and nearly 20 senior officers, not to mention thousands of tank crews and riflemen. XV Mechanised Corps lost three-quarters of its strength, while VIII Mechanised Corps left behind upwards of 90 per cent of its equipment on the field of battle (Nikolai Popel's group of a few hundred men finally reached Soviet lines 100 miles east of Dubno in the fourth week of July). But that is only half the story of the Red Army's failure. Some units desperate to take part never joined battle. Perhaps half of VIII Mechanised Corps was sent scurrying to and fro on the lanes and highways of Galicia by orders and counter-orders. In his after-action report on the defeat, Major General Rodion Morgunov, in charge of Southwestern Front's armour, blamed a litany of failings: the heavy armour had come straight from the factories, untested, dogged by faults, with no spare parts and few, if any, armour-piercing shells to combat enemy tanks. Crews had little or no time to get used to the new machines before war broke out, and when they went into action they did so with little reconnaissance and subjected to constant German air attacks.[62]

According to German sources, fewer than 80 panzers were destroyed, although a couple of hundred did need repairs behind the lines. Some divisions had suffered more than others – 11th and 16th Panzer, which claimed to have destroyed more than 400 enemy tanks – especially, with nearly 1,900 casualties between them. 'Every enemy attack had been smashed with heavy losses, despite the partial material superiority of Russian tanks and the fighting spirit of the Russian soldiers,' wrote a satisfied Gustav Schrodek of 15th Panzer Regiment. Me109 pilot Heinz Sannemann downed three obsolescent DB-3 and a modern Pe-2 bomber over the Dubno pocket. 'You'll be amazed how quickly we'll finish things off here in the East,' he assured his girlfriend Marlies. 'We've got elite Bolshevik troops facing us who will fight until they're wiped out. A struggle between two ideologies is nevertheless different than an ordinary conflict! We can only be grateful to our Führer that he struck at the right time!' As far as Franz Halder was concerned, Mikhail Kirponos had done exactly what the Germans wanted: throwing his armour at *Panzergruppe* 1 'pell-mell' and frittering it away. Following the flags and markers being moved across the situation maps produced for him each day at the army's field headquarters in the gloomy forests of East Prussia, the Chief of the General Staff believed there was a good chance that Kleist's men had 'destroyed everything that can be brought to bear against Army Group South in Ukraine'. Wolfgang Werthen, 16th Panzer Division's chronicler, gave a far more realistic assessment of the titanic clash of armour, comparing the advance in Ukraine with that across France and Belgium 12 months before. 'After ten days in France German panzers stood on the Atlantic following an 800-kilometre journey, driving terrified French and Englishmen before them,' he wrote. 'After ten days in the East, 100 kilometres had been covered and the German armoured spearheads faced an enemy who was technically and numerically superior and who often used hitherto unknown yet effective fighting methods.' Put simply, after ten days of bitter fighting, there had been no collapse on the Southern Front.[63]

'LEMBERG WILL FALL INTO OUR LAP LIKE A ROTTEN APPLE...' 29–30 JUNE

At dusk on Saturday 28 June, Yefim Pushkin gathered the commanders of his 32nd Tank Division in a cottage on the edge of the village of Ryasna, half a dozen miles from the heart of Lvov. The city, he told them, would fall. The hour had come to make a stand in Złoczów, 40 miles to the east. Two armoured regiments would cover the withdrawal. He turned to his friend Alexander Yegorov. 'One of them is yours.'

Yegorov protested. 'Do we have to abandon Lvov?'

His commander paused before responding quietly: 'We have to…'

Alexander Yegorov's regiment moved through the western outskirts of Lvov at dawn the next day. Tall columns of smoke were already rising above the city. His men were dejected. 'I could see how much it weighed on everyone's hearts,' he wrote. 'It wasn't fatigue. No, it was the awareness that the enemy was at the gates of the city.'[64]

The rising smoke Alexander Yegorov saw was caused by the guns of Hans Kreppel's artillery battalion, which unleashed a ten-minute barrage at first light. After marching and fighting their way across 60 miles of Galicia, the mountain infantry of 1st *Gebirgs* Division were finally in a position to attack the region's capital. As Kreppel's guns fell silent, the *Jäger* left their jump-off positions and began to move forward through the dense morning mist. Progress was rapid, the Red Army's defence disorganised, but dogged when they chose to fight. In Bryukhovychi, just half a dozen miles northwest of the city centre, the mountain men surprised a Soviet troop train about to pull out, taking a rifle battalion eastwards. '*Los, Jäger, drauf!*' – 'Go *Jäger*, at them!' battalion commander Josef Salminger urged his men, expecting an easy fight. But the thousand Russians chose to fight rather than surrender – a decision which would cost the lives of 800 men. They charged the German lines in groups, running straight into machine-gun fire and 'were mown down as if by a scythe'. A bus carrying commissars and Red Army officers tried to drive through the German lines but was brought to a halt by the *Gebirgsjäger*. Once again, instead of giving themselves up, the Russians opted to fight. Every man on the bus was killed.[65]

By mid-morning the mist had been burned away by the searing sun of a mid-summer's day. The attacking *Gebirgsjäger* sweated profusely in their heavy jackets. 'Why do we have to traipse around in these lousy plains anyway?' one complained, longing for the mountains. The best Lvov could offer was the high ground a couple of miles north of the city centre in Holosko. The scene of several days of ferocious fighting in September 1939, the hills were in German hands by early afternoon. The *Jäger* simply bypassed scattered Soviet artillery units, cavalry and infantry moving through the woods to the north of the city. Struggling to keep pace with the infantry, Hans Kreppel found the road to Lvov straddled with 'tanks, horse-drawn vehicles with dead horses and smouldering vehicles'. The houses of Rynesa – where the commanders of 32nd Tank Division had met just the previous evening – now burned. Dead Soviet soldiers lay next to dead horses. But there were dead *Gebirgsjäger* as well.

Early in the evening a reconnaissance patrol was sent into the northern outskirts of the city. It found no Russians, but plenty of enthusiastic Leopolitans decorated their 'liberators' with flowers. In 1939 1st *Gebirgs* Division had been forced to hand over Lvov to the Red Army after a week of intense fighting for the city. Its fall would have been the last major act of the Polish campaign. Twenty months later, the mountain troops were not to be denied their victory – but this time, as one officer realised, 'it was only a minor prelude. The expanse of Russia still lay ahead of us.'[66]

———

Non-commissioned officer Emilian Hindelang served in an infantry unit following the mountain troops advancing on Lvov. The road to the Galician capital was a never-ending scene of death and devastation. 'I've never seen anything like it,' he recorded in his diary. 'The Russians' retreat must have been mad chaos.' Cars, tanks and tractors lay in a tangled mass, entire batteries of howitzers lay abandoned, their barrels pointing west, their ammunition scattered around. The German dead had already been buried, but not the Russian. 'They lie around in every possible position'; many were badly burned and almost all were 'badly bloated – due to the heat, the smell is foul'. That didn't deter the Ukrainian populace from depriving the Red Army dead of their shoes and boots. Hindelang and his comrades donned gas masks, dug mass graves and began collecting the corpses.

> Some of the dead are terribly ripped to pieces. One Russian consists only of his lower body with intestines and thousands of maggots. Of another, despite a thorough search, all we find is part of a foot. I got a rope, which is wrapped around the feet of the dead, so they can be dragged to a suitable spot. There you can see what man is, a heap of stinking dirt.

And then there were the cadavers of horses, similarly bloated, the bodies so rigid their legs had to be chopped off to make burial easier. The gruesome work lasted a week. 'We are delighted when the bloody task is finished,' Hindelang wrote with relief. 'We lie down to rest, tired and full of revulsion.'[67]

In Lvov, Leopolitans who had benefitted from Soviet patronage either fled with the retreating Red Army or disappeared into the shadows. The remainder of the city's inhabitants pondered their fate: which language should they use? Ukrainian? Polish? German? 'Certainly not Russian,' wrote Polish-born Stanisław Różycki. Many fellow Jews had attempted to flee Lvov, but not the 36-year-old university assistant, nor most of the city's Jewish inhabitants. 'We are sad and helpless, depressed and resigned,' he wrote. 'I said quite a long time ago that we must endure everything in life. We cannot escape from the Germans. We must be prepared for the worst and stoically accept everything which will happen to us.'[68]

As night fell, Hubert Lanz mulled over the possibility of sending his men into Lvov. The resistance the Red Army had offered his division that Sunday persuaded him otherwise. Rather than embroil his troops in house-to-house fighting, Lanz decided to 'build a golden bridge' for the Red Army so that it could continue to withdraw to the east. 'Tomorrow Lemberg will fall into our lap like a rotten apple. Victory is surely ours,' he assured his operations officer, Hans Steets, before sending a curt message to his superior, Ludwig Kübler – the man denied victory in September 1939: *The city of Lemberg will be taken tomorrow, June 30th.*[69]

Hans Kreppel spent the night deploying his guns in the Jewish cemetery on a hillside in Holosko – almost precisely the same spot where they had been located in September 1939. He ordered the barrels trained at Lvov's citadel complex, situated on a hill just south of the city centre. His gunners waited for the order to fire. 'Thank God I do not need to give it,' Kreppel wrote. At dawn on 30 June battalion commander Josef Fleischmann and his reconnaissance party raised the German battle standard, the *Reichskriegsflagge*, on the old citadel. 'The beautiful city lies before us in the early morning mist,' an overjoyed Kreppel noted. 'Lemberg belongs to 1st *Gebirgs* Division!'

Fleischmann's battalion had penetrated the city in the small hours. The entering Germans found the final Soviet troops preparing to torch Lvov's warehouses and depots – and stopped them. By 4am, the detachment had reached the city centre where it found the metropolitan Archbishop Septyckyi sheltering in his residence next to the burning cathedral. Fifteen minutes later and Lvov's ornate city hall and market square had been seized. At 4.20am, the citadel, then the central station, the radio station – partially damaged but on air again before the day's end – the post office, the NKVD headquarters with its files still intact, the arsenal with vast quantities of weaponry, the barracks with 30 working tanks, including a dozen heavy models, the tannery, the chocolate factory, and warehouses and depots containing 'items worth millions'. By 7am, all the strategic points in Lvov were in the hands of 1st *Gebirgs* Division. It had taken the Galician capital at a cost of 800 casualties, 229 of them dead.[70]

By the time the bulk of 1st *Gebirgs* Division began marching into Lvov mid-morning, the entire city was on its feet. The yellow-blue Ukrainian flag was flying from the town hall tower and civic theatre alongside the German ensign while the windows of houses were dressed in the national colours and the swastika. 'Under a beaming morning sun,' the entering soldiers were hailed as liberators, greeted with applause and cries of '*Sieg Heil*', and decorated with flowers 'by women who have literally stripped their gardens bare'. Many Ukrainian women put on their finest dresses, 'greeting their saviours and liberators with smiles, joy, full of good hopes and illusions,' Pole Stanisław Różycki wrote. After the ragged, nervous, trigger-happy Red Army, 'the arrival of the Germans was a pleasant surprise,' Różycki noted. 'The Germans came to us as friends. Smiling, confident, rifles on their backs, usually with just a revolver, similarly hidden in its holster, and did not spread fear or panic.' German vehicles moved through 'a sea of flowers,' one Ukrainian woman wrote. 'The cars were open and officers stood erect in them.' While the officers studied maps, she watched as ethnic Germans, Poles and Ukrainians – all her friends and neighbours – walked up to the conquerors and tossed bouquets at them.

'I felt like I was in a liberation army,' one Norwegian volunteer with the SS *Wiking* Division wrote. 'The people were wild with enthusiasm.' The columns of 71st Infantry Division struggled to force their way through the city centre. 'Every soldier was festooned with flowers by the populace, who lined the road in dense rows,' junior officer Manfred *Freiherr* von Plotho wrote to his family in Potsdam. 'Every vehicle, every horse received flowers. Many women cried with joy. We really have come here as liberators from an unbearable yoke.'

The celebrations reached a hedonistic climax in the market square around 8am when the vanguard of the Nightingale Battalion – Ukrainian nationalist volunteers under German leadership – marched in singing patriotic songs. The troops were enthusiastically received not just by Ukrainians but some Poles – 'who had suffered under the Bolshevik terror and had not yet come to know the Germans,' Pole Jan Rogowski observed – and even the occasional Jew. A crowd several thousand strong roared its approval; some people even dropped to the ground and prayed.

Yet there was a darker side to the arrival of the German Army. As he and his 257th Infantry Division comrades entered Lvov, Herbert Schrödter noticed 'people are restless. Excitement, horror, anger and despair lie in the air like some explosive tension.' While Ukrainians and Poles were 'insane with joy,' one Jewish inhabitant observed, Lvov's Jews remained in their homes 'full of anxiety, fearing every minute'. And the sea of flowers and flags could not hide the damage the city had suffered. Houses burned. Dense palls of smoke drifted over the city. Shops were closed. Emil Klein – a veteran of Hitler's 1923 Munich Putsch now serving with 1st *Gebirgs* Division – found Lvov 'badly scarred by the fighting.

Entire house fronts are still burning, abandoned and shot up tanks are left in the streets. Everywhere you can see traces of the rapid flight of Soviet tanks, guns and ammunition which are strewn along the empty streets in vast numbers.' Among the blackened buildings still burning which was passed by Klein and his company was Brygidki prison. 'We want to hold our breath,' he wrote, 'but it's impossible. The entire district smells of fire and corpses.'[71]

'The Bolshevik hangmen literally waded in blood...' Lvov, 24–30 June

Dominating an entire block just five minutes' walk from Lvov's most fashionable street, Brygidki had begun life in the 17th century as a nunnery. But for the past 150 years, the city's inhabitants had come to fear the three-storey building as one of Lvov's main prisons. And in the final week of June 1941, it became the scene of some of the most bloodthirsty atrocities committed by the NKVD as they carried out Moscow's orders and eliminated 'enemies of the state' across Ukraine.

The murder had begun around dusk on Tuesday, when NKVD troops returned to Brygidki having initially abandoned the prison. Forty men were singled out at roll call. Ninety minutes later, two pistol shots fired by guards on the prison roof announced the beginning of the massacre. Wild shooting and grenades exploding followed for more than two hours. After each roll call for the next couple of days – morning, afternoon and evening – the killings continued. Bohdan Shtyha and 100 other inmates in his cell were led to one of the cellar rooms. Some men thought it was for their protection against German air raids. The terrible truth was soon revealed. Prisoners near the cellar door could hear dull hammer blows and trowels applying mortar to bricks. 'Friends, we're being walled in,' someone called out. 'It became clear,' Shtyha recalled, 'that the cellar would become our tomb.' One prisoner found the stub of a pencil; it was passed around as the condemned wrote their personal details and addresses of relatives on their shirts – until the electricity was turned off and the cellar was plunged into darkness. 'Minutes seemed like hours,' Shtyha remembered. 'One man went mad and began to scream frantically. Others were unconscious by the door. The air became harder to breathe. Blood streamed from my neighbour's nose.' Seconds later, Bohdan Shtyha passed out. Above ground, Polish prisoner Zygmunt Cybulski awoke in the small hours of Thursday to the cries of a Ukrainian farmer 'begging for her life in the inner courtyard. To save herself, she cried that she had worked for Stalin and had children.' A shot rang out. The cries ceased. Those left behind in the cells were tormented by the agonising cries and final last words of the condemned. 'Where are you taking me?' 'Give me life and freedom.' 'What do you intend to do with me?' Motor engines tried to disguise the screams and gun shots, while a large grave was dug in the courtyard; those executed simply toppled into it. One inmate watched as a family were led to the side of the pit by the guards. 'Take everything, just spare the children,' the mother implored. As she cried, the guards opened fire and all four bodies slumped into the grave. As the cells emptied and the dead piled up, one of Cybulski's fellow inmates overheard one side of a telephone conversation. 'And shoot the rest as well? Good.' But time was running out for the executioners. When one Ukrainian political prisoner was led out of Cell No.84 at 3am on Saturday morning, the Germans were at the gates of Lvov. The final victims were taken down to the cellars, their arms tied behind their backs using wire. 'A dreadful sight met my eyes: countless corpses of prisoners who had been shot and their bodies maimed with all sorts of instruments,' he testified two decades later. 'We were ordered to face the wall. On seeing the pile of bodies with smashed skulls, I fainted and fell on top of the corpses.' The remaining prisoners – about 600 – were locked in their cells, prompting fears Brygidki was about to be set alight. But the guards formed up in the courtyard and marched out. Silence descended upon the prison, but no inmate dared to make a tentative break for freedom until mid-day, seeking shelter in the crypt of St George's Cathedral. As they moved furtively through Lvov's streets, they noticed Red Army units abandoning the city. When Bohdan Shtyha regained consciousness, he found he was lying in the prison courtyard, surrounded not by NKVD guards but Ukrainian militia who offered water from their canteens to the prisoners and handed out clothes to those, like Shtyha, who were able to stand. 'Friend, run. Run away as soon as possible,' one of the militiamen told him. He did, but when he reached his home near the huge Lychakov cemetery a couple of miles away, his wife slammed the door in his face because she no longer recognised him.[72]

For those who dared to venture inside Brygidki – it was probably sometime on Sunday 29 June before the first anxious Leopolitans began to look for relatives – the horrors within almost defied description. Farmer's wife Warwara Soziada headed there hoping to find her husband Josefa. She did not. But she did find 'a mass of corpses lying butchered on a table', the body of one man sitting in an armchair with a bayonet driven into his mouth, and a girl, aged about eight, hanged by a towel attached to a lamp in one cell. 'The sight was so dreadful that I almost fainted,' she recalled. 'I had to be taken home by several people.' Some prisoners were decapitated with an axe; others were set on fire after their hands had been tied behind their backs. Women's breasts were sliced off. Children were found hung up on meat hooks like cattle in the slaughterhouse, or found nailed to walls. A young Ukrainian who'd escaped the prison guided senior military doctor Georg Saeltzer around. He found four cells filled with bodies – the most recently slain on top, the corpses at the bottom of the pile already beginning to decompose badly. Worst of all, the cellar, its floor 'swimming with blood'. One reservist officer donned a gas mask to search the basement of the 330-year-old building. 'In one corner of the vault there was a mountain of corpses piled on top of each other more than one metre high and covered with a thin layer of sand,' he reported. His men urged him to inspect the neighbouring cellar where a hole had been cut. He shone his torch through 'and saw several corpses on the floor'. It would take three days to recover all the bodies from the basement – Georg Saeltzer counted 423, boys as young as ten, teenage girls, and elderly men and women. All had been shot in the back of the head or neck, or else badly beaten, their mouths wide open, their eyes popping out. Another German officer reported women and children 'with their tongues cut off, eyes gouged out, nailed to doors and the floors'. Several inmates had been scalped, while the genitalia of some men were cut, the wounds sprinkled with salt. In all, 739 people were murdered by the Soviet authorities in Brygidki prison at the end of June 1941. Its horrors were repeated in Lvov's other two main prisons – and the tally of dead surpassed.[73]

Georg Saeltzer's gruesome tour continued with a visit to the military prison in Zamarstynów Street, ten minutes' walk north of the city centre. 'Entering the cellars there was such a foul smell of decomposition and so much blood in the mountains of corpses that we all had to put on a Polish gas mask to carry out the necessary investigation,' he reported. Saeltzer and his colleagues found two cellars filled to the ceiling with corpses – 'young girls, women and men, in layers, stacked on top of each other'. Saeltzer ordered them removed to receive a proper burial in Lvov's Catholic cemetery. He stopped counting at 460. The remaining 511 bodies had decayed too severely to allow recovery. The cellars were covered with chlorinated lime and bricked up. The corpses which were brought out of Zamarstynów were 'almost impossible to identify,' Jan Maksymilian Sokołowski, one of the leaders of the Polish underground movement in eastern Galicia, recalled. 'The sight of them was shocking: bloated, faces without eyes, covered in blood, juices streaming out of them, probably gnawed by rats.'[74]

Nowhere in Lvov at the end of June and beginning of July 1941 were there more horrific – and heartrending – scenes than at the city's main prison, Lvov No.1, the NKVD's principal interrogation centre. Located halfway up a hill between the university district and the old citadel and overlooked by Habsburg-era apartment blocks with ornate façades, Lontskoho Street had been built by the Austro-Hungarians towards the end of the 19th century at the rear of the new police station to hold 1,500 prisoners over three floors of cells. In June 1941 it held an estimated 3,500 inmates, with just six toilets and nine wash basins serving their most basic needs. Almost half of them would be murdered in a four-day frenzy of killing.

The ceilings of the cells were smeared with blood, while in the interrogation room there was a crust of blood 20cm above the floor. 'So the Bolshevik hangmen literally waded in blood,' an official German report observed. 'From the faces of the dead, their torn clothes, as well as other signs, it is clear that those arrested suffered terribly. Every one was literally beaten to death.' In the guardroom – a large hall – bodies were stacked 'like blocks of wood' up to neck height. A non-commissioned officer found 'pregnant women hanged by their feet. Someone had cut off noses, ears, eyes, fingers, hands, sometimes the arms and legs, and in some cases the hearts, from women.' He claimed 300 children aged between two and 17 had been nailed to the courtyard wall where they were tortured. Two decades later, one horrific sight was still fixed in the memory of soldier Herbert Gierschke: the corpse of a pregnant woman. 'Her unborn child had been cut out of her body and someone had placed this child in the body of a priest lying beside her and sewn it up again.' Gierschke's comrades took photographs. 'I probably still have one of the pictures in my home.' Another eyewitness claimed to have seen the head of a child jutting out from the cut-open stomach of a pregnant woman, a girl who'd been raped, leaving her genitalia smeared in blood. One Polish woman found the corpse of her friend who'd been arrested just three days before the German attack 'for political reasons'. The body was in a dreadful condition: 'The back of her head was smashed so that the brain mass was visible. The right half of her was blue, the left streaming with blood. Her right thigh was completely blue.' Next to her lay the body of another women who had clearly been burned on her thigh, while the left breast had been cut off and bandaged using a torn shirt. Her skull looked 'as if it had been beaten with a chisel'. There were men without genitals – cut off then wrapped in newspaper and stuffed in a jacket pocket in one instance. And in the cellar, the worst sight of all: a 12-year-old girl hanging on an iron bar; her face and dress were covered in blood after a meat hook was driven into her mouth. Georg Saeltzer found the cap of a German airman with the name sewn into it, plus a parachute belt. As bodies were disinterred, the corpses of four Luftwaffe personnel were recovered. As at Brygidki, most victims had been killed by shots to the neck, but female prisoners suffered particularly brutal treatment: their hair was tousled, their thighs scratched, one with a right breast cut off. Austrian Lance Corporal Paul Rubelt spared no details for his girlfriend at home in the mountains of Styria. 'Many people had been skinned, the men had their genitals cut off, eyes gouged out, feet or arms hacked off, nailed to the walls, or 30 or 40 people were locked in a room which was then bricked up so they all suffocated in a wretched situation,' he told her. And Edward Chruslicki, a 39-year-old Polish caretaker, testified seeing a naked priest nailed to the wall of a cell. 'He had literally been crucified. They had beaten nails through his hands and feet, which formed a cross.' A red strip of cloth hung from his feet with an inscription in Russian: *Christ will save you!* On closer inspection, Chruslicki noticed a cross had been carved in the priest's forehead. With the help of several other people searching the prison, the body was cut down – revealing another cross, this time carved in his back. It wasn't the only horror in this cell. The floor was littered with corpses, many of them mutilated: a woman with a breast cut off, another with both her ears chopped off, on a third a strip of skin torn off the face. And finally there were bodies with mouths sewn up. The caretaker saw three corpses mutilated thus. He could bear no more and left the prison 'filled with horror'.

Chruslicki refused to believe rumours about atrocities at a nearby orphanage – until he visited it. 'In one room I saw the corpses of 30 children hanging – children aged six to 15. They'd hanged the children using a pickaxe through the mouth.' Dressed or undressed, the corpses hung from the walls and ceiling.[75]

The prison courtyard soon became the focal point of all Lvov's grief and sorrow as relatives moved among corpses which had been disinterred or recovered from the cells. There were two mass graves: one full of corpses and covered with earth, a second half-filled with bodies which had only a sprinkling of soil on them. A father pointed to bloody nails in a wooden fence where his 18-year-old daughter had supposedly been crucified. Reservist officer Captain Hans Kondruss, a veteran of World War I, came across the body of a Ukrainian Girl Guide whose heart had been cut out, while old men and boys had 'literally been butchered'. 'Legs and arms had been deftly cut off and were lying around. Ukrainian priests had been deliberately targeted – strapped to boards and three-inch nails bashed into their heads. Others had been hanged with their heads facing down, nails driven into the soles of their feet – and all while they were still alive.'

Though no-one in his family had been arrested, German teenager Georg Jestadt still felt drawn to the site. 'People stumbled around the lines of butchered corpses with handkerchiefs in front of their faces,' Jestadt remembered. The sight of the bodies and the forlorn relatives moving among them made his skin crawl, yet he too walked up and down the rows of the dead, looking for friends or neighbours. Suddenly there was a terrible scream and a woman collapsed – a neighbour. 'I hurried to her and then I saw the men in her life – father and son beside each other, faces to the ground and with huge bloody holes in the backs of their heads,' the schoolboy wrote. 'They'd been finished off from behind at close range. We stood in front of them as if turned to stone.'[76]

Of the 5,424 people incarcerated in Lvov's prisons on 22 June 1941, the NKVD claimed 2,464 had been put to death by the 28th. Recent research places the death toll somewhere between 3,100 and 3,500, while historians at the memorial museum which now occupies Lontskoho prison came up with the precise total of 3,391 dead. Many were never identified – relatives were unable to put a name to fewer than half of the 1,681 people executed in Lontskoho. Someone found the NKVD ledger – running to more than 190 pages – and stood outside the jail reading the names out. With each announcement, there were loud wails followed by a push towards the cellars or courtyard. The future politician Franz-Josef Strauss, a 25-year-old Bavarian serving with an artillery battery, was repeatedly accosted in the streets by hysterical Polish or Ukrainian women, who grabbed his arm and showed him the photographs of missing husbands or sons. Yet so badly beaten, mutilated or decomposed were the corpses that a month later, people could still be found outside the prisons begging for news of their relatives.

The dead were either political prisoners – Ukrainian and Polish intellectuals, nationalists, capitalists – or petty criminals. Many had been arrested since 22 June, denounced by neighbours, concierges and janitors in apartment blocks – as had been the case in Kaunas and Vilnius – prompting their disappearance 'with lightning speed'. But above all, the German military investigators blamed Lvov's Jews – 'particularly willing tools' of the Soviet authorities. They believed fewer than one per cent of the dead were Jewish – the true figure was nearly seven per cent – and these, the Germans concluded, were Zionists. 'It is clear that here in Lvov the Jews made an intimate pact with the Bolsheviks and hence at the very least indirectly sent some victims to their doom at the hands of the hangmen.'[77]

With the bodies of more than 3,000 people decaying in Lvov's prisons, 'the stench of the plague hung over the city' as the German Army entered. Soldiers felt compelled to put handkerchiefs over their mouths so overwhelming was the smell of decay and decomposition. It was too much for one battle-hardened officer who collapsed when subjected to the sights, sounds and smells of Lvov. Revulsion quickly turned to anger. Here on the last day of June 1941 was confirmation of all the Nazis' horror stories about Bolshevism. Until now, Manfred *Freiherr* von Plotho had dismissed them as 'a primitive appeal to basic instincts. Today I know better,' he told his family.

> Up to now in my life, I've not known what hate means. But as of today I know this feeling. Here there can be no compromise, here we are the tough soldiers of Adolf Hitler, either leading European culture to new heights or dragging it with us into the abyss of total destruction. Well, our past successes against tough and dogged opponents give us confidence to be victors here too.

'The Jews are at the forefront of all these shameful deeds,' Norwegian war correspondent Per Asbjørn Pedersen, accompanying the SS *Wiking* Division, wrote. 'And I can tell you right now: not a single Norwegian will return as a friend of the Jews. You'll never hear us say one good word about the Jews – we've seen too much.' After what Pedersen and his countrymen had experienced in Lvov, 'there was no one who felt sorry for the Jews, on the contrary'.

Hans Kondruss had seen 'thousands of dead' on the fields of Byelorussia in 1916 – 'bodies torn apart and battered by our barrage' – and 'war in its most terrible forms' at Verdun and Flanders. 'What I saw here surpasses everything!' he told his family. 'There, war was war, always something impersonal, a type of natural disaster, which provoked terror but here it was beasts in human form on a killing spree. Never in the history of nations have there been such atrocities, has the animal instinct in man revealed itself as clearly as here.'

'A dark chapter of human history was written here,' Kondruss concluded. 'Shaken to the core, we observed everything, dominated by a single thought: *if these beasts were given a free hand to deal with our people at home. Ja,* that's not worth thinking about.'

One non-commissioned officer agreed:

All this would have been visited upon the German people had Bolshevism stolen a march on us. Those constant whingers and philistines that we still have in the Reich should listen up. They should see what Bolshevism in its purest form means, then they would fall to their knees and thank the Führer for sparing Germany this. I've seen it as have many other German soldiers. We all thank the Führer for allowing us to see the Bolshevik 'paradise'. We swear that this plague must be destroyed root and branch.[78]

In Zolkiev, just up the road from Lvov, signaller Wilhelm Moldenhauer watched the mutilated corpses of two dozen women and children being disinterred. 'It's unimaginable that men can carry out such atrocities,' he seethed as he stood at the prison entrance. 'The horror of death was etched on the faces of the people standing in front of the gate. Once again it was the Jews who had their hand in the terrible business. The Bolsheviks have carried out these terrible murders in every town.'[79]

As in the Baltic States and Byelorussia, so too in Ukraine. *Barbarossa* began to assume the form of a modern-day holy war. 'They talk of the struggle against Bolshevism as if it's a crusade,' Roman Catholic priest Arnold Brinz, serving with 132nd Infantry Division, wrote. 'Will our victory – which I do not doubt – re-open the doors of churches and chapels? Can we get the resurrection bells tolling again in a land which has become godless? Is the war a holy one?' The merest sight of Soviet prisoners – 'mostly Mongolians' – appalled Berlin infantryman Herbert Schrödter. 'Mongols in Galicia,' he fumed. 'The hordes from the Asian steppe once again stand at the gates of Europe! Now I realise the objective of my war: saving European culture from cultureless steppe, saving Western Christianity from godless Bolshevism.' A Stuttgart doctor serving with 25th Infantry Division told his wife: 'We have begun the final battle with Jewish Bolshevism. A ruthless, bitter life and death struggle will rage everywhere. Just don't let me fall into Bolshevik captivity!' One Norwegian volunteer wrote to his family: 'The German people know what they are fighting for, and they are fighting with a fanatical, burning hatred of their Jewish adversaries.' A medic in 125th Infantry Division wrote enthusiastically: 'Adolf and I are marching against our great enemy, Russia. One of my great wishes has thus been fulfilled.' And 1st *Gebirgs* Division battalion commander Josef Salminger felt compelled to address an order of the day to his men:

When we began our attack on the Bolshevik Army by crossing the demarcation line on June 22nd 1941, many soldiers in my battalion did not understand the reasons for this struggle. They did not understand that this struggle was essential for our people and that we had to destroy an enemy whom we can only describe as an animal and beast. This Communist cabal of criminals must be completely wiped out and destroyed. I recommend that every soldier in my battalion to take the opportunity to inspect the prisons in Lvov to finally grasp the type of beasts we face…

Every sceptic would be won over by the sight of these inhuman atrocities. Then he will understand the necessity of this struggle against the horde of Jewish-Bolshevik criminals and realise that every German soldier who has to shed blood and lose his life in this decisive struggle between order and chaos must be avenged a thousand times over. This will be – and remain – the oath of III Battalion until the annihilation and elimination of the Bolshevik Army.[80]

As afternoon turned to evening in Lvov, intelligence officers Ernst zu Eickern and Hans Koch raced through the city centre streets determined to reach the meeting rooms of the Provitsa cultural group and cork the bottle of the genie released earlier in the day. They were too late. Ukrainian nationalist Yaroslav Stecko was proclaiming the country's independence to an ecstatic audience. The decree by independence leader Stepan Bandera announcing the formation of a Ukrainian government and 'the re-establishment of the Ukrainian State, for which entire generations of the best sons of Ukraine have made sacrifices', had already been read out. The hall filled with the sound of applause before Koch took to the stage to address the audience first in German, then in Ukrainian. Koch made no mention of liberation or a new government. War was still raging – 'there was no time at all for politics'. For now the Germans – and the Germans alone – were in charge in Ukraine. The intelligence officer closed with a '*Sieg Heil*' for Hitler, enthusiastically acknowledged by the audience. As the cries faded, the crowd began to sing. '*Shche ne vmerla Ukraïna*' – Ukraine Has Not Yet Perished – the national anthem, filled the hall. Posters quickly appeared across the city featuring Bandera's proclamation. They lasted no more than an hour, hurriedly torn down by Lvov's 'liberators'.[81]

There was a strange mood in the Galician capital this Monday evening. Euphoria at liberation, yes. But also a rising tide of anger. At the newly established military commandant's headquarters in a four-storey townhouse on the north side of the market square, one staff officer observed that the 'atrocities carried out by the Reds have inflamed people', while another, Eugen Meyding, noticed 'the faint whiff of a pogrom' in the air. It was far from faint.[82]

'WELL, JEWS, REVENGE IS SWEET…' LVOV, 1 JULY

By mid-morning on Tuesday 1 July, the mood in Lvov had turned ugly. For days – even when the Soviets still ruled the city – the underground Ukrainian nationalist movement had distributed leaflets, fanning hatred. 'Do not throw your weapons away now,' they urged. 'Seize them. Destroy the enemy. People! Know! Moscow, Poles, Hungarians, Judaism – these are your enemies. Destroy them.' Now these same nationalists emerged from the shadows, grabbed whatever weapon was to hand, perhaps slipped on a yellow-blue armband, and began to patrol the streets. One Jew stumbled into one such group as he made his way into the city centre. As soon as the militiaman realised he was dealing with a Jew, he began yelling, 'Go to work in Brygidki prison.' A group of Ukrainians began to gather – and then began to 'bloodily beat' any Jew who refused to follow the 'orders' issued by the militia. Norwegian SS volunteer Ørnulf Olav Bjørnstad rode through the city centre in a truck. As it stopped in heavy traffic, he watched a smartly dressed gentleman in a blue suit being harangued by a couple. 'Bandit, Jew,' they yelled, before the husband grabbed a shovel and began attacking the man in the suit, who ran between the trucks in a bid to escape. All he succeeded in doing, however, was run into the Ukrainian militia who beat him to a pulp. Convinced he was dead, Bjørnstad watched the attackers dig a shallow grave, toss the body in then cover it with a thin layer of soil. 'When they've finished, we can see that the man isn't dead – the grave rises with his breath,' Bjørnstad wrote. 'I think this is dreadful to look at and ask our squad leader to do something. Even he thinks it's bad and finishes the man off with a shot.' Another Norwegian soldier claimed to have seen 'Jews hanging in the trees', while a comrade watched 'Poles' chase 'Jews in front of German military vehicles and the vehicles drove over them'.[83]

Soon, rather than individual Jews, entire groups were being attacked, driven by club and whip towards Brygidki by men wearing armbands in the Ukrainian colours. A Ukrainian mob burst into the apartment of Rabbi Jecheskiel Lewin. They found only his 16-year-old son Kurt. The teenager was grabbed by the collar and led into the street, kicked and punched all the time by his abductor. 'The Ukrainian and Polish population greeted every Jew with a wild howling in the street,' the rabbi's son remembered. The baying soon turned into acts of violence. 'They beat us with sticks and umbrellas, kicked and scratched us. It wasn't just men who did this but women too who went crazy.' German soldier Fritz Spod saw animated young men – teenagers through to some in their mid-30s – armed with sticks forcing their way into the homes and apartments of Jews, emerging a few minutes later with a family who joined other prisoners in ever-growing numbers. 'As the groups formed columns, the civilians armed with sticks handled the Jews particularly roughly, striking them when they failed to follow instructions quickly enough.' From the window of his apartment near the prison, law professor Maurycy Allerhand could see Jews being beaten. 'If someone fell down, someone kicked him with his boots. Many Jews bled, and, if somebody who had fallen got up again, he was beaten again and driven in the direction of Brygidki prison.' Men jumped on the backs of Jews, hitting them with sticks – as if they were riding horses – or else simply beat their heads to a pulp. Wilek Markiewicz heard the voice of a woman pleading for mercy as a mob dragged her through Smolki Square, no more than five minutes' walk from Brygidki. 'People, let me go,' she begged. 'I've never done anything bad to anyone.' Next came the voices of men. 'Don't listen to her! Finish her off!' What especially shocked Markiewicz, however, was the sight of Ukrainian women, many young farmers' wives, 'who were every bit as cruel as the men'.

But this was also pogrom as spectacle, almost entertainment. As in Vienna in 1938, Jews were made to clean the streets as bystanders cajoled them. One man was forced to remove horse dung from the highway by shovelling it into his cap; elsewhere Jews were given toothbrushes or handkerchiefs to scrub the pavement. 'What a terribly debasing feeling it was when doctors and professors cleaned the streets with shovels in their hands,' Lilith Stern recalled. Groups of female Jews were forced to wash German trucks rolling through Lvov bound for the front to the east. The enormous poster of Stalin near the city's central post office was ripped down. Jubilant Ukrainians danced on its remnants to the applause of onlookers, while just a few feet away Jews were beaten in the same street by a mob brandishing shovels and screaming: '*Jude, Jude!*' Some columns of Jews were forced to move along on their knees, others made to crawl on all fours. The militia made their prisoners sing Russian songs, give three cheers for Stalin, or else chant 'We want Stalin!' Jakub Dentei saw 'thousands of Jews beaten and cruelly mutilated, completely naked women and children streaming with blood, I saw old men bleeding to death in the street, and German "heroes" who rejoiced at this awful spectacle and took photographs.' Jacob Gerstenfeld watched a group of elderly, women and children forced to remove paving stones from a bomb crater with their bare hands 'under a hail of blows'. And all while life in Lvov seemingly went on as normal. 'Passers-by stopped for a moment or two, some to laugh at the "ridiculous" look of the victims, and went calmly on.' To Jewish lawyer Edmund Kessler it seemed as if Judgment Day had come, with judgment passed – and punishment meted out – by the mob in an 'orgy of bloodshed'. Occasionally someone in the crowd might protest at the horror before them, or even intervene to try to save the unfortunate Jew being butchered. The mob quickly silenced them.[84]

As for the victims, most seemingly accepted their terrible fate 'with a dumb resignation'. Rarely did they fight back. Those who dared to escape were quickly hunted down and forced back into the ranks of unfortunate souls being hounded towards Brygidki. Bystanders struck out at the Jewish columns with whatever weapon they had to hand: brooms, carpet-beaters, stones. The streets leading to the prison soon filled with the howls and screams of dying Jews – and the triumphant cheers of Ukrainian nationalists, while the pavement and cobbles were rapidly stained with blood.

By the time Jews reached the prison entrance, many were 'already half-dead'. In the courtyard, where Kurt Lewin found the stench of decomposition almost overpowering, the Jews were split into two groups: one to work outside bricking up the windows, the other to haul corpses from the cellar and lay them out on the grass in the yard – by far the worst job, as the teenager remembered: 'Liquid flowed from the corpses and sometimes a decomposed hand or leg came off the body. The faces were terrible, they were distorted by the contortions of death. The skin came off some of them. When you carried the bodies, the flabby, feeble arms slumped against our legs, leaving behind a damp mark which smelled.'

The work, Lewin concluded, 'was already sufficiently macabre'. Now it became sadistic as Germans and Ukrainians landed blows on the Jews. 'They beat us with rifle butts, iron bars, whips,' the 16-year-old recalled. 'If somebody fell under the blows, they put their foot on his face, thorax or stomach until the victim exhaled his last breath.' One of the tormentors stood out: an elegantly dressed Ukrainian wearing a beautifully embroidered shirt who fixed an iron bar to a stick and timed his beatings to coincide with the clock, striking his victims on the head. Lewin continued:

He ripped the eyes out of several people or tore their ears off. Finally the stick broke. He didn't stop to think for long. He reached for a half-burned piece of firewood and hit my neighbour on the head. His skull shattered, his brain splashed everywhere, splattering my clothes and face. The unfortunate soul died immediately. The Ukrainian yob breathed heavily, leant against the wall to rest for a moment. The horrible, brutish face of this sadist, pale, with bloodshot protruding eyes, aroused disgust and horror.

By late morning, the emphasis at Brygidki began to change from 'cleaning up' and arbitrary beatings to plain killing. The freshly arrived ranks of *Einsatzgruppe* C ordered Jews to face the prison wall, then opened fire. Lewin observed as his school friend Henryk, his older brother and their father were forced into the yard. The eldest son was shot first – the burst of fire from a submachine-gun ripped the boy apart. The Germans then ordered the dead boy's father and younger brother to remove the corpse and toss it onto a growing mound of other Jewish bodies. 'When they came back, they were separated and Henryk was shot. He just about managed to shout out to his father with a breaking voice: "Goodbye!"' And there the shooting stopped. The father was spared – though he gradually went out of his mind and died the following year in the Jewish ghetto the Germans would establish in the city.

Some time before mid-day, Lewin's father Jecheskiel, a well-known and respected rabbi, was brought to Brygidki in his regalia. 'It is hard to describe my despair, the despair of a child who cannot help his father,' Kurt wrote. 'The powerlessness and the pain suffocated me. I pulled my hair out, ripped my shirt collar off as if I was going to suffocate. Something was tearing at my soul at this moment. I turned to stone. I watched, but my eyes didn't take in what happened next.'

Under pain of blows from the butts of German rifles, the rabbi was forced to join a group of Jews already standing next to the wall. He led them in prayer. First, the Confessions of Sin. Then, in a loud voice, *Shema Yisrael*. 'Hear, O Israel, the Lord our God, the Lord is one…' The Germans opened fire.

At one point, the distraught Lewin remembered a senior German officer striding into the prison and demanding an end to the massacre. And the shootings did indeed stop. But the terrible task of removing the corpses continued. As did the insults and abuse. 'Well, Jews, revenge is sweet,' one German snarled. Others photographed the tormented Jews. Every now and then, the SS officer seemingly orchestrating the massacre would remove his mask and address the unfortunate Jews in the courtyard. 'The whole world is bleeding because of you. Look what you've done!'

It went on like this until dusk, when the surviving Jews were ordered to go home but report for further work duties at 4am. Kurt Lewin reckoned 2,000 Jews had passed through the gates of Brygidki on Tuesday morning – probably double the actual figure. When the last were marched out of the prison grounds as darkness fell, there were just 80 still alive.[85]

In the largely Jewish quarter around Zamarstynów prison, Rózia Wagner was among hundreds of people hauled out of their homes and pushed and kicked towards the nearby jail where a line of baying men, women and children – 'the scum of the city' – lashed out at the passing Jews, punching and kicking them, pulling at hair. Far worse lay in store in the courtyard. While most Jews were forced to exhume the bodies of inmates killed by the NKVD, some, like Wagner, were made to build small piles of sand in the courtyard, allowing them to observe what happened:

> Inhuman cries, heads beaten in, abused bodies and ghostly, disfigured faces of the
> beaten, streaming with blood and dirt, helped unleash bloodthirsty instincts and

a mob howling with excitement. Unconscious women and old people, who lay on the ground close to death, were covered with bruises from sticks, kicked and dragged across the ground... The blood in our veins froze. When the still-unsatisfied hangmen ripped the clothes from the body of one woman and beat her naked body mercilessly with sticks, we begged German soldiers who were crossing the courtyard to intervene. They replied in a tone which showed they approved what was happening: 'This is the revenge of the Ukrainians.'

German troops passing Zamarstynów prison took photographs, promising '*Das wird im Stürmer sein*' – 'They'll appear in *Der Sturmer*', the most virulent of antisemitic rags.[86]

Curiosity drew 20-year-old Bavarian Heinrich Heimkes, serving with a mountain infantry signals unit, to Lontskoho prison. He watched a priest, accompanied by altar boys carrying burning candles, moving among the rows of the dead, blessing the fallen. But in the neighbouring yard, SS troops were at work. One of the firing squad relished his task. 'He pulled an old man by his beard and shot him personally,' Heimkes recalled. 'I could not understand how a man could be capable of something like that.' A teenage Jew who spoke good German pleaded for his life. The German troops were inclined to let him go, but not the mob. Heimkes considered intervening to save the boy, but feared 'they'd put me up against the wall as well. So, I left him – that still haunts me today,' he wrote decades later.

The courtyard, remembered Jan Rogowski, searching for a friend, presented 'a terrible sight. On the grass in the courtyard lay around 200 corpses of men, gruesomely murdered'. Rogowski could see bodies being removed from a large pit by a group of Jews, including Jakób Birkenfeld, who were at the mercy of the Ukrainians. 'They struck with anything to hand – knives, axes and shovels,' Birkenfeld recalled. 'They beat me unconscious. They knocked my teeth out and struck my head with an iron bar. I had a hole in my head large enough to fit two fingers in. I had wounds on my arms and legs and was completely covered in blood.'

After the Jews had finishing recovering the dead, they were forced 'to jog around the inner courtyard keeping our hands above our heads,' said Abraham Goldberg. Some, the elderly especially, collapsed and were simply left lying in the yard. When the running stopped, the torture did not. Someone yelled: 'Run the gauntlet', and Ukrainian militiamen fixed bayonets and fell into line in two columns. Jews were forced to pass between the ranks as the Ukrainians struck out at them. The first men to attempt to run the gauntlet almost all died. 'Those who followed had to run over those who were lying on the ground,' Goldberg recalled. He threw himself to the ground almost immediately when his turn came and pretended to be dead. He only escaped after being loaded onto a truck with the other corpses.

By the afternoon, the attacks of the mob began to be replaced by a more organised torment as Lvov's Jews were rounded up and force-marched to the three prisons. Edmund Kessler watched one group sullenly march uphill towards Lontskoho, hounded by a rabid crowd who jeered their disapproval, while children spat and the militia lashed out. 'All they lack are crowns of thorns and crosses,' Kessler observed. 'Their pain is the pain of the Jewish nation, their blood is its blood.' One elderly man collapsed, unable to take the beatings any more. His fellow Jews tried to help him up until a German soldier fired a shot in the air, strode over and finished the old man off with his rifle butt. When the Jews entered the prison courtyard, they ran a gauntlet of German soldiers and Ukrainian militia who beat them with iron bars, or were showered by stones hurled by the furious crowd. 'The manner in which the Jews endured this catastrophe was truly admirable,' Berliner Herbert Schrödter noted. He watched as a giant of a Ukrainian picked up a board, swung it over his head and brought it crashing down on the head of a Jew. The victim fell to his knees, recovered his composure and stood upright once more, slightly stunned, but still calm. Schrödter saw only one person break down: a Jewish teenager. She threw herself at a German soldier, wrapped her arms around his neck and shouted: 'Help me, help me, I am innocent.' Slightly embarrassed, the German did not react. The mob seized the girl and forced her into the prison. In the grounds, some were shot at random; most were ordered to bury – or re-bury – inmates murdered by the NKVD. Some had to dig graves with their bare hands; others were given children's shovels. All were subject to arbitrary acts. And almost every one faced a German bullet at the end of their purgatory.[87]

———

For the most part, German soldiers watched rather than participated in the pogrom. They took photographs, posed for the newsreel cameras, lapped up the public adulation as liberators and largely supported the acts of vengeance committed before them. Jews had 'acted like Asiatic beasts', 21-year-old mountain infantryman Werner Jacobi wrote – he never actually ventured into any of the prisons, but lapped up the stories of women with breasts cut off, priests with crosses carved in their bodies and other tortures – 'all carried out on living bodies'. It justified the actions of Ukrainian nationalists 'scouring the city for perpetrators and eradicating them without mercy'. Soldier Lothar Hochschulz was appalled by the scenes unfolding before his eyes – but not for any moral reasons. 'I was quite happy if Jews were killed,' he wrote home. 'I simply didn't want to see it.' But after visiting one of Lvov's prisons, he was 'shaken to the very core' and became convinced that, even though they were acting 'like rabid dogs', the Ukrainians' actions were justified. When Hochschulz stopped a Jewish looter, he chose not to shoot the man, but draw the attention of the mob. When the Jew tried to flee, the soldier put his foot out. The man fell. The mob pounced. 'He was beaten to death,' Hochschulz wrote. 'Like a fly, a pesky insect.' To Finnish chaplain Ensio Pihkala, serving with the *Wiking* Division, the horrors of Lvov confirmed to him that this 'is a holy war – the Bolsheviks and the dreadful terror of the secret police in this country must be stopped'. For one anti-tank gunner in 1st *Gebirgs* Division, the Ukrainians had not gone far enough. 'We should put many more of these spawns of the devil up against the wall than we've done to date,' he told his family. Yet fellow *Gebirgsjäger* Fritz Gradner was horrified by the sight of Jews being 'dragged out of their houses and beaten in a god-awful manner. This afternoon these acts became so bad that we had to step in.' Such interventions were rare and spontaneous. Not one senior officer on the staff of 1st *Gebirgs* Division issued orders to put an end to what the unit's diarist called 'a proper pogrom'. Instead, at last light, just ten minutes' walk from the horrors of Lontskoho, the division's staff gathered on the terrace of the citadel which offered a fine view of the city. Lvov had been captured, the mountain infantry granted 48 hours' rest. Satisfied with their work, the officers watched darkness fall this Tuesday. 'A fire flares up,' artillery officer Hans Kreppel noted. 'Thanks to its red glow you can clearly see the silhouette of a church.'[88]

———

Herbert Schrödter quickly left Lontskoho and continued through the city. The men had not marched far before the scene changed completely:

> On the left side of the street there is a park, on the right side there is a row of houses. On the balcony on the first floor of a house an elderly gentleman sits in a deck chair and reads his newspaper calmly. On the second floor of the next house, two blonde teenage girls stand on the balcony in flowery summer dresses and wave happily to us. What a contrast! Still filled with the gruesome overabundance of inhuman brutality, I now stare at this image of peace. Just around the street corner, horror hangs over the city, raging hatred and death. And here is peace, tranquillity and cheerfulness! How close life and death, love and hate, peace and turmoil, war and peace live together![89]

Nearby – and shortly before a curfew came into effect – Edmund Kessler risked a stroll through the city. The gutters of Kopernika Street, leading to Lontskoho, were brimming with bodies, 'some of them still alive and scarcely breathing'. The Poles and Ukrainians who ventured into the streets this evening walked past these poor souls with indifference, but a few Jews who'd been spared the day's horrors, like Kessler, tried to help some survivors. Most of those still alive dragged their beaten bodies into Lvov's side streets in the hope no-one would find them there. 'In tattered rags,' Edmund Kessler observed, they resembled 'ghosts more than humans.'[90] Somewhere between 7,000 and 8,000 Jews died in the streets and prison courtyards of Lvov this day. Barely 100 of them were Communists, informers or Party functionaries.

'IT'S NOT WAR ANY MORE...' GALICIA, LATE JUNE, EARLY JULY

The pogrom in Lvov was no anomaly. Galicia at the end of June and beginning of July 1941 was ablaze as Ukrainians exacted revenge in nearly three dozen towns and villages. Almost without fail, the catalyst was the discovery of butchered prisoners in the abandoned NKVD jails. And the victims of the revenge were almost exclusively Jewish.

Złoczów was in German hands by the small hours of 1 July. The highway from the Galician capital was littered with 'an unholy mess' of wrecked and abandoned vehicles: 'trucks with ammunition, guns pulled by tractors, signals vehicles, cars and tanks'. As for Złoczów itself, 'things look wild,' company commander Sigismund von Gemmingen noted. The streets were littered with rubble, shattered beams, destroyed vehicles, craters and dead Russians. And, above all, knocked-out Soviet tanks, 'dozens of them', their barrels uselessly pointing skywards. A strong smell of burning filled the air. Złoczów was 'an inferno of destruction'.[91]

The mob were on the streets at first light. Rolling through the town centre, the crews of 9th Panzer Division's tanks watched inhabitants trying to topple an oversized statue of Lenin – they'd already deprived it of his head. Samuel Tennenbaum watched crowds raid government warehouses until two German non-commissioned officers drew up in a staff car and began to fire into the mass, killing one Jew, a Ukrainian peasant girl and several more. The mob scattered, only to re-form around the bodies a few minutes later when the Germans drove off. Members of the Jewish community carried away the body of their compatriot. The remaining corpses were left on the pavement as a pool of crimson grew around them.[92]

There were even grimmer sights in Złoczów's prison, located in the 17th-century citadel on the city's eastern outskirts: 649 corpses buried in mass graves. Adjutant Bruno Brehm ran into 'one long procession of weeping women' outside Złoczów. As he and a fellow officer approached the citadel, they were struck by a 'sweetish, nauseating smell', quickly followed by the sight of corpses being recovered from the moat and laid out on the reverse slope. In the castle grounds, crying women and children ignored the thousands of flies and moved among ten rows of bodies, looking for husbands, sons and fathers. An elderly lady grabbed Brehm by the arm. 'My husband was a senior doctor in the Austrian Army. He's lying over there with his two sons!' she told him. 'Before they pulled out they killed the entire Ukrainian intelligentsia – and mutilated almost every one!' Infantryman Fritz Wittke immediately blamed the 'sadistic bloodlust' of the town's Jews – they accounted for three out of every four of Złoczów's inhabitants. 'They rounded up these poor, amicable people, dragged them into the citadel and murdered them in a bestial manner,' he wrote. These latest 'crimes' were 'a new link in a chain of evidence – a fire which will burn inside us until the last Jew has disappeared from Europe. This war means the end of Judaism in Europe.'[93]

By mid-day Złoczów was a divided town. Ukrainians were in the streets, flying their national flag, waving swastikas. A legless man, pushing himself forward on a little board with wheels, raised his right hand in a Hitler salute. The city's Jews were in hiding – but young Ukrainians were all too eager to identify Jewish apartments for Złoczów's new masters. German troops soon burst into Samuel Tennenbaum's flat – looking not for its Jewish residents, but plunder. They seized two cameras and a Japanese silk raincoat before leaving. Other Jews were not so fortunate. Rumours began to spread through the city that male Jews were being rounded up and sent to the citadel. Tennenbaum decided to run the gauntlet and hide in the pharmaceutical factory he managed. The streets swarmed with surly young Ukrainians wearing yellow and blue armbands which appeared to give them the authority to molest the town's Jewish populace. Tennenbaum passed several Jews lying on the pavements bleeding and one sorely beaten Jew being dragged through the town by a youth. Despite being accosted at least once, the 32-year-old reached his factory and was soon joined by the rest of the family. They hid in the attic. 'We heard people running, screaming, cursing, and we heard shooting, but were unable to see what was going on,' he recalled nearly half a century later. The statue of Lenin in the market square was toppled. Fires were widespread. Jews dashed to the main synagogue to recover the Torah scrolls before fire took hold – the flames had already devoured all the houses on the same road.[94]

By the time pioneer Paul Kaesberg, a platoon leader in 295th Infantry Division, entered Złoczów, there was 'shooting everywhere'. He continued:

The SS shoot everyone who falls into their hands. It's awful – mass murder. The pure horror of it all affects me. Yesterday Jews and Bolsheviks murdered around 1,000 Ukrainians in a castle. We saw children with their throats slit, long nails driven through their chests, mutilated corpses, bound by barbed wire, nailed to barn doors. Now the Ukrainians take terrible revenge – the SS armed them. Everywhere there are half-dead bodies, Jews and Bolsheviks were driven to the citadel by the Ukrainians and have to dig up the corpses of the interred and are then beaten to death.[95]

On 2 July, posters appeared across the city ordering Jews to report to the main square at 8am the next day. Despite the threat of being shot, most of Złoczów's male Jews did not muster at the appointed time. But a large crowd of Jews – mostly women and the elderly – did. From the window of his apartment, Samuel Tennenbaum watched a German officer address the crowd. Złoczów's Jews would have to wear armbands and a curfew would be imposed under penalty of death. Despite these impositions, Tennenbaum strangely felt reassured. 'We believed the worst was over,' he wrote. 'The Germans were, after all, civilised people, the nation of Kant, Schiller and Goethe…'[96]

Anna Ulrich watched the work details driven towards the citadel by Germans and Ukrainians who 'ran along the roadside beating them with anything to hand: rifles, sticks, iron bars and stones. Many Jews collapsed on the way, streaming with blood. Seriously-injured Jews lay along the entire route leading to the citadel.'

In the prison courtyard, Jewish men removed bodies from a mass grave, loading them onto horse-drawn carts which were driven to the cemetery by Ukrainians. Teenager Shlomo Wolkowicz was forced to join them.

It was a hot day and many lost consciousness as a result of the pungent smell of the corpses, but our guards didn't mind. SS men stood around the pit and, from time to time, they ordered someone – particularly men with beards and earlocks – to climb out and throw themselves on their knees in front of them. With sadistic pleasure they then hit out at their victim until they lay unconscious on the ground and then they kicked them back into the pit.

Any relative who tried to intervene suffered terribly. Occasionally men were hauled out of the grave by the guards and beaten savagely before 'the murderers let the wounded slowly and painfully succumb to their injuries,' Wolkowicz recalled. 'It went on like this all day.' As the exhumations neared their conclusion, it became increasingly difficult to recover the bodies – so decomposed were the dead 'that the skin came off the bones when they tried to pull them out'.

Eighteen-year-old Pole Maria Rogowska had gone to the prison hoping for news of her father, arrested three days before the German invasion. She watched Jews toil in the grave. 'They looked so dreadful that if you'd placed them side-by-side with the corpses, they would have looked very similar,' she recalled. 'Pushed and beaten by the Germans, covered with earth and dirt. They exhumed the corpses using any hook or bar, they stepped on the corpses and were intimidated to breaking point.' It was more than the teenager could bear:

I felt dizzy from fear and pain, tears streamed from my eyes, it was hard to breathe, I felt sick. It was all terrible, horrifying, hellish, a horror you couldn't comprehend. I saw the reason for this hell. There was a terrible groaning coming from every direction. People holding pieces of wood stood by the corpses which had been hauled out of the pits and removed the excrement, dirt and filth from the dead bodies. You hoped you might find a single face with a grain of hope among these beaten, scalded and decomposing faces. I wanted to find the body of the person I loved, 'liberate' it from the filth of the other corpses and bury it on its own. Unfortunately, the efforts of hundreds of people were in vain. Only occasionally did somebody recognise the tortured body of a loved one, usually thanks to what was left of their clothing.

Soldier Hans Kessel watched 'a rowdy Ukrainian beat the kneeling Jews with an iron bar – after they'd been allowed to recite a prayer – and broke the back of their necks. The people tumbled head-first into the ditch where many corpses already lay.' Kessel was appalled by what he saw but forbidden to intervene by a military policemen who explained that events in the citadel were 'a Ukrainian matter'. Paul Kaesberg did intervene, however, having observed two men from the *Wiking* Division force three teenage Jewish girls to dig a grave in the garden. 'They wanted to shoot these girls,' Kaesberg wrote. 'I threatened the men with my pistol and let the girls go.' The episode made the young officer mull over the war in the East. 'It is no longer human,' he concluded. 'The Russians brought these murders upon themselves with their bestial actions. It's not war any more.'

The maltreatment and murders were still under way when Otto Korfes arrived and found German troops gawping at a terrible spectacle in one corner of the prison courtyard: upwards of 80 Jews – not just men as on the first day, but women and children as well – in a large pit which SS troops and Ukrainian nationalists tossed grenades into. As one civilian stepped up to the lip of the pit and prepared to pull the pin, Korfes tore the grenade from his hand and screamed at the men to cease the slaughter immediately. The German soldiers quickly scattered, while the regimental commander assured the survivors in the pit they were now under the protection of the German Army. The Jews refused to believe him, sank to their knees and begged, 'Mercy, mercy, *Herr Offizier.*' Only one man clambered out of the hole, a well-dressed former soldier who'd earned the Iron Cross for his service in World War I – and fled to Poland when the Nazis came to power. He persuaded his fellow Jews that they were safe.

Otto Korfes saw to it that the survivors were accommodated in the vaults of the citadel, received food, straw, beds and blankets and had his regiment's doctors treat the wounded. Korfes himself inspected a line of corpses, piled five and six high – there were perhaps 600 dead. He hoped to find the occasional soul still living. 'Most of them had either received a pistol shot, or others, children for example, had been torn apart by hand-grenades, and the rest had their heads split open,' he remembered. 'The civilians had pickaxes, axes and spades. They used them to smash in the heads of the badly wounded in the pit.'[97]

In the oil town of Drohobycz, 15-year-old Pole Henryk Czarkowski watched in horror as the mob – many of them farmers who'd plundered Drohobycz's warehouses during the night and now sought some new 'amusement' – dragged Jews from their homes. 'They beat them mercilessly,' he recalled.

> Accompanied by the general laughter of the mob, they broke their sticks on the bare heads of Jewesses – they'd already deprived them of their wigs. They dragged terribly frightened, defenceless men behind them, kicked them, and tore them to shreds as they sought new victims.
>
> All this occurred with the consent of the Germans who photographed and filmed it laughing. The crowd became intoxicated with the massacre and called out: 'You betrayed people to the Bolsheviks and the NKVD. You have to be blamed and killed for what you have done…'[98]

When Bremen's 303rd Police Battalion marched into the town, the pogrom was in full swing. Enormous piles of corpses, some freshly killed, others – the dead recovered from the cellar of the NKVD prison – decaying badly, grew on two sides of the market square. 'Jewish commissars' were to blame for the massacre in the jail, townsfolk told the Germans' interpreter, 'So, we'll kill every Jew.' For

24 hours they acted with impunity. The police battalion commander, Heinrich Hannibal, did not order his men to halt the pogrom; instead, he confined them to quarters for the rest of the day. Bernhard Sintek helped a father carrying a small child to escape by halting his three rabid pursuers. 'Otherwise, we didn't intervene,' he remembered. 'The order of the day was: the inhabitants should restore order themselves.'[99]

Twenty miles away, the first German troops to march into Sambor were immediately warned about horrific sights in the prison – locals had found at least 500 corpses, perhaps as many as 800. Still, it took two more days for anger at supposed 'Jewish' crimes to boil over, perhaps aided by an inflammatory article in *Ukrainski scodenni visti*, the town's Ukrainian-language newspaper – produced under German oversight. A Polish former inmate told the editor that for weeks, prisoners had been fed 'suspicious white meat' which did not taste like chicken, beef or pork, nor were there ever any bones. 'Boiled arms and legs were found in the vats in the prison kitchen,' he claimed. His friends were sceptical – they stared into the vat and saw some meat, but not necessarily human flesh. The man was insistent. This was human flesh – leg and buttocks, but chopped into pieces. 'I remember that the pieces of meat really did look like those body parts,' one of the Poles recalled.

Once again, the task of removing decomposing corpses – 'the stench around the prison was unbearable,' one signaller recalled, and the bodies 'already had black faces' – was energetically tackled by nationalists who began rounding up local Jews, assisted by German troops. Entire families were driven towards the jail, such as Herman Rieger, forced along with his wife and five-year-old son, all 'terribly beaten by Ukrainians with iron bars'. Dulek Frei remembered 'incited groups of Ukrainians in a state of wild excitement, driving thrashed Jews, streaming with blood' towards the jail. He continued:

> The gates of the prison opened and then closed behind us. An indescribable, terrible, hellish sight presented itself: Ukrainians hit out at dozens of Jews with iron bars and rifle butts. Corpses of Ukrainians – victims of Stalin's murderers as they pulled out – were piled up at the end of the prison yard. A dreadful smell which truly took our breath away came from the decomposing corpses. The blood that flowed from the beatings our heads and faces suffered impeded us seeing what was happening around us.[100]

Fewer than 2,000 people lived in the town of Bóbrka, 20 miles southeast of Lvov, but it still had a prison. A German investigator found 16 bodies inside;

the inmates' final hours must have been dreadful, he concluded. 'Some of the corpses had been scalded, others soaked in petrol and set alight after being mutilated such as skulls smashed in, eyes gouged out, fingers cut off, tongues cut out.' Yet again it was the Jews who were blamed for the atrocities, dragged from their homes and forced to exhume the bodies. 'Lying and sitting in the round pit were around 30 to 40 Jews, men and women,' the investigator reported. 'They were sworn at and pelted by the populace standing around the pit – some of them relatives of the murdered. Every Jew was injured.' Lothar Hochschulz watched as a family of five Jews was beaten to death by Ukrainians. 'Never before have I heard such animal-like death cries. Strange! It no longer bothered me.' Later he confided his feelings to a Polish teacher who spoke excellent German. 'We talked about the Jews, about those who'd been murdered, about everything,' Hochschulz wrote. As far as he was concerned, 'every Jew should simply be killed. Nothing could persuade me otherwise after all I'd seen and experienced. She said: "You have beautiful eyes, but a stony, ice-cold heart." And she was right.' Berliner Herbert Schrödter arrived in Bóbrka with the pogrom in full swing. He watched the local populace stone one Jew to the point of death, while others torched a house where half a dozen Jews had locked themselves in. A community leader appeared and demanded an end to the outrage. The attackers put out the fire, but then forced their way into the building.

Soon we hear blows and the screams of women. I look through the broken windows into the living room. There is an old Jew with a long grey beard sitting in an armchair, rigid and upright, looking at me with a piercing gaze. Another Jew, also with a long grey beard, tries to leave the house. He's spotted, and some men grab him by the kaftan, laughing, knock him to the ground and then run away because other events have attracted their attention. The Jew remains lying in the street with his face in the dirt and looks around carefully with just one eye, looking for his tormentors. But they suddenly come back and attack him again with stones and kicks. They drag the now-unconscious man into a meadow and leave him there. In the meadow there's a civilian, wearing the armband of an auxiliary policeman and armed with a shotgun. A German militia man joins him. I gather from his gestures that he wants to persuade the policeman to give the Jew the *coup de grâce*. The young man obviously refuses, but his compatriot refuses to stop pestering him until the boy goes up to the Jew, puts the gun on him and misses. But the stubborn compatriot persuades him until the auxiliary policeman finally holds the shotgun to the Jew's head for a second time, hesitantly and reluctantly, and pulls the trigger.

None of Schrödter's 257th Infantry Division comrades attempted to intervene; they had received strict instructions not to. 'When I leave I remind myself of the dreadful crime of the Jews when they cried out to Pilate as Christ was condemned: "His blood be on us and our children!" The Lord has paid them back.'[101]

Rumours that corpses had been found in the former offices of crude oil firm FANTO – since September 1939 the NKVD headquarters – sparked the pogrom which raged through Boryslav, just down the road from Drohobycz, on 3 July. An ever-growing crowd gathered outside the building and discovered that the rumours were true, as 18-year-old Pole Alfred Jasiński remembered:

> The entrances to the building were wide open, young men came out of them one after another carrying the corpses of young men and women. They lay them down in the square beside each other. Others – Jews – washed the corpses. There were visible signs on the corpses which were cleaned that they had been restrained with barbed wire and suffered inhuman torture, including broken limbs and women's breasts cut off.

In the midst of this recovery of corpses, a staff car carrying senior German officers pulled into the square. One climbed onto a balcony and addressed the crowd, giving them free rein for the next 24 hours to avenge all the injustices they had suffered under the Soviets. His words were the spark to the powder keg. The square emptied almost immediately. The crowd ripped up boards and posts, wrenched branches from trees, picked up stones and headed into the town centre, determined to have their vengeance. 'The air smelled of blood and bloodthirsty anti-Jewish propaganda,' one observer recalled. 'The Jews were publicly accused of the most profane crimes and blamed for every misfortune, including the outbreak of war. "The Jews are to blame for everything! Jews, they are hyenas, barbarians, murderers, they murder Aryan children so they have blood for Passover."' Within half an hour all of Boryslav was on its feet, as Koppel Holzman later testified.

> They expected plenty of booty and set about their work – nothing would slow them down... Now it was a case of unrestrained envy, hysterical ambition and the wish to avenge the Jews for restricting their lives... They did not confine themselves to taking Jewish men prisoner, rather they maltreated them, drove entire families out of their homes and robbed their apartments. They loaded what they could onto carts. If they didn't know what to do with an object, they smashed it with

axes. They eagerly smashed mirrors, tore pictures and feather beds and smashed up slabs or marble. But there was nothing they enjoyed destroying more than Jewish books. This malicious gang possessed an astonishing, incomprehensible fear of collections of Jewish books and the Torah scrolls in the synagogues, a fear they tried to quell through the complete destruction of Jewish houses.

Holzman himself was pelted with stones by youths who screamed at him in Ukrainian: 'This is a Jew! Arrest this Jew! Arrest him!' One yob stood in front of him brandishing a large stick, threatening to kill him. Holzman escaped by fleeing through a stream polluted by oil – only to be arrested as he tried to return to his apartment via the town centre. Outside the former NKVD headquarters, a macabre party now seemed to be in full swing, an orgy of death and violence. 'There was widespread joy,' Holzman observed. 'To them, it was one big celebration, a celebration of the murder of Jews.' He managed to wrestle free from his guards and, with the help of a Polish stranger, eventually reached his home.

Having been confined to quarters for 24 hours, German police restored some semblance of order to Boryslav the next day. When Alfred Jasiński returned to the prison square, the streets were clear. Had it all been a bad dream, the teenager wondered? But then, down a narrow alley, he spied 'a pile of naked red bodies'. Muffled groans came from some of them.[102]

In Lutsk, the newly arrived German security forces brought death, not order. Nearly 1,500 Jews had already been executed by the time posters appeared across Lutsk calling on all Jewish males aged 16 to 60 to report to the citadel. As he carried out an inventory of a nearby pharmaceutical warehouse, medic Alois Kräutle watched Jews report to be registered – the 44-year-old sergeant estimated around 1,300 came forward. Before 3 July, 1,180 of those men were dead. Lined up in groups of 30 to 50 on the edge of three huge pits, the Jews were dispatched with rifle shots to the back of the head. The bodies slumped forward, face down in the soil. The SS officer in charge of the killings strode among the victims, delivering the *coup de grâce* with a pistol to any still alive. When he saw Kräutle, he ordered him to grab his rifle and join the executions. The medic refused – his membership of the Red Cross meant he could not bear arms. 'He told me to go to Hell with the words: This here is not some show.' The victims went to their deaths passively, save one Jew who turned to face his executioners, removed a French Army pamphlet from his pocket, waved it in the air and declared that he had fought for Germany on the Western Front. 'Turn around, you bastard!' the SS officer snarled. Seconds later a volley of fire rang out.[103]

After Lvov and Złoczów, the next major city in the Wehrmacht's path as it pushed into the Ukrainian heartland was Tarnopol. In the nearby village of Dobropol, Polish priest Józef Anczarski found its Jews terrified of the impending German occupation. With trembling hands, one middle-aged Jewish friend told him: 'Hitler is coming. He will murder the Jews, there is no salvation for them.' Anczarski tried to calm the man down, but deep down he knew his friend was correct. 'If the Germans come here, they could fare badly.'[104]

'THERE ARE WHOLE VILLAGES AND TOWNS THAT YOU CAN ERASE FROM THE MAP...' UKRAINE, BEGINNING OF JULY

The twin defeats of Lvov and Dubno precipitated chaos and panic far behind the front. Party leaders in a string of towns and villages as far as 250 miles east of Lvov abandoned their posts and fled eastwards – not with official documents or valuable items of machinery, but with their families and personal possessions. In Proskurov, 150 miles from the Galician capital, the power station and water works were destroyed by withdrawing Party officials, leaving inhabitants and troops without electricity or water. Nor was the Red Army exempt from this panic. Desertion was rife – some men simply failed to respond to the call-up; others fled at the first sign of enemy action – especially among troops drawn from Ukraine who either did not wish to fight for a regime they hated, or wished to run from the advancing Germans with their families. A railway unit which claimed 40 per cent casualties during bombing raids on Rovno in fact lost just ten men; the rest had simply deserted. Similarly, Twenty-Sixth Army, which had defended the southernmost stretch of the Eastern Front between Przemyśl and the Carpathian mountains, suffered 6,000 casualties, but two out of three of those were deserters. Special blocking detachments had to be formed to stop deserters far behind the front and return them to their units. In just three days at the end of June, 697 deserters were rounded up. It was the tip of the iceberg. VI Rifle Corps, defending the area around Rava-Ruska when the Germans attacked, had simply melted away since 22 June. Five thousand of its men deserted – though almost all were subsequently caught and sent back to the front. Serial offenders and ringleaders were shot on the spot: 100 men in VI Rifle Corps alone. A company commander in 139th Rifle Division pulled his men out of the line during battle without orders and tried to withdraw. The division's commander, Major General Fedor Smekhotvorov, had him shot on the spot. Eighty men in 99th Rifle Division – mostly composed of conscripts from

Byelorussia and Ukraine – refused to shoot in battle. Every one of them was promptly executed in front of their comrades. And ten deserters from 41st Rifle Division were arrested and shot. 'This action was unequivocally supported by the men,' an official report noted. 'Troops and leaders say: enemies and cowards need to be exterminated ruthlessly.'[105]

Battered Soviet units joined the torrent of refugees and carts streaming eastwards. Having somehow extricated some of his VIII Mechanised Corps from encirclement at Dubno, Dmitry Ryabyshev was now entwined with an endless line of refugees and their carts on the Tarnopol–Proskurov road, constantly harassed by German dive-bombers. After a while, this column of the damned finally ground to a halt. Ryabyshev drove forward in his KV tank and found the cause of the traffic jam: four ammunition trucks ablaze, the shells they carried exploding, terrifying the civilians. With a swamp to the left and the steep slope of a hill to the right, the route was blocked. Ryabyshev realised he could not allow the vehicles to burn until the flames died down. As he pondered the fate of his corps, his driver yelled: 'Comrade General, better close the hatch!' The tank picked up speed and rammed all four trucks, pushing them to the side. The civilians and soldiers continued eastwards.[106]

Snapping at their heels, the advancing Germans were horrified by the sights on the main highway between Lvov and Tarnopol – nothing but 'a road of destruction and death', wrote 20-year-old Ernst Günter Merten:

> Guns of all types and calibres lay twisted on the roadside, all painted in that indescribable Russian green, the only colour of paint they produce in Russia evidently. Next huge, partially burned-out tractors, next to them charred corpses – we found the burned head of one 50 metres away in the field.
>
> Countless crates of ammunition with their contents strewn all over the place, in some places a slew of pages from pamphlets spread out, and spilled herrings in a ditch. All charmingly mixed with the dirt on the rain-sodden ground. On top of all this, the foul stench of corpses.[107]

It wasn't merely the highways of Ukraine which were charnel houses. Passing through the remains of one town, signaller Richard Rommel observed that nothing was still standing except 'blackened chimneys cruelly rising into the sky! Not one house was spared! There's the smell of burning and carcasses in the air.' A junior officer in 25th Infantry Division found 'destruction everywhere… There are whole villages and towns that you can erase from the map… Just smoking ruins.' As night fell, the terrain assumed ghostly forms which mesmerised Friedrich Sachsse:

It's wild and beautiful when you march at night in the middle of a road lined by houses which are reduced to red wooden skeletons – they groan in the raging inferno and collapse with a crash. Then sparks are thrown up into the night sky and the outlines of the vehicle columns glow in the flickering red light. It's also beautiful when there's a brief howling in the air and then there's a crash with thunderous force somewhere, like God's fist. It's followed by a breathless silence from your head through your entire body down to your heels. And the entire body utters a silent prayer: God protect me![108]

And yet signals officer Ivan Tseloyko was struck by the peace of night in Galicia. 'The sky was clear and starry, no clouds,' he wrote. 'Myriads of heavenly stars stared at us from the firmament. We had the impression that each of them was looking at us, sympathising with us or following us.'[109]

This was the *other* Ukraine. An endless land of fields peacefully tilled by farmers, seemingly as they had done for centuries. 'Now we're beginning to grasp what "Europe's breadbasket" means when we can see across the ripening fields of rye and wheat,' Ernst Günter Merten noted in his diary. 'There's hardly a metre of earth that's not tilled. There's clover as well, rape or flax.' Staff officer Udo von Alvensleben agreed. 'This land is infinite yet doesn't seem desolate. We constantly come across villages and individual cottages, built of clay or wood, with thatched roofs, very poor, but which fire the imagination. Such primitive little houses make you think you've reached the end of the earth.' The *Landser* had been told the Ukrainian was not Russian – their culture, language, history, even racial composition were different. They were a staunchly religious people, optimistic, hard working, hardy, their hospitality 'legendary'. Alvensleben found the Ukrainians to be 'hard, patient, fatalistic souls who endure an horrific existence in fear, caution and stoic dignity as world events are played out at their expense'.[110]

Otherwise, impressions of the Soviet Union mirrored those of German soldiers advancing on the central and northern axes: run-down cottages, poorly clothed and ill-fed children, primitive living conditions and, in the towns, 'kitsch Party and factory buildings'. The onion-domed church – if it was still standing – invariably dominated every village, but most had fallen into a state of neglect after a quarter of a century of Soviet rule. 'So now we're in the true "Soviet paradise",' former SA trooper Hermann Beyer, now a chaplain with 294th Infantry Division, noted in his diary. 'The first impressions are immediately devastating. The grain in the fertile fields is wretched. The houses are untidy wooden buildings with thatched roofs. There's hardly a church to be found in the villages. Where they're still standing, they serve other purposes.'[111]

Paved and cobbled roads in towns quickly gave way to dirt tracks which became quagmires in the rain, or were rutted by the deep grooves of cart wheels and vehicle tyres which created an almost lunar landscape when dry. 'We continued over bogs, fields, dusty roads. You cannot imagine what we look like,' one sergeant in 93rd Infantry Regiment wrote to his family in Wolfsburg. 'The dust is as fine as flour.' Vehicles often drove through the fields to escape the dust or mud. The dust, Friedrich Sachsse told his wife, was 'the worst feature'. He continued:

> It sticks to our faces like a grey mask, leaving just our eyes peering out. It clings to eyelashes and eyebrows and gets in your ears. We hardly notice it. It's only bad when you have to overtake the column at night on these unimaginable roads on a motorcycle without any lights. Then you can't see your hands in front of your face, you gasp for air and your eyes burn with the dust.[112]

No man behind the front line felt safe with thousands of Russian troops hiding in Galicia's woods and fields. Snipers, excellently camouflaged in bushes, only picked off 'profitable targets', aiming at the head or chest – 'and always with success', the staff of the SS *Wiking* Division lamented. 'Pursuit is not easy because death lurks in every grain field,' an ethnic German serving in the *Wiking* wrote. A Dutchman in the same division agreed: 'It was as if a Russian with a gun was hiding in every corner of the cornfields.' Behind the front, 'a proper guerrilla war' was being waged, 'skilfully aimed at the army's Achilles heel, the supply line,' a supply officer in 25th Infantry Division noted worriedly on the last day of June. 'This war of snipers gets on your nerves,' Ernst Günter Merten wrote. 'Lying for hours on end in the corn under the blazing sun – you only have to raise your head and there's a whistling in the trees in front of us.' The men were nervous. 'Anyone not wearing a scrap of uniform is shot as a last resort,' Merten continued. 'You can't even go for a shit without your steel helmet any more, otherwise you'll be shot at as a spy or sniper.' Motorcycle messengers behind the front were particularly susceptible to being ambushed or seized and tortured by Russian stragglers. 'This Asian mob is sly and cunning,' 299th Infantry Division's Hans Roth recorded in his diary. 'Every hour brings an evil surprise – a large pile of shit. We are no longer safe anywhere.'[113]

'OUR REVENGE WILL BE TERRIBLE!'
UKRAINE, JUNE–JULY 1941

They were certainly not safe in Red Army hands. Time and again captured German troops were killed, often butchered. Three Waffen SS men were captured by 40th Tank Division and paraded before its commander, Colonel Mikhail Shirobokov.

'They lined up with typical German-Prussian precision, their eyes never moving,' communications officer Lieutenant Ivan Tseloyko observed.

'Who will win this war?' Shirobokov asked as he eyed up his prisoners.

One immediately gave the Nazi salute and shouted: '*Heil* Hitler!'

He was shot on the spot.

Shirobokov asked the remaining two prisoners the same question; they immediately flashed back: 'Stalin!'

Tseloyko was not impressed. 'These two young men immediately turned from imaginary victors to sheep, forgetting their loyalty to Hitler and their oath,' he wrote. 'They lost the belligerent appearance of invaders and were sent to corps headquarters for questioning.'[114]

Hundreds of captured German soldiers never made it beyond the battlefield. 36th Infantry Regiment came across the bodies of an entire reconnaissance unit sent to scout a border village. Two of the men had been tied to trees, the rest driven into the main square after they had been captured by the Soviets. 'Every man had one arm and his genitals cut off, the eyes of others had been gouged out or they had suffered bayonet wounds to the chest, their arms and legs pulled out of their sockets,' an official report noted. On 26 June, Heinrich Raegener surveyed the field of battle where the previous day his 518th Infantry Regiment had fought. The doctor hoped to find wounded. He found only the dead – perhaps 100 corpses – all killed after falling into Red Army hands, some bayonetted, others with their skulls smashed in by rifle butts, shovels, even a blood-spattered potato masher. In Lutsk, 14th Panzer Division found the bodies of four German aircrew in the abandoned Communist Party headquarters. 'Unless you'd seen it, you wouldn't believe it,' Franz Siebeler, a gunner with 14th Panzer Division, told his family. 'Some had their eyes gouged out, legs and hands chopped off, they'd been burned by red-hot irons in many places. Tears of anger welled in my eyes. War against the Soviets is hard and cruel, no mercy is shown.' In Tarnopol, Klaus Häberlen, an adjutant in *Kampfgeschwader* 51, located some of his comrades who'd crash-landed and been taken to the NKVD prison, where they suffered almost identical torture. They were identifiable only from their dental records. Emilian Hindelang was told that 'Jews and Communists' killed 17 German prisoners in Berezhany, 50 miles southeast of Lvov. 'Eyes gouged out, ears, noses and genitals cut off.' The town's Ukrainian residents now turned on the Jews, first forcing them to dig graves, before tossing them in the holes and killing them. 'Given the murders, the punishment was just,' Hindelang concluded. Outside Berezhany, he encountered a German soldier escorting a Jewish prisoner. 'It's only a pity that I drove by so fast, I would have shot him.'[115] No atrocity angered the Germans more than the fate of 35th Infantry Regiment, overrun near the village of Broniki on 1 July. At least 132 of the 153 dead subsequently found on the battlefield had been killed after capture (the rumour mill would quickly increase the death toll to 250). 'The majority were half-naked, some had their hands bound behind their backs,' one report noted. Most men had been stripped of their dog tags; all had been deprived of their weapons and often their boots and jackets. And every man had either been stabbed to death by bayonet or beaten to death with rifle butts and spades. Mutilations were commonplace: medic Franz Wagner came across a non-commissioned officer with his genitals cut off and a rifleman who had bled to death after being stabbed. Many more corpses were branded by a Soviet star burned onto the chest. Broniki, wrote Erwin Boehm, 'introduced us to a new dimension in war. We shielded ourselves with several pieces of armour around our heart, tightened our helmets and swore that we would never be without one last round.' His comrade Erich Dürr was incensed. 'It almost turned my blood to stone in my veins,' he wrote. 'These are no longer human beings but criminals and pitiless murderers. Our revenge will be terrible!'[116]

It frequently was. It was typically arbitrary and rarely just. Following a brief skirmish in a cornfield outside Lutsk, 62nd Infantry Division captured 42 Russian troops. As he moved around the battlefield looking for stragglers, a non-commissioned officer found the body of a German soldier lying in a field, a knife stuck in his throat. Another soldier reported a second German corpse had been found. This was sufficient for the sergeant to order six men to shoot every prisoner. They did so 'very quickly because we had to hurry behind the company'. The actions of 124th Rifle Division seemed to invoke particular fury. Its ranks consistently 'mistreated, tortured, mutilated and murdered German soldiers' who fell into its hands, wounded or not. When officers from the division were captured, Sixth Army's commander Field Marshal Walther von Reichenau ordered their immediate execution.[117]

If the atrocity occurred in a town or village, the Jewish populace was almost always singled out. When the Wehrmacht entered Klevan – just up the road from the massacre at Broniki – they acted 'like hyenas and any Jew they came across was killed on the spot'. Assisted by Ukrainian nationalists, and one of Klevan's butchers, they began rounding up every one of the town's Jews. If anyone refused to leave their home or hiding place, the troops simply tossed a grenade inside. Those who did surrender were driven into the market square where, fuelled by vodka 'liberated' from a Communist warehouse, German soldiers shot an estimated 150 men, women and children. By the time the invaders' bloodlust was satiated, around 700 Jews were dead. 'For three days, the corpses of those murdered lay unburied on the streets,' recalled Abraham Kirschner, one of the few of Klevan's Jews to survive the massacre. 'Dogs and pigs ripped them apart.' When the corpses began to decompose, the Germans ordered the remnants of the Jewish community to carry the corpses to the synagogue, where they poured petrol on the bodies and set them alight. After being ambushed in a small town outside Tarnopol, Dutch troops in the SS *Wiking* Division traced the culprits to the cellar of a ruined house. Twenty litres of petrol and two hand-grenades were used to smoke them out. 'In a few minutes, 12 civilians emerged, seven of them Jews,' Dutch volunteer Pieter Willems wrote. 'The Jews first had to dig their own grave and were then executed. Of the 12 civilians, three were women – if you could call these beasts that. A Jewish commissar made the noose with which he was hanged.'[118]

In the summer of 1941, few fighting units could compete with the *Wiking* Division when it came to arbitrary brutality. The SS troops – ethnic Germans, Finns, Norwegians, Danes, Swedes, Dutch and Belgians – arrived on Soviet soil having been warned about 'the terrible methods used by the Bolsheviks' and determined to mete out revenge. 'Woe betide the Russian who fell into our hands,' one Dutchman wrote. 'It is a privilege and at the same time a duty to help the struggle.' Captured Soviet soldiers bore the brunt of the *Wiking*'s fury. 'From the beginning we knew almost no compassion for prisoners,' another volunteer from the Netherlands recorded. The personal diaries of these men frequently refer to prisoners being executed or 'suspicious-looking civilians' being shot on the spot. 'Fortunate' captives might be ordered to render unexploded bombs safe. An hour-long halt in a village outside Tarnopol was sufficient for three prisoners – a Mongol and two Jews – to be shot. The Jews were forced to dig the graves, then lie in them to measure them for size, before all three men were shot and the grave filled in. When one company commander tried to put an end to such killings, there was uproar – 'the men wanted to continue'.[119]

Nothing incensed the men of the *Wiking* more than the death of a brutal but evidently popular regimental commander, Hilmar Wäckerle. As he visited his troops in Olszanica, east of Lvov, late in the morning of 2 July, Wäckerle was killed in an ambush ... or was shot by the surviving crew members of a seemingly abandoned Soviet tank he inspected ... or was picked off by a Soviet sniper hiding in a tree. His death, wrote Marinus Weers, was 'a tremendous blow. For a year we've shared joy and pain with him and when he's finally able to lead his regiment into action, he's one of the first to be killed.' The 23-year-old Amsterdamer was a fanatical National Socialist who viewed his enemy as 'hordes'. After Hilmar Wäckerle was buried with full military honours, Weers and his comrades were given free rein to seek revenge. 'Until an order instructs us to uphold the law again, no quarter is given to the Russians who fall into our hands today,' Weers noted. Wäckerle's supposed executioner was hanged, a captured commissar shot. Olszanica was torched – 'all night long we could see the glow of flames,' one anti-tank gunner recorded – cattle slaughtered and Jewish inhabitants lined up in rows by the road, where they were made to first hand over their money, which was greedily seized by the remaining villagers, then bury the decomposing cadaver of a horse – having mostly dug the grave with their bare hands. Now the Jews were made to strip, their clothes distributed among Olszanica's other residents. The humiliation was far from over. The SS men fetched crowbars and spades, thrust them into the Jews' hands and forced them to perform military drills, fight each other or pretend to shoot one another. Any man who stopped through exhaustion was forced to continue at bayonet point. The 'games' lasted for three hours, until the exhausted Jews dug a mass grave as company commander Alfred Schade formed a firing squad. Two Finns refused to take part. One was engaged to a Jew, while his friend Sakari Lappi-Seppälä had no intention of shooting someone who'd caused them no harm. Schade 'bristled with anger,' Lappi-Seppälä recalled. 'He said he never thought we were such cowards. He would show us that his men were truly worthy of the title "men".'

Eight times Jews lined up on the edge of the freshly dug pit. Eight times a firing squad of Germans took aim and fired. A couple of Jews who had the misfortune to walk down the road at that moment suffered the same fate until there was 'a proper mountain of naked, bloody bodies'. When it was over, prisoners of war were ordered to fill the grave, while Alfred Schade rewarded his men with cognac and cigarettes, recorded their names and thanked them 'for their work as avengers. The new Europe would need more men like them, men with the character of true Germans.' Between 36 and 150 Jews were captured and shot until the *Wiking* was ordered – reluctantly – to send prisoners to the rear for processing, rather than execute them, and resume its march towards Złoczów.[120]

'LONG LIVE THE ROMANIAN ARMY!' NORTHERN BUKOVINA AND BESSARABIA, 2–5 JULY 1941

At first light on the second day of July, the River Prut erupted along a 130-mile front as the second stage of Romania's great war of liberation began. The first stage – the recapture of Bukovina – was progressing rapidly; Bucharest's troops already stood just outside the region's greatest city, Czernovitz – Cernăuți to Romanians. Now came the liberation of Bessarabia. To the north of Iași, Germany's Eleventh Army struck; to the south, Romanian Fourth Army.

On the left wing of the German assault, a wave of Stukas hammered Soviet defences, followed by an artillery barrage and an 'abrupt, hellish storm shattered the silence of the sleeping morning'. Under the cover of the shellfire, pioneers hauled their rubber boats down to the water's edge, then paddled the infantry over the Prut at a steady pace. 'The inferno of fire-spewing weapons turned into a hissing, roaring, raging, swirling rumble in the air, making it impossible to distinguish between shells being fired and impacting,' one observer wrote, while the river itself 'seemed to boil from the impacts of enemy artillery and mortars'. As the rubber boats reached the right bank, a curtain of fog and smoke came down, and German observers on the other side only caught fleeting glimpses of the battle: fountains of earth thrown up into a morning sky blackened by smoke, the occasional jet of fire from a flamethrower, chunks of concrete spinning through the air as charges took out bunkers. And then flares went up to signal that the assault had succeeded and the first line of defence had been overrun.

'The moment when we crossed was impressive,' the diarist of Romania's 5th Infantry Division wrote as its men assaulted the Prut in the direction of Bălți in Bessarabia. 'Contrary to orders to maintain silence, officers and the band on the first boats began to cross singing patriotic hymns.' The theatrics understandably attracted the attention of the Soviet troops on the far bank, who immediately subjected the attackers to a ferocious bombardment. It did not, the diarist continued, 'unduly interfere with the assault by the officers and band'.[121]

Once over the Prut, the lead elements of 76th Infantry Division advanced 25 miles, despite Soviet armoured counter-attacks – one involving more than 150 tanks. Heavy rain turned the terrain and the mud tracks especially into a morass, which left the supply train far behind the fighting troops – and left the fighting troops without ammunition at critical moments. After the battle, Italian war correspondent Curzio Malaparte was struck by the melancholy of the German soldiers he accompanied through Bessarabia. Having liberated one Romanian village 50 miles north of Iași, the men sat on a patch of grass, eating bread and marmalade, talking quietly. 'They do not speak of the war,' Malaparte wrote. 'I have noticed that they never speak of the war. They sing – but to themselves, not in chorus.' One Romanian major was choked with emotion. 'You know, I can't imagine anything more impressive than the scenes of this day!' he commented to a German comrade.[122]

Downstream, 198th Infantry Division broke out of its bridgehead at Sculeni, determined to reach Bălți – 40 miles away – then the Dniester, another 40. It struggled to make headway initially in the face of rain-soaked ground and dogged Soviet artillery. The battle was chaotic: a terrified team of horses ran around the battlefield hauling the command truck of a machine-gun company. The rear wall of the truck had fallen off and the contents spilled out, piece by piece. Soviet tanks appeared and disappeared in the tall fields of corn and sunflowers. Anti-tank and tank guns duelled with 'ear-splitting bangs and crashes'. Clouds of black smoke rose above the fields. A German medic who'd temporarily lost his mind wandered around repeating: 'Blood is flowing in torrents. Blood is flowing in torrents...'

More typically it was the rain, not blood, which ran in torrents. 'Soldiers fought harder with the terrain than with the enemy,' the diarist of Romanian 8th Infantry Division commented. Frequent downpours brought the advance to a standstill for hours on end. 'The sights on the roads of Bessarabia became increasingly impressive: carts from Romanian units mingled with those from German units, bogged down in the mud, and there was no chance of extricating them.' Motor vehicles revved their engines in vain as groups of soldiers tried to push them out of ditches and streams. But when the clouds passed and the tracks dried, progress was rapid – although as one Romanian platoon leader recalled, 'the Russians sacrificed rearguards'. Well-camouflaged, they were left behind to ambush the Romanians after they'd passed over the battlefield. 'Many of them surrendered eventually, but some of them could only be knocked out by grenades exploding in their foxholes.'[123]

By the second day of the offensive, the bridgehead at Sculeni was deemed to be safe enough for Ion Antonescu to visit. The *conducător* crossed the repaired bridge over the Prut and set foot in Bessarabia, driving about ten miles to the village of Chirileni, inspecting a captured Russian tank, interrogating some Soviet prisoners and talking with local inhabitants. The people invariably welcomed the Romanians as their liberators. Priests and teachers approached the men of 39th Infantry Regiment 'with the Cross in their hands, celebrating their liberation from the Bolsheviks. Church bells sounded continuously, proclaiming the victory of the Cross over Bolshevism, and the people, dressed in festive clothing, greeted soldiers with bread and salt.' The joy of the populace in the village of Bogdăneşti was 'indescribable'. The chime of church bells announced the return of Christianity to the region. 'God cannot help those who attacked the Church and degraded the Cross,' the war diary of 14th Infantry Division observed. Further south, Romanian 7th Infantry Division was welcomed by villagers dressed in their finest clothes, teachers and clergy, who immediately held services of thanksgiving for their deliverance. All the time, people brought flowers, water, milk and bread for the soldiers passing through. 'Things are changing,' one infantryman wrote, 'and the terrible Bolshevik oppression of the Romanian populace can be felt.'[124]

Captain Vasile Scârneci led the first Romanian troops into Cernăuți shortly after 9am on 4 July. The veteran officer was not impressed by the city and its 'dirty, foul-smelling slums'. The march continued through a landscape dominated by small villages and windmills – it reminded Scârneci 'of the stories of Don Quixote'. What struck him most, however, was the attitude of the liberated Romanians. 'There is so much melancholy, so much sadness after just one year of Bolshevik rule,' he observed. 'People are afraid.'[125]

The mountain troops following in the wake of Scârneci's reconnaissance unit found the Romanian flag and national colours of blue, yellow and red in every village they marched through in northern Bukovina. One battalion was greeted by:

> ... elderly people, women and children, their arms full of flowers, tears in their eyes, joy in their hearts, shouting: 'Long live the Romanian army! Long live Romania!' kissing the rifles of Romanian soldiers. There were moments of exaltation, moments that gave fresh courage and emboldened Romanian soldiers. In every village we entered, the same joy, the same delight, the same Romanian joy.

Junior officer Dumitru Toedorescu watched as his men were quickly surrounded by inhabitants who brought food, while young men and women put flowers in the barrels of their rifles. A single cry accompanied the columns moving through the lanes of liberated Bukovina: 'Our army! Our army!' The liberators also found, as one officer observed, that the enemy had acted 'full of anger against the civilian populace'. Outside Cernăuți, several hundred Romanians 'were tied to each other and placed face down on the ground in a field on the banks of the Dniester. After this "living bridge" had been built, Soviet tanks passed over the bodies... Dust was then cast over the bodies, which had been turned into a heap of deformed flesh.' It was 5 July before the Romanian troops entered Cernăuți in force. They found that the retreating Russians had destroyed 'everything of military value or which might support the people's livelihood'. Administrative buildings had been destroyed, churches devastated and defiled by Soviet soldiers, and the population left hungry. The sight of the metropolitan church was especially painful: the eyes of statues of saints had been speared by bayonets, a wall of icons was peppered with bullet holes, and ornate wooden crosses, decorated with pure gold and silver, had been used as firewood. The similarly intricate priests' robes had been ripped to shreds and used as toilet paper. 'The church was transformed into a closet and the Bolshevik soldiers desecrated the altar in particular; it was covered with excrement.' Otherwise, Cernăuți's liberation was the catalyst for celebration 300 miles away in Bucharest. There was 'indescribable joy in the capital', a reporter for the national newspaper *Timpul* noted, while readers of *Universul* were urged to 'kneel in worship, with deep gratitude and sincere piety before all those who, through their sacrifice, gave us this moment. We are faced with serious tasks now and for the future: to prevent for all time one of the most Romanian of provinces being taken away from us.' Romanians hung out their national colours across the land. They were soon joined by the swastika and, eventually, the Italian tricolore. As allies in the campaign against the Soviet Union, Hungary demanded the same honour. Bucharest was in no mood to appease its arch enemy. It decreed the period of national celebration over and all flags should be removed.[126]

'IT'S NOT GOOD FOR JEWS TO STAY HERE...' BUKOVINA AND BESSARABIA, LATE JUNE AND EARLY JULY 1941

Continuing his battlefield tour, Ion Antonescu was just 15 miles from Cernăuţi in the ancient town of Storojineţ, where the occasional sound of gunshots announced the discovery of Soviet stragglers found hiding in attics and cellars. Antonescu was delighted by the reception he and his men received – the latter were cheerful, their morale high. But evidently, reports of the atrocities Romanian soldiers were committing had reached his ear, for wherever he visited troops across Bukovina and Bessarabia, he told them: 'We are not invading hordes. We are the army of law and justice, of order, of honesty, of humanity. Everyone caught committing acts of vandalism will be shot... Order, order, order!'[127]

Except that all too often Romanian troops *were* invading hordes, especially in Bukovina – urged on by no lesser a figure than Antonescu's namesake and deputy, though no relation, Mihai. 'It doesn't matter whether we go down in history as barbarians,' he declared. 'So please be implacable. Please be implacable.' Implacable they were. In Ciudei, two dozen miles outside Cernăuţi, Moses Eisig failed to heed the warning of his older brother Osias. 'It's not good for Jews to stay here when the Romanians and Germans are on the advance,' he told Moses. 'They will be bloodthirsty and we are the first Jews in their path.' Moses Eisig, like most of Ciudei's Jews, chose to stay. But when the Romanian Army's 16th Infantry Battalion marched in on 3 July, 27-year-old Moses decided to flee. One year before the same battalion – with the same commander, Valeriu Carp – had murdered several Jews as it surrendered the region to the Soviet Union. Twelve months later and Carp's men were far more bloodthirsty. Hiding in the woods outside Ciudei, Moses Eisig claimed he could hear the sound of gunfire three or four miles away, then 'terrible cries and yelling. We thought that they would shoot the men, but not the women and children.' By the time Carp's battalion was finished 'settling accounts' with Ciudei's Jews, more than 500 were dead. As they were laid to rest in six mass graves, their apartments were plundered by their neighbours.

The next day, Romanian troops marched into Storojineț, the heart of Bukovina's Jewish community, and killed upwards of one in ten of its 2,500 Jews. The killings were repeated in the surrounding villages, the perpetrators mostly Romanian soldiers, aided by liberated countrymen and even some Ukrainians, the victims always Jews. The largely Ukrainian populace of Stăneștii de Jos did not wait to be freed from the Soviet yoke to begin exacting their revenge. A mob roamed the streets, following a list to hunt down male Jews, who were then detained in the saw mill and gradually beaten or tortured to death. Between 80 and 130 men were killed before a Romanian police officer put an end to the bloodbath. In Banila on the River Siret, the Romanian mayor led a pogrom so brutal – the corpse of one Jew was supposedly cut into pieces and his blood used to grease the axes of carts – that the village priest refused to hold a service on the following Sunday. Kosov, a small town close to the Romanian border, was 'teeming with Jews'; every one of them was put to work. 'Some have to sweep the streets, others have to carry out repairs,' a German junior officer wrote. 'The young women have to wash and mend clothes, youths clean boots.' Kosov was, he observed, 'now cleaner than it has ever been' – although only one building in four was still standing. When the town's new rulers ordered every Jewish inhabitant to wear a yellow star, one elder 'declared that there was no hurry. When challenged again, he gave the same response. We had to shoot him.' In Herța, 20 miles southeast of Cernăuți, 1,500 Jews were immediately rounded up by soldiers and by a newly formed militia. Women, children and the elderly were led to a mill on the edge of town, where they were shot – twice or more if the initial volley from the three-strong firing squad failed to finish them off. Young female Jews were frequently raped, while 'suspicious' Jews were shot, usually having dug their own graves. At the northwestern tip of the region, in Kyseliv, an estimated 150 Jews were butchered. The methods of killing were invariably crude – and often ineffective. According to one account, 'some Jews managed to escape from the mass graves, alive but streaming with blood, saving themselves in the neighbouring woods, before reporting the massacre'. And in Sadagura, on the outskirts of Cernăuți, a baying mob 'dragged 86 Jews out of their beds' and led them to specially dug pits in the nearby woods where most were shot, their bodies tumbling into the mass grave.[128]

The route of 6th Mountain Infantry Regiment through Bessarabia was marked by massacres. Supposedly attacked by Jews in Sculeni, it singled out the village's

Jewish inhabitants and shot 311, robbing the corpses of anything valuable. In Mărculeşti, the regiment again came under attack from 'armed Jewish civilians'. 'The Jewish population, whom we have protected for more than 20 years, has taken revenge on us,' the regiment's commander sneered. He had around 400 executed.[129]

THE 'CITY OF THE DEAD...' LVOV, 3–5 JULY

Jewish blood was still flowing in Lvov, but the 'spontaneous' pogrom of 1 July was giving way to a more organised, systematic round-up of opponents of the city's new masters. They began with Polish academics, rounding up three dozen university professors over three days, among them the mathematician and former Polish prime minister Kazimierz Bartel. All but one was shot – either in the courtyard of a university building or in the woods on the southwestern outskirts of Lvov.[130]

Most Ukrainians were still convinced they had been 'liberated' by the Germans – city leaders even thanked Hitler for freeing them:

> The city of Lvov, which was liberated from Bolshevik terror by the victorious advance of the German armies, sends grateful greetings to the Führer of the Greater German Reich. The innocent inhabitants of the city who were murdered by Moscow's henchmen will forever remind us of the fulfilment of our pledge. We are certain that over the graves of these victims and under the victorious sword of the German Army, the Ukrainian people will achieve their ultimate freedom.[131]

But to polytechnic assistant Stanisław Różycki, liberation looked more like occupation. To be sure, the hammer and sickle had been quickly replaced by the swastika, the Ukrainian trident and flags in blue and yellow. But the slogans and banners appearing across the city – 'liberation from the knout', 'the down-trodden Ukrainian nation', 'the brilliant leader', 'invincible army' – bore a remarkable similarity to those the Soviets had pasted in September 1939.[132]

And instead of the NKVD, there was the SS. Felix Landau's *Einsatzkommando* – a small, mobile killing squad which carried out the murderous tasks of the *Einsatzgruppen* – had arrived in Lvov on the afternoon of 2 July and began killing Jews immediately. Landau, a former cabinet maker from Vienna, worked for the security service in occupied Poland before volunteering to join the crusade in the Soviet Union. As he wrote his first letter of the campaign in the East to his mistress Gertrude from his fine quarters in Lvov's southern suburbs, Landau was handed 30 rounds of ammunition for his carbine and ordered to get ready for the day's work: 500 Jews were lined up to be shot. He returned a few hours later to finish the letter. 'The mood is rather tense,' he recorded in his diary. 'Shooting defenceless people – even if they are Jews – isn't really my thing.'

Landau did not desist, however. Shortly after dawn on the fifth, his unit was ordered to kill 32 Poles – 'intelligentsia and the resistance movement' – barely 200 yards from his quarters. 'One of them did not want to die,' Landau wrote. 'The first layer of sand had been tossed on the first group of victims when a hand shot out of the sand, waved and pointed to a spot – presumably his heart. Another couple of shots sounded, then someone cried out – the Pole himself: "Shoot faster!"'

The killings continued in the afternoon – 'around 300 Jews and Poles finished off'. In the evening, the SS men headed into the city centre, where they encountered 'hundreds of Jews, their faces streaming with blood, their heads bashed in, hands and eyes hanging out, running along the street. Several blood-soaked Jews carried fellow Jews who'd collapsed.' Landau and his comrades traced the source of the battered Jews: the citadel. 'There we saw things the likes of which people have rarely witnessed,' he recorded. 'At the entrance to the citadel soldiers were standing with sticks as large as a fist, striking anyone they encountered. At the entrance Jews were pouring out – rows of Jews lying on top of each other like pigs and whimpering like nothing I've ever experienced. We repeatedly ran into Jews getting to their feet, streaming with blood.'[133]

It wasn't the beatings that troubled Felix Landau, rather that bloodied and battered Jews were running around the streets of Lvov. There was no hiding the massacre. Military chaplain Alfons Satzger, passing through Lvov with 132nd Infantry Division, was appalled by the 'city of the dead' with its 'blood, murder, bestiality and tears!' Fires still raged. Jews were still being rounded up and forced to bury the bodies in the courtyard of Lontskoho prison with their bare hands. Dead for at least a week now, the corpses were hideously bloated and swarming with flies. Two hours after the Jews had finished their work, they were beaten to death. Most were killed instantly; a few lingered for a couple of hours. When Satzger left Lvov, the stench of death clung to his uniform for several days.[134]

'THERE WILL ALWAYS BE GOOD AND EVIL...'
TARNOPOL, 2–5 JULY

Eighty miles to the east, Felix Landau's comrades were now at work in Tarnopol. Once again, the flight of the Soviet authorities had revealed a prison massacre – some 2,000 dead – followed by a round-up of the city's Jews in revenge. At least 180 had been killed by the time *Einsatzkommando* 4b arrived. Posters immediately began to appear on billboards and hoardings across Tarnopol assuring the Jewish populace that they had nothing to fear; the German authorities were restoring order. 'Jews began to emerge from their hiding places,' housewife Janett Margolies wrote. 'When they had all returned home, Ukrainian nationalists entered the homes to reassure Jews, telling them that the massacres were over and that now they were taking only people for work duties.' Her husband and son were taken by SS troops to carry crates of ammunition. She did not believe the posters and followed them into the city – only to notice her mother hauling a corpse through the streets of Tarnopol, before suddenly disappearing into a house which Jews entered one-by-one with their arms raised. 'Suddenly, I heard a burst of machine-gun fire,' Janett Margolies remembered. 'After a few minutes, the Germans were gone. One of them said they were all bumped off in there.' The next day she returned to the building and a found a huge pit in the garden 'full of corpses and, on top, my poor mother, on her knees, her upper body sagging, already stiffened.' German troops stood around the mass grave taking photographs. One asked Margolies who was responsible, unaware she was Jewish. 'Unable to control myself, I yelled at them: "You and your lot!"'

Despite her mother's murder, Margolies' son and husband reluctantly reported for labour duties that same day as ordered – but failed to return in the evening. It took her several days to discover their fate.

> They had been forced to transport the corpses of Ukrainians from the prison to the cemetery. While my husband was working on the truck, my son and other Jews were pulled from the truck, chased and beaten with sticks and boards. It seems that my son cried out, 'You have no right to beat and torture us, we're not guilty. Kill us but stop torturing us!' In response, he was beaten to death. My husband, seeing his dead son, fainted. The Germans noticed that he had stopped work and started beating him ferociously until he stopped moving. A little later, they shot him.

The corpses of Jews lying in Tarnopol's streets became as commonplace as shot-up Soviet tanks at every road junction. The dead were piled up against walls in squares, along bridges, or were tossed into the River Seret. The first victims were killed by bullet; those murdered later were butchered by picks and spades to spare ammunition. Dutchman Marinus Weers was 'delighted' that Tarnopol's Jews were being 'held to account'. The Russians had 'acted like animals' in the city. 'Like everywhere, the Jews ran everything and subjected the people to their carnal desires,' the 23-year-old noted. 'The Jews played a major role in these killings,' Weers sneered. 'They are being punished in the same place. An eye for an eye and tooth for a tooth!' A comrade told his family back in the Netherlands 'how nice it was to hang a Chief Rabbi from the tower of his synagogue – and then set the building on fire'.

Outside the city, the vanguard of 9th Panzer Division waited for the ground to dry after a cloudburst so its reconnaissance vehicles could push east. A commander told junior officer August von Kageneck to speak to one of his men who'd returned from Tarnopol with 'funny stories'. The *Wiking* Division, said the soldier, had made use of its two-day halt in the city to murder all its Jews.

'Every Jew?' Kageneck quizzed him.

'Yes, every Jew.'

'How did you know they were Jews?'

'It was obvious, wasn't it? Their noses, their beards, their strange clothes...'[135]

The pogrom spread to the surrounding villages. In Dobropole, Polish priest Józef Anczarski looked on as the joy and excitement of 'liberation' almost immediately gave way to more base instincts. 'Enemies are listed on leaflets: Bolsheviks, Poles, Hungarians and Jews. They will be destroyed,' the clergyman noted. Ukrainians barged into the homes of Poles at gunpoint. 'An armed snotty-nosed kid kidnapped my landlord a few minutes ago,' Anczarski wrote. 'Behind him an entire group of rabid Ukrainians.' The Pole called this 'liberation frenzy'. And Ukrainians exercised their newly found freedom by butchering Jews first, then Poles. The mob moved through the streets singing: 'Death, death, death to the Poles, death to the Jewish-Muscovite communes' or chanting, 'Slaughter the Poles'. South of Tarnopol, Emilian Hindelang watched a group of Jews 'atone' for their crimes as Ukrainian militia led them into a courtyard at dusk.

> The Jews were driven naked into a corner of the yard where there was dirt up to their knees. The Ukrainians had armed themselves with all kinds of weapons and were now attacking the Jews. They were horribly beaten, so that skin and flesh hung in shreds from their bodies. The screams were terrible. Then they were made to kneel down in the mud and had to sing – I don't know the song. After about half an hour they were shot.

When Hindelang and his comrades awoke early the next day to resume their march, the bodies still lay in the courtyard 'covered all over in blood, lying in the mud. One was still twitching.' As the infantrymen set off, Jews armed with spades were marched in. 'They had to bury their kinfolk,' Hindelang wrote.

'Anyone who knows how this murderous rabble acted in Ukraine can understand all this. In any case, I felt no sympathy.'

Frequently, German troops either encouraged or took part in the atrocities. In a village just east of Tarnopol, the *Wiking* Division joined in a pogrom already under way. 'We seized a couple of Jews and had our car polished until it glistened,' Marinus Weers recorded in his diary. The SS men were not done, however. The Dutchman continued:

> First, we shaved the Jews. We left half their beard and cut off the other half with scissors. Some beards we burned off using petrol. Later we handed them over to the commander. They were driven through the gate into a pond, and then *prrt prrt* from carbines and the shot Jews fell into the water. I saw the pond the following morning. It was full of the dead and half-dead. Groaning and a foul smell. I put my handkerchief over my mouth because I had to throw up.[136]

Finn Ensio Pihkala found the pond in Grymailov filled with several hundred corpses. Grymailov's surviving Jews fared no better; they were forced to clean courtyards by hand before being led away for execution. 'One German tried to shoot a 62-year-old Jewish man four times without hitting him,' the Finnish chaplain observed. 'He ran out and smashed the Jew's head to smithereens.' Pihkala noted that many German officers voiced their disgust at such acts. They did not, however, punish the offenders. When Norwegian SS troops came across the bodies of three Ukrainian women – 'mutilated in the most bestial and cruelest way – eyes sticking out and so on' – they searched a neighbouring house, where they found another half dozen corpses, 'and, under a blanket, a Jew who was alive. When he realised that he had been found, he bleated us: "I did not do that. I'm hurt. I live nearby." A short trial. He was shot in front of the house at point-blank range – his head blew apart and the mass of his brain spilled out.'

Junior officer Walter Melchinger could have intervened to prevent such atrocities, but did not. 'You must be amazed that I coldly stand by and watch,' he conceded to his wife. 'I'm usually filled with rage at the murderers. Don't believe that war makes someone brutal and insensitive. There will always be good and evil. We are grateful that we are fighting for good to eliminate the bad. The new era marches with us.'[137]

What happened around Tarnopol was the last major pogrom of around three dozen anti-Jewish riots which swept through Lvov and upwards of three dozen Galician villages and towns in late June and early July 1941. No toll of the dead was kept. Only the advancing *Einsatzgruppen* and *Einsatzkommandos* were methodical as they carried out arrests and executions in the soldiers' wake, 'cleansing' the Galician heartland. In Dobromil, 132 Jews were shot. In Yavorov, a 'mere' 15. The killings in Sokal lasted several days, the toll rising above 300. The figure was similar in Lutsk – until the bodies of ten German soldiers were found, and a further 1,160 Jews were shot in 'retaliation'. In the first two weeks of the war in Ukraine, German security forces estimated they'd executed 7,000 Jews in revenge 'for the inhuman atrocities'.[138]

In the first two weeks of the war, Army Group South had pushed a good 150 miles into Soviet territory. Kiev lay just 250 miles to the east. Ahead, the panzers continued through the steppe, followed almost wearily by the infantry. 'The daily routine was basically always the same,' reservist non-commissioned officer Herbert Schrödter wrote. In the morning, units threaded their way into the marching columns and headed in the direction of their destination – typically 15 to 20 miles away. 'It went on and on, day after day, week after week,' Schrödter noted. 'But the mood was good. We were advancing!' Emilian Hindelang was struck by the 'huge grain fields everywhere – you can see that here we are in the granary of Europe'. And to Erich Drechsler, serving in 530th Infantry Regiment, the advance was both monotonous and mesmerising:

> Now we're advancing on a better road, under a blazing sun, sweaty, covered in dust, or in thunderstorms which leave us completely soaked, water in our boots. Sometimes motorised columns overtake us. Every now and then they throw cigarettes at us. Oh how we envy them! Far ahead in the distance we're greeted by a field of hops – it's on fire and tells us that war is already here. But there are often places that do not show the slightest trace of an army passing through. Distant and endless, the fertile terrain of Ukraine spreads out. Golden wheat, fields of sunflower, cucumbers, tomatoes – these are the fruits of this land, and occasionally in between there's corn. The earth is black, there are no stones, fertility wherever you look. Our panzers cut wide roads through the golden grain. The heart shudders at such a sight.[139]

6

VICTORY DENIED

I feel that the war will continue somewhere from the depths of this endless land, even if Moscow is occupied.

Gotthard Heinrici

'LET THE PEOPLE HEAR HIS VOICE...' MOSCOW, 3 JULY, 6.30AM

It was nearly midnight on Wednesday 2 July and David Ortenberg was still at the offices of *Krasnaya Zvezda*, making the final touches to the Thursday edition of the official organ of the Red Army. The phone rang. On the other end was the bespectacled alcoholic Aleksandr Shcherbakov, head of the newly created Soviet Information Bureau news agency.

'How's the newspaper going?'

'Finished. It'll soon be rolling off the presses,' a pleased Ortenberg reported.

'Hold the front page. There's some important news coming.' With that, Shcherbakov put the phone down.

Ortenberg immediately called the editors of *Pravda* and *Izvestia* to see if they knew what the 'important news' was. They did not. David Ortenberg drew the only conclusion he could based on previous experience. Joseph Stalin was about to speak.

It was what the people of the Soviet Union needed in July 1941. For nearly a fortnight, since Molotov's speech on the opening day of the war, Soviet citizens had heard nothing from their leaders. To be sure, there had been proclamations and declarations, resolutions by this arm of the

Communist Party or that. But apart from the occasional – and highly inaccurate – official communiqué, the loudspeakers on street corners across the Soviet Union merely spewed out music. 'Knowing that people are dying and all we hear is music merely makes us want to throw up,' one Leningrader fumed. People wanted news, they wanted encouragement – and they wanted to hear from their leader. 'We are waiting for Comrade Stalin,' the same Leningrad citizen complained to local Party leader Andrei Zhdanov. 'He is the head of government and he has to speak to the people about our current situation.' His continued silence played into the hands of the panic mongers. 'Where is he? Is he afraid of his people? Let him approach the radio, let the people hear his voice, the voice of the one in whose honour we sing so many songs.'[1]

Night in Moscow had turned to day. It was now gone 5am on Thursday 3 July and still David Ortenberg's front page was blank. The *Krasnaya Zvezda* editor picked up the telephone again, this time to call the head of the TASS news agency, Yakov Havinson. Havinson responded to Ortenberg's enquiry with a single word: *wait*.

While David Ortenberg waited, Yuri Levitan was being frisked in a Kremlin anteroom in the presence of Stalin's police chief Lavrentiy Beria and head bodyguard Nikolai Vlasik. No voice in the land – not even that of the *vozhd* – was better known than the deep, clear but rather stern tone of the 26-year-old radio announcer. 'Answer all Comrade Stalin's questions with "yes" or "no",' Beria and Vlasik told him. 'Don't ask him anything.'

Levitan found Joseph Stalin rather warmer than his henchmen. 'So that's what you look like – just as I'd imagined you,' the Soviet leader greeted the young broadcaster. He had brought Levitan to the Kremlin for advice – it had been more than two years since the Soviet leader had spoken publicly.

'How should I speak?'

'Like you always do, Comrade Stalin,' Levitan told him.

'And where should I pause?'

'Where you always pause, Comrade Stalin.' The *vozhd* laughed.[2]

It had turned 6.30am before Joseph Stalin was ready to address the nation. As a burst of classical music ended, Yuri Levitan seized the microphone.

Attention! Attention!

Listen! Moscow is speaking!

Moscow is speaking!
All radio stations of the Soviet Union are broadcasting.
Listen to the speech by the Chairman of the State Committee of Defence,
  Comrade Stalin.

The slow, rather monotone voice which those awake at this hour next heard was nervous, the Georgian accent more pronounced than usual. 'Comrades, citizens, brothers and sisters, soldiers of our Army and Navy, I turn to you, my friends...' This was a new vocabulary for Stalin, addressing the Soviet peoples as their father rather than their *vozhd*. For the first time, too, he conceded that Soviet forces had been defeated and Soviet soil was now in German hands: Lithuania, 'a considerable part of Latvia', western Byelorussia and western Ukraine. The Soviet Union was 'in grave danger': 'In spite of the heroic resistance of the Red Army, and despite the fact that the enemy's finest divisions and finest air force squadrons have been smashed and met their doom on the field of battle, the enemy continues to push forward, hurling fresh forces to the front.'

How could this be? Stalin asked his people. How could the Red Army surrender sacred soil to the invader? Was the German Army invincible? 'Of course not!' the *vozhd* said forcefully:

> History shows that there are no invincible armies and never have been. Napoleon's army was considered invincible, but it was beaten in turn by the armies of Russia, England and Germany. Kaiser Wilhelm's army was also considered invincible, but it was beaten several times by Russian and Anglo-French troops, and was finally smashed by the Anglo-French forces.

Hitler's army, Stalin promised, would suffer the same fate. Only on Soviet soil had it actually encountered serious resistance. 'This means that it too can be smashed and will be smashed, as were the armies of Napoleon and Wilhelm.'

Smashed, yes, but Stalin did not play down the threat posed to the Soviet Union. 'Our country is locked in a life-and-death struggle with its bitterest, most cunning foe, German Fascism.' It was essential, the *vozhd* underlined, that the Soviet people understood this:

> At stake is the life or death of the Soviet state, the life or death of the peoples of the Soviet Union. The question is whether those people shall be free or become slaves. The Soviet people must realise this... The Red Army, Red Navy and every citizen of the Soviet Union must defend every inch of Soviet soil, must fight to

the last drop of blood for our towns and villages, must display the daring, initiative and mental alertness that are inherent in our people.

Should the enemy prevail on the battlefield, he was to be left nothing. No locomotives or wagons in railway stations, no petrol in fuel tanks, no crops, no cattle, no machinery on the collective farms. The occupier should find nothing more than a wasteland – and partisan units and saboteurs, 'fomenting guerrilla warfare everywhere' by destroying bridges, railway, telephone and telegraph lines. Life in the occupied territories must become 'unbearable' for the enemy.

After nearly 20 minutes at the microphone – punctuated by the occasional pouring of water into a glass – Stalin's delivery had become faster, more confident.

> Comrades, our forces are limitless. The arrogant foe will soon learn this to his cost. Side by side with the Red Army, thousands of workers, collective farmers and intellectuals have risen up to fight the enemy. The people will rise up in their millions… Every worker must put their lives on the line to defend their freedom, their honour and their Motherland in this patriotic war against German Fascism…
>
> Rally around the Party of Lenin and Stalin and around the government. Give unselfish support to the Red Army and to the Red Navy to wipe out the enemy and achieve victory.
>
> All our efforts to support our heroic Red Army and our glorious Red Navy!
>
> All efforts by our people to destroy the enemy!
>
> Forward to victory![3]

As the *vozhd* finished, the rousing chorus of the *Internationale* rang out twice:

> This is our final, decisive battle
> With the Internationale
> Humanity will arise!

In his office, David Ortenberg felt moved like never before after a speech by the leader. 'Stalin's first words literally pierced my soul,' he wrote. 'The bitter truth could be heard in his words. He answered the burning questions that worried all our people back then very frankly.' The speech 'shone clear light on what was happening and, most importantly, it strengthened the Soviet people's sense of optimism, confidence in their own strength'.

Within an hour, a transcript of Stalin's address was in Ortenberg's hands. It would lead not just *Krasnaya Zvezda*, but every Soviet newspaper this Thursday.[4]

'PUT A WEAPON IN MY HANDS TO DEFEND THE GREAT HOMELAND...' REACTION TO STALIN'S SPEECH

Throughout the day, Stalin's speech was repeated on the radio – read by Yuri Levitan, no recording was made of the *vozhd's* early morning address – and read out to gatherings of workers, Party rallies and patriotic demonstrations. Thirty-year-old history teacher Vasily Savchenko had just received his call-up papers when he heard his leader's appeal. 'We will remember his words and vow to fight for our homeland to the last drop of blood,' he recorded.

As they had done during the first couple of days of the war, Communist Party spies and NKVD agents moved among the workers and crowds, noting their reaction. 'The speech on the radio by Comrade Stalin provoked a new surge of patriotism, energy and will to strive for victory over Fascism among the working people of Moscow and the Moscow Region,' one report noted. 'His words – brothers and sisters – reach the heart of everyone,' an employee at a Moscow plastics factory declared. 'I want to work even harder, giving all my strength and energy to my beloved Motherland.' It was a common reaction. A worker at a carburettor factory noticed that immediately after the speech 'the mood of the people lifted. Our people believe in their leader. If Comrade Stalin said that victory is assured, then we will win.' In Leningrad, 70-year-old artist Anna Ostroumova-Lebedeva felt Stalin's words 'pour feelings of calm, hope and cheer into the soul'. A composer at the Moscow Conservatory was convinced the address would prove to be 'a turning point in the entire war. Today or tomorrow our troops will halt the Germans and go over to the counter-attack.' A machine-tool operator immediately stopped work, realising his place was at the front as a machine-gunner. He signed up for the Moscow militia there and then. One trolleybus conductor felt equally strongly, handing in his notice, and volunteering for the Red Army 'where I will risk my life to destroy the Fascist reptiles'. An employee in a leather factory in Novgorod, south of Leningrad, felt similarly inspired: 'When brutal fascists are trampling Soviet soil, when the blood of Soviet patriots is being shed protecting the Motherland, the peaceful lives and work of our wives, children, sisters and brothers, I beg you Comrade Commissar to send me to the front as a volunteer, put a weapon in my hands to defend the great homeland, the USSR.' And from an insurance inspector: 'If I am honoured enough to be given a rifle, I will defend my Fatherland to the last drop of blood. As long as the enemy lives, I will not surrender.' She was 50 years old.

'Today you have to stretch your imagination that people truly believed in Stalin – it wasn't mythical, the masses believed,' one listener recalled half a century later. 'Naturally propaganda and agitation played a huge role, but people believed in Stalin as someone whose will and mind would help all of us defeat Fascism and restore our peaceful lives.' But not every Soviet citizen was rallied by Joseph Stalin's words. 'Everything is crashing down. The situation at the front is hopeless,' a literary researcher commented, while an engineer named Perelman remarked: 'All these speeches, the mobilisation of the people, the organisation of the militia in the rear will not save the situation.' One academic was overheard remarking – with remarkable prescience: 'Our leadership has failed, broken away from the people, and when the people are victorious, this mob will reappear and claim the victory for itself.' And in Moscow, one citizen assured comrades that they faced 'inevitable' defeat and the occupation of their capital. 'Everything that we have spent the past 25 years creating, it's all turned out to be a myth.'[5]

Few men at the front heard their leader's words on 3 July. But they learned of them in the days that followed. 'Our most important work is making Stalin's speech clear to every Soviet soldier,' one commissar, killed later in the summer, wrote. When the situation at the front allowed, *politruks* gathered platoons and companies explained the meaning of Stalin's speech, how the entire nation was responding to his and the Party's appeal to wage a great patriotic war. 'They stressed that the struggle would be bitter and difficult, that there would be many setbacks, there would be hardship and sacrifice, but the Fascist invader could never defeat our mighty, hard-working peoples,' rifle corps commander Ivan Fedyuninsky remembered 20 years later. 'It's difficult to describe the great enthusiasm and the patriotic lift this appeal aroused. It was as if we had greater strength.'[6]

'IN A FEW WEEKS WE'LL BE IN MOSCOW...'
THE GERMAN ARMY, EARLY JULY 1941

While Joseph Stalin nervously addressed his nation, in the humid pine forest on the western shore of the Mauersee in East Prussia staff officers were collating the morning situation reports arriving at two partially buried concrete bunkers which served as the German Army's communications link with the armies and army groups on the Eastern Front. At 8am, their work done, they briefed the German Army's operations officer, Major Adolf Heusinger, on the situation so he, in turn, could report to the Chief of the General Staff, Franz Halder. The highly strung Bavarian was pleased with progress this Thursday morning. In the south, he brushed aside warnings of substantial Soviet forces hiding in the Pripet marshes, waiting to strike into the ever-lengthening German bulge extending across Ukraine. In the centre of the front, Heinz Guderian's panzers were over the Beresina, while the infantry armies were making good progress in crushing the westernmost of the two enormous pockets of Soviet forces trapped between Białystok and Minsk. And in the north, Erich Hoepner's armour was on the move for Leningrad once again – despite heavy rain which turned the roads into a mudbath. Eberhard Kinzel, the army's head of intelligence for the Eastern Front, and Rudolf Bogatsch, the Luftwaffe's reconnaissance chief, brought similarly encouraging news. They reckoned upwards of 20 divisions had been wiped out at Białystok, another 15 divisions smashed in the north, while in Ukraine the Red Army had been 'torn apart and scattered'. All the information Franz Halder possessed suggested the Red Army was beaten and the Soviet Union was on the verge of collapse. 'It is therefore probably no overstatement to say that the campaign in Russia has been won inside two weeks,' he recorded in his diary, before adding a caveat: 'Of course this does not mean that it is over – the sheer geographical size of the land and the stubbornness of the resistance, which continues unabated, will demand our time and effort for many more weeks to come.'[7]

A few miles away at the Wolf's Lair, Hitler's staff were counting the days until victory. 'We've already covered two-thirds of the distance to Leningrad and are half the way to Moscow,' the Wehrmacht's official diarist Helmuth Greiner wrote. 'I think we'll be there in 14 days. The Russians seem to be weakening, there are many reports of signs of disintegration. They've lost so many aircraft and tanks (4,600) that they can't have many more left.' His confidence stemmed from the pronouncements of his leader, who spent his days attending military briefings and situation conferences, receiving occasional guests – such as successful U-boat commanders to whom he gave awards – and especially subjecting his entourage to an insight into his world view with monologues extending into the small hours. The heat and humidity were stifling. The Führer's audience struggled to remain awake, despite the enthralling subject matter: the importance of religion, the origins of man, the need for a network of Autobahns across the new German empire. At times he railed against the Jews – 'the bacillus and stimulant to all human social decomposition'. He had demonstrated, so he claimed, 'that a nation can live without Jews, that the economy, culture, art, and so on can exist without Jews, in fact they're even better. That is the gravest blow I have dealt the Jews.' At other times he ruminated about Russia. The land would become a German colony, its people reduced to servitude, its capital erased from the surface of the earth. 'I will stand before history as a destroyer of Bolshevism,' he boasted to Walther Hewel, veteran of the 1923 Munich Putsch and now the Foreign Office's man at the Führer's headquarters. 'He is absolutely convinced of victory,' Hewel added in his diary. Secretaries overheard their leader brag: 'In a few weeks we'll be in

Moscow', while he assured his recently returned former ambassador to the Soviet Union that German soldiers would be parading through Red Square by 15 August, and the entire campaign would be won by the beginning of October.[8]

In July 1941, many ordinary German soldiers shared their Führer's confidence. A non-commissioned officer in 18th Infantry Regiment assured his family that 'the campaign here in the East will only last a little longer'. Motorcyclist Albert Frank agreed: 'This war can't last much longer. We'll soon march into Moscow.' Radio operator Wilhelm Moldenhauer told his wife Erika that 'I'm certain that this campaign won't last much longer.' Tank gunner Karl Fuchs reckoned that 'within eight to ten days this campaign will be over', telling his family, 'You can be proud of the German soldiers and the military accomplishments of our men.' The date passed, but still Fuchs remained certain of victory. 'We're all of the opinion that it is merely a matter of weeks before these Russians will have to give up.' A Stuttgart doctor serving with 25th Infantry Division who had predicted the struggle in the East would reach its climax 'by 10 July' revised his estimate to 'a few weeks' two days before his self-imposed deadline. 'Hopefully the Bolsheviks will soon start running – then there'll be no stopping them,' he wrote home. 'They'll be pursued relentlessly until they're completely beaten.' He was still confident at the beginning of August. 'The Russians cannot offer really serious resistance anywhere, to say nothing of mounting an offensive anywhere! They're far too weak for that...' A junior officer in 36th Infantry Division assured his family in Worms on the Rhine that 'the bulk of the work up here has been done. In a couple of weeks [Saint] Petersburg will fall into our laps like a ripe fruit.' Fighter pilot Erbo von Kageneck could picture nothing but a triumph of German arms. 'The Russian Army is already beaten and breaking apart,' he assured his family on 6 July. 'By the time you receive this letter everything will probably be settled. The question remains: can the remnants of the Red Army still withdraw as far as the Urals? Well, perhaps another 14 days, and I shall be back home. It's the English Channel that will be calling me from now on.' One week later he was still in Russia, physically and mentally exhausted by the strain of constant action, yet upbeat all the same. 'The goal and success are everything,' he told his parents. 'The most glorious victory will be our victory over Bolshevism.'[9]

'FAREWELL, VILLAGE, PERHAPS I WILL NEVER SEE YOU AGAIN...' THE USSR MOBILISES, SUMMER 1941

While Erbo von Kageneck dreamed of victory, the Soviet Union was mobilising its human and material resources. Just three days into the war, a commission was established to move key industries from the great cities of Ukraine and European Russian and out of reach of the grasping pincers of the panzers, or even the Luftwaffe, to the depths of the Soviet Union, beyond the Ural mountains, to Siberia, Kazakhstan. In just four months, more than 1,500 factories were relocated, four out of five of them armaments works. Despite the loss of land, resources and workers, despite the chaos and disruption caused by uprooting industry, Soviet factories produced twice the number of aircraft and two and a half times the number of tanks in the second half of 1941 than they did in the first six months.

It would be 1942 and beyond before the material losses of the first months of the war – tanks, artillery, rifles and aircraft – were rectified. It proved far easier – and quicker – to fill the gaps torn in the ranks of the Red Army. Five million men received call-up papers before the end of June alone as the Red Army's mobilisation apparatus swung into action, the first of 14 million men of military age – 16 to 50 – who had received some form of training to be drafted. Law professor Tamurbek Davletshin and Jewish reservist Lieutenant Yevtushevich were two such men among millions hastily pitchforked into battle in the summer of 1941. To Yevtushevich, called up to join 64th Pioneer Battalion, it all seemed 'rather rushed' as he left his mother, wife and daughter behind.

> With a sad feeling I looked into the face of my poor mother, a face that is indescribably dear to me, and thought: What a hard life she's had, what good things has life given her? Here she is, sitting beside me, my old mother, holding the turmoil deep down inside her in check, barely managing to stop the tears from flowing. She made the sign of the cross and thrust a piece of paper into my hand at the gate of the barrack square. I want to show that I'm strong, hold her poor little hands, but there are tears and gratitude in my heart for her worries. I quickly said goodbye to my mother and, with a lump in my throat, choking back the tears, I kissed all of them.[10]

Identical scenes were played out in towns, cities and villages across the Soviet Union in the summer of 1941. In one village, 'people stormed the shops and took all the bottles of Moscow Special [vodka],' the son of one conscript recalled:

> Everyone was drinking – those who were being taken away, those who were staying. And they were all in tears, as though they were saying goodbye forever. Father turned around, took a deep bow and spoke with a quavering voice. 'Farewell, village, perhaps I will never see you again. Farewell fields. Farewell everyone.' Then he came to us, kissed us one by one and said to mother: 'Go home and take care of the children.'

'Everywhere you looked, our beloved Russia was crying its heart out,' a villager in Drankovo, just outside Moscow, observed. 'People made no effort to restrain themselves, but mourned freely and without shame. Women wailed and lamented, howling inconsolably as if for the dead, knowing in their heart of hearts that this was the final farewell.'[11]

They were right to weep. Most of the men mobilised in the summer of 1941 would be dead or in German hands before the year's end, thrown into battle with few thoughts of tactics and none for human life. On the day of Joseph Stalin's speech alone, 75 military trains left the capital for the front, some carrying material, food and ammunition, but three dozen of them packed with fresh recruits – upwards of 80,000 men. Those bound for the Western Front got no closer to the battlefield than Smolensk. From there they continued by truck or on foot. When men finally reached their units, they found plenty of fellow draftees – but little else. There were shortages everywhere: rifles, uniforms, helmets and canteens. There were too few horses, too few radios, insufficient artillery support, insufficient ammunition. The rear services – transport, medical provision, field kitchens – were particularly bereft. Most men received only the most rudimentary military instruction, while their officers were ill-trained, with little or no combat experience. Thus was the Red Army able to raise enough new divisions to throw 13 fresh armies into the fray by the end of July. They flowered briefly, withered, then died. Take the case of Thirteenth Army. Nothing but a name on paper on 22 June, in a matter of days it was three rifle corps strong. It was all but destroyed in the Minsk pocket, only to be re-formed in the first week of July with two entire new corps.[12]

Lieutenant Yevtushevich's pioneers passed through Leningrad on their way to serve with the shattered Western Front. 'The city's inhabitants warmly welcomed us,' the junior officer wrote. 'Their honesty and their wishes of a happy return were particularly noticeable as they accompanied us. But in the eyes of everyone there was concern, concern for us, concern in us.' The battalion was marched from one location to the next with little aim or direction until finally being committed, where it was wiped out at the end of August. Called up at the end of June in Kazan, 500 miles east of Moscow, lawyer Tamurbek Davletshin was assigned to an infantry regiment in Novgorod, south of Leningrad. It did little fighting, only retreating and attempting to save itself from Luftwaffe attacks. The men were driven on by a reservist officer and Party fanatic who threatened them with being shot if they fled the field of battle – 'Better to be dead than a coward!' – and spurred them on with promises which could not be fulfilled: 'The Red Army's great attack has begun. In three days we'll be lying in bed with young German girls in Berlin.'[13] Tamurbek Davletshin was taken prisoner in his first encounter with the enemy.

Company commander Peter Sebelev received his baptism of fire outside Smolensk. Sebelev watched his men run at German panzers armed only with Molotov cocktails – knocking out the enemy armour but killing themselves in the process. Several more panzers ran over mines, but still the attack continued until Sebelev's lines crumbled and the enemy ranged at will in his rear. The company retreated, but not in panic and not disheartened. It had, Sebelev told his family, 'put up a good fight... After this first encounter, our soldiers cheered up and were certain that we would beat the Fascists. They strutted around Europe and no-one punched them in the face.'[14]

Similar resolve is expressed time and again in letters sent home by Soviet soldiers in the summer of 1941. They believed their land had been violated, despised Fascism and were convinced that whatever defeats they were suffering were only temporary. If Mother Russia stood firm, she would triumph. 'Our people will never forgive Hitler's thieves for the crimes they are committing in our homes and for mocking the Soviet people,' Vladimir Meladze, senior navigator in a bomber squadron, told his family. His men faced fearful odds flying round-the-clock missions trying to stop the invader – all too often the Luftwaffe prevailed. 'Nevertheless, the men remain resolute and, most importantly, believe in victory.' Quartermaster Fedor Chernikov, in charge of providing the units of Southwestern Front with food, urged his wife to 'stick it out: victory will be ours – the entire world is on the side of the Soviet Union. Now all the people will have to rise up to defend their Motherland.' A soldier in 836th Motorised Rifle Regiment promised his wife: 'The enemy will be defeated, victory will be ours. Lyenusya, do not worry, I will return and we will have a happy life...' Boris Oskarovich Rauschenbach, a 31-year-old gunner in a tank regiment in Ukraine, reassured his parents: 'The enemy is strong, but we'll beat him, it cannot be otherwise... It is time to teach these Fascists – Hitler and his mob – a good lesson. They've gone too far.' Rauschenbach had not yet seen action, 'but I soon will'.[15]

Yet there were also soldiers prepared to betray the Soviet Union. Peter Sebelev watched 20 men throw away their rifles, clamber out of their trench and dash towards the German lines waving white strips of cloth torn from their shirts. 'Everywhere there were shouts: "Shoot at the traitors of the Motherland!" I too gave my men the same order. The traitors were shot with machine guns.'

It failed to deter three more of Sebelev's men from abandoning their position and running to the rear. 'Brothers, where are you going? Are we not Russians!' one soldier shouted at them. Several more left the trench and chased after the deserters, beating them with their fists and eventually driving them back into the trench. Sebelev was appalled by such cowardice:

> In peacetime, we all wore the same uniform, seemed to be all the same Russian people and nobody knew what was in the soul of the other. And it turned out that not all of them were the same. Among those who walked in the same uniform, ate the same Russian bread, breathed the same air and sang the same Red Army songs were traitors, treason was buried deep down in their souls.[16]

'I HAVE COMMITTED NO TREASON OR TREACHERY...' SOVIET SCAPEGOATS, JULY 1941

It's estimated 300,000 Red Army soldiers – perhaps more – deserted in 1941. But desertion alone could not explain the scale of the Soviet defeat that summer. The supreme leader could, of course, not bear the blame. Instead, scapegoats were sought – and found.

In mid-July 1941, submariner Peter Grishchenko ran into his old friend Yuri Afanasiev at the naval headquarters in Tallinn.

'What happened? Why are you here?' Grishchenko asked.

'I'm a defendant,' Afanasiev sobbed. 'In two hours' time I'll face the Revolutionary Tribunal. But believe me, I am not guilty. So tell our classmates: "Yuri Afanasiev is not guilty. He acted on the orders of the commander of Liepāja naval base."'

Afanasiev stood accused of prematurely destroying ships and submarines in Liepāja, including the destroyer he commanded, *Lenin*. His fate was sealed by the naval base commander Mikhail Klevensky. Afanasiev, he lied to interrogators, had 'panicked, demonstrated cowardice and acted on his own initiative'.

The tone and outcome of Afanasiev's trial was set by the prosecutor's opening gambit: 'In hard times, the Fleet needs ships. And you blew them up!'

'I had to choose the lesser of two evils,' the defendant pleaded. 'It would have been worse had the ships fallen into enemy hands. I am proud that the ships and stores did not fall into enemy hands. History will absolve me.'

Yuri Afanasiev was sentenced to death and executed on 29 July. Fifteen years later, the navy reappraised his actions in June 1941 and decided they had been correct; the judgment against the destroyer captain was overturned.[17]

The command of the Western Front bore the brunt of the blame for the catastrophe, led by its commander. A general without an army, Dmitry Pavlov hung around the headquarters of Western Front for several days until NKVD troops arrested him on 4 July. Three days later, he was in Moscow, facing several hours of interrogation. He had been plotting against his Motherland for six years, his questioner argued: the collapse of the Western Front was due solely to his 'criminal actions'. At least five times, the general denied being a traitor. He bore no guilt for the disaster which had befallen his forces. 'I have committed no treason or treachery,' he protested.

Two weeks later, Dmitry Pavlov, his deputy Vladimir Klimovskikh, Fourth Army commander Aleksandr Korobkov and his senior communications officer, Major General Andrei Grigoriev, faced a military tribunal accused variously of cowardice, inaction, alarmist behaviour, spinelessness and criminal inaction. For good measure, trumped-up charges of collaboration – Pavlov, for example, was accused of betraying the Communist cause going all the way back to his time commanding tanks in Spain five years earlier – were added. Above all, each man had 'violated the military oath, dishonoured the high rank of the Red Army soldier and forgotten their duty to the Motherland'. All four were stripped of their rank and sentenced to death – a sentence carried out the same day. The bodies were tossed on a rubbish dump on the outskirts of Moscow, the men's closest families sent to the Gulag.

The purge continued later in the month: Major General Sergei Chernykh's 9th Mixed Air Division based near Białystok had been equipped with more than 200 of the latest MiG-3s and lost 350 aircraft on 22 June alone, though Chernykh's crime was fleeing the battlefield with his staff. Western Front's artillery commander Nikolai Klich survived a little longer – he wasn't shot until September. XIV Mechanised Corps' commander Stepan Oborin, gravely wounded on the fourth day of the war, was arrested on 6 July for supposedly fleeing the front, sentenced to death a month later and executed in October. Perhaps the saddest fate is that of the man thrust into Ivan Kopets' shoes as commander of Pavlov's air forces on the eve of battle. Andrei Taiurskii was in command no more than a fortnight before he was arrested for 'failings'. He was incarcerated for more than six months before being shot in a wave of fresh executions of military leaders in February 1942.

The punishment of such men, Joseph Stalin ordered, should serve as a warning to 'all cowards and panic mongers'.[18]

None of the senior commanders executed on Stalin's orders in summer 1941 had made contact with the enemy. The only man to entertain the idea was the Soviet leader himself, who buttonholed his security chief Lavrentiy Beria – possibly at the end of June, more likely late July. Was, the *vozhd* wanted to know, Ivan Stamenov still in Moscow? He was, Beria told his leader, who now wanted the Bulgarian ambassador – for nearly a decade a Soviet spy – to put his feelers out: 'What is

Hitler doing, what does he want?' More specifically to Pavel Sudoplatov, Stamenov's 'handler', Beria wanted to know how Moscow might end the war. It was prepared to cede Ukraine, Bukovina and Bessarabia and the Karelian isthmus to Berlin, perhaps other territories too. Sudoplatov floated the 'peace offer' – which Beria had assured his man was merely a ruse to buy the Soviet Union time – over dinner at Beria's favourite Georgian restaurant. Despite the Germans' startling progress, Ivan Stamenov was convinced the Soviet Union would 'win in the end, even if you retreat to the Urals'. His host persisted. 'War is a war,' Pavel Sudoplatov told his guest. 'Maybe it is worth putting out a feeler about negotiations.' The Bulgarian was not hopeful. 'I doubt anything will come of it.'

And nothing did. Soviet intelligence monitored all post and radio communications leaving Ivan Stamenov's embassy. There was not a single reference in them to any form of peace offer or negotiations.[19]

Adolf Hitler was offered no olive branch by Moscow. Had it come, he told Joseph Goebbels, he might have considered it 'provided, of course, that he had very extensive territorial safeguards in his hands and that he had smashed the Bolshevik armed forces to the last rifle'.[20]

'MY DAYS ARE NUMBERED...' RED ARMY PRISONERS OF WAR, SUMMER 1941

Whether they deserted or surrendered, few Soviet soldiers who fell into German hands in the summer of 1941 would survive the year, let alone the war. Their ordeal began the moment they were captured and marched off the field of battle to a *Dulag* – *Durchgangslager*, or processing camp – from where officers would be sent to an *Oflag* (*Offizierslager*), the rank and file to a *Stalag* (*Stammlager*). They were to be denied 'luxuries' such as coffee, tea and tobacco, and fed 'the most basic means' – meaning horsemeat. The reality was even bleaker, as Tamurbek Davletshin found when he was marched for three days in the broiling heat after his capture outside Novgorod. The 37-year-old and his fellow prisoners were given no food, only the occasional sip of water. Finally, when there was a protracted halt in a village's vegetable garden, the prisoners fell upon the grass, pulled it up, mixed it up with whatever food they had been able to hide on them – kale, potatoes, barley and bread – and boiled it with water provided by the local populace, to create what Davletshin called 'grass soup'. Such scenes were commonplace on the lanes of occupied Byelorussia, Ukraine, Latvia and Russia that summer. It was easy to trace the route a column of prisoners took from the detritus left behind: leaves, discarded turnip stalks, half-eaten potatoes or slices of melon – food tossed to the men by local inhabitants toiling in the fields. 'The sight of these debilitated prisoners, with hunger staring from their eyes, must surely damage the feeling of the population towards the Germans,' one officer noted. Cavalry regiment commander Friedrich von Broich passed a column of 6,000 'tottering figures, completely emaciated'. Every couple of hundred yards, two or three prisoners collapsed through exhaustion. Their guards – German soldiers on bicycles – made no attempt to get the men on their feet. They shot them on the spot and had the bodies tossed into the roadside ditch.[21]

After a journey of 90 miles – the second half of it, unusually, in trucks – Tamurbek Davletshin's column reached a makeshift prison camp centred on the former Red Army barracks in Porkhov, holding around 15,000 men. Each new arrival was rigorously interrogated – not by the guards, but by those held captive, desperate for news from the outside world.

'Where did they capture you?' one inmate asked Davletshin.

'At Lake Ilmen.'

'When?'

'Seven days ago.'

'Really? And you were at the front the rest of the time?'

'*Da.*'

'What's happening there … how are things … tell us…'

'Are aircraft in action?' another chipped in.

'Germans, yes, not ours,' Davletshin told them.

'What? Not one of ours all this time?'

'Not one…'

'And the Germans are advancing?'

'Very rapidly.'

'And we're retreating without a fight?'

'Well you could call it fighting…'

There was no meal that first night. The prisoners were left to sleep under the stars before settling in to the camp's routine.

They were roused for breakfast at 6am: bread and soup; the bread 'was usually stale and often covered in green mould', the latter was watery, bulked out with millet and poured into bowls, tin cans, helmets, even field caps. Given the number of inmates, it could take until mid-day to dish out 'breakfast'. Any man who attempted to obtain second helpings was hauled out of the line and beaten by guards – normally Ukrainian prisoners, armed with clubs – until he could stand no more.

The rest of the day was spent wandering around the camp. The men talked, played cards, read, shaved, trawled the black market, where they might pick up a daily ration of bread for 25 roubles, thin soup for 10 roubles, a roll-up cigarette for just 3 roubles. Some prisoners found freedom in the camp – freedom to practise their Christianity, denied them in Stalin's Russia. Davletshin listened to them discussing their faith

'We are all in the hands of God, everything happens according to His will,' said one.

'He has foreseen everything, taken care of everything. Everything has been created so wisely, so sensibly...' the other agreed.

'People should stop wanting more and they should remember the words: "So, do not worry about tomorrow, for tomorrow will worry about itself."'

'I am glad that we met and had such a pleasant talk. God brought us together...'

Nearby a group of junior officers sat around. 'Everything that awaits us is in the Bible,' said one prisoner, fixing the buttons on his jacket.

'Everything?' his comrade asked.

'Of course,' a third man confirmed.

'Is there anything about war?'

'Oh yes, it is written that two roosters will fight and the red rooster will win.'

'That means the Red Army will win! That's right, isn't it?'

'The war will end in 1941, and those who survive 1941 will be happy... That's what it says...'

With no radios, no newspapers, no contact with the outside world, prisoners seized upon the most meagre of information. 'The war is over,' a former interpreter assured the men around him. 'I heard it on the radio this morning: Molotov went to Berlin and signed a truce with Germany.'

'And what about us, will we be released?'

'Yes, lists are being prepared now, and in a week all prisoners will be able to go home,' the interpreter said earnestly.

'What? What? Prisoners will be able to go home, where has this news come from?' asked a prisoner who joined the growing crowd around the translator.

Another left the group to begin packing his belongings and wait for his captives to send him home.

The interpreter's news was, of course, false, but it didn't seem to matter. Twenty-four hours later the rumour had been superseded by more outlandish gossip.

Come evening, soup was issued again – there was no bread for supper, only breakfast. It was dark when the last prisoners ate. Then cries began to ring across the camp: 'Chapiigaa!' 'Androkhin!' 'Maklakov!' 'Filimonov!' as soldiers sought comrades or friends and prepared to settle down for the night, 15,000 men lying head to head or head to toe, perhaps using their jackets as makeshift pillows and pulling coats or cloaks over their heads to keep the warmth in.

And at 6am the prisoners were standing in line again for their soup and bread.[22]

Given the diet, the inactivity, the exposure to the elements, prisoners soon began to starve, to lose their minds, to die. While billeted near one camp holding 20,000 men, Friedrich von Broich was haunted at night by the sound of the inmates who 'howled like wild beasts. They hadn't got anything to eat.' While he passed one transit camp outside Lvov, Wehrmacht officer Edwin Grützner watched as a 'dead horse was devoured raw by prisoners inside 15 minutes, using just their hands and mouths'. A Ukrainian soldier being held in one of Kaunas' 19th-century forts slipped a note out of the camp in the hope it might reach his family in Chernigov. 'I asked many people for salvation, I've promised all my possessions, but there is no salvation,' the prisoner wrote. After two months unshaven, unwashed, undressed, undernourished, cold, plagued by lice and surrounded by the dead – 200 to 300 men perished daily – he had lost hope: 'So that's the situation I find myself in. My days are numbered. So live a good life, my dear ones, live well my loves, my friends, my acquaintances. If a good person finds this letter and sends it on, you at least know where I found a wretched, difficult end.'[23]

'HITHERTO WE WERE HUMAN BEINGS...'
OCCUPIED RUSSIA, SUMMER 1941

Those outside the camps in the newly occupied territories fared no better. After the soldiers and *Einsatzgruppen* had passed through, the occupational authorities began establishing German rule – immediately dashing hopes of an independent Lithuania, Latvia or Ukraine as one authoritarian regime replaced another. Two huge new administrative regions – *Reichskommissariat* – were created: the *Ostland*, encompassing the Baltic states plus Byelorussia, renamed White Ruthenia by the Nazis; and Ukraine, which stretched from Brest-Litovsk – one of several regions of Byelorussia swallowed by the new empire – to the shores of the Sea of Azov. Each *Reichskommissariat* required a *Reichskommissar*, one of Hitler's paladins: in the *Ostland* Heinrich Lohse, in Ukraine the particularly brutal Erich Koch. Ukraine was especially fertile ground – literally and politically. 'The vast majority of the population has turned out to be anti-Bolshevik,' a German Army intelligence officer who travelled extensively around the 'liberated' land reported at the end of September. Ukrainians sided with Berlin, not Moscow, hailed Hitler as their liberator, regarded German soldiers as their friends. Erich Koch had no intention of exploiting that goodwill. 'We didn't liberate Ukraine to please Ukrainians but to ensure Germany has the necessary living space and food supplies,' Koch told his staff. 'We really did not come here to distribute manna, we came here to create the conditions for victory.' Koch did not merely dismiss notions of Ukrainian independence; he crushed them. 'We are the master race and must remember that the lowliest German worker is a thousand times superior racially and biologically to the native population,' he declared, while on another occasion he was overheard remarking: 'If I find a Ukrainian who is worthy of sitting at the same table as me, I must have him shot.'[24]

The two Nazi fiefdoms would not be established until late July (*Ostland*) and the beginning of September (Ukraine). The civilian populace felt the impact of their new masters' rule long before then, Jews especially. Within a week of the Germans entering Lvov, its Jewish populace had been deprived of many of its rights. A curfew had been imposed. Jews were forced to wear armbands. They could no longer use non-Jewish stores or shop at the market. 'As a result they are practically condemned to starve,' observed Edwin Grützner, a Wehrmacht officer dispatched to Ukraine to exploit its economy for the German war effort. 'Thinking about it is dreadful. Devising something like this is dreadful.' Work parties moved wearily through the streets 'beaten, starving, carrying heavy loads, tortured, humiliated and ridiculed,' polytechnic assistant Stanisław Różycki wrote. A Jew's home offered no sanctuary, for the mob simply smashed their way in, looted at will and subjected the inhabitants to beatings. 'They are fair game,' Grützner wrote, before correcting himself. 'These people are actually worse than fair game. Even fair game is killed according to the rules of hunting. Here there is no law, no justice any more, and no longer the law of humanity, human rights.' To prove the point, a large crowd had gathered around a poster erected outside the Café Lux demanding one million Reichsmarks from Lvov's Jews to pay for the destruction of the city at the beginning of July. 'This sudden change of fortunes, from one extreme to another, is too hard a blow to take,' Różycki continued. 'A gloomy chapter of Jewish suffering in the Lvov area is beginning.'

> Hitherto we were human beings, treated as the equivalent of every other citizen in the Soviet Union. Suddenly we've been turned into sub-humans, slaves, deprived of all rights, in the course of a single day we no longer have rights. We've become the plaything of beasts, who rule over our freedom and health, our lives and possessions at will.

To Stanisław Różycki it was if he was 'living through a long period of history at an accelerated, insane, unreal pace. And yet it's true. And there's still this emptiness in the stomach.'

Otherwise, life in the Galician capital began to resume some form of normality. The market traded as usual – vegetables, fruit, every kind of berry, meat, chickens, ducks, geese, milk, cream, curd, flowers in the most beautiful blaze of colour. Except that it wasn't like the old Lvov. The smell of fire from the fighting at the end of June lingered. Prices had risen threefold since the beginning of the war.

Minsk too bore the scars of fighting long after its fall. The Byelorussian capital was still largely devastated when junior artillery officer Fritz Kalsche passed through the city in mid-August. The electricity and water supplies were working again, but otherwise the city was still devastated: the opera house burned out; tram and telegraph lines still hanging limply from wrecked poles; posters for *Tanker Derbent* – showing on 21 June – still on display in the ruins of a cinema; apartment blocks and houses little more than façades, bent, rusting bedsteads in some rooms; piles of rubble and shot-up trams in the streets; and the great statue of Lenin, toppled from his pedestal in front of the Communist Party headquarters where there were still no window panes. The bronze heel had smashed its way through the asphalt, the legs cut off, Lenin's face shattered with an axe. There was a proliferation of military signposts directing German troops to supply dumps, hospitals, railway stations and airfields, and numerous unit headquarters. Children begged for bread while prisoners worked to clear the streets. As Kalsche passed from the centre to the suburbs and finally into the Byelorussian countryside, everyday scenes changed from war to peace. 'Countless women work with sickles in the fields and mow,' he observed. 'The harvest has to be brought in.'[25]

These farmers were promised a better life under Hitler than Stalin. 'We come to you not as foes rather as liberators from Bolshevik oppression,' one poster proclaimed. 'We bring you a new order without Bolsheviks and without landowners.' They were allowed to tend to their own fields – but they were also expected to work in collective farms as they had done before the invasion; only now they would be rewarded with better pay, security and bread. It was an offer which proved more popular than Soviet rule in many parts of the occupied territories, particularly the former Polish lands of western Galicia and western Byelorussia seized in the autumn of 1939. Here the 'joy of liberation' persisted well into mid-August; the populace was described as 'pro-German' by the land's new masters, despite repeated plundering and looting by passing troops.[26]

The blunt methods employed by the Germans would soon turn this fertile ground fallow as they began rounding up scattered Soviet soldiers or Communist functionaries. A junior officer in 293rd Infantry Division received orders to seize every man aged between 17 and 60 in Wysokie Litewski, a couple of dozen miles north of Brest, in the hope of rooting out soldiers in hiding.

We surround the village with an outer ring and close the circle, gradually tightening it as we move in on the village. The local priest informs his parishioners. A church service had just taken place – the first since the land was occupied by the Soviets. The men pulled long faces, the women were desperate. When the long column was ready, the women came out with blankets and food. I stood to one side; seeing civilians being rounded up was not a pretty sight.[27]

In the village of Kabi outside Minsk, every Communist Party activist was immediately rounded up, taken to the outskirts and machine-gunned. Shenya Selenya's uncle, a member of the local soviet, was clubbed to death. 'They bashed his head in and I picked up his brain with my hands,' her aunt Katya told the five-year-old. 'It was completely white.'[28]

Such ruthless actions would, in time, turn the populace against their new masters. But in the summer of 1941 Ivan Poznyakov, the former head of the Communist Party in Grodno, found Byelorussians far more ambivalent. Poznyakov spent a month moving through the country trying to reach Soviet lines. The people, he reported, disliked their new rulers – understandably, for they seized potatoes, cattle and poultry and 'even take pieces of bread from the hands of children'. But they were evidently unwilling to take up arms against the Germans. 'When the Red Army attacks, then we'll help in the rear,' they promised. It was a far cry from the guerrilla war Panteleimon Ponomarenko intended to wage now most of his domain was occupied. Byelorussia's Communist Party leader appealed to farm labourers and villagers to rise up against the invader in visceral language:

Destroy all communications in the enemy's rear, blow up and damage bridges, roads, set fuel and food depots, cars and aircraft ablaze, cause trains to crash.

Destroy your enemies, do not give them any rest, day or night. Kill them wherever you find yourself with whatever is to hand: an axe, scythe, crowbar, pitchfork, knife… Attack airfields at night, set aircraft ablaze, slaughter pilots.

Do not wait one moment, start acting now, quickly and decisively.

Do not hesitate to resort to any means to wipe out the enemy: choke, chop, burn, poison the Fascist reptile.

Let the enemy feel the earth burning beneath his feet.

Act boldly, decisively, victory is ours. There is no such force that could conquer the Soviet people.[29]

It would be well into 1942 before an organised partisan movement truly began to disrupt the German war effort in the East.

'Think of the worst exhaustion you've felt...' German infantry in Russia, summer 1941

Never again did the German advance match the pace of the heady days of late June and early July. There were short spells – such as on the road to Moscow in early October, when the panzers once again punctured Red Army defences and raced seemingly unhindered towards the capital. And never did the advance make simultaneous progress on all three axes: Leningrad, Moscow and Kiev. The deeper German arms pushed into the Soviet Union, the more their advance stuttered and slowed – there was no 'flow' to the attack, as Johann Adolf Graf von Kielmansegg, 6th Panzer Division's operations officer, noted just days after *Panzergruppe* 4 finally resumed its drive on Leningrad. After every attack or advance, the troops stopped – sometimes to regroup, sometimes out of exhaustion. 'There's no joy of victory, to say nothing of a "victory high" as there was in France.' The demands of the new campaign – the vastness of the land, the ferocity of its defenders, the primitive conditions – quickly took their toll. 'The war has only lasted eight days, but I have the feeling that weeks have passed since we left Germany and civilisation,' 7th Panzer Division's Hans Riederer von Paar wrote on 30 June. He and his comrades 'had pretty much reached the end of our strength. The vehicles are almost all unserviceable; the men were so overtired that they could hardly go on.' When the armour did move out again, Erich Hoepner found the renewed advance 'a struggle', he conceded to his wife. 'The Russians offer dogged resistance on the few major roads and blow up every bridge, slowing our tempo considerably,' he continued. 'Today I doubt that I'll be in Leningrad on 13 July as I'd planned.' Far more confident was Army Group North's commander Ritter von Leeb. The field marshal had already selected the locations of his headquarters on his triumphal march to the Gulf of Finland, predicting the demise of the Red Army by the end of July.[30]

If the motorised divisions stuttered and lurched towards their objectives, the infantry marched robotically. To the ordinary soldier, Mother Russia appeared as much an enemy as the men defending her. Twenty-one-year-old Berliner Harald Henry wrote:

The hours when we advance are endless, 25 or 30 kilometres past smashed and burned-out tanks, vehicle after vehicle, past the outlines of villages which have been shot up or set afire. Eerie, blackened walls stand out, all alone, and in the small gardens a couple of tiger lilies still bloom in a quite sinister manner. You notice a strange smell which will probably remain with me as an indelible memory of this campaign – that mix of fire, sweat and the cadavers of horses. All of us have 'masks of dust': those who are blond have white hair with something of a dull sheen; those with black hair look like the soldiers of Frederick the Great, brightly powdered, on others the hair curls like it does on negroes, and the martial moustaches which many of us have allowed to grow – me too – turn grey. Our entire bodies are damp. Broad streams run down our faces. Not just sweat, sometimes tears too – tears of helpless fury, of despair and pain, which these tremendous efforts demand of us. No-one can tell me that someone else, that someone who isn't an infantryman, can imagine what we're going through here. Think of the worst exhaustion you've felt, the searing pain of open, festering wounds on your feet – and that's not at the end of but the beginning of a 45-kilometre march. Only gradually, after several hours, with each step along this road does your foot gradually become inured to the pain.[31]

Hartmut Petri and his comrades marched 500 kilometres in a fortnight. There was the occasional skirmish or encounter with Russian troops, but otherwise Petri's diary is a chronicle of the drudgery of incessant, monotonous marching, day after day. The men no longer surveyed the world around; their heads were lowered, eyes fixed on the ground. They unbuttoned the top button on their tunics and even several on their trousers 'to bring a little freshness'. There was no singing, none of the regular banter between comrades. 'We rarely hear a word,' Petri wrote. 'Everything is impulsive, automatic. No more jokes, no more encouragement; from time to time we hear a monotonous "get up" or "five kilometres to go".' The infantry began to dread each coming day and the exertions it might bring, especially carrying the machine-guns – weighing around 14kg. After a 22-mile march on 9 July, the regiment had reached 'the end of its tether'. The men hobbled rather than marched uniformly and collapsed instantly every time a halt was ordered. 'No-one drags themselves to the river to bathe, even though this was the dream during the march,' Petri noted.

We fall down and want to sleep, just sleep, but then comes the plague which allows us no rest and no sleep. Hundreds of flies attack us, it's dark, fires are lit, the smoke should chase the mosquitoes away; after the damned watch, I at least want to get some sleep after these exhausting days, but it's too hot under the blanket and if you leave your head outside, you're eaten alive. You don't know what to do, you have the feeling that it's all over.[32]

Man and beast longed to rest. Helmut Breymayer, marching through Ukraine with 125th Infantry Division, watched comrades 'dragging themselves forward on their own feet. The vast majority of marchers are suffering the worst effects of foot sores! Soles are painful with each footstep and in the morning some men don't know how to put their boots on.' And when the 125th clashed with its foe, the men 'limped rather than strode into battle'.[33]

The *Landser* did not question the outcome of the war, but he did wonder when it might end. As his 299th Infantry Division advanced into the heart of Ukraine, anti-tank gunner Hans Roth observed: 'The same subject dominates our conversations: When will this campaign be over?' His officers were convinced the division would be home in Erfurt by the end of September. Roth disagreed. 'I think that the Russian campaign will last much longer.'[34]

A weary Adolf Scheuer, advancing with 197th Infantry Division, believed his regiment was 'marching itself to death – almost every day we cover 45 kilometres,' he told his family.

> What it means to take part in a campaign in Russia as a simple soldier can only be measured by those who were there themselves or know the conditions here. If I didn't have a family at home for whom I live, a family that is my whole happiness in life, sometimes dying would have been easier for me than living.

And yet Scheuer maintained his faith in victory, convinced that the 'decision will fall' before the end of August and that he would 'come out of this struggle well and return home jubilant'.[35]

More insightful soldiers, like 87th Infantry Division junior officer Siegfried Knappe, noticed a growing melancholy in the German Army in the East. 'Nothing could have prepared us for the mental depression brought on by this realisation of the utter physical vastness of Russia,' Knappe recalled. 'As we marched, low hills would emerge from the horizon ahead of us and then slowly sink back into the horizon behind us. It almost seemed that the same hill kept appearing in front of us, kilometre after kilometre. Everything seemed to blur into uniform grey because of the vastness and sameness of everything.'

Plateaus 'extended as far as the eye could see' and huge fields of corn and sunflowers which 'stretched for kilometre after weary kilometre'. Tiny doubts began to creep into the men's minds, Knappe wrote. 'Was it even possible that such vast emptiness could be conquered by foot soldiers?'[36]

Helmuth Groscurth thought not. The bespectacled operations officer of 295th Infantry Division was a long-time opponent of the Nazi regime. Two months of campaigning through Ukraine convinced him not only that the war would go on far longer than expected but also 'that its outcome is extremely doubtful', he told his brother Reinhard.

Should I keep on alarming you with stories of graves, battlefields with dead and burned Russians, gutted and stinking horses, desolate columns of prisoners, transports for wounded, people with their nerves shattered, SS hordes and more? Rather, should one ignore or best of all close one's eyes completely and preserve his nerves for the pressing daily tasks, sleep on supplies and enjoy the fact that the mood of the troops is not bad yet?[37]

Helmuth Groscurth penned his letter in Bila Tserkva, just 50 miles outside Kiev. His division had advanced nearly 400 miles in under two months.

Corps commander Gotthard Heinrici had reached a similar conclusion. 'No campaign to date can be compared with this one,' he wrote in mid-July.

Our men are physically extremely exhausted. Yesterday I found the drivers of carriages sleeping like the dead in front of their horses. The tremendous marches, the unimaginable tracks – no-one in Germany has the slightest idea of what they're like – the extreme tension, not only due to the ever-changing situations, but also the danger everyone faces of being attacked – all these things are more than debilitating, nor have we seen them in any campaign to date. No-one knows how long this campaign will last. There's no end in sight at present, despite all the successes which have been achieved.

Hopefully one day Russian resistance will collapse because the situation which they find themselves in is far from pleasant. Far from it – it's actually pretty bad, but you certainly don't get the impression that the Russians' determination to resist is broken – or that the people want to get rid of their Bolshevik leaders. Right now I feel that the war will continue somewhere from the depths of this endless land, even if Moscow is occupied.[38]

After days of sluggish progress in the face of a stubborn foe who demolished every bridge on the few roads which cut through the marshland and forests of northern Russia, Erich Hoepner was forced to call off his attack on Leningrad. His *Panzergruppe* simply did not have the strength to continue. 'We are now into our fourth week in action without a day's rest, the heat is punishing, in terrain almost impassable for vehicles,' he told his wife. 'The men are growing tired, losses are rising, as is the number of vehicles out of action.' It took until mid-August for Hoepner's armour to finally puncture the Red Army's defences on the road to Leningrad. But by now, the general had one eye on his objective, the other on the Russian winter, barely six weeks away. 'We can only hope that it will soon end,' he told his wife. 'The campaign must be concluded by the end of September.'[39]

A 'SMOULDERING AND FOUL-SMELLING DESERT OF RUBBLE AND RUINS', BREST-LITOVSK, JULY AND AUGUST 1941

Although the German ensign now flew over the citadel, Brest fortress was still not entirely subdued. Each day more than 100 soldiers combed the ruins of the fortress to root out stragglers, while Soviet prisoners performed the grim task of recovering bodies. Their fallen comrades were simply tossed in the nearest shell crater – no attempt was made to identify the corpses or record where they lay. Not so the German dead. Despite a terrible state of decomposition, the bodies were searched, documents, personal effects and dog tags removed and handed to an officer, and the dead piled up awaiting a formal burial in 45th Infantry Division's cemetery. Senior Sergeant Sergei Kavalin was at work around 14 or 15 July when a group of 50 Germans marched past him, singing. As they passed under the ruins of the Terespol Gate on the west of the citadel island, there was suddenly a huge explosion. The gate – and the soldiers – were shrouded in smoke. When it cleared, ten Germans were dead and many more wounded. The perpetrator, a member of the garrison, had hidden in the remains of the tower for several days, waited for the opportunity to kill as many Germans as possible, then blown himself up.

Prisoners were brought in on a regular basis – usually from the outlying forts rather than the central citadel. Nikolai Tarasov, a sergeant in 84th Rifle Regiment, was wounded and taken prisoner on 12 July. Two nights later his regimental comrade Anatoly Petrovich Bessonov was also seized after being wounded. And Private Ivan Petrovich Oskirko from 455th Rifle Regiment succeeded in breaking out of the fortress with a small group on the night of 13–14 July. The most determined resistance came from the remains of the Eastern Fort, led by 40-year-old Major Pyotr Gavrilov, commander of a motorised rifle regiment which no longer existed. He rallied around a dozen men hiding in the catacombs of the fortification, then picked off German troops whenever the opportunity arose, waiting for the right moment to slip out of the fortress and somehow reach Soviet lines through the woods northeast of Brest – unaware that the front was now 250 miles to the east. Living on just 100g of biscuits per day, the group survived until mid-July when they stumbled into an enemy detachment and were mostly wiped out. Gavrilov fled the encounter and hid in a covered passage near the fortress's North Gate. By day he buried himself under a pile of dry horse manure, eating fodder from a neighbouring stable. He survived for ten days, surrendering on 23 July – the 32nd day of the war – after a final clash with German troops. He was taken to the prison camp at Biała Podlaska, where the Russian doctor who treated him found a man 'so weak that he could barely turn on his side'. The face of the normally clean-shaven Gavrilov was covered by a thick, unkempt beard; his skin was smeared with mud and dust. Where he'd been wounded, he had used blood-stained pieces of cloth and underwear as makeshift bandages. 'He looked awful,' the doctor recalled. 'I cannot imagine how we managed to save him.'[40]

The city itself resembled a frontier town in the Wild West through much of the summer of 1941. German officers were shot in the city centre. Men of the *Reichsarbeitsdienst*, the German labour service, regularly found the roads around their barracks littered with nails – and regularly found themselves repairing the tyres on their trucks. This lawlessness concerned Theodor Stahr, commander of the newly arrived 307th Police Battalion. There were hundreds of dispersed Soviet soldiers in the countryside outside Brest, while in the city there were stockpiles of weapons and ammunition which needed dealing with, not to mention more than 500 railway wagons packed with valuable items awaiting transportation to Germany in the goods yard. In mid-July, Stahr resolved to act – but almost exclusively against Brest Jews. His men sealed off several blocks, systematically searching houses for any Jewish men aged between 16 and 60 supposedly for a work detail. Instead, the Jews were driven in trucks to sandy terrain about 15 minutes' drive south of the city. There they were lined up in groups of ten on the edge of a huge pit before facing a volley from a firing squad of 20 police officers. Sometimes wives refused to be separated from their husbands; at least a dozen shared their fate in the mass grave. Some policemen refused to take part in the shootings; one suffered a mental breakdown. 'Many said that they never again wanted to experience something like that in their entire lives,' one officer testified two decades later. 'Others were content with saying "an order is an order". With that the matter was settled for them.' The killings continued until nightfall each day for at least one week. Occasionally there was a reward for the killers at supper time: strawberries and cream, in addition to the usual fare of smoked ham, tinned milk, bread and butter, and schnaps. When the battalion's work was done, they continued their murderous advance eastwards.[41]

Theodor Stahr's actions brought no law to Brest. All he succeeded in achieving was reducing its Jewish populace by 4,000. When the city's new military commandant, Walter von Unruh, arrived a fortnight later, he was appalled by what he found. Unruh was convinced that there were still Soviet troops shooting from the 'smouldering and foul-smelling desert of rubble and ruins' in the fortress. 'All public life had come to a standstill,' he recalled. The roads were blocked. There was no street lighting, no running water – the city's inhabitants fetched buckets from the filthy Mukhavets – windows were smashed and there were no suitable medical facilities. Unruh immediately set military and civilian authorities, as well as cityfolk, to work clearing up Brest, cleaning its streets, getting the market and main hospital running again, and combing out the fortress and military installations once more. Prisoners from Brest were delivered to Biała Podlaska in early August. 'They were all in rags,' one fellow captive remembered, 'with bloodied, filthy bandages. They were so weakened that they could hardly stand.' After a month in charge, Walter von Unruh felt it safe enough to walk the streets of Brest unarmed. 'Quiet and security reigned,' he wrote.[42]

Only now was Brest fortress deemed sufficiently safe for one final humiliation. Nearly two months after its fall, the German ensign was raised once again above the citadel. For three hours, Brest would be the focus of world attention once more as Hitler showed his prize to Mussolini. After a 20-minute briefing from army and Luftwaffe commanders at the airfield in Terespol, the two dictators climbed into open-top staff cars for the 30-minute drive over the Bug. Every Polish male who lived on the road leading to the fortress was rounded up and detained throughout the visit, while German troops searched every home and lined the route, leaving a few vantage points for local German officials and the female Polish populace, should they wish to watch. The tour of the fortress was timed to the minute; the two leaders spent five or ten minutes talking with some of the heroes of the battle, inspecting some of the weaponry used and seeing some of the destruction, 'to give the impression of the severity of the fighting for the citadel, the fighting spirit of German troops and the quality of German arms'. There was to be no mention of the heavy mortars employed, or the heavy bomb which brought organised resistance to an end. Mussolini was drawn to the large artillery pieces. How heavy were the shells? the Duce enquired. 'Rather heavy,' the battery commander responded. And the gun itself? 'Very heavy.' The Italian leader smiled. And what about the range? 'Very long, but not too long.' It was clear to Mussolini that he would glean nothing from the Germans and stopped his questioning. 'I could not help thinking that the Axis partners did not trust each other very much,' Walter von Unruh observed. The two dictators spent just 80 minutes in the ruins of Brest fortress before returning to their vehicles for the short ride back to Terespol and lunch from a field kitchen.[43]

NO LONGER CERTAIN OF VICTORY...
GERMANY, LATE SUMMER 1941

It was the beginning of September before the German public saw Hitler and Mussolini touring the ruins of Brest citadel on the newsreel. On screen, the

Führer exuded 'certainty in victory and calm confidence'. But the people he led did not. In mid-July rumours had circulated that German troops were already in Leningrad and Kiev and stood just 20 kilometres from Moscow. But no longer. As death notices began to grow in number in newspapers, as letters from the front were passed around families, and as men returned home on leave, disquieting rumours which had begun to circulate – the struggle was much harder and losses much heavier than they had been in France, many hospitals were already overcrowded – were confirmed. Consumed by the burdens of everyday life in wartime Germany such as shortages of fruit and veg and, for inhabitants of cities in western Germany, the increasing – and increasingly heavy – air raids by the British, the public quickly tired of the fanfares, the bursts of Liszt blaring from loudspeakers, the special announcements. 'Even the greatest military success' – such as breaking through the Stalin Line or the crushing of the Białystok pocket – no longer sparked the enthusiasm and excitement they had 12 months earlier in France, the official observers of public opinion noted. As July and August progressed and the fanfares and *Sondermeldungen* dried up, people began to question how long the war might last, until the majority doubted a victory for German arms in 1941. They suspected the Russians possessed 'inexhaustible masses of soldiers and material', believed the battle of France had been 'child's play' compared with the campaign in the East, and feared the true death toll on the Eastern Front was actually closer to a million men.[44]

It wasn't. It was nowhere near. But war in the East was far harder than any of Germany's previous, victorious campaigns. The first ten days of *Barbarossa* had cost the Reich 54,000 casualties, 11,822 of them dead. Every day 1,161 German soldiers had died on the nascent Eastern Front – a higher rate than in any of Hitler's military adventures to date. The Officer Corps was hit particularly hard: 61 were killed daily, double the losses of the western campaign 12 months earlier. 'Our best officers are fading away in this cruel war, which is so very different from that against Poland or even that in the West,' XXXXVII Panzer Corps' commander Joachim Lemelsen complained in mid-July. As the vanguard of the advance into the Soviet Union, corps like Lemelsen's invariably suffered the heaviest losses. When its 29th Motorised Infantry Division was pulled out of the line after a month's fighting, it had lost more than 2,600 men, nearly 700 of them dead or missing, while just 12 of the 212 tanks with which 18th Panzer Division had crossed the Bug on 22 June were still in working order. It had suffered 3,100 casualties, including 750 dead and upwards of 400 men thought to have fallen into enemy hands.[45] The latter probably survived no more than a few days in Soviet hands – as the advancing Wehrmacht all too often discovered. Perhaps as many as three-quarters of Germans captured in 1941 were killed or died of maltreatment.

By mid-August 1941, one in every ten German soldiers in the East had become a casualty – more than 375,000 men killed or wounded. Infantry divisions possessed perhaps two-thirds of the strength they enjoyed when the invasion began, panzer divisions perhaps half. No division would ever make good the losses it suffered during the opening weeks of *Barbarossa* – replacements did not even half-fill the denuded ranks.

Such a rate of attrition in the East meant that barely six weeks into the campaign, German arms could no longer attack on every axis simultaneously. 'We cannot do everything at once,' Franz Halder conceded; the Wehrmacht had to pick and choose its battles. In France, Halder had boasted that the campaign he choreographed ran 'like a well-edited film'. His diary entries through July and early August 1941 suggest nothing of the case in the East. The 57-year-old envisaged great sweeping operations to smash the Red Army en masse. Hitler fretted about the slightest enemy concentration along the front and demanded it eliminated. The constant, costly fighting was taking its toll on the men at the front; progress slowed, and there was no repeat of the vast number of prisoners seized in the opening battles of encirclement. It all led to widespread depression in the East Prussian headquarters. Just five weeks after declaring the campaign in the East 'won', the Chief of the General Staff re-assessed the situation:

> It is increasingly clear that we underestimated the Russian colossus... At the beginning of the war we reckoned with around 200 enemy divisions. We've already counted 360. Of course, they're not armed and equipped according to our standards and their tactical leadership is often poor. But there they are – and if we destroy a dozen of them, the Russians simply throw another dozen into the line. Time favours them – they are near their own resources, while we are moving further and further from ours.[46]

Franz Halder did not write it, but inwardly he knew. *Barbarossa* had failed.

EPILOGUE: *BARBAROSSA*'S LONG SHADOW

They stood unto death. Glory to the heroes.

Inscription at Brest fortress

It is a sultry Sunday morning in Iași in late June 2016 when a taxi pulls up outside my hotel – the last remnant of *fin de siècle* grandeur in Piața Unirii, a large square now dominated by brutalist Communist architecture.

'*Cimitirul Evreiesc*,' I tell the driver as I climb into the back of his yellow cab. He looks at me quizzically.

I show him my notebook with the cemetery's name written down. He nods, mutters something in Romanian and we head off.

Halfway towards our destination, he turns around and looks at me.

'Israeli?'

'*Nul, Engleza*,' I say, attempting pidgin Romanian again. '*Istorie*' – not knowing the word for historian.

'No Israeli,' he says. 'All dead. Hitler shot.'

He makes a pistol shape with his right hand and proceeds to tell me: 'Hitler kill all Israeli.'

I nod politely. '*Da, da*, Hitler.'

We continue to the northwestern edge of Iași, past an English-language school and affluent town houses, each with a new 4x4 on the driveway, which line a narrow road climbing a slope to the Jewish cemetery.

Somehow the ornate gateway at the entrance survived the pogrom of 1941 and Antonescu's anti-Jewish regime. Perhaps it was fiercely guarded then, as now, by the elderly concierge and her pack of dogs, which bark ferociously at the merest sight of anyone approaching.

The cemetery sits on a dusty hilltop – locals say Iași is built on seven hills, but it falls far short of Rome's magnificence.

The graves of the pogrom victims can be found in the cemetery's western corner: four concrete sarcophogi which step down the hillside with a memorial tablet at the end in Romanian and Hebrew. Like most things erected during Communist rule, the surroundings are crumbling, the blue paint on the star of David fading.

Before the war, the cemetery was served by more than 100 synagogues, of which just two survive today. In front of the oldest, the restored Great Synagogue, stands a small obelisk, adorned with the Jewish candle and a plaque in Hebrew, Romanian and English. It is the only memorial in commemorating the atrocities of June 1941 in Iaşi.

It is the same across much of the Eastern European borderlands where fire and fury raged for a few terrible days in late June and early July 1941. There are monuments, memorials and museums to the thousands of people deported under the Stalinist yoke and the systematic murder of the Jewish populace by the Germans. But the interregnum between Soviet and Nazi occupations is a blind spot, a gap in the public consciousness.

Take Lviv. As it did in 1941, Brygidki dominates the cobbled main thoroughfare leading from the city centre to the railway station on which trams, battered old Ladas and sparkling new Mercedes-Benz vie for space. The frosted or shuttered windows are either all closed or hang off, revealing the grills of the cells – the three-storey structure remains a prison, Detention Facility No.19, to this day.

There is no memorial at Brygidki but there is at Zamarstynivska, just north of the city. The building has reverted to its original scholastic role. A plaque recalls 'the Ukrainian Calvary' on a 'wall of memory and grief from September 1939–June 1941'. 'Over the course of six days in 1941, 7,348 prisoners were executed here: Ukrainians, Poles, Jews. Remember and pray for the victims.'

Lontskoho prison still stands, halfway up a hill from Lviv's university, a good 15 minutes' walk from the city centre. It has changed little in eight decades: the sandstone façade still faces Habsburg-era apartment blocks; there are still three floors of spartan cells, two above ground, one below. But today Lontskoho is mostly a monument and memorial – though only to the estimated 24,000 souls murdered by the NKVD in the prisons of western Ukraine between 22 June and 4 July 1941, not the Jews and Communists butchered in the subsequent wave of 'spontaneous' violence. It's the same in the city's famous Lychakiv Cemetery, where mass graves are marked with a plain white cross and simple inscription: 'Burial of the victims of the Communist regime, 1941, among them many children.'

Where there are monuments to the Jewish victims of the first days of Operation *Barbarossa*, it is all too easy to overlook them. The garage forecourt where the 'Death-dealer of Kaunas' once bludgeoned the innocent to the sound of applause and accordions has long gone. In its place, a nondescript courtyard sandwiched between a volleyball court and a faceless office block. In the middle, beneath a tree and largely hidden from view by parked cars, is a gravestone, inscribed in Yiddish and Lithuanian, with a few pebbles placed at its base. The monument to Białystok's *Shvartser Fraytik* is more substantial – a sculpture depicting the warped and broken metal frame of the burned-out dome on the site of the Great Synagogue – but no more visible. Though barely five minutes' walk from the city's main square, it occupies a drab patch of open ground between a block of flats and the car park of a utilitarian bank building. The ruins of Riga's Great Choral Synagogue were demolished by the Soviets when they re-occupied Latvia. It was nearly half a century before the Communist authorities acknowledged the site had once been a place of worship. It took Latvian independence to turn the foundations into a memorial site, though the plaque lays the blame for the massacre at the feet of Viktors Arājs and his small band of nationalist collaborators, who have become convenient scapegoats for actions and atrocities of broader Latvian society during the tumultuous few days spanning the end of June and beginning of July 1941.

Kaunas' Fort VII is the exception. It may be eclipsed as a site of pilgrimage for Lithuanians by the memorial museum to German crimes at the city's Fort IX, but no attempt is made to gloss over what happened here in the summer of 1941 – nor turn a blind eye to the perpetrators. By the time the killings came to an end on 10 August, between 3,000 and 5,000 Jews had perished. As of 75 years later, a mere 93 victims had been identified – no formal records were kept. Most of the dead came from the city, but there were some brought here from further afield: Jonava, Tauragė or Biržai in northern Lithuania, from where 66-year-old Elchonon Wasserman, one of the older victims, hailed. The youngest was possibly Josef Yosef Brojda, not yet two. Three members of the Wolpert family perished: Khaia Ana, Khana Khane and Aide Yehudit. They perished at the hands of their fellow countrymen – something the small museum in the fort makes quite clear. All are remembered by a memorial in the northeastern corner of the grounds – now covered in grass rather than gravel – which bears an inscription in Yiddish.

Lithuanians had largely welcomed the Germans into their land in June 1941. So too Latvians and Ukrainians. All would suffer as much, or worse, under Hitler than they had under Stalin. Lithuania lost around 700,000 dead, displaced, deported and missing – perhaps one-third of its pre-war population. Its northern neighbour fared slightly better, losing about 30 per cent of its people, nearly 600,000 Latvians. And then there was Ukraine. Though no extermination camps were established on its soil, it still became a land of death: it lost between eight and ten million souls between 1941 and 1945, accounting for two in every five Soviet citizens killed in the Great Patriotic War as the conflict is known in the former USSR. An estimated two million prisoners of war died across some 180 camps. The

Nazis deported nearly two and a half million Ukrainians to the Reich as forced labourers, while a further three and a half million were evacuated beyond the Urals with key industries by the Soviet authorities in the face of the German advance.

Byelorussia's losses were just as grievous. The population fell by three million between 1941 and 1944. Discounting military dead on Byelorussian soil, the Germans killed 2,357,000 people in Byelorussia – 1,547,000 civilians, perhaps half of them Jews, and around 810,000 prisoners of war. No-one and nowhere in Byelorussia was not touched by the war. In a partisan conflict which became increasingly brutal from 1942 onwards, more than 5,000 towns and villages were partially or completely erased from the map by German forces. Fewer than 200 were fully restored. By the time the Red Army returned in summer 1944, sweeping west across Byelorussia almost as quickly as it had retreated three years earlier, the damage inflicted on the country amounted to 35 times its budget in 1940.

One day in April 1942, a German staff car pulled up alongside violinist Zalman Stavsky as he trudged to work from Brest's Jewish ghetto to the city hospital, where he and other prisoners tended to wounded Germans. Before the war, Stavsky had entertained diners at a Brest restaurant. Now, for some reason, Brest's masters thought the musician would be able to draw out a Russian soldier hiding in the ruins of 333rd Rifle Regiment's barracks. As armed German soldiers ringed the entrance to an underground passage, Stavsky went down the steps and soon found the man, then succeeded in encouraging him to surrender. Above ground, the Germans were presented with a thin, heavily bearded man, his blond hair in a ponytail, his uniform reduced to rags. It was impossible to determine his age. An officer asked if there was anyone left below. 'I am alone,' the prisoner told him before collapsing on a pile of bricks through exhaustion. He was offered bread and a tin of food, but declined. 'Look,' said the German officer, turning to his men, 'this is how you defend your land. This soldier is a hero – neither death, nor hunger, nor deprivation broke his will. This is an extraordinary act.'[1] The story has never been verified, the defender never identified, but no more Soviet soldiers were discovered alive in Brest fortress.

Unlike the men of 1941, the Germans made no concerted effort to defend the fortress in 1944 as the Red Army swept westwards. Bricks from the ruins would help to rebuild the nearby city. As teams began to excavate the fortress, they continually came across the bones of soldiers given a hasty burial in 1941 – either by their fellow defenders or the Germans. They unearthed fragments of letters, orders, personal effects. In September 1956 Junior Sergeant Rodion Semenyuk returned to the casemate where he and two comrades had tried to keep the Luftwaffe at bay. He recovered the banner of the 393rd Independent Anti-Aircraft Artillery Unit – to date the only regimental standard from 1941 found on the site – and presented it to the fortress's small museum. Others carved their defiance into the brickwork and plaster, probably using the sharp edge of a stone. A decade later, these now-fading inscriptions were found by historians and battlefield archaeologists: 'Death to the German invaders', 'We will die but we will not abandon the fortress', 'There were three of us from Moscow: Ivanov, Stepanchikov, Zhuntyaev defending this chapel. We vowed never to surrender, July 1941.' A few days later, Ivanov added a postscript: 'I'm the only one left. I've one grenade left, but will not surrender. Avenge us comrades. 1941.' As late as 1952, historians researching the site discovered the most recently dated inscription: 'I am dying, but I won't surrender. Farewell, Motherland. 20/VII/41.' Barely legible, its author unknown, it was scrawled on the plaster three days before the fortress's last verified defender, Pyotr Gavrilov, was captured.

Having survived four years in German captivity, Gavrilov sought to resume his military career at the age of 45. Instead, as a former prisoner of war, he found himself shunned in the post-war Stalinist Soviet Union, dismissed from the Communist Party, stripped of his rank. He struggled to eke a lowly existence for his family as a cleaner and factory worker in Krasnodar in the Caucasus. And there he might have spent the rest of his life, but for the labours of writer Sergei Smirnov who spent the early 1950s scouring the Soviet Union for the defenders of Brest fortress. He found more than 200, organised a much-publicised reunion in the grounds of the citadel, then a reception in Moscow and appearances on state television, wrote articles, a play and a history of the fortress's defence, which became the bedrock of Soviet historiography of the Great Patriotic War. By the time the revised edition of Smirnov's account was published in 1965, the fortress's defence was enshrined in Soviet mythology and Pyotr Gavrilov had been made a Hero of the Soviet Union. Now he became an ambassador for the Soviet cause, sought out by historians, journalists, film crews eager to hear his story, a story he eventually put down on paper. When he died in 1979, he was buried in the cemetery of Brest's garrison.

The fortress itself was granted 'hero' status alongside half a dozen cities such as Stalingrad and Leningrad which had defiantly withstood the Nazi storm. In the late 1960s and beginning of the 1970s, the site was turned into a vast memorial complex, complete with oversized realist statues and installations. The citadel grounds are dominated by a 500ft-tall obelisk, a traditional Russian four-sided bayonet made of titanium – visible, fortress guides will proudly tell you – in Terespol, a couple of miles to the west, and 'Courage', a monolithic grey slab of concrete rising 100ft over a series of mass graves, depicting a grim-faced defender, his head bowed in defiance, his eyes hollow.

Beneath him, several banks of black granite tombs. Most of the Soviet dead were incinerated by the Germans in the aftermath of battle, but some bodies were not located or were buried in the ruins. Some 962 cadavers were uncovered after liberation and reinterred in these communal graves: Armenians, Georgians, Jews, Communists, Christians, Russians, Belarussians, Ukrainians. Most are marked Неизвестный (unknown); just 273 bodies were identified, among them Akakiy Ambrosievich Shevardnadze – elder brother of Eduard, the last foreign minister of the USSR – a German Communist named Meier, and Lieutenant Alexsei Maximovich Bobkov, his wife Raisa, and their daughter Azalda.

Nearby, local schoolchildren provide a guard of honour for 15 minutes at a time between 9am and 6pm at the Eternal Flame, which is bordered by earth from all the USSR's hero cities. Стояли насмерть, the inscription reminds visitors. *They stood unto death.* Героям слава. *Glory to the heroes.* From loudspeakers dotted around what is now known as the ceremonial square, there is constant choral music, Robert Schumann's *Träumerei* (Dreaming).

Of the once almost-continuous red-brick barrack blocks and imposing gates which ringed the citadel island, no more than half survive, almost entirely on the south side. The engineers' barracks, close to the northern – or Brest – gate, where defenders met on 26 June to discuss the garrison's fate, were never rebuilt, nor the gate, but there's still a bridge across the northern arm of the Mukhavets; young couples fix padlocks to the railings as a sign of their love for each other.

Peppered around the site are monuments, statues and memorial plaques to individuals, specific groups or handfuls of men, such as the border guards of Frontier Post 9, 17th Border Station, who died defending the partly demolished Terespol Gate. Nearby, at Kholmsky Gate, the sole-surviving historic entrance which has become the iconic symbol of Brest fortress, there's a relief of Commissar Yefim Fomin, posthumously awarded the Order of Lenin for his actions in June 1941. On a still day, or if the wind is in the right direction, you might hear the strains of the choral music from the ceremonial square.

St Nicholas' Garrison Church – turned into the officers' club by the Soviets – sits on slightly raised ground in the centre of the island. Restoration as a house of worship only began under *perestroika* in the mid-1980s and is still incomplete. Outside it is still pockmarked by bullets. Inside, despite being filled with icons, much of the building remains gutted. The bell tower has never been rebuilt.

Nor too the White Palace, where Germans and Bolsheviks signed their peace treaty in 1918. Destroyed on 1 July 1941, all that remains today are a few vaults of the basement and the red-brick foundations.

A couple of hundred feet away, close to the spot where the Mukhavets branches around the citadel island, another drab, realist monument, 'Thirst': a desperate soldier clutching a machine-gun in one hand and his helmet in the other to scoop water from the river.

From 'Thirst', a wide tree-lined avenue leads for several hundred yards past where many of the garrison's families once lived – the homes were never rebuilt. The boulevard continues past a handful of armed vehicles from Brest's liberation in 1944, to the main entrance to the complex, arch Soviet propaganda: a 35ft-high rampart partly obliterated by a gigantic slab of concrete with a large Soviet star carved through the middle.

There's a constant soundtrack as you pass: the loud ticking of a clock, symbolising night in the fortress, gives way to the jarring sound of engines and explosions, then the infantile jingle of Radio Moscow and the lugubrious voice of Yuri Levitan – invited back in the early 1970s to re-record the news – announces that war has broken out with Germany. As Levitan fades, the rousing patriotic song *Sacred War* resounds before the recording restarts, running in a continuous loop.

Those who fought here in June and July 1941 are now all gone. The 45th Infantry Division was wiped out in Byelorussia in the summer of 1944, destroyed in the same offensive which liberated Brest. Of the 400 or so fortress defenders believed to have survived the German onslaught, from the mid-1950s onward they returned each year, perhaps on the anniversary of the attack, or for Victory Day celebrations on 9 May, in dwindling numbers until, by 2011, they came no more.

The families of the defenders have passed into history too. A surprising number of those who lost husbands in June 1941 chose to remain in – or return to – Brest in peacetime. Arshinova Anastasia Antonovna lost her husband in the fortress, her entire family in the war. 'When I walk through the streets of Brest today, I can still see destroyed Brest in my mind and feel the pain,' she told German journalist Paul Kohl nearly half a century later. 'And yet at the same time I see a city which is flourishing, houses rebuilt, people laughing.' She could not, however, bring herself to look at the fortress.[2]

Had she done so, she might have seen children scampering over the ramparts, or riding around on bicycles and scooters, young families with prams, grandparents posing for a photograph next to a statue, fishermen hoping for a bite at the confluence of the Bug and Mukhavets, while couples stroll along the riverbank.

For somewhere which has seen so much war, few places today are so peaceful.

NOTES

Acronyms

BA-MA	Bundesarchiv-Militärarchiv, Freiburg
DDRZW	*Das Deutsche Reich und der Zweiten Weltkrieg*
DGFP	*Documents on German Foreign Policy*
GASWW	*Germany and the Second World War*
ID	Infantry Division
JG	Jagdgeschwader
JSMS	*Journal of Soviet Military Studies*
KG	Kampfgeschwader
KTB	Kriegstagebuch
NARA	US National Archives and Records Administration
NSR	*Nazi–Soviet Relations*
Pz	Panzer
TB	Tagebuch
VEJ	*Der Verfolgung und Ermordung der europäischen Juden*

Chapter 1: One More Blitzkrieg

1 Based on Kohl, p.32; Suvarov, p.145; Oberleutnant Walter Loos 'Die Einnahme von Brest-Litowsk am 22 Juni 1941', BA-MA MSg 2/5384; Ganzer, p.446; Sandalov, pp.68–9; Aliev, *Brestskaya krepost*, p.248; *Posledniy Pis'ma s Fronta*, Vol.1, 1941, p.19.

2 Knopp, p.44; 45th ID, p.204; Überschär, pp.319–23; KTB 45 ID, 21/6/41 in BA-MA RH 26-45/20; and KTB 45 ID Sonstige Ausgänge, 21/6/41–17/11/41 in BA-MA RH 26-45/27.

3 *Steh auf*, pp.13–14; Bunke, p.216; Aliev, *Siege*, pp.57–8.

4 Based on the diaries of Bock, Halder, von Waldau and Hoth; KTB OKW 3/3/41; Wilhelm, *Rassenpolitik und Kriegführung*, pp.133–4.

5 Bagramjan, pp.62–4 and Khrushchev, *Khrushchev Remembers*, p.141.

6 Besymenski, pp.373–93. See also Kotkin, pp.860–2.

7 Glantz, *Stumbling Colossus*, pp.242–4; NSR, pp.324, 328, 330; KTB Halder, 5/5/41 and Hilger, pp.305–7.

8   KTB Halder, 5/5/41; KTB Engel, 9/2/41; Speer, p.250 and Fritz, p.76; Warlimont, p.140; Suchenwirth, p.254; Guderian, p.142; Moritz, pp.258–9 and Wilhelm, *Rassenpolitik und Kriegführung*, p.141.

9   Osterkamp, p.385; GASWW, iv, pp.343, 372; Muller, *The German Air War in Russia*, p.36; Plocher, 1941, pp.16–20.

10   Luther, pp.118–22; Forczyk, pp.22–5; Hartmann, *Wehrmacht im Ostkrieg*, pp.57–61, 232–4; Guderian, pp.139 and 143; Rosen, pp.14–32.

11   Bagramjan, pp.68–70.

12   Wegner, p.385; Forczyk, pp.30–2; Glantz, *Stumbling Colossus*, p.155; Lelyushenko, pp.12–13; Rokossovsky, p.11 and Bellamy, p.200.

13   Mawdsley, pp.20–1; Sandalov, p.421; Glantz, *Stumbling Colossus*, p.57.

14   *Pravda*, 25/2/39; Reese, pp.18, 41–70; Glantz, *Stumbling Colossus*, pp.110–16, 152.

15   Reese, pp.17–24; Heydorn, p.54; Sherstnev, p.191 and Sandalov, p.421.

16   Merridale, pp.56–8; instructions issued in July 1941, cited in Hill, *The Great Patriotic War of the Soviet Union 1941–45*, p.54; Heysing (ed), 'Aus dem Tagebuch eines Sowjetkommissars' 10/9/41; and Besymenski, pp.439–40.

17   Hürter, *Hitlers Heerführer*, p.220; 'Kennt ihr den Feind?', undated, in BA-MA RH 26-102/7; *Barbarossa* jurisdiction decree, 13/5/41 in author's papers; Guidelines for the behaviour of troops in Russia, 19/5/41, in KTB 4th Panzer Division Anlagen, NARA T315 R205, ff88–90; BA-MA RW 4/578, Bl.42–44; 'Rettung aus schwerster Gefahr', *Mitteilungen für die Truppe*, No.116, June 1941, cited in Messerschmidt, *Die Wehrmacht im NS-Staat*, p.327 and Manoschek, *Die Wehrmacht im Rassenkrieg*, p.63.

18   Röw, p.413; Mende, pp.150–1; 32ID, p.75; "*Die Angehörigen der Truppe sind keine Henkersknechte!*" in BA-MA RH 26-102/6. Cited in Römer, *Kommissarbefehl*, p.176; Stahlberg, p.159; KTB XXVI Korps, 21/6/41 in BA-MA RH 24-26/62, p.9; Schlussansprache des Kdr der 134 ID, 16/6/41 in BA-MA RH 26-134/5; Wilhelm, *Rassenpolitik und Kriegführung*, p.140.

19   Based on Buchbender, *Das tönende Erz*, pp.56–8, 61 and Kirchner, pp.6–7; Streit, pp.75, 79, 131, 332; KTB 134 ID, 16/6/41 in BA-MA RH 26-134/5.

20   Kay, 'The Purpose of the Russian Campaign is the Decimation of the Slavic Population by 30 Million', in Kay (ed), *Nazi Policy on the Eastern Front 1941*, p.122n44; Backe, '12 Gebote', 1/6/41, Dok. 089-USSR in IMT, xlix, pp.367–71; Wirtschaftspolitische Richtlinien für die Wirtschaftsorganisation Ost, Gruppe Landwirtschaft, 23/5/41, Dok. 126-EC in IMT, xxxvi, pp.135–57.

21   Moritz, p.305; Hartmann, *Wehrmacht im Ostkrieg*, p.789; Angrick, Andrej et al., 'Da hätte man schon ein Tagebuch führen müssen: Das Polizeibataillon 322 und die Judenmorde im Bereich der Heeresgruppe Mitte des Sommers und Herbstes 1941', in Grabitz, Helga (ed), *Die Normalität des Verbrechens*, p.330.

22   KTB Halder, 3/7/40 and 31/7/40; Müller, *Enemy in the East*, p.229.

23   Hans Steets, 'Die Grosse Marsch nach Osten', pp.1–2 in BA-MA MSg 2/13984 and Hartmann, *Halder*, p.269.

24   Leeb, pp.58–9; *Wegner*, p.181; DDRZW, 5/1, p.553; Wegner-Korfes, p.88.

25   Knopp, p.31; Vopersal, Band 2a, p.15; Freitag, pp.49–50; Hossbach, p.37.

26   Hans-Günther Seraphim, 'Erinnerungen aus dem Jahren des zweiten Weltkriegs',
      Band 2, p.92, in BA-MA MSg 2/12198; Kuehn, p.172; Freund, pp.102–3; TB Haape,
      2/5/41 in Luther papers; Prien, JG53, i, pp.252–3.

27   KTB 20 ID, 5/6/41 in BA-MA RH 26-20/11; IR62, pp.5–6; Nayhauss, p.125;
      Luther, p.188; Kuehn, p.172; Buchbender and Sterz, p.67; Frauer, p.40; *Soldiers of
      Barbarossa*, p.18; TB Haape, 20/5/41 in Luther papers; Petri, p.43; Steiniger, p.100;
      Ruville, p.32; Alfred Opitz in Wette, *Der Krieg des Kleinen Mannes*, p.233.

28   Knyshevskii, pp.42–7; Voronkov, *Minsk*, pp.43, 81; BA-MA RH 21-1/472, 24/8/41;
      NARA T315 R205 Frame 183; Hill, p.204; Hoffmann, pp.74–7.

29   Hoffmann, p.33; Voronkov, *Minsk*, p.80; Sherstnev, p.197; Gotzes, p.41; Rentrop,
      p.59.

30   Bagramjan, pp.70–3.

31   Sherstnev, p.196; NSR, pp.345–6.

32   Based on Besymenski, pp.436–7, 443; Zhukov, i, pp.275–6; Kumanev, p.311; JSMS,
      Vol.4, No.2, pp.234–5; Gorodetsky, pp.298–9.

33   Fedyuninsky, pp.10–12; Moskalenko, pp.30–1.

34   Life in Minsk on the eve of war is based on Voronkov, *Dvadtsat'*, pp.35–40 and
      Voronkov, *Minsk*, pp.12–24, 76–7.

35   Stankiewicz, pp.194, 199–200.

36   Based on Glantz, *Stumbling Colossus*, pp.189–90, 192–3; GASWW, iv, p.351 and
      Sherstnev, p.192–3.

37   Schäufler, *So lebten*, p.51; Buchbender and Sterz, p.68.

38   *Meldungen aus dem Reich* No.183, 185 and 194, 5/5/41, 12/5/41 and 16/6/41.

39   Hitler even claimed it 'bought a little extra breathing space'. See TB Goebbels,
      14/6/41–16/6/41.

40   *Pravda*, 20/6/41; Gorodetsky, p.306.

41   Moorhouse, *Devil's Alliance*, pp.96–7.

42   Information provided by Fort VII, Kaunas; Dieckmann, pp.156–7, 163.

43   Holzman, pp.7–8.

44   Based on the author's visit to Lviv and Lontskoho prison, October 2014; diary of
      Stanisław Różycki, 12/6/41 and 20/6/41 in VEJ, Band 7, pp.121–4; Gross, *Revolution*,
      p.223; Jestadt, pp.29–41; Wells, p.27; Musial, *Konterrevolutionäre*, pp.54, 72–3.

45   TB Habicht, 20/6/41 in Römer, *Die narzisstische Volksgemeinschaft*, pp.303–5.

46   Erlebnisse von Soldaten der I/Stukageschwader 77 in BA-MA MSg2/4219.

47   Maligin, pp.5–6.

48   Based on Dinglreiter, p.39; Drabkin, p.113; JSMS, Vol.4, No.1, pp.158–9.

49   Kumanev, p.24.

50   Gushchin, pp.39–46.

51   TB Hewel, 20/6/41; KTB OKW, 21/6/41.

52   *Völkischer Beobachter*, 21/6/41; TB Goebbels, 22/6/41.

53   Sandalov, pp.74–5.

54   Rosen, p.42.

55   Ryabyshev, p.8.

56   Petrow, pp.14, 41.

57   Yegorov, pp.5–6.

58   BA-MA MSg 2/13984, pp.3–4.

59   Trautloft, pp.84–5.

60   Seraphim, pp.100–1 in BA-MA MSg 2/12198; 18th Pz Div, p.12.

61   Boehm, p.78; Riederer von Paar, p.417; Reinhardt to his wife, 19/6/41 in BA-MA N 245/2.

62   Meyer, p.53; KTB Panzergruppe 4 Anlagen, 21/6/41 in BA-MA RH 21-4/16; Bartov, *Hitler's Army*, p.129; Haupt, *134 ID*, p.28; Schrodek, *11 Pz*, p.116; Paul, *18 Pz*, p.12.

63   Wette, *Der Krieg des Kleinen Mannes*, pp.236–7; Freund, p.104; Prien, JG53, i, p.255.

64   Keubke, pp.271–2; TB Maresch, 21/6/41 in Ganzer, pp.378–9; Uffz Fr Schaback 'Der Todesmarsch nach Leningrad', BA-MA MSg 2/2580, p.19; Ruville, p.33; Hartmann, *Wehrmacht im Ostkrieg*, p.248; Beevor, p.190; Buchbender and Sterz, p.72.

65   Rosen, p.42.

66   Freitag, p.50.

67   *Leto 1941, Ukraina: dokumenty, materialy: khronika sobytii Ukraina*, p.97.

68   Ryabyshev, pp.8–9; Popjel, p.12.

69   KTB Halder, 30/3/41; Axworthy, p.39; Balta, pp.185–6 and Brief Assessment of the Romanian Army, 22/5/41 in BA-MA RH 31-I/93; Letter from Hauffe, 22/9/41 in BA-MA RH 31-I/93; Emilian, pp.31–5.

70   Kiehl, p.136.

71   Waiss, KG27, 3, p.84.

72   Sandalov, pp.77–9.

73   Kumanev, pp.474–5.

74   Sherstnev, p.199.

75   Grupe, pp.150–1.

76   Voronkov, *Dvadtsat'*, pp.40–1.

77   Erickson, i, p.145, Heydorn, p.144.

78   Ryabyshev, pp.8–9 and Popjel, p.9.

79   Besymenski, p.416; DGFP, D, xii, Doc.662; NSR, pp.355–6; Hilger, pp.311–12.

80   Tennenbaum, pp.159–60.

81   Petrov, *Pogranichniki*, p.48; Matonin, pp.93–4, 97, 108–9.

82   *Organy gosudarstvennoy bezopasnosti SSSR v Velikoy Otechestvennoy voyne*, Documents 287 and 342; Petrov, *Pogranichniki*, p.212; Drabkin, p.30.

83   Erickson, i, p.150–1.

84   Sherstnev, p.204; Zhukov, i, p.277.

85   Bagramjan, p.89.

86   DGFP, D, xii, Doc.658; NSR, pp.353–5 and Berezhkov, *History*, p.74.

87   Knyshevskii, pp.330–1.

88   Mauss, p.114; Haape, *Endstation Moskau*, pp.10–11 and TB Haape, 21/6/41 in Luther papers; Heer, 'Und dann', pp.138–9; Bauer, p.48; Selz, pp.55–6; Luther, p.202; Feldpost von Plotho, 21/6/41.

89   TB Goebbels, 22/6/41.

90   Yegorov, p.10.

91 Sandalov, pp.77–9.
92 Petrow, pp.46–7.
93 Erickson, pp.157–8; Volkogonov, p.401.
94 Allmayer-Beck, pp.170–1.
95 Uffz Fr Schaback 'Der Todesmarsch nach Leningrad', BA-MA MSg 2/2580, p.28 and Bauer, p.50.
96 Freter, i, p.277; Kippar, pp.772–3.
97 Mende, pp.151–2.
98 Reinecke, pp.59–60.
99 Krupinski, pp.46–7.
100 Ott, p.30.
101 Chaldej, p.55.
102 Popjel, pp.11–12.
103 Fedyuninsky, pp.12–13.
104 Freitag, pp.50–1.
105 Heydorn, pp.155–6.
106 Yegorov, pp.12–14.
107 Mahlke, p.138.
108 Reimer, p.96.
109 Kirstein, p.199.
110 TB Goebbels, 22/6/41.
111 Braatz, *Gott oder ein Flugzeug*, p.248.
112 Uffz Fr Schaback 'Der Todesmarsch nach Leningrad' in BA-MA MSg 2/2580, p.29.
113 Jacobsen, pp.106–9; Weinmann, pp.20–35; and the author's papers.
114 *Organy gosudarstvennoy bezopasnosti SSSR v Velikoy Otechestvennoy voyne*, Document 342.
115 TB Maresch, 20-21/6/41 in Ganzer, pp.378–9.
116 Habedanck, Gerd, 'Nacht vor Brest-Litowsk' in *Deutschland im Kampf, Juli 1941*, pp.27–8

CHAPTER 2: THE GATES OF HELL OPENED IN FRONT OF US

1 Mahlke, p.139; Bergström, *Black Cross*, pp.29–30.
2 Schwabedissen, p.54.
3 Mahlke, p.139.
4 Knyshevskii, pp.330–1; JG77, ii, pp.636–7.
5 Trautloft, pp.85–6.
6 Braatz, *Walter Krupinski*, p.48.
7 'Aus dem Kriegstagebuch: Tatschenbericht und Erlebnisse eines ehemaligen Frontsoldaten im Russlandfeldzug 1941–43' in BA-MA RH 41/702.
8 Allmayer-Beck, p.172.

9   Uffz Fr Schaback 'Der Todesmarsch nach Leningrad' in BA-MA MSg 2/2580, pp.29–31; Ruville, p.35.

10 Kippar, pp.772–3.

11 Bergström, *Black Cross*, pp.33–4 and Kamenir, p.95.

12 Drabkin and Isayev, pp.358–9.

13 Yegorov, p.14.

14 Based on Habedanck, p.28; Erickson, p.168; Loos, in BA-MA MSg 2/5384; 'Die 45 Infanterie Division im Kampf um Brest-Litowsk, Juni 1941' in *Linzer Turm*, 35 Jahrgang, Nummer 138, März 1992 in BA-MA MSg 3/2083; Hans Wiesinger, 'Es begann in Wels: Eine Biographie aus der Zeit von 1935–1947' in *Linzer Turm*, 42 Jahrgang, Nummer 168, September 1999 in BA-MA MSg 3/2083; Aliev, *Siege*, p.79; Prien, JG53, i, p.260; *Steh auf*, p.1; TB Arnreiter, 22/6/41 in Ganzer, pp.400–3.

15 Luther, p.209; Schäufler, *Der Weg war Weit*, p.9; BA-MA MSg 2/13906; *Ukrayina: 100 dniv viyny*, pp.30–1; Petrov, *June 22 1941*, p.219.

16 Maligin, pp.7–8; Ryabyshev, pp.9–10; Bagramjan, p.90.

17 Gschöpf, p.211 and Hartmann, *Wehrmacht im Ostkrieg*, p.261.

18 The account of Josef Kremers' assault is based on Loos in BA-MA MSg 2/5384; KTB 45ID, 0328 Hours, 22/6/41, in BA-MA RH 26-45/20; KTB 45ID Anlagen, 21/6/41–17/11/41, in BA-MA RH 26-45/27; and 45th Infantry Division's casualty list in the author's papers.

19 Freund, pp.105–6.

20 Moskalenko, pp.32–3.

21 Spaeter, *Brandenburger*, pp.152–3.

22 Inozemtsev, pp.23–4.

23 Pokryschkin, pp.18–19.

24 Based on Prien, JG3-1, pp.153–5; www.acestory.elknet.pl/rubstov/rubstov.htm; and Weal, p.15.

25 Kiehl, pp.141–2.

26 Kieffer, Egon, 'Über dem brennenden Litauen' in Heintze and Wiedemann (eds), *Wir kämpften gegen die Sowjets 1941/42*.

27 Bialer, pp.224–5 and Sandalov, pp.83–4.

28 Statsenko, pp.18–20.

29 https://iremember.ru/en/memoirs/others/nikolai-dupak/, accessed March 2024.

30 Zhukov, i, p.281.

31 Ortenberg, p.6.

32 Based on Schmidt, pp.234–5; Knopp, pp.42–3; Berezhkov memoirs in *History in the Making*, pp.76–9 and *At Stalin's Side*, pp.52–3.

33 Based on DGFP, D, xii, Doc.659; Hilger, pp.312–13; *Organy gosudarstvennoy bezopasnosti SSSR v Velikoy Otechestvennoy voyne*, Document 281, p.12 and Sebag-Montefiore, p.372.

34 *Jurnalul mareşalului Ion Antonescu*, Vol.1, 1940–41, p.321 and Solomovici, p.353.

35 GR315, p.57.

36 Matonin, p.138.

37 Grupe, pp.155–6.

38   Paul, *18 Pz*, p.16.

39   Voronkov, p.57; Kumanev, pp.139–40.

40   Bialer, pp.229–30.

41   Ibid, pp.225–6.

42   Based on *Deutsche Wochenschau*, 25/6/41; TB Goebbels, 22/6/41 and *Völkischer Beobachter*, 23/6/4. Goebbels' propaganda machine would, accurately, describe those Berliners who heard the appeal – and a subsequent, leaden address by von Ribbentrop to foreign correspondents – listening 'with breathless tension'.

43   Mahlke, pp.139–40; Knoke, pp.40–1.

44   Based on author's visit to Brest and Abaturov, p.50; Petrov, *Pogranichniki*, p.51; Ganzer, pp.457–8; TB Arnreiter, 22/6/41 in Ganzer, pp.400–3; Gschöpf, pp.222–3; Kohl, pp.30–1; *Steh auf*, pp.22–3; KTB 45ID, 0625 Hours, 22/6/41 in BA-MA RH 26-45/20; Aliev, *Siege*, pp.7–9, 24, 28–37.

45   KTB 45ID, 0730–0840 Hours, 22/6/41 in BA-MA RH 26-45/20; Wiesinger in BA-MA MSg 3/2083.

46   Brandišauskas, Docs 5 and 129; Grossman, p.621.

47   Ibid, Doc 70.

48   Ibid, Doc 36.

49   VEJ, Band 7, pp.149–50.

50   Chaldej, p.14 and *Pravda*, 22/6/41.

51   Ortenberg, p.6.

52   Tennenbaum, pp.160–1.

53   Skrjabina, pp.3–4.

54   Alexijewitsch, p.18; Stimme, pp.93–4; Kumanev, pp.141–2.

55   Based on Dmytro Malakov, 'Kyiv, June 22 1941' at www.day.kiev.ua/en/article/history-and -i/kyiv-june-22-1941; Drabkin and Isayev, pp.365–66 and *Ukrayina: 100 dniv viyny*, p.28.

56   Voznesensky, pp.206–7.

57   Karpow, p.34 and Petrov, *Pogranichniki*, p.55 and author's papers.

58   Yegorov, pp.19–20.

59   Erickson, pp.176–7.

60   Popjel, pp.25–7.

61   Sachsse, p.99; Freitag, p.52; BA-MA MSg 2/2580, pp.36–8 and Ruville, p.36.

62   The corpses were found that evening by advancing German soldiers. The priests received a proper burial in Lakštučiai four days later. BA-MA RW 2/149, p.416.

63   BA-MA RW 2/150, p.47.

64   BA-MA RW 2/150, p.65.

65   Voznesensky, p.208; KTB 35ID, 22/6/41 in BA-MA RH 26-35/35; Pfau, p.130; Petrov, *Pogranichniki*, p.56.

66   Romanian reactions based on Emilian, pp.39–40; *Völkischer Beobachter*, 23/6/41; Balta, p.195; *Jurnalul mareşalului Ion Antonescu*, Vol.1, 1940–41, p.321; Cornel Jurju, 'Opinia publică şi intrarea României În al doilea război mondial (22 iunie 1941)', *Revista Bistritei*, No.15, 2001, pp.298–318; Duţu, p.17; Solomovici, p.355; Arma, p.18; *Veteranii pe Drumul Onoarei şi Jertfei*, Spre Cetăţile de pe Nistru, pp.111, 384–5 and Deletant, pp.81–2.

67 Kumanev, pp.25–6; Radzinsky, p.447.
68 Alexijewitsch, p.13; Rentrop, p.61 and Voronkov, pp.70–1.
69 Skrjabina, pp.3–4. *Blokada Leningrada: Dnevniki 1941–1944 godov*, pp.7–8.
70 https://iremember.ru/en/memoirs/others/nikolai-dupak/, accessed March 2024. *Taras Bulba* would never be finished and Nikolai Dupak would train as an infantry officer before the year ended.
71 *Ukrayina: 100 dniv viyny*, p.32; *Ljubimye, zhdite!*, p.307.
72 Chaldej, p.14.
73 Smirnov, pp.59–60, 61–2; KTB 45ID, 22/6/41 in BA-MA RH26-45/20; Aliev, *Siege*, pp.126–8.
74 Loos in BA-MA MSg 2/5384; Erich Maresch's diary in Ganzer, pp.379–81; and Gschöpf, p.206.
75 Based on TB Arnreiter, 22/6/41 in Ganzer, pp.400–3; Loos in BA-MA MSg 2/5384; Ganzer, pp.272–3, 322, 324; and Sandalov, p.95.
76 Based on Johannes Kaufmann, pp.98–9 and Starinov, pp.172–3.
77 Stimme, p.95; Voronkov, pp.71, 72.
78 Sutzkever, p.9 and Brandišauskas, Doc 37.
79 Holzman, pp.9–10.
80 Brandišauskas, Doc 71.
81 Tory, p.3; Brandišauskas, Docs 8 and 71; Levinson, pp.168–9.
82 Levinson, pp.100, 124.
83 Dieckmann, p.361; Frank, pp.84–5; Rosowski, p.132; Forczyk, p.44–5; *Initial Period*, pp.173–5; Manteuffel, pp.136–7.
84 Slesina, pp.39–42; Grupe, pp.158–9; and Sherstnev, p.222.
85 Sherstnev, pp.219–20.
86 *Strana v Ogne*, Vol.1 Pt 2, pp.402–4; Musial, *Sowjetische Partisanen*, p.39.
87 Yegorov, p.21.
88 Based on KTB 45ID, 1200–1350 Hours, 22/6/41 in BA-MA RH 26-45/20; John, MS D-239, p.8; Aliev, *Siege*, pp.130–2.
89 Pokryschkin, pp.23–4 and Bergström, *Black Cross*, pp.45–6.
90 Arkhipenko, pp.29–31.
91 Bialer, p.230.
92 Bekker, p.389; and diary of Uffz Christian Luibl in BA-MA MSg 2/4219.
93 Wawrzyński, pp.224–30. Soviet accounts, including the 1985 film *Bitva za Moskvu*, claim Kopets shot himself in his office in Minsk as the scale of the disaster which had befallen his aerial forces became known. It was only in 2008 when Ponomarenko's diary was published that Kopets' true fate was revealed. On 23 June, Stalin told the Byelorussian Party chief: 'Oh, I almost forgot. Smushkevich revealed that Kopets turned out to be a German spy. I had his deputy take over. Look into his actions. Tell Pavlov about this.' Kopets' wife Nina Pavlovna was told that her husband had flown to Białystok to direct the battle before she was evacuated to Moscow, where she tried – unsuccessfully – to find out about her husband's fate. Her enquiries led to her arrest and she was swiftly sentenced to five years in the Gulag for 'anti-Soviet agitation'. She fared

better than the wives of other Red Air Force officers seized during the purge; they died alongside their husbands as 'relatives of traitors of the Motherland'. Nina Kopets was finally released in the summer of 1946. Her husband was either executed – or committed suicide – on 23 July. Andrei Taiurskii, the man who succeeded him, was arrested on 8 July and shot the following February for his 'failings' during the first fortnight of the invasion.

94 Based on *Völkischer Beobachter*, 22/6/41 and 23/6/41; DDRZW, 9/2, pp.264–5; *Deutschland im Kampf*, Juni 1941, p.99; Flannery, p.259 and SD Meldung Nr.196, 23/6/41. The observations of both are confirmed by Leland B. Morris, the US Chargé d'Affaires, in his report of 23 June. See FRUS, 1941, I, p.153.

95 Based on *Pravda*, 23/6/41; Voronkov, *Dvadtsat'*, pp.73–4; *Novgorodskaya zemlya v epokhu sotsial'nykh potryaseniy. 1941–1945*, Docs 1 and 11; *Kyiv: Viina, vlada, suspil'stvo 1939–1945*, pp.243–52; VEJ, Band 7, p.133; Marples, p.55; *Moskva Voyennaya 1941–1945*, pp.42–52 and J. Barber, 'Popular Reactions in Moscow to the German Invasion of June 22 1941', in Wieczynski, p.2.

96 *Pravda*, 23/6/41; Voronkov, pp.75–6.

97 VEJ, Band 7, pp.149–50 and Jestadt, p.42.

98 Slesina, pp.46–53.

99 Mende, pp.153–4.

100 KTB 45ID, 1830 Hours, 22/6/41 in BA-MA RH 26-45/20 and 45ID, p.208.

101 Martin, pp.15–16.

102 Nearly 30 years later, Bedin was awarded the Order of the Patriotic War of the 1st Rank, while a memorial to the deeds of the 12 men – who had supposedly killed 250 enemy soldiers and held up the advance of two battalions – was erected on the site of the former headquarters. Petrov, *Pogranichniki*, p.63.

103 Matonin, p.138.

104 Oblt. Richard D., 7th Pz Div, 22/6/41; TB Haape, 22/6/41; IR77 chronicle – all in Luther papers.

105 Based on BA-MA MSg 2/13984, pp.18–19; KTB 1 Geb Div, 22/6/41 in NARA T351 R039 f310; Kaltenegger, *Stammdivision*, pp.210–11; Meyer, pp.54–5; and Burdick, pp.103–4.

106 The stadium was eventually opened under German rule in 1942 and, once restored after Kiev was liberated in 1943, tickets for the 1941 ceremony were honoured for the belated rededication. Based on Statsenko, p.32; Dmytro Malakov, 'Kyiv, June 22 1941' at www.day.kiev.ua/en/article/history-and-i/kyiv-june-22-1941; Drabkin and Isayev, pp.365–66 and *Ukrayina: 100 dniv viyny*, p.28.

107 Maligin, p.9 and Fedyuninsky, pp.16–17.

108 Ryabyshev, pp.14–15.

109 BA-MA RH 26-123/143, Bl. 5–7; DDRZW, 9/1, pp.524–5.

110 *Strana v Ogne*, Vol.1 Pt 2, pp.402–4; Sherstnev, pp.223, 225.

111 Sandalov, p.456.

112 Werth, pp.156–7; Bialer, pp.231–2; and *Strana v Ogne*, Vol.1 Pt 1, p.325.

113 Stimme, p.94; Voronkov, *Dvadtsat'*, pp.71–2; Alexijewitsch, p.14.

114 Knoke, p.43.

115 Braatz, *Werner Mölders*, p.314; Trautloft, p.87; JG53, i, p.264; Bergström, *Black Cross*, p.47; KG51, p.158; Bergström, *Operation Barbarossa*, p.63.

116 Bergström, *Black Cross*, pp.36, 41. The Soviet official history credits Kokorev with the first *taran* – and also claims he brought down a Dornier. Soviet OH, ii, p.20.

117 Wawrzyński, p.155.

118 Pokryschkin, pp.25–7.

119 Mölders, pp.314, 316; Tilitzki, p.156; IR90, p.31.

120 Arkhipenko, p.31; Pokryschkin, pp.25–7.

121 Dierich, p.158.

122 Brandišauskas, Doc 8.

123 Holzman, pp.11–13; Tory, p.4; Ganor, pp.53–4.

124 Events of 22 June in Przemyśl are based on Jacobsen, pp.106–9; Weinmann, pp.20–35; Błonski and Cieplińska, pp.29–31; diary of Lieutenant Oleksandr Patarikin in *Ukrayina: 100 dniv viyny*, p.31; *Leto 1941, Ukraina: dokumenty, materialy: khronika sobytii Ukraina*, pp.166–7; and the author's papers.

125 Kaltenegger, *Stammdivision*, p.212.

126 Grupe, pp.160–1.

127 Kempowski, p.59; Wiesinger, in BA-MA MSg 3/2083; TB Arnreiter, 22/6/41 in Ganzer, pp.400–3; TB Maresch 22/6/41 in Ganzer, pp.379–81; Gschöpf, p.223 and Aliev, *Siege*, p.135.

128 Voznesensky, pp.208–10.

129 Chaldej, p.16.

130 Bagramjan, pp.120–6.

131 Rosen, pp.43–4.

132 Sutzkever, p.10.

133 BA-MA MSg 2/2580, p.38; Allmayer-Beck, pp.176–7.

134 Frank, pp.88–9.

CHAPTER 3: TO LENINGRAD

1 Raus, p.16.

2 Grossmann, p.622.

3 *Ich werde es nie vergessen*, p.94. JSMS, Vol.4, No.4, p.721.

4 Based on Brandišauskas, Docs 6, 7, 8, Doc 129; Dieckmann, p.418; Bartusevicius, p.41; and Grossmann, p.623.

5 *Clandestine History of the Kovno Jewish Ghetto Police*, pp.65–6; Grossmann, p.622; Tory, p.6.

6 Schur, pp.36–7.

7 Rolnikaitė, pp.37–8.

8 Ganor, p.57.

9 Raus, pp.17–19.

10 Riederer von Paar, p.429.

11 JSMS, Vol.4, No.4, p.729.

12   Schur, p.37; Brandišauskas, Doc 37.

13   Riederer von Paar, pp.429–31.

14   Chernyshev, pp.68–9; JSMS, Vol.5, No.2, p.290.

15   Benz, *Bombennächte und Frontschicksale*, pp.182–3.

16   Based on Testimony of Dr Antanas Garmus in BA-MA RW2/149, pp.393–4; Seydlitz, p.98; author's papers and Dieckmann, pp.301–2. Communist accounts claim partisans ambushed the firing squad, the prisoners tried to flee and were either shot escaping or captured and executed once Soviet armour had eradicated the rebels. Account by Domas Ročius in Brandišauskas, Doc 154.

17   Seydlitz, p.98; Karpow, p.29; 7th Pz, pp.138–9; Schur, pp.37–9; Kruk, pp.47, 49; Mallmann, *Ereignismeldungen*, pp.97–8; Brandišauskas, Doc 37; Dieckmann, pp.339–40; Rolnikaitė, pp.41–2.

18   Based on the Judgment of Ulm district court, 29/8/58, on the Garsden massacre in Lichtenstein, pp.35–9 and Curilla, *Die deutsche Ordnungspolizei*, pp.138–42.

19   Grossmann, p.625; Holzman, pp.14–15.

20   Tory, p.6; Sutzkever, pp.10–12.

21   Zvyagintsev, pp.259–64.

22   Based on BA-MA MSg 2/2580, pp.53–5; 'Marschweg und Kämpfe des III/IR405' in BA-MA RH 37/3095; Kirchbach in BA-MA RH 37/3096; IR89, p.140; and Grossmann, p.626.

23   Grossmann, pp.626–7.

24   The account of the fighting at Raseiniai is based on Paul, *Brennpunkte*, pp.108–9; Schadewitz, pp.278–82; Glantz, *The Battle for Leningrad*, pp.32–3; Feldmeyer and Meyer, p.18; Stoves, pp.192–3, 195; *Initial Period*, p.114; Raus, pp.21–4; Forczyk, pp.41–2; letter dated 5/7/41 in Eiber, p.69; letter from Reinhardt to his wife, 26/6/41 in BA-MA N 245/2; Bücheler, p.134; Isaev, *Ot granitsy do Leningrada*, pp.96–117; and the memoirs of Dmitry Osadchy in the author's papers.

25   Dieckmann, pp.385–6 and Levinson, pp.98–9.

26   Holzman, pp.15–18.

27   *Į laisvę*, 24/6/41.

28   Based on Dieckmann, pp.319–20; *Clandestine History of the Kovno Jewish Ghetto Police*, pp.13, 69; Kirchbach, in BA-MA RH 37/3096; Mallmann, *Deutscher Osten*, p.63.

29   Dieckmann, pp.313–14.

30   Mallmann, *Deutscher Osten*, pp.63–4.

31   *Clandestine History of the Kovno Jewish Ghetto Police*, p.70; Grossmann, pp.626–7; and Krausnick, pp.205–6.

32   Lopez, pp.388–9.

33   Weber, pp.22–3; Brandišauskas, Docs 36, 71.

34   TB Beyer, 26/6/41 in Ruville, p.40; Mauss, p.123.

35   Brandišauskas, Docs 148, 150.

36   Wette, *Karl Jäger*, p.66; Letter, circa 24/6/41 in BA-MA N756/126a; Luther, p.283; Brandišauskas, Doc 70; Bartusevicius, p.41.

37   Sasse, p.51; Pichler, p.75; IR77, p.56 in Luther papers; Schadewitz, p.302; KTB 20 ID, 24/6/41 and 26/6/41 in BA-MA RH 26-20/11 and letter from an SS man in 3rd SS Div, circa 24/6/41 in BA-MA N 756/126a.

38 VEJ, Band 7, p.130; Letter to the Commander of Rear Area Army Group North, 10/7/41 in BA-MA RH 26-281/25.

39 Based on Allmayer-Beck, p.184; Schadewitz, p.301; BA-MA MSg 2/2580, pp.63, 65; KTB 20 ID, 23/6/41 in BA-MA RH 26-20/11; Letters dated 3/7/41 and 5/7/41 in Eiber, pp.68–9; *Soldiers of Barbarossa*, p.38; Kempowski, p.98; KTB Gruppe Schmidt, 26–27/6/41 in BA-MA RH 26-253/20; TB Habicht, 25/6/41 in Römer, *Kameraden*, p.423; IR18, p.58; Letter from an unnamed SS trooper, 3rd SS Division, 6/7/41, in BA-MA N 756/126a; Leeb, p.280.

40 The capture of the bridges at Daugavpils is based on Cavaleri, pp.124–31; Haupt, *8 Pz*, pp.146–7; Kindel, pp.450–1, 467. A similar attempt by Brandenburgers to seize the road bridge over the Daugava downstream at Jēkabpils, roughly halfway between Riga and Daugavpils, was foiled by the crossing's defenders who wiped out the entire detachment with the exception of the driver, then demolished the bridge. See Spaeter, *Brandenburger*, pp.146–7.

41 Karpow, p.41; JSMS, Vol.5, No.2, p.294; Isaev, *Ot granitsy do Leningrada*, pp.138–9; *World War II and the Occupation of Latvia*, p.27; and Manstein, p.184.

42 Neiburgs, *Grēka un ienaida liesmās*, pp.18–23; Isaev, *Prigranichnoe srazhenie 1941*, pp.121–4; JSMS, Vol.5, No.2, p.292; Chernyshev, p.76; *Strana v Ogne*, Vol.1 Pt 2, pp.92–3; Conze, pp.21–3; Benz, *Marineinfanterie*, p.110.

43 Grossmann, pp.628–32, 636; *Clandestine History of the Kovno Jewish Ghetto Police*, p.68; Bartusevicius, pp.43–4; Benz, *Reichskommissariat Ostland*, p.176; and Brandišauskas, Doc 129.

44 Brandišauskas, Doc 37; Schur, pp.42–5; Dieckmann, p.340; Sutzkever, pp.12–16.

45 Levinson, pp.166–7; Bartusevicius, p.43; Dieckmann, pp.375–7.

46 Based on Dieckmann, pp.321–5; Klee, pp.32–42; Mallmann, *Deutscher Osten*, pp.64–5; Wette, *Karl Jäger*, p.72; Holzman, pp.24–5; and *Clandestine History of the Kovno Jewish Ghetto Police*, p.68. News of the Lietūkis garage massacre reached the city's Archbishop, Juozapas Skvireckas. A delegation pleaded with him to halt the killings. He promised he would – but did nothing. Brandišauskas, Doc 129.

47 Based on Benz, *Marineinfanterie*, pp.110–12; Heer, *War of Extermination*, p.220; *Deutschland im Kampf*, Juli, pp.36–7 and Neiburgs, *Grēka un ienaida liesmās*, pp.20–4.

48 Isaev, *Prigranichnoe srazhenie 1941*, pp.124, 126; Waltereck, pp.220–2; Heer, *War of Extermination*, pp.225–6 and Neiburgs, *Grēka un ienaida liesmās*, pp.20–4.

49 BA-MA RH 26-1/6 and Lasch, pp.17–18.

50 Allmayer-Beck, 21 ID, pp.122–3.

51 JSMS, Vol.5, No.1, pp.139–40; Buldygin, pp.118–19.

52 Buldygin, pp.96, 122; Isaev, *Ot granitsy do Leningrada*, pp.168–9.

53 Lasch, pp.18–20; Action of the advanced regiment of I Corps between 27 June and 1 July 1941, in BA-MA RH 26-1/6.

54 Based on Gushchin, pp. 59–60, 64–9, 71–5, 79, 87 and *Nacionālā Zemgale*, 1/7/41, 3/7/41.

55 Manstein, pp.185–6; Forczyk, pp.42–3. 6th Panzer Division's operations officer Johann Adolf Graf von Kielmansegg was highly critical of Manstein's post-war stance, convinced his plan to attack alone 'would have been out-and-out recklessness'. See Bücheler, p.136.

56   Lelyushenko, pp.15–20; Manstein, p.184; and Isaev, *Ot granitsy do Leningrada*, pp.140–2.

57   BA-MA MSg 2/12198, p.137; Reichelt, p.87; Ullrich, ii, p.100; Bauer, p.68.

58   Isaev, *Ot granitsy do Leningrada*, p.176 and Buldygin, p.124.

59   Angrick, *Final Solution in Riga*, p.85n22; Report on the fighting in Riga, 30 June– 1 July 1941 in BA-MA RH 26-1/6.

60   KTB XXVI Korps, Anlagen 22/6/41–12/7/41, BA-MA RH 24-26/64.

61   BA-MA RH 26-1/6; KTB XXVI Korps, Anlagen 22/6/41–12/7/41 in BA-MA RH 24-26/64; Neiburgs, *Dievs*, pp.18–20; *Final Solution in Riga*, pp.63–5 and Ezergailis, pp.214–15. Several accounts claim the *Horst Wessel* song was played after the Latvian anthem although the radio library did not even contain a copy of *Deutschland über alles*. Otto Lasch was rather the forgotten man in the celebrations, but his unit received a special mention on German radio and he was subsequently awarded the Knight's Cross.

62   Lumans, pp.158–9; *Deutschland im Kampf,* Juli 1941, p.31; 'Das Infanterieregiment 151 1939–1942', p.173 in BA-MA RH 37/2785.

63   Neiburgs, *Dievs*, p.23 and *Brīvā Zeme*, 1/7/41.

64   Pesendorfer, p.38; Neiburgs, *Dievs*, p.22.

65   Buldygin, pp.130–1 and information supplied by the Occupation Museum, Riga.

66   Press, p.44 and *World War II and the Occupation of Latvia*, p.13.

67   Holzman, pp.17–21; Umansky, pp.189–91.

68   Three officers resigned in protest at the killings, while the commander of one company, Lt Bronius Kirkila, shot himself.

69   Based on Dieckmann, pp.327–31; Mallmann, *Deutscher Osten*, pp.66–7; and the author's visit, June 2014.

70   Holzman, pp.25–6.

71   BA-MA RH 41/702; Angrick, *Final Solution in Riga*, p.76; Press, p.47; Grossmann, pp.682–5.

72   Letter from *Obergefreiter* J. L., 10th Machine Gun Battalion, 14/7/41 in Kawka, p.13.

73   Max Kaufmann, pp.37–8.

74   Based on Angrick, *Final Solution in Riga*, pp.72–3; Max Kaufmann, pp.37–8; Press, p.46; Grossmann, pp.680–1; and Ezergailis, pp.219–21.

75   Greiner letter, 29/6/41 in Greiner papers; KTB OKW, I, pp.1019–20; 6th Pz, p.113; Melvin, pp.210–11 and Schadewitz, p.304.

CHAPTER 4: TO MOSCOW

1   Rosen, p.44.

2   Ellis, *Barbarossa 1941*, p.474.

3   Hoffmann, *Stalins Vernichtungskrieg 1941–1945*, p.61; Mende, pp.154–5.

4   KTB 45 ID, 0500 and 0745 Hours, 23/6/41 in BA-MA RH 26-45/20 and BA-MA RH 26-45/27; Aliev, *Siege*, pp.148–50 and information provided by the Brest Fortress Museum.

5   Voronkov, *Dvadtsat'*, pp.81–2; Stimme, p.95.

6   Voronkov, *Dvadtsat'*, pp.59–62.

7   *Steh auf*, pp.17–19; Voronkov, *Dvadtsat'*, p.100; Stimme, p.96.

8   Schäufler, *Der Weg war Weit*, p.13; 3 Pz, pp.146–8.

9   Ellis, *Barbarossa 1941*, pp.475–7; JSMS, Vol.4, No.1, pp.182, 187–8.

10 Vasily Bitko was killed leading his men the following day. Ganzer, p.372; Aliev, *Siege*, pp.154–5, 157–8; Smirnov, pp.93–4 and KTB 45 ID, 1700 Hours, 23/6/41 in BA-MA RH 26-45/20.

11 Forczyk, p.50; TB Richthofen, 24/6/41 in BA-MA N671/8 and Boldin, p.98.

12 8th ID, p.69.

13 Based on KTB 45 ID, 24/6/41, in BA-MA RH 26-45/20; BA-MA RH 26-45/27; Gefechtsbericht I/AR98 in BA-MA RH 41/1040; TB Dr Leo Losert, 24/6/41 in BA-MA RH 26-45/154; and Gschöpf, p.224.

14 Stölten, pp.122–3; Hager, p.32.

15 TB von Barsewisch, 7–11/7/41 in BA-MA N 802/189; Guderian, p.156.

16 Based on Kempowski, pp.76–7; Humburg, p.131; Kuehn, pp.178–9; and Bergström, p.75.

17 Aliev, *Siege*, pp.180–7.

18 Events in Minsk on 24 June based on Stimme, pp.96–9; JSMS, Vol.4, No.2, p.334; Gotzes, pp.39–40, 42; Alexijewitsch, pp.19–20, 41; Rentrop, p.63; Kohl, p.68; *Strana v Ogne*, Vol.1 Pt 1, p.462; Voronkov, *Dvadtsat'*, pp.111–22, 187, 188, 198–9, 200, 206; and Manley, p.48.

19 Stankiewicz, pp.201, 204–5; Musial, *Konterrevolutionäre*, pp.132–4 and Voronkov, *Dvadtsat'*, pp.169–71.

20 Knyshevskii, p.113.

21 Based on Sherstnev, pp.258–9; Forczyk, pp.50–1; Gefechtsbericht über den Feldzug in Russland 1941 in BA-MA RH 24-8/253, p.8; KTB TB Richthofen, 25/6/41 in BA-MA N 671/8; 8 ID, p.72; Boucsein, pp.19, 21; and Boldin, pp.99–100.

22 Based on Gotzes, p.42; Voronkov, *Dvadtsat'*, pp.202–5; *Strana v Ogne*, Vol.1 Pt 1, p.477; Alexijewitsch, pp.14–15.

23 The anonymous Minsk inhabitant's life on the road was indeed brief. After five days on the move, his family awoke in the town of Dukora, three dozen miles southeast of Minsk, on the morning of 30 June to find it occupied by the enemy. Based on VEJ, pp.134–6; Report by the Head of Logistics, Fourth Army, 29/6/41 in Knyshevskii, p.149; Voronkov, *Dvadtsat'*, pp.189, 192, 196; *Strana v Ogne*, Vol.1 Pt 1, pp.472, 476; Bender, p.90; and *Ich werde es nie vergessen*, p.53.

24 Based on Aliev, *Siege*, pp.146, 171, 182 197–203; an account by Fomin's son, http://mishpoha.org/6/fomin.html, accessed January 2017; Letter Baumgartner (135 IR) an Bünau, 7/7/41. Cited in Hartmann, *Wehrmacht im Ostkrieg*, p.263; Ganzer, pp.162–3; KTB 45ID, 2200 Hours, 25/6/41 in BA-MA RH 26-45/20; and KTB 45 ID, 26/6/41 in BA-MA RH 26-45/27; Kohl, pp.26, 30–1; Smirnov, pp.101–2, 113–15, 120–2, 137, 183–5; Knopp, p.60; *Steh auf*, pp.22–3; TB Erich von dem Bach-Zalewski, 30/6/41 in BA R 20/45b; Ganzer, pp.146, 334, 405, 409; and the author's visit to Brest fortress.

25 JSMS, Vol.4, No.2, p.344; Hoth, p.77 and KTB Bock, 25/6/41.

26 Gerhard Möws, 'Meine Erinnerungen als Kradschütze und Panzeraufklärer von September 1940 bis Januar 1943'. Author's papers.

27 *Pravda*, 9/7/41; *Pisma pogibshikh geroev*, p.29.

28 Kageneck, *Erbo*, pp.212–13.

29 Stankiewicz, p.208; Musial, *Konterrevolutionäre*, pp.132–4 and Voronkov, *Dvadtsat'*, pp.169–71.

30 The fall of Białystok is based on Wilhelm Müller, pp.11–14; *Strana v Ogne*, Vol.1 Pt 1, p.88 and *Strana v Ogne*, Vol.1 Pt 2, pp.401–2; Hartmann, *Wehrmacht im Ostkrieg*, pp.272–3; and BA-MA RH 26-221/24.

31 The Białystok massacre is based on the combat report of 309th Police Battalion, 1/7/41 in BA-MA RH 26-221/24; KTB 221 Sicherungs Division, 27/6/41 in *Verbrechen*; KTB Ic, 221 Sicherungs Division, Tätigkeitsbericht 10/5–14/12/41, Anlage in BA-MA RH 26-221/70; Curilla, *Judenmord*, pp.247–54; Lichtenstein, pp.74–8; Mallmann, *Deutscher Osten*, pp.71–4; Schulenburg, pp.279–80; Hartmann, *Wehrmacht im Ostkrieg*, pp.272–6; and www.zchor.org/Białystok/testimony.htm accessed January 2017.

32 Gross, *Neighbours*, pp.59–60; Bender, p.90; Dmitrow, pp.68–70; and Mallmann, *Deutscher Osten*, pp.77–8.

33 Based on author's visit to the Stalin Line Museum; http://stalin-line.by/en/nashi -proekty/istorii/boi-na-linii-stalina, accessed April 2017; Isaev, *Prigranichnoe srazhenie 1941*, p.412; Akalovich, pp.56–62; Panzer Pionier Bataillon 32, 'Bericht über den Einsatz des Bataillons im Feldzug gegen Russland, 15/8/41' in BA-MA RH 12-5/375 and Wittek, p.34.

34 When he visited the city a few days later, Second Army commander Maximilian von Weichs was particularly impressed by the House of the Red Army with its spacious club rooms, theatre, cinema and swimming pool. 'There was also a large map of Germany, with all objects, namely industrial plants, which were suitable for air attack marked on it,' he wrote. 'From this you could follow the plans of a Russian attack.' See BA-MA N 19/9. The fall of Minsk is based on 'How Minsk fell into German hands', by Rasso Königer, in *Minsker Zeitung*, 28–29/6/42, cited in Lenhard, pp.74–6; Wittek, pp.34–7; Hinze, pp.32–3; BA-MA RH 26-23/91; Rosowski, pp.136–40; and Voronkov, *Dvadtsat'*, p.221.

35 Meyer-Detring, pp.27–8.

36 Gefechtsbericht über den Feldzug in Russland 1941 in BA-MA RH 24-8/253, p.10 and Bergner, pp.79–81; Sherstnev, p.269; Haupt, 134ID, pp.38–50; KTB Schulze, 27–29/6/41.

37 *Flugblätter aus Deutschland*, p.11; Hertlein, p.65; Heinrici, 4/7/41; Dokument 16, p.64.

38 Based on KTB 45ID, 27/6/41 in BA-MA RH 26-45/20; KTB 45ID, 0800 Hours, 29/6/41 in BA-MA RH26-45/20; BA-MA RH 26-45/27; KTB 45 ID, 1730 Hours, 29/6/41 in BA-MA RH 26-45/20; BA-MA RH 26-45/27; Aliev, *Siege*, pp.211–13; Ganzer, pp.412–13.

39 Based on KTB 45ID, 29–30/6/41 in BA-MA RH 26-45/27; KTB 45ID, 29–30/6/41 in BA-MA RH 26-45/34; Ganzer, pp.412–13; Aliev, *Siege*, p.202; and Gschöpf, pp.225–6.

40 Based on *Deutsche Wochenschau*, 29/6/41; SD *Meldungen*, Nr 197–200, 26/6/41, 30/6/41, 3/7/41 and 7/7/41; *Freiburger Zeitung*, 30/6/41; *Völkischer Beobachter*, 30/6/41; TB Goebbels, 30/6/41 and 1/7/41; and Flannery, pp.262–3.

41 Heinrici, Dokument 15, 24/6/41, p.63; Römer, *Kommissarbefehl*, p.209.

42 See, e.g., KTB 10 Pz Div, 3/7/41 in BA-MA RH 27-10/49 and Bericht des Kdrs. der 20. Inf.Div. (mot.), 'Unsere Erlebnisse in Rußland 22/6–31/7/41' in BA-MA RH 26-20/145.

43 KTB 125 ID, 25/6/41 in BA-MA RH 26-125/3.

44 Bergström, *Operation Barbarossa*, p.83; KTB Schulze, 2/7/41; Mende, p.158; Braatz, *Werner Mölders*, pp.316–17.

45 Lopez, pp.398–9; BA-MA RW2/150, pp.63–4.

46 Meldung, 28/6/41, BA-MA RH 26-299/118 and KTB Ic 56 ID, 28/6/41 in BA-MA RH 26-56/18; Heer, 'Und dann', p.148; TB Richthofen, 4/7/41 in BA-MA N 671/8; TB Benno Wundshammer, 24/6/41; Bericht 99ID/Abt Ic, 2/7/41 in BA-MA RH 26-99/21; Gerlach, p.775; Hammer, pp.227–8.

47 Hammer, pp.227–8; Heinemann, p.73; Befehl, 25/6/41 in BA-MA RH 26-29/60; KTB Ic XLVII Corps, 26/6/41 in BA-MA RH 24-47/108; BA-MA RH 24-47/4.

48 TB Benno Wundshammer, 24/6/41; TB Habicht, 28/6/41. Cited in Quinkert and Morré, p.105; Hammer, pp.227–8; Römer, *Kommissarbefehl*, p.482.

49 BA-MA RH 20-2/1433; Von Weichs memoirs in BA-MA N 19/9; DDRZW, 5/1, p.83; Römer, *Kommissarbefehl*, pp.580–3.

50 TB Hanns-Adolf Munier, 30/6/41 in BA-MA MSg 2/4651; Luther, p.426; BA-MA RH 26-23/91.

51 Based on Diewerge, pp.19, 59–60; Mallmann, *Deutscher Osten*, pp.24–5; Manoschek, *Rassenkrieg*, p.63; Pöpping, p.41; Krause, p.176; and author's papers.

52 Letter, 23/6/41, in Frank, p.78; Luther, p.379; TB Mauss, 30/6/41 in Mauss, pp.131–2; Luck, p.70.

53 TB Gercke, 11/7/41 in BA-MA RH 26-23/91; TB Farnbacher, 29/6/41 and 1/7/41 in BA-MA MSg 2/13906; Moutier, pp.127–9.

54 Based on Hamm, p.27; Kohl, pp.59, 65, 69; *Steh auf*, pp.29–30; *Ich werde es nie vergessen*, p.60; VEJ, Band 7, Dokument 72, pp.274–5; DDRZW 9/2, p.85; Lopez, p.399; 'How Minsk fell into German hands', by Rasso Königer in *Minsker Zeitung*, 28–29/6/42, cited in Lenhard, pp.74–6; and letter from Dorsch to Rosenberg, 10/7/41 in Lenhard, p.167.

55 KTB Schulze, 1/7/41; Knyshevskii, p.65; Hammer, p.234; BA-MA MSg 2/4434.

56 Rhein, p.58; Oehmichen, p.90.

57 Gercke, *Nach Hause geschrieben*, p.22 and Paul, *IR9*, p.176; Petri, pp.47, 48; TB Bock, 30/6/41; Heinrici, 4/7/41. Dokument 16, p.64.

58 Lemelsen, pp.111–14; Stühring, pp.57–8.

59 Bunke was wounded the following day during another tank attack in the same woods. Bunke, pp.259–63.

60 Spaeter, *Grossdeutschland*, i, pp.188–90.

61 Rees, p.44; Musial, *Sowjetische Partisanen*, p.40; NARA T315 R205, frames 183–4.

62 DDRZW, 9/2, p.271; Hans Bayer, p.69; Bähr, pp.69–70.

63   Reinecke, p.75.

64   Braatz, *Krupinski*, p.49; TB Richthofen, 1/7/41 and 3/7/41 in BA-MA N 671/8.

65   Heinrici, 4/7/41. Dokument 16, p.64; Moutier, pp.127–9; Hager, pp.34–5.

66   TB Dr Jürgen Nicolas, 1/7/41 in BA-MA MSg 2/19485.

67   Based on Bopp, p.70; Selder, pp.47–8; Mayerhofer, pp.61–2; Oehmichen, p.81; 8 ID, p.84 and 258 ID, p.32.

68   Based on Ganzer, pp.325, 548 and TB Erich von dem Bach-Zalewski, 30/6/41 in BA R 20/45b.

69   Based on TB Maresch, 1/7/42 and TB Arnreiter, 1/7/42 in Ganzer, pp.382, 413–14.

70   Zeigert, pp.97–103; Schroeder, pp.86–91, 94–6; Greiner letters, 27/6/41; TB Hewel, 23/6/41–2/7/41; Leyen, p.14; *Initial Period*, p.342; Morell, p.81; IR11, p.90; and KTB OKW, I, p.1020.

71   Kumanev, pp.30–1, Mikoyan, pp.390–1; Volkogonov, p.410.

72   *Na zemle Belarusi*, Document 226–7; Musial, p.40; *Knyshevskii*, pp.118–20; Cohen, p.50.

73   Stankiewicz, pp.213–16.

74   *Geschichte des Grossen Vaterländischen Krieges der Sowjetunion*, Band 2, pp.60–1.

75   *Leningradskaya Pravda*, 28/6/41; *Blokada Leningrada: Dnevniki 1941–1944 godov*, pp.11–12; *Organy gosudarstvennoy bezopasnosti SSSR v Velikoy Otechestvennoy voyne*, Documents 313 and 323, pp.75, 86.

76   Karpow, p.37.

77   Mikoyan, pp.390–1 and Kumanev, pp.32–3.

78   Eremenko, pp.50–1, 63–6 and the interrogation of Pavlov reproduced in Ellis, pp.465–85.

79   Aaken, p.27; Luther, p.274; Paul, *18 Pz*, pp.25–32; Paul, *Nehring*, pp.119–20.

80   Paul, *18 Pz*, p.28.

81   Röw, p.215; Hamm, p.27.

82   JSMS, Vol.4 No.3, pp.531, 532; 3 Pz, pp.154–5; Munzel, pp.70–1; *Panzerkeil im Osten*, p.48.

83   Based on Sandalov, pp.135–6; TB Hanns-Adolf Munier, 30/6/41 in BA-MA MSg 2/4651; Munzel, p.71; Braatz, *Werner Mölders*, p.315; *Panzerkeil im Osten*, pp.50–1; and 3 Pz, pp.156–7.

84   Eremenko, p.69; *Posledniy Pisma s Fronta*, Vol.1, 1941, p.50; and Bergström, *Black Cross*, pp.84–6.

85   BA-MA RH 12-5/375.

86   Lubs, pp.296–7.

87   TB Dr Karl Mauss, 1–2/7/41 in BA-MA RH 82/169.

88   Luther, p.291.

89   Hamm, p.28; Hossbach, p.64.

90   TB Bock, 8/7/41; Krivosheev, p.111 and Abaturov, pp.111–12.

91   Gercke, 1/10/41 in BA-MA RH 26-23/91.

92   KTB Schulze, 6/7/41.

93   Möws, in author's papers.

CHAPTER 5: TO KIEV

1 Schrodek, *Ihr Glaubte*, pp.124–6.
2 Khrushchev, *Memoirs*, i, p.257; Hürter, *Hitlers Heerführer*, pp.137, 290.
3 Christoforow, p.25.
4 Moskalenko, pp.41–3; Maligin, pp.10–11.
5 Kirstein, pp.219–20.
6 KTB XLVIII AK, 25/6/41 in BA-MA RH 24-48/10; Hartmann, *Wehrmacht im Ostkrieg*, pp.267–8.
7 Petrow, pp.73–5.
8 Schrodek, *Ihr Glaubte*, pp.124–7; Isaev, *Dubno*, p.83; Ganz, pp.63–5.
9 Kiebuzinski and Motyl, pp.215–16; Musial, *Konterrevolutionäre*, pp.115–17, 148–9; Berkhoff, pp.14–15.
10 Events in Lvov are based on Musial, *Konterrevolutionäre*, pp.103–4, 106–8; Struve, pp.248–51 and Mick, p.468.
11 Bagramjan, p.135.
12 Isaev, *Dubno*, pp.91–2; 97ID, pp.35–7; Kempowski, p.56.
13 Khorochounova, pp.28–32 and *Ljubimye, zhdite!*, p.331.
14 Berkhoff, p.15; Krausnick, pp.303–4; Novak, pp.55–7, 64–5; BA-MA RH 24-48/198, 1/7/41; and BA-MA RH 21-1/148 (b), Bl. 213–14.
15 Based on 1st Geb Div (Lanz), p.215; Lanz, pp.106–7; and 1st Geb (Meyer), p.55.
16 *Leto 1941, Ukraina: dokumenty, materialy: khronika sobytii Ukraina*, pp.138–40; Ryabyshev, pp.22–5.
17 Daines, pp.274–5; Isaev, *Dubno*, pp.123–6; *Leto 1941, Ukraina: dokumenty, materialy: khronika sobytii Ukraina*, pp.156–8; Schrodek, *Ihr Glaubte*, p.131; and author's papers.
18 Slyusarenko, pp.12–14 and 297ID, pp.46–9.
19 Popjel, pp.109–11; 16th Pz, pp.44–5.
20 Ryabyshev, p.28.
21 Isaev, *Dubno*, p.139; Slyusarenko, p.14.
22 Isaev, *Dubno*, p.138; Popjel, p.132; Ryabyshev, pp.25–30; Munzel, pp.20–2.
23 Bagramjan, pp.150–1.
24 KTB 13 Pz Div, 27/6/41 in BA-MA RH 27-13/12.
25 Popjel, pp.164–5.
26 Kubik, pp.21–2; *Soldiers of Barbarossa*, p.53; Popjel, p.168.
27 Kempowski, p.123.
28 Knopp, p.65.
29 Khorochounova, p.34; Wischnewski, pp.16–18.
30 *Posledniy Pisma s Fronta*, Vol.1, 1941, pp.58–9. Ivan Bokov was mortally wounded a fortnight later trying to defend his hometown, by which time his family had been evacuated to the Stalingrad area.
31 Bagramjan, pp.169–70.
32 Political report on the political-moral situation of 131st Mechanised Division, 27/6/41 in NARA T315 R656 f.625.

33   Popjel, p.168.

34   Isaev, *Dubno*, pp.151–2.

35   Based on Bagramjan, pp.159–60; *Der Spiegel*, 16/8/1961, p.62 and Khrushchev, *Khrushchev Memoirs*, Vol.1, p.310.

36   BA-MA RH 37/7693.

37   Based on Błonski and Cieplińska, pp.30–1; www.przemysl24.pl/historia/barbarossa -nad-sanem-1941.html, accessed April 2018; Zając, p.189; and information provided by the Kaponiera 8813 museum.

38   Maligin, p.17; Inozemtsev, p.29.

39   Karl von Roques, 'Was ich in den ersten 4 Monaten des Ostfeldzuges in Sowjet-Russland erlebt habe', in BA-MA N 152/10.

40   Knopp, *Verdammte Krieg*, p.71.

41   TB Reichold, 30/6/41 and 3/7/41 in BA-MA N 314/2; TB Hindelang, 7/7/41; Sørlie, p.219; Sannemann, p.104; Kaltenegger, pp.233–4; Musial, *Konterrevolutionäre*, p.217.

42   Gross, *Revolution*, p.182; Kiebuzinski and Motyl, pp.335–8; BA-MA RW2/150, p.37.

43   Sandkühler, p.113; Pohl, pp.40, 48; Struve, p.239.

44   Sebastian, pp.372–4; Ioanid, *Holocaust*, pp.7–9; Deletant, p.129.

45   Carp, p.269; Zwieback, p.24; Ancel, pp.76, 79, 80; Ioanid, *Iași Pogrom*, p.30; Eaton, p.92.

46   Ancel, pp.94–9 and Stoenescu, pp.369–73.

47   Based on Ioanid, *Holocaust*, pp.73, 75, 78–9; Ancel, pp.127, 137; Geissbühler, pp.55–6; Zwieback, pp.25–6; Ioanid, *Iași Pogrom*, p.37.

48   Based on Ancel, pp.156, 157, 167, 182, 184, 193; Ioanid, *Holocaust*, pp.76–7; Zwieback, pp.26–7; Eaton, p.90; Carp, p.272.

49   VEJ, Band 13, pp.391–4; Angrick, pp.141–3.

50   Based on Ancel, pp.290, 301; Eaton, pp.97–101, 114; Ioanid, *Holocaust*, pp.80, 83; the testimony of Nathan Goldstein in VEJ, Band 13, pp.398–400; and Carp, pp.273–6.

51   Ioanid, *Holocaust*, p.85; Eaton, p.114; Ancel, p.475; Ioanid, *Iași Pogrom*, p.114.

52   Ancel, pp.83, 270–9, 282; Eaton, p.114.

53   Ancel, p.561.

54   Stoenescu, pp.351–3, 369–72, 397–8.

55   Memminger, p.D308; KTB *Panzergruppe* 1, 30/6/41 in BA-MA RH 21-1/50; Popjel, pp.195–6.

56   Schimak, pp.140–1.

57   Popjel, pp.196–201, 214–16.

58   Boehm, p.87.

59   Maligin, pp.15–16.

60   TB Drechsler, pp.46–7.

61   Maligin, pp.15–16. Maligin mis-dates the counter-attack to 28 June rather than 1 July. See Isaev, *Dubno*, pp.177–8.

62   Sæther, p.90; Glantz, *Stumbling Colossus*, pp.138–9.

63   Sannemann, p.104; KTB Halder, 27/6/41; Werthen, p.48.

64   Yegorov, pp.58–9.

65   The word the division's war diarist used was 'massacred'. BA-MA MSg2/13984, pp.55–6 and Meyer, p.56.

66   BA-MA MSg2/13984, p.55; 'Kämpfe bis zur Einnahme von Lemberg' in BA-MA RH 28-1/284.

67   TB Hindelang, 26/6/41–1/7/41.

68   VEJ, Band 7, pp.150–1.

69   BA-MA MSg 2/13984, p.57.

70   TB Hans Kreppel, 30/6/41 in BA-MA MSg 2/97; BA-MA MSg 2/13984, p.59; NARA T315 R040 f303; and BA-MA RH 28-1/266.

71   Based on BA-MA MSg2/13984, pp.59–60; VEJ, Band 7, p.152; Klein, pp.20–1; Sæther, p.93; Feldpost von Plotho, 30/6/41; Struve, pp.260–1, 262; Jones, pp.78–9; TB Schrödter, 22/6/41; Kaltenegger, *Gefangen im russischen Winter*, p.68.

72   Musial, *Konterrevolutionäre*, pp.106–11; Kiebuzinski and Motyl, pp.292–7 and Zwart, pp.38–9, 44–45.

73   BA-MA RW 2/149, pp.339–40, 346, 373; Struve, pp.273, 278.

74   BA-MA RW 2/149, pp.340–1; Struve, p.280.

75   BA-MA RW2/149, pp.340–1, 362–3, 380–3; Diewerge, pp.44–5; Struve, p.278; Seidler, pp.339, 340–1.

76   Zwart, p.40; Diewerge, pp.41–2; Jestadt, pp.45–51.

77   Sandkühler, p.116; BA-MA RW2/149, pp.380–3.

78   Kaltenegger, *Gefangen im russischen Winter*, p.68; Sandkühler, p.116; Feldpost von Plotho, 30/6/41; Veum, pp.58–9; Diewerge, pp.41–2, 44–5.

79   Ebert, pp.123–4.

80   Pöpping, p.41; TB Schrödter, 22/6/41; Adolf B., Feldpostbrief, 23/6/41 in Stader, pp.16–17; Sørlie, p.238; Manoschek, *Es gibt nur*, p.31; BA-MA RH 28-1/284.

81   Struve, pp.292–4; Rossoliński-Liebe, pp.198–9; Mick, p.479.

82   NARA T315 R040 f304 and Feldpostbrief Eugen Meyding, 30/6/41 in Struve, p.305.

83   Pohl, p.57; Veum, pp.59–60; Sæther, p.94.

84   Himka, pp.212, 214; Mick, p.473; Rossoliński-Liebe, p.209; Struve, pp.308–9; Musial, pp.176–7.

85   Jones, pp.80–1; Struve, pp.307–8, 311–14.

86   Struve, pp.337–8; Cüppers, pp.203–5.

87   Heimkes, p.13; Struve, pp.326–35; Mallmann, *Deutscher Osten*, pp.81–2; TB Schrödter, 22/6/41.

88   Jacobi, p.18; Heer, 'Und dann', pp.150–1; Swanström, p.229; Manoschek, *Es gibt nur*, p.41; Mallmann, *Deutscher Osten*, p.81; KTB 1st *Gebirgs* Division, 1/7/41 in NARA T351 R039 f444; TB Hans Kreppel, 1/7/41 in BA-MA MSg2/97.

89   TB Schrödter, 22/6/41.

90   Kessler, pp.33–40.

91   BA-MA RH 26-295/22; TB von Gemmingen, 1/7/41.

92   Tennenbaum, pp.167–8.

93   Musial, *Konterrevolutionäre*, pp.212–13; BA-MA RH 26-295/22.

94   Tennenbaum, pp.169–73; Kempowski, p.227.

95   Kirstein, p.250.

96 Tennenbaum, p.175.

97 Based on Kirstein, p.251; Korfes, pp.90–1; and Struve, pp.567–82.

98 Struve, p.447.

99 Schneider, pp.432–3.

100 Struve, pp.434–9; Musial, *Konterrevolutionäre*, p.268.

101 BA-MA RH 24-49/161; Heer, 'Und dann', p.151; TB Schrödter, 22/6/41.

102 Struve, pp.468–77; Kiebuzinski and Motyl, pp.326–9.

103 Umansky, pp.195–7.

104 Musial, *Konterrevolutionäre*, p.216.

105 *Knyshevskii*, pp.121, 263–6.

106 Ryabyshev, p.50.

107 Kempowski, p.226.

108 Frauer, p.41; Shepherd, *Hitler's Soldiers*, p.138; Sachsse, pp.147–9.

109 *Ukrayina: 100 dniv viny*, p.425.

110 Kempowski, p.172; Alvensleben, p.187; Buchbender, *Tönende Erz*, pp.32–3.

111 Benary, pp.31–2; Kempowski, p.172; Pöpping, p.143.

112 Moutier, p.125; Sachsse, p.147.

113 Vincx, iv, pp.103, 120; Feldpost from a member of 13 *Kompanie*, *Nordland* Regiment, 29/7/41 in BA-MA N 756/144b; 25 ID, p.87; Kempowski, p.120; Roth, p.31.

114 *Ukrayina: 100 dniv viny*, p.432.

115 BA-MA RW2/150, p.62; BA-MA RW2/149, p.187; Feldpost Siebeler, 2/7/41; TB Hindelang, 7/7/41.

116 BA-MA RW2/149, p.211; KTB 14 Pz Div Anlagen, 2/7/41 in NARA T315 R656, f57; 25ID, pp.84–6; Heuer, pp.207–8.

117 Manoschek, *Rassenkrieg*, pp.95–7; BA-MA RH 20-6/489.

118 Burds, p.32; Seberechts, p.157.

119 Roekel (Kindle edition).

120 Based on Seberechts, pp.149–54; Dagboek Marinus Weers 21/6/41, 1–2/7/41; Struve, pp.563–6, 572; and Manoschek, *Es gibt nur*, p.31.

121 Constantiniu, p.394.

122 Löser, p.80; Leutnant Mende, 'Der erste Tag' in *Die Soldatische Tat: Der Kampf im Osten 1941/42*, pp.14–17; Malaparte, p.43.

123 Graser, pp.58–9; Duțu, p.40.

124 *Jurnalul mareșalului Ion Antonescu*, p.327; Duțu, pp.35, 40, 42.

125 Scârneci, p.113.

126 Voicu, pp.342–3; Duțu, pp.32, 35; VEJ, Band 13, pp.400–1.

127 *Jurnalul mareșalului Ion Antonescu*, p.328; Solomovici, p.356.

128 Constantiniu, pp.392–3; DDRZW, 9/2, p.81; Geissbühler, pp.61–7.

129 Carp, p.228.

130 Pohl, p.69.

131 Musial, *Konterrevolutionäre*, p.259.

132 VEJ, Band 7, p.153.

133 Kempowski, pp.216, 243–5.

134 Ibid, pp.227–8.

135 Events in Tarnopol are based on Mallmann, *Ereignismeldungen*, pp.86, 132–3; Manoschek, *Rassenkrieg*, pp.102–3; Kiebuzinski, *Great West Ukrainian Prison Massacre*, pp.368–72; Pohl, pp.63–4; Prazan, pp.60–2; Roekel (Kindle edition); Dagboek Marinus Weers, 4/7/41; Kageneck, *Examen de Conscience*, pp.38–40.

136 Musial, *Konterrevolutionäre*, pp.278–9; TB Hindelang, 17/7/41; Dagboek Marinus Weers.

137 Swanström, p.242; Sørlie, pp.292–3; Kempowski, p.245.

138 Pohl, p.64; and Mallmann, *Ereignismeldungen*, pp.132–3.

139 TB Schrödter, 9/7/41; TB Hindelang, 7/7/41; KTB Erich Dreschler, 4/7/41

CHAPTER 6: VICTORY DENIED

1 Lopez, p.433.

2 Guslyarov, p.352.

3 Author's papers.

4 Ortenberg, pp.21–4.

5 Based on Vasily Savchenko's diary held by prozhito.org; reports published in *Moskva Voyennaya 1941–1945*, pp.66–9; Reid, p.40; Docs 1 and 11 in *Novgorodskaya zemlya v epokhu sotsial'nykh potryaseniy 1941–1945*; Khristoforov, pp.453–4; and Vihavainen and Manninen, p.145.

6 Heysing, *Die Wehrmacht*, Vol. 5, No.19, 10/9/41; Fedyuninsky, p.32.

7 TB Halder, 3/7/41. Such sentiments were echoed in a letter to his former secretary at the beginning of July: 'The Russians have lost the war within the first eight days. Their losses in men and equipment are inconceivable. The size of Russia will allow them to fight on for a long time yet, but they will not be able to change their destiny any more.' Jodl, p.55.

8 Greiner, 4/7/41; TT, 5–6/7/41 and TB Hewel, 29/6/41–11/7/41.

9 Martin, 18 IR, p.72; Frank, p.78; Ebert, p.136; Fuchs, pp.118, 122; Adolf B., letters 27/6/41 and 8/7/41, 3/8/41 in Stader, pp.17, 23; Heyl, p.77; Kageneck, *Erbo*, pp.213–14.

10 Dollinger, pp.81–2.

11 Broekmeyer, p.48.

12 Bellamy, p.233; Glantz, *Stumbling Colossus*, pp.206–11.

13 Dollinger, p.88; Dawletschin, pp.29, 35.

14 *Po Obe Storoni Fronta*, pp.153–5.

15 Vladimir Meladze was killed over Ukraine on 5 July. *Posledniy Pis'ma s Fronta*; *Ukrayina: 100 dniv viyny*, p.229; Lehasova, p.181.

16 *Po Obe Storoni Fronta*, pp.153–5.

17 Edele, p.33; Zvyagintsev, pp.263–5.

18 Based on Ellis, pp.261–77, 465–85; and *Strana v Ogne*, Vol.1 Pt 2, pp.133–4.

19 Based on Sudoplatov, Vol.2, pp.60–5 and https://novayagazeta.ru/articles/2016/06/17/68966-stalin-v-1941-godu-byl-gotov-otdat-gitleru-pribaltiku-i-ukrainu, accessed 22 December 2019.

20   TB Goebbels, 19/8/41.

21   BA-MA RH 20-4/877; Dawletschin, pp.56–7; WiStabOst, report 27/11/41, cited in GASWW, iv, pp.1175–6; Neiztel, p.189

22   Dawletschin, pp.62–9.

23   Müller, *Deutsche Wirtschaftspolitik*, p.595.

24   Berkhoff, pp.37, 115; Meindl, pp.338, 339.

25   TB Fritz Kalsche, undated, *c*.mid-August 1941 in Heikens.

26   BA-MA RH 26-221/19; AOK9 Ic 18/8/41 in BA-MA RH 26-6/63. Bl.45–6.

27   TB Leutnant, 293 ID, 30/6/41 in BA-MA MSg 2/10411.

28   Alexijewitsch, p.38.

29   *Strana v Ogne*, Vol.1 Pt 2, pp.402–4; *Na zemle Belarusi*, Document 235, pp.457–8.

30   Paul, *Brennpunkte*, p.115; Riederer von Paar, p.443; Brief, 5/7/41 in Bücheler, p.136; Leeb, p.283n.

31   Bähr, pp.70–1.

32   Petri, pp.50–1.

33   Breymayer, pp.39–40.

34   Alexander, p.65.

35   Letters, 26/7/41, 7/8/41 and 15/8/41 in Scheuer, pp.26–7, 30, 31.

36   Knappe, pp.213–14, 222.

37   Brief, 14/8/41 in Krausnick, *Tagebücher eines Abwehroffiziers*, pp.522–3.

38   Heinrici letter, 22/7/41. Dokument 24, p.70.

39   Letters, 13/7/41, 16/7/41 and 15/8/41 in Bücheler, pp.137–8, 140.

40   Bieszanow, pp.229–30.

41   Hammer, p.129; Curilla, *Die deutsche Ordnungspolizei*, pp.571–4; Browning, pp.121–3.

42   Bieszanow, p.230; Unruh in MS D-052; Aliev, *Siege*, p.218.

43   MS D-052; BA-MA RH 20-4/1210.

44   *Meldungen aus dem Reich*, Nr.200–203, 207, 212, 219, 7/7/41–17/7/41, 31/7/41, 18/8/41, 11/9/41.

45   TB Lemelsen, 16/7/41 in Luther papers; Haupt, *8 Pz*, pp.46, 48.

46   TB Halder, 5/8/41, 11/8/41.

EPILOGUE: *BARBAROSSA*'S LONG SHADOW

1   Bieszanow, p.231. Smirnov gives a similar account, without identifying the violinist.

2   Kohl, p.26.

BIBLIOGRAPHY

Personal diaries

Bock, Fedor von, *Zwischen Pflicht und Verweigerung. Das Kriegstagebuch*, Herbig, 1995

Drechsler, Erich, *Von Ohrdruf bis Orel*, Selbstverlag

Engel, Gerhard, *Heeresadjutant bei Hitler 1938–1943. Aufzeichnungen des Majors Engel*, DVA, 1974

Gemmingen, Sigismund von, author's papers

Goebbels, Joseph, *Die Tagebücher von Joseph Goebbels*, K. G. Saur, 1993–1996

Greiner, Helmut, David Irving papers, Microform Ltd

Haape, Heinrich, Luther papers, kindly provided by Craig Luther

Halder, Franz, held by the Imperial War Museum, London

Hewel, Walther, https://fpp.co.uk/Hitler/Hewel/Tgb_1941.html (accessed March 2024)

Hindelang, Emilian, *Über Nacht war Krieg: Mein Weg nach Russland 1941*, BoD, 2019

Hoth, Hermann, BA-MA RH 21-3/40

Leeb, Wilhelm Ritter von, *Generalfeldmarschall Wilhelm Ritter von Leeb. Tagebuchaufzeichnungen und Lagebeurteilungen aus zwei Weltkriegen*, DVA, 1985

Schrödter, Herbert, courtesy of the Schrödter family

Schulze, Hans, Kriegstagebuch, März bis Dezember 1941 in author's papers

Waldau, Otto Hoffmann von, David Irving papers, Microform Ltd

Wundshammer, Benno, *Propaganda-Fotograf im Zweiten Weltkrieg*, Ch Links, 2014

Feldpost, Das Museum für Kommunikation Berlin

Plotho, Manfred *Freiherr* von

Siebeler, Franz

Unpublished sources

Bundesarchiv, Berlin

R 20/45b TB Erich von dem Bach-Zalewski

BUNDESARCHIV-MILITÄRARCHIV, FREIBURG

OFFICIAL RECORDS

RH 12-5/375 Panzer Pionier Bataillon 32, 'Bericht über den Einsatz des Bataillons im Feldzug gegen Russland, 15/8/41'

RH 20-4 Papers of Fourth Army

RH 20-6 Papers of Sixth Army

RH 21-1 Papers of *Panzergruppe* 1

RH 21-4 Papers of *Panzergruppe* 4

RH 24-8 Papers of VIII Corps

RH 24-26 Papers of XXVI Corps

RH 24-47 Papers of XLVII Corps

RH 24-48 Papers of XLVIII Corps

RH 24-49 Papers of XLIX Corps

RH 26-1 Papers of 1st Infantry Division

RH 26-20 Papers of 20th (Mot) Infantry Division

RH 26-23 Papers of 23rd Infantry Division

RH 26-29 Papers of 29th Infantry Division

RH 26-35 Papers of 35th Infantry Division

RH 26-45 Papers of 45th Infantry Division

RH 26-56 Papers of 56th Infantry Division

RH 26-6/63 Papers of 63rd Infantry Division

RH 26-99 Papers of 99th Infantry Division

RH 26-102 Papers of 102nd Infantry Division

RH 26-123 Papers of 123rd Infantry Division

RH 26-125 Papers of 125th Infantry Division

RH 26-134 Papers of 134th Infantry Division

RH 26-221 Papers of 221st Security Division

RH 26-253 Papers of 253rd Infantry Division

RH 26-281 Papers of 281st Infantry Division

RH 26-299 Papers of 299th Infantry Division

RH 27-10 Papers of 10th Panzer Division

RH 27-13 Papers of 13th Panzer Division

RH 28-1 Papers of 1st *Gebirgs* Division

RH 31-I/93 Papers of the Deutsche Heeresmission Rumänien, 1941–42

RH 37/2785 'Das Infanterieregiment 151 1939–1942: Geschichte des Regiments in den Feldzügen in Polen, Holland, Belgien, Frankreich, Baltenland und Russland'

RH 37/3095 'Marschweg und Kämpfe des III/IR405'

RH 37/3096 *Oberst* von Kirchbach, 'Mein Regiment'

RH 37/7693 Infanterie Regiment 519 in Ostfeldzug

RH 41/702 Aus dem Kriegstagebuch: Tatschenbericht und Erlebnisse eines ehemaligen Frontsoldaten im Russlandfeldzug 1941–43

RH 82/169 TB Dr Karl Mauss

RW 2/149 Wehrmacht Untersuchungsstelle für Verletzungen des Völkerrechts: Anlagen zu der Denkschrift 'Kriegsverbrechen der russischen Wehrmacht 1941'

RW 2/150 Wehrmacht Untersuchungsstelle für Verletzungen des Völkerrechts: Kriegsverbrechen der russischen Wehrmacht

RW 4/578 Operative Entscheidungen des Rußland-Feldzuges: Sammlung von Niederschriften über Besprechungen, Vorträge und Weisungen Hitlers für das Kriegstagebuch des Wehrmachtführungsstabes, Dez. 1940 – Aug. 1941

PERSONAL PAPERS

MSg 2/97 TB Hans Kreppel

MSg 2/2580 Uffz Fr Schaback 'Der Todesmarsch nach Leningrad'

MSg 2/4219 Erlebnisse von Soldaten der I/Stukageschwader 77

MSg 2/4434 Max Dörfler, 'Einsatz beim Kessel von Białystok'

MSg 2/4651 TB Hanns-Adolf Munier

MSg 2/5384 Walter Loos 'Die Einnahme von Brest-Litowsk am 22 Juni 1941'

MSg 2/10411 TB Leutnant, 293rd Infantry Division.

MSg 2/12198 Hans-Günther Seraphim, 'Erinnerungen aus dem Jahren des zweiten Weltkriegs', Band 2

MSg 2/13906 TB Fritz Farnbacher

MSg 2/13984 Hans Steets, 'Die Grosse Marsch nach Osten: Weg und Kampf der ersten Gebirgsdivision im Sommer 1941 von Lemberg bis Winnica'

MSg 2/19485 TB Dr Jürgen Nicolas

MSg 3/2083 *Linzer Turm*

PERSONAL PAPERS OF SENIOR FIGURES

N 19/9 Papers of Maximilian von Weichs

N 152/10 Karl von Roques, 'Was ich in den ersten 4 Monaten des Ostfeldzuges in Sowjet-Russland erlebt habe'

N 245/2 Papers of Georg-Hans Reinhardt

N 314/2 Rolf Reichold, 'Mit einem Artillerie Regiment im Russland-Feldzug'

N 671/8 TB Wolfram von Richthofen

N 756 Papers of Wolfgang Vopersal

N 802/189 Guderian papers

US NATIONAL ARCHIVES AND RECORDS ADMINISTRATION (NARA)

T315 Roll 039 KTB 1st *Gebirgs* Division

T315 Roll 040 KTB 1st *Gebirgs* Division

T315 Roll 205 KTB 4th Panzer Division

T315 Roll 656 KTB 14th Panzer Division

NIOD, AMSTERDAM

244/1073 Dagboek Marinus Weers

PUBLISHED SOURCES

NEWSPAPERS AND MAGAZINES

Brīvā Zeme
Die Wehrmacht
Į laisvę
Leningradskaya Pravda
Nacionālā Zemgale
Pravda
Völkischer Beobachter, Berlin edition

NEWSREELS

Deutsche Wochenschau

PRIMARY SOURCES

DOCUMENTS

Boberach, Heinz, *Meldungen aus dem Reich: Die geheimen Lageberichte des Sicherheitsdienstes der SS 1938–1945*, Pawlak, Herrsching, 1984

Christoforow, Vasilij (ed), *Verhört: Die Befragungen deutscher Generale und Offiziere durch die sowjetischen Geheimdienste 1945–1952*, De Gruyter Oldenbourg, 2015

Deutschland im Kampf, Stollberg, 1941

Documents on German Foreign Policy, Series D, Volume XII, HMSO, 1962

Hill, Alexander, *The Great Patriotic War of the Soviet Union 1941–45: A Documentary Reader*, Routledge, 2009

Hoppe, Bert, and Glass, Hildrun, *Der Verfolgung und Ermordung der europäischen Juden durch das nationalsozialistische Deutschland 1933–1945*, Band 7 and 13, Sowjetunion mit annektierten Gebieten I, Oldenbourg Verlag, 2011

Kiebuzinski, Ksenya and Motyl, Alexander, *The Great West Ukrainian Prison Massacre of 1941: A Sourcebook*, Amsterdam University Press, 2017

Knyshevskii, P. N. (ed), *Skrytaia pravda voiny: 1941 god: neizvestnye dokumenty*, Russkaia kniga, 1992

Kyiv: Viina, vlada, suspil'stvo: 1939–1945: Za dokumentamy radians'kykh spetssluzhb ta natsysts'koi okupatsiinoi administratsii, Tempora, 2014

Mallmann, Klaus-Michael, Angrick, Andrej, Matthäus, Jürgen and Cüppers, Martin (eds), *Die Ereignismeldungen UdSSR 1941: Dokumente der Einsatzgruppen in der Sowjetunion*, Wissenschaftliche Buchgesellschaft, Darmstadt, 2011

Mallmann, Klaus-Michael, Riess, Volker and Pyta, Wolfram, *Deutscher Osten 1939–1945: Der Weltanschauungskrieg in Photos und Texten*, Wissenschaftliche Buchgesellschaft, Darmstadt, 2003

Moritz, Erhard (ed), *Fall Barbarossa: Dokumente zur Vorbereitung der faschistischen Wehrmacht auf die Aggression gegen die Sowjet Union 1940–41*, Deutscher Militärverlag, 1970

Na zemle Belarusi: kanun i nachalo voiny: boevye deistviia sovetskikh voisk v nachal'nom periode Velikoi Otechestvennoi voiny, Belta, 2006

Nazi–Soviet Relations 1939–1941, US Department of State, 1948

Neiztel, Sönke (ed), *Tapping Hitler's Generals*, Frontline, 2013

Novgorodskaya zemlya v epokhu sotsial'nykh potryaseniy. 1941–1945, Nestor-Istoriya, 2008

Organy gosudarstvennoy bezopasnosti SSSR v Velikoy Otechestvennoy voyne. Sbornik dokumentov. Volume 2, *Nachalo*, Part 1, 2000

Overmans, Rudiger, Hilger, Andreas and Polian, Pavel, *Rotarmisten in deutscher Hand: Dokumente zu Gefangenschaft, Repatriierung und Rehabilitierung sowjetischer Soldaten des Zweiten Weltkrieges*, Ferdinand Schöningh, 2012

Schramm, Percy E. (ed), *Kriegstagebuch des Oberkommandos der Wehrmacht*, 8 Volumes, Herrsching, Manfred Pawlak, 1982

Seidler, Franz (ed), *Verbrechen an der Wehrmacht: Kriegsgreuel der Roten Armee 1941/42*, Pour le Mérite, Selent, 1997

Trevor-Roper, Hugh (ed), *Hitler's Table Talk*, Oxford University Press, 1988

PERSONAL ACCOUNTS

Alexander, Christine, *Eastern Inferno: The Journals of a German Panzerjäger on the Eastern Front*, Casemate, 2010

Alexijewitsch, Swetlana, *Die letzten Zeugen: Kinder im Zweiten Weltkrieg*, Hanser Berlin, 2014

Allmayer-Beck, Johann Christoph, *Herr Oberleitnant, det lohnt doch nicht: Kriegserinnerungen an die Jahre 1938 bis 1945*, Böhlau, 2013

Alvensleben, Udo von, *Lauter Abschiede: Tagebuch im Kriege*, Ullstein, 1979

Arkhipenko, Fyodor, *Zapiski letchika-istrebitelya Podrobneye*, Eksmo, 2007

Bagramjan, I. Ch., *So begann der Krieg*, Militärverlag der DDR, 1979

Bähr, Walter aı   ʿeds), *Kriegsbriefe Gefallener Studenten 1939–1945*, Rainer Wunderlich

Bender, Sara, *The   ʝ…ok During World War II and the Holocaust*, Brandeis, 2008

Benz, Jörg, *Bombennächte und Frontschicksale: Briefwehsel einer Kieler Familie 1939–1945*, Husum, 2008

Berezhkov, Valentin, *At Stalin's Side*, Birch Lane, 1994

Berezhkov, Valentin, *History in the Making*, Progress, 1983

Bialer, Seweryn (ed), *Stalin and his Generals*, Souvenir, 1970

Boldin, *Stranitsy Zhizni*, Voenizdat, 1961

Bopp, Gerhard, *Kriegstagebuch: Aufzeichnungen während des II Weltkrieges 1940–1943*, Timon, 2005

Brandišauskas, Valentinas (ed), *1941m Birželio Sukilimas*, Lithuanian Centre for Genocide and Resistance Research, 2000

Buchbender, Ortwin and Sterz, Reinhold, *Das andere Gesicht des Krieges: Deutsche Feldpostbriefe 1939–1945*, CH Beck, 1982

Bunke, Erich, *Der Osten blieb unser Schicksal 1939–1945*, Selbstverlag, 1991

Buzatu, Gheorghe, Cheptea, Stela and Cîrstea, Marusi (eds) *Pace și război (1940–1944): jurnalul mareșalului Ion Antonescu*, Vol. 1, 1940–41, Tipo Moldova, 2011

Chaldej, Jewgeni, *Kriegstagebuch*, Das Neue Berlin, 2011

Clandestine History of the Kovno Jewish Ghetto Police, Indiana University Press, 2014

Dawletschin, Tamurbek, *Von Kasan nach Bergen-Belsen: Erinnerungen eines sowjetischen Kriegsgefangenen*, Vandenhoeck & Ruprecht, 2005

Diewerge, Wolfgang (ed), *Deutsche Soldaten sehen die Sowjet-Union*, Wilhelm Limpert, 1941

Dollinger, Hans (ed), *Kain, wo ist dein Bruder?*, Fischer, 1987

Drabkin, Artem, *Barbarossa Through Soviet Eyes: The First Twenty-Four Hours*, Pen and Sword, 2012

Ebert, Jens (ed), *Im Funkwagen der Wehrmacht durch Europa: Feldpostbriefe des Gefreiten Wilhelm Moldenhauer 1940–1943*, Trafo, 2008

Emilian, Ion Valerian, *Der phantastische Ritt*, Verlag KW Schütz, 1977

Eremenko, Andrey, *The Arduous Beginning*, University Press of the Pacific, 2003

Fedyuninsky, Ivan Ivanovich, *Podnyatyye po trevoge*, Voenizdat, 1961

Flannery, Harry, *Assignment to Berlin*, Michael Joseph, 1942

Foreign Relations of the United States, US Government, 1941, Volume I

Frank, Walter, *Verführt, verheizt: Auszüge aus den Feldpostbriefen meines Bruders Albert Frank*, Deutsche Kriegsgräberfürsorge, 2006

Frauer, Hans-Dieter (ed), *Signale an der Front: Das geheime Kriegstagebuch von Funker Richard Rommel*

Freitag, August, *Aufzeichnungen aus Krieg und Gefangenschaft (1941–1945)*

Fuchs, Karl, *Sieg Heil!: War Letters of Tank Gunner Karl Fuchs 1937–41*

Ganor, Solly, *Light One Candle: A Survivor's Tale from Lithuania to Jerusalem*, Kodansha America, 2003

Ganzer, Christian (ed), *Brest. Leto 1941 goda. Dokumenty. Materialy. Fotografii*, Inbelkult, Smolensk, 2016

Gercke, Fritz, *Nach Hause geschrieben – Aus dem Feldzug 1941 gegen Sowjet-Rußland*, Zander Druck- u. Verlagshaus, 1941

Grossman, Wassili, and Ehrenburg, Ilja (eds), *Das Schwarzbuch: Der Genozid an den sowjetischen Juden*, Rowohlt, 1994

Grupe, Friedrich, *Jahrgang 1916: Die Fahne war mehr als der Tod*, Universitas, 1989

Guderian, Heinz, *Panzer Leader*, Michael Joseph, 1952

Haape, Heinrich, *Endstation Moskau*, Motorverlag, 1980

Habedanck, Gerd, 'Nacht vor Brest-Litowsk', *Deutschland im Kampf, Juli 1941*

Hager, Erich, *The War Diaries of a Panzer Soldier Erich Hager with the 17th Panzer Division on the Russian Front 1941–1945*, Schiffer, 2010

Hamm, J. A., *Als Priester in Russland: Ein Tagebuch*, Johann Josef Zimmer, 1959

Hammer, I. and Neiden, Suzanne zu, *Sehr selten habe ich geweint*, Schweizer, 1993

Hanxleden, Eberhard von, '*22 Juni 1941. Brest. 31.5 Uhr beginnen die Batterien*': *Kriegstagebuch Eberhard von Hanxleden*, Minsk, 2011

Heikens, Stefan, *Du wirst mich doch nicht vergessen? Briefe und Schriften von Leutnant Fritz Kalsche*

Heimkes, Heinrich, *Ein Münchner als Gebirgssoldat im Kaukasus und auf dem Balkan*, Selbstverlag, 2000

Heinemann, Ulrich, *Ein konservativer Rebell: Fritz-Dietlof Graf von der Schulenburg und der 20 Juli*, Siedler, 1990

Heintze, *Freiherr* von and Wiedemann, Ludwig (ed), *Wir kämpften gegen die Sowjets 1941/42*, Fliegerkorps VIII, 1942

Heuer, Edith, *Im Vertrauen auf Gott und den Führer: Die Tagebücher meines Vaters 1935–1945*, Books on Demand, 2015

Heyl, Ludwig, *Wie ich den Krieg erlebte*, Weber, 1984

Heysing, Günther (ed), 'Aus dem Tagebuch eines Sowjetkommissars: Mit Lüge und Genickschuss,' *Die Wehrmacht*, Vol.5, No.19, 10/9/41

Hilger, Gustav, *Wir und der Kreml: Deutsche sowjetische Beziehungen 1918–1941 – Erinnerungen eines deutschen Diplomaten*, Athenäum, 1955

Holzman, Margarete and Kaiser, Reinhard, *Dies Kind soll leben: Die Aufzeichnungen der Helene Holzman 1941–1944*, List Taschenbuch, 2001

Hossbach, Friedrich, *Infanterie im Ostfeldzug 1941/42*, Giebel and Oehlschlägel, 1951

Hürter, Johannes, *Ein deutscher General an der Ostfront: Die Briefe und Tagebücher des Gotthard Heinrici 1941–1942*, Edition Tempus, 2001

Ich werde es nie vergessen: Briefe sowjetischer Kriegsgefangener 2004–2006, Ch Links, 2007

International Military Tribunal, *Trial of the Major War Criminals before the International Military Tribunal*, 42 volumes, 1947

Inozemtsev, N. N., *Tsena pobedy v toi samoi voine: Frontovoi dnevnik*, Nauka, 1995

Irrgang, Astrid, *Leutnant der Wehrmacht Peter Stölten in seine Feldpostbriefen: vom richtigen Leben im falschen*, Rombach Historiae, 2007

Jacobi, Werner, *Jugend im Krieg: Kriegstagebuch 1939–1945*, Selbstverlag, 1995

Jacobsen, Otto, *Erich Marcks, Soldat und Gelehrter*, Musterschmidt, 1971

Jestadt, Georg, *Ohne Siege und Hurra*, Buch&Media, 2005

Jodl, Luise, *Jenseits des Endes: Leben und Sterben des Generaloberst Alfred Jodl*, Molden Taschenbuch, 1978

John, Friedrich, 'Forced Crossing of the Bug River, Advance through the Russian Border Defences and Capture of the Fortress Brest-Litovsk', MS D-239

Kageneck, August von, *Erbo: Pilote de chasse*, Editions de la Loupe, 2004

Kageneck, August von, *Examen de Conscience*, Tempus Perrin, 2004

Kaufmann, Johannes, *Flugberichte 1935–1945*, Journal Verlag Schwend, 1989

Kaufmann, Max, *Churbn Lettland: The Destruction of the Jews of Latvia*, Hartung-Gorre, 1947

Kawka, Zbigniew, *Menschen zwischen Hoffnung und Angst: Feldpost 1939–1945*, Opolgraf, 2020

Kempowski, Walter, *Das Echolot: Barbarossa '41 – Ein kollektives Tagebuch*, Albrecht Knaus, 2002

Kessler, Edmund, *The Wartime Diary Of Edmund Kessler*, Academic Studies, 2010

Khorochounova, Irina, *Carnets de Kiev 1941–1943*, Calman Levy, 2018

Khrushchev, Nikita, *Khrushchev Remembers*, Sphere, 1971

Khrushchev, Nikita, *Memoirs of Nikita Khrushchev*, Volume 1, Penn State University Press, 2013

Kirchner, Klaus, *Flugblattpropaganda im 2 Weltkrieg: Flugblätter aus Deutschland 1941*

Klein, Emil, *Aus dem Tagebuch eines Gruppen und Zugführers, Russland 1941*, Selbstverlag, 1979

Knappe, Siegfried, *Soldat*, Dell, 1993

Knoke, Heinz, *I Flew for the Führer*, Corgi, 1966

Krause, Joachim, *Fremde Eltern: Zeitgeschichte in Tagebüchern und Briefen 1933–1945*, Sax, 2016

Krausnick, Helmut (ed), *Tagebücher eines Abwehroffiziers 1938–1940*, DVA, 1970

Kruk, Hermann, *The Last Days of the Jerusalem of Lithuania*, Yale University Press, 2002

Kubik, Willi, *Erinnerungen eines Panzerschützen 1941–1945: Tagebuchaufzeichnung eines Panzerschützen der Pz.Aufkl.Abt.13 im Russlandfeldzug*, Flechsig, 2007

Lasch, Otto, *So fiel Königsberg*, Motorbuch, 2002

Lehasova, L. V. (ed), *Neprochytani lysty 1941-ho: doslidzh., dok., svidchennya*, Aerostat, 2012

Lelyushenko, Dmitry, *Moskva-Stalingrad-Berlin-Praga*, Nauka, 1985

Lenhard, Hartmut, *Lebensraum im Osten: Deutsche in Belorussland 1941–44*, DKV, 1991

Leto 1941, Ukraina : dokumenty, materialy: khronika sobytii Ukraina, 1991

Leyen, Ferdinand Prinz von der, *Rückblick zum Mauerwald*, Biederstein, 1965

Ljubimye, zhdite! Ja vernus… Frontovye pisma 1941–1945, Veche, 2019

Luck, Hans von, *Mit Rommel an der Front*, Mittler & Sohn, 2007

Mahlke, Helmut, *Stuka: Angriff – Sturzflug*, Mittler, 1993

Malaparte, Curzio, *The Volga Rises in Europe*, Redman, 1957

Maligin, Konstantin, *V tsentre boyevogo poryadka*, Voenizdat, 1986

Manoschek, Walter (ed), *Es gibt nur eines für das Judentum: Vernichtung: Das Judenbild in deutschen Soldatenbriefen 1939–1944*, Hamburger Edition, 1995

Manstein, Erich von, *Lost Victories*, Greenhill, 1987

Martin, Helmut, *Weit war der Weg: An der Rollbahn 1941–1945*, Universitas, 2002

Mauss, Hans-Jörg, *Als Sanitätsoffizier im II Weltkrieg: Das Kriegstagebuch des Dr Wilhelm Mauss*, Verlag Dr Köster, 2008

Mende, Erich, *Das verdammte Gewissen: Zeuge der Zeit 1921–1945*, Herbig, 1982

Mikoyan, Anastas, *Tak bylo: Razmyshleniia o minuvshem (Moi 20 vek)*, Vagrius, 1999

Morell, Theo, *Die geheimen Tagebücher des Dr Morell*, Goldmann, 1983

Moskalenko, K. S., *In der Südwestrichtung*, Militärverlag der DDR, 1975

Moskva Voyennaya 1941–1945: Memuary i Arkhivnyye Dokumenty, Izdatelstvo Obyedineniya, Mosgorarkhiv, 1995

Moutier, Marie, *Liebste Schwester, wir müssen hier sterben oder siegen: Briefe deutscher Wehrmachtssoldaten 1939–45*, Blessing, 1945

Müller, Wilhelm, *22 Juni 1941: 40 Jahre danach*, Selbstverlag, n.d.

Ortenberg, David, *Iyun' Dekabr' Sorok Pervogo*, Moscow, 1984

Osterkamp, Theo, *Durch Höhen und Tiefen jagt ein Herz*, Vowinckel, 1952

Panzerkeil im Osten: Gedenkbuch der Berlin-Märkischen Panzer-Division, Die Wehrmacht, 1942

Pesendorfer, Franz, *Sturm zum Finnenmeer: Baltikum 1941*, Stadtdruckerei, 1943

Petri, Hartmut, *Journal de marche d'un fantassin allemand 1941–1945*, L'Harmattan, 2006

Petrow, Vassili Stepanowitsch, *Kanoniere*, Militärverlag der DDR, 1986

Pichler, Hans, *Truppenarzt und Zeitzeuge: Mit der 4 SS Polizei Division an vorderster Front*, Winkelried, 2006

Pisma pogibshikh geroev, Ast, 2023

Po Obe Storoni Fronta, 1995

Pokryschkin, A. I., *Himmel des Krieges*, Militärverlag der DDR, 1981

Popjel, Nikolai Kirillowitsch, *In schwerer Zeit*, Militärverlag der DDR, 1975

Posledniy Pis'ma s Fronta, Vol.1, 1941, Voenizdat, 1991

Press, Bernhard, *The Murder of the Jews in Latvia, 1941–1945*, Northwestern University Press, 2000

Prüller, Wilhelm, *Diary of a German Soldier*, Faber, 1963

Raus, Erhard, *Panzer Operations*, Da Capo, 2003

Riederer von Paar, Johannes (ed), *Die Kriegstagebücher des Hans Riederer v. Paar: Ergänzt durch Briefe, Dokumente und Erläuterungen*, Selbstverlag, 1979

Rokossovsky, Konstantin, *A Soldier's Duty*, Progress, 1985

Rolnikaitė, Mascha, *Ich muss erzählen: Mein Tagebuch 1941–45*, Rowohlt, 2010

Römer, Felix, *Die narzisstische Volksgemeinschaft: Theodor Habichts Kampf 1914–1944*, S. Fischer, 2017

Rosen, Richard *Freiherr* von, *Als Panzeroffizier in Ost und West*, Flechsig, 2013

Rosowski, Udo, *Die Kriegstagebücher des Feldwebels Kurt Pfau 1939–1945*, Literates, 2013

Ruville, Hubertus von, *Durch die Hölle: 1896 Tage Krieg Russlandkrieg bis zum bitteren Ende. Aus deutschen Fronttagebüchern 1941–1945*, Agenda, 2008

Ryabyshev, Dmitry, *Pervyy god voyny*, Voenizdat, 1990

Sachsse, Friedrich, *Roter Mohn*, Schild, 1973

Sandalov, Leonid, *1941. Na moskovskom napravlenii*, Veche, 2010

Sasse, Hans-Heinrich, *Zwei Spätsommer vor Leningrad*, Books on Demand, 2005

Scârneci, Vasile, *Viața și moartea în linia întâi: jurnal și însemnări de război 1916–1920, 1941–1943*, Editura Militara, 2013

Schäufler, *Der Weg war Weit*, Vowinckel, 1972

Schmidt, Paul, *Hitler's Interpreter*, Heinemann, 1951

Schroeder, Christa, *Er war mein Chef*, Herbig, 1985

Schur, Grigorij, *Die Juden von Wilna: Die Aufzeichnungen des Grigorij Schur 1941–1944*, DTV, 1999

Seydlitz, Walther von, *Stalingrad: Konflikt und Konsequenz*, Gerhard Stalling, 1977

Skrjabina, Elena, *Siege and Survival: the Odyssey of a Leningrader*, Southern Illinois University Press, 1971

Slesina, Horst, *Soldaten gegen Tod und Teufel*, Völkischer Verlag, 1942

Slyusarenko, *Posledniy vystrel*, Voenizdat, 1974

Soldiers of Barbarossa, edited by Craig Luther and David Stahel, Stackpole, 2021

Speer, Albert, *Inside the Third Reich*, Sphere, 1971

Stahlberg, Alexander, *Bounden Duty*, Brassey's, 1990

Stader, Ingo (ed), *Ihr daheim und wir hier draussen: Ein Briefwechsel zwischen Ostfront und Heimat*, Juni 1941–März 1943, Böhlau, 2006

Stankiewicz-Januszczak, Joanna, *Dziś mówię ludziom, co mówiłam Bogu*, Asp Rymsza, 2002

Starinov, Ilya, *Over the Abyss*, Ballantine, 1995

Statsenko, Aleksei, *Kiev bombili... Oborona stolitsy Sovetskoj Ukrainy*, Pyatiy Rim, 2020

Steh auf, es ist Krieg: Der Deutsche Überfall auf die Sowjetunion, TR Verlagsunion, 1991

Steiniger, Erhard, *Als Funker an den Brennpunkten der Front*, Flechsig, 2019

Die Stimme des Menschen: Briefe und Aufzeichnungen aus der ganzen Welt, 1939–1945, Piper & Co, 1961

Sudoplatov, Andrei, *Tainaia zhizn Generala Sudoplatova: Pravda i vymysli o moem ottse*, Seriia 'Dose', 1998

Sutzkever, Abraham, *Wilner Getto 1941–1944*, Ammann, 2009

Tennenbaum, Samuel, *Złoczów Memoir: 1939–1944*, iUniverse, 2001

Tilitzki, Christian, *Alltag in Ostpreussen 1940–45: Die geheimen Lageberichte der Königsberger Justiz*, Flechsig, n.d.

Tory, Avraham, *Surviving the Holocaust: The Kovno Ghetto Diary*, Harvard University Press, 1991

Trautloft, Hannes, *Kriegstagebuch von Hannes Trautloft: Grünherzjäger im Luftkampf 1940–1945*, VDM Heinz Nickel, 2006

Ukrayina: 100 dniv viyny. 22 chervnya-29 veresnya 1941 r.: doslidzhennya, dokumenty, svidchennya, Aerostat, Kiev, 2016

Unruh, Walter von, MS D-056 'War Experiences in Russia', author's papers

Veteranii pe Drumul Onoarei și Jertfei, Spre Cetățile de pe Nistru, Editura Vasile Cârlova, 1996

Waiss, Walter, *Heinz Sannemann: Ein Jagdfliegerleben: in Berichten, Dokumenten*, Helios, 2018

Warlimont, Walter, *Inside Hitler's Headquarters*, Presidio, 1991

Wells, Leon, *The Janowska Road*, Jonathan Cape, 1966

Wischnewski, Alexander, *Tagebuch eines Feldchirurgen*, Militärverlag, 1978

Wittek, Erhard, *Die Soldatische Tat: Der Kampf im Osten 1941/42*, Deutscher, 1943

Woltereck, Heinz (ed), *Seekrieg im Osten: Der Kampf der deutschen Kriegsmarine gegen die Sowjets*, Quelle & Meyer, 1943

Yegorov, A. V., *S veroy v pobedu (Zapiski komandira tankovogo polka)*, Voenizdat, 1974

Zhukov, Georgy, *Reminiscences and Recollections*, 2 volumes, Progress, 1985

Zwieback, Jacques, *Der Todeszug von Iasi 1941: Ein Überlebender des größten Pogroms in Rumänien erinnert sich*, Hartung-Gorre, 2002

UNIT HISTORIES
ARMY

Allmayer-Beck, Christoph *Freiherr* von, *Die Geschichte der 21 (ostpr/westpr) Infanterie Division*, Schild, 1990

Asmus, Dietwart, *Die 20.Inf.Div.(mot) Chronik und Geschichte*, Band 4, Selbstverlag

Bauer, Josef, *290 Infanterie Division*, Selbstverlag Kameraden-Hilfswerk 290 ID eV, 1960

Beck, Alois, *Bis Stalingrad*, Helmuth Abt Verlag, 1983

Benary, Albert, *Die Berliner 257. Bären-Division*, Podzun, 1957

Bergner, Romuald, *Schlesische Infanterie; Grenadier-Regiment 7*, Pöppinghaus, 1980

Boehm, Erwin, *Geschichte der 25 Division*, Selbstverlag, 1983

Boucsein, Heinrich, *Halten oder Sterben. Die hessisch-thüringische 129. Infanterie-Division im Rußlandfeldzug und Ostpreußen 1941–1945*, Vowinckel, 1999

Breymayer, Helmut, *Das Wiesel: Geschichte der 125 Infanterie Division 1940–1944*, Armin Vaas, 1983

Cavaleri, Leo, *Das 2 Regiment der Division Brandenburg*, Helios, 2017

Conze, *Die Geschichte der 291. Infanterie-Division 1940–1945*

Die Geschichte der 8 Infanterie/Jäger Division, Selbstverlag, 1979

Dinglreiter, Joseph, *Die Vierziger: Chronik des Regiments*, Selbstverlag, n.d.

Donat, Gerhard, *Lützows wilde verwegene Schar: Das mecklenburgische Grenadier Regiment 89 in beiden Weltkriegen*, Biblio, 1990

Freund, Gerhard, *Die Panzer Abwehrabteilung 9 in Gelnhausen und ihr Schicksal 1935–1945*, Märchenstrassen, 1996

Ganz, A. Harding, *Ghost Division – The 11th 'Gespenster' Panzer Division and the German Armored Force in World War II*, Stackpole, 2016

Geschichte der 3 Panzer Division 1935–1945, der Buchhandlung Günter Richter, 1967

Geschichte der 258 Infanterie Division, Band 2, Vowinckel, 1978

Geschichte des 11 (Sachs) Infanterie Regiments, späteren Infanterie Regiments 11 und Grenadier Regiments 11 von 1918–1945, Selbstverlag, n.d.

Graser, Gerhard, *Zwischen Kattegat und Kaukasus: Weg und Kämpfe der 198 Infanterie Division*, Kameradenhilfswerk und Traditionsverband der ehemaligen 198 Infanterie Division, 1961

Gschöpf, Rudolf, *Mein Weg mit der 45 Infanterie Division*, Buchdienst Südtirol, 2002

Haupt, Werner, *Die 8. Panzer- Division im 2. Weltkrieg*, Podzun Pallas, 1987

Haupt, Werner, *Geschichte der 134 Infanterie Division*, Selbstverlag, 1971

Hertlein, Wilhelm, *Chronik der 7. Infanterie-Division München*, Bruckmann, 1984

Hinze, Rolf, *Hitze, Frost und Pulverdampf: Der Schicksalsweg der 20 Panzer Division*, 5th Ed, Selbstverlag, 1994

Hoffmann, Dieter, *Die Magdeburger Division: Zur Geschichte der 13 Infanterie und 13 Panzer Division 1935–1945*, Max Schlutius, 1999

Kaltenegger, Roland, *Die Stammdivision der deutschen Gebirgstruppe: Weg un Kampf der 1 Gebirgs-Division 1935–1945*, Leopold Stocker, 1981

Keubke, Klaus Ulrich, *Zur Geschichte der 12. (Meckl) Infanterie-Division*, Schriften zur Geschichte Mecklenburgs, 2013

Kindel, Richard, *Die 8 Panzer Division der Deutschen Wehrmacht 1939–1945*, Band I, Sammlung Alte Armee und Deutsche Wehrmacht, 2004

Kippar, Gerhard, *Das Kampfgeschehen der 161 (ostpr) Infanterie Division*, Selbstverlag, n.d.

Kirstein, Wolfgang, *Rekonstruktion eines Tage-Buches: Die 295. Infanterie-Division von 1940 bis 1945*, Selbstverlag, 1999

Knecht, Wolfgang, *Die Geschichte des Infanterie-Regiments 77*, Selbstverlag, 1964

Kuehn, Dietrich, *Geschichte des Reiter Regiments 1*, Teil II, 1939–1941, Selbstverlag, n.d.

Kurowski, *Schlesische Infanterie*

Lanz, Hubert, *Gebirgsjäger: Die 1. Gebirgs-Division 1935–1945*, H. H. Podzun, 1954

Lemelsen, Joachim and Schmidt, Julius, *29 Division, 29 Infanterie Division (mot.), 29 Panzergrenadier Division*, Podzun Pallas, 1960

Löser, Jochen, *Bittere Pflicht: Kampf und Untergang der 76. Berlin-Brandenburgischen Infanterie-Division*, Biblio, 1986

Lubs, Gerhard, *IR5 – Aus der Geschichte eines Pommerschen Regiments 1920–1945*, Berg, 1965

Manteuffel, Hasso von, *Die 7. Panzer-Division im Zweiten Weltkrieg: Einsatz und Kampf der Gespenster-Division 1939–1945*, Traditionsverband ehem. 7 Panzer Division Kameradenhilfe, 1965

Mayerhofer, Franz, *Geschichte des Grenadier Regiments 315 der bayerischen 167 ID – Almhütten Division – 1939–1944*, Kameradschaft ehemaliges Grenadier-Regiment 315, 1977

Memminger, Fritz, *Die Kriegsgeschichte der Windhund Division*, Heinrich Pöppinghaus, n.d.

Meyer, Hermann Frank, *Blutiges Edelweiss: Die 1 Gebirgs-Division im Zweiten Weltkrieg*, Ch Links, 2008

Meyer-Detring, Wilhelm, *137. Infanterie-Division im Mittelabschnitt der Ostfront*

Nayhauss-Cormons, Mainhardt Graf von, *Zwischen Gehorsam und Gewissen: Richard von Weizsäcker und das Infanterie Regiment 9*

Oehmichen, Hermann and Mann, Martin, *Der Weg der 87 Infanterie Division*

Ott, Ernst, *Jäger am Feind*

Paul, Wolfgang, *Brennpunkte: Die Geschichte der 6 Panzerdivision (1 leichte) 1937–1945*

Paul, Wolfgang, *Das Potsdamer Infanterie Regiment 9 1918–1945*

Paul, Wolfgang, *Geschichte der 18 Panzer Division 1940–1943*

Reimer, Hans, *Erinnerungen an das Infanterie-Regiment 36*

Reinicke, Adolf, *Die 5 Jäger Division*

Rhein, Ernst Martin, *Das Infanterie-Grenadier Regiment 18*

Schadewitz, Michael, *Panzerregiment 11, Panzerabteilung 65 und Panzerersatz und Ausbildungsabteilung 11*, Band 1

Schäufler, Hans, *So lebten und so starben sie: Das Buch vom Panzerregiment 35*

Schimak, Anton, Lamprecht, Karl and Dettmer, Friedrich, *Die 44 Infanterie Division: Tagebuch der Hoch und Deutschmeister*

Schrodek, G. W., *Die 11 Panzerdivision 'Gespensterdivision'*

Schrodek, G. W., *Ihr Glaube galt dem Vaterland: Geschichte des Panzer-Regiments 15*

Selder, Emanuel, *Der Krieg der Infanterie dargestellt in der Chronik des Infanterie Regiments 62 (7 Infanterie Division) 1935–1945*, Teil IV, *Unternehmen Barbarossa – Der Russlandkrieg*, Kameradschaft ehem Angehöriger des Inf.Rgt 62, 1985

Selz, Barbara, *Das Grüne Regiment: Der Weg der 256 Infanterie Division aus der Sicht des Regiments 481*, Otto Kehrer, 1970

Spaeter, Helmuth, *Die Brandenburger: eine deutsche Kommandotruppe*, Dissberger, 1994

Spaeter, Helmuth, *The History of the Panzerkorps Grossdeutschland*, Volume 1, JJ Fedorowicz, 1992

Stoves, Rolf, *1 Panzer Division 1935–1945: Chronik einer der drei Stamm Divisionen der deutschen Panzerwaffe*, Podzun Pallas, 1961

Stühring, Henning, *Die Falke-Division an der Ostfront*, epubli, Berlin, 2017

Weber, Helmut, *122 Infanterie Division: Erinnerung der Pommersch-Mecklenburgischen Greif Division*, Selbstverlag, 1988

Weinmann, Willi, *Die 101 Jäger Division in Dokumente, Berichten und Bildern*, Selbstverlag, 1966

Werthen, Wolfgang, *Geschichte der 16 Panzer Division*, Podzun, 1958

WAFFEN SS

Ullrich, Karl, *Wie ein Fels im Meer: Kriegsgeschichte der 3 SS Panzerdivision Totenkopf*, Band 2, Munin, 1987

Vopersal, Wolfgang, *Soldaten, Kämpfer, Kameraden: Marsch und Kämpfe der SS-Totenkopf Division*, Band IIa, Biblio, 1984

LUFTWAFFE

Dierich, Wolfgang, *Chronik Kampfgeschwader 51 'Edelweiss'*, Motorbuch, 2011

Freter, Hermann, *Fla nach vorn! Die Fliegerabwehr-Waffe des Heeres und ihre Doppelrolle im Zweiten Weltkrieg*, Im Eigenverlag der Fla-Kameradschaft, 1973

Kiehl, Heinz, *Chronik Kampfgeschwader 53 'Legion Condor'*, Motorbuch, 2010

Novak, Dr Hugo, *Geschichte der ostpreussischen leichte Flakabteilung 71*, Teil II, Im Verbande der 11 Panzer Division, Selbstverlag, 1980

Prien, Jochen, *Einsatz des Jagdgeschwaders 77 von 1939 bis 1945*, Teil 2: Juni 1941 bis November 1942, Selbstverlag, 1993

Prien, Jochen, *Jagdgeschwader 53: A History of the Pik As Geschwader*, Volume 1, Schiffer, 2004

Prien, Jochen and Stemmer, Gerhard, *Messerschmitt Bf109 in Einsatz bei Stab und I/ Jagdgeschwader 3 1938–1945*, Struve, n.d

Waiss, Walter, *Chronik Kampfgeschwader Nr.27 Boelcke*, Band 3, Teil 2, 01.01.1941- 31.12.1941, Selbstverlag, n.d.

NAVY

Benz, Jörg, *Deutsche Marineinfanterie 1938-1945,* Husum, 1996

SECONDARY SOURCES

Aaken, Wolf van, *Hexenkessel Ostfront: Von Smolensk nach Breslau*, Erich Pabel, 1964

Abaturov, Valeriy, *1941. Na Zapadnom napravlenii*, Eksmo, 2007

Akalovich N. M., *Oni zashchishchali Minsk*, 1982

Aliev, Rostislav, *Brestskaya krepost*, Veche, 2013

Aliev, Rostislav, *The Siege of Brest 1941*, Pen and Sword, 2013

Ancel, Jean, *Prelude to Mass Murder*, Yad Vashem, 2014

Angrick, Andrej, *Besatzungspolitik und Massenmord: Die Einsatzgruppe D in der südlichen Sowjetunion 1941–1943*, Hamburger Edition, 2003

Angrick, Andrej, *The Final Solution in Riga*, Berghahn, 2012

Arma, Alexandru, *Bucurestiul sub bombardamente 1941–1944*, Editura Militara, 2015

Axworthy, Mark, *Third Axis, Fourth Ally, Romanian Armed Forces in the European War 1941– 1945*, Weidenfeld Military, 1995

Balta, Sebastian, *Rumänien und die Grossmächte in der Ära Antonescu 1940–1944*, Franz Steiner, 2005

Bartov, Omer, *Hitler's Army*, Oxford University Press, 1991

Bartusevicius, Vincas, Tauber, Joachim and Wette, Wolfram (eds), *Holocaust in Litauen: Krieg, Judenmorde und Kollaboration im Jahre 1941*, Böhlau, 2003

Beevor, Antony, *The Second World War*, Weidenfeld & Nicolson, 2014

Bekker, Cajus, *Angriffshöhe 4000*, Buch und Welt, 1964

Bellamy, Chris, *Absolute War*, Pan, 2009

Benz, Wigbert, *Der Hungerplan im Unternehmen Barbarossa 1941*, Wissenschaftlicher Verlag, 2011

Benz, Wolfgang, Kwiet, Konrad and Matthäus, Jürgen (eds), *Einsatz im Reichskommissariat Ostland: Dokumente zum Völkermord im Baltikum und in Weissrussland 1941–44*, Metropol, 1998

Bergström, Christer, *Black Cross/Red Star: Operation Barbarossa 1941: The Air War Over the Eastern Front*, Pacific Military History, 2000

Bergström, Christer, *Operation Barbarossa*, Casemate, 2016

Berkhoff, Karel, *Life and Death in Ukraine Under Nazi Rule*, Belknap, 2008

Besymenski, Lev, *Stalin und Hitler: Pokerspiel der Diktatoren*, Aufbau, 2002

Bieszanow, Władimir, *Twierdza Brzeska*, Bellona, 2012

Blokada Leningrada: Dnevniki 1941–1944 godov, Eksmo, 2023

Błonski, Jacek and Cieplińska, Anna, *Przemyśl w czasie II wojny światowej*, Muzeum Narodowe Ziemi Przemyskiej, 2015

Braatz, Kurt, *Gott oder ein Flugzeug: Leben und Sterben des Jagdfliegers Günther Lützow*, Neunundzwanzigsechs, 2005

Braatz, Kurt, *Walter Krupinski*, Neunundzwanzigsechs, 2010

Braatz, Kurt, *Werner Mölders: Die Biographie*, Neunundzwanzigsechs, 2008

Broekmeyer, Marius, *Stalin, the Russians, and Their War: 1941–1945*, University of Wisconsin Press, 1998

Browning, Christopher, *Nazi Policy, Jewish Workers, German Killers*, Cambridge University Press, 2000

Buchbender, Ortwin, *Das tönende Erz: Deutsche Propaganda gegen die Rote Armee im Zweiten Weltkrieg*

Bücheler, Heinrich, *Hoepner: ein deutsches Soldatenschicksal des 20 Jahrhunderts*, Mittler, 1980

Buldygin, S. B., *Borba za Rigu v 1941 godu*, Gangut, 2013

Burdick, Charles, *Hubert Lanz: General der Gebirgstruppe. 1896–1982*, Biblio, 1988

Burds, Jeffrey, *Holocaust in Rovno*, Palgrave, 2016

Carp, Matatias, *Cartea neagra: Le Livre noir sur la destruction des Juifs de Roumanie (1940–1944)*, Denoel, 2009

Chernyshev, Aleksandr, *1941 god na Baltike – podvig i tragediia*, Eksmo, 2009

Cohen, Laurie, *Smolensk under the Nazis*, University of Rochester Press, 2013

Constantiniu, Florin, *O Istorie sinceră a poporuliu roman*, Univers Enciclopedic Gold, n.d

Cüppers, Martin (ed), *Naziverbrechen: Täter, Taten, Bewältigungsversuche*, WBG, 2013

Curilla, Wolfgang, *Die deutsche Ordnungspolizei und der Holocaust im Baltikum und in Weissrussland 1941–1944*, Ferdinand Schöningh, 2006

Curilla, Wolfgang, *Der Judenmord in Polen und die deutsche Ordnungspolizei 1939–1945*, Ferdinand Schöningh, 2011

Daines, Vladimir, *Komandarmy 1941 goda. Doblest i tragediya*, Veche, 2017

Das Deutsche Reich und der Zweite Weltkrieg, 10 volumes, DVA, 1979–2008

Deletant, Dennis, *Hitler's Forgotten Ally: Ion Antonescu and his Regime*, Palgrave, 2006

Dieckmann, Christoph, *Deutsche Besatzungspolitik in Litauen 1941–1944*, Wallstein, 2011

Dmitrow, Edmund, Machcewicz, Pawel and Szarota, Tomasz, *Der Beginn der Vernichtung: Zum Mord an den Juden in Jedwabne und Umgebung im Sommer 1941*, Fibre, 2004

Drabkin, A. and Isayev, A., *22 iyunya Chernyy den' kalendarya*, Eksmo, 2011

Duțu, Alesandru, *Armata Română in Război*, Editura Enciclopedica, 2016

Eaton, Henry, *The Origins and Onset of the Romanian Holocaust*, Wayne State University Press, 2013

Edele, Mark, *Stalin's Defectors*, Oxford University Press, 2017

Eiber, Ludwig, 'Ein bisschen die Wahrheit: Briefe eines Bremer Kaufmanns von seinem Einsatz beim Reserve-Polizeibataillon 105 in der Sowjetunion 1941', in *1999 Zeitschrift für Sozialgeschichte des 20 und 21 Jahrhunderts*, Heft 1, 1999, pp.67–83

Ellis, Frank, *Barbarossa 1941: Reframing Hitler's Invasion of Stalin's Soviet Empire*, University Press of Kansas, 2015

Erickson, John, *The Road to Stalingrad*, Harper Collins, 1985

Ezergailis Andrew, *The Holocaust in Latvia, 1941–1944*, Latvijas Vestures Indtituts, 1996

Feldmeyer, Karl and Meyer, Georg, *Johann Graf von Kielmansegg 1906–2006: Deutscher Patriot, Europäer, Atlantiker*, Mittler & Sohn, 2007

Forczyk, Robert, *Tank Warfare on the Eastern Front 1941–1942: Schwerpunkt*, Pen and Sword, 2014

Fritz, Stephen G., *Ostkrieg*, University Press of Kentucky, 2011

Geissbühler, Simon, *Blutiger Juli: Rumäniens Vernichtungskrieg und der vergessene Massenmord an den Juden 1941*, Ferdinand Schöningh, 2013

Gerlach, Christian, *Kalkulierte Morde: Die deutsche Wirtschafts- und Vernichtungspolitik im Weissrussland 1941 bis 1944*, Hamburger Edition, 1999

Germany and the Second World War, Volume IV, Oxford University Press, 1998

Geschichte des Grossen Vaterländischen Krieges der Sowjetunion, Band 2, Deutscher Militärverlag, 1963

Glantz, David, *The Battle for Leningrad*, University Press of Kansas, 2002

Glantz, David, *Stumbling Colossus: Red Army on the Eve of World War*, University Press of Kansas, 1998

Gorodetsky, Gabriel, *Grand Delusion: Stalin and the German Invasion of Russia*, Yale University Press, 1999

Gotzes, Andrea, *Krieg und Vernichtung: Sowjetische Zeitzeugen erinnern sich*, Wissenschaftliche Buchgesellschaft, Darmstadt, 2006

Grabitz, Helga (ed), *Die Normalität des Verbrechens*, Edition Hentrich, 1994

Gross, Jan T., *Neighbours: The Destruction of the Jewish Community in Jedwabne, Poland*, Arrow, 2003

Gross, Jan T., *Revolution from Abroad: The Soviet Conquest of Poland's Western Ukraine and Western Belorussia*, Princeton University Press, 2002

Gushchin, Viktor, *Istoriya Yelgavy 1940–1991. Chast' chetvertaya. Kniga 2. V gody nemetsko-fashistskoy okkupatsii*, Baltijas vēsturisko un sociālpolitisko pētījumu centrs, 2020

Guslyarov, Evgeniy, *Stalin v Zhizni*, Olma, 2003

Hans Bayer: Kriegsberichter im Zweiten Weltkrieg, Stiftung Topographie des Terrors, 2014

Hartmann, Christian, *Halder: Generalstabschef Hitlers 1938–1942*, Ferdinand Schöningh, 2010

Hartmann, Christian, *Wehrmacht im Ostkrieg: Front und militärisches Hinterland 1941/42*, Oldenbourg, 2009

Heer, Hannes, 'Und dann kamen wir nach Russland: Junge Soldaten im Krieg gegen die Sowjetunion', in Herrmann, Ulrich and Müller, Rolf-Dieter (eds), *Junge Soldaten im Zweiten Weltkrieg: Kriegserfahrungen als Lebenserfahrungen*, Juventa, 2010

Heer, Hannes (ed), *War of Extermination: The German Military in World War II*, Berghahn, 2000

Heydorn, Volker Detlef, *Der sowjetische Aufmarsch im Bialystoker Balkon*, für Wehrwissenschaften, 1989

Hill, Alexander, *The Red Army and the Second World War*, Cambridge University Press, Cambridge, 2016

Himka, John-Paul, 'The Lviv Pogrom of 1941: The Germans, Ukrainian Nationalists, and the Carnival Crowd', *Canadian Slavonic Papers*, No.53, 2011

Hoffmann, Joachim, *Stalins Vernichtungskrieg 1941–1945*, Herbig, 1999

Humburg, Martin, *Das Gesicht des Krieges: Feldpostbriefe von Wehrmachtssoldaten aus der Sowjetunion 1941–1944*, Westdeutscher, 1998

Hürter, Johannes, *Hitlers Heerführer: Die Deutschen Oberbefehlshaber im Krieg gegen die Sowjetunion 1941–1942*, Oldenbourg, 2006

The Initial Period of War on the Eastern Front, 22 June–August 1941: Proceedings of the Fourth Art of War Symposium, Garmisch, October 1987, Frank Cass, 1997

Ioanid, Radu, *The Holocaust in Romania: The Destruction of Jews and Gypsies Under the Antonescu Regime, 1940–1944*, Ivan R. Dee, 1999

Ioanid, Radu (ed), *The Iaşi Pogrom, June–July 1941: A Photo Documentary from the Holocaust in Romania*, Indiana University Press, 2017

Isaev, Aleksei, *Dubno 1941*, Helion, 2017

Isaev, Aleksei, *Ot granitsy do Leningrada. Pravda protiv mifov o 1941 gode*, Juaza, 2020

Jurju, Cornel, 'Opinia publică și intrarea României În al doilea război mondial (22 iunie 1941)', *Revista Bistritei*, No.15, 2001, pp.298–318

Kaltenegger, Roland, *Blutende Fronten: Truppenärzte, Sanitäter und Rotkreuzschwestern im Zweiten Weltkrieg*, Flechsig, 2018

Kaltenegger, Roland, *Gefangen im russischen Winter: Unternehmen Barbarossa in Dokumenten und Zeitzeugenberichten 1941/42*, Rosenheimer, 2007

Kamenir, Victor, *The Bloody Triangle: The Defeat of Soviet Armor in the Ukraine, June 1941*, Zenith, 2008

Karpow, Wladimir, *Russland im Krieg 1941–1945*, Weltbild, 2009

Kay, Alex J. (ed), *Nazi Policy on the Eastern Front 1941*, University of Rochester Press, 2014

Khristoforov, V. S. (ed), *Velikaya Otechestvennaya Voyna, 1941 god: Issledovaniya, dokumenty, kommentarii*, 2011

Klee, Ernst (ed), *'Schöne Zeiten' – Judenmord aus der Sicht der Täter und Gaffer*, Fischer, 1997

Kohl, Paul, *'Ich wundere mich, dass ich noch lebe': Sowjetische Augenzeugen berichten*, Gütersloher Verlagshaus Gerd Mohn, 1990

Kotkin, Steven, *Stalin: Waiting for Hitler, 1928–1941*, Penguin, 2018

Knopp, Guido, *Der Verdammte Krieg*, Vol.1, Orbis, 1998

Krausnick, Helmut and Wilhelm, Hans-Heinrich, *Die Truppe des Weltanschauungskrieges: Die Einsatzgruppen der Sicherheitspolizei und des SD 1938–1942*, DVA, 1981

Krivosheev, G. F., *Soviet Casualties and Combat Losses in the Twentieth Century*, Greenhill, 1997

Kumanev, G. A., *Ryadom so Stalinym*, Rusich, 2001

Levinson, Joseph, *The Shoah in Lithuania*, Vaga, 2006

Lichtenstein, Heiner, *Himmlers grüne Helfer: Die Schutz und Ordnungspolizei im Dritten Reich*, Bund, 1990

Lopez, Jean and Otkhmenzuri, Lasha, *Barbarossa: 1941. La guerre absolue*, Passes Composes, 2019

Lumans, Valdis, *Latvia in World War II*, Fordham University Press, 2006

Luther, Craig, *Barbarossa Unleashed*, Schiffer, 2014

Manley, Rebecca, *To the Tashkent Station: Evacuation and Survival in the Soviet Union at War*, Cornell University Press, 2009

Manoschek, Walter (ed), *Die Wehrmacht im Rassenkrieg*, Picus, 1996

Marples, David, *'Our Glorious Past': Lukashenka's Belarus and the Great Patriotic War*, Ibidem, 2014

Matonin, Evgeniy, *22 Iiunia 1941 goda: den, kogda obrushilsia mir*, Komsomolskaya Pravda, 2021

Mawdsley, Evan, *Thunder in the East*, Hodder and Arnold, 2005

Meindl, Ralf, *Ostpreußens Gauleiter Erich Koch: eine politische Biographie*, Fibre, 2007

Melvin, Mungo, *Manstein: Hitler's Greatest General*, Weidenfeld & Nicolson, 2010

Merridale, Catherine, *Ivan's War*, Faber and Faber, 2005

Messerschmidt, Manfred, *Die Wehrmacht im NS-Staat*, R. V. Decker, 1969

Mick, Christoph, *Kriegserfahrungen in einer multiethnischen Stadt: Lemberg 1914–1947*, Harrossowitz, 2010

Moorhouse, Roger, *The Devil's Alliance*, Bodley Head, 2014

Muller, Richard, *The German Air War in Russia*, Nautical & Aviation Pub Co of America, 1992

Müller, Rolf-Dieter, *Die deutsche Wirtschaftspolitik in den besetzten sowjetischen Gebieten 1941–1943*, Harald Boldt, 1991

Müller, Rolf-Dieter, *Enemy in the East: Hitler's Secret Plans to Invade the Soviet Union*, I. B. Tauris, 2014

Munzel, Oskar, *Panzer-Taktik*, Kurt Vowickel, 1959

Musial, Bogdan, *Konterrevolutionäre Elemente sind zu erschiessen: Die Brutalisierung des deutsch-sowjetischen Krieges im Sommer 1941*, Propyläen, 2000

Musial, Bogdan, *Sowjetische Partisanen 1941–1944: Mythos und Wirklichkeit*, Ferdinand Schöningh, 2009

Neiburgs, Uldis, *Dievs, Tava zeme deg! Latvijas Otra pasaules kara stasti*, Lauku avize, 2014

Neiburgs, Uldis, *Grēka un ienaida liesmās! Latvijas Otrā pasaules kara stāsti*, Latvijas Mediji, 2018

Paul, Wolfgang, *Panzer-General Walter K. Nehring. Eine Biographie*, Motorbuch, 2002

Petrov, Igor, *1941: Pogranichniki v boiu*, Eksmo, 2008

Petrov, Vladimir, *June 22 1941: Soviet Historians and the German Invasion*, University of South Carolina Press, 1968

Plocher, Hermann, *The German Air Force Versus Russia 1941*, US Air Force Historical Research Agency, 1965

Pohl, Dieter, *Nationalsozialistische Judenverfolgung in Ostgalizien 1941–1944: Organisation und Durchführung eines staatlichen Massenverbrechens*, Oldenbourg, 1997

Pöpping, Dagmar, *Kriegspfarrer an der Ostfront*, Vandenhoeck & Ruprecht, 2017

Prazan, Michaël, *Einsatzgruppen: Les commandos de la mort nazis*, Éditions du Seuil, 2010

Projektgruppe Belarus (ed), *Existiert das Ghetto noch? Weissrussland: Jüdisches Überleben gegen nationalsozialistische Herrschaft*, Assoziation A, 2003

Quinkert, Babette and Morré, Jorg (eds), *Deutsche Besatzung in der Sowjetunion 1941–1944: Vernichtungskrieg, Reaktionen, Erinnerung*, Ferdinand Schöningh, 2014

Radzinsky, Edward, *Stalin*, Sceptre, 1997

Rees, Laurence, *The War of the Century: When Hitler Fought Stalin*, BBC Books, 1999

Reese, Roger, *Stalin's Reluctant Soldiers: A Social History of the Red Army, 1925–41*, University Press of Kansas, 1996

Reichelt, Katrin, *Lettland unter deutscher Besatzung 1941–1944: der lettische Anteil am Holocaust*, Metropol, 2011

Reid, Anna, *Leningrad*, Walker, 2011

Rentrop, Petra, *Tatorte der Endlösung: Das Ghetto Minsk und die Vernichtungsstätte von Maly Trostinez*, Metropol, 2011

Roekel, Evertjan van, *Veldgrauw: Nederlanders in de Waffen-SS*, Spectrum, 2017

Römer, Felix, *Kameraden: Die Wehrmacht von innen*, Piper, 2012

Römer, Felix, 'Der Kommissarbefehl bei den Frontdivisionen des Ostheeres 1941–42' in Quinkert, Babette and Morré, Jorg (eds), *Deutsche Besatzung in der Sowjetunion 1941–1944: Vernichtungskrieg, Reaktionen, Erinnerung*

Römer, Felix, *Der Kommissarbefehl: Wehrmacht und NS Verbrechen an der Ostfront 1941/42*, Ferdinand Schöningh, 2008

Rossoliński-Liebe, Grzegorz, *Stepan Bandera*, Ibidem, 2014

Röw, Martin, *Militärseelsorge unter dem Hakenkreuz: Die katholische Feldpastoral 1939–1945*, Brill Schöningh, 2014

Sæther, Vegard, *En av oss: Norske frontkjempere i krig og fred*, Cappelen Damm, 2011

Sandkühler, Thomas, *Endlösung in Galizien*, Dietz, 1996

Schneider, Karl, *Auswärts eingesetzt: Bremer Polizeibataillone und der Holocaust*, Klartext, 2011

Schroeter, Gudrun, *Worte aus einer zerstörten Welt: das Ghetto in Wilna*, Röhrig Universitätsverlag, 2008

Schwabedissen, Walter, *The Russian Air Force in the Eyes of German Commanders*, unpublished US Air Force study in the author's papers

Sebag-Montefiore, Simon, *Stalin: The Court of the Red Tsar*, Orion, 2007

Seberechts, Frank, *Drang naar het Osten: Vlaamse soldaten en kolonisten aan het oostfront*, Polis, 2019

Shepherd, Ben, *Hitler's Soldiers: The German Army in the Third Reich*, Yale University Press, 2016

Shepherd, Ben, *War in the Wild East*, Harvard University Press, 2004

Sherstnev, Vladimir, *Tragediya sorok pervogo. Dokumenty i razmyshleniya*, Rusish, 2005

Smirnov, Sergei, *Heroes of Brest Fortress*, Progress, 1960

Solomovici, Teşu, *Mareşalul Ion Antonescu*, Editura Teşu, 2011

Sørlie, Sigurd, *Sonnenrad und Hakenkreuz: Norweger in der Waffen-SS 1941–1945*, Ferdinand Schöningh, 2019

Stoenescu, Alex Mihai, *Armata, Mareşalul şi Evreii*, Editura RAO, 2010

Strana v Ogne, 1941, 2 volumes, Olma, 2011

Streit, Christian, *Keine Kameraden*, Dietz, 1997

Struve, Kai, *Deutsche Herrschaft, Ukrainischer Nationalismus, Antijüdische Gewalt: Der Sommer 1941 in der Westukraine*, De Gruyter, 2015

Suchenwirth, Richard, *Command and Leadership in the German Air Force*, unpublished US Air Force study in the author's papers

Suvarov, A. M., *Brestskaia krepost': voina i mir*, Poligrafika, 2012

Swanström, André, *Hakaristin ritarit: Suomalaiset SS-miehet, politiikka, uskonto ja sotarikokset*, Atena, 2019

Überschär, Gerd and Wette, Wolfram, *Unternehmen Barbarossa: Der deutsche Überfall auf die Sowjetunion 1941*, Schöningh, 1984

Umansky, Andrej, *La Shoah a l'Est: regards d'allemands*, Fayard, 2018

Veum, Eirik, *Deres ære var troskap*, Vega Forlag, 2017

Vihavainen, Timo and Manninen, Ohto (eds), *Stalinin Salainen Jatkosota*, Docendo, 2014

Vincx, Jan and Schotanius, Viktor, *Nederlands vrijwilligers in Europese krijgsdienst 1940–1945*, Deel 4, 5 SS Pantserdivisie Wiking, Etnika, 1991

Voicu, Marin, *Pentru Neam şi Ţară*, Miidecărţi, 2019

Volkogonov, Dmitri, *Stalin: Triumph and Tragedy*, Grove, 1991

Voronkov, Irina, *'Dvadtsat' vtorogo iyunya, rovno v chetyre chasa': Minsk i minchane v pervyye dni Velikoy Otechestvennoy voyny*, Belaruskaja navuka, 2011

Voronkov, Irina, *Minsk: leto 1941, leto 1944*, Belaruskaia navuka, 2014

Voznesensky, V., *Perviy udar Barbarossy. Brest-Litovskiy ukreprayon*, Veche, 2022

Wawrzyński, Mirosław, *Powietrzny Pogrom ZSRR: 22 czerwca 1941*, Bellona, 2015

Weal, John, *Bf109 Aces of the Eastern Front*, Osprey, 2001

Wegner, Bernd (ed), *From Peace to War: Germany, Soviet Russia, and the World, 1939–1941*, Berghahn, 1997

Wegner-Korfes, Sigrid, *Weimer, Stalingrad, Berlin: Das Leben des deutschen Generals Otto Korfes*, Verlag der Nation, Weiden, 1994

Werth, Alexander, *Russia at War*, Pan, 1965

Wette, Wolfram, *Der Krieg des Kleinen Mannes: ein Militärgeschichte von Unten*, Piper, München, 1992

Wette, Wolfram, *Karl Jäger: Mörder der litauischen Juden*, Fischer, 2011

Wieczynski, Joseph L. (ed), *Operation Barbarossa: The German Attack on the Soviet Union, June 22, 1941*, Charles Schlacks Jr, 1993

Wilhelm, Hans-Heinrich, *Rassenpolitik und Kriegführung: Sicherheitspolizei und Wehrmacht in Polen und Sowjetunion 1939–1945*, Wissenschaftsverlag Richard Rothe, 1991

World War II and the Occupation of Latvia, Latvian War Museum, Riga, n.d.

Zając, Tomasz, *W szponach Barbarossy: Działania wojenne w 1941 r. na terenie 8 Przemyskiego Rejonu Umocnionego*, Muzeum Narodowe Ziemi Przemyskiej, Przemyśl, 2021

Zeigert, Didier and Siedler, Franz, *Hitler's Secret Headquarters: The Fuhrer's Wartime Bases from the Invasion of France to the Berlin Bunker*, Greenhill, 2004

Zvyagintsev, Vyacheslav, *Voina na vesakh Femidy*, Terra, 2006

Zwart, Joop (ed), *Lemberg 1941 und Oberländer: Das Ergebnis einer Untersuchung*, Selbstverlag, Amstelveen, 1960

INDEX

Note: page numbers in **bold** refer to illustrations.